Thoughts from a Bridge

Thoughts from a Bridge

A Retrospective of Writings on New Europe and American Federalism

Eric Stein

With a Foreword by
Joseph H. H. Weiler

Ann Arbor

THE UNIVERSITY OF MICHIGAN PRESS

Published in the United States of America by
The University of Michigan Press
Manufactured in the United States of America
♾ Printed on acid-free paper

2003 2002 2001 2000 4 3 2 1

A CIP catalog record for this book is available from the British Library.

Library of Congress Cataloging-in-Publication Data

Stein, Eric.
Thoughts from a bridge : a retrospective of writings on new Europe and American federalism / Eric Stein ; with a foreword by Joseph H.H. Weiler.
p. cm.
Includes bibliographical references and index.
ISBN 0-472-11059-4 (acid-free paper)
1. Federal government—European Union countries. I. Title.
KJE5076.S73 1999
321.8′094—dc21 99-39240
CIP

To Michel Gaudet, Conseiller d'État and the unsurpassed Director General of the Legal Service of the Commission of the European Community, and to my many European friends dedicated to European peace and unity

O, rejoice
Beyond a common joy! and set it down
With gold on lasting pillars

—William Shakespeare, *The Tempest,* act 5, sc. 1

Contents

Foreword: Eric Stein's Bridge—A Retrospective ix
Joseph H. H. Weiler

Acknowledgments xvii

Introduction
Five Variations on a Theme: Divided-Power Systems 3

Part 1. Constitutionalizing, Harmonizing

Lawyers, Judges, and the Making of a Transnational Constitution 15

Excerpt from *Harmonization of European Company Laws—The Making of the First Coordination Directive: A Case Study* 50

Part 2. European Integration and the American Federal Experience

Uses, Misuses—and Nonuses of Comparative Law 89

Excerpt from *Courts and Free Markets—Perspectives from the United States and Europe* 112
On the Two Systems: An Overview 115

Citizen Access to Judicial Review of Administrative Action in a Transnational and Federal Context 161

Towards a European Foreign Policy? The European Foreign Affairs System from the Perspective of the United States Constitution with Excerpts from *External Relations of the European Community: Structure and Process* 191

and

Foreign Policy at Maastricht: "Non in Commotione Dominus" 304

Uniformity and Diversity in a Divided-Power System: The United States' Experience 309

Panel Statement on "Democracy without 'a People' " 335

Part 3. Europe's Burden of History

History against Free Speech: German Law in European and American Perspective 347

and

On the "Auschwitz Lie"—Correspondence 410

Excerpts from *Czecho/Slovakia: Ethnic Conflict, Constitutional Fissure, Negotiated Breakup* 417
- Preface 418
- A Framework 420
- An Overview: Some Answers and Some Reflections at the End of the Day 423

Coda

Reminiscences of the Embryonic EEC 471

and

A Million Footnotes 476
Virginia Stein

Index 479

Foreword: Eric Stein's Bridge—A Retrospective

Joseph H. H. Weiler

I

There are at least two ways in which works of art are thought to be classics—recognized as having a value and retaining a power that lasts beyond the moment or period of their creation. Consider two artists much beloved and admired by Eric Stein and his valorous wife, Virginia.

The first is Duccio, the Sienese painter, born sometime between 1250 and 1260. His most famous works beautified the Cathedral of Siena and are now housed in the adjacent Cathedral Museum—the Museo dell'Opera del duomo. His altarpiece containing a *Maestà* and the *Storie della Passione* is among the most celebrated—and rightly so. Exhibited in a darkened room with the spots directed exclusively at the elements of the painting—replicating perfectly the darkened interior of the duomo with the sunshine falling on the altar—the *Maestà* and *Storie* emerge with mesmerizing luminosity, a gilded beauty that no reproduction can adequately capture. Even in Italy, a country that has no equal in the splendor of its artistic treasures, Duccio's altar leaves a lasting, indelible impression. This is a classic—moving us today as much, perhaps, as it moved Duccio's contemporaries when it was revealed between 1308 and 1311. And yet, the painting is clearly dated. Perspective, foreshortening, coloration are all "hopelessly" pre-Renaissance with that "clumsiness" that we associate with medieval art in the period before the revolution that was beginning to burgeon just fifty kilometers to the north. Despite this, our appreciation of Duccio's creation is not archaeological—the way we often appreciate the art in certain archaeological sites as part of our general admiration for an ancient culture; it is not even anthropological—in which we attempt to the best of our ability to internalize the

Joseph H. H. Weiler is Manley Hudson Professor of Law and Jean Monnet Chair, Harvard Law School.

sensibilities of the epoch in order to try and live the beauty as experienced through the eyes of its contemporaries. In the case of Duccio and works such as his, our appreciation is measured by our current yardsticks, and the breathtaking pleasure we receive is because of the impact of the picture on our present-day sensibilities. It belongs to an earlier period, but it has qualities that transcend its time.

Fra Angelico, born sometime between 1386 and 1400, is, if anything, even more famous than Duccio. A visit to San Marco in Florence is de rigueur for even the casual visitor. He, too, in style and technique is pre-Renaissance or, at best, early Renaissance and is, thus, dated in a way similar to Duccio. None of his paintings, altarpieces, and *affreschi* have quite the same dramatic luminosity of Duccio's though the unsurpassed delicacy of line and coloration combined with his forceful themes clearly places him among the greats. And yet a closer look at a few of Angelico's masterpieces reveals a timelessness of an altogether different sort. Consider the *Crocifisso e Santi* at the San Niccolò del Ceppo Church in Florence or the *Cristo deriso* and a number of other items of the San Marco *Affreschi* and the *Armadio degli Argenti*. Despite their early style and technique, in their conception and creative imagination they transcend space and time. In my personal and unorthodox perception they could be by a Bosch who was born shortly before Angelico's death or, say, by our contemporary Dalí. These works of Fra Angelico are in various ways utterly modern, leapfrogging centuries of transition in the history of art.

II

Eric Stein would be embarrassed reading this foreword if he thought that his work was being compared to these timeless Italian masters. Such a comparison is not, needless to say, my purpose. We lawyers have a hefty measure of conceit, but we are not quite so reckless. But reflecting on Duccio and Fra Angelico does give us some keys to understanding the power, within its own domain, of this volume and also a way not only of learning and becoming wiser by reading the essays but also of enjoying the volume in its totality.

The essays collected here cover a generation of scholarship. Indeed, some of them, though published in, say, the 1970s find their origin in earlier research and work. And, yet, one cannot approach any of these essays as archaeology or anthropology. Each, in one of the two ways suggested previously, has the power to assault our present day sensibilities with their abiding relevance to the most current debates. "Harmonization of European Company Laws" will not, of course, give you chapter and verse on the latest nuance of this or that directive. In that respect it is dated. But read it with the recent debates about harmonization v. coordination, about subsidiarity, about the appropriate level of Union intervention in member state legal culture and you will find its calm insights, well, illuminating if not luminous. By contrast, read (or reread!) the famous "Citizen Access" coauthored with Vining. The piece spawned controversy and response and became a classic. After all these years it is thoroughly modernist: it is a legal essay and an essay about the law at one and the same time. It seeks to elucidate and explicate; it is comparative and sociological. In its open-endedness it even has a tinge of the postmodern.

As remarkable as the classical power of some of the earlier essays is the poignancy of the more recent ones. I know of no better analytical framework for the understanding of the European foreign policy apparatus covering both external relations and Political Cooperation and its aftermath than in this book. Here there is nothing dated. The work is contemporary and fully usable. The new cases just fit into their anticipated slots. Likewise the sad work in post–cold war Czecho/Slovakia displays youthful freshness with the wisdom of age. It is as insightful as anything in the recent avalanche of writing on Eastern Europe and the breakup of the Soviet empire.

Though difficult, I have my favorite in this retrospective, and I make no apologies that it is, arguably, the most celebrated of his essays.

"Tucked away in the fairyland Duchy of Luxembourg and blessed, until recently, with benign neglect by the powers that be and the mass media, the Court of Justice of the European Communities has fashioned a constitutional framework for a federal-type structure in Europe." This is the famous opening line of the 1981 article "Lawyers, Judges, and the Making of a Transnational Constitution" in the *American Journal of International Law.* It is a landmark in the literature on European integration and is among those works that ushered in the most important conceptual innovation of the field—the constitutional paradigm. It is interesting to locate the importance of this piece in the intellectual history of European integration.

What, then, are the roots of the constitutional paradigm?

In the beginning there was doctrine: the disparate legal doctrines of the court grappling to interpret the treaties, to solve concrete legal conundrums before it. Schuman said:

> Europe will not be made all at once, or according to a single, general plan. It will be built through concrete achievements, which first create a *de facto* solidarity.

This prediction—or prescription—certainly fits the first stages in constitutionalization. The first steps were just that—concrete steps. Momentous? Sure. But hardly part of a general plan and certainly not all at once. There is even truth to the de facto solidarity part of the Schuman declaration that fits constitutionalization. The success of the constitutional construct would depend not only, or even primarily, on the utterances of the European Court but on their acceptance by national actors, mainly courts, and principally national constitutional courts. That solidarity of national legal actors was achieved through concrete achievements, as the neo-neo functionalists were to argue convincingly, and has remained to this day in many cases more de facto than de jure.

For its part, the first *intellectual* stratum was the more traditional analysis of the judicial developments qua "doctrine": working out their contours, examining their reach, trying to understand their rationale and their legal significance. Some might dismiss this kind of work as intellectually empty, without systemic significance, and so on. And yet, this doctrinal work is the foundation for all that came after. Clever archaeologists may through flights of creative imagination construct rich interpretative narratives from fragments of pottery, debris of buildings, remnants of documents. But someone must have dug the fragments up, exposed the debris, salvaged the remnants. The original doctrinal work is truly foundational in this sense.

It is at this point that Eric Stein shifts the paradigm, for he realized that beyond the doctrine what was happening was the fashioning of a constitutional framework for a federal-type structure in Europe and he was bold enough to state this. It is a prime example of the second stratum in academic constitutional discourse about Europe. What this type of remarkable work did (and it, and some others like it, did a lot more besides) was to take disparate legal doctrines, to baptize them as "constitutional," and to put them together with the bold assertion that the whole was greater than the parts—that a constitutional framework had come into being long before the Court was willing to use that vocabulary or, arguably, even think in those terms.

The intellectual feat here was not simply one of conceptualization. There was already in that early work an interesting working out of relationships that involved legal and other actors. The work clearly understood that the constitutional framework was not primarily a doctrinal construct but that if it was to become a reality, it would depend on the construction of a political interpretative and epistemological community that would align itself with the constitutional paradigm. The work also understood that the emergence of such a construct was to be the subject of an empirical investigation, not of doctrinal exegesis. Today, with hindsight, we can quibble or even quarrel with the early description and analysis. But it does not take particular generosity of spirit to confess that much of the most contemporary work is erecting a tower to the scaffolding that Eric Stein had already put in place.

III

The final, obvious, lesson from the initial foray into the world of Italian art is not to approach this book simply for the learning and wisdom that its individual essays impart. Unfolding in this volume is the intellectual life of a master Europeanist, internationalist, and comparatist. Each essay is a picture in a carefully selected human and scholarly retrospective and should be read as such. Each is worthy of study not only in terms of the information and insight it contains but also in its lessons about approach, perspective, and style. Several can be used, with only slight modifications, as models for the endless stream of students who find fascination in European-American comparative analysis. The approach and conclusions of Stein will not necessarily appeal to all tastes, but in its lucidity, huge erudition, and analytical sharpness, the work displays timeless virtues.

But this is not simply a collection of essays. It is a retrospective wherein the whole is, and is meant to be, greater than the parts. There is one clear aspect of the collection that can be gleaned only from the whole and not from its parts. Eric Stein belongs to that severe school of scholarship that privileges moderation of tone, prudence of content, and the careful forensic investigation of the dramas of life to which the law is so often a mouthpiece. This approach (and style of writing) has, at times, been accused of simply burying its prejudices below its severe rhetorical surfaces and smuggling its moral normativity instead of declaring it at the frontier. It contrasts sharply with more overtly *engaged* and openly ideological scholarship that has become fashionable recently. Of course the latter often suffers from excessive narcissism and, not infrequently, a maddening intellectual and scholarly thinness when its ideas are exposed as banalities masquerading through the use of opaque language as profundities. Still, the dichotomy in its extreme polemical presentation is, naturally, false; but there is no point in trying to paper over clear differences in academic approaches or in engaging in futile apologetics. The work of Stein provides powerfully probative evidence for the qualities of temperance, suppression of the personal and the subjective in favor of a disciplined, rational discourse that is never naive but never pompous and self important either. That these classical virtues can be welcomed, let us admit it, as the proverbial breath of fresh air is a sign—maybe a sad sign—of the times.

And yet, from the whole rather than from each individual essay emerge clearly the deontological foundations on which practically all the essays are premised. Consider the emotive power achieved through the studied, glacial coldness—perhaps the only way to deal with that subject—of his narrative and analysis in the "Auschwitz Lie" essay. Consider the carefully hidden passion in his work on Czecho/Slovakia and his barely hidden sadness at the failure of the federal constitutional construct. Consider the very lifelong fascination with European integration. Consider the enigma of a life and an opus that are at one and the same time so American and yet so European. Consider the almost obsessive leitmotiv of reaching beyond boundaries that animates most of his essays. And, finally, consider the title he has given to the retrospective: *Thoughts from a Bridge.*

Eric Stein explains the whole as an intellectual fascination with divided power systems—with American federalism and European integration. We could add that it is the fascination of a human being whose own identity and very persona—utterly at home in America, utterly at home in Europe—is the bridge from whence the thoughts emerge.

But in the essays themselves, in their moral and spiritual content, what bridge is it that we are invited to traverse? It is a hallmark and strength of the person and of the work that these considerations are left unstated. But we may be free to speculate on these dimensions. This is how I, forever a student of Eric Stein, have tried to express what for me is the noble neo-Kantian sensibility underlying the entire work.

Europe was built on the ashes of World War II, which witnessed the most horrific alienation of those thought of as aliens, an alienation that became annihilation. The European construct was not simply about the prevention of another such carnage—that has been the easy part—but about dealing at a deeper level with the source of such attitudes. In the realm of the social, in the public square, the relationship to the alien is at the core of such decency. It defines the very self, collective and individual. Living in bounded identities, individual and social, the alien is not only ontologically constitutive of the self but deontologically as well. It is difficult to imagine something normatively more important to the human condition.

There are, it seems to me, two basic human strategies of dealing with the alien, and these two strategies have played a decisive role in Western civilization. One strategy is to remove the boundaries. It is the spirit of "come, be one of us." It is noble since it involves, of course, elimination of prejudice, of the notion that there are boundaries that cannot be eradicated. But the "be one of us," however well intentioned, is often an invitation to the alien to be one of us by being us. The strongest manifestation of this has been in the supersessionist version of

Christianity. Vis-à-vis the alien, it risks robbing him or her of identity. Vis-à-vis one's self, it may be a subtle manifestation of intolerance. If I cannot tolerate the alien, one way of resolving the dilemma is to make the alien like me, no longer an alien. This is, of course, infinitely better than the physical annihilation. But it is still a form of dangerous internal and external intolerance.

The alternative strategy is to acknowledge the validity of certain forms of bounded identity but simultaneously to reach across boundaries. We acknowledge and respect difference (and, no less importantly, what is special and unique about ourselves as individuals and groups), and yet we reach across differences in recognition of our essential humanity of being all born in the image of God. This, I think, is the essence of Mosaic law on this issue. It is not surprising that, according to tradition, the most ubiquitous norm in the Pentateuch is that which is designed to shield the alien. Here are some expressive examples: "And a stranger shalt thou not wrong, neither shalt thou oppress him; for ye were strangers in the land of Egypt" (Ex. 22:21); "And a stranger shalt thou not oppress; for ye know the heart of a stranger, seeing ye were strangers in the land of Egypt" (Ex. 23:9); "And if a stranger sojourn with thee in your land, ye shall not do him wrong" (Lev. 19:33).

Hermann Cohen (1842–1918), the great neo-Kantian philosopher of religion, in an exquisite modern interpretation of the Mosaic law on this subject captures its deep meaning in a way that retains its vitality even in today's "Ever Closer Union." It has been usefully summarized as follows: "This law of shielding the alien from all wrong is of vital significance. . . . The alien was to be protected, not because he was a member of one's family, clan, religious community or people; but because he was a human being. In the alien, therefore, man discovered the idea of humanity" (J. H. Hertz, The Pentateuch and Haftorahs, 313, 2d ed. [London: Soncino Press, 1980]). What is significant in this are the two elements I have mentioned: on the one hand, the identity of the alien, as such, is maintained. One is not invited to go out and say 'save him' by inviting him to be one of you. One is not invited to recast the boundary. On the other hand, despite the boundaries which are maintained, and constitute the I and the Alien, one is commanded to construct a bridge so as to reach over the boundary and accept him, in his alienship. The alien is accorded his essential human dignity.

This is, precisely, Eric Stein's bridge.

Acknowledgments

It is perhaps not surprising that the idea for this collection first surfaced in Europe rather than on this side of the Atlantic. Professor Cosimo Marco Mazzoni of the University of Siena, Italy, was instrumental in having a selection of my writings translated into Italian and published in the series of Guiristi Stranieri di Oggi (Foreign jurists of today), which he has been editing with Professor Vincenzo Varano. Professor Francesco Capotorti, then Advocate General at the Community Court of Justice, wrote an impressive introduction. Through some mysterious way, the handsome Italian volume published by Giuffrè of Milano found its way to the desk of Colin Day, the director of the University of Michigan Press. It was he who first suggested an English version, a curious inversion of the normal process. I am most grateful to him as well as to my friend Cosimo Mazzoni.

My warmest thanks go to Professor Louis Henkin of the Columbia University Law School and to my colleagues Professors Terrance Sandalow and Joseph Vining for authorizing the inclusion of the essays that they coauthored.

I doubt that this undertaking would have come to fruition without the persistent urging and advice of Professor Joseph H. H. Weiler of the Harvard Law School.

I am deeply grateful to my wife, Virginia, for her intelligent criticism and enthusiastic support, particularly during our at times exacting peregrinations.

Barbara Shapiro, Barbara Žežulka Brown, and Janis Proctor worked efficiently on the manuscript.

The excellent staff members of the University of Michigan Law Library under the leadership of Barbara Garavaglia-Vaccaro and Jonathan Franklin were most helpful.

Elisha Hadar helped greatly with the index.

Introduction

Five Variations on a Theme: Divided-Power Systems

Commonly, an aspiring young scholar receives his or her first lodestar from a mentor. In my case, on the contrary, it was the working experience that determined my orientation. Kurt Lipstein of Cambridge University has written in a survey of his lifetime scholarship: "The combination of doctrinal interest and, what may seem to be, antiquarian learning, which is in reality an attempt to comprehend any principle of permanence and universal validity, directed my early work." I was able to follow a like path only upon entering academia, much later in my life.

If I am pressed to encapsulate my central intellectual interest in a single phrase, I would say it has been the art of governance or the management of power in more or less complex divided-power systems. These systems range from a highly centralized federation on one end of the spectrum to a loose intergovernmental regime on the other. In between these two poles there is a multiplicity of "unions," confederate structures, and international organizations in an increasingly globalized international order. This line of inquiry responded also to my intuitive inclination to view law in a broad context since each such system is brought to life by a legal instrument, a constitution, a treaty, but its "living law" is shaped by the metalegal environment.

1. In a Divided Italy

My first working assignment after graduating from the Michigan Law School in 1942 was as a soldier-lawyer with the Allied Commission for Italy during World War II. The principal legal-political questions were posed by the division of power between the Italian king and his government on one hand and the Allied "belligerent occupant" on the other, in a novel situation of "co-belligerency" not contemplated by the current international law of war. As an aspect of the division of jurisdiction, a procedure was devised in the Legal Subcommission of the Allied Commission that made it possible for the king's government to legislate in the area returned by the Allied powers to Italian sovereignty, but the application of that legislation in the zone of operations controlled by the Allied military command was subject to approval by the Allied Commission.

This legal conceit proved baleful for a group of Italian partisans who had been fighting the retreating German army. In a newly liberated village they had shot a number of suspected fascist collaborators without even the semblance of a trial. When the case came before the Allied Military Tribunal, it transpired that had the killings occurred just a short distance south of the dividing line in the territory restored to Italian authorities, the partisans would not have faced a death penalty. In one of its first acts the new Italian government had abolished the ultimate penalty, which it viewed as a fascist excess contrary to an Italian tradition reaching deep into the nineteenth century. However, the relevant law was not extended to the Allied-controlled zone of operations because of military security needs. The case became a "cause célèbre," and on my return from Italy, I analyzed it within the framework of the international law of war in my first ever scholarly publication.[1]

In the Italian version of this collection, which includes this piece, I also describe other aspects of the work in the Legal Subcommission, such as the selection of the undersecretary for justice in the first post-fascist government of experts, the opening of Italian courts in the war torn areas, and later in Rome the liaison with the successive ministers of justice. I learned a great deal about the process of restoring democracy and a rule of law after the defeat of the fascist regime. The experience was comparable in some aspects to my encounter, half a century later, with the post-Communist transformation in central Europe, the last subject in this book.

2. In the Conflicted United Nations and NATO

During my postwar service with the Bureau of United Nations (later the Bureau of International Organizations) of the U.S. Department of State, I was asked in 1955 to discuss "the constitutional developments" of the UN political organs. Somewhat defensively, I said:

> Being a lawyer I must make it clear that I am using the term "constitutional" in the broadest sense . . . the UN is a loose association of sovereign states in a world fundamentally dominated by power considerations. We cannot analyze its problems in terms of an orderly community operating under a rule of law.[2]

In contrast, a quarter of century later, following the seminal rulings of the Court of Justice of the European Communities, I had no hesitation in styling the treaty establishing the European Economic Community as a "transnational constitution."

The core legal issues in the early years of the United Nations stemmed from a division of power vertically, between the United Nations organization and the member states, and horizontally, between the principal organs of the organization, not to speak of the tension within the power structure of the United States related to the problems on the UN agenda.

All that I wrote at the time—and the talks I gave—reflected the concerns of the working day, dominated by problems of decolonization and the emerging cold war. A series of challenging, novel interpretations of the UN Charter culminated in the controversial Uniting for Peace Resolution of 1950, which was designed to mobilize the vetoless all-member General Assembly when the Security Council was blocked by a Soviet veto. John Foster Dulles argued in the assembly that the principle of "balance of power" among the UN organs must be complemented by the principle of "compensation of power" so that if one organ is incapacitated another must take over. On its face a horizontal, interorgan confrontation, in reality the resolution raised serious national power concerns on the parts of all the permanent members of the Council endowed with the privilege of the veto. I looked back at this encounter in a piece for a symposium at the Heidelberg Max Planck Institute for Foreign Public and International Law.[3] In a similar vein, I speculated on the far-reaching implications of the enlargement of United Nations membership.[4]

Analyzing Secretary General Hammarskjöld's important report on the situation in the Congo, I noted his concern about the scope of his discretion, large enough to expose the international Secretariat to heated political controversy and to accusations of lack of neutrality. At a time when the Security Council and the General Assembly showed decreasing interest in law-oriented charter interpretation, the Secretary General displayed a great skill in legal reasoning as a method for reducing the area of his discretion.[5]

An interpretive issue that occupied the UN Assembly for weeks and months at a time turned on the conflict, insoluble on its face, between the broad powers of discussion and recommendation granted the assembly by the UN Charter and the charter prohibition of intervention in matters "essentially within the domestic jurisdiction of any state." "In terms of raw reality," I wrote in 1955:

> the problem is to reconcile, on the one hand the forces of change, i.e. nationalism, anti-colonialism, anti-westernism, with the forces of status quo. . . . In an important measure the maintenance of

> peace depends upon the reconciliation of these forces. The problem is complicated for the free world because the Soviet Union is all out for change in the free world [Tunisia, Morocco, Indonesia, Greece, South Africa] but firmly committed to the unhappy status quo behind the Iron Curtain [the case of human rights clauses in the Peace Treaties with Bulgaria, Hungary and Romania].[6]

In the last mentioned case concerning the state of basic human rights in Eastern Europe, the Soviet Union and its allies fought in vain to keep the General Assembly from dealing with the matter; the assembly decided to ask the International Court of Justice for an advisory opinion on the interpretation of the relevant treaty clauses. In its first appearance ever before that Court, the United States presented its view on the case. I was adviser to the U.S. representative, Benjamin V. Cohen, a brilliant Washington lawyer and member of President Roosevelt's "brain trust."

Those of us who witnessed the bitter controversies over the assembly's authority to include a matter on its agenda could not foresee that within a decade the issue would vanish into thin air and the reach of the domestic jurisdiction article would be drastically reduced. This was due not only to the end of the decolonization era but also to the emerging international law on individual basic rights.

The problems of unanimity as against majority voting, defining the limits of jurisdiction, and membership enlargement resonated later, albeit in a radically different context, in the emerging European divided-power system.

In one instance I was actually present at the creation of a divided-power system. As a member of a small international team, I participated in turning a blank piece of paper into the charter of the UN-linked International Atomic Energy Agency. This was at a time when the demand for control over military uses of the new technology and the deceptively alluring potential of its peaceful application posed a Faustian dilemma.[7]

In the whirlwind of "parliamentary democracy" (Dean Rusk) in New York and in Washington, DC, there was little chance for a doctrinal or theoretical exploration of the changing international system. But I had no question where I stood in the quarrel between the "realists" of the Hans Morgenthau persuasion centering on preponderance of national power and those like Philip Jessup, then U.S. Ambassador at Large,[8] advocating collective security and the international rule of law through the UN and related instrumentalities. In fact, the staff of the UN Bureau in the Department of State, drawn from outside the traditional diplomatic service, enthusiastically pursued the vision of such a global system. Yet in the face of the emerging postwar power play, this utopia soon gave way to what I would best describe as enlightened "functional pragmatism" (Martti Koskenniemi).

Some years later, I returned briefly to the issues of international arms control in a book on the crucial negotiations for a ban on testing nuclear weapons and in my Hague Academy lectures exploring the impact of arms control measures on general international law.[9]

When the North Atlantic Treaty was negotiated in 1948 it was conceived as a collective defense agreement pure and simple, within the meaning of the much discussed Article 51 of the UN Charter; after its ratification and proclamation, it would be placed on a shelf as a clear warning to a potential aggressor against Western Europe. At the time it was not expected that the treaty would give rise to the most elaborate multinational military command structure since the end of World War II. When de Gaulle's France decided to withdraw from the integrated command while remaining a party to the North Atlantic Treaty, I became interested in the complex issues of international treaty law and the law of international organization within that divided-power system and the significant security and political implications of the withdrawal. I wrote a study on the subject with a French graduate student, now an established member of a Paris University law faculty.[10]

I left the Department of State with a sense of disillusion over the failure of the member governments to make the United Nations, the first truly global divided-power system, live up to its shining promise. When I went to say good-bye to Secretary of State John Foster Dulles, he left me with the following advice: "Until now, when you spoke you were listened to because you spoke for the United States, but in the classroom you will be speaking for yourself only"—the implication being that I had better know my subject. Yet I soon found out that whatever I expounded in class was promptly inscribed in class notes with only an occasional challenge.

3. In an Integrating Europe

It is easy to understand—and I tell the story in the "Coda" section of this book—why I became intrigued from the very outset by the European Community experiment, the most advanced divided-power system in the international arena.

At the beginning I faced problems on how to organize the brand new subject for research and for teaching in an American law school. The challenge was to devise a conceptual framework that would meet the doctrinal standards while respecting the needs of professional training for an expanding international legal practice. I learned quickly that I needed a great deal of advice and assistance.

In 1957–58, before the Rome treaties establishing the European Economic Community and EURATOM had come into force, I commissioned a series of essays by European and American scholars to which I contributed a chapter on the overview, institutions, and (with Peter Hay) the new legal remedies. The principal purpose of the collection, published in two volumes, was to provide a picture of the new legal structure and project the treaty text against national legislation of the member states apt to be affected as the Common Market moved forward.[11] The most important by-product of this work was the setting up of a dense network of European scholars, officials, judges, parliamentarians, and practitioners whose cooperation became essential for the Michigan program. This collection was followed two decades later by the "Bellagio papers" excerpted in Part 2 of this book.

Beginning in 1963, we published a series of volumes designed to serve as guides to research and law teaching. They reflect a strong influence of Ernst Haas's innovative early version of neofunctionalism. If I were to identify a pervading doctrinal theme, it would be the Court of Justice's own vision of the Community as I described it in the first essay of this collection, "Lawyers, Judges, and the Making of a Transnational Constitution"; and, as a corollary, an emphatic rejection of formalist legal positivism that contrasts sharply with the Court's teleological jurisprudence. I kept in mind what a lawyer should know as government adviser and negotiator, diplomat, and corporate counsel and, last but not least, as an attorney in international practice. The multiple objectives necessitated drawing upon concepts, materials, and methodologies of several legal disciplines, international law, conflict of laws, national public and private law, and the "law of international transactions," and also upon sources in political science, economics, and history.

The principal theme of the first two editions was a systematic projection of the European Community and other regional institutions and their goals against the worldwide institutions and their goals. This we sought to accomplish in a trilevel scheme by observing the judicial, quasi-judicial, or coordinating processes in national (West European and American), regional (Atlantic), and global structures. The principal sectors of activities included the movement of goods, factors of production, foreign commercial policies, protection of basic rights, and defense cooperation.[12]

A new edition of this work was published four years later in 1967.[13]

By that time the grid of Community law had become substantially denser as the construction of the internal common market progressed, and the Community began to emerge as a significant actor on the international scene. This meant that the Community and European integration became the centerpiece, commanding most of the space in the book. It meant also narrowing the scope of the worldwide coverage, but we added for purposes of comparison the tentative moves toward integration in Latin America, influenced by the European model. The book was adopted widely, and for some two decades it was the only work of its kind on the market.

Over the years, I have published some sixty pieces on a variety of aspects of European integration with the ubiquitous divided-power theme at the center or lurking in the background. For me, the European Community offered a compensation—intellectually, professionally, emotionally—for the "failure" of the United Nations. Scaled down from the worldwide to a regional dimension, the vision of a multinational order under a rule of law appeared within the realm of possibility. In fact, I became a firm believer in, if not a protagonist of, the European integration process, although aware of the danger of seeing only what I wanted to see, not unlike Wallace Stevens's famous blue guitar player.

> They said, "You have a blue guitar,
> You do not play things as they are."
> The man replied, "Things as they are
> Are changed upon the blue guitar."

It is perhaps both naive and immodest to ask whether the guitar players on both sides of the Atlantic, intoning the European unity theme, could and did—in some measure at any rate—"change the things" as they were.

4. In a Mature Federal System

On joining the University of Michigan law faculty in 1956, I found myself once more in an environment where divided-power topics—this time in an academic context within the framework of a centralized federation—have been the subject of a day-to-day intense discourse. In fact, most of the essays in this book reflect this atmosphere, but they also illustrate the perils of viewing contemporary Europe through the prism of the American federal experience.

Along with federalism came thoughts about constitutionalism and democracy, unity and diversity, the individual and the community, and the individual in the changing international system, as well as an exposure to more recent theories and methodologies and the links of the law to other disciplines.

My colleague William W. Bishop's innovative casebook, from which I was teaching my course in international law, aroused my interest in the use of international law in domestic legal orders and in particular the right of an individual to rely directly on a treaty before a domestic tribunal. I participated in comparative studies designed to explore the extent to which national constitutions and practices open their domestic courts to international law.[14] In the regional context, at any rate, suits by individuals and companies pursuing their claims under the Common Market Treaty in member state courts have proved to be the most effective instrumentality for enforcing the treaty-constitution canon. At the global level, the right of an individual to pursue a claim under a treaty in domestic courts is as important for the strengthening of the rule of law in an essentially state-based international system as it is for the enhancement of the status of an individual in that system. I returned to the topic in connection with my incursion into post-Communist Europe, and I have noted a number of the new constitutions that provide generous openings for international law into the national legal orders, affirming a worldwide trend diagnosed earlier by Antonio Cassese.[15]

Endemic to systems composed of two or more component units is the problem of harmonization or unification of laws and policies. A prior condition to such activities is a comparative study of the laws and policies prevailing within the discrete units. The comparative legal method becomes a standard tool for the central regulator, lawmaker, and judiciary, as well as for the scholar-observer. And one becomes easily enticed into comparing corresponding processes in other divided-power systems. Thus I was drawn into comparisons in such areas as constitutional, administrative, company, and foreign affairs law, happily with the indispensable assistance of experts in the fields concerned.

5. In the Czech-Slovak Federation

In part 3 of this collection, I describe the circumstances under which I was lured back to central Europe after more than half a century—to be confronted again with a divided-power dilemma, this time in the context of the faltering Czech-Slovak federation. What began as negotiations on a full range of issues of federalism, constitutionalism, and democracy against the background of deep political, societal, and economic transformations turned into an exercise in ethnic conflict resolution through a uniquely orderly separation. In addition to a book, I have published a series of articles based on this experience.

That chance (or predestination?) plays a major role in human destiny is a common experience. What gives my story a particular twist is the persistent congruence between the chance opportunities that opened at critical stages and my intellectual interest and bent. I confess to having become fully conscious of this correlation only on writing this introductory section.

Note: No effort was made to update the republished pieces. In a number of instances, however, I thought it necessary to add a new footnote or to insert new information into an existing footnote. "Update:" precedes each such addition.

The brief introductions preceding each chapter also refer to some major developments that occurred after the publication of the individual essays.

Notes

1. "Application of the Law of the Absent Sovereign in Territory under Belligerent Occupation: The Schio Massacre," 46 MICH. L. REV. 341 (1948).
2. "Constitutional Developments of United Nations Political Organs," in INTERNATIONAL LAW AND THE UNITED NATIONS, Eighth Summer Institute, University of Michigan Law School, June 23–25, 1955, 347.
3. "Collective Enforcement of International Obligations," 47 ZEITSCHRIFT FÜR AUSLÄNDISCHES ÖFFENTLICHES RECHT UND VÖLKERRECHT 56 (1987).
4. "Some Implications of Expanding United Nations Membership," Carnegie Endowment for International Peace (1956); also in 12 EUROPA ARCHIV (1957).
5. "Mr. Hammarskjöld, the Charter Law, and the Future Role of the United Nations Secretary General," 56 AJIL 9 (1962).
6. "Constitutional Developments of United Nations Political Organs," *supra* note 2, 352.
7. "Atoms for Peace: The New International Atomic Energy Agency" (with B. G. Bechhoefer), 55 MICH. L. REV. 747 (1957); "The New International Atomic Energy Agency," 51 Proceedings, AM. SOC. INT'L L. 158 (1957).
8. As an adviser to the U.S. delegation to the UN General Assembly I had the privilege of working with Ambassador Jessup in New York. I wrote a foreword to his Cooley lectures delivered at the University of Michigan Law School. Philip C. Jessup, THE USE OF INTERNATIONAL LAW: FIVE LECTURES DELIVERED AT THE UNIVERSITY OF MICHIGAN, FEBRUARY 27, 28, MARCH 3, 6, AND 7, 1958 (University of Michigan Law School, Ann Arbor, 1959), vii.
9. DIPLOMATS, SCIENTISTS AND POLITICIANS: THE UNITED STATES AND THE

Nuclear Test Ban Negotiations (with Harold K. Jacobson) (Ann Arbor, University of Michigan Press, 1966); Impact of New Weapons Technology on International Law: Selected Aspects (Hague Academy of International Law, Recueil des Cours, 1971), vol. 1, 225.

10. "Law and Peaceful Change in a Subsystem: 'Withdrawal' of France from the North Atlantic Treaty Organization" (with Dominique Carreau), 62 AJIL 577 (1968).

11. American Enterprise in the European Common Market—A Legal Profile (with T. L. Nicholson, ed.), 2 vols. (Michigan Legal Studies, University of Michigan Law School, Ann Arbor, 1959, 1960).

12. Law and Institutions in the Atlantic Area—Readings, Cases and Problems (with Peter Hay), (Indianapolis: Bobbs-Merril Co., 1963, 1967).

13. European Community Law and Institutions in Perspective—Text, Cases and Readings (with Peter Hay and Michel Waelbroeck (Indianapolis: Bobbs-Merril Co., 1963, 1967, 1976). Supplement (with Joseph H. H. Weiler added as coeditor) (1985).

14. Reports given at the International Academy of Comparative Law: Sixth International Congress, Hamburg, August 1962, and General Report pp. 1–27 for the Ninth International Congress of Comparative Law, 1974.

15. "International Law in Internal Law: Toward Internationalization of Central-Eastern European Constitutions," 88 AJIL 428 (1994).

PART 1

Constitutionalizing, Harmonizing

Lawyers, Judges, and the Making of a Transnational Constitution

By "constitutionalizing" the European Community Treaty, I mean attributing certain prerogatives to that treaty that are germane to a modern federal constitution, such as broad direct effect of Community law on citizens and its supremacy over members' state law. I ask in this essay who are the principal actors in this process and how far has it advanced.

*For international lawyers born and bred in the positivist and dualist tradition, turning an international treaty into a "quasi-constitution" is an oxymoron. For national constitutional lawyers of the same bent of mind, the supremacy of a "foreign" canon in internal law signaled a breach of the internal constitutional order. For some scholars in the United Kingdom, where there is no written constitution and statutory interpretation is the tradition, the Community Court of Justice has exceeded its powers beyond redemption. The German Constitutional Court—which, paradoxically, was the first tribunal to speak of the Community Treaty as a constitution—insists on retaining ultimate control over the impact of the constitutionalizing process on the German legal order. Yet, the constitutional structure of the European Community erected in the early decisions of its Court of Justice has met the test of time and has been broadly accepted by national judiciary.**

In the "Coda" section of this collection I relate the early debate on these issues within the Legal Service of the Community Commission as it was

---

Reprinted from 75 AMERICAN JOURNAL OF INTERNATIONAL LAW 1 (Jan. 1981). I wish to acknowledge with appreciation the research assistance of Sabine Hackspiel, Cologne University, LLM University of Michigan.

A version of this article was prepared as a contribution to a volume in honor of Prof. Dr. Konrad Zweigert, Director of the Max Planck Institute for Foreign and Private International Law in Hamburg.

*See also on this topic "Toward Supremacy of Treaty Constitution by Judicial Fiat: On the Margin of the Costa Case," 63 MICH. L. REV. 491 (1965), also in XLVIII Rivista di diritto internazionale 3 (1965); "The Emerging European Constitution," in Proceedings of the 72nd Annual Meeting of the American Society of International Law, April 1978, 166 *passim;* "Treaty-Based Federalism, A.D. 1978: A Gloss on Covey Oliver at the Hague Academy," 127 U. OF PENN. L. REV. 897 (1979); Development of Judicial Control of the European Communities, by Gerhard Bebr, book review, 78 AJIL 692 (1984).

developing the positions for presentation to the Court. Subsequent events have confirmed my conclusion that without the Commission's stand, embraced in substance by the Court, the Community might well have turned into "little more than a regional General Agreement on Tariffs and Trade," with its rules "observed more in the breach."

But even GATT, reincarnated in the World Trade Organization, has embarked on a modicum of "constitutionalization" in its novel dispute settlement system. Not surprisingly, the innovation raised questions in the United States about the compatibility with the federal constitution of the potential intrusion into the American legal order. This poses an interesting question: the Community was spawned by international law; will its constitutional doctrine (direct effect, supremacy, preemption, and judicial review) have a boomerang effect on international law and on the thinking of international lawyers?

I might add a comparative observation illustrating a difference between the European and American judicial cultures. Only rarely would an American sitting judge comment on an issue involved in a case in which he or she participated, or expatiate on controversial legal-political questions of the day; the European Court judges (and German judges as well) have been doing it with some frequency. Earlier European practice, noted in note 4 of this essay, has continued as exemplified by Judge Federico Mancini, mentioned in the closing section of the essay in Part 2 entitled, "Panel Statement on Democracy without 'a People' " and Judge Paul Kirchhoff of the German Constitutional Court in Frankfurter Allgemeine Zeitung of December 4, 1996, Wirtschaft, p. 11.

Tucked away in the fairyland Duchy of Luxembourg and blessed, until recently, with benign neglect by the powers that be and the mass media, the Court of Justice of the European Communities has fashioned a constitutional framework for a federal-type structure in Europe. From its inception a mere quarter of a century ago, the Court has construed the European Community Treaties in a constitutional mode rather than employing the traditional international law methodology. Proceeding from its fragile jurisdictional base, the Court has arrogated to itself the ultimate authority to draw the line between Community law and national law. Moreover, it has established and obtained acceptance of the broad principle of direct integration of Community law into the national legal orders of the member states and of the supremacy of Community law within its limited but expanding area of competence over any conflicting national law.

The European judicial process, characterized by a symbiotic relationship between national courts and the Court of Justice, is a complex dialectic process—even more intricate than that of a divided-power national judicial system such as in a federation. A great variety of participants interact in a number of fora, but the dominant groups are clearly the legal elite:

1. The judges of the Court of Justice, acting as a *collegium.*[1]
2. The Advocates General of the Court, "officers of the Court" assigned the principal task of stating in a public session their personal, independent opinion for the benefit of the Court, not unlike the Commissaires du Gouvernement at the French Conseil d'Etat.
3. The Legal Service of the executive Commission of the Communities, headed by the Director General, which determines the position of the Commission as plaintiff, defendant, or "*amicus curiae*" before the Court.[2]
4. The Legal Counsel and Director General at the Council of Ministers with his staff, performing corresponding tasks for the ministers and for the complex committee system under the Committee of the Permanent Representatives.
5. Lawyers in the national ministries and other offices of the member states, who advise their governments, and in effect formulate the positions taken in the governments' name as plaintiffs, defendants, "*amici curiae,*" or intervenors.
6. Judges on national courts and attorneys appearing before them in litigation that involves Community law and is referred to the Court of Justice for a "preliminary ruling."[3]
7. Legal scholars and writers. The great influence traditionally exerted on the continental judiciary by legal doctrine has been somewhat overshadowed by the growing impact of, and respect for, the case law. However, the judges and the Advocates General of the Court of Justice often assume the role of scholarly writers. Their publications and speeches on issues facing the Court and the seminars they offer for members of national judiciaries greatly facilitate the propagation and acceptance of the Court's rulings.[4]
8. The "legal establishment" in political arenas at the national and European levels, where laws and policies are made, influences the judicial process indirectly.

It would exceed the scope of this essay to undertake a comprehensive inquiry into the roles of all the participants and—the notorious quantifiers should beware!—to attempt to measure their relative impact. I have limited my task to a study of the positions of the Commission, the member governments and the Advocates General before the Court, and of the opinions of the Court itself, as stated in the official published case reports. It is reasonably safe to assume that although the issues determined in the judicial process often have significant long-term implications, the political decision makers view them mostly as "technical," and thus lawyers are given a more or less free hand to speak for the Commission, the Council, and the national governments.

A major purpose of this study has been to observe whether, in advancing the legal integration of the Community, the Court has followed the lead of the Commission or, to the contrary, whether it has pressed the frontiers of the constitutional development without the support, or even against the advice, of the Community's "executive-political" branch. Similarly, I have attempted to discern the relationship over time between the Court's position and that of the Advocates General. The attitudes of national governments are also of considerable interest to the extent that they can be determined from the Court's reports.

I have selected from among more than a thousand cases a small sampling of major opinions in which "constitutional law was made." The chosen cases deal with four categories of legal issues: the power of the Court of Justice to decide which provisions of Community law are to be given "direct effect" in national law and the consequences of such decisions; the supremacy, or—to use the more modest term preferred by the Court—the "precedence," of Community law over national law, including national constitutions; the extension of the "direct effect" principle in three important directions; and the scope of the Community's treaty-making power.

On "Penetrating" National Law: The "Direct Effect" Principle

The cornerstone for the constitutional evolution was the Court's judgment in the celebrated *van Gend* case,[5] which arose during the early stages of formation of the customs union, before internal tariffs within the Community were completely dismantled. Article 12 of the European Economic Community Treaty[6]—the so-called standstill provision—required the member states to refrain from increasing customs duties on imports from other member states. A Dutch firm that imported chemicals from the German Federal Republic sued the Dutch Tax Administration before the Tariefcommissie, a Dutch tribunal, alleging that the customs duty it had been required to pay was imposed in violation of this article. After the

Treaty had come into effect, the Netherlands implemented a Benelux[7] Protocol, with the result that the chemical in question was reclassified and charged with a higher duty. The Tariefcommissie then asked the Court of Justice for a ruling on whether Article 12 "has direct application within the territory of a Member State, in other words, whether nationals of such State can, on the basis of the Article in question, lay claim to an individual right which the courts must protect."[8]

The views pressed upon the Court of Justice reflected the full spectrum of attitudes regarding the division of power between the Community and the member states. The Belgian, Dutch, and German Governments, appearing in the case,[9] took the position most solicitous of national sovereignty, while the Commission advocated the most advanced "pro-Community" posture, with the Advocate General choosing a position closer to that of the member state governments.

Who Decides? The Problem of Jurisdiction

The Governments denied the jurisdiction of the Court to deal with the request from the Dutch tribunal at all.[10] They relied both on an interpretation of the Treaty and on international law practice with respect to treaties. In the Community system, the argument went, a charge against a member state of Treaty infringement as was involved in this case might be brought before the Court only by the Commission or by another member state pursuant to the procedure specifically made available in Articles 169 and 170; it could not be referred to the Court of Justice by a national court under Article 177 lest "the legal protection" of the state be "considerably diminished."[11] Moreover, the jurisdictional argument continued, even if such a reference was admissible in principle, the issue was the effect in Dutch internal law of an international treaty; according to established international law practice, this issue must be determined exclusively by Dutch constitutional law. Consequently, because the question was one of "application" and not of "interpretation" of the Treaty and also because the ruling was not "necessary" for the adjudication of the case in the Dutch tribunal, it was not appropriate for the Court of Justice to consider the matter in an Article 177 procedure. Neither Advocate General Roemer nor the Commission was prepared to follow the Governments on the question of lack of jurisdiction.[12]

The Commission insisted that the effect of a Treaty provision in national law is a question of interpretation of the Treaty to be determined without regard to the respective national law. The Commission was also concerned that if the Court were to refuse to entertain a reference from a national court, individual rights would have no protection under Community law in cases of a Treaty infringement by a member state.[13]

The Court might have chosen, in the interest of safeguarding the integrity of the national legal orders, to embrace the position urged by the Netherlands and Belgium, refusing jurisdiction, with the result that only the Commission or the member states could have brought actions against a member state's infringement of Community law before the Court in accordance with Articles 169 and 170. The Court, however, declined to do this and instead upheld its jurisdiction. The Court appeared primarily concerned with effective enforcement of the Treaty and with the protection of individuals whose "vigilance" in pressing their own rights adds to "effective supervision."[14]

It is safe to say, with the benefit of hindsight, that had the Court followed the Governments, Community law would have remained an abstract skeleton, and a great variety and number of Treaty violations would have remained undisclosed and unredressed. To date, only a single case has been decided by the Court upon the complaint of a member state under Article 170, and a relatively limited number were instituted by the Commission under Article 169.[15] Until quite recently, the Commission obviously hesitated to aggravate its fragile relationships with member governments by bringing them into the Court—and a decision by a member government to sue another posed political difficulties of a similar nature. In contrast, most of the "constitutional" cases, as well as the cases in which the Court fashioned such concepts as illegal "charges equivalent to customs duties" or "measures equivalent to quantitative restrictions" into tools for striking down national protectionist legislation, were referred to the Court under Article 177 as a result of litigation instituted by individuals or companies against their governments, as, for example, in *van Gend.* Similarly, it is unlikely that the Court would have had the opportunity to develop the extensive case law on discriminatory state taxation if it had accepted the arguments against its jurisdiction.

By What Criteria and with What Effect?

On the merits of the issue, the three Governments as well as the Advocate General proceeded from the basic assumption that the Treaty was no different from any "standard international treaty." According to the traditional international law analysis applicable to such a treaty, it is the intention of the parties that determines whether any of its provisions should be attributed "internal" effect.[16] In the case of Article 12, the actual wording was clear enough to establish the intention of the parties only to impose an international obligation on member states,[17] which had to be implemented subsequently by national legislative authorities before it became a part of national law.[18] But even if Article 12 had been intended by the parties to have "internal effect," the decision would be made under Dutch constitutional law whether it would be given "direct effect" in the sense of enabling the plaintiff to assert a subjective right in a Dutch court.[19]

The Advocate General accepted essentially the same doctrinal basis, but his criteria for treaty interpretation were somewhat broader. In his view, an analysis of the Treaty based on "the wording," "material content and its context" disclosed the intention of the parties that only certain provisions of the Treaty (such as the prohibitions against anticompetitive practices in Articles 85 and 86, and Article 177) were designed to produce direct effect, with the understanding that only in those member states whose constitutional law makes international treaties directly applicable ("self-executing") could such Treaty provisions be directly enforced even if contrary to local law. Many other Treaty provisions, however, including Article 12, that "expressly refer to the obligations of Member States" and do not contain such unambiguous terms as "prohibited," "without effect," or "inadmissible" were not intended to have such effect, "in particular insofar as they are not addressed to nationals."[20] Judged by its "content" and "object," Article 12, if directly applied, would infringe on the legislative powers still retained by member states in customs matters; it would make possible judicial review of legislation by national courts in member states in which such review in principle does not exist; and, contrary to the Commission's view, it would increase legal uncertainty in the complex and continually changing customs law system.

Although accepting the intention of the parties as a point of departure, the Commission's argument turns in a radically different direction. An analysis of the legal structure of the Treaty and of the legal system it establishes shows that not only did the member states intend to undertake mutual obligations, but—unlike parties to ordinary treaties—they aimed at establishing a system of Community law which must be applied effectively and uniformly throughout the Community. As a result, the effect of Community law (including the Treaty) in national law cannot be determined by reference to the respective national laws but only by Community law itself; and national courts are bound not only to apply directly the rules of Community law but also to ensure that the rules prevail over conflicting national law even if the national law is later in time. Moreover, a Community rule, such as Article 12, even if it is formally addressed only to member states, must nevertheless be given direct effect and allowed to penetrate into the national legal order, providing that it is capable of being effectively applied by national courts, that it is "perfectly clear" in the sense of creating for the member states "a specific unambiguous obligation" in a matter affecting their nationals and not qualified by any other provision of the Treaty, and that it is "complete and self sufficient" in that it does not require any Community measure making the obligation concrete.[21]

On this issue, the Court followed the lead of the Commission, with one, or perhaps two, qualifications discussed below. The Court discarded the criterion of subjective intention of the parties and offered instead a criterion that appears to provide a somewhat broader framework for analysis than the contextual, object-and-purpose-oriented indicia specified in the Vienna Convention on the Law of Treaties.[22] To ascertain whether a provision of an international treaty gives nationals of the state party a right which national courts must protect, it is necessary to consider, the Court stated, "*the spirit, the general scheme and the wording of these provisions,*"[23] a formula that the Court invoked subsequently with some variations in all the major constitutional pronouncements. Applying this formula to the EEC Treaty, the Court held, echoing the Commission, that the Treaty objectives, the "institutions endowed with sovereign rights," and the significant role assigned to individual citizens imply that "this Treaty is more than an agreement which merely creates mutual obligations between the contracting parties."[24]

> The conclusion to be drawn from this is that the Community constitutes a new legal order of international law for the benefit of which the states have limited their sovereign rights, albeit within limited fields, and the subjects of which comprise not only Member States but also their nationals. Independently of the legislation of Member States, Community law therefore not only imposes obligations on individuals but is also intended to confer upon them rights which become part of their legal heritage. These rights arise not only where they are expressly granted by the Treaty, but also by reason of obligations which the Treaty imposes in a clearly defined way upon individuals as well as upon the Member States and upon the institutions of the Community.[25]

The "general scheme" of the Treaty concerning intra-Community customs duties, according to the Court, postulates the essential prohibition of these duties which is "applied and explained by Article 12." The wording of that article contains "a clear and unconditional prohibition" which is framed not as a "positive" obligation to act but as a "negative" obligation to refrain from acting and which is "not qualified" by any reservation by a member state that would make its implementation conditional upon national legislation, and thus is "ideally adapted to produce direct effects."[26]

It may be of interest to compare the Court's criteria with those applied by the Permanent Court of International Justice in 1928 in determining whether an agreement between Poland and Danzig was intended to create individual rights enforceable in national courts. Parting from the "well established principle of international law" that an international agreement "cannot, as such, create direct rights and obligations for private individuals," the Permanent Court nevertheless held that "it cannot be disputed that the very object of an international agreement, according to the intention of the contracting Parties, may be the adoption by the Parties of some definite rules creating individual rights and obligations and enforceable by the national courts."[27] The intention of the two parties in question would be determined from the *contents,* the *wording,* and the *general tenor* of the agreement and from the *manner in which it was applied.* On that basis the Permanent Court concluded that certain provisions of the agreement did indeed have direct effect in the above sense, although the particular obligations were addressed only to a governmental agency of the state that was a party to the agreement. The majority of international law scholars[28] read this opinion as creating a presumption against direct effect, to be rebutted only by explicit evidence of the intention of the parties to the contrary. If that is the correct interpretation of the Permanent Court's view, the Court of Justice may be said to have taken a different position: because of the particular character of the Community Treaty, any presumption must be held to work in favor of, rather than against, direct effect. In any case, as Professor Waelbroeck rightly observes, the *Danzig* case reasoning would hardly fit modern conditions since it arose at a time when government intervention in national economies was still limited, when treaties intended to affect private parties were relatively rare, and agreements designed to harmonize and even integrate national economic and social policies were nonexistent.[29]

In the crucial part of the *van Gend* holding, the Court ruled that Article 12 "produces direct effects and creates individual rights which national courts must protect."[30] In effect, the Court has established the "direct effect" concept as a general operational principle of the Community system with the result that in due course most of the substantive provisions of the Treaty, although addressed to member states, have been turned into rules that individual plaintiffs may invoke—and have invoked on numerous occasions—in national courts. The Courts, however, stopped short of taking the next step, which the Commission viewed as a necessary and logical consequence of the direct effect principle: the Court failed to say that a Treaty provision which is entitled to direct effect must by the same token prevail over any national law, regardless of the constitutional practice followed in a given member state in this respect. Clearly, the court exercised "judicial restraint" since the questions put to it by the Dutch judge did not require it to take a position on the "supremacy" issue. The strong opposition from member governments and its own Advocate General may have convinced the Court that its ruling affirming the direct effect principle in broadest terms was "sufficient for the day," as far as it went.

In one other respect the Court appeared to qualify its ruling: Article 12 has direct effect because, *inter alia,* its prohibition entails not a "positive" but a "negative" obligation, an obligation *not* to act. This limitation, as we shall see, proved of short duration.

On Supremacy without a "Supremacy Clause"

The Principle

A year after *van Gend,* the Court was faced squarely with the issue left unresolved in that case, *i.e.,* whether a directly applicable Treaty provision must *ipso jure* prevail in national courts over conflicting national legislation. In *Costa v. ENEL,*[31] a case originating before a justice of peace in Milan, Italy, a customer and shareholder of a nationalized power company challenged the Italian law nationalizing the electric power industry as being contrary to both the Italian Constitution and the EEC Treaty. The justice of peace referred the allegations respectively to the Italian Constitutional Court and to the Court of Justice. The Constitutional Court ruled that because the nationalization law was adopted by the Parliament after the law approving the EEC Treaty, in any conflict between the two the former must prevail according to the principle *lex posterior derogat priori.* Consequently, there was no basis for the Milan justice to appeal to the Court of Justice.[32]

In line with this decision, the Italian Government claimed in the proceeding before the Court of Justice that the reference to that Court was "absolutely inadmissible" since the Italian lower court must apply the nationalization law only as the latest expression of the parliamentary will and "cannot avail itself of Article 177."[33] In addition, the Government revived the Dutch-Belgian argument previously rejected in the *van Gend* case that only the procedures in Articles 169 and 170 may be invoked against Treaty infringement by a member state. The Commission, the Advocate General, and the Court again rejected the jurisdictional argument and agreed that, as in *van Gend,* the Court should rule on whether the Treaty articles that were allegedly infringed must be interpreted as having direct effect in Italian law. And the Court proceeded to give such a ruling on the four Treaty articles listed by the referring Italian judge.

The Commission, having urged the concept of supremacy of Community law in *van Gend,* here limited itself—if the published record tells the full story—to observations on the issues of relevance and jurisdiction and on the interpretation of the Treaty articles in question. It manifested its concern, however, about the repercussions of the judgment of the Constitutional Court "on the future of Community law as a whole."[34] With an eye on that judgment, the Court, this time supported by Advocate General Lagrange, held that a national law, whether adopted before or after the effective date of the Treaty, "cannot take precedence over Community law."[35] Pointing again to the characteristics that distinguish the EEC Treaty from "ordinary international treaties,"[36] in particular to the Community's "real powers stemming from the limitation of sovereignty or a transfer of power from the States," the Court declared that "the integration" of the Community's own system into the laws of each member state, "and more generally the terms and spirit of the Treaty, make it impossible for the States, as a corollary, to accord precedence to a unilateral and subsequent measure over a legal system accepted by them on a basis of reciprocity."[37]

One may discern some differing nuances between the reasoning of the Advocate General and that of the Court. While the Advocate General speaks of the Community system as "separate but nevertheless intimately and even organically tied" to member states' systems, the Court stresses the nature of the Community system as an "integral part" of the member states' legal orders.[38] What is perhaps more important, on one hand, the Advocate General suggests that since in Italy and in the German Federal Republic treaties are not accorded precedence in national courts over subsequent national law, the two states may have to amend their Constitutions to conform to the Community supremacy principle or terminate their participation in the Treaty. The Court, on the other hand, perhaps unconsciously anticipating its holding in the *Simmenthal* case,[39] considered that the supremacy rule had already become a part of the national legal systems "on the entry into force of the Treaty," in the sense that the completion of the ratification process according to national constitutional procedures was the one and only requirement for the application of the rule by national courts and authorities.[40]

The implications of the supremacy principle did not become fully apparent until 1978 when the Court decided the *Simmenthal* case,[41] also referred to it by an Italian court. By that time, the Italian Constitutional Court, faced with the rulings of the Court of Justice, had retreated from the position it had taken in *Costa v. ENEL* and accepted both the direct effect and the supremacy principles. However, the Constitutional Court still insisted that in the case of a conflict between Community law and a subsequent national act of Parliament, the problem becomes one of constitutional law and, unless the Parliament repeals the law, the principle of separation of powers requires that only the Constitutional Court itself may declare the national law invalid.[42] *Simmenthal* raised the ultimate question whether an ordinary Italian court, faced with such a conflict, must refer the issue to the Constitutional Court in accordance with Italian law, or whether it must refuse to apply the national law without such reference.[43] It was not surprising that the Italian Government argued strongly in favor of the position formulated by the Constitutional Court, while the Commission, Advocate General Reischl, and the Court took the opposite view. As a logical consequence of the principles of direct effect and supremacy of Community law, the Court reasoned, "current national law" that is incompatible with Community law is rendered "automatically inapplicable" upon the entry into force of conflicting Community law, and any legislative measures in conflict with Community law that are subsequently enacted have no legal effect since member states are precluded from "the valid adoption" of such measures. Consequently, the Court declared, a national court, in a case before it, must refuse "of its own motion" to apply a conflicting provision of national law, whether prior or subsequent to the Community norm. The effectiveness of Community law would be impaired if the resolution of the conflict were deferred to a court other than the one with initial jurisdiction, "even if such an impediment to the full effectiveness of Community law were only temporary,"[44] as was the case in Italy. The language of the Court seems to suggest that upon the coming into force of the Community law the member states lose the competence to enact conflicting legislation which, if nevertheless adopted, would be automatically null and void.[45]

The Supremacy Principle and the Protection of Basic Rights

The conceptual framework for the principle of supremacy does not allow any distinction regarding the hierarchical status of the national law that must bow to conflicting Community law: according to *ENEL,* national constitutions are clearly included. But what if a Community citizen, instead of challenging a national law conflicting with Community law, as in *van Gend, ENEL,* and *Simmenthal,* asserts that Community law and, more specifically, an act of a Community institution, has deprived him of a fundamental right protected by his national constitution? Logically, on the *van Gend-ENEL* theory of Community law as a distinct, "independent" legal system, national law, including national constitutional law, is entirely irrelevant to measuring the legality of a Community act. This, in fact, had been the position of the Court of Justice when the issue had arisen in 1960.[46] In the *Stauder* case [47] almost a decade later, the Court of Justice was able to avoid the problem in its holding by interpreting the Community act (a Commission decision) in a way that precluded conflict with any basic right. However, since the referring German court specifically raised the question and also perhaps because of the new emphasis on basic human rights and the litigation in German and Italian courts raising the issue of the constitutionality of the Community Treaties, the Commission, Advocate General Roemer, and the Court itself (in the reasoning part of the opinion) were moved to deal with the protection of the basic rights in Community law. They agreed that although the Community institutions cannot apply national constitutions, they are bound to protect individual fundamental rights as a matter of "general principles" which form an unwritten part of Community law.[48]

It was, however, only in the *Internationale Handelsgesellschaft* case[49] that the Court identified, albeit in very general terms, the source on which to draw in defining the content of the general principles of Community law. At issue was a Council regulation of some importance for the enforcement of the common agricultural policy. The regulation requires importers, as a condition for obtaining an import license, to deposit a certain amount, which is forfeited if the licensed import transaction is not carried out. The regulation system was contested on the ground that it imposed a disproportionate burden upon the importer in violation of his fundamental rights, which were protected by the principle of proportionality in the German Basic Law (*Grundgesetz*).[50] The Commission, Advocate General Dutheillet de Lamothe, and the Court again rejected any attempt to subject Community law to a national constitution, but they concurred that the principle of proportionality was a part of unwritten Community law to which the regulation must (and did) conform. According to the Court—and the Commission took essentially an identical view—the respect for fundamental rights forms an integral part of the general principles of law protected by the Court, and this protection, "whilst inspired by the constitutional traditions common to the Member States, must be ensured within the framework of the structure and objectives of the Community."[51] The Advocate General urged the Court to draw upon the "fundamental principles of national legal systems" forming "a philosophical, political and legal substratum common to the Member States"—"the common heritage."[52] The German and Dutch Governments found no violation of the proportionality principle, which, according to the German Government, was at any rate already established in previous case law as a part of Community law; thus, there was no need to explore any constitutional issues. It is interesting that the Commission found it necessary, evidently for reasons of prudence and political advisability, to discuss the question of conformity of the contested regulation with the German Basic Law.[53]

Despite the assurances of Community law protection, however, both the German and the Italian Constitutional Courts, while accepting the supremacy and independence of Community law in principle, nevertheless insisted on reserving their own power to protect basic rights of their citizens against violations by the Community institutions, at least until the democratic features and individual protection are strengthened in the Community by the transfer of Community lawmaking to the European Parliament and by the adoption of a "codified catalogue of human rights."[54]

The Triple Expansion

1. From "Negative" to "Positive" Obligations

After *van Gend,* the Court proceeded to expand the impact of the direct effect principle in three significant directions. First, only 3 years later, the Court, urged by the Commission and Advocate General Gand, drastically reduced, if not eliminated, the scope of the one limitation it had seemingly grafted onto the direct effect concept in *van Gend.*

In the *Lütticke* case,[55] the Court held that even though Article 95 imposed on the member states a "positive" obligation to remove discriminatory internal taxes on imports (as distinguished from a "negative" obligation to refrain from action) within a specified period, an individual plaintiff might invoke its direct effect in a national court against the delinquent member state, provided the period within which the state was required to act had lapsed. The Court was not impressed by the arguments that within the elapsed period the member states had discretion to choose the appropriate action and that national legislatures were better equipped to define the scope of the prohibition of discrimination in the complex field of indirect taxation than were national courts. It was no coincidence that the German Government, here directly concerned (and the referring German court), as well as the Dutch and Belgian Governments, opposed such an extension of the direct effect principle because it constituted encroachment on national "tax sovereignty."

The Court applied the same rationale in a subsequent series of cases decided in 1974 (*Reyners, van Binsbergen, van Duyn*),[56] with the effect that the myriad of discriminatory restrictions on freedom of movement of workers, and on the establishment and supply of services that were to be abolished by the member states before the end of 1969, became inapplicable—as by the touch of a magic wand—when the clock struck midnight on Saint Sylvester day of 1969. Thus, individual plaintiffs have been able to challenge national discriminatory legislation in national courts by invoking the direct effect of the respective Treaty provisions despite the fact that under the Treaty itself, the Council was to have issued implementing measures before 1969, and failed to do so. In these cases, also, the Court followed the conclusions of the Commission and the Advocate General, while the Governments, with some exceptions, remained adamantly opposed to such an extension.[57]

2. From "Vertical" to "Horizontal" Effect

The second significant line of case law has expanded the direct effect of Community law from situations where an individual invokes a Community law provision against governmental action ("vertical" dimension) to instances where such provision is invoked by one individual against another ("horizontal" dimension). In *Walrave* the question was whether a professional "pacemaker" employed in bicycle races may invoke the Treaty prohibition of discrimination in employment and supply of services as against an "alien clause" in the articles of a private bicycle association that would exclude him from such employment because of his nationality.[58] The Court, supported by Advocate General Warner, agreed that the prohibition not only is applicable "to the action of public authorities but extends likewise to rules of any other nature aimed at collectively regulating gainful employment and services." The Commission agreed with respect to discrimination in employment but opposed such extension with respect to the supply of services because of the specific wording of the Treaty article in question,[59] which requires the abolition of discriminatory measures by *public* authorities only; the resulting gap, however, would be filled by the general prohibition of discrimination on nationality grounds in Article 7.[60] The Government of the United Kingdom, the only government to intervene, admitted expressly only the vertical direct effect in the supply of services area.[61] Brushing aside the Commission's textual argument, the Court reasoned that the "fundamental objectives of the Community contained in Article 3(c) [freedom of movement for persons, services and capital] would be compromised if the abolition of barriers of national origin could be neutralized by obstacles resulting from the exercise of their legal autonomy by associations or organizations which do not come under public law."[62]

The widely discussed holding in the *Defrenne* case[63] may be viewed as carrying the extension of direct effect to private relationships a step further. In contrast with *Walrave,* the provision involved, Article 119, is expressly addressed to the member states and does not fall within the "fundamental objectives of the Community" enumerated in Article 3 but is contained in the Treaty part on social policy. Article 119 provides that "[e]ach Member State shall [before 1962] ensure and subsequently maintain the application of the principle that men and women should receive equal pay for equal work," and it describes the meaning of this principle in general terms. Relying on this article, a Belgian "air hostess" sued SABENA, a private Belgian airline,[64] demanding compensation on the ground that although her work was identical to that of a male cabin steward, she was paid a lower salary.

The Governments of the United Kingdom and of Ireland opposed giving direct effect to the article because it failed to satisfy the Court's criteria of clarity and precision and contained merely a "principle" to be implemented by national legislation. This view appeared to conform to earlier measures, such as a resolution adopted by the member states extending the Treaty deadline for compliance and a Council directive purporting to harmonize divergent national laws and allowing more time for full application of the article. Pointing to the diversity in job classification, methods of wage formation, etc., in the private sector, the Commission argued (in line with its view in *Walrave*) that the "principle" in Article 119 cannot be invoked before the courts by employees in the private sector; however, in the public and semi-public sectors, where job classification and other relevant aspects are fixed by law, the uncertainties of interpretation do not arise, and workers in that sector may rely on the principle against their public employers. In other words, the Commission would have attributed to Article 119 vertical but not horizontal direct effect.

Drawing on the extensive opinion of Advocate General Trabucchi, and exploring the "nature of the principle of equal pay, the aim of this provision and its place in the scheme of the Treaty," the Court considered that the principle serves the social objectives and thus forms a "part of the foundations of the Community."[65] Admittedly, Article 119 may require implementation by Community or national legislation to define "indirect and disguised discrimination"; but in case of "direct discrimination which may be identified solely by reference to the criteria laid down by Article 119" and "which may be detected on the basis of a purely legal analysis of the situation,"[66] the article gives rise to rights that individuals may assert against their employers in both the public and the private sectors. In the private sector, the application by a national court of the equal pay principle would amount to a modification of an individual employment contract or of a collective bargaining agreement.

The Court, as in *Walrave,* thus refused to follow the Commission's position, which would limit the horizontal direct effect to the public sector, and it agreed instead on this point with the Advocate General. However, in contrast with the Advocate General, the Court found it quite appropriate to take into account "the practical consequences" of a retroactive application of the equal pay principle for national treasuries and economies as well as for the financial situation of private employers. Consequently, the Court ruled that Article 119 cannot be relied on to support claims for back pay arising prior to the date of the judgment except as regards claims already pending.[67]

The Court did not follow the Advocate General in still another respect. Because the principle of equal treatment of men and women has been enshrined in the legal systems of member states (albeit in varied form and with uncertain success), Mr. Trabucchi urged the Court to include it among the fundamental human rights that the Community must protect as one of the general principles of unwritten Community law and to give full direct effect to it. The Court, however, obviously did not wish to go as far as to read into Article 119 a general prohibition of sex discrimination in working conditions other than unequal pay.[68]

3. From Treaty Law to Community Legislation

The third and, in some respects, the most radical extension of the direct effect principle concerns its application to Community legislation. By virtue of Article 189 only a "regulation" is made *expressis verbis* "directly applicable"[69] in all member states, while a "directive" is "binding, as to the result to be achieved upon each Member State to which it is addressed," leaving to the national authorities "the choice of form and methods," and a "decision" is "binding in its entirety upon those to whom it is addressed." In *Franz Grad,*[70] the question was whether a plaintiff before a national court might challenge the validity of a national law imposing a special transportation tax on the ground that it violated a Council *decision* which required member states to replace any such taxes by a common value-added tax system not later than by the date set in a Council *directive.* The Commission, Advocate General Roemer, and the Court supported the plaintiff's position, while the German Government opposed it on the ground that a regulation was the only Community act that had direct effect in national law. The Court saw no reason why a decision addressed to a member state, which by its "nature, background and wording" was "unconditional and sufficiently clear and precise to be capable of producing effects in the legal relationship between the Member States and those subject to their jurisdiction," could not be invoked by an individual.

A contrary conclusion, the Court held, would weaken the "*effet utile*" of the decision in Community law and was not mandated by the language of Article 189.[71] Moreover—and this appears to be the Court's own argument—since Article 177 empowers national courts to refer to the Court questions regarding the validity and interpretation of *any* Community act without distinction of form, it is clear that individuals may rely in appropriate circumstances on any such acts (including presumably directives and decisions) before national courts.[72]

In the *van Duyn* case,[73] the United Kingdom Government, relying on Article 189, argued that in principle an individual might not invoke a right based on a directive, and it sought to limit the reach of *Franz Grad* to its specific, rather unique, facts. Neither the Commission, nor Advocate General Mayras, nor the Court accepted this argument and the Court's holding dispelled any doubt that the *Franz Grad* rationale did include directives as well as decisions addressed to member states. The Court held that a Council directive purporting to limit the discretion of national authorities to apply the public order exception as a bar to free movement of workers had direct effect in national law and thus could be invoked by a Dutch national who was denied entry into the United Kingdom. The Court's disregard of the text of Article 189 distinguishing between the effects of a regulation and a directive is perhaps the most striking example of its teleological method of interpretation. It was in this context that for the first time in the Court's history its authority was openly defied by a high national tribunal.[74] The French Conseil d'Etat refused in 1978 to allow a German national, Daniel Cohn-Bendit of May 1968 fame, to rely on the same Council directive against an order by French authorities expelling him from France. The Conseil justified the refusal on the ground that according to Article 189, in principle, no directive could have direct effect in a national legal order.[75] There is no evidence that the Commission will want to stage a confrontation with the French Government by making use of its authority to hold France responsible before the Court of Justice for violating Community law.

On Community Treaty-Making Power

The *ERTA* case,[76] in which the Court addressed for the first time the scope of the community power in the sensitive field of foreign relations, is a worthy counterpart to the *van Gend* case dealing with Community authority in the "domestic" field. In both cases, separated by a lapse of 8 years, the principal actors took similar positions with respect to Treaty interpretation and definition of Community authority. In *ERTA,* however, although formally the controversy was between the Commission and the Council, the real parties in interest were the Community, represented by the Commission, and the member state governments whose independent treaty-making power was at stake.[77]

In only two instances does the Treaty expressly empower the Community to enter into international agreements with third states. It may conclude agreements in the field of foreign commercial policy (Article 113) and also so-called association agreements with an undefined content (Article 238).[78] The procedure prescribed is that the Commission negotiates and the Council "concludes" the agreement (Article 228).

Since 1967 member state governments had been negotiating with other governments for a new European Road Transport Agreement.[79] In 1970, over the Commission's objection, the Council adopted "conclusions" in which it defined the position member governments should take in the continuing negotiations with a view to harmonizing the prospective agreement with a 1969 Council regulation on the same subject.[80] The Commission, claiming exclusive power to negotiate on behalf of the Community, asked the Court to annul the Council action. The Council, supported by the Advocate General, opposed the claim and contended that the Community treaty-making power was confined to the two specifically identified areas; thus, in the field of transportation the member states had retained their power to negotiate, which they were free to exercise in this instance under the guidance of the Council. The Commission responded with the far-reaching proposition that the Community power to formulate common transport policy for the interior of its territory could not be fully effective without "conferring on the Community the means of taking appropriate action in respect of external relations," and, therefore, since the adoption of a Council regulation the negotiations "could only be carried out by the Community."[81]

The Court upheld the Commission's interpretation on the basis of "the general system of Community law in the sphere of relations with third countries."[82] The bland provision in Article 210 that "[t]he Community shall have legal personality" meant, according to the Court, that "the Community enjoys the capacity to establish contractual links with third countries over the whole field" of the general objectives listed in the introductory articles, including the formulation of a common transportation policy. The Community's *authority* in a particular case to enter into a treaty not only arises

> from an express conferment by the Treaty . . . but may equally flow from other provisions of the Treaty and from measures adopted . . . by the Community institutions. In particular, each time the Community, with a view to implementing a common policy envisaged by the Treaty, adopts provisions laying down common rules, whatever form these may take, the Member States no longer have the right, acting individually or even collectively, to undertake obligations with third countries which affect those rules.[83]

On the merits of the case, however, the Court refused the Commission's claim. Because the negotiations had been initiated before the adoption of the Council regulation, the member states were free to conclude the negotiations, provided they coordinated their action in the interest of the Community.

Although "momentarily persuaded" by the Commission's view, Advocate General Dutheillet de Lamothe "with some regret" rejected "the argument of implied and automatic transfer of authority outside the cases laid down by the Treaty" as a "very daring exercise in legal construction which indeed I consider too audacious for reasons of principle. . . ."[84] In his interpretation, the general scheme of the Treaty shows that "its authors intended strictly to limit the Community's authority in external matters to the cases which they expressly laid down."[85]

It has not come as a surprise that the application of the *ERTA* ruling has encountered some opposition in national foreign ministries, but in subsequent cases the Court has reaffirmed and clarified its definition of the Community foreign relations power.[86]

Summary and Some Conclusions

The data harvested in this survey of eleven significant cases may be illustrated in a simple table in which "yes" indicates support for, and "no" opposition to, a position advancing the legal integration of the Community in a given case. (See table 1.)

As is necessarily the case with a schematic presentation of complex phenomena, the table does not bring out the differential impact of the individual items—in particular, the overriding importance of *van Gend,* the first in the series of major constitutional cases. In that case, a group of lawyers at the Commission's Legal Service, headed by its Director General, fashioned the argument based on the uniqueness of the Community Treaty which has made it possible for the Court to elude the strictures of international treaty law and to deal with the Treaty as a constitution.[87] The Advocate General, on the other hand, remained in that case a prisoner of the traditional doctrine. Starting with *van Gend*, the international law concept of the "self-executing" treaty has been replaced by the "direct effect" principle, with the result that Community law has progressively acquired the status of quasi-federal law in terms of its impact on individual citizens. As a necessary corollary, the authority of the Community and of the Court itself has grown substantially at the expense of national governments and courts.

TABLE 1. Position of Principal Actors on Major "Constitutional" Issues

Issue and Case	Governments	Commission	Advocate General	Court
direct effect: *van Gend* 1963	no: Belg:, Neth., Lux., Germany	yes	no (Roemer, German)	yes
supremacy: (1)*Costa v. ENEL* 1964	no: Italy	yes	yes (Lagrange, French)	yes
(2) *Simmenthal* 1978	no: Italy	yes	yes (Reischl, German)	yes
(3) human rights: *Internationale Handelsges.* 1966	unnecessary to decide: Germany, Neth.	yes	yes (Dutheillet de Lamothe, French)	yes
expanding direct effect: (1) *Lütticke* 1966	no: Belg., Neth., Germany	yes	yes (Gand, French)	yes
(2) *Reyners* 1974	no: Belg., Lux., Ire., UK yes: Germany, Neth.?	yes	yes (Mayras, French)	yes
(3) *Walrave* 1974	no position: UK	no	yes (Warner, British)	yes
(4) *Defrenne* 1976	no: UK, Ire.	yes on public empl., no on private	yes (Trabucchi, Italian)	yes
(5) *Franz Grad* 1970	no: Germany	yes	yes (Roemer, German)	yes
(6) *van Duyn* 1974	no: UK	yes	yes (Mayras, French)	yes
treaty-making power: *ERTA* 1970	no: Council	yes	no (Dutheillet de Lamothe, French)	yes

The third and fifth columns in the table disclose that since *van Gend,* with two important exceptions, the Court has been led by the Commission in the inexorable progression toward more legal integration and more Community power. The close alliance between the Court and the Commission, the "executive-political" branch of the Community, has probably alleviated some of the concern members of the Court may have felt regarding the legitimacy and acceptance of its rulings. Such concern has no doubt been fanned by the consistent opposition to increased integration on the part of the member governments, registered in the second column of the table.

The Court ventured beyond the Commission's lead only when it ruled to extend the direct effect of the Treaty-constitution to govern private law relationships between individuals. Although in this instance, the Commission's lawyers invoked a textual interpretation against the Court's usual reliance on the "spirit" of the Treaty, they may have been motivated as much by national constitutional practices as by their political judgment against pressing the legal integration process too far too fast. The spurt of criticism following the ruling in the *Defrenne* case may be viewed as a justification of the Commission's sensitivity.[88]

In only one instance may the Court be said to have temporarily stopped short of the Commission's "prointegration" position. In *van Gend* it did not deal expressly with the supremacy issue which was pressed by the Commission, but it did resolve that issue a year later in *Costa v. ENEL,* reacting to the unacceptable holding of the Italian Constitutional Court.

The fourth and fifth columns show that since *van Gend,* with the important exception of *ERTA,* dealing with the sensitive foreign affairs power, the Court's holdings have generally paralleled the conclusions of its Advocates General. The support by these officers of the Court, enjoying in most instances an established reputation in their national professional circles, may have discouraged some opposition to the far-reaching decisions. In *Defrenne,* the Court was not prepared to elevate the "equal pay for men and women" principle to a directly effective general prohibition against discrimination on the ground of sex, as urged by the Advocate General, and, contrary to his advice, it gave its ruling prospective application only. The nationality and the background of the successive Advocates General may have affected their style of expression, but there is little evidence that these factors determined their ultimate conclusions in the cases considered here. Nor is there any evidence in these cases that changes in the membership of the Court—or for that matter of the Commission—have had any noticeable effect on the general trend favoring ever closer legal integration.

The only participants in the process opposing the trend have been the national governments. Although all member governments have a legal right to be notified of any proceeding referred to the Court under Article 177 and to state their views, relatively few have taken advantage of the opportunity, and they did so in most instances only if their national law or other interest was directly involved. In the *ENEL* case, for instance, despite its obvious importance, only the Italian Government appeared. The French Government was conspicuously absent, which may suggest a policy decision of unclear motivation. A member of the Commission's legal staff considers it regrettable that the Court's rules do not "guarantee" the participation in Article 177 proceedings even of the member state "affected by the case."[89]

One may speculate why the "legal establishment," particularly in the Belgian and Dutch Ministries, chose for example in *van Gend* a course of action that would have stunted the Community at a crucial stage of building the customs union and turned it possibly into little more than a regional General Agreement on Tariffs and Trade whose principles "are observed more in the breach."[90] In striking contrast, at the political level, those two Governments, in particular the Netherlands, have been in the forefront of the European integration movement, if only because, as small countries, they have depended on effective Community law in their relationships with their more powerful partners. One reason for the attitude of these Governments may be the consideration that the Court's rulings, although based on ingenious interpretations of the Treaty rather than on unambiguous wording, required abandonment of hallowed national constitutional practices. Such sacrifice would not come easily to any lawyer born and bred in a national system. Again, it may be too much to expect a national lawyer-bureaucrat, however enlightened, to preside with any degree of enthusiasm over a steady erosion of national power and his own vested career interests. These lawyers may also have been concerned about a possible negative reaction on the part of their national parliaments. Finally, in the context of contentious proceedings, it is a more or less ironclad rule that a lawyer must press any available legal argument that may "win the case" of his client, and the lawyers before the Court of Justice are no exception when they defend national law and authority against the intruding Community power.[91]

Notes

1. No dissenting or other separate opinions are allowed.
2. On the use of the term "*amicus curiae*" in this essay, see the penultimate paragraph of note 3 *infra*.

3. Article 177 of the Treaty Establishing the European Economic Community (EEC) provides:

> The Court of Justice shall have jurisdiction to give preliminary rulings concerning:
>
> (a) the interpretation of this Treaty;
> (b) the validity and interpretation of acts of the institutions of the Community;
> (c) the interpretation of the statutes of bodies established by an act of the Council, where those statutes so provide.
>
> Where such a question is raised before any court or tribunal of a Member State, that court or tribunal may, if it considers that a decision on the question is necessary to enable it to give judgment, request the Court of Justice to give a ruling thereon.
>
> Where any such question is raised in a case pending before a court or tribunal of a Member State, against whose decisions there is no judicial remedy under national law, that court or tribunal shall bring the matter before the Court of Justice.

See the corresponding Article 41 of the Treaty Establishing the European Coal and Steel Community and Article 150 of the Treaty Establishing the European Atomic Energy Community. For a handy volume of the text of these Treaties, see OFFICE FOR OFFICIAL PUBLICATIONS OF THE EUROPEAN COMMUNITIES, TREATIES ESTABLISHING THE EUROPEAN COMMUNITIES (1978). EEC Article 177 is at p. 348.

Article 20 of the Protocol on the Statute of the Court of Justice of the European Economic Community requires that in cases governed by Article 177, when a national tribunal refers the case to the Court of Justice, the parties to the case, the member states, and the Commission (and also the Council if its act is involved) must be notified and they are *entitled* to submit oral statements or written observations to the Court. *Id.* at 525. The term "*amicus curiae*" is used in the text in a general sense only. According to Article 37 of the same Protocol, member states may "intervene" in cases before the Court. *Id.* at 529.

This essay deals exclusively with the Treaty Establishing the European Economic Community, March 25, 1957, 298 UNTS 11 (*in force* Jan. 1, 1958). For an authoritative English text, see [1973] Gr. Brit. TS No. 1, pt. II (Cmd. 5179 II), at 1.

4. For examples of writings by judges and Advocates General of the Court of Justice, see L. DELVAUX, LA COUR DE JUSTICE DE LA COMMUNAUTÉ EUROPÉENNE DU CHARBON ET DE L'ACIER (1956); A. M. DONNER, THE COURT OF JUSTICE AS A CONSTITUTIONAL COURT OF THE COMMUNITIES—THE EXETER LECTURE IN EUROPEAN LAW (1978); Donner, *The Constitutional Powers of the Court of Justice of the European Communities,* 11 COMM. MKT. L. REV. 127 (1974); R. LECOURT, L'EUROPE DES JUGES (1976); LORD MACKENZIE STUART, THE EUROPEAN COMMUNITIES AND THE

RULE OF LAW (1977); P. PESCATORE, THE LAW OF INTEGRATION (1974); Hammes, *Gedanken zu Funktion und Verfahren des Gerichtshofs der Europaeischen Gemeinschaften,* [1968] EUROPARECHT [EUR] 1; Kutscher, *Der Gerichtshof der Europaeischen Gemeinschaften,* [1978] EUROPAEISCHE GRUNDRECHTE-ZEITSCHRIFT [EuGRZ] 503; Lagrange, *La Cour de Justice des Communautés européennes: du plan Schuman à l'union européenne,* [1978] REVUE TRIMESTRIELLE DU DROIT EUROPÉEN [REV. TRIM. D.E.] 1: Mertens de Wilmars, *La jurisprudence de la Cour de Justice comme instrument de l'intégration communautaire,* [1976] CAHIERS DE DROIT EUROPÉEN [CAH. DR. DE EUR.] 135; Touffait, *La Cour de Justice des Communautés européennes,* [1978] REV. INTERNATIONALE DE DROIT COMPARÉ 363; Trabucchi, *L'effet ⟨⟨erga omnes⟩⟩ des décisions préjudicielles rendues par la Cour de Justice des Communautés européennes,* [1974] REV. TRIM. D.E. 56; Warner, *The Relationship between European Community Law and the National Laws of Member States,* [1977] L. Q. REV. 349.

5. Case 26/62, N. V. Algemene Transport—en Expeditie Onderneming van Gend & Loos v. Nederlandse Administratie der Belastingen, [1963] EUROPEAN COURT REPORTS [ECR] 1. *See,* among the many comments on this case, Hay, *Federal Jurisdiction of the Common Market Court,* 12 AM. J. COMP. L. 21 (1963); and Riesenfeld & Buxbaum, *N. V. Algemene Transport—en Expeditie Onderneming van Gend & Loos c. Administration Fiscale Néerlandaise: A Pioneering Decision of the Court of Justice of the European Communities,* 58 AJIL 152 (1964). *See also* Amphoux, *A propos de l'arrêt 26/62 (Société N. V. Allgemene [sic] Transport en Expeditie Onderneming van Gend et Loos contre Administration fiscale néerlandaise) rendu le 5 février 1963 par la Cour de Justice des Communautés européennes,* 68 REVUE GÉNÉRALE DE DROIT INTERNATIONAL PUBLIC [RGDIP] 110 (1964); Catalano, *L'inserimento diretto delle disposizioni contenute nel trattato istitutivo della Comunità Economica Europea negli ordinamenti giuridici degli Stati membri,* 18 IL FORO PADANO, parte quinta, col. 33 (1963); Jeantet in 37 JURIS-CLASSEUR PÉRIODIQUE, LA SEMAINE JURIDIQUE, II Jurisprudence No. 13177 (1963); Marsh, *Some Reflections on Legal Integration in Europe,* 12 INT'L & COMP. L.Q. 1411 (1963); Wengler in 16 NEUE JURISTISCHE WOCHENSCHRIFT [N.J.W.] 1751 (1963).

6. Unless otherwise indicated, "the Treaty" in this essay refers to the Treaty Establishing the European Economic Community, *supra* note 3.

7. Belgium-Netherlands-Luxembourg.

8. For this and the second question, Case 26/62, [1963] ECR at 3.

9. Art. 20 of the Protocol on the Statute of the Court of Justice of the European Economic Community, *supra* note 3.

10. The Belgian and Dutch Governments challenged the jurisdiction expressly, the German Federal Republic by implication with respect to the second, and possibly also the first, question.

11. Case 26/62, [1963] ECR at 6–9.

12. The Advocate General felt that

> [i]t is impossible to clarify exhaustively the real legal effects of an international agreement on the nationals of a Member State without having regard to the constitutional law of that Member State. But, on the other hand, it is

clear that the question does not refer exclusively to problems of constitutional law.

The question whether the Treaty, and especially Article 12, was intended by the parties to be "self-executing" (or have "direct effect") in their national legal systems was relevant for the decision in the case; the Court of Justice may "extract" from the Dutch tribunal's request an appropriate issue of interpretation, and in principle, at any rate, it is for the national court and not for the Court of Justice to inquire into the relevance of the question for the decision in the principal case. *Id.* at 18–19. The Advocate General seems to have come close to accepting the "fall-back" position of the Netherlands. This option would have recognized the jurisdiction of the Court to rule on the effect of Article 12, but even if the Courts should have found that the article was intended to have direct effect, the application of such ruling for the purpose of determining whether an individual might invoke it in a Dutch tribunal would still have been a matter of national constitutional law. *Id.* at 8.

13. *Id.* at 6.

14. To confine the "guarantees against infringement of Art. 12" by the member states to the procedures under Articles 169 and 170 would remove all direct legal protection of the individual rights of their nationals. There is a risk that recourse to the procedure under these articles would be ineffective if it were to occur after the implementation of a national decision taken contrary to the provisions of the Treaty. *Id.* at 13. The Court's interest in broadening an individual's access to national courts as a basis for a reference under Article 177 became particularly acute when, starting with the cases decided in December 1962, the Court laid down an extremely narrow and technical interpretation of the important Article 173(2) and thus severely restricted the direct access of the individual to the Court itself in case of an infringement of Community law by Community institutions, as compared with the broad access accorded to member states. Cases 16 and 17/62, [1962] ECR 471; 19–22/62, [1962] ECR 491; 25/62, [1963] ECR 95. For subsequent cases, see Stein & Vining, *Citizen Access to Judicial Review of Administrative Action in a Transnational and Federal Context,* 70 AJIL 219, 222–27 (1976). In view of the questionable chance for an individual to obtain satisfaction through an action for damages against the Community under Article 215, the procedure under Article 177 has been crucial in ensuring an individual's protection under the Community system, including cases where a member state acts to implement an act of a Community institution that violates Community law. In Joined Cases 261 & 262/78, Interquell StaerkeChemie GmGH & Co. KG and Diamalt AG v. Council and Commission of the European Economic Community, [1980] ECR 3045, the Court of Justice held the Community liable for damages.

15. There were 106 cases brought under Articles 169 and 93, as compared with 764 cases initiated by private parties under Article 177. Thirteenth General Report on the Activities of the European Communities, Feb. 1980, at 340, updated by EC BULLETIN, Nos. 1–6, 1980.

16. Case 26/62, [1963] ECR at 8 (Netherlands) and 19 (Advocate General).

17. *Id.* at 8 (Netherlands). Article 12 states: "Member States shall refrain from introducing between themselves any new customs duties on imports or exports or any charges having equivalent effect, and from increasing those which they already apply in their trade with each other." OFFICIAL PUBLICATIONS, TREATIES, *supra* note 3, at 203, 230.

18. Case 26/62, [1963] ECR at 8 (Belgium and Germany).

19. According to the Dutch Government, any other conclusion would "upset the system the authors of the Treaty intended to establish"; it would create uncertainty with respect to many Community norms expressly imposing obligations on member states—as does Article 12—and it would reduce the willingness of member states to cooperate; and finally it would provide an inappropriate way of testing the responsibility of member states. *Ibid.* In German law, the German Goverment pointed out, a national provision that laid down a customs duty contrary to the provisions of Article 12 would be "perfectly valid." *Ibid.*

20. *Id.* at 19–22. Advocate General Roemer may have reflected the view of the German courts, which recognize treaty-derived rights of individuals only if the intention to that effect appears "with full clarity" *(mit voller Klarheit)* from the content, purpose, and scheme *(Inhalt, Zweck und Fassung)* of the treaty. Reichsgericht. March 29, 1928, 121 RGZ 7, 9. Prof. Waelbroeck cautions, however, that in practice the German courts have not been as restrictive as the above wording would indicate. M. WAELBROECK, TRAITÉS INTERNATIONAUX ET JURIDICTIONS INTERNES DANS LES PAYS DU MARCHÉ COMMUN 185 (1969).

21. Case 26/62, [1963] ECR at 7.

22. Arts. 31 and 32 of the Vienna Convention on the Law of Treaties, UN Doc. A/CONF. 39/27 (1969), *reprinted* in 63 AJIL 875, 885 (1969).

23. Emphasis added.

24.

> The objective of the EEC Treaty, which is to establish a Common Market, the functioning of which is of direct concern to interested parties in the Community, implies that this Treaty is more than an agreement which merely creates mutual obligations between the contracting states. This view is confirmed by the preamble to the Treaty which refers not only to governments but to peoples. It is also confirmed more specifically by the establishment of institutions endowed with sovereign rights, the exercise of which affects Member States and also their citizens. Furthermore, it must be noted that the nationals of the states brought together in the Community are called upon to cooperate in the functioning of this Community through the intermediary of the European Parliament and the Economic and Social Committee.
>
> In addition the task assigned to the Court of Justice under Article 177, the object of which is to secure uniform interpretation of the Treaty by national courts and tribunals, confirms that the states have acknowledged that Community law has an authority which can be invoked by their nationals before those courts and tribunals.

Case 26.62, [1963] ECR at 12.

25. *Ibid.*

26. *Id.* at 12–13. *Cf.* Chief Justice Marshall's definition of a self-executing treaty in Foster & Elam v. Neilson, 27 U.S. (2 Pet.) 253, 314 (1829).

27. Advisory Opinion on the Jurisdiction of the Courts of Danzig, March 3, 1928, PCIJ, ser. B, No. 15, at 4, 17 and 18.

28. M. WAELBROECK, *supra* note 20, at 165. It is safe to say that the subjective interpretation principle based on intention of the parties has been losing support in international law. *See, e.g.*, Bleckmann, *Teleologie und dynamische Auslegung des Europaeischen Gemeinschaftsrechts,* [1979] EuR 239.

29. M. WAELBROECK, *supra* note 20, at 185–86.

30. Case 26/62, [1963] ECR at 16.

31. Case 6/64, Flaminio Costa v. ENEL, [1964] ECR 585. Of the many comments on this case, see Frowein, *Zum Verhaeltnis zwischen dem EWG-Recht und nationalem Recht aus der Sicht des Gerichtshofes der Europaeischen Gemeinschaften,* [1964] AUSSENWIRTSCHAFTSDIENST DES BETRIEBS-BERATERS [AWD] 233; Kovar, *Chronique de la jurisprudence de la Cour de Justice des Communautés européennes,* 92 JOURNAL DU DROIT INT'L 697 (1965); Monaco, *Diritto comunitario e diritto interno avanti la Corte costituzionale,* 116 GIURISPRUDENZA ITALIANA I COL. 1312 (1964); Sasse, *The Common Market: Between International and Municipal Law,* 75 YALE L.J. 695 (1965–1966); Stein, *Toward Supremacy of Treaty-Constitution by Judicial Fiat: On the Margin of the Costa Case,* 63 MICH. L. REV. 491 (1964–1965).

32. Costa c. E.n.el. & Soc. Edisonvolta, Judgment No. 14 of March 7, 1964, 87 FORO ITALIANO [FORO IT.] I, at 465.

33. Case 6/64, [1964] ECR at 589 and 593.

34. *Id.* at 589.

35. *Id.* at 599.

36. The Court said:

> By contrast with ordinary international treaties, the EEC Treaty has created its own legal system which, on the entry into force of the Treaty, became an integral part of the legal systems of the Member States and which their courts are bound to apply.
>
> By creating a Community of unlimited duration, having its own institutions, its own personality, its own legal capacity and capacity of representation on the international plane and, more particularly, real powers stemming from a limitation of sovereignty or a transfer of powers from the States to the Community, the Member States have limited their sovereign rights, albeit within limited fields, and have thus created a body of law which binds both their nationals and themselves.

Id. at 593.

37. *Id.* at 593–94. The Court relied here on the provision of Article 5(2), requiring member state cooperation and loyalty in very general terms, on Article 7, prohibiting discrimination on the ground of nationality, and on Article 189,

which makes "regulations" issued by the Community institutions directly applicable in all member states. *Ibid.*

38. If a "supremacy clause" is to be read into the Treaty, the Court's formulation appears more appropriate. *See* Casper, in ASIL, 72 PROC. 169, 172 (1978). Sasse, *supra* note 31, at 720, calls Advocate General Lagrange's attitude "rather dualistic," as opposed to the "definite monistic" view taken by the Court.

39. *See infra* note 41.

40. Case 6/64, [1964] ECR at 593. In June 1965, the Court refused to suspend the proceeding before it pending the consideration by the Italian Constitutional Court of the constitutionality of the Italian law ratifying the European Coal and Steel Community Treaty. Case 9/65, Order of the Court, Acciaierie San Michele SpA (in liquidation) v. High Authority of the ECSC, [1967] ECR 27, 29. (The Report of the Interim Order does not give the position of either the Commission or the Advocate General.) In December 1965, the Constitutional Court rejected the claim made in the *Acciaierie San Michele* case that the transfer of judicial power to the Court of Justice deprived the Italian plaintiff of his constitutional right to be judged in an Italian court. The basis for upholding the transfer was that the Community system was distinct from, but "internally effective," in the internal system (shades of Advocate General Lagrange) and that it assured individual legal protection through its own judicial process. Soc. Acciaierie San Michele v. C.E.C.A., No. 98 of Dec. 27, 1965, 89 FORO IT. I, at 8 (1966), 6 COMM. MKT. L.R. 160 (1967).

In Case 14/68, *Walt Wilhelm and Others v. Bundeskartellamt* ([1969] ECR 1), the *Commission,* the *Court,* and *Advocate General Roemer* concurred in allowing simultaneous application of national and Community competition laws, but the Court took what may be viewed as a middle position on the extent of deference national authorities must accord to Community action in case of a possible conflict with national action.

41. Case 106/77, Amministrazione delle Finanze dello Stato v. Simmenthal SpA, [1978] ECR 629.

42. Update: Judgment No. 232 of October 30, 1975, 98 FORO IT. I, at 2662 (1975); Judgment No. 205 of July 28, 1976 and Order No. 206 of July 28, 1976, 99 FORO IT. I, at 2298 (1976); *see also* Judgment No. 183 of Dec. 27, 1973, 97 FORO IT. I, at 314 (1974), 14 COMM. MKT. L.R. 372 (1974). In 1984, responding to the ruling of the Court of Justice in the Simmenthal case, the Italian Constitutional Court held that any ordinary Italian Court faced with an irreconcilable conflict between an Italian law and a Community regulation must disregard the Italian law even in the absence of a decision by the Constitutional Court holding that law invalid. S.p.a. Granital v. Amministrazione delle Finanze dello Stato, Decision No. 170 of June 1984, FORO IT. I, at 2062 (1984).

43. Case 106/77, [1978] ECR 629. *See* Barav, *Observations. Les Effets du Droit Communautaire directement applicable,* [1978] CAH. DR. EUR. 265; Carreau, *Droit communautaire et droits nationaux: concurrence ou primauté?,* [1978] REV. TRIM. D.E. 381; IL PRIMATO DEL DIRITTO COMMUNITARIO E I GIUDICI ITALIANI (Angeli ed. 1978).

44. [1978] ECR at 643–45. In *Simmenthal,* the *Commission* and the *Advocate General* engaged in an elaborate debate with the *Italian Government* on the advantages and disadvantages of an ad hoc decision of "invalidity" by an ordinary judge, which would be applicable only to the particular case, as compared with a ruling by the Constitutional Court entailing an impact *erga omnes* with a retroactive *ex tunc* effect. For better or for worse, the Court refused to grasp this particular thicket, apparently because it was not specifically asked by the Italian court to address it. There is no indication that as a result of the Court's ruling Italian administrative authorities or courts were swamped with requests for refunds of payments exacted on the basis of the law held invalid in the *Simmenthal* case context or of any other law held invalid, so that the question of the reach of the retroactive effect and its impact on completed transactions has apparently not arisen thus far.

45. Barav, *supra* note 43, at 279, concludes that national measures conflicting with Community law do not exist from a legal point of view. Therefore, there is no conflict, and the national judge has to apply the only valid law which is Community law. Carreau, *supra* note 43, at 404, sees in the Court's words only a forceful statement of the inapplicability of conflicting national law. This interpretation does not admit the "invalidity" of subsequent conflicting law, but he views it as "inapplicable." *Id.* at 403–4. *See also* Ipsen, *Die Rolle des Prozessrichters in der Vorrang-Frage,* [1979] EuR 223, 233–37.

46. Joint Cases 36–38/59 and 40/59, Präsident Ruhrkohlen-Verkaufsgesellschaft etc. [Geitling] v. High Authority of the ECSC, [1960] ECR 423.

47. Erich Stauder v. City of Ulm, Sozialamt, [1969] ECR 419. For a comment, see Ehlermann, *Anmerkung,* [1970] EuR 41.

48. The Community act in question was a decision of the Commission, which was intended to help reduce surplus stocks of butter by allowing retailers to sell at reduced prices to welfare recipients in exchange for "individualized coupons" that would make sure that the system was not abused. The German administrative court felt that the decision made it impossible to avoid revealing the name of the beneficiary to the retailers and thus was contrary "to the German concept of social welfare and to the German system of protection of fundamental rights which must, at least in part, be guaranteed equally by the Community institutions as a part of protection afforded by the provisions of Community law." [1969] ECR at 421. The *Commission,* the *Advocate General,* and the *Court* interpreted the Commission's decision as not necessarily requiring identification *by name* so that the question of a conflict with the general principles of Community law did not arise. The *Commission* opined that even the identification by name would be proper because it was a necessary means, proportionate to the desired end; thus, the principle of proportionality which was repeatedly applied by the Court of Justice (and was part of German constitutional law) had not been violated. According to the Commission, the general principles of Community law were derived from the general principles of law in force in the member states. *Id.* at 422–23. The *Advocate General* would follow "many writers' " views that "general qualitative concepts of national constitutional law, in particular

fundamental rights recognized by national law, must be ascertained by means of comparative evaluation of laws, and that such concepts which form an unwritten constituent part of Community law, must be observed in making secondary Community law." *Id.* at 428. The *Court* did not identify the source of the general principles. It confined itself to the statement that the Commission decision, as properly interpreted, "contains nothing capable of prejudicing the fundamental human rights enshrined in the general principles of Community law and protected by the Court." *Ibid.*

49. Case 11/70, Internationale Handelsgesellschaft mbH v. Einfuhr- und Vorratsstelle für Getreide und Futtermittel, [1970] ECR 1125. *See* Pescatore, *The Protection of Human Rights in the European Communities,* 9 COMM. MKT. L. REV. 73 (1972); and Zuleeg, *Fundamental Rights and the Law of the European Communities,* 8 *id.* at 446 (1971), both also dealing with the *Stauder* case, *supra* note 47. *See also* most recently, Case 44/79, Liselotte Hauer v. Land Rheinland-Pfalz, [1979] ECR 3727.

50. The German court claimed that the system of deposits runs counter to the principles of freedom of action and of disposition, of economic liberty, and of proportionality arising from the *Grundgesetz* and that the "primacy of supranational law must yield before the principles of the German Basic Law." [1970] ECR at 1133.

51. *Id.* at 1131. The definition of the actual content of these general principles of law is up to the Court of Justice. Pescatore, *supra* note 49, at 78. According to Pescatore (at 79), the Court will have to apply the highest standard of protection for the Community citizen found in the law of any member state.

52. [1970] ECR at 1146–47.

53. *Id.* at 1131. *See also* Case 4/73, J. Nold Kohlen- und Baustoffgrosshandlung v. Commission, [1974] ECR 491.

54. Internationale Handelsgesellschaft mbH v. Einfuhr- und Vorratsstelle für Getreide und Futtermittel, 37 B VerfGE 271 (1974), 14 COMM. MKT. L.R. 540 (1974); Italian Constitutional Court Judgment No. 183 of Dec. 27, 1973, *supra* note 42. However, in a recent order the German Constitutional Court left open the question whether or to what extent the reservation in the 1974 judgment should continue to apply "in view of the political and legal developments in the European sphere" that had taken place since 1974. Order of July 25, 1979, 2 BvR 6/77, [1979] EuGRZ 547, 551. Update: In 1986, the German Constitutional Court held that since all the principal organs of the Community, and particularly the Court of Justice, have now firmly committed themselves to a high degree of protection of basic human rights and all Member States were parties to the European Convention on Human Rights, as long as such protection exists the Constitutional Court will no longer exercise its jurisdiction to review Community acts for alleged violations of basic rights guaranteed by the German Constitution, except in a hypothetical extreme case of a fundamental conflict. Decision of the Second Senate of 22 Oct. 1986, 2 BvR 197/83. Two years earlier, the Italian Constitutional Court affirmed a similar conclusion. S.p.a. Granital v. Amministrazione delle Finanze dello Stato, Decision No. 170 of 8 June 1984,

FORO IT. I, at 2062 (1984). However, in a judgment of Oct. 12, 1993, upholding the constitutionality of the Maastricht Treaty, the German Constitutional Court asserted its power to review acts of the European Union organs for compatibility with the basic rights guaranteed in the German Constitution and with the German acts transferring power to the Union. 2 BvR 2134/92-2 BvR 2159/92.

55. Case 57/65, Alfons Lütticke GmbH v. Hauptzollamt Saarlouis, [1966] ECR 205. *See* Ipsen, *Anmerkung,* [1966] EuR 356; Mailänder, *Annotation,* 4, COMM. MKT. L. REV. 330 (1966–1967); Waelbroeck, *Observations. L'Applicabilité directe de l'article 95 du traité CEE,* [1967] CAH. DR. EUR. 184. On the impact of the *Lütticke* case in Germany, see Wägenbaur, *The Elimination of Tax Discrimination in Intra-Community Trade,* in COURTS AND FREE MARKETS — EUROPEAN AND UNITED STATES PERSPECTIVES (Sandalow & Stein eds., 1982, Oxford University Press).

56. As to Art. 48: Case 167/73, Commission v. French Republic, [1974] ECR 359, April 4, 1974; and Case 41/74, Yvonne van Duyn v. Home Office, [1974] ECR 1337, Dec. 4, 1974. As to Art. 52: Case 2/74, Jean Reyners v. Belgian State, [1974] ECR 631, June 21, 1974. As to Arts. 59 and 60: Case 33/74, J. H. M. van Binsbergen v. Bestuur van de Bedrijfsvereniging Metaalnijverheid, [1974] ECR 1299, Dec. 3, 1974. For a list of Treaty articles imposing obligations on member states that the Court held to have direct effect and the relevant case law, see H. G. SCHERMERS, JUDICIAL PROTECTION IN THE EUROPEAN COMMUNITIES §187, at 105–7 (2d ed., 1979). For comments on *Reyners* and *van Binsbergen,* see Leleux, *La libre circulation des avocats. Problèmes actuels. Premier rapport,* [1976] CAH. DR. EUR. 676; and Bronkhorst, *Freedom of Establishment and Freedom to Provide Services under the EEC Treaty,* 12 COMM. MKT. L. REV. 245 (1975); on *van Duyn,* see *infra,* text at note 73 and literature cited in that note. Generally, see Leleux, *The Role of the Court of Justice in Protecting Individual Rights in the Context of Free Movement of Persons and Services,* in Sandalow & Stein eds., *supra* note 55.

57. In the *Reyners* case, *Luxembourg, Belgium, Ireland,* and the *United Kingdom* opposed direct effect of Article 52, while *Germany* accepted it in view of the Court's case law; the *Netherlands* is reported also as accepting in Hirsch, *Un arrêt fondamental de la CJCE—la liberté d'établissement dans le Marché Commun,* [1975] SCHWEIZERISCHE JURISTENZEITUNG 37, 38. In *van Duyn,* the *United Kingdom* made "no submission" on the issue of direct effect of Article 48 "in the light" of the previous case law (*i.e.,* Case 167/73). In *van Binsbergen, Ireland* opposed the direct effect of Articles 59 and 60; the *United Kingdom* and *Germany* accepted it in principle but suggested that the difficulties encountered by direct application could be solved only by enacting Community directives.

58. Case 36/74, B. N. O. Walrave and L. J. N. Koch v. Association Union Cycliste Internationale, [1974] ECR 1405. The prohibitions in question are contained in Articles 48, 59, and 7 (general prohibition of discrimination based on nationality). For comments, see Delannay, *Observations,* [1976] CAH. DR. EUR. 209; and Ubertazzi, *Le domaine matériel du droit communautaire,* [1976] REV. TRIM. D. E. 635.

59. According to the published record, the Commission referred here to

Article 54(3)c, which concerns freedom of establishment. The correct reference in this context indicated by the Court is to Articles 60, 62, and 64, which deal with the supply of services. [1974] ECR at 1419.

60. *Id.* at 1410 and 1412.

61. *Id.* at 1415.

62. *Id.* at 1419. According to Delannay, *supra* note 58, at 221, it is an innovation that this judgment recognizes obligations imposed on individuals not by an express Treaty provision—as Articles 85 and 86—but derived from the very breadth of the provisions' wording and from the lack of evidence to the contrary.

63. Case 43/75, Gabrielle Defrenne v. Société Anonyme Belge de Navigation Aérienne Sabena, [1976] ECR 455. For a criticism, see, *e.g.,* Prof. C. J. Hamson in Court of Justice of the European Communities, Judicial and Academic Conference 27–28 September 1976, 2 Reports 10 and 15 (1976); *see also* van Gerven, *Contribution de l'arrêt Defrenne au développement du droit communautaire,* [1977] Cah. dr. eur. 131, 141–43; and Grisham in 14 Comm. Mkt. L. Rev. 108 (1977).

64. The fact that "a great majority of shares" in SABENA are held by the Belgian state was held irrelevant by the Advocate General, since, as the SABENA representative pointed out, the company was organized under private law and its relations with the staff are governed by private law contracts. [1976] ECR at 470 and 488.

65. *Id.* at 471–72. The question may be raised whether the interpretative criteria are identical with those in *van Gend* and *Costa v. ENEL,* or whether they are somewhat modified.

66. [1976] ECR at 473.

67. Van Gerven, *supra* note 63, at 136, compares the factors used by the European Court with those used by the U.S. Supreme Court in cases of prospective overrulings: the practical consequences, the degree of reliance by authorities and individuals on the law as it seemed to be, and legal certainty. Van Gerven suggests that judgments bringing about as radical a change as did *Defrenne* should be treated like legislation, that is, they should not be given any retroactive effect. *Id.* at 137.

68. In the Case 149/77, *Gabrielle Defrenne v. Société Anonyme Belge de Navigation Aérienne Sabena* ([1978] ECR 1365), the Court refused to extend the equal pay principle of Article 119 to equality in other working conditions; although elimination of sex discrimination is a part of fundamental human rights and thus forms a part of general principles of Community law, in the absence of further action by the Community, the Court cannot enforce its observance in relationships between employer and employee, which are exclusively a matter of national law.

69. *See infra* note 71.

70. Case 9/70, Franz Grad v. Finanzamt Traunstein, [1970] ECR 825. For a comment, see Wägenbaur, *Zur Wirkung von Entscheidungen und Richtlinien des EWG-Rats,* [1970] AWD 481.

71. [1970] ECR at 837–38. The *Court* considered that the clause in Article 189 making regulations "directly applicable," and *therefore* capable of producing

direct effect, does not mean that the other legal forms mentioned in that article could never produce a similar effect. *Id.* at 837. To buttress this argument, the *Commission* suggested that a distinction be made between "direct applicability" in the sense of Article 189, meaning "in particular" that no national legislation is required to make a Community measure effective, and "direct effect," meaning that an individual may derive a right from the measure "in spite of the absence of national implementing legislation." *Id.* at 832. For the Advocate General's view on this distinction, see *id.* at 847. *See also* Brinkhorst, *Annotations,* 8 COMM. MKT. L. REV. 386, 391 (1971).

72. How convincing is the argument in the light of the opinion in the Case 111/75, *Impresa Costruzioni Comm. Quirino Mazzalai v. Ferrovia del Renon* ([1976] ECR 657), in which the Court held that under Article 177 it has jurisdiction to interpret Community acts regardless of whether they are directly applicable? In *Franz Grad,* the Court appears to have left open the question whether the direct effect would come into play in case of a positive as well as a negative obligation imposed in a decision or a directive on the addressee member state, and there is no indication that it meant to deal with the "horizontal" direct effect of such measures on private relationships between individuals. Wägenbaur, *supra* note 70, at 482, concludes that the direct effect of decisions and directives is of a lesser kind than the direct effect accorded to Treaty articles and regulations. Whereas the latter immediately replace national law, directives and decisions only give a defense to individuals which they can invoke in national courts. R. LAUWAARS, LAWFULNESS AND LEGAL FORCE OF COMMUNITY DECISIONS (1973), states at p. 36 that directives cannot be given "horizontal" direct effect; *but see* Easson, *Can Directives Impose Obligations on Individuals?,* 4 EUROPEAN LAW REVIEW [E.L.R.] 67, 79 (1979), who considers this an "open question."

73. Case 41/74, *supra* note 56. *See* Barav, *La Libre Circulation des travailleurs, l'ordre public et le pouvoir de sanctions des états membres,* [1977] REV. TRIM. D.E. 721; and Simmonds, *Van Duyn v. the Home Office: The Direct Effectiveness of Directives,* 24 INT'L & COMP. L.Q. 419 (1975).

74. More recently, the French Government refused to respond to the Court's judgment holding its restrictions on lamb meat imports from the United Kingdom contrary to the Treaty. Case 232/78 of Sept. 25, 1979, [1979] ECR 2729.

75. Ministre de l'Intérieur c. Sieur Cohn Bendit (Daniel), No. 11604, Dec. 22, 1978. Excerpt in [1979] CAH. DR. EUR. 265.

76. Case 22/70, Commission of the European Communities v. Council of the European Communities, [1971] ECR 263. *See* Constantinesco, [1971] REV. TRIM. D.E. 796; Ganshof van der Meersch, *Les Relations extérieures de la CEE dans le domaine des politiques communes et l'arrêt de la Cour de Justice du 31 mars 1971,* [1972] CAH. DR. EUR. 127; Kovar, *La Contribution de la Cour de Justice au développement de la condition internationale de la Communauté européenne,* [1978] CAH. DR. EUR. 527; Raux, *La Cour de Justice des Communautés et les relations extérieures de la C.E.E.,* [1972] RGDIP 36; Sasse, *Zur auswaertigen Gewalt der Europaeischen Wirtschaftsgemeinschaft,* [1971] EUR 208; Tizzano, *La controversia tra Consiglio e Commissione in materia di competenza a stipulare della C.e.e.,* 94 FORO IT. IV, at 339 (1971); Waelbroeck, *L'arrêt A.E.T.R. et les*

compétences externes de la Communauté économique européenne, [1971] INTEGRATION 79.

77. This was the first case in which an intrainstitutional dispute between the Commission and the Council was brought before the Court.

78. *See also* Art. 111, applicable during the transitional period.

79. An earlier agreement, negotiated within the UN Economic Commission for Europe in 1962 and signed among others by the six member states, failed to enter into force for want of ratifications. The negotiations were resumed in 1966. Case 22/70, [1971] ECR at 284–85.

80. Reg. No. 543/69, 12 J.O. COMM. EUR. (NO. L 77) 49 (Mar. 29, 1969), [1969] O.J. EUR. COMM. (Spec. Ed. I) 170.

81. [1971] ECR at 269.

82. *Id.* at 274.

83. *Ibid.*

84. *Id.* at 290–91.

85. *Id.* at 293.

86. Riesenfeld in ASIL, 72 PROC. 185–89 (1978); Pescatore, *External Relations in the Case-Law of the Court of Justice of the European Communities,* 16 COMM. MKT. L. REV. 615 (1979).

87. For an early reference to the EEC Treaty as—"in a sense"—a constitution, see Advocate General Lagrange in Costa v. ENEL, [1964] ECR at 605.

88. *See supra* note 63.

89. Wägenbauer, *supra* note 55. In a note submitted on September 20, 1978, the Government of the United Kingdom made a number of suggestions purporting to bring about an improvement in the proceedings under Article 177, but thus far no action appears to have been taken to implement these suggestions. According to Mortelmans, in the 346 cases decided by the Court between 1962 and 1978 under Article 177, member states submitted observations on cases referred from their own respective courts in 37.5% of the cases, while the Commission did so in all the cases. The percentages vary considerably from one member state (*e.g.,* Denmark, 100%) to another (the Federal Republic of Germany, 27.3%). However, in cases referred from courts other than their own, member states submitted observations in only 5.59% of cases. Mortelmans, *Observations in the Cases Governed by Article 177 of the EEC Treaty: Procedure and Practice,* 16 COMM. MKT. L. REV. 557, 572–77 (1979). For a discussion of the United Kingdom suggestions mentioned earlier in this note, see *id.* at 585–87.

90. Jackson, *Governmental Disputes in International Trade Relations: A Proposal in the Context of GATT,* 13 J. WORLD TRADE L. 1, 2 (1979), quoting a document of a U.S. Senate committee.

91. This rule may be illustrated by an example drawn from the American legal folklore. Lawyers defending the United States in a case before the International Court of Justice felt compelled to invoke, quite unnecessarily as it turned out, the notorious "self-judging" reservation against the jurisdiction of the Court even though the President and the executive departments were on record as urging the Senate to drop it. Interhandel Case (Switzerland v. U.S.), [1959] ICJ REP. 6.

Excerpt from *Harmonization of European Company Laws*—The Making of the First Coordination Directive: A Case Study

*In the European Community, harmonization of member state laws was given a distinct goal: to remove differences among national rules that burden the functioning of the Common Market. In 1964 I published a study entitled "Assimilation of National Laws as a Function of European Integration" in which I sought to define the concept, establish some categories, examine the early trends, and offer some policy ideas.**

After a massive attempt extending over some three decades to harmonize the minute details of national economic regulations, major obstacles remained. In a radical change of policy, following the path signaled by the Court of Justice, the Community introduced a system requiring the member states mutually to recognize each other's rules despite the differences in their content, subject only to national limitations in defined public policy interest. This has made it possible to confine Community measures to serious problems.

The harmonization, or, more accurately, the "coordination" of company laws that is the subject of the book excerpted in this essay, has been treated as a special subunit of the overall harmonization scheme. It aims at removing differences among national legislations relating to the level of protection of shareholders as against the managers and of the creditors as against the company, which could distort decision making by managers and investors in intra-Community intercourse. Here again, the original grandiose scheme was scaled down to reflect more realistic business needs. Nevertheless, at this writing more than two dozen Community laws ("directives") coordinating national rules on company laws, securities regulations, and accounting systems have become a part of Community law, in addition to special directives on banking, other financial institutions, and insurance companies.

Reprinted from HARMONIZATION OF EUROPEAN COMPANY LAWS — NATIONAL REFORM AND TRANSNATIONAL COORDINATION, chap. 6, 195–235 (Indianapolis, Kansas City, New York, Bobbs-Merrill Co., 1971). Reprinted with permission of Prentice Hall Company, Upper Saddle River, N.J.

*58 AMERICAN JOURNAL OF INTERNATIONAL LAW 1–40 (1964).

In my book, which appeared in 1971, I considered the function of harmonization of laws in the Community system and the position of commercial companies within the treaty framework. In three "interludes" (which had given me a particular pleasure to write with my colleague Alfred F. Conard as a tutor) I asked first whether a company law in the American "common market" could be viewed as a paradigm for the Community; I then observed briefly company law as a subject of unification in federal, regional, and global contexts; and, finally, I contemplated the problem of law reform in modern company law. Turning to the specific company codes in the original "six," I found them "divergent but converging" with a dynamic interplay between national reform and Community coordination, a novel way of reconciling national diversity with perceived need for greater uniformity in an enlarged market. I then explored in some detail the coordination process itself, centering on the making of the first directive and its impact on national legislation. I analyzed other projects on the table at the time and their prospects of realization, including the convention on recognition of companies and the ill-fated draft for a "federal-type" European stock company. Reexamined after a quarter-of-a-century effort, the European company scheme remains thwarted primarily by the disagreement over worker representation in the organs of the proposed form. Some conclusions are offered in the last chapter of the book.

I was drawn to this subject by a variety of motives: It was not only the impact on the private sector and the intriguing interaction between national law reform and the Community action but more generally again the reach of central power in a divided-power system. As an auditor in one of the working groups composed of national company law experts and chaired by Commission staff, I was captivated by what turned into a sophisticated seminar. A company as a system of competing and cooperating constituencies came to life for me. And the "birth" of the first directive in this field, designed to coordinate national rules on publicity, validity of undertakings, and nullity of companies, offered an appealing topic not only as a study of harmonization but also as an illustration of the early phase legislative process in general.

Searching behind the façade of technical argumentation, I discerned a colorful world of public and private groups pressing a variety of political, economic, professional, and class interests, fiercely protecting institutional "turfs" and indigenous legal traditions, as well as private individuals with their own ambitions. The core of the law-making process has remained as I describe it in this excerpt, but it has undergone important changes noted "Panel Statement on 'Democracy without "a People" ' " (in Part 2). I might add that I return to the European company law story briefly in the piece on "Uses, Misuses—and Nonuses of Comparative Law" in the next essay.

In the normal course of the Community lawmaking process, a working-group draft of a directive is approved by the Commission after consultation with interested nongovernmental groups. The Commission transmits the approved text to the Council of Ministers which consults formally with the Economic and Social Committee and with the European Parliament. The Council may then adopt the Commission's proposal by a qualified majority vote, but if it wishes to modify the proposal it may do so by a unanimous vote only, unless the Commission is prepared to accept the modification.[1]

1. The Hobson's Choice: What Topics to Coordinate?

If coordination was to embrace practically the entire company law (and this was a part of the Community mythology), the working group of Directorate General (D.G.) III would have been faced with a sisyphian task, a monumental study of six legal systems, which would have to be completed within a brief period of time.[2] If, on the other hand, the group decided "to begin at the beginning" by singling out several more or less specific problems for treatment in a series of directives, it opened itself to the objection of a "piece-meal" approach which presumably was not acceptable either to the national parliaments or to the business community and was viewed as destructive of the coherence of the legal systems. Nevertheless, the decision was made to seek some practical results as rapidly as possible[3] and to proceed with a first directive that would be limited both horizontally to certain company forms and vertically with respect to subject matter.

(a) Horizontal Limitation: Only "Capital" Companies Covered

The first directive was to apply not to all companies which according to Article 58 of the Treaty were to benefit from the freedom of establishment, but only to those which were "most prominent in the international sphere" (and thus most likely to seek the benefit of freedom of establishment abroad),[4] and in which individual liability was limited so that the company assets were the only "guarantee" with respect to creditors,[5] that is, stock companies, limited partnerships with shares and limited

Flow Chart of Directives on Coordination of Company Laws

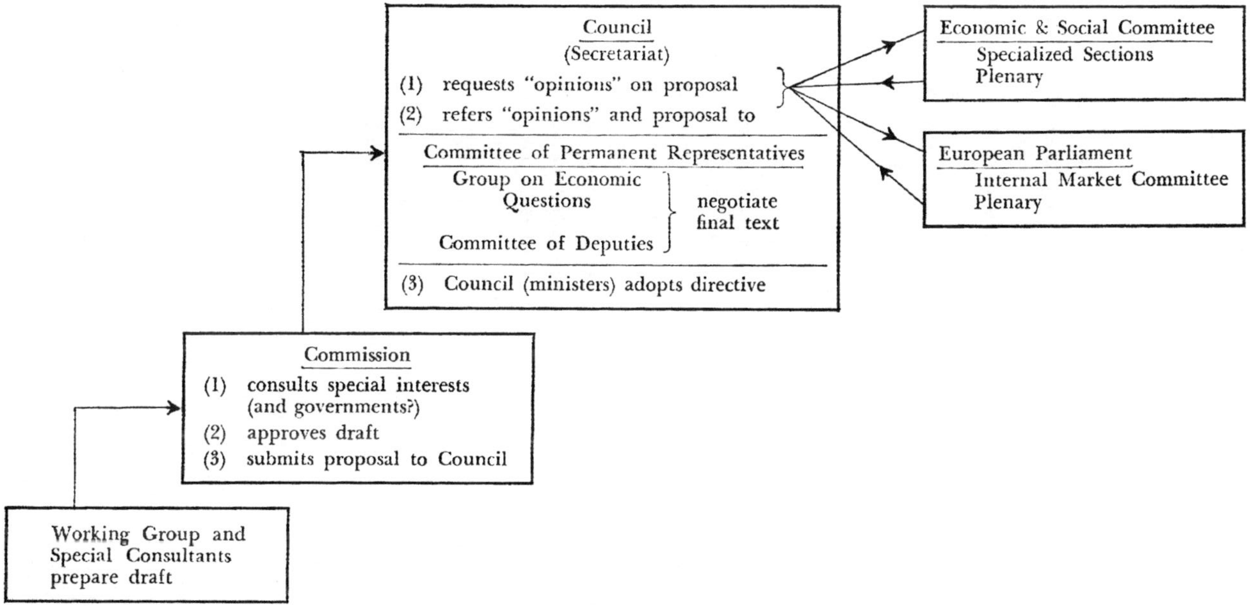

liability companies.[6] Other reasons for selecting these companies were that "their purposes are practically the same or that on certain points they are subject to identical or similar national rules," and last, but not least, to include some, but not all, company forms in this group might encourage "getting round the law."[7]

This selection, dictated by a sense of urgency,[8] was applauded by some[9] and only reluctantly accepted—for practical reasons—by others, including the majority of the Economic and Social Committee.[10] In accepting the limitation, the Committee urged that the coordination be extended as quickly as possible to other types of legal persons, including cooperatives and "foundations" *(fondations, Stiftungen)* some of which play an important role in national economies.[11]

(b) Vertical Limitation: Only Three Subjects Chosen

When it came to choosing the specific subjects the ideas on priorities differed widely. Theoretically, the discussion was of course in the context of what coordination was "necessary" in the sense of Article 54.[11a] In reality, most of the individual national experts wished to focus first either on those aspects which in their own company law were deficient and required reform, or on those areas where less strict provisions in other Member States posed a potential problem. Thus Dr. Gessler, obviously concerned at the loss of power by the German authorities to keep out foreign undercapitalized "dwarf" companies,[12] urged concentrating first on provisions governing the minimum required company capital, availability and maintenance of the capital, but also the rules concerning the authority of company organs to act on its behalf and publication of information on the legal status of companies, all of which called for a reform in *other* Member States.[13] The Belgian delegation laid particular emphasis on strengthening the protection of minority shareholders. The Netherlands experts continued to assert that no coordination was necessary; they argued that although the Netherlands company law was much less elaborate there have not been any more numerous bankruptcies under that law than under the strict legislation of its neighbor to the East.[14] However, a French civil service official employed in D.G. III, brought with him to Brussels a draft of a questionnaire prepared originally, as reported by Professor Houin, by the so-called Hamel Committee at the Secretariat of State for Economic Affairs in Paris. This paper was limited to three topics: publication of information in connection with the formation of companies, the extent of the authority of company organs in relation to third parties, and circumstances under which a company was considered invalid ("null and void"). The same questionnaire, designed to elicit information on national rules governing these topics, was sent by the EEC Commission to the Member Governments. The responses were submitted to the working group which in the end embraced a somewhat broadened version of the original French selection of topics.[15] The idea apparently was that the three topics lent themselves to a treatment separate from other aspects of company law, since the coordinating rules could be designed so as to apply to the entire group of the companies concerned, while subsequent directives would coordinate separately other aspects (such as minimum capital requirements).[16] In effect, the first directive was to serve as a "trial run" for the coordination process and was to be dealt with quickly on a priority basis. This, we shall see, proved to be an illusion.

The selection of the topics was criticized both within and outside the working group because, so went the argument, on one hand, it did not include the truly urgent matters, and on the other hand, it exceeded the authority under Article 54, par. 3(g).[17]

Nevertheless the working group proceeded with the drafting of the coordinating rules in these three areas, and the draft was formally approved by the Commission, published and transmitted to the Council on February 19, 1964,[18] and the Council then instituted the next phase in the lawmaking process, consultation with the Economic and Social Committee and the European Parliament.

2. Consultations with Transnational Economic and Political Groups

These consultations begin as a rule, when a working group of national experts and Commission staff reaches a more or less general agreement on a draft of a directive—and prior to the submission of the draft to the Commission for formal approval. The multiphased consultation process of mutual enlightenment and persuasion broadens the circle of the elite beyond the national and transnational bureaucracy directly concerned, and beyond the group of scholars linked with it.

(a) "Bilateral" Consultations with Economic Interest Groups

Perhaps because this process had not been firmly established as yet at the time when the first draft of the first coordination directive became available, the Commission staff omitted the first stage—that is, "bilateral" consultation with the interested economic and professional groups organized on the Community level. By contrast, in 1968 the draft of the second coordination directive[19] was submitted, with a request for an opinion, to the three professional "summit" organizations grouping together national associations of industry, banking and the legal professions, that is, the Union of Industries of the European Community *(Union des Industries de la Communauté, UNICE),* the Federation of Banks of the EEC *(Fédération Bancaire de la C.E.E.),* and the Consultative Commission of the Bar of the Six Countries of the EEC *(Commission Consultative du Barreau des Six Pays de la CEE)* established for this purpose by the International Union of Attorneys *(Union Internationale des Avocats).* These three organizations are now regularly consulted on matters of company law.[20] Yet the number of persons in the transnational secretariats and committees of these nongovernmental organizations, who actually become familiar with the complex technical texts and directly involved in the preparation of the opinions on behalf of the organizations, is quite limited. Thus, the opinion of the *Fédération Bancaire* on the second coordination directive was drafted by a house counsel of a leading national bank who (in addition to his law faculty position and law practice) has served simultaneously on the national company law reform commission and also was a national expert on the Commission's working group. This may be perhaps an extreme, if not unique, instance illustrating the dearth of expert talent in this field.

The impact of the "summit" organizations on lawmaking in the Community has often been reduced by their inability to arrive at a common position. This probably would have been the case with respect to the first directive's provisions on financial disclosure where divisions were clearly along national lines. However, the effort itself to agree on a common posture has probably had some integrating impact on the professional organizations, particularly since the Commission has consistently made it clear that it will attribute little weight to divided counsel, and also has refused to have relations with *national* interest groups, lest it come into conflict with Member Governments.[21]

(b) Institutionalized Consultations: The "Opinion" of the Economic and Social Committee

(i) Committee Structure

When the Commission's proposal for the first coordination directive was received by the President of the Council of Ministers, his first move was, in letters dated March 25, 1964, to request the Economic and Social Committee and the European Parliament to render their "opinions" on the proposal in accordance with Article 54 of the Treaty. This marked the beginning of the second, highly formal and institutionalized, phase of consultations with both the economic and the political quarters in the Community. The "opinions" *(avis)* of the two bodies are not "binding" in the normative sense either upon the Commission or the Council who together hold the power to "make" Community law. The actual influence of these opinions upon the lawmakers has varied, although in this particular instance it was probably greater than has been usually the case.

The Economic and Social Committee's one hundred and one members are appointed by the Council of Ministers according to a nationality key fixed by the Treaty[22] from lists compiled by the Member Governments, and they are to represent the numerous categories of economic and social life in the Community.[23]

The Committee does most of its work in eight specialized sections dealing with the main fields covered by the Treaty which in effect function as parliamentary committees. In order to reflect the transnational socio-economic reality, the Committee members have formed three groups: employers, workers and the heterogeneous "general interest" group.[24] The "general interest" group has been viewed by the workers with considerable suspicion, as in effect concealing additional representatives of employers. With some exceptions, as in the case of transport policy, the alignment in the Committee has generally followed group loyalty rather than national allegiance. The specialized sections are serviced by the Committee secretariat counting some 100 personnel, while the groups must rely on outside organizations (the first group relies on UNICE, the second group on the "summit" labor union organizations) for staff assistance.

The first coordination directive was assigned to the Specialized Section on Economic Questions whose President, M. de Précigout of the employers' group, was persuaded to assume also the office of section rapporteur, an unusual cumulation of functions which obviously would not remain without effect on the tenor of the final opinion.[25] M. de Précigout, a lawyer connected with the textile industry in France and Vice-President of the influential national association of French industry *(Conseil National du Patronat Français,* CNPF), also served as a member of the French Economic and Social Council, and in both capacities had an opportunity to speak with authority on the French national reform. To avoid ruffled feathers and a jurisdictional controversy, the Specialized Section on Non-Wage-Earning Activities and Services was asked to provide a supplementary report on four specific questions, considered to fall within its particular competence.

(ii) Minority Opposition by Dutch-German Industry

In the deliberations of the two Sections, and for that matter in the plenary of the Committee as well, two issues proved sharply controversial: first, the legality and wisdom of the directive in general, and second, the provision concerning financial disclosure. Even those members who did not possess any expertise in company law were able to understand some aspects of these questions, and it is not surprising that those who opposed the second expressed also their doubts, in more or less emphatic terms, on the first issue.

In this first exposure to the "private sector," the Commission's draft encountered a determined opposition by a small minority alliance of Dutch and German industrial interests. While the Dutch industry presented a united front and its spokesman went so far as to formally propose recommittal of the draft to the Commission,[26] there were minor defections from the German employers' group and only a mild support for the opposition from a spokesman for the Federation of Belgian Industries.[27] The workers' group was solidly with the majority which favored the directive, and this included all the German and Dutch members of the labor group; the third or "general interest" group, with one exception to be noted below, also formed a part of the majority.

The opposition was led by Mr. van de Woestijne, a professor at the Technical College in Delft who, although a member of the "general interest" group, succeeded another Dutch professor who had maintained close ties with the Dutch oil industry.[28] The dissenters demanded to know in what respect the divergence of national company laws had jeopardized the exercise of the freedom of establishment, so as to make coordination "necessary," within the meaning of Article 54. Moreover, "partial" harmonization without a "complete view" of the intended "global harmonization" was improper and risked introducing new discriminations.[29] The majority of the Section on Economic Questions, after hearing the staff member of the legal service of the Commission expound on the problem, chose to assume the legality of the proposal by implication (recognizing that the Court of Justice would have the last word). However, the other Section, perhaps under the "law oriented" influence of its rapporteur, Sig. de Cesare, a former member of the Italian Consiglio di Stato, dealt with the question of legality in some considerable detail without any hesitation and rejected the minority onslaught on the legality in ringing terms.[30] In its final opinion, the majority of the plenary Committee upheld the legality of the directive but suggested that since the divergence of national laws could affect not only the exercise of the freedom of establishment but also the competitive conditions as well, "the legal bases of the directive" might be enlarged, implying no doubt a possible recourse to Article 100.[31]

More significant, however, was the policy posture of the Committee majority which urged the Commission to proceed energetically beyond the first directive toward the coordination of other topics, toward clear-cut rather than compromise solutions, even if this meant more far-reaching "harmonization," in the interest of clarity and simplicity. Even a "harmonization" of the general principles of civil, commercial and criminal law was "desirable," but it required "careful study and great prudence." Several provisions of the Commission proposal were criticized as not going far enough and indulging in an "appearance of harmony," only to conceal persisting "different realities." Moreover, the majority desired to strengthen the arrangement for assuring the Commission's coordinating role in the adoption of national reform laws.[32]

(iii) The Showdown on Financial Disclosure—The Outcome

There was unanimous agreement, M. de Précigout explained, on requiring "publicity" for the financial statements of those companies which "draw upon public capital markets"—a criterion first employed in French law—and a "rather large majority" was ready to go further and to support the original stance of the Commission which would have extended this obligation to all capital companies.[33] However, since such extension would result in flooding the public repositories of information with data on economically insignificant companies and thus reduce the efficacy of the "publicity" system, a large majority was ready to accept the exception for companies with assets of not more than one million dollars as proposed by the Commission, but only if the exception was broadened to cover not solely small limited liability companies, but small stock companies as well.[34] This was a concession to the Dutch view pressed by the spokesmen not only for the Dutch industry, but for the Dutch labor unions as well[35] who pointed out that, since the limited liability company form did not exist in Dutch law, the small "close" stock companies which took its place in the Netherlands would be subject to discrimination, unless they were given the same treatment. It was also argued that confining the exception from the disclosure obligation to limited liability companies would encourage an "escape" from the stock company to the limited liability company form.[36] The view was also advanced that it would be possible for a company to manipulate its balance sheet so as to show assets below the minimum level in order to remain within the exception,[37] and there was a general feeling that the exemption criterion based on the amount of the assets ought to be reviewed.

The most noteworthy feature of the relatively brief debate was a confrontation between two German nationals, Mrs. Hesse, a member of the workers' group and official of the German white-collar workers' union,[38] and Mr. Seibel, a member of the employers' group connected with the Chamber of Industry and Commerce in the Federal Republic. The issues were the same as those debated hotly in the Federal Republic in connection with the national disclosure legislation, and concerned both the rationale and the criteria for the disclosure obligation.[39] Reflecting the position of the Social Democrats and labor union spokesmen in Bonn, Mrs. Hesse asserted[40] in the Committee debate that disclosure must serve not only to protect creditors and shareholders, but must also assure the transparency of the national economy in the public interest. Mr. Seibel, on the other hand, took the view that, at the Community level at any rate, the consideration of any interest beyond that of creditors and shareholder-investors exceeded the powers of the Community institutions. This view, we shall see, was echoed by the German Christian Democratic voices in the European Parliament. Similarly, the divergence among the Dutch employers and workers reflected the corresponding debate in the Netherlands, surrounding the Verdam Commission Report.

On one aspect, however, there was general agreement in the Economic and Social Committee: whatever the scope of the disclosure obligation, the content of the financial statements and the procedure for their preparation and verification, which differed greatly from one Member State to another, must be coordinated to assure comparability. This position became the central point in the next phase of the consultation process, the proceeding before the European Parliament, and in addition to presenting a weighty question for which the Commission had no immediate answer, it was employed by the opponents of the coordination as a handy delaying device.

In the final Committee vote—at the end of a single plenary session devoted to the subject—67 members voted in favor of the "opinion" supporting the directive subject to the qualifications indicated earlier, and 7 opposed it. The negative votes were cast by four Dutch and two German members of the employers' group,[41] and by Professor van de Woestijne.

The tenor of the Committee "opinion" reflects substantial French influence, exerted very likely in no small measure through the able French Section President and rapporteur. In contrast with the proceedings of the European Parliament, one discerns little impact of the spokesmen for the German industry, perhaps because those circles have attributed little importance to the Committee This generally skeptical attitude might be explained in part by the fact that although the Committee has its national counterparts in Belgium, France, Italy and the Netherlands, no comparable body exists in Germany, and in fact the Federal Government originally was opposed to its establishment as a Community institution. Germany industry is thus accustomed to pressing its interests directly with the Government or with the members of the Parliament. The German workers, on the other hand, have consistently selected top union talent for service on the Committee, and seem to pay considerable attention to its work.

(iv) The EEC Commission's Response

The Commission staff that labored assiduously to help indoctrinate the Committee members in the mysteries of company law and Treaty interpretation was evidently pleased by the outcome, particularly since the affirmative opinion of the Committee provided a welcome compensation for the widespread criticism which the draft had encountered in professional literature. The energetic Dr. Bruns expressed this sentiment when he addressed the Committee plenary session immediately after the vote. He announced that in view of the "particularly valuable" opinion of the Committee, the Commission would deviate from the established procedure and return the draft to its working group before the institution of the proceeding within the Council of Ministers; this move would enable the group to review the proposal in the light of the modifications proposed by the Committee. This promise was fulfilled and—as we shall see—the First Draft was modified substantially. However, not all the modifications proposed by the Committee or by the European Parliament were accepted.

(c) Institutionalized Consultations Continued: The "Opinion" of the European Parliament

If the Commission's proposal fared reasonably well in its first confrontation with organized economic interests, it sailed into stormy weather when it came before the "transnational politicians." To start with, it met with the most common and yet the most exasperating maneuver in parliamentary practice, a thinly disguised but effective delaying tactic.

(i) The Composition of the European Parliament

Like the Economic and Social Committee, the European Parliament must be heard but need not be obeyed by the lawmakers in the Community.

Each national parliament sends a specified number of its own members to the European Parliament, and the national contingents more or less accurately mirror the power positions of the national political parties in the national arenas, except that until very recently Communists were kept out.[42] The Italian contingent now includes Communist Party members. The deputies are organized in four transnational political groups, the Christian-Democrats, the Socialists, and the Liberals (with affiliates), and the French *Union Démocratique Européenne* (U.D.E.), comprising the Gaullist supporters. The positions on more important matters are determined as a rule in group caucuses, and—as in national parliamentary bodies—most of the work is done in standing committees of limited membership.[43]

(ii) The Labors of the Internal Market Committee

The request for the Parliament's opinion on the first coordination directive was received by the "Bureau" in late March 1964, and it was assigned to the Internal Market Committee. As is the case with all the official positions in the Parliament, the crucial jobs of rapporteur are distributed in equal proportion among the four political groups; within each group, the most interested deputy is given the assignment. In this instance, by a decision of the Internal Market Committee of April 23, 1964, the rapporteurship went to the Committee Vice President, Mr. Berkhouwer, a member of the "liberal" group and of a Netherlands conservative party, and a law-trained spokesman for the Dutch industry.[44] Mr. Berkhouwer succeeded, very likely with some assistance from his Christian-Democrat colleague and co-national, the Committee President Mr. Blaisse, whose ties with the industry were, if anything, even closer,[45] to delay the submission of the report for more than two years—a feat which is quite uncommon in the annals of the Parliament. This delay was made subject to a rare public criticism in the plenary debate.[46] Mr. Blaisse did not return to the European Parliament after 1966.

The Internal Market Committee met nine times between December 1964 and April 1966. Initially, the Committee had before it only the proposed text of the directive with a brief "motivation" (statement of reasons) prepared by the Commission staff. In view of this scanty information, the rapporteur first addressed a questionnaire to the Commission—a procedure that is not common but was employed in several instances before—intended to elicit further data on the proposed directive, and on the Commission's current and projected work in the company law field generally. The Commission replied on May 6, 1965, to the twenty-three questions posed to it; these answers and a brief sketch of the pertinent national laws, prepared by the Committee Secretariat,[47] apparently constituted the only written information made available to the Committee as a basis for its deliberations on this complex technical subject. Several members of the Commission staff appeared before the Committee and gave a detailed oral explanation of the proposed text but no "independent" company law experts were heard. On March 21, 1966, and on April 25, 1966, the Committee finally approved the report and a resolution with an "opinion" proposed for adoption in the plenary, by a vote of 20 with two abstentions.[48] The vote evidently did not reflect the sharp controversy within the Committee.

Paradoxically, the report did not support, and in fact was in conflict with, the proposed "opinion," and this was a cause of an understandable bafflement for the Commission.[49] The report was strongly critical of the proposed directive and stated that in several respects the Commission exceeded the legal basis of Article 54 of the Treaty.[50] Some of the legal arguments advanced to show that the proposed directive was illegal were more convincing than others.

In the first place, the report relied on the traditional rule laid down by the Permanent Court of International Justice to the effect that treaties limiting state sovereignty must be given a restrictive interpretation. This is only one of the principles of interpretation, and one may wonder how relevant it is when it comes to interpreting the EEC Treaty which differs in many respects from the common variety of treaties.

Second, it was said in the report that some articles in the directive were so detailed and specific as to leave hardly any freedom to the national legislator, and this feature was contrary to the Treaty which defined directives as "binding upon the Member States as to the result to be achieved, but the form and means of enforcing them shall be left to the national authorities";[51] in effect, the proposed text would require Member States to adopt a "uniform law" whereas Article 54 authorizes "coordination" only. There is some support for this criticism in the literature.[52] On the other hand, other writers have pointed out that the directives of the Community, generally speaking, have been becoming progressively more specific;[53] some felt that the "equivalence" of guaranties required in Article 54 may in certain instances be achieved only when "form and substance" are connected so closely as to become merged, and that the Community institutions were given the necessary range of power in the interest of achieving substantial equivalence;[54] thus even a uniform law could be imposed in a directive if the only means to achieve effective harmonization was through "uniformity of time, means and forms";[55] in any event, after a directive is adopted the Member States would still be free to transform it into national law through means of their choice, that is, by a statute, a government decree or administrative order.[56]

Finally, the report attempted to draw certain conclusions from a judgment of the Court of Justice of the Communities in the widely discussed case of *Costa v. E.N.E.L.* In the plenary debate of the Parliament, a deputy characterized these conclusions as "slightly erroneous," a description apparently tempered by parliamentary courtesy.[57]

In a more weighty observation, based as much on policy as on legal considerations, the report castigated the Commission for having failed to offer any evidence, obtained through inquiries from banking, industrial or commercial quarters, that decisions concerning the location of company facilities and activities were in fact influenced by differences in national company laws rather than by considerations relating to taxes, foreign exchange restrictions and transport cost. Another objection was that the Commission appeared to proceed "in slices" rather than first evolving an overview, a "*conception d'ensemble,*" based on a thorough comparative study of "the legal problems in general, and the administrative, commercial and accounting practices in the Member States."[58]

(iii) A Paradox, a Paradox . . .

Along with the negative report, the Internal Market Committee adopted a resolution containing the proposed "opinion" in which the European Parliament was to express its pleasure ("*se félicite*") at the Commission's initiative and approve the draft directive, subject to certain modifications. The principal modification, again reflecting the Netherlands-German coalition of interests, aimed at broadening still further the exemption from financial disclosure and postponing the disclosure obligation for limited liability companies and Dutch close companies, pending coordination of provisions prescribing the content of the financial statements. The resolution asked that the Parliament be advised of the other sectors of company law earmarked for coordination, and it stressed the need for an overview.

The contradiction between the report and the resolution can be explained if one reconstructs the happenings in the Internal market Committee which began its difficult, and in many respects painful, proceedings in Rome during December 1965. Of the more than twenty Committee members, apart from Mr. Berkhouwer who obviously set the tone, only Mr. Blaisse and Mr. Deringer, a member of the Federal Parliament, and to a lesser degree his socialist colleague, Mr. Seuffert, were actively interested in this aspect of the Committee's work. The first draft of the report was prepared by Mr. Berkhouwer alone, and was said to have been replete with factual errors; the author proposed to say flatly that the disclosure provisions were illegal and that no action should be taken on the directive—a view reminiscent of the position taken by Professor van de Woestijne in the Economic and Social Committee. Moreover, a move developed in the Committee to refer the legal aspects to the Legal Committee of the European Parliament which would have meant another postponement, as well as a danger that a restrictive interpretation of Article 54, par. 3(g) would be "frozen" at this early junction. The members of the Commission staff who arrived in Rome from Brussels succeeded in persuading the Committee to forego this move. If the Commission officials and the sympathetic members of the Internal Market Committee had attempted to modify the text of the report radically enough to reflect their own views, still another year's delay would no doubt have been inevitable. Consequently, the tactical decision was made to concentrate on the more important of the two documents, the resolution with the "opinion." The Commission staff had the difficult task of instructing the Committee members in the technicalities of company law, and the painful nature of this process is illustrated by the fact that it took four long meetings of the Committee to deal with just the first four articles of the draft.

(iv) Profile of a Community Lawyer

Perhaps the most active participant in the parliamentary proceeding was Mr. Deringer of the Christian Democratic group in the European Parliament, a deputy for the Christian Democratic Party in the Bundestag and member of its Legal Committee, and last but not least, a successful attorney, representing substantial corporate clients and trade organizations particularly in matters of the new European law, including antitrust law and agricultural regulations. He has been engaged in practice before the German authorities and courts, and before the EEC Commission and Court of Justice; at the same time, he has played a role in the framing of national legislation in the Bundestag and in the formation of the Community policy in the European Parliament. He was able—for instance—to address the Commission in the European Parliament on matters of interest to industry in the form of parliamentary questions which, according to the Treaty,[59] the Commission was required to answer. Moreover, as an effective chairman of the newly created Legal Committee of the European Parliament, he sought to explore ways of increasing the power and influence of that body.[59a] Keeping in mind the rather negative attitude of important sectors in his own Parliament and of the German industry toward breaching the privacy of limited liability companies,[60] Mr. Deringer may well have been inclined to join Mr. Berkhouwer in seeking the recommittal of the draft directive to the Commission. But a realistic appraisal of the parliamentary situation convinced him that a majority (including his own German Socialist colleagues) would not be amenable to such an unprecedented rebuff to the Commission. Nor was he prepared to carry the opposition so far as to cause serious prejudice to the Commission's standing. Thus he disassociated himself from Mr. Berkhouwer in a statement made on behalf of the Christian Democratic group in the plenary. In that statement he criticized the delay in the completion of the Committee report on the ground that it had damaged the reputation of the Parliament, and he also took issue with some of the legal arguments in the report.[61] He concentrated on two points which he considered essential for his objectives—the postponement of the effective date of the disclosure obligation for limited liability companies, and the preservation and extension to other Members, to the greatest extent possible, of the German rule excluding the "*ultra vires*" doctrine. He succeeded in carrying with him an "almost unanimous" Committee,[62] and eventually the plenary as well.

(v) Plenary Debate: The "Groups" Speak

The plenary debate extended over three sessions, and it was much more lively and better attended than an average debate in the European Parliament. In the opening summary of his report Mr. Berkhouwer, the rapporteur, sought to explain the delay and dispel any possible impression of partiality; but his position on the substance of the directive was quite negative.

In accordance with the established pattern, he was followed by the spokesmen for each of the four political groups, starting with Mr. Deringer who spoke in the name of the Christian Democratic group within which there was relatively little interest in this subject. He carefully rejected the implication in the rapporteur's speech that either he, Deringer, or the opinion of the Legal Committee of the Bundestag (on which Mr. Berkhouwer also relied) had reached the conclusion that the directive exceeded the legal basis in the Treaty. He made it clear that the Christian Democratic group did not take a position on the issue of legality—very likely because it was divided on the disclosure provision—and proceeded to state his personal opinion to the effect that disclosure by limited liability companies was not required for the protection of either the creditors or the investor-shareholders; whether it was necessary for the protection of workers or the public was a political question unrelated to the freedom of establishment, and the protection of these interests was not a proper basis for a directive. He also adumbrated that one of the reasons why "certain Member States" were so vigorously opposed to some provisions in the directive was that the Commission relied on Article 54, allowing majority vote on such an important matter, rather than on Article 100 requiring unanimity—an argument advanced earlier by the staff of D.G. IV. He pressed for the modification of the Commission's text on the two issues described above which were close to his heart; he urged the Commission to present promptly and at one time all the provisions which unquestionably required coordination; and he pointedly enumerated what he considered the advantages of a "European company" form as compared with the coordination of company law, particularly if it was to occur "by little slices."

The position of the Socialist group was stated in a brief (five paragraph), perfunctory, and ambiguous statement by Mr. Seuffert, a successful German attorney with a corporate practice in the tax field who has since become a judge and Vice President at the Federal Constitutional Court. While mildly praising the directive as "a first step on a long and difficult journey" and finding Mr. Deringer's proposal to postpone the disclosure for limited liability companies "regrettable" (this would presumably be expected from him as a member of the Socialist group), he found the reasons motivating the proposal for a delay "perfectly well founded."

It was perhaps not a coincidence that many of the deputies actively interested in this subject were members of the Liberal group whose views were presented by M. Jozeau-Marigné, a notary representing the Independent Republican Party in the French Senate. Yet neither he nor M. Pleven, his group and party colleague, and chairman of the important French national committee on company law reform, who also intervened vigorously in the plenary debate, was a member of the Internal Market Committee. Their absence from the Committee was perhaps the reason why the Liberal group submitted a series of amendments as late as at the plenary stage of the proceeding. M. Jozeau-Marigné indicated that his group also had considered proposing that the directive be referred back to the EEC Commission because it wished to avoid "multiple consultations of our national parliaments" on piecemeal coordination measures, but decided against such a move for fear of jeopardizing two years of work. Instead, the group decided to propose specific improvements of the text, including one designed to "assure" that it remained within the scope of Article 54.[63] The most important two amendments, however, were, *first,* to eliminate the postponement in the disclosure obligation (and here the speaker pointedly referred to the remarks in the German Federal Parliament that protection of third parties can no longer be delayed); and, *second,* to limit this obligation further, so as to exempt not only the Dutch "close" stock companies with assets of not more than one million dollars but *all* stock companies of that size "that do not draw upon public savings"—which has been the yardstick employed by French law.[64]

In a spirited discussion Mr. Colonna di Paliano, a member of the Commission, supported the first amendment and urged that the postponement provision be dropped; Messrs. Deringer, Berkhouwer and Blaisse argued that it should be maintained, and the plenary followed their view and rejected the amendment.[65] But the other Liberal amendment, which sought to introduce the French law criterion into the exemption from the disclosure and was strongly pressed by M. Pleven, was adopted despite the negative posture by Commissioner Colonna di Paliano and sharp opposition by the German deputies, both Socialist and Christian Democrat, who argued that this criterion had no legal meaning in German law. Another Liberal amendment advanced by the French deputies that would have required every Member State to assure publication of data on companies in a *local* newspaper and a reference to such publication in a single centralized file maintained for the entire country, again in the French image, was not accepted.[66]

The last of the four groups to present its view was the Gaullist *Union démocratique européenne.* M. Drouot L'Hermine, carefully avoiding what he called the "technical content" of the directive, criticized the Berkhouwer Report as not going far enough and called for as rapid a harmonization of legislation as possible, "if we want really to build a Europe which, sooner or later, will turn into a political Europe."[67] He asserted that of the six Member States, the Federal Republic and France were the two countries which proved by their acts that they took very seriously the importance of evolving a European commercial law. Recalling that France was often blamed for not being "European" enough, he referred to the massive effort, led by M. Pleven, to fit the French company law into a "European plan" and he stressed, "in the name of my group," the French origin of the proposal for a European company. Having delivered his address, which was as eloquent as it was general, M. Drouot L'Hermine left the hall, as Mr. Berkhouwer regretfully observed, not to return for the rest of the debate.

The most emphatic individual defense of the legality of the directive came, as in the Economic and Social Committee, from Italian quarters. Sig. Battaglia of the Liberal group, a member of the right-of-center Italian Liberal Party in the Italian Senate, stressed an argument particularly germane to Italian law, that coordination of national legislation was necessary in order to reduce the tendency—prevalent in Italy—to impose local law on foreign companies.[68]

Commissioner Colonna di Paliano restated the position of the Commission on the legal issues, in addition to commenting on the amendments.[69] As a member of a collegiate body, he was in a difficult position when urged to take a position on new amendments, submitted on the floor, that would modify the text approved by the Commission. In general, when pressed he took a negative view of amendments that would substantially deviate from the Commission's text, and supported those amendments that sought to restore the original Commission text, modified in the Parliamentary Committee.

The plenary debate and the attitudes taken on the amendments were, at least in some measure, instructive in revealing the alignment of the groups and individuals. However, the final vote on the resolution and "opinion" was anticlimactic and without much interest. The only negative vote was cast by Sig. Carboni, a professor of maritime law from Cagliari, Sardinia, a Christian Democrat in the Italian Senate. The good law professor dissented because of his passionate attachment to the *ultra vires* doctrine[70] which he was prepared to defend single-handedly to the last drop of his southern blood.[71]

(vi) Aftermath: The "Second Draft"

With the consultation stage completed, the Commission's working group—as anticipated by Dr. Bruns—reopened its discussion on those aspects of the directive raised in the consultation proceedings. However, the Commission staff alone prepared a new draft, which the Commission approved without prior reference to the working group and which it forwarded to the Council of Ministers in October 1966.[72] This Second Draft reflected a number of suggestions made by the Economic and Social Committee and some, but not all, amendments proposed by the European Parliament. Above all, the Commission did not embrace the European Parliament's view on financial disclosure. Although it agreed to extend the exemption from disclosure so as to cover not only *small* limited liability companies but also the Dutch close stock companies, the Commission did not agree to broaden the exemption still further to all small stock companies that did not draw upon public capital markets. In addition to the fact that the latter concept was unfamiliar outside the French system, such broadening of the exemption, the Commission explained, would free from disclosure "too many stock companies whose financial situation is of interest to third parties"; it would constitute "a step backward" from the level of the law in Germany, Belgium, Luxembourg, and Italy, and it was not acceptable to the majority of governmental experts.[73] It soon appeared, however, that the acute disagreement on this major political issue remained unresolved and would cause further delay and controversy.

3. The Final Stage of Lawmaking: The Council of Ministers

(a) The Committee of Permanent Representatives: Conflict or "Collusion" with the Commission?

The preparatory work for the busy Ministers is done within the multi-tiered framework of the so-called Committee of the Permanent Representatives[74] which on its highest level consists of the Ambassadors heading the national Permanent Missions of the Six to the Communities in Brussels. The Ministers in the Council have a dual responsibility, first, as "representatives of the Member States" and, second, as members of a Community institution;[75] and the members of the Committee of Permanent Representatives have the same dual status. However, since in theory at any rate all the decisions must be made by the Council itself, actual decision-making cannot be delegated to the Committee. This principle is to assure that the power of final decision remains in the hands of the politically "responsible" Ministers, and is not usurped by "faceless bureaucrats." With the exception of the Permanent Mission of Luxembourg which is quite small (three persons), each Permanent Mission maintains a staff of twenty to twenty-five officials drawn mostly from the Ministries of Foreign Affairs, but also included are officials on detached service from Ministries for Economic Affairs, Finance and other departments. Only the Federal Republic maintains a careful balance between diplomats and officials of the Ministry of Economic Affairs which reflects the division of responsibility for Common Market matters in the Federal Government, a source of continuing difficulty in the formulation of German policy. In the German Mission, a high ranking member of the Foreign Office acts as the Permanent Representative, but his deputy is a senior official of the Ministry of Economic Affairs.

The Committee meets weekly both at the ambassadorial level of the Permanent Representatives themselves and at the level of the Deputies who, with the one exception noted above, are also career diplomats of superior rank. The Ambassadors deal with matters of substantial political significance, including those concerning foreign relations of the Community. The Deputies handle all the other matters, and these comprise not only "routine business" but also "technical" proposals which, however, may have also certain political implications, as in the case of the first coordination directive. It is noteworthy that the conclusions of the

Deputies are not reviewed by the Ambassadors but are submitted directly to the Ministers.[76] Some fifteen permanent working groups, staffed by the Permanent Missions and national officials commuting from the capitals, prepare the work for the Committee sessions, with the assistance of the Secretariat of the Council of Ministers. The Secretariat is composed of some 500 persons who, like the Commission staff, are transnational "civil servants" employed by the Communities.

As one could expect, tension has existed between the Commission complex and the Permanent Representatives' "establishment" which in principle is expected to act as "the eyes and ears of the national governments"[77] and to defend their prerogatives and those of the Council, as against the Commission's assertions of power. The influence of the Committee has clearly grown at the expense of the Commission in certain matters which did not require the Commission's formal initiative. Thus for instance the preparatory work for the "European company" was entrusted by the Ministers, at the insistence of France, to the Committee rather than to the Commission. However, the Permanent Representatives have gradually become more "Community conscious." What initially may have been described as a "conflict" relationship between the "supranational" Commission and the nationally instructed Committee, has progressively evolved into a cooperation, albeit an uneasy one, at least when the power relationship between the two is not directly involved. The Committee not only influences the Commission but it also interprets and defends the Commission's positions in national capitals.

(b) The Directive before the Committee of Permanent Representatives

(i) The Actors

When the Commission submitted the 1966 text (Second Draft) of the directive to the Council it in effect exercised its Treaty authority to withdraw its proposal at any time before the "final action" by the Ministers[78] and substitute a new one. When the new text reached the Council of Ministers, it was first referred, along with the two "opinions" of the European Parliament and the Economic and Social Committee, to a standing working group of the Committee of Permanent Representatives, the Group on Economic Questions. In this Group were some familiar faces from the national Ministries of Justice that appeared earlier as national experts in the Commission's working group.

In a great number, if not in most instances, an agreement is reached by the Six Governments and the Commission on the substance of the

Commission's text before it reaches this final phase in the lawmaking process. At times, however, when agreement cannot be reached—and this was the case with our directive—significant questions are left open for resolution in the Council framework. Moreover, the full impact of pressures, exerted locally on the national governments by economic interest groups, often becomes felt at this stage of the proceeding only and must be taken into account. Again, the clearance process within the national governments moves in this phase, as a rule for the first time, vertically to the highest echelons and horizontally to all the interested departments other than that with primary competence. Finally, the seasoned "old hands" in the Permanent Missions review the proposal for its compatibility with more general national policies toward the Community and with Community precedents in the same or related fields, and also weigh its effect as a precedent for the future. No wonder therefore, that new solutions and significant modifications are often brought about by the national representatives.

The actors in this phase of the proceeding may be grouped into four categories. First, the national delegations primarily press the postures determined in their respective capitals and reflecting "national interest." Second, the Commission staff, also bound at least in a general way by instructions, aims at preserving the Commission text and particularly those aspects of the proposal that in their view best advance Community interests. Third, the Secretariat of the Council of Ministers poses as a "neutral" and "administrative" factor; but at times it is capable of suggesting new avenues, precisely because it enjoys a degree of freedom from any instructions. Last but not least, the Chairman of the Group and the Chairman of the Committee assume the position of "Presidential impartiality" by relinquishing their posts on their respective national delegations to other national officials; they exert pressure on the national delegations and on the Commission's staff toward advancing the negotiations and disposing of the matter as promptly as possible. Under this pressure, the effectiveness of which varies depending upon the energy and ingenuity of the Chairman, national instructions are loosened, new alliances created, and "Presidential compromises" are considered. The national delegations of course are in the best bargaining position because they are capable of trading concessions. The Commission has little to bargain with beyond the implied threat of withholding consent to the modification of its text.[79] In theory, if the Commission refused to accept a modification the text could not become law unless approved by a *unanimous* Council, and in most cases the Commission would be able to enlist the support of at least one Member Government for its position. Moreover, if the modification of the Commission's text, made without its consent, should be so radical as to constitute in effect a new solution, the Council act might be subject to annulment by the Court of Justice.[80]

(ii) A Partial Consensus

In the case of our directive, the process was simplified on the one hand by the fact that the senior officials of the Ministries of Justice who did most of the negotiating at this stage had been involved in the enterprise from the very outset, starting at the Commission working group level, and no other Ministries claimed substantial concurrent interest. On the other hand, the thorny "political" problem of financial disclosure remained unsettled because of the German and Dutch opposition; and—as we shall see—the Italian delegation introduced a series of new demands in the field of company invalidity which it was not prepared to abandon at least as long as the German delegation maintained its negative stand on the disclosure.

The Group on Economic Questions met throughout the first part of 1967, with the Commission staff present as active participants since the proceeding was based on a formal Commission proposal. The Belgian chairman, a high official of the Ministry of Justice, working closely with the Commission's legal advisor, also a Belgian national, played a prominent part at this stage in reducing the area of disagreement. However, in June 1967 the Group, unable to make further progress, decided to pass on to the higher echelon the two problems on which the deadlock persisted. Considerable pessimism prevailed in the Group at that time, and it was felt more or less generally that the matter might have to go as high up as the Council of Ministers itself, possibly with the participation of the Ministers of Justice.

When the proceedings began before the Committee of Permanent Representatives at the Deputies' level, the German officials were on one extreme end of the spectrum. They were unalterably opposed to any provision imposing a disclosure obligation upon limited liability companies, pending coordination at the Community level of the content of the financial documents; but at the same time they insisted that the directive must exempt from any obligation whatsoever all such companies which fall below a specified minimum size. It may be relevant to note here that the draft of the new Federal law subjecting German limited liability companies for the first time to a limited disclosure requirement was not to be published until some two years later.[81] At the other extreme were the Belgian and Italian officials who opposed any delay or exemption from the disclosure duty. The Commission representatives made every effort to maintain the Commission's 1966 formula which, they claimed, had the support of five delegations, and they were particularly opposed to fixing the floor for the disclosure obligation—at one time the then German Chairman proposed the figure of $2,500,000 of assets as a "Presidential compromise" that did not prove particularly helpful—and at the same time deferring the effective date of the obligation.[82] A series of compromise proposals was suggested by several delegations designed to conciliate the divergences.[83] The chairmanship passed to the German delegation on July 1, 1967, and in the ensuing difficult negotiations a compromise gradually emerged with respect to the Italian and German demands in the field of invalidity of companies.

(iii) Disclosure Problem "Resolved"

It took another six months before the Deputies reached a unanimous agreement on the disclosure provision in early December 1967. Thereafter they referred the text back to the Group with instructions to adjust the remaining differences and to complete the redrafting. The final text imposed the general disclosure obligation on all the companies covered by the directive, but it postponed the disclosure obligation of limited liability companies and Dutch close stock companies (which were defined in the directive) until the effective date of a further directive. This additional directive was to (a) coordinate the content of the balance sheet and the statement of profit and loss, and (b) relieve some of these companies, whose assets were less than the minimum amount to be fixed in that directive, of the obligation to publish "all or a part of" these documents. The Council of Ministers was to adopt the second directive within two years—and in a separate declaration the Council of Ministers directed the Commission to submit an appropriate draft before December 31, 1968. The compromise satisfied the German insistence on the delay and the Commission's opposition to a fixed floor for an exemption.

Just before Christmas 1967, a consensus was confirmed on the entire directive, except that the Commission continued to insist on its own text of the article relating to its coordinating role with respect to prospective changes in national company laws. Finally, this issue also was resolved[84] and the text became Community law upon approval by the Council on March 9, 1968.[85] The Member States became obligated to effect all the necessary modifications in their laws and regulations within eighteen months and to inform the Commission thereof at once.[86]

Along with the directive, the Council approved seven interpretative declarations which were proposed to it by the Committee of Permanent Representatives.

Since a consensus had been reached in the Committee of Permanent Representatives among the national delegations and the Commission, the proposal appeared on the Council's agenda as one of the so-called "items A" which are disposed of by a formal approval and without any debate, unless a Minister or a member of the Commission should demand a discussion, in which case the item is taken up in the next meeting. Since no such demand was made, the approval by the Council became a formality, and one may wonder to what extent the Foreign Ministers were aware of the content of the directive. For all practical purposes the final decision on the directive, including the solution of the "political" problem of financial disclosure, had been made before the matter reached the "political forum" of the Ministers.

This procedure obviously enhances the status and the power of the Committee of Permanent Representatives.[87] In order to be able to exercise this power effectively, the Permanent Representatives, and particularly the Deputies, must be in position to comprehend the technical aspects of a proposal without becoming lost in the technicalities. They must avoid the impression that they seek to replace the experts on the subject, and at the same time they must be able to identify, and deal with, the political problems involved—obviously no mean task for professional diplomats, if one considers the wide range and technical complexity of the subjects on their agenda.

Two characteristics of this phase in the lawmaking should be noted. First, the process of broadening the circle of actors which begins immediately after a "pre-draft" is prepared by the Commission staff is dramatically reversed in this final stage, and only the miniscule, intimate group of national and Community officials, mostly diplomats (and in our case senior law officials), remains in the arena. Second, in contrast to the previous proceedings, this phase takes place without any publicity whatsoever, in an atmosphere amounting almost to mystery, where abstract legal argument is eschewed, bargaining is the order of the day, and solutions at times are reached in the privacy of the chairman's office.

Notes

This is a list of full citations to the literature cited in this excerpt in abbreviated form.

Von Arnim, *Das Niederlassungsrecht für Gesellschaften im Gemeinsamen Markt und die Pläne zur Schaffung einer "europäischen" Handelsgesellschaft,* 1965 AWD 221,
cited as von Arnim, *Das Niederlassungsrecht.*

Bruns, in ENTWICKLUNGSTENDENZEN DES HANDELS- UND STEUERRECHTS, BERICHT ÜBER DIE FACHTAGUNG DES INSTITUTS DER WIRTSCHAFTSPRÜFER IN DEUTSCHLAND e.V., München, Jan. 30–31, 1965 (Düsseldorf 1964),
cited as Bruns, in ENTWICKLUNGSTENDENZEN.

Conard, *Organizing for Business,* in 2 STEIN & NICHOLSON (eds.), AMERICAN ENTERPRISE IN THE EUROPEAN COMMON MARKET 1 (Ann Arbor, 1960),
cited as Conard, *Organizing for Business.*

Dorat des Monts, *Vers un droit européen des sociétés commerciales,* 1965 JUR.-CL.PÉR. DOCTR. 1896,
cited as Dorat des Monts, *Vers un droit européen.*

Everling, *Niederlassungsfreiheit und freier Dienstleistungsverkehr in der EWG,* 1961 BB 1257,
cited as Everling, *Niederlassungsfreiheit.*

Fikentscher & Grossfeld, *The Proposed Directive on Company Law,* 2 C.M.L. Rev. 259 (1964–65),
cited as Fikentscher & Grossfeld, *The Proposed Directive.*

Gessler, *Ziele und Methoden der Harmonisierung des Gesellschaftsrechts der GmbH,* in HARMONISIERUNG DES GESELLSCHAFTSRECHTS UND DES STEUERRECHTS IN EUROPA 9, BERICHT ÜBER DEN VII. INTERNATIONALEN GMBH-KONGRESS IN KÖLN, April 24–26, 1962,
cited as Gessler, in HARMONISIERUNG.

Goldman, COURS DE DROIT DU COMMERCE ET DE LA CONCURRENCE DANS LES COMMUNAUTÉS EUROPÉENNES (Paris 1964–65),
cited as GOLDMAN, COURS.

Houin, *Le Régime juridique des sociétés dans la Communauté économique européenne,* 1965 REV. TRIM. DROIT EUR. 11,
cited as Houin, *Le régime.*

Leleux, *Harmonisation des droits des sociétés,* in VON CAEMMERER (ed.), EUROPÄISCHE HANDELSGESSELSCHAFT UND ANGLEICHUNG DES NATIONALEN GESELLSCHAFTSRECHTS, WISSENSCHAFTLICHES KOLLOQUIUM DER FACHGRUPPE EUROPARECHT 7, Bad Ems, May 5–6, 1967 (Frankfurt a.M., Berlin 1968),
cited as Leleux, *Harmonisation des droits.*

Rodière, *L'harmonisation des législations européennes dans le cadre de la C.E.E.,* 1965 REV. TRIM. DROIT EUR. 336,
cited as Rodière, *L'harmonisation des législations.*

Le Tallec, *Koordinierung des Gesellschaftsrechts in der Europäischen Wirtschaftsgemeinschaft,* 1963 AWD 114,
cited as Le Tallec, *Koordinierung des Gesellschaftsrechts.*

Uniken-Venema, *Coordination du droit des sociétés dans la Cee,* 1966 RIVISTA DELLE SOCIETÀ 994,
cited as Uniken-Venema, *Coordination du droit des sociétés.*

1. EEC Arts. 51, 1–18, 1–19.

2. According to Art. VI of the General Program for the Removal of Restrictions on the Right of Establishment, and General Program for the Removal of Restrictions on the Free Supply of Services, [1962] J.O. 32–46, p. 25, in STEIN, HARMONIZATION OF EUROPEAN COMPANY LAWS — NATIONAL REFORM AND TRANSNATIONAL COORDINATION (Indianapolis, Kansas City, New York, 1971), the national laws of the Member States were to be coordinated before the expiration of the second year of the second stage of the transitional period, that is, according to Art. 8 of the Treaty, before December 31, 1963. Everling, *Niederlassungsfreiheit* at 1259; LeTallec, *Koordinierung des Gesellschaftsrechts in der EWG,* 1963 AWD 114. The time limit set forth in the General Program has been greatly exceeded. In the first draft of the first directive on the coordination of company law ([1964] J.O. 3245), the Commission set as a deadline for the Member States to enact the necessary changes in their national laws the 1st of January, 1965. After that date had passed without the adoption of the directive by the Council, the Commission considered that it should be possible to adopt the directive before the end of 1966 (BERKHOUWER REPORT at 9). The hope to meet this deadline was indicated in the second draft of the Commission (Proposition revisée d'une Directive du Conseil, COM (66) 366 final Oct. 3, 1966) which fixed the 1st of July, 1967, as the date by which the changes in national laws were to be executed. However, the directive was not adopted until March 9, 1968, and the final deadline for modification of national laws was set eighteen months after the notification of the Member States.

3. Bruns, in ENTWICKLUNGSTENDENZEN at 27.

4. Explanatory Memorandum (at 14) to the first draft of a Proposal for a Council Directive to Coordinate and Render Equivalent the Guarantees Required in the Member States of Companies Defined in Art. 58, Second Paragraph of the Treaty, to Protect the Interests of the Members of Such Companies and of Third Parties, Submitted to the Council on Feb. 21, 1964, [1964] J.O. 3245; unofficial English text in 1964 Bull. E.E.C. Supp. No. 3, at 10. Cited as "*First Draft,*" reproduced with the Opinion of the Economic and Social Committee (AVIS). Revised proposal of the directive dated Oct. 3, 1966, in Commission Doc. 1966, COM (66) 366 final of the same date, cited as "*Second Draft.*" *Final Text,* as adopted, on Mar. 8, 1968, in [1968] J.O. L65 (Mar. 14) at 8–12. English text in the Annex p. 515, HARMONIZATION OF EUROPEAN COMPANY LAWS and also in CCH COMM. MKT. REP. ¶ 6083.

According to Uniken-Venema, *Coordination du droit des sociétés* at 1004, the argument of the Commission in the text above did not carry any conviction, for "activity" did not mean "establishment." *But see* M. Molle, Reapporteur de la Commission des lois, DÉB. PARL., SÉNAT, [1966] J.O. (France) at 117.

5. Eighth preambular para. of the proposed directive, *First Draft,* in Avis at 3246; *Final Text,* [1968] J.O. L65 (March 14), at 8.

6. Art. I enumerates specifically the company forms in the national laws included. This means exclusion from coordination, for the time being, of partnerships and limited partnerships, e.g., "sociétés en nom collectif" and "sociétés en commandite simple" in France (see Conard, *Organizing for Business* at 50) and of "foundations" and cooperatives.

7. Working paper 456/III/C/63-F, at 9. 1968 Bull. E.C. No. 3, at 14, II. CCH COMM. MKT. REP. ¶ 1375.02.

8. Sixth preambular paragraph, [1964] J.O. 3245, [1968] J.O. L65, (March 14), at 8.

9. Fikentscher & Grossfeld, *The Proposed Directive* at 265–66, welcomed particularly the inclusion of the limited liability company because it is "very widely interchangeable" with the stock company, and "a transformation into a limited liability company is able (sic) to produce only too easily an escape from the provisions laid down in respect of the joint stock company." Similarly, approving at least temporary limitation, GOLDMAN, COURS at 215, and Dorat des Monts, *Vers un droit européen* at par. I, 3.

10. Avis du Comité économique et social at 3249–56, approved in the 41st session held at Brussels, Oct. 27–28, 1964, by a vote of 68 to 7. Dorat des Monts, *Vers un droit européen* at par I.

11. Avis at [1964] J.O. 3250. The Specialized Group for Non-Salaried Activities and Services, a subsidiary body of the Committee, actually urged that the Commission's proposal be amended to include foundations organized for profit, but the Committee did not accept this view. ZUSÄTZLICHE STELLUNGNAHME, July 30, 1964, CES 195/64 fin. at 3. The Committee stated that, if foundations were not included, this would be an inducement to abuse this legal form. [1964] J.O. 3250, par. II, 2. Dorat des Monts, *Vers un droit européen* at par. I, 3 urged that the problem of the scope of the application of the proposed directive be viewed more from the economic than the legal viewpoint. He suggested that any obligation (such as disclosure) imposed on an association should not be linked to its legal form but to the actual importance it has in the economy. This criterion, employed in the First Draft with respect to the limited liability company which was to be required to disclose its financial situation only if its balance sheet total exceeded one million units of account ($) (Art. 2, par. 1, sect. 1), should be determinative for all associations. Le Tallec, *Koordinierung des Gesellschaftsrechts* at 114, thought that the decision to include only the three mentioned companies was made on the assumption that other types of associations would not be interested in international business activities. But consider the German Zeiss Foundation and its worldwide business. For the structure of this Foundation and its legal and economic aspects see Mayer, *The Carl Zeiss Foundation,* 10 J. PUB. L. 384 (1961).

11a. Art. 54 sets forth a program for implementing the freedom of establishment by, i.a., "coordinating to the necessary extent the safeguards which, for the protection of the interests of Members and others, are required by Member States of companies and firms . . . with a view to making such safeguards equivalent throughout the Community." (par. 3(g)).

12. HARMONIZATION OF EUROPEAN COMPANY LAWS p. 40.

13. Gessler, *Ziele und Methoden,* in HARMONISIERUNG at 18; Gessler pointed out that it was possible, before the enactment of the new French Company Law (Loi No. 66-537 of July 24, 1966), to derive from the prescribed minimum number of incorporators and minimum face amount of a share the minimum capital of 700 French francs, Art. 23 of the Law of 1867, and Art. 28 of the Décret of August 4, 1949. Bruns, in ENTWICKLUNGSTENDENZEN at 17; similarly EVERLING at 84 n.63. The 1966 Company Law introduced the concept of a minimum capital by requiring in its Art. 71 that all stock companies which make public offering must have 500,000 francs ($100,000) minimum capital; for all other stock companies a minimum of 100,000 francs ($20,000) is required. This new law brings the French law in line with the German law (not considering recent changes in monetary values), except that the German stock company law does not employ the distinction between companies which do and which do not make public offering, and thus provides only for a 100,000 DM ($27,300) minimum for all stock companies. The similarity also prevails with respect to the limited liability company for which in both countries 20,000 francs or marks is necessary. Art. 35 of the French Law of July 24, 1966; §5 of the Law on Limited Liability Companies (Gesetz über die Gesellschaften mit beschränkter Haftung). In Luxembourg the required capitalization is still minimal. The minimum number of incorporators taking one share each of the minimum face amount would bring the total capital to 350 Luxembourg francs ($77). Loi sur les sociétés commerciales of Aug. 15, 1915, Arts. 26, 27, 37. In the Netherlands, apparently the Ministry of Justice allows not infrequently incorporation of stock companies with a capital amounting to not more than 1,000 guilders (about $276); an actual minimum amount is not required. Art. 36d of the Netherlands WETBOEK VAN KOOPHANDEL. Belgium has no minimum capital requirement as yet, but one million francs ($20,000) is contemplated to be the requirement in the reform law. In Italy one million lire (about $1,600) is the minimum required to form a stock company. Art. 2327 CODICE CIVILE.

14. Bruns, in ENTWICKLUNGSTENDENZEN at 26.

15. Houin, *Le régime* at 14. Paul Leleux, a legal advisor at the Legal Service of the Commission, writes that the selection was based substantially on "studies made in France where there were complaints of a certain degree of legal chaos" in two of the three areas selected, to wit: " 'publicity' which was extremely insufficient, and the causes of 'nullity,' which, until the adoption of recent French law [of 1966], represented a puzzle for lawyers and business men." Leleux, *Harmonisation des droits des sociétés,* in EUROPÄISCHE HANDELSGESELLSCHAFT UND ANGLEICHUNG DES NATIONALEN GESELLSCHAFTSRECHTS, WISSENSCHAFTLICHES KOLLOQUIUM DER FACHGRUPPE EUROPARECHT, WISSENSCHAFTLICHE GESELLSCHAFT FÜR EUROPARECHT, 5/6 Mai 1967, Bad Ems, 37, at 47 (Frankfurt/M.-Berlin 1968). Houin who prepared the questionnaire in the Hamel Committee disagrees with this analysis. He asserts that the choice of subjects was not based on considerations of French law but rather on an effort to identify, *in the laws of the Six,* important points, affecting interests of third parties, on which a

first study could be usefully focused, as is contemplated in Art. 54, par. 3(g). First, "publicity" appeared important, he reports, not because the French legislation was defective (such legislation was not substantially modified by the Law of 1966 and to a large measure it served as a basis for the First Directive) but because purely local publicity, effected in a variety of different forms, did not appear suitable for an enlarged Common Market. Second, as regards the power of management with respect to third parties, the German system which had already been in effect in France for limited liability companies appeared worthy of general acceptance. Third, the Hamel Committee was aware of the criticism abroad of the French system of "nullities" of companies, and it appeared useful to study how this problem was solved in the other Member States.

16. Bruns, in ENTWICKLUNGSTENDENZEN at 27. See for additional explanation Leleux, *Harmonisation des droits* at 47–48.

17. Leleux, *Harmonisation des droits* at 47, Uniken-Venema, *Coordination du droit* at 1008–9. The Economic and Social Committee also suggested a number of other rules which it thought ought to be coordinated: payment of capital, audits of accounts, number of shareholders. Avis at 3250.

18. [1964] J.O. 3245–48, *First Draft.* Until 1964 the working group met not more than three times a year for sessions of 2–3 days. However, in 1964 it had already met six times. BERKHOUWER REPORT at 8, par. 19.

19. *See* p. 316 in HARMONIZATION OF EUROPEAN COMPANY LAWS.

20. Initially, labor unions were not included in the consultation process in this field. But labor unions were consulted on the proposed directive concerning "internal fusion" of companies. *See* p. 382 in HARMONIZATION OF EUROPEAN COMPANY LAWS. On the role of the unions see generally BEEVER, EUROPEAN UNITY AND THE TRADE UNION MOVEMENT (Leyden 1960).

21. Pryce, *Interest Groups in the Community,* EUROPEAN COMMUNITY at 13 (London, May 1968). According to this author there are now some three to four hundred Community-wide associations of national groups. On the interest groups in the Community generally see FISCHER, DIE INSTITUTIONALISIERTE VERTRETUNG DER VERBÄNDE IN DER EUROPÄISCHEN WIRTSCHAFTSGEMEINSCHAFT (Hamburg 1965); RITTSTIEG, WIRTSCHAFTSVERBÄNDE UND EUROPÄISCHE GEMEINSCHAFTEN, EINE UNTERSUCHUNG ZUR INSTITUTIONALISIERTEN INTERESSENVERTRETUNG (Hamburg 1967).

22. 24 members from each of the Federal Republic, France, and Italy, 12 from Belgium and the Netherlands, 5 from Luxembourg. Art. 193.

23. Art. 193 states that the Committee is to include, in particular, representatives of producers, farmers, transport operators, workers, merchants, artisans, the professions and representatives of the general interest.

24. Vanhaeverbeke & Genton, *The Economic and Social Committee,* EUROPEAN COMMUNITY at 14 (London, May 1968). *See generally* Genton, *La représentation et l'influence des opérateurs économiques dans la Communauté européenne,* in INSTITUTIONS COMMUNAUTAIRES ET INSTITUTIONS NATIONALES DANS LE DÉVELOPPEMENT DES COMMUNAUTÉS 75 (Bruxelles 1968); LES GROUPES DE PRESSION DANS LA C.E.E. (Europa Instituut, Université d'Amsterdam, 1965); ZELLENTIN,

Der Wirtschafts- und Sozialausschuss der EWG und EURATOM (Leyden 1962). In 1968, there were 27 members in the employers' group, 34 in the workers' group, 40 in the general interest group including farm producers, craftsmen, tradesmen, journalists, and members of liberal professions.

25. Actually M. de Précigout took over the rapporteurship only after the originally appointed rapporteur resigned his function.

26. Prof. van de Woestijne, Comité Écon. et Soc., CES 316/64, *Compte rendu des déliberations* Nov. 20, 1964, 41ème Session plénière, Oct. 27 and 28, 1964, at 13.

27. M. de Bièvre, *id.* at 19.

28. The Netherlands Government as a matter of policy discusses the appointments to the *Community* Economic and Social Committee with the *national* Social and Economic Council and sees to it that, in the case of a resignation, the successor reflects the views of the same interests and organizations.

29. Van de Woestijne, in *Compte rendu des déliberations* at 12; Bölger, *id.* at 16–17; Seibel, *id.* at 20.

30. Rapport de la Section spécialisée pour les questions économiques sur la Proposition d'une Directive du Conseil tendant à coordonner pour les rendre équivalentes, les guaranties qui sont exigées dans les États membres, des sociétés au sens de l'article 58, alinéa 2 du Traité, pour protéger les intérêts tant des associés que des tiers, Rapporteur: M. de Précigout, Sept. 28, 1964; Rapport complementaire, July 31, 1964, and Avis complementaire, July 30, 1964 de la Section pour les activités non salariés et les services sur quelques points relatifs à la Proposition de directive, etc.

31. Avis du Comité Economique et Social at 3249; on this point see also Rodière, *L'harmonisation des législations* at 336, 343 ff. Update: In its original version Art. 100 provided for directives "for approximation of such laws, regulations and administrative provisions of the Member States as directly affect the establishment or functioning of the Common Market." The original requirement of unanimous approval in the Council was later replaced—with some exceptions—by a qualified majority voting formula.

32. Avis, *passim.*

33. Van de Woestijne, in *Compte rendu des déliberations* at 10.

34. *Id.* at 11.

35. Prof. van de Woestijne, *id.* at 12; Mr. ter Heide, *id.* at 24.

36. M. de Précigout, *id.* at 13.

37. Prof. van de Woestijne, *id.* at 12.

38. Union of German Employees (Deutsche Angestelltengewerkschaft).

39. Harmonization of European Company Laws p. 247.

40. Compte rendu des déliberations at 14–17. She was supported by Mr. Brand of the "general interest" group, at 17–19, Mr. ter Heide of the workers' group, at 23–24, and basically also by Mr. Rollinger of Luxembourg, who is close to small business groups in that country, at 17.

41. Messrs. Bölger, Jonker, Kuipers, and Schrijvers of the Netherlands; Messrs. Kley and Seibel of the Federal Republic. *Id.* at 26.

42. The "Big Three" Parliaments send 36 deputies each, Belgian and Dutch Parliaments send 14 each, and 6 come from Luxembourg. EEC Treaty Art. 138.

43. The number of members of 1966 was as follows: Christian Democrats 61, Socialists 35, Liberals with affiliates 26, UDE 15.

44. The official biography provides the following data on Mr. Berkhouwer: doctor of law, attorney, member of the board of directors of two stock companies, substitute member of the Consultative Council of Benelux, member of the Chamber of Deputies since 1956 for the Popular Party for Freedom and Democracy (V.V.D.). PARLEMENT EUROPÉEN, ANNUAIRE 1965–66, at 32 (Luxembourg 1966).

45. The official biography contains the following data on Mr. Blaisse: doctor of law, Institute of Technology, Hanover, secretary of the Philips Gloeilampentabriek at Eindhoven, Secretary of the Federation of Industry, director at the directorate general of foreign relations at the Ministry for Economic Affairs, economic consultant since 1952, member of the second chamber from 1952 for the Popular Catholic Party (K.V.P.). PARLEMENT EUROPÉEN, ANNUAIRE 1965–66, at 36. Most recently Mr. Blaisse has become part-time professor at the Technical College at Delft where he lectures on legal and economic aspects of international organizations.

46. Deringer, in [1966–67] PARL. EUR., DÉBATS, *Compte rendu in extenso des séances,* Doc. No. 85, at 56.

47. The Parliament has its own staff and each Committee is assigned several staff members.

48. BERKHOUWER REPORT at 2. The vote on Mar. 21, 1966 was subject to further consideration of the statement of reasons to be included in the report. This vote took place on Apr. 25, 1966 but there is no indication of the outcome.

49. Commissioner Colonna di Paliano, in [1966–67] PARL. EUR., DÉBATS, Doc. No. 85, at 69.

50. BERKHOUWER REPORT at 35, par. 74. Specifically, the report raised the question whether the problem of invalidity ("nullity") of companies was outside the scope of recognition of companies because the effect of invalidity was territorially limited. The report apparently confused the two provisions of the EEC Treaty which are often mentioned together, namely, Art. 220 and Art. 54; only the former deals with recognition of companies, but the latter, on which the directive was based, does not. Although one may argue about the urgency of coordinating the rules on invalidity in the first coordination attempt, it is hardly possible to contend that the rules specifying the grounds on which a company may be declared not validly constituted do not concern the protection of especially third persons who would want to be certain about the legal status of the company with which they deal.

51. Treaty Art. 189. BERKHOUWER REPORT at 25.

52. Rodière, *L'harmonisation des législations* at 340.

53. Sohier & Mégret, *Le rôle de l'executif national et du législateur national dans la mise en oeuvre du droit communautaire,* SEMAINE DE BRUGES, 1965, 107, at 114. *See generally* Waelbroeck, *The Application of EEC Law by National*

Courts, 19 STAN. L. REV. 1248, at 1272–75 (1967); OLDEKOP, DIE RICHTLINIEN DER EWG at 178–90 (Göttingen 1968); Ipsen, *Richtlinien-Ergebnisse,* in HALLSTEIN (ed.), FESTSCHRIFT FÜR OPHÜLS 67 (Karlsruhe 1965).

54. Lutter, *Die Angleichung des Gesellschaftsrechts nach dem EWG-Vertrag,* 1966 NJW 273, at 274.

55. Zweigert, *Der Einfluss des europäischen Gemeinschaftsrechts auf die Rechtsordnungen der Mitgliedstaaten,* 1964 RABELS ZEITSCHRIFT 601, at 643. *See also* Zweigert, *Grundsatzfragen der europäischen Rechtsangleichung, ihrer Schöpfung und Sicherung,* in VON CAEMMERER, NIKISCH, ZWEIGERT (eds.), 2 FESTSCHRIFT FÜR DÖLLE 401, at 418 (Tübingen 1963). Von Arnim, *Das Niederlassungsrecht* at 347, although preferring clear and definite unification of law over mere approximation with its necessarily uncertain results, doubts whether Zweigert's opinion would be upheld. Houin, *Rapport général sur la fusion des sociétés, in* FÉDÉRATION INTERNATIONALE DE DROIT EUROPÉEN, 3ème Colloque international de droit européen, Paris, Nov. 1965, 9, at 22.

56. RABE, DAS VERORDNUNGSRECHT DER EUROPÄISCHEN WIRTSCHAFTSGEMEINSCHAFT at 42 (Hamburg 1963); Gaudet, *Rechtliche Aspekte der Niederlassungsfreiheit im Gemeinsamen Markt,* 1961–62 ZHR 66, at 87.

57. BERKHOUWER REPORT at 26, par. 24, 25. Costa v. E.N.E.L., Case No. 6/64, 10 Recueil de la Jurisprudence 1141, at 1163 (1964). The statement in the plenary was by Deringer, in [1966] PARL. EUR., DÉBATS, No. 85, at 56–57.

In the *E.N.E.L.* case the Court held that Art. 58, prohibiting new restrictions on the freedom of establishment, must be interpreted in the light of Art. 52 requiring no better than national treatment. The argument in the *Report* was that Art. 54 must also be interpreted in the light of Art. 52. Referring to the *Report,* Scholten concluded that the Court's decision points to a restrictive interpretation of Art. 54. Scholten, *European Company Law,* 4 C.M.L. REV. 377, at 391 (1967). One may wonder how relevant this argument is to the problem of the legality of the First Directive.

58. BERKHOUWER REPORT at 35, par. 78.

59. EEC Art. 140.

59a. Mr. Deringer was defeated in the 1969 election for the Bundestag by a Social Democrat.

60. The changes in the Federal law imposing disclosure on certain large limited liability companies were still three years off, as was the publication of the new draft law on limited liability companies requiring these companies to make their balance sheet publicly available.

61. [1966] PARL. EUR., DÉBATS, No. 85, at 56 rejecting the relevancy of the *E.N.E.L.* case.

62. *Id.* at 58.

63. *Id.* at 62–84.

64. *Id.* at 62. *See* Art. 72 of the Law of July 24, 1966.

65. *Id.* at 91.

66. *See id.* at 91–93, 99–100. Commissioner Colonna di Paliano did not accept the amendment. It was supported by Pleven and Armengaud.

67. *Id.* at 68.

68. *Id.* at 65–66.

69. *Id.* at 69–73; 86; 90; 92; 93; 99; 100.

70. *See* p. 292 in HARMONIZATION OF EUROPEAN COMPANY LAWS.

71. [1966] PARL. EUR., DÉBATS, No. 85, at 95.

72. COM (60) 366 final (Oct. 3, 1966).

73. *Second Draft,* EXPOSÉ DES MOTIFS, COM (66) 366 final (Oct. 3, 1966) at 2.

74. EEC Art. 151, EURATOM Art. 121, *Merger Treaty* Art. 4. The latter Treaty speaks expressly of "permanent representatives." Thus their appointment now takes place in execution of the "Merger Treaty" and not in execution of an intergovernmental agreement as was the case before. Noël, *Le Comité des représentants permanents,* in INSTITUTIONS COMMUNAUTAIRES ET INSTITUTIONS NATIONALES DANS LE DÉVELOPPEMENT DES COMMUNAUTÉS 9, at 10, 24 (Brussels 1968).

75. Noël, *Le comité des représentants permanents* at 41.

76. Noël, *Le comité des représentants permanents* at 25.

77. HOUBEN, LES CONSEILS DE MINISTRES DES COMMUNAUTÉS EUROPÉENNES at 142 (Leyden 1964), *quoting* HANDELINGEN TWEEDE KAMER DER STATEN GENERAAL II, Dec. 10, 1958, 454.

78. Art. 149 (2).

79. EEC Arts. 149 par. 1, 173.

80. In fact, in case of such a radical modification, even if it is approved by the Commission, it is probably necessary for the Council to refer the new text again to the Economic and Social Committee and to the European Parliament, if consultation on the matter involved is prescribed by the Treaty.

81. *See* p. 248 in HARMONIZATION OF EUROPEAN COMPANY LAWS.

82. The Commission staff argued that when the coordinated content of the balance sheet and the profit-and-loss statement shall have been worked out, it might well be that all Governments would agree to remove the floor entirely and impose disclosure on *all* companies or at least reduce the floor to, say, $500,000. Thus this question must not be prejudiced in the first directive.

83. The first such proposal, while imposing a general disclosure obligation, would have allowed Member States to delay compliance for companies presently not subject to disclosure until after about 1969, with an instruction to the Commission to propose a further directive coordinating the content rules and to examine whether a distinction should be made among the various types of companies. The second variant would have provided in effect for a delay in the disclosure by limited liability companies and the Dutch close companies until the effective date of the other directive which would not only coordinate the content of disclosure but also "the conditions and details" thereof for these companies. The Belgian and Italian delegations did not consider this a compromise since no legal obligation would be imposed with respect to the exempted companies. Finally, the Italian delegation proposed a third variant which would have imposed the obligation to publish the balance sheet upon *all* companies but postponed obligatory disclosure of the profit-and-loss statement pending further coordination.

84. Harmonization of European Company Laws p. 166.

85. [1968] J.O. I.65 (Mar. 14) at 8–12.

86. Art. 13. For a longer period afforded to certain Dutch stock companies see Art. 13, par. 2. The eighteen months' period lapsed on Sept. 14, 1969 and only the Federal Republic completed the national modification process by adopting an appropriate law. *See* p. 311 *in* Harmonization of European Company Laws.

87. Noël, *Le comité des représentants permanents* at 41.

PART 2

European Integration and the American Federal Experience

Uses, Misuses—and Nonuses of Comparative Law

The comparative perspective has been an integral part of my writing. However, neither I nor most of the current practitioners of the comparative legal method have dwelt upon the doctrine and theory behind it. The essay that follows is a rare if not the only piece in which I attempted to explore the doctrinal underpinnings of the method, taking as a point of departure a juxtaposition of the conflicting perceptions by two virtuoso players of the comparative game. The piece is in effect a by-product of the book Harmonization of European Company Laws—National Reform and Transnational Coordination, *excerpted in Part 1.*

I have no explanation for the current dearth of new ideas on methodology not only in comparative law but in comparative politics as well, but I return to the question later on in this collection.

The state of the "use," or, more appropriately, "nonuse," of the comparative method in American legal education and lawmaking has not improved appreciably since the original publication of this essay.

If I were to write this piece today, I would eschew any reference to "law as a science" and "scientific research in law."

This essay is intended to serve three objectives. The first is to honor a friend and esteemed colleague upon his retirement from teaching. Professor MacChesney belongs to the select circle of American scholars who recognized at an early date the existential relationship between domestic and international law. His course combining "American" conflict-of-laws with international law was an innovation in a field largely devoid of experimentation. As Director of International Legal Studies at Northwestern University Law School, he perceived the importance of a systematic study and comparison of different legal systems. He also saw to the strengthening of his faculty in the field of comparative law.

The second objective of this article is to draw the attention of the American audience to an exchange between an English legal comparatist, Professor Otto Kahn-Freund, and a Scottish comparative legal historian, Professor Alan Watson, on the subject of "transferability" or

Reprinted by special permission of Northwestern University School of Law, from 72 *Northwestern Law Review* 198–216 (1977).

"transplantability" of legal norms from one system to another in the process of law making and particularly law reform.[1] The debate raises the significant question of the extent to which a law maker should take into account foreign legislative solutions and thereby add another dimension—and complication—to the already complex process of law making in a modern participatory democracy. If comparative law—or more accurately, the comparative method in the sense of German *Rechtsvergleichung*—is the chosen instrumentality, the specific question of how the law maker should employ this method to suit his purpose remains.

Finally, as a third objective of this paper, I propose to add a few observations on the current practice in the use of the comparative method on both sides of the Atlantic, and to note the implications this practice holds for the science of law and legal education in the United States.

Transfer or Transplant? A Thesis of a Lawyer-Sociologist

Kahn-Freund distinguishes three purposes that may be pursued by those who use foreign law in law making: first, international unification of law; second, "giving adequate legal effect to a social change shared by the foreign country with one's own country";[2] and third, "promoting at home a social change which foreign law is designed either to express or produce."[3] He then evokes a continuum of legal rules, the terminal points of which are, on one end, a rule which can readily be "transferred" by mechanical insertion (not unlike a carburetor or a wheel transferred from one car to another) and, on the other end, a rule comparable to a living organism which can be "transplanted" only by a surgical operation comparable to a transplant of a kidney, with the attendant risk of rejection by the home environment. Any given rule or institution may be placed at an appropriate point in this continuum.

As the next step, Kahn-Freund proposes a set of criteria to assist the law maker in determining the degree of transferability of any such rule or institution. In this, he relies heavily on "the first of all comparative lawyers," Montesquieu, who believed that it was only in the most exceptional case—"un grand hazard," a great coincidence—that the law of one country could serve that of another at all.

In Montesquieu's view (according to Kahn-Freund), transferability stands in an inverse relation to the closeness of the local institution to its habitat. This closeness is determined by two groups of variables: *environmental factors,* geographical (such as size and geographic position of a country, climate, fertility of the soil), social and economic (such as occupation, density, wealth of the population, trade), cultural (such as religion, traditions, customs); and "*purely political*" *factors* such as the nature of the government.[4]

It is Kahn-Freund's central thesis that in the course of the more than two hundred years since Montesquieu's time, the geographical, social, economic and cultural factors have greatly lost, but the political factors have equally greatly gained, in importance. Industrialization, urbanization, the development of communications and the increased mobility of people have set in motion a "process of economic, social and cultural assimilation or integration among the developed countries (and also the dominant classes of the developing countries)"[5] which has greatly reduced the environmental obstacles to legal transplantation.[6] But this process—Kahn-Freund continues—has been accompanied by a process of political differentiation: first, between the communist and the noncommunist world and between dictatorships and democracies in the noncommunist world; second, between the presidential (United States–type) and the parliamentary type of government;[7] and third—and in many ways most important—"the enormously increased role which is played by organised interests in the making and in the maintenance of legal institutions."[8]

> Anyone contemplating the use of foreign legislation for law making in his country must ask himself: how far does this rule or institution owe its existence or its continued existence to a distribution of power in the foreign country which we do not share? How far would it be accepted and how far rejected by the organised groups which, in the political sense, are part of our constitution? And if I say "organised groups" I am not only thinking of groups representing economic interests: big business, agriculture, trade unions, consumer organisations, but equally of organised cultural interests, religious, charitable, etc. All these share in the political power, and the extent of their influence and the way it is exercised varies from country to country. Here perhaps is the strongest organic element in the law today: its close link with the infinite variations of the organisation of power in culturally, socially, economically very similar countries.[9]

Kahn-Freund offers several examples to support this point. For instance, the law of divorce and alimony would prima facie appear to be most closely linked to local environmental factors such as moral and religious convictions, mores and the social structure. Yet fundamental rules and even details of divorce laws have been transplanted successfully from Australia and New Zealand to England. Radical changes in the same direction have occurred in Canada and in New York, and even earlier, in Japan and in the Scandinavian countries. But, if divorce "as a relief from misfortune" rather than "redress for fault or sin" is now accepted in all these legal systems, will it ever be accepted in Dublin? The Irish rejection of divorce can be explained only by the central importance of the power factor—the political power of the Catholic Church.

As a second example involving rules of an institutional nature where the power factor looms much more strongly than in divorce law, Kahn-Freund cites the futile attempts to export British parliamentary institutions to African territories and the abortive attempt to transplant the English jury system to the Continent in the nineteenth century. The latter failed because of the opposition of the legal profession. It was quietly replaced by a mixed-bench system in Germany in 1924 and in France in 1932 and 1941. On the other hand, the model of the Conseil d'État—an important institutional system—has been one of the great French exports to several Continental countries, presumably because it was congenial with the power structure in the recipient countries.

Kahn-Freund does not want to deter legislators from using the comparative method, but he warns that any attempt to use a pattern of law outside the environment of its origin continues to entail a serious risk of rejection. As a principal instance of rules which are closest to the "organic" end of his continuum and thus most resistant to transplantation, Kahn-Freund points to the labor laws dealing with collective bargaining, the closed shop, trade unions and strikes. He offers the 1971 British Industrial Relations Act, most strongly influenced by foreign (particularly American) patterns, as an egregious exhibit of misuse of comparative law. The Act invited "rejection" both because of the peculiarities of the recipient habitat and the differences in the distribution of institutional powers. As it turned out, in the 1971 Act, which was adopted by the Conservative majority over the opposition of the trade unions, was in fact repealed in 1974 after the Labor Party's election victory.[10]

Kahn-Freund's final point is addressed not only to law makers but to those who teach the comparative method as well, and in this respect it is also apposite to my concluding comments on legal research and training:

> All I have wanted to suggest is that [the use of the comparative method] requires knowledge not only of the foreign law, but also of its social, and above all, its political context. The use of compara-

tive law for practical purposes becomes an abuse only if it is informed by a legalistic spirit which ignores this context of the law.[11]

A Legal Historian's Antithesis

Professor Watson challenges the three basic tenets of Kahn-Freund's thesis:[12]

1. The pessimistic view of legal transplants is not borne out by history. Successful transplanting from a very different legal system, even from one at a much higher level of development and of a different political complexion, has frequently been accomplished.
2. Systematic knowledge of the donor system is not necessary. "What . . . the law reformer should be after in looking at foreign systems was an idea which could be transformed into part of the law of his country." Successful borrowing could be achieved "even when nothing was known [by the recipient] of the political, social or economic context of the foreign law."[13]
3. It is at least questionable whether environmental factors are today less important than political factors.

Montesquieu, according to Watson, "badly—very badly" underestimated the amount of successful borrowing which had taken place up to and including his time. The reception of Roman law in Western Europe is a prime illustration. Although, of course, not every Roman legal institution was adopted and many were profoundly modified, the reception constituted "such a massive transfusion" that "one simply cannot accept Montesquieu's claim that it is 'un grand hazard' if the rules of one nation can suit another."[14] Moreover, this successful transplant occurred where the environmental as well as the political circumstances of the recipient were very different from those of the donor, and where the recipient did not require any real knowledge of the social, economic, geographical and political context of the origin and growth of the original rule. "How otherwise could one explain the use made of Roman law by fifth-century Germanic tribes, the acceptance of so much Roman law dating from different periods and different political circumstances in the Middle Ages and later by so many diverse States in Western Europe, in monarchies, oligarchies and republics alike?"[15] Watson concedes that the chances of a reception were greatly reduced where the rule of Roman law was inimical to the political and environmental factors in the recipient, but argues that this was not the case where the Roman context of the rule was merely different from the context of the recipient. From the influence of Roman law he deduces the proposition that "[h]owever historically conditioned their origins might be, rules of private law in their continuing lifetime have no inherent close relationship with a particular people, time or place."[16]

Successful modern borrowings, Watson argues, also support his view. For example, the Japanese Penal Code and Code of Criminal Procedure of 1882 was modeled after French law, and the Japanese Civil Code of 1898 contains basically German law of contract, delict and property. Watson also mentions the Turkish Civil Code of 1926 and the Ethiopian Civil Code of 1960 as instances of acceptance of codes based on developed Western law by developing countries, and he questions the assertion that in rural areas these codes, although on the books, have in effect been rejected.[17]

Although he agrees with Kahn-Freund that a foreign legal rule will not easily be borrowed successfully if it does not fit into the domestic political context, Watson does not agree that the degree to which any rule can be borrowed depends on how closely it is linked with the foreign power structure. He challenges Kahn-Freund's assertion that the effective use of the comparative method depends upon knowledge, not only of the foreign rule, but also of its political context. In order to know that an English-style divorce could not be successfully introduced into Ireland, it would be enough, he maintains, to look at the Irish power structure. Knowledge of the power structure in England is quite irrelevant. Again, the success of the transplant of Western law in Japan was due to the "Japanese desire for it, not their knowledge of the French and German political context or any similarity of that political context with what existed in Japan."[18]

In his earlier work on "Legal Transplants," Watson appears to go even a step or two further:

> [T]he transplanting of legal rules is socially easy. Whatever opposition there might be from the bar or legislature, it remains true that legal rules move easily and are accepted into the system without too great difficulty. This is so even when the rules come from a very different kind of system. The truth of the matter seems to be that many legal rules make little impact on individuals, and that very often it is important that there be a rule; but what rule actually is adopted is of restricted significance for general human happiness. . . . [U]sually legal rules are not peculiarly devised for the particular society in which they now operate and also . . . this is not a matter for great concerns.[19]

A Synthesis?

On the "Ease" of Transplants

Viewing the two sides of the exchange, one may wonder if the different perceptions of the ease of transplants, and of the importance of environmental over political factors, are simply in the eye of the beholder, or if they are due rather to the particular focus of his inquiry. Watson, the historian, takes a "macro-legal" view that contemplates the massive transplants that loom as milestones on the large-scale canvas of world history. Most if not all of these transplants involve en bloc receptions of sophisticated systems by less developed societies pursuant to a basic modernization decision made by an authoritarian elite.

In contrast to Watson, Kahn-Freund, the lawyer-sociologist, takes a "micro-legal" view. He concentrates primarily on pieces of more or less modern reform legislation in developed countries where differences in environmental factors have been substantially blunted by a process of assimilation. Differences in political factors, on the other hand, which determine the distribution of power, have become increasingly important because law in modern democracies is made by a consensus of a variety of constituencies, representing conflicting interests, rather than by fiat of a small elite. From this perspective, the transplant—and the law reform process in general—appears in quite a different light.[20]

An historian sees a wealth of receptions and his vista across centuries is bound to blur the detail and soften the difficulties. A lawyer-sociologist who is close to the contemporary scene, and who views the law in its operational context, has a different interpretation. He is likely to disagree with the historian on what is or is not "socially easy," and he may also question whether the significance of a rule can be measured by the Olympian test of "general human happiness."

Roman law "receptions," it may be argued, are not a typical case of "easy" transfers because Roman law, as it was received in the Middle Ages and thereafter, was a self-contained system which had been richly elaborated by generations of scholars and completely detached from the original political institutions and cultural setting. One of the many possible contemporary examples of the difficulty of transplants can be seen in the efforts of industrialized countries to reform their company laws. Here is a subject that presumably would be particularly susceptible to "easy" transplants in view of the high degree of assimilation of environmental conditions resulting from high mobility and transfrontier commercial intercourse among developed countries. Yet the 1966 French

Law on Commercial Companies, a consolidation and reform which borrowed substantially from foreign — particularly German — law, was in the making for no less than a quarter of a century. It purports to transplant to France the German two-tier company-board system, consisting of a supervisory board and a management board, but it does so only as an optional form of corporate organization. The transplant has not been successful since the vast majority of French companies continue to prefer the old single board pattern.[21] Despite the pressure from the Gaullist left, the more radical German innovation of worker "codetermination" in company administration was dropped from the draft of the 1966 law, and the existing provision for employee representation on the board without the right to vote was left unchanged. The resulting text represented a mild reform — a limited "transplant" — with the bulk of the rules hardly affecting "general human happiness." Nevertheless, despite the immense amount of preparatory work,[22] the draft in the end became embroiled in an acute power conflict between the French executive and the Parliament. The executive, asserting its law-making power under the recent constitution, stripped the Parliament's draft of almost one third of its articles, thus defeating a major objective of the reform — the consolidation of the rules in a single codification.

Elsewhere in Western Europe, the process of assimilation[23] towards the German corporation law — the *Aktiengesetz* — has been equally time consuming and laborious, despite the fact that the institutions of the European Economic Community are required by the constitutive treaty to see to the "coordination" of Member States' company laws, to facilitate company mobility throughout the Community. After some fifteen years of extensive efforts by multinational expert groups, only two of the seven partial coordination drafts which have been presented by the executive Commission have become Community law thus far. Yet the treaty itself, reflecting a Watson-type optimism, contemplated the completion of the entire process within not more than twelve years, a deadline which expired at the end of 1969.[24] The Commission's mandate in this field was directed toward greater uniformity among national company laws, which was considered necessary for the freedom of establishment of business enterprises. The Commission, however, broadened its mandate so as to encompass important policy objectives. In the context of the industrial policy, the Commission proposed facilitating the adjustment of industrial structures to the new Community-wide market by modernizing national legislation and establishing a new "European" Company Statute for European multinationals.[24a] As an aspect of social policy, the Commission sought to advance social harmony by pressing for employee participation in corporate decision making on a modified German model.[25] In terms of the three uses of foreign law described earlier,[26] the Commission has moved in fact from the first purpose, "unification of law," to the third, "promoting . . . social change which foreign law is designed either to express or produce." The principal factors that have stalled the current "transplant" effort are all of the "political" type. The most important of these factors are dissimilarities between donor and recipient countries in the attitudes of the business communities and in the status, ideology and power of the national labor unions. Nevertheless, if we assume, as we may, that the Commission's projects will eventually become Community law in one form or another, a Watson disciple, writing in the twenty-first century, may well view the phenomenon as yet another "easy" or "common" transplant.

Anyone searching for instances of conscious transfers or transplants ought to keep in mind one caveat. A germ of a rule or of an institution may surface more or less simultaneously in widely divergent geographic areas in response to parallel social demands and without any evidence that the law makers concerned "borrowed" or were even aware of the solution adopted elsewhere. It was no doubt the impact of the world-wide economic and financial crisis on trade in corporate securities that brought about the establishment of the Securities and Exchange Commission in the United States in 1934, and of the Belgian Commission Bancaire in 1935. Perhaps also the same crisis was responsible for the administrative reorganization in Chile, resulting in the Superintendencia de compañias de seguros, sociedades anónimas y bolsas de comercio in 1931. I was unable to find any indication of borrowing either in the East-West or North-South direction. By contrast, in organizing the French Commission des Operations de Bourse in 1967, the law maker reportedly drew upon the American and Belgian experience.[27]

On the Relative Importance of Environmental and Political Factors

The disagreement on the relative impact today of the two categories of factors on transplant feasibility raises the problem—recognized by Watson[28]—of how to measure the effect of these factors. Assuming that the concepts of "environmental" and "political" can be defined and delineated with some precision—and this obviously may not be an easy task—any scientific measurement of the degree of their importance would present a more than usual challenge to even the most adventurous "quantifiers" of the new political science.[29]

Returning to the example of contemporary company law reform in Western Europe, it should be recognized that the reluctance of certain sections of the bar to accept "transfers" of even unimportant technical rules has definitely been an inhibiting factor. To the extent that the opposition of lawyers was based on their passionate attachment to national legal doctrines and traditions[30] rather than on vested professional interests, one may say their resistance was due to "environmental factors rather than power factors," but it is not always easy to draw the line. For example, in 1975 the British financial and business community opposed the transplant of the German-type two-tier system because it viewed that system as the first step toward worker codetermination leading ultimately to worker control (a political factor) and also because it considered the old-type single board with outside directors to be better suited to local conditions (an environmental factor).[31]

Similarly, certain structural differences which may be classified as "environmental" persist among the several states of the European Community and have posed difficulties for legal transplants. For example, there are divergent degrees of concentration of national industries and disparities in the use of comparable corporate forms.[32] But in the more significant transplants the principal factors have been political: the relative power and institutional arrangements of business and labor, of the management and the shareholders, of the bar, of the banks, and of the national and transnational bureaucracy.[33]

On the Depth of the Required Knowledge

The last and, in a way, the most interesting point of disagreement is Watson's challenge to Kahn-Freund's conclusion that the use of the comparative method by the law reformer-transplanter requires knowledge not only of the foreign law but also of its political context.[34] I find it somewhat difficult to conjure up an image of a law reformer on a *tour d'horizon* of foreign legal systems, plucking ideas from "black letter" rules in complete ignorance of how such rules operate as "living law" and where they fit into the legal system—not unlike a romantic lass crossing a spring meadow and plucking any flower which strikes her fancy. Suffice it to say that Watson himself admits that a "systematic knowledge of the donor system" would make a law reformer "more efficient."[35] It was precisely Kahn-Freund's point that had the British law maker understood—and taken into account—the status of collective agreements and the nature of the collective bargaining process in the American legal and political context, he might have avoided transplanting certain American concepts into the British Industrial Relations Act at a risk of their rejection.[36]

It would be interesting indeed to investigate, for example, how much the Japanese and Turkish experts knew about the Western systems which they recommended for reception to their law makers. It may well be that where the law maker lacks private or governmental institutional arrangements for a systematic use of the comparative method, his way of drawing on foreign law, if he considers it at all, corresponds to Watson's idea.

On Uses and "Nonuses" of Comparative Law

In Law Making

The debate on the relative ease of transplants and on the risk of misuse of the comparative method would make little sense without a tacit assumption that a law maker does in fact use the method and considers foreign law models. The question then arises as to the extent to which today this assumption is warranted on either side of the Atlantic.

On the Continent any codification or major legislative revision "normally results in the type of comparative law studies that would delight the most learned professor of that subject in the universities."[37] Such studies are usually conducted or commissioned by officials of the Ministry of Justice. Legal research centers staffed with experts on foreign law, such as the Max Planck Institutes in the German Federal Republic, are available in some countries to do the spade work. More recently, at the transnational level, the European Community Commission staff has performed a function somewhat similar to that of a Ministry of Justice. National law makers are increasingly compelled—by the operation of the Common Market—to take into account each other's systems.

Long before the Common Market, British legislation, according to Kahn-Freund, had become open to a degree unknown in previous times to foreign influences. In fact, the Law Commission Act of 1965 requires that both the English and the Scottish Law Commissions "obtain such information as to the legal systems of other countries as appears to the Commissioners likely to facilitate the performance of any of their functions."[38] Many of the published reports and the Working Papers show that the Commissioners have met their obligation.[39] These materials also bear witness to the usefulness of the comparative method in law making.

There is no evidence of any comparable mandate in the charters of the state law revision commissions established in the United States or in other institutions connected with law making or law reform such as the National Conference of Commissioners on Uniform State Laws or the American Law Institute.[40] As for the actual consideration of foreign law, the New York State Commission apparently went about as far as any in the course of preparing the enactment of the Uniform Commercial Code when it obtained a report from its expert consultants on the experience with codification in foreign legal systems.[41]

The draft of the Uniform Commercial Code, clearly the most successful instance of American legal unification, was elaborated jointly by the American Law Institute and the National Conference of Commissioners on Uniform State Laws. The preparatory working papers contain scattered references to foreign—mostly British—law,[42] and some of the Reporters brought their comparative skills to bear on the text. But there is no trace of systematic comparative studies in a field that by its very transnational nature invites creative comparison, not only among the state laws but with foreign laws as well.

Similarly, the drafts of the Model Penal Code, another product of the American Law Institute, has exerted considerable influence on state legislation in a field where consideration of foreign solutions would be obviously useful. However, these drafts contain only scattered references, mainly to English and Commonwealth laws.[43] No comparative monographs or studies appear among the published materials. In the field of criminal procedure, Professor Schlesinger observes,

> our reformers' approach . . . remains essentially parochial. . . . This is regrettable, because the most casual observations suggest, at least prima facie, that some other countries facing comparable problems have been conspicuously more successful in developing an efficient and yet civilized system of repression of crime, and in curbing lawlessness on the part of the police without resorting to jail deliveries of the *Mapp* and *Miranda* type.[44]

The Model Corporation Act, which also has had some impact on state laws, has been prepared by an American Bar Association committee without the benefit of studies of modern foreign legislation which, in many respects, offers superior solutions to corporate problems common to technologically advanced societies.

Judging from published materials and responses to private inquiries, the National Conference of Commissioners on Uniform Laws—and for that matter state legislatures—have limited their more or less systematic comparisons to the laws of sister states. In the few instances where National Commissioners took notice of a foreign rule—generally where the subject contained an inherently foreign element[45]—they did so in an episodic manner.[46]

At the federal level, there appear to be no institutional arrangements or procedures for regular recourse to foreign law in the executive departments, where most bills originate. The same is true in the congressional committees, even though these committees are endowed with ample staff and have access to the unique facilities of the Library of Congress.[47] With rare exceptions, attention is given to foreign legislation only in such inherently "international" matters as the operation of antitrust law, sovereign immunity of foreign governments, foreign criminal courts proceedings under the "Status of Forces" treaties or international judicial assistance.[48]

At the international level, the United States joined the two organizations dealing with unification of private law only in 1964.[49] Of the 140 conventions on uniform labor standards adopted by the International Labor Organization, the United States has ratified only seven, as compared, for example, with ninety-six accepted by France, and sixty-eight accepted by the United Kingdom.[50]

In Legal Research and Education

Contemporary comparative legal scholarship in Europe has produced a harvest of systematic doctrinal treatises in the Continental tradition,[51] as well as numerous specialized comparative studies in private and public law. A new, seventeen-volume encyclopedia comparing private laws on a worldwide basis is being edited in the German Federal Republic.[52] This flowering of comparative legal studies is due only in part to the impact of the European Communities, although the myriad of Brussels working groups composed of national governmental and academic experts and the establishment of some forty-five university centers for European studies have provided a powerful impulse for comparative work.

In the United States, no systematic doctrinal treatise in the Continental mode has appeared since Dean Wigmore's three-volume *Panorama of the World's Legal Systems* was published in 1928. In the last three decades the number of comparative articles published in American legal periodicals has greatly increased,[53] and there have been several imaginative casebooks and a number of competent monographs. The *American Journal of Comparative Law* has provided a useful outlet. However, the mushrooming student international law journals have concentrated primarily on problems of international law and organization and on international trade.[54]

Although individuals knowledgeable in various foreign legal systems are scattered through major law faculties, no centers for systematic comparative legal research exist. The influx of foundation funds in the nineteen-fifties and sixties has had an enriching effect on law faculties primarily in the field of international law, but in the long run, the impact of foundation money has become questionable because of its termination with no replacement in sight.[55] Natural attrition has been taking its toll of European-trained law teachers, and young faculty members are not turning toward comparative law even if they possess the necessary (and rare) linguistic skills. Similarly, in the few law schools where comparative training and foreign law library facilities are available, qualified students are often not encouraged to take advantage of the opportunity to do intensive work in this field.

More than twenty years ago, Hessel E. Yntema surveyed the state of legal research and education as it existed in this country, and, drawing on a Platonic simile, he urged American lawyers to "look out of the cave." His appeal has a curiously timely ring today.[56] Legal education, he wrote, clearly has the vital function of transmitting existing legal knowledge and developing the skills needed by practitioners: but

> legal education is something more than indoctrination in what has been or acquirement of technical expertise. It also contemplates that at least the principal centers of legal education have in effect a scientific mission, a responsibility for the constant refinement of our knowledge of law, regarded as the practical realization of justice.[57]

He accepted as necessary the bulk of contemporary legal production, "the purpose of which is not to extend, but to brief our knowledge of law, whether to support a client's claim, to facilitate legal instruction, or to transmit information to students or practitioners."[58] Scientific research in law, however, as employed in other branches of knowledge requires more than that. It involves two lines of action: the formulation of more or less general propositions and the verification of these propositions. The principal techniques employed in verification are controlled experimentation (and, one may add, empirical inquiry in general), and comparison of the relevant events. Considering the difficulty and high cost of experimentation, comparison of existing laws becomes an essential, if not primary, tool of scientific study of law: "[E]ven if the existing experimental knowledge of how law operates were less fragmentary than it is . . . it would still have to be comparative, if only to make sure that what happens in Ann Arbor is duplicated in Ruritania."[59]

In one respect the prospects for the scientific study of law have improved since Yntema's time. Faculties at major law schools have added a number of younger members with advanced training in social sciences and history. Joint appointments in law and other university departments have promoted this trend, which is reflected favorably in the current research product. But we see no such broadening of interest in the systematic use of the comparative method. In that respect, the "professional and practical introversion" of legal education and most of the research persists unabated. Paradoxically, the realist school of jurisprudence has also had a territorially confining effect on legal scholarship.

In England and on the Continent—and for that matter in Japan and elsewhere—theoretical legal training is followed by apprenticeship in practice, so that the scientific and professional phases of legal education are differentiated. In the United States, on the other hand, the professional law school must serve both purposes. Because of the complexity of the American legal system, the growing mass of legal materials, the ever increasing specialization and the proliferation of courses, legal research and training in Yntema's sense have been neglected to meet the demands of "practical" instruction. Another factor contributing to this result has been the career perceptions of the faculty and of the students, strongly influenced by pressures from the more articulate sectors of the Bar and the judiciary. The President of the Association of American Law Schools, Professor Francis A. Allen, recently felt compelled to respond to these pressures:

> [T]here has been injected into these discussions [of legal education] a disquieting element, one that I have described as the "new anti-intellectualism in legal education." These attitudes are characterized by a loss of interest in substantive issues, a disposition to devalue course offerings not promising immediate pragmatic gains in lawyer skills (often accompanied by very fallible judgments about the pragmatic utility of many of these offerings), and a general skepticism of course offerings directed to policy evaluation and value analysis.[60]

Properly conducted training in the comparative method not only advances the basic "lawyer skills" of writing and reasoning, but also leads to controlled policy evaluation and value analysis when solutions in different systems are compared at various levels of analysis in the Kahn-Freund style. There is thus no incompatibility between "effective professional training" and scientific legal study. The current three-year law school curriculum can accommodate both. Moreover, there is always the possibility for graduate study. Whereas graduate studies in other disciplines have increasingly gained recognition in university faculty appointments and in the market place generally, they have for most practical purposes been discontinued or sharply reduced in most law schools.

Conclusion

In the changing international system, new centers of economic and political power arise and new institutions are built—quite different from the symmetrical, global-type organizations built under American leadership after the Second World War. Any major business enterprise is bound to reach across national frontiers. In a world that has become so much more complex, the United States remains the most powerful nation, but it is no longer able—or willing—to "carry the burden" of freedom everywhere. Those who speak abroad on behalf of American interests—governmental and private—must now rely on their art of persuasion rather than on the imperial voice from Washington. For this purpose lawyers require better knowledge and deeper understanding of the international scene and particularly of the foreign legal systems within which their counterparts function. The law schools have the responsibility to provide the necessary research and training. Moreover, the time has come for the American institutions concerned with law revision and for the legislatures at the state and federal levels to institutionalize and make systematic the study of foreign legal solutions in law revision and law making generally. The time of "non-uses" of comparative law has passed in this country as it did in Western Europe.

Notes

I wish to acknowledge the research and editing assistance by George A. Lehner and R. B. Drubel of the Michigan Law School. I am indebted to Mr. Mark Sandstrom of the District of Columbia Bar for some of the information regarding the practices employed in the Congress and in the executive departments of the federal government.

1. Kahn-Freund. *On Uses and Misuses of Comparative Law,* 37 Mod. L. Rev. 1 (1974) [hereinafter cited as Kahn-Freund]; Watson, *Legal Transplants and Law Reform,* 92 Law Q. Rev. 79 (1976) [hereinafter cited as Watson].
2. Kahn-Freund, *supra* note 1, at 2.
3. *Id.* at 3.
4. Kahn-Freund interprets Montesquieu as formulating the "political factor" in terms of principles rather than institutions, *id.* at 7, but Watson disagrees, Watson, *supra* note 1, at 80.
5. Kahn-Freund, *supra* note 1, at 8.

6. Kahn-Freund documents the impact of this "flattening out of economic and social diversity" by examples from the law of tort. In Montesquieu's day, tort liability centered upon situations arising from personal relations ("rivalry, whether sexual or commercial, family ties, ties of neighborhood") where the attitude of the law is bound to vary from nation to nation. Today attention is focused on accident liability, problems of insurance, producer's liability and the relation between private liability and social security; and the same ideas are explored in all the developed countries. *Id.* at 9–10.

7. I would agree with Kahn-Freund that this differentiation is often underestimated. Yet the responsibility of the executive toward the parliament, which is the fundamental characteristic of the parliamentary system, is at times quite illusory. The legislature is often unable to respond speedily and effectively to the needs of a rapidly changing society or to assure individual justice. This is one reason for the vital role of the judicial branch. We touch upon this problem in Stein & Vining, *Citizen Access to Judicial Review of Administrative Action in a Transnational and Federal Context,* 70 AM. J. INT'L L. 219 (1976), and EUROPEAN LAW AND THE INDIVIDUAL 113 (F. Jacobs ed. 1976). Update: This article is republished *infra* in Part 2.

8. Kahn-Freund, *supra* note 1, at 12.

9. *Id.*

10. Trade Unions and Labor Relations Act, 1974. *See* Wedderburn, *The Trade Union and Labour Relations Act 1974,* 37 MOD. L. REV. 525 (1974). On the 1971 Act, see Gould, *Taft-Hartley Comes to Great Britain: Observations on the Industrial Relations Act of 1971,* 81 YALE L.J. 1421 (1972); Kahn-Freund, *Das britische Gesetz über die Arbeitsbeziehungen von 1971—Eine kritische Würdigung,* in BEITRÄGE ZUM ZIVIL-UND WIRTSCHAFTSRECHT, FESTSCHRIFT FÜR KURT BALLERSTEDT (W. Flume, P. Raisch & E. Steindorff eds. 1975).

11. Kahn-Freund, *supra* note 1, at 27.

12. Watson, *supra* note 1, at 79.

13. *Id.*

14. *Id.* at 80.

15. *Id.* at 81. For other illustrations see *id.*

16. *Id.* at 81.

17. *Id.* at 83, n.17.

18. *Id.* at 83.

19. A. WATSON, LEGAL TRANSPLANTS 95–96 (1974).

20. When he looks beyond the "Western" orbit, Kahn-Freund sees a mixed picture: the success of Western transplants in Africa and Asia depended on the degree of local social change and the assimilation of Western urban conditions in the recipient states. Such transplants were rejected where differences in environmental factors were not sufficiently taken into account. Thus, German family law, even as modified in the Japanese reception, "largely failed to mold the 'law in actual operation,'" and the Swiss Civil Code adopted in Turkey was "clearly rejected," at least in rural areas. Kahn-Freund, *supra* note 1, at 16–17. As mentioned in the text accompanying note 17 *supra,* Watson questions this.

21. Of the 2,187 new stock companies formed in 1968, 29 chose the new two-tier system, as did 13 of the 1,256 established during the first six months in 1969. No figures are available for transformations of the "old" companies into the new type, but according to one estimate a total of some 300 companies, old and new, including some large concerns, had adopted the new form by 1970. E. STEIN, HARMONIZATION OF EUROPEAN COMPANY LAWS—NATIONAL REFORM AND TRANSNATIONAL COORDINATION 124 (1971) [hereinafter cited as E. STEIN]. The Association Nationale des Sociétés par Actions of Paris, which originally supplied these figures, has now indicated that the figures may not be quite accurate, and it has discontinued publication of statistics for subsequent years.

Professor Roger Houin of the Université de droit, d'économie et des sciences sociales de Paris, a leading expert in French company law, confirms that no accurate figures are available and that the two-tier form has not gained acceptance in French practice. According to his estimate not more than three percent of new companies select this form annually, and of the more than 90,000 stock companies existing today not more than 1,000 are organized in that form. Letter from Roger Houin to the author (December 18, 1976).

22. In 1961–1962, the Ministerial Committee concerned held no less than 63 meetings, and it heard 48 groups and individuals from all walks of life, including attorneys, law professors, representatives of banks, chambers of commerce, employers, labor unions and even "two foreigners," members of the British and American organizations of accountants. Yet when the governmental draft came before the Parliament, more than 400 amendments were tabled in the National Assembly and 548 in the Senate. For a study of the French reform and of the national reform efforts in the other five original Member States of the European Communities, see E. STEIN, *supra* note 21, at 108–26.

23. In my writings on the European development I have used the term "assimilation" which does not appear in the European Economic Community (EEC) Treaty. Theo Vogelaar, former Director General of the Commission of the European Communities, wondered why I would add still another term to the multiple terminology employed in the EEC Treaty. Vogelaar, *The Approximation of the Laws of Member States under the Treaty of Rome,* 12 COMM. MKT. L. REV. 211, 213 (1975). I have used the term for two reasons. First, the terms "approximation," "harmonization," "coordination," etc. are used quite indiscriminately in the Treaty. Introducing a defined, general term would, I had hoped, reduce confusion. Second, the term "assimilation" has been traditionally more familiar to the English-speaking audience. *See, e.g.,* Wigmore, *International Assimilation of Law—Its Needs and Its Possibilities From an American Standpoint,* 10 ILL. L. REV. 385 (1916), and the quotation from Kahn-Freund in the text accompanying note 5 *supra.*

24. The end of 1969 marked the end of the "transitional period" at which time the Common Market was to be fully in place.

24a. Update: In early 1999, the European Company Statute remains in draft form, and there is no present prospect for its adoption.

25. COMMISSION OF THE EUROPEAN COMMUNITY, EUR. COMM. BULL., Supp. No. 4/75, STATUTE FOR EUROPEAN COMPANIES: AMENDED PROPOSAL FOR A REGULA-

TION; *Id.*, Supp. No. 8/75. EMPLOYEE PARTICIPATION AND COMPANY STRUCTURE IN THE EUROPEAN COMMUNITY. *See generally* E. STEIN, P. HAY & M. WAELBROEK, EUROPEAN COMMUNITY LAW AND INSTITUTIONS IN PERSPECTIVE 609–62 (1976).

26. *See* text accompanying note 2 *supra.*

27. R. CAÑAS LASTARRIA, LA SOCIEDAD ANÓNIMA EN CHILE (1967); J. OLVARRÍA A., MANUAL DE DERECHO COMERCIAL (1970); D. PONLOT, LE STATUT LÉGAL DES BANQUES ET LE CONTRÔLE DES EMISSIONS DE TITRES ET VALEURS xvi (1969); E. STEIN, *supra* note 21, *passim;* Huyck, *The French Capital Market: Institutions and Issues,* 16 AM. J. COMP. L. 219 (1968). Huyck points out that as in the United States, economic "trouble bred reform in France," *id.* at 230, but "[v]iewing the success enjoyed by the American Securities and Exchange Commission and the Belgian Banking Commission during three decades of operation, the French authorities decided to introduce a similar administrative body into their system," *id.* at 244.

28. Watson, *supra* note 1, at 83 n.18.

29. *See, e.g.,* L. LINDBERG & SCHEINGOLD, EUROPE'S WOULD-BE-POLITY—PATTERNS OF CHANGE IN THE EUROPEAN COMMUNITY (1970).

30. Many instances illustrating such attachment emerged and greatly complicated the Brussels negotiations for the coordination of company laws, *e.g.,* differences in the concepts of ultra vires and of declaratory versus constitutive effect of publication of company formation, as well as differences in the attachment to various methods of publication of basic information on companies. The lingering devotion on the part of some Italian and French lawyers to the theoretical concept of a company as a contract (as distinguished from the modern concept of a company as a legal person) "seemed to have played a greater role than any policy differences" in determining the parameters for the "one-man" company or the circumstances under which a company may be declared null and void. *See* E. STEIN, *supra* note 21, at 274ff. In this respect, the accession to Community membership of the three new members (the United Kingdom, Ireland and Denmark) has caused additional complications. For instance, the Continental systems view a number of decisions, such as the decision to increase company capital, as "constitutional" and therefore requiring shareholder consent by a high majority vote. This concept is unknown and apparently difficult to accept in the United Kingdom. Also, where British practice has been to rely on guidelines and flexible principles (*e.g.,* the take-over code, the format for company accounts), the Continental systems call for more or less detailed, enforceable norms.

31. *See, e.g.,* LONDON CITY COMPANY LAW COMMITTEE, FIRST REPORT: EMPLOYEE PARTICIPATION (1975); Schmithoff, *Company Structure and Employee Participation in the EEC—the British Attitude,* 25 INT'L COMP. L.Q. 611 (1976). *See also* DEP'T OF TRADE COMMITTEE OF INQUIRY, REPORT ON INDUSTRIAL DEMOCRACY, CMD. No. 6706 (1977).

32. *E.g.,* in 1960 there were 37,984 limited liability companies (GmbH) and only 2,573 stock companies in the Federal Republic of Germany. Comparable figures in Belgium were 31,000 to 18,000. E. STEIN, *supra* note 21, at 134, 244.

33. In seeking to refute Kahn-Freund's view by his own example. Watson

states that in Catholic German states of the sixteenth and seventeenth centuries, divorce would be just as inconceivable—despite the example of the Protestant neighbors—as in modern Ireland, "and for similar reasons." All the example seems to sustain is that in this instance the political factor—the power of the Catholic Church—has remained decisive in certain areas from the sixteenth to the twentieth centuries. One could argue, however, that Ireland's rejection of divorce in the final analysis is due to the deeply felt religious belief and tradition of its people (an environmental factor) and that the power of the Church (a political factor) is only a necessary derivative.

34. Watson asserts:

> Now, should an attempt be made to introduce English-style divorce law into Ireland, it would be enough on my view to look at the Irish power structure to know that the attempt would fail. For that success or failure in Ireland, the power structure in England and any knowledge or appreciation of it is quite irrelevant. A similar example can be found in the Industrial Relations Act of 1971. The prospects for its success or failure were determined by the power structure in British industry. The knowledge would not have been particularly helpful that in America, a major source of influence on the Act, the industrial power structure was different from in Britain.

Watson, *supra* note 1, at 82.

35. *Id.* at 79.

36. *See* Kahn-Freund, *supra* note 1, at 24–26. Professor Gould characterizes the transplant in the following terms:

> Thus, from an almost exclusive reliance on "voluntarism," *i.e.,* the promotion of negotiating procedures drawing at most indirectly upon law, Great Britain has now imposed upon the conduct of unions and employers more formal and far-reaching regulations than those characterizing the U.S. system, a system which British experts traditionally regarded as excessively law-ridden. Moreover, where the U.S. system represents a gradual accretion of statutory and ever-changing case law, and where gradualness has allowed labor and management here to adapt to the system, the British have attempted an abrupt, mammoth, one-step codification. The suddenness of change contributed to causing political and social upheaval. The summer of 1972 in Great Britain was one of nearly unprecedented bitterness and tumult.

Gould, *Taft-Hartley Comes to Great Britain: Observations on the Industrial Relations Act of 1971,* 81 Yale L.J. 1421, 1424 (1972).

37. Stone, *A Primer on Codification,* 29 Tul. L. Rev. 303, 307 (1955). *See also* Houin, *Reform of the French Civil Code and the Code of Commerce,* 4 Am. J. Comp. L. 485, 491 (1955).

38. Law Commission Act of 1965, c. 22, § 3(*l*)f.

39. Kahn-Freund, *supra* note 1, at 2 n.3. "When the Scottish Law Commission considers any question of major reform the first instinct is to look at solutions in other jurisdictions." LEGAL TRANSPLANTS, *supra* note 19, at 91.

40. *See, e.g.,* the California Law Revision Commission Statute, CAL. GOV'T CODE §§ 10300, 10330 (West 1966); the Michigan Legislative Council Act, MICH. COMP. LAWS §§ 4.322, 4.324 (1970); the New York Law Revision Commission Statute, N.Y. LEGIS. LAW §§ 70, 72 (McKinney 1952); NATIONAL CONFERENCE OF COMM'RS ON UNIFORM STATE LAWS, A MODEL ACT TO PROVIDE FOR THE CREATION OF A COMM'N ON UNIFORM STATE LAWS (1944). *See also* NATIONAL CONFERENCE OF COMM'RS ON UNIFORM STATE LAWS, 1975 HANDBOOK 342 (1975) (Constitution and By-Laws); 52 ALI PROCEEDINGS 769, 773 (1975) (Certificate of Incorporation and By-Laws).

41. *See* E. PATTERSON & R. SCHLESINGER, PROBLEMS OF CODIFICATION OF COMMERCIAL LAW, N.Y. LEGIS. DOC. NO. 65 (A), *reprinted in* NEW YORK STATE LAW REVISION COMM'N REPORT 31 (1955). For another example of an effective employment of the comparative method, see R. SCHLESINGER, THE NOTARY AND THE FORMAL CONTRACT IN CIVIL LAW, N.Y. LEGIS. DOC. NO. 65 (M) app., at 59–70 (1941), *reprinted in* NEW YORK STATE LAW REVISION COMM'N REPORT 403–14 (1941). *See generally* R. SCHLESINGER, COMPARATIVE LAW 14–21 (3d ed. 1970).

42. *E.g.,* U.C.C. art. 3, §1, Comment at 7 (Tent. Draft No. 1, 1946); U.C.C. art. 3, §1, Comment at 4 (Tent. Draft No. 3, 1947). *See also* U.C.C. §3-410, Comment 3 (1972) (citing English Bills of Exchange Act); *id.* §3-417, Comment 4, in which the case of Price v. Neal, 3 Burr. 1354 (K.B. 1762), is discussed.

43. *See* MODEL PENAL CODE art. 206, app. A, at 102 n.3, 103 (Tent. Draft No. 1, 1953) (referring to the French and German Penal Codes); *id.* § 3.02, Comment 2, note 3 (Tent. Draft No. 8, 1958) (referring to the British Code for Cyprus, the Canadian Criminal Code, the Criminal Codes of Queensland and Western Australia, the Indian Penal Code, the Italian, German, Yugoslav and Philippine Penal Codes); *id.* § 3.08, Comment 3, note 7 (referring to Canadian, New Zealand and Indian legislation); *id.* § 5.03 app., at 159 (Tent. Draft No. 10, 1960) (quoting from the Australian Crimes Act, 13 ACTS AUSTL. P. 16 (1914)); *id.* §§ 5.06, 5.07 app., at 80 (Tent. Draft No. 13, 1961) (quoting extensively from the Prevention of Crime Act, 1953, 1 & 2 Eliz. 2, c. 14, § 1).

Among the most recent texts produced by the American Law Institute is the Model Land Development Code (Proposed Official Draft, 1975). In defining "development," it refers to English legislation and case law. *Id.* § 1-202, Note. Isolated references to foreign, predominantly English and British Commonwealth, laws are also found in the drafts of the various Restatements prepared by the American Law Institute.

44. SCHLESINGER, COMPARATIVE LAW, *supra* note 41, at 20. *See also* Schlesinger, *Comparative Criminal Procedure: A Plea for Utilizing Foreign Experience,* 26 BUFFALO L. REV. 385 (1977).

45. *E.g.,* uniform acts on enforcement of foreign judgments, interstate and international procedure, reciprocal enforcement of support.

46. *See* UNIFORM MARRIAGE AND DIVORCE ACT, prefatory note, at 5 & § 207,

Comment (referring to English divorce laws). *See also* NATIONAL COMM'RS ON UNIFORM STATE LAWS, 1972 HANDBOOK 74 (1972) (Report to the Ford Foundation Concerning Work on Private International Law). Note also that the *Uniform Consumer Credit Code,* prefatory note, indicates that a special study of consumer credit laws was undertaken by a select committee of the American Bar Association. *Id.* at xvii. The result of this study, B. CURRAN, TRENDS IN CONSUMER CREDIT LEGISLATION (1965), is a comprehensive and comparative review of state legislation. There is no indication in the published study that foreign legal systems were examined. I am advised, however, that Canadian legislation was considered in connection with the Consumer Credit Code.

47. The requested appropriations for fiscal year 1977 for professional and clerical assistance to the standing committees of the United States Senate and House of Representatives are over 30 million dollars. This figure does not include appropriations for administrative staff. U.S. OFFICE OF MANAGEMENT AND THE BUDGET, THE BUDGET OF THE UNITED STATES GOVERNMENT, FISCAL YEAR 1977 app., at 14, 16. Members of Congress and Committee staff may also call on the experts in the Library of Congress who provide, among other things, advice on questions of foreign law and bibliographic assistance.

48. For examples of the exceptions and instances mentioned above, see *Hearings before a Special Subcomm. on Air and Water Pollution of the Senate Comm. on Public Works,* 89th Cong., 1st Sess., pt. 3, at 941–53 (1965) (documented testimony of Dr. Allen Kneese on the German model for effluent taxes); *International Aspects of Antitrust Laws: Hearings before the Subcomm. on Antitrust and Monopoly of the Senate Comm. on the Judiciary,* 93d Cong., 1st & 2d Sess. (1973–1974); SUBCOMMITTEE ON ANTITRUST AND MONOPOLY OF THE SENATE COMM. ON THE JUDICIARY, 88TH CONG. 2D SESS., ANTITRUST DEVELOPMENTS IN THE EUROPEAN COMMON MARKET (Comm. Print 1964); *Status of Forces Agreements: Hearings before the House Comm. on Foreign Affairs,* 84th Cong., 1st Sess., pt. 1 (1955). In connection with the Trade Act of 1974, the Senate Committee consulted the French Embassy on French experience with adjustment assistance; policies of other states were considered on such matters as preferences for undeveloped states, expropriation, reciprocity, etc.

As an example of a valuable comparative study commissioned by an executive department, see J. SWEENEY, THE INTERNATIONAL LAW OF SOVEREIGN IMMUNITY, U.S. Dep't of State Policy Research Study (1963) (bringing up to date a 1949 version). *See also* U.S. DEP'T OF TRANSP., COMPARATIVE STUDIES IN AUTOMOBILE ACCIDENT COMPENSATION (1970) (describing laws of France, Germany, Great Britain, Sweden and Canada).

On the impact of ignorance of other legal systems on the current copyright revision proposals before Congress, see Merryman, *Bernard Buffet's Refrigerator and the Integrity of the Work of Art,* 76 ARTNEWS 38, 42 (Feb. 1977), and *The Refrigerator of Bernard Buffet,* 27 HASTINGS L.J. 1023 (1976).

49. Statute of the Hague Conference on Private International Law, *formulated* Oct. 9–31, 1951, 15 U.S.T. 2228, T.I.A.S. No. 5710 (entered into force for the U.S. on Oct. 15, 1964); Charter of the International Institute for the Unifica-

tion of Private Law, March 15, 1940, *as amended by* 15 U.S.T. 2494, T.I.A.S. No. 5743 (entered into force for the U.S. on March 13, 1964).

50. INTERNATIONAL LABOUR OFFICE, INTERNATIONAL LABOUR CONVENTIONS: CHART OF RATIFICATIONS, (1975). It cannot be seriously argued that the Federal Constitution would prevent the United States from adhering to the I.L.O. Conventions.

51. *E.g.*, R. DAVID, LES GRANDS SYSTÈMES DE DROIT CONTEMPORAINS (6th ed. 1974); R. DAVID & J.E.C. BRIERLY, MAJOR LEGAL SYSTEMS IN THE WORLD TODAY (1968); W. FIKENTSCHER, METHODEN DES RECHTS IN VERGLEICHENDER DARSTELLUNG (Vols. 1–4, 1975–1977). K. ZWEIGERT & H. KÖTZ, EINFÜHRUNG IN DIE RECHTSVERGLEICHUNG AUF DEM GEBIETE DES PRIVATRECHTS (Vols. 1 & 2, 1969, 1971).

52. INTERNATIONAL ENCYCLOPEDIA OF COMPARATIVE LAW, (Vols. 1–17, 1971–).

53. A comparison of the *Index to Legal Periodicals* for 1946–1949 and 1970–1973 reveals a more than twofold increase in the number of comparative or foreign law items published in U.S.-English language periodicals.

54. For example, the *Harvard International Law Journal* published 110 articles and comments in its first 15 volumes (1959–1974). Of the 110 items, some 24 could be even remotely classified as centering on comparative or foreign law. The remaining items deal with international law and organization (including European Community law), international trade and American regulations of foreign trade and investment. Similarly, of the 42 articles, notes and comments published in the first five volumes (1968–1972) of the *Cornell International Law Journal,* eight might be considered in the foreign-comparative law category.

55. In an address delivered on the occasion of the "International Law Weekend" at the Association of the Bar of the City of New York, November 13, 1976, Professor Richard R. Baxter, former President of the American Society of International Law and Editor-in-Chief of the *American Journal of International Law,* noted the absence of any modern systematic treatise on international law in this country. He indicated that despite the many articles (of varying quality) in the many student international law journals, there have been very few monographs dealing in a scientific manner with important general themes of international law.

56. Yntema, *Comparative Legal Research—Some Remarks on "Looking out of the Cave,"* 54 MICH. L. REV. 899 (1956).

57. *Id.* at 901.

58. *Id.* at 902.

59. *Id.* at 903.

60. Association of American Law Schools News Letter No. 76-2 (May 12, 1976).

Excerpt from *Courts and Free Markets—Perspectives from the United States and Europe*

Isaiah Berlin was skeptical about comparing complex social phenomena. Indeed, to undertake a comparison between a centralized mature federation encompassing one nation and a regional regime of states in a fluctuating process of integration is to embark on a venturesome journey, particularly in the absence of a reliable methodological guide. The success of a comparison depends on a clear perception of the "tertium comparationis" (the subject of the comparison) and on sufficient points of similarity, at a level of abstraction high enough to avoid the purely technical but still in contact with reality.

Thus a comparison between methods of interpretation employed by the highest courts is more compelling than a juxtaposition of the institutional structures on the two sides of the Atlantic. As regards the latter, a more definite study would call for an interdisciplinary inquiry into the history and political, social, and economic conditions underpinning the vastly different constitutional schemes.

The piece in this chapter, written with my colleague Terrance Sandalow, forms an introductory essay to a collection of parallel European and American papers published under the title Courts and Free Markets—Perspectives from the United States and Europe. *It reflects the discussion of a group that met in the enchanting environment of the Villa Serbelloni at Bellagio in July 1979. The group of twenty-five included members of the highest American federal and state courts, judges of the Court of Justice of the European Communities and an Advocate General at that Court, heads of the legal departments of the Community Commission and Council of Ministers, and a member of the French Conseil d'État, as well as Belgian, Danish, English, German, Italian, and American academics.*

Judge Pierre Pescatore, himself a "bold constructionist" during the early halcyon days of the Community Court, offered the following aperçu of the Bellagio enterprise in the foreword to our book.

Reprinted from Terrance Sandalow and Eric Stein, COURTS AND FREE MARKETS—PERSPECTIVES FROM THE UNITED STATES AND EUROPE, 2 vols., vol 1, 3–45 (Oxford, Clarendon Press, 1982).

The European participants in the Bellagio Conference felt a delight not unlike that of Monsieur Jourdain, Molière's famous character, when he discovered that he had been speaking prose for years without even being aware of it. To them came the realization that they have been practicing federalism on lines not unlike those of the United States, and that they too, have a Supreme Court of their own, with even some Marshalls and other bold constructionists sitting on it.

The striking thing is that all this was by no means a matter of imitation, but a discovery *a posteriori.* Though the United States have from the outset taken a sympathetic attitude towards European integration, there was never on our side any question of taking American federalism and the experience of the Supreme Court as examples in European affairs. Only American antitrust law has furnished a pattern for the Communities' competition rules, as it did for the relevant statutes of many countries, but that was indeed all. How then shall we explain the many coincidences which a comparative study of the case law of the Supreme Court and the Court of the European Communities has enabled us to discern in the various fields which have been explored on the basis of parallel investigations: growth of central power and determination of power relationship between the whole and its parts; free movement of goods and incidence of state taxation on interstate commerce; free movement of persons and services and the right of establishment?

The outstanding reports published in this book [*Courts and Free Markets—Perspectives from the United States and Europe*] and the introductory essay reflecting the exchange of views show that comparable problems have arisen in the United States and the European Community, and that, while allowing for the difference of legal techniques, solutions reached and achievements made are remarkably similar. This is the more striking as these developments have taken place at different periods of history and in contexts which varied widely from both a political and legal standpoint . . .

How then can these analogies be explained? I think that our study, conducted as it was in a spirit of comparison and mutual understanding, has made us aware of the fact that the methods of federalism are not only a means of organizing states. It would rather seem that federalism is a political and legal philosophy which adapts itself to all political contexts on both the municipal and the international level, wherever and whenever two basic prerequisites are fulfilled: the

> search for unity, combined with genuine respect for the autonomy and the legitimate interests of the participant entities . . .
>
> It is to be hoped that the reader of these studies will experience in turn some of the amazement which was felt by those who had the privilege of first exchanging their ideas on this basis. It might be a psychological advantage to all concerned that during a full generation we have been working in a sort of splendid mutual ignorance. But now has come the time to take note of the experience gathered on both sides of the Atlantic, and, on our part, to recognize that on many issues arising in a federal context the United States have the advantage of some hundred and fifty years of a highly diversified judicial development from which many useful lessons may well be learned by the Jourdains of Europe.

Almost two decades have elapsed since the Bellagio adventure. While the American system has continued working as described in this essay (with some of the modifications mentioned in the newly added footnotes), its European counterpart has taken several steps in the process of integration. The Community's competence has been substantially extended beyond the original traditional areas, and it has advanced from the "common market" closer toward a "single market" with a common currency and the European Central Bank. The unanimity requirement in the Council has been curtailed, particularly by the Single European Act of 1987, thus reducing the veto power of the individual member states. The European Parliament now shares legislative power with the Council.

With the extension of power came significant structural change. Thus, by virtue of the Maastricht Treaty of 1992, the Community has become the first of the three components ("pillars") of the new, overarching European Union. The second and third pillars included in the European Union were originally conceived as intergovernmental arrangements for cooperation within the European Council (the highest political organ comprised of heads of member states and governments) and in the Council of Ministers. The executive Commission and the European Parliament played a marginal, informational role, and the Court of Justice was expressly excluded. The competences within these two pillars touch most directly upon the "national sovereignty" of the members. The second pillar deals with the "common foreign and security policy," and I shall return to the subject of foreign affairs in some detail later in part 2. The third pillar covers immigration, border and alien control, asylum, drug traffic, international fraud, and judicial and police cooperation. By the Amsterdam Treaty signed in October 1997, most of the "sensitive" competences in the third pillar had been transferred to the first pillar and made subject, with some significant qualifications, to the jurisdiction of the Court of Justice.

We wrote in this essay that no separate citizenship existed in the Community. Yet the Maastricht Treaty introduced this concept superimposed on national citizenship. It comprises a bundle of rights, such as the right to vote in local elections anywhere in the Community area and the right of free movement and residence throughout the Community territory, no longer tied to the requirement of an economic activity in the host state.

Unlike the structural modification, the core case law of the Court of Justice has not been subject to dramatic changes, and the same may be said about the U.S. Supreme Court.

On the Two Systems: An Overview

I. Introduction

A. The Rationale

The United States and the European Economic Community (ECC)[1] are systems in which governmental power is divided between central and local ("state") authorities. Because of this common characteristic, and despite vital contextual and institutional differences, the two systems share certain problems that must be faced by every divided-power system. In every such system there must be, first, criteria for determining, at any moment, which issues come within the respective domains of the central and state authorities; and, second, a mechanism for resolving disputes that may arise concerning this allocation of competencies. Moreover, to preserve its vitality over time, every such system must have a mechanism for reallocating central and local authority in response to changing conditions.

The common problems facing the two systems suggest the possibility that, at the appropriate level of analysis, each system may draw on the other's experience. We should not, of course, expect to find that either system has developed "solutions" to these problems that are readily transferable to the other. But an examination of the manner in which each has responded and the reasons that it has responded as it has may suggest hitherto unseen opportunities for the other. Whether or not such opportunities emerge, the perspective gained from comparing a system with another facing similar issues is likely to provide students of each system with a new insight into its workings. In this light, similarities and differences in the principles and mechanisms developed by the two systems are of equal interest.

Two additional considerations support a comparative examination of the European and American systems, one relating to the similarity of their objectives and the other to a similarity of means by which they have sought to achieve those objectives. First, both the Constitution and the EEC Treaty superimposed central institutional frameworks upon existing state structures with the objective of forming "a more perfect union." To be sure, the Constitution was intended to establish a nation, while the immediate purpose of the Treaty was limited to economic objectives, including a customs union and a "common market." But it is also true that, in the United States, a central reason for establishing the nation was to promote a "common market"; and among the animating impulses for creating the European common market was the vision of an economic and political union as the culmination of the integration movement.

Comparative study of the two systems is also suggested by the reliance of each upon courts to advance their objectives. The Community is the only treaty-based system equipped with a court which may be approaching the role of a constitutional court in a federal system.[2] The United States Supreme Court is, of course, the best known of such tribunals. By acquiescence of the political institutions, if not by design of the architects of the two systems, the courts in each have come to play a major role in defining the boundaries of central and local authority. The interpretative techniques and the principles that the Supreme Court and the Court of Justice have developed in performing that role provide a fertile field for investigation.

B. The Risks: Contextual and Institutional Differences

Any attempt to press the American federation as a general model for the new Europe would fly in the face of both history and present-day reality. The United States is the product of two centuries of nationhood. "Europe" is barely a quarter-century old. There is also a vast disparity in the quantum of the powers conferred on the central institutions of the two systems. In the United States, the federal government holds the exclusive powers of immigration and naturalization, monetary management, defence, and political foreign policy. It also has the power to tax. In Europe, these powers remain in the state governments, with only modest advances thus far towards a common monetary system and co-ordination of general economic policies; although the Community has important powers in foreign economic policy, political foreign policy and defence remain in the hands of the Member States, subject only to cooperation through instrumentalities outside the Community structure.[3] Moreover, any vision of a United States of Europe "just around the corner" underestimates the centrifugal forces at work, the effectiveness of the European "Jeffersonians" of the 1980s and, above all, the divergent economic, political, social, and cultural conditions of the nations that compose the Community.

Even a comparison between contemporary Europe and the young American Republic of Chief Justice Marshall's days must be accompanied by a recognition of immense differences. Although the American colonial communities differed in religion and way of life, they were of common stock, spoke one official language, shared the same legal institutions and colonial government, and had fought a war of independence on the same side. At the time of the adoption of the Constitution, the thirteen states were already tied loosely together in a Confederation and, though they were endowed with their own constitutions and governments, had no history as independent nation-states. Even so, it took a brutal civil war to contain, if not resolve, the differences between the North and South within the union. Moreover, the new Republic, endowed with natural resources vastly superior to those of Western Europe, functioned in a *laissez-faire* market economy that offered substantially fewer opportunities for confrontations between state and central institutions than are generated by "welfare state" economies. Finally, the "splendid isolation" of the North American continent, much freer than Europe from foreign policy pressures, allowed for a leisurely progress in the "nationalization" of the economy and of political life.

In Europe, the six founding Member States of the Community (Belgium, Federal Republic of Germany, France, Italy, Luxembourg, and the Netherlands) have had long histories as proud nation-states on the world scene. The history, traditions, culture, and laws of their people differ dramatically, and they speak four different languages. With the accession of four new Members (Denmark, Ireland, United Kingdom in 1973 and Greece in 1981), four additional languages and cultures were added, and the mosaic of the continental civil law systems was enriched by common law and Scandinavian law in a Community of some 270 million citizens.[4]

In contrast with the early American experience, the contemporary European welfare state systems postulate intensive governmental intervention in the economy that magnifies the role of public institutions and adds tensions between the new "European" and nation-state institutions. On the other hand, the awareness that the solutions of many problems facing the modern European nation-state (monetary management, energy, and environmental protection, to mention a few) are beyond its individual capacity has worked in favour of unification. Similarly, in the international arena, the political-military pressures from the East and the economic competition with other industrialized countries have increased the need for Europe to speak with one voice. Nevertheless, Europe is not on the way to becoming a federal system in the United States' image, but is likely to evolve its own indigenous design for a divided-power system through an arduous process marked by limited steps forward, alternating with disappointing setbacks.

The contextual differences between Europe and the United States are reflected in the differing designs of the central institutions of the two systems. The institutions of the federal government, based upon Montesquieu's model of division of powers among the executive, legislative, and judicial branches, are constituted independently of the state governments. In the Community system, by contrast, the tripartite institutional pattern was replaced by a quadripartite scheme in which the "branches" of "the central government" are linked more or less closely to the constituent state governments. The four principal Community institutions are:[5]

(a) *The intergovernmental organ,* "the Council," consists of representatives of the Member governments, usually foreign ministers, who are assisted or replaced, depending on the subject-matter, by ministers heading other executive departments.

(b) *The common executive body,* "the Commission," consists of fourteen members who are appointed by common agreement of the national governments but can be dismissed only by a motion of censure of the European Parliament, which has not yet invoked this authority. The Commission members are, however, appointed for a relatively short term of four years, and, although the term is renewable, there are at least two well-known cases in which a government prevented a reappointment.[6] The President and Vice-Presidents of the Commission are selected from among its members also by the Member governments rather than by the Commission itself. These arrangements clearly assure that in principle all Commissioners will be acceptable to each government. Nevertheless, it is specifically provided that the Commissioners are "completely independent" and "shall neither seek nor take instruction from any Government" — and a corresponding obligation "not to seek to influence" the Commissioners is imposed on the Member States.[7]

(c) *The parliamentary organ,* "the Assembly," which christened itself "the European Parliament," was composed originally of deputies from the national parliaments. Since 1979, however, the members are elected directly by the citizens of each state.

(d) *The judicial organ,* the "Court of Justice," consists of ten members, also appointed by common agreement of the Member governments but assured of judicial independence. The Advocates General, currently four in number, assist the Court by stating in each case their independent, reasoned opinion in open court.

In 1974 the heads of state and government institutionalized their summit meetings in the form of the "European Council," which was to provide highest-level policy direction and a stimulus to the slow-moving Community machinery. This institution does not have any basis in the Treaty.

To initiate the law- and policy-making process, the Commission, with a staff of some 8,000,[8] prepares the necessary studies and, after consulting a variety of special interest groups,[9] submits a formal proposal to the Council, which also has a substantial staff of its own. The Commission's role is important because, in most instances, the Council cannot act without a proposal from the Commission and cannot modify a proposal except by unanimous concurrence of all the ministers. Before acting on the proposal, however, the Council must often obtain "opinions" from the European Parliament and from the Economic and Social Committee, a large advisory body representing the principal economic and social groups in the Member States. These opinions, however, are advisory and the Council may, and often does, disregard them. The proposal, with the opinions, is then examined and more often than not it is substantially rewritten in secret negotiations in which the Commission staff participates. These negotiations take place within the framework of the so-called Committee of Permanent Representatives, a body of high-level diplomats, accredited by the Member State governments to the Community. They are assisted by a complex network of specialized working groups of national officials who do the preparatory work for the Council. Since all but the most important "political" issues are resolved in this forum, the final adoption by the ministers often amounts to a formality.

In this scheme, the Council is the true "legislator." According to the Treaty, the Council may act in a number of instances by a weighted majority vote, but as a result of the informal "Luxembourg agreement" which France imposed on the other Member States in 1965, voting has disappeared for all practical purposes (except in the budgetary procedure) and issues are generally negotiated until all ministers agree.

The formal law-making procedures of the Community have at best a superficial similarity to the procedure for enacting legislation in the

United States. In the United States, a legislative bill must originate in the Congress. Frequently, especially since the turn of the century, bills are drafted in one of the federal executive departments under the direction of the President. The "Administration bill" is then "sponsored" by one or more members of the House of Representatives and the Senate. Not unlike a proposal of the Commission, a bill is invariably modified in the powerful congressional committees after negotiations with the "Administration" and in response to special interest group pressures. It must then be adopted by the Congress and approved by the President before it becomes law.

It is apparent that there are profound differences between the law-making process of the United States and those of the Community. Although legally the Congress legislates by majority vote, students of the Congress have often observed that important legislation is rarely adopted if supported only by a bare majority. Nevertheless, Congress's enactment of legislation does not depend upon its ability to achieve unanimity, as is now, in effect, required in the Community. Moreover, members of Congress, unlike members of the Council, do not represent their state governments. Indeed, often — perhaps even typically — the political base of members of Congress from a given state is quite different from that of the state's chief executive who, in turn, may belong to a different party from the one that controls one or both houses of the state legislature. In consequence, Congress may, and often does, enact legislation opposed by state governments, even by a majority of state governments.

There are differences of at least equal magnitude between the executive branches of the two systems. The Commission, "the conscience and the organized impulse of the Community," in addition to its exclusive power of legislative initiative, acts as an "executive": it exercises delegated rule-making power, takes care of administrative tasks, operates a variety of funds and centres, and, upon prior authorization from the Council, negotiates international agreements which are then "concluded" by the Council. Finally, in its "watchdog" function, it supervises compliance with Community law.

In performing its purely "executive" functions, the Commission is responsible for numerous administrative activities similar to those performed by the elaborate bureaucracy that constitutes the Executive Branch in the United States. The differences of scale are, of course, very great, reflecting the vastly greater range of activities of the central government in the United States. Although both the Commission and the Executive Branch bear primary responsibility for administering central policy, both systems also rely heavily upon state governments to execute important areas of central policy. The Community, indeed, must rely upon the Member States to act for it in such important areas as customs inspection and collection at Community frontiers.

Community law consists of the Treaty; supplementary agreements; "Community acts" adopted by the Council or the Commission, which are commonly (but somewhat loosely) described as "secondary legislation";[10] and "general principles" derived from the legal orders of the Member States. Americans may be surprised to learn that the Court of Justice has held legislation adopted by the Council invalid for violating "general principles" that state norms of fundamental fairness regarding the treatment of private interests.

Community acts are divided by the Treaty into four classes—(1) regulations, (2) directives, (3) decisions, and (4) recommendations and opinions.

According to Article 189 of the Treaty "[a] regulation shall have general application. It shall be binding in its entirety and directly applicable in all Member States." Since a regulation not only binds the Member State governments, but also binds directly all persons within the jurisdiction of the Community and does not require any national implementing measures, it is comparable, in this respect, to a federal statute, administrative agency rule, or executive order in the United States.

A "directive," in contrast with a regulation, "shall be binding, as to the result to be achieved, upon each Member State to which it is addressed, but shall leave to the national authorities the choice of form and methods." The directive, which is reminiscent of the German Federal *Rahmengesetz* (framework law), has no direct American counterpart, but may be likened, at least functionally, to federal grants-in-aid conditioned upon acceptance by the states of federal standards or policies.

While regulations and directives provide norms of general application, a "decision" deals with a specific situation and may be addressed to one or more governments or individuals. It is "binding in its entirety upon those to whom it is addressed."

Recommendations and opinions "have no binding force" and enable the Commission in its discretion to provide guidance and express its views for the benefit of the Member States. The Council may also adopt this form of acts.

Although not mentioned in Article 189, international agreements concluded by the Community constitute a specific type of Community act.

II. Judicial Review

In every system of divided power, some means must exist to resolve controversies arising out of the allocation of authority between central and local institutions. Meaning must be given to the provisions of fundamental law that define the limits of central and local authority and a mechanism established for enforcing those limits. Both the United States and the Community have come to rely heavily upon courts to perform these functions.

The primary means by which American courts perform these functions is the power they exercise to determine the constitutionality of legislation. The Constitution did not expressly confer upon the Supreme Court the power to determine the constitutionality of acts of Congress, nor is it entirely clear that the framers intended the Court to exercise that power. Nevertheless, the Court asserted the power early in the nation's history. In *Marbury* v. *Madison,*[11] Chief Justice Marshall justified it on the grounds that the Constitution is a paramount law and that courts are obligated to decide cases conformably to law. It follows from these propositions, he argued, that courts could not give effect to legislation forbidden by the Constitution. Critics of Marshall's argument have maintained that it begged the question by assuming that the Court is the ultimate authority on the meaning of the Constitution. Marshall's response to that criticism was to assert that "It is emphatically the province and duty of the judicial branch to say what the law is."[12]

Although constitutional scholars continue to debate the persuasiveness of Marshall's argument and, more generally, the legitimacy of judicial review of the constitutionality of federal legislation, the existence of the power has not for many years been open to serious question. In the years since *Marbury,* the Court has reviewed the constitutionality of many hundreds of federal statutes and has held more than one hundred invalid. It is worth noting, however, that the Court does not have a commission to pass judgment upon the constitutionality of all acts of Congress. Marshall rested the argument for judicial review on the obligation of courts to decide "cases" in accordance with the law. It follows that the Court may rule upon the constitutionality of legislation only if such a determination is necessary to dispose of a "case" properly before it. Over the years, the Court has expanded the definition of a "case" in response to an evolving consensus that the validity of legislation should be subject to judicial review. Nevertheless, it remains true that the constitutionality of many federal statutes will never be judicially determined because the issue cannot arise in a form that meets the constitutional requirements for a "case."

Although the Constitution is explicit in declaring that the "Constitution, and the Laws of the United States which shall be made in pursuance thereof" are the "supreme Law of the Land,"[13] it does not expressly confer upon the Supreme Court the power to review state legislation for consistency with federal law. The logic of Marshall's argument in *Marbury,* however, applies with equal force to state legislation, and the Court has from the very beginning routinely exercised the power to review such legislation for conformity with federal law. Such questions may arise initially in either lower federal courts or state courts. In the early years of the nation's history, it was occasionally argued that the Court lacks power to review state court judgments, even though the correctness of the judgment depends upon an interpretation of federal law. The Court held otherwise, and the issue has not been raised for many years. Advocates of "states' rights" have been more persistent in claiming for the states a power of "interposition," i.e. a power to "interpose" their own interpretation of the Constitution as a bar to the contrary interpretation of the federal government. The doctrine of interposition does not, it will be noted, deny the supremacy of the Constitution; it merely asserts that each state may determine for itself the meaning to be given to the document. Although the doctrine has been asserted throughout American history, most recently in the aftermath of the Court's decision prohibiting the maintenance of racially segregated public schools, it has been consistently rejected by the Court and may confidently be said to have no present significance.[14]

The discussion thus far has been cast in terms of the Supreme Court's power to determine the constitutionality of legislation. Marshall's justification for that power does not, however, establish a unique role for the Supreme Court; it applies equally to all courts, imposing upon them the obligation to give effect to the Constitution whenever a justiciable claim is made that its provisions have been transgressed by legislation. With respect to state courts, indeed, the Constitution expressly establishes that duty, requiring that they give effect to its provisions "any Thing in the Constitution or Law of any State to the Contrary notwithstanding."[15] Since the Supreme Court has only a very limited original jurisdiction—confined by the Constitution to "Cases affecting Ambassadors, other Public Ministers and Consuls, and those in which a State shall be a Party"[16]—nearly all claims that legislation violates the Constitution arise initially in state or federal courts. The entire state and federal judiciaries thus share in the responsibility for ensuring the conformity of legislation to the Constitution. The role of the state and lower federal courts is of critical importance, since the Supreme Court can hear only a fraction of the cases raising constitutional issues, and even in those cases in which it does assert jurisdiction, its power is confined by the limitations implicit in its role as an appellate court: that is it may decide only questions of law and is bound by the determination of facts by the trial court.

The EEC Treaty differs substantially from the Constitution in its treatment of judicial review, but the power exercised by the Court of Justice is in many respects similar to that exercised by the Supreme Court. Perhaps because the drafters were afraid of the "tyranny" of the new institutions, Article 173 grants the Court express and broad power to review Community legislation for conformity with the Treaty. The Member States, the Commission, the Council, and even individuals or companies (if they can meet strict standing requirements)[17] are authorized to institute an original action in the Court for review of an act of a Community institution. If the Court holds that the claim is well-founded, the Treaty directs that it "shall declare the act concerned to be void" and further directs the "institution whose act has been declared void . . . to take the necessary measures to comply with the judgment of the Court of Justice."[18]

The Court may also exercise original jurisdiction to review Member State law for conformity with Community law, but only at the request of a Member State or the Commission. An individual party plaintiff is not permitted to maintain such an action. In contrast with the procedure for review of Community legislation, the Court is not authorized to declare state law void if it finds that such law violates Community law. The Treaty provides only that upon such a finding "the State shall be required to take the necessary measures to comply with the judgment of the Court of Justice."[19]

In the history of the Court to date only a single case has been decided on a complaint by a Member State, and until 1978 only a limited number were brought by the Commission. Since that time the Commission's initiative has increased,[20] but it has become obvious that the Commission is reluctant to bring an action against a Member State whose support it may need in the Council negotiations and, for similar political reasons, a Member government hesitates to sue another for a violation of Community law. If judicial review of state action depended solely on these procedures, many protectionist and discriminatory state measures would go unchallenged and the effectiveness of Community law would be seriously impaired.

In practice, control of state laws that violate Community law has come chiefly from a source that probably was not anticipated by the founding fathers of the Community. This source is Article 177 of the Treaty. It is addressed to state courts and is predicated upon the symbiotic relationship between those courts and the Court of Justice. When, in a case before it, a state court needs to apply a provision of Community law, it may suspend the proceeding and refer any questions of interpretation of that law, or of the validity of a Community act, to the Court of

Justice for a "preliminary ruling." If it is a court of last resort, it is required to do so. Unlike the right of appeal in the United States, this procedure may be suggested by the parties to the case, but they cannot demand it. Unlike the American certiorari procedure, it does not give the Court an option to accept or refuse the reference. The Court's ruling is binding upon the requesting state court, but it is for the latter court to apply it to the specific factual situation and to decide the case. Since, in line with the continental doctrine, the Court does not follow the *stare decisis* rule of binding precedent, the preliminary ruling applies only to the case in which it was rendered. However, the referring court and all other state courts must follow the preliminary ruling if they are faced with the same question of interpretation unless they again refer the question to the Court of Justice.

The Article 177 procedure was clearly intended, first, to ensure a uniform interpretation of Community law throughout the Community territory, and second, to reinforce the effectiveness of judicial review of Community acts in the context of private litigation. In the celebrated *van Gend en Loos* case,[21] however, over the strong objection of the state governments, the Court allowed this procedure to be turned into a device approaching judicial review of state legislation. According to the holding in that case, an individual plaintiff may sue his government before a state court and ask the court to strike down a state law which he claims violates his personal right derived from a provision of a Community law. It will then be for the Court of Justice to decide—on reference from the state court—whether the right exists (in other words, whether the provision in question must be given "direct effect" in the state legal order) and, if so, to interpret the content and the reach of the provision. In *Costa* v. *ENEL,*[22] the next most important case, the Court of Justice wrote into the Treaty "a supremacy clause" by making explicit what it had implied in *van Gend,* that Community law, within its limited sphere, is superior to conflicting state law, including state constitutions. In *Simmenthal,*[23] the last of the triad, the Court completed the supremacy clause equivalence by ruling that a state judge must refuse to apply a state law which conflicts with a "directly effective" Community law, since the Member States have given up the power to adopt such a law upon ratifying the Treaty. This line of cases has imposed in effect a form of "constitutional review" on Member States in which this institution was unknown because of a strong attachment to the doctrine of separation of powers or to "parliamentary sovereignty." In Italy and Germany, where the central Constitutional Courts had previously had the exclusive power to declare an act of Parliament unconstitutional, it introduced a decentralized form of judicial review.

In a series of major constitutional cases, the Court broadened the concept of "directly effective" provisions in such a way that individual plaintiffs are now able to claim "constitutional-level" rights on the basis of practically all the substantive provisions of the Treaty that govern the establishment of the customs union; prohibit discriminatory state taxes; and guarantee the freedom of movement of workers, the freedom of establishment, and the right to supply services. The end result has been that any such provision of the Treaty may be relied upon by an individual plaintiff who challenges a conflicting state law in a state court. Some Treaty provisions, such as that guaranteeing equal pay for men and women, may be invoked by an individual not only against a state law, but also against private contracts—including collective bargaining agreements. If one may recall American constitutional parlance, the Court of Justice has in these cases dispensed with the "state action" prerequisite, according to which a citizen may invoke the direct protection of the Constitution against state actions but not against private conduct. This dispensation contrasts with the American doctrine according to which federal protection against private action cannot be derived directly from the Constitution but requires an implementing act of Congress.

The Court has also extended the right of private parties to claim rights under Community legislation. Although the Treaty stipulates only that a regulation shall be "directly applicable," the Court has held that directives and decisions are to be given similar effect if they are complete enough for judicial application. In consequence, the Article 177 procedure may now be employed to achieve a ruling by the Court of Justice upon claims of rights under appropriate provisions of Community legislation as well as under the Treaty.

The significance of these seminal rulings can hardly be overstated. In the aggregate, they must be taken as establishing a nascent federal system. The linchpin of the emerging system is the Court's expansion of the direct effect of Community law and, as a corollary, its fiat declaring the supremacy of that law. Although the Community was established by Treaty, as early as 1962 the Court refused to treat it "as an ordinary international agreement" governing relations among sovereign states and insisted instead on interpreting it as creating "a new legal order,"[24] one in which Community law, within its proper sphere, was paramount over national law. It is interesting to note that a similar issue arose early in American history. The Constitution was regarded by many as essentially an agreement among sovereign states. The "compact" theory, which provided the underpinnings for the doctrine of interposition and for other efforts to limit federal power, was rejected by the Supreme

Court in *McCulloch* v. *Maryland* and also, at a much later date, in the context of Justice Sutherland's theory of undivided national sovereignty over foreign affairs.[25] Although the legal consequences of the "compact" theory were never very clear, it served as an important political symbol until the Civil War.

If confronted directly with the assertion that the Treaty is tantamount to a constitution, most if not all Member governments would be likely to demur. Nevertheless, the Court's "constitutionalizing" decisions have received general acceptance by state courts. Community law is routinely given "direct effect" by those courts and accorded precedence over inconsistent state law. In a recent case,[26] however, the French *Conseil d'État,* which traditionally has been unfriendly to the Community, flatly refused to follow an established Court of Justice rule and insisted on its own authority to interpret the effect of a Community act, employing language reminiscent of the American doctrine of interposition.

It is often said by Americans that the crucial decision of the 1787 Constitutional Convention was the decision to establish a federal government with power to act directly upon individuals. The existence of direct relations between individuals and central institutions is, indeed, generally taken to be a defining characteristic of a federal system. The importance of such relations is illustrated by the effect that it has had in facilitating the enforcement of Community law. Through the medium of private actions, the Court has enlisted the state judiciaries in the enforcement of Community law. Moreover, with the gates of access opened via Article 177, the Court has been flooded by references from state courts. The expansion of its caseload has enabled it to identify a multitude of discriminatory state laws and practices, afford protection to individuals harmed by these state measures, and develop a substantial body of law, implementing the policies expressed by the Treaty and acts adopted by Council and the Commission. The experience in the United States is similar. Actions for judicial review are instituted in an overwhelming majority of cases by private plaintiffs; a suit by one state against another is a rarity and an action by the federal government against a state is also uncommon. Similarities between the two systems must not, of course, be overstated. The Court of Justice, in an Article 177 proceeding, has less control over national courts than the Supreme Court has over state courts when reviewing their judgments. Moreover, the Community lacks any counterpart to the system of lower federal courts, which plays so vital a role in securing recognition of federal rights in the United States, and must, therefore, rely on state authorities for the enforcement of Community law. These differences serve to remind us that "Europe" is not a mature federal system. They do not disturb the earlier suggestion that the decisions of the Court of Justice create the possibility that it may become one.

III. The Legislative Power of the Central Institutions

A. "The Living Law"

It is commonly accepted that the authority of the central institutions in both systems is limited to the exercise of enumerated powers. Neither the original Constitution nor the Treaty expresses such a limitation, but there is general agreement that it was contemplated by the framers of both documents. A textual foundation for the limitation was provided by the Tenth Amendment, which was adopted two years after the ratification of the Constitution.

There are, of course, as we pointed out earlier, very great differences between the legislative authority conferred upon the Congress and that which is conferred upon the Council. The former was intended to serve as the legislature of a nation; the powers of the latter are confined to the much more limited objectives of the Community. Another reason for the differences is the different eras in which the two documents were adopted. The Constitution was written prior to the industrial revolution; the Treaty was drafted at a time when men were beginning to herald the arrival of the post-industrial age.

Such differences have had a significant effect in shaping the questions that have arisen under the two documents. Thus, the perceptions of a need for federal economic legislation evolved gradually in the United States as the industrial revolution created novel social and economic problems. The constitutional question posed was whether the requisite powers could be found in a document drafted to deal with the problems of an earlier and very different time. The Community, by contrast, was born at a time when many of the problems confronted by a highly complex industrial society were fully in view; it was created, indeed, precisely for the purpose of dealing with those problems. As a result, the question that bedevilled the United States for a half-century, whether federal power over interstate commerce extended to production activities (manufacturing, mining, and agriculture) as well as to interstate trade, was never an issue in Europe.

Despite these differences, there are interesting similarities in the interpretative problems that have arisen under the Treaty and the Constitution, in the techniques of construction that the Court of Justice and the

Supreme Court have employed to resolve those problems, and more generally in the role that the two courts have played in defining the legislative power of the central institutions. Needless to say, there are also important differences.

In interpreting the reach of a Treaty provision defining the power of the Community, the Court of Justice looks to "the spirit, general scheme and the wording" ("*esprit, économie, texte*"),[27] or, in other terms, to "the objects and purposes."[28] The formula bears considerable resemblance to the approach adopted by Chief Justice Marshall in the important early case of *McCulloch* v. *Maryland.*[29] The question whether the Constitution conferred one or another power, Marshall wrote, depends upon "a fair construction of the whole instrument." A constitution, he suggested, should not be interpreted with the literalness appropriate to a statute. Reference must be made to "its great outlines" and "its important objects."[30] The Court of Justice, similarly, looks beyond the "text" of a particular provision and it gleans the "spirit," "objects," and "general scheme," first, from the underlying Community objective of economic integration and the unique institutional system; second, from the preamble and the tasks broadly stated in the introductory articles of the Treaty (such as freedom of intra-Community trade); and third, from the location of the provision in the Treaty and the function assigned to a power in the over-all scheme. The Court's broad reading of Community power rests in part upon its own vision of the Community as a living and dynamic whole with a purpose and values presumably supported by a consensus of its constituency.

In the earliest opinions of the Court of Justice there were occasional references to the "intention of the parties to the Treaty," but reliance upon such intention seems to have been abandoned in favour of the purpose-oriented formula. The use of an "intention" criterion in this context is problematic, if for no other reason than that the founding governments agreed not to publish the legislative history of the Treaty. The current approach of the Court of Justice is in line with the continental tradition of interpreting broad general clauses in comprehensive codes and written constitutions, but understandably it has caused no small measure of bewilderment among British lawyers accustomed to a "faithful" textual interpretation of statutes.

Marshall's determination in *McCulloch* v. *Maryland* to read the provisions of the Constitution broadly is demonstrated in part by the fact that he was willing to sustain Congressional authority to create a federal bank even though that power is not expressly conferred in the Constitution, without reliance upon the "necessary and proper clause" of the Constitution.[31] In the Community, Article 235 is the Treaty equivalent of that clause, but in sharp contrast with the United States practice, it has played a crucial role in Community law-making, as illustrated below.[32]

The American experience over the course of nearly two centuries demonstrates the latitude conferred by interpretative techniques such as those employed by the two courts. In the early years of Marshall's strongly nationalistic views, the Supreme Court read Congressional power very broadly. Thus, in an early case involving the reach of Congressional power under the interstate commerce clause, Marshall, while not repudiating the theory of enumerated powers, wrote for the Court that the "genius and character of the whole government" is that its powers extend "to those internal concerns [of the nation] which affect the states generally, but not those which are completely within a particular state [and] . . . do not affect other States. . . ."[33] However, beginning in 1895, and for some forty years thereafter, the Court found the Constitution to be animated by a very different spirit, one far more restrictive of federal power. Thus, the mere fact that production activities had consequences beyond the borders of the states in which they were carried on was held to be insufficient to justify federal regulation. The "great outlines" and "important objects" of the Constitution, its "general scheme" and "spirit," required that such activities remain within the exclusive control of the states. In the 1930s the Court returned to Marshall's capacious view of federal authority. Although the Supreme Court continues to pay lip-service to the theory of enumerated powers, its decisions in practical effect sanction plenary Congressional authority in the economic sphere and nearly plenary authority beyond that sphere. At the present time, in consequence, there are few, if any, issues that can confidently be asserted to be beyond the reach of federal authority. In brief, the limits of Congressional power are now determined almost entirely by political rather than by legal considerations.

The extent to which both courts have been influenced by their understandings regarding the objectives of union is illustrated by their decisions regarding external relations. The Supreme Court has considered the power to conduct foreign relations, including the treaty-making power, as one of the exclusive powers of the nation and thus not limited by the Tenth Amendment. Similarly, beginning with the celebrated *ERTA* case,[34] the Court of Justice has construed the Community power to deal with the outside world on economic matters in the broadest terms, even though the specific grant of foreign affairs power in the Treaty is quite limited. Such power, according to the Court, does not depend only on the specific Treaty provisions but may be found in the general provisions as viewed in the over-all Treaty system. Thus the Community has the power to enter into international agreements with a third country or an international organization on any matter which falls within its internal competence if such agreement is necessary for the achievement of a Community objective. As in the United States, the need for the Member States of the Community to speak with a single voice in international economic negotiations has been thought to require a broad interpretation of the Community treaty-making power. However, the Court's posture has caused tension with the Member governments, who are jealous of their authority in this sensitive field and who remain in full control of their political and military foreign policies, which still vary considerably.

Outside the area of external relations, the powers of the Community have also grown beyond those that would be suggested by a strict construction of the language of the Treaty. In those areas in which the Treaty confers powers on the central institutions to form "common policies," that is, in agriculture (including fishing), transportation, and foreign economic policy, the Court and a majority of commentators tend to view the Community's powers as plenary, for all practical purposes. The Council has engaged in massive law-making in agriculture and to an important degree in foreign economic policy (common customs tariff, trade negotiations, anti-dumping, etc.) as well. The reasons it has largely failed in the transportation field have been political rather than "constitutional." The Treaty also reflects modern Europe's compassionate concern for social welfare, as manifested in the sections on social policy and social security for migrant workers, and the Council has been able to invoke its law-making powers in agriculture and transportation to protect workers in these fields. Even where the Treaty does not call for common policies, its provisions conferring power upon the Council are interpreted broadly enough to allow the conclusion that in the economic sphere the limits of the Council power are determined, as are those of the Congress in the United States, predominantly by political rather than legal considerations.

The strong tendency in both courts to defer to the decisions of the central legislative institutions regarding the extent of the latter's powers *vis-à-vis* the states is most vividly demonstrated by the fact that the Supreme Court has only rarely, and the Court of Justice never, invalidated central legislation on the ground that it encroached upon state power. An overwhelming percentage of decisions in which the Supreme Court declared a Congressional act unconstitutional rested on constitutional provisions aimed at protecting individual rights; a few rested on constitutional provisions concerned with the separation of powers. However, since the aberrational episode of some forty years duration mentioned above, in which the Court spasmodically attempted to curb the growth of central power, only two Congressional acts have been invalidated on the ground that they interfered with state power.[35] Both decisions were rendered during the past decade, and though it is certain they will not have the effect of sharply contracting federal power, constitutional scholars wonder whether the decisions represent a new trend or a temporary deviation from the consistent case law that has enabled the Congress, at least in the field of economic regulation, to exercise what are in effect plenary powers tantamount to those of a legislature in a unitary nation.[36]

The decisions of the Court of Justice reveal a similar pattern. By the end of 1979, the Court had "annulled" provisions of Council regulations in some twenty-five cases, the majority on the ground of infringement of individual rights protected either by a broadly interpreted Treaty provision, or by a "general principle" common to and gleaned from the legal orders of the Member States or from international human rights agreements. In the remaining cases, a regulation was invalidated because it was inconsistent with a prior regulation on which it was based[37] or with the basic free trade provisions of the Treaty. In no case thus far has the Court annulled an act on the ground that it encroached upon the powers retained by the Member States. Generally, the invalidated legislation was of minor importance from the viewpoint of Community policy, but imposed considerable costs upon the individuals concerned.

B. The Dialectics of Law-Making

Although the Supreme Court has very largely abandoned the attempt to limit Congressional power on "states' rights" grounds, questions concerning the appropriate limits of federal power continue to be debated within the Congress. Typically, such debates are cast in political terms, but occasionally (as was the case with the Civil Rights Act of 1964) the issue is also considered in constitutional terms. Whether the issue is cast in political or constitutional terms, it has typically been true that Congress has been more respectful of "states' rights" than the Executive Branch and that, within the Congress, senators and representatives from Southern (and to a lesser extent Western) states have been more concerned with them than those from other parts of the country.

In the Community, similarly, the decisive debate on the Council's legislative authority takes place within the Council's own confines, closed to public scrutiny. In using its exclusive authority to propose legislation, the Commission invariably presses for maximum power for the Community and for itself, and it is supported more often than not by the majority in the European Parliament, which has been predominantly composed of "pro-European" politicians. The state officials within the

Council complex on the other hand seek to retain as much state control as possible. Even where a consensus is reached on the need for Council legislation, an effort is made to reduce the Commission's executive role to a minimum by surrounding it with "management" committees of national experts.

Congress's ability to cope with issues involving the relationship between the federal and state power, whether they are cast as issues of policy or of constitutional law, has over the years been materially aided by the alternative techniques it can employ to deal with a problem that is thought to require federal attention. The power of Congress to regulate a particular subject depends, in theory, upon whether its enumerated powers extend to that subject. Federal spending power, however, is not confined to particular subjects; Congress may appropriate funds from the federal treasury for "the general welfare."[38] Congressional inability to achieve consensus on the question whether a particular regulation would be an appropriate exercise of federal power need not, thus, prevent all federal action. Congress may employ "the power of the purse" to deal with the problem. It may, for example, offer the states financial inducements to adopt policies that it wishes to promote. At an earlier time, when federal powers were read more restrictively than they have been in recent years, Congress's authority to spend for the general welfare was an important vehicle for expanding federal power. Even now, when Congressional powers are interpreted very broadly, the spending power permits Congress to exert significant influence in areas in which a sufficient political consensus cannot be achieved to permit detailed federal regulation.

The opportunity that the spending power has afforded Congress for expanding federal influence has no direct analogue in the Community. Although the Community does have its "own resources"—derived from customs duties and agricultural levies on third-country products and from a fixed percentage of proceeds from the harmonized state value-added taxes—its budget is dwarfed by the state budgets, and the funds that it has available to influence state policies are quite limited. Some 70 per cent of Community revenue is expended to subsidize the common agricultural policy. Efforts by the Commission, supported by the European Parliament, to reduce the expenditure on agriculture, so as to free additional funds for other common programmes, have been thwarted in the Council, which controls the bulk of the budget. The European Parliament disposes of only a small fraction of the revenues, although it has the option to reject the draft budget and ask for a new draft to be submitted. With the continuing increase of agricultural costs, the Community will face a financial crisis unless the present percentage from the state value-added taxes is increased, a difficult process requiring approval by economy-minded national parliaments.

Although the central institutions have been unable to employ the "power of the purse" to increase significantly the Community's influence, two provisions of the Treaty have enabled the Council to extend its law-making in response to changing conditions, only one of which has a counterpart in the Constitution: Article 100 requires the Council to issue directives for the harmonization ("approximation") of state laws that "directly affect the establishment or functioning of the common market," and Article 235 (reminiscent, as mentioned above, of the "necessary and proper clause" in the Constitution) empowers the Council to claim any power not granted by the Treaty but "necessary to attain, in the course of the operation of the common market, one of the objectives of the Community." Both provisions may be invoked only by the unanimous decision of the Council. When there is a choice of founding legislation either on an article allowing majority vote or on Article 100, state officials tend to insist on the latter; the resulting conflict with the Commission, which generally seeks to establish precedent for majority voting, may delay action for months if not for years. Similar conflicts have arisen with respect to Article 235. However, the Commission has maintained—and the Court of Justice has agreed—that recourse to the "necessary and proper clause" in Article 235 is proper only if other articles do not provide the necessary law-making power.[39]

Although, as we pointed out earlier, the Congress for all practical purposes now exercises plenary legislative powers, custom and tradition compel it to leave a wide spectrum of subjects to state governments. Thus, the Congress could, in the exercise of its commerce power, build national highways, and indeed it could enact a national speed limit for automobiles on highways as a gasoline conservation measure. In fact, for historical and political reasons, it chose the policy of granting money to states on condition that they build highways to certain federal specifications and enact the national speed limit. Similarly, the Uniform Commercial Code has been left for adoption by state legislatures even though it could have been enacted as a federal code which would have obviated the variations in the state-adopted texts and facilitated uniform application. On the other hand, Congress has not hesitated to regulate specific aspects of commercial transactions even though such regulations supersede conflicting provisions of Uniform Commercial Credit Codes in each of the separate states.

Although policy and politics both dictate that many subjects constitutionally subject to federal authority remain within the control of the states, there are today very few areas of life touched by government that are not subject in some measure to federal legislation. Congress relies for authority on many different constitutional specifications of power, but during the past fifty years it has relied especially heavily upon the Commerce Clause as a source of power, often to deal with matters that seem quite far removed from those that the framers had in mind in conferring the power. Thus, Congress has relied upon the Commerce Clause as the source of its authority to enact legislation for the protection of the environment and of civil rights, and for the suppression of immoral acts and of organized crime.

In the Community, as in the United States, the power to regulate economic issues has been employed to justify legislation in noneconomic areas, including environmental and consumer protection and some aspects of education. The Treaty does not even mention these "second generation" areas, which surfaced only after it had been negotiated. Some Member governments have been sensitive to what they view as excessive reliance on the "necessary and proper clause" of Article 235 to justify regulation in these areas. The Danish government, for instance, blocked the establishment of the European Foundation[40] because it was given mainly educational tasks. In proposing legislation in these areas, the Commission faces something of a dilemma. On the one hand, it is eager to stress to the Parliament and the public at large its concern for the noneconomic values of individual life. On the other, it is compelled to justify its proposals on economic grounds in order to carry along the "strict constructionists" in the Council. As a result, Council directives for the improvement of the quality of air and water, although obviously not primarily economically motivated, had to be justified on economic grounds.

The Community undertaking to harmonize national laws and regulations by central legislation (directives), particularly in the area of technical standards, company laws, indirect taxation, and professional qualifications, has no counterpart in the United States. The American effort at harmonization and unification of state laws presents a mosaic of uncoordinated activities including regulations by federal agencies, federal grants to states conditioned upon acceptance of certain standards, uniform or model laws offered for adoption to state legislatures (and often modified and ignored by them), and standard-setting activities by hundreds of professional and trade organizations and insurance groups. The states of the Union have not employed their constitutional authority to negotiate interstate "compacts" in a way comparable to the important interstate Conventions that the Member States have concluded within the framework of the Community on such important subjects as Community patent, and jurisdiction and recognition of judgments in civil and commercial matters.[41]

Despite the great mass of Council legislation already on the books—the bulk in the agricultural area—it is generally felt that the law-making process is too slow and burdensome to meet Community needs. Apart from the bureaucratic complexity, a major obstacle has been the fundamental reluctance on the part of governments to surrender powers traditionally exercised by nation-states—even in areas where common action is clearly necessary and which in the United States are fully federalized. Thus, even though the new European Monetary System is viewed by the governments as the only feasible means to improved monetary stability in Europe, the progression towards the system has been delayed because the governments have been unwilling to transfer the necessary powers of control over their reserves and currencies to the central institutions. Such a transfer—and any major assertion of central law-making—entails a transfer of power and responsibility from national parliaments to what is essentially a conference of national ministers.

Among the grounds on which such transfers are opposed, one of the most common is the so-called "democratic deficit," resulting from the Council's lack of direct electoral responsibility. The response sometimes made to this argument is that the ministers who sit in the Council, although not responsible to the European Parliament for their actions, must answer to their own parliaments, and some national parliaments, including the House of Lords, have designed rather effective procedures for keeping abreast of Community activities. The Council, some argue, represents Member State interests more directly than would individual members of an elected legislature, and the current Council practice, requiring unanimous consent, fully protects the interests of each state. Apart from history, tradition and strong nationalist feelings, restraints on Council law-making derive from vested interests of the national bureaucracies, from a distrust of the "distant" Commission "Eurocrats," and from the weakness of a number of the national governments, often dependent on fragile majorities and therefore reluctant to assume responsibility for controversial policies.[41a]

IV. The Free Movement of Goods

A. "Self-Executing" Limitations on State Power

1. The Principles

The Supreme Court views the Commerce Clause not just as a source of Congressional power to regulate interstate commerce, but also as a direct restraint on state power to affect such commerce. The Treaty articles on free movement of goods serve as the source of a corresponding restraint on Member State action affecting movement of goods within the Community. It has been suggested that in reviewing the compatibility of state action with these "constitutional" restraints, the Court of Justice is less tolerant of state restrictions than the Supreme Court. Whether or not that is so, a question we shall consider presently, it is plain that in many respects there are significant similarities in the restrictions that the two courts have placed on state legislation that would impede the interstate movement of goods.

The principles developed by both courts demonstrate steadfast opposition to "protectionist" policies. Legislation that in terms discriminates against goods from other states, by imposing restrictions that are not equally applicable to domestic goods, is invalid except in rare circumstances. The same is true of legislation that in terms attempts to restrict exports. Not surprisingly, both courts have had greater difficulty fashioning principles to deal with legislation that does not on its face reveal a protectionist aim, but that has a disparate effect on domestic and foreign goods. Both have refused to adopt either of the extreme positions that might have been put forward, i.e. that all such legislation is either valid or invalid. In adjudicating the validity of such legislation, both courts have, rather, looked primarily to the aims of the legislation to ascertain whether it serves a protectionist policy or whether it promotes a legitimate interest of the state.

The suggestion that the Court of Justice has adopted principles more restrictive of state power than those adopted by the Supreme Court rests upon an assessment of the attitudes of the two courts towards legislation that does not express a protectionist policy, but that nonetheless restricts the free movement of goods across state boundaries. The Court of Justice, it is argued, has held such legislation generally incompatible with the Treaty, while the Supreme Court has held that it is not proscribed by the Constitution. Support for this intriguing thesis can be found in the case law of the two courts, but it is not free of difficulty and it rests upon an interpretation of the American decisions that is highly controversial.

The Court of Justice has on a number of occasions rendered opinions requiring the invalidation of legislation that could not fairly have been characterized as protectionist. Thus, the Court held that "a national provision which requires, even purely as a formality, import or export licenses or any other similar procedure"[42] (such as an export declaration endorsed automatically by state customs authorities) was inconsistent with the Treaty. The Court also has ruled that the holder of a patent or trademark may not invoke a standard state industrial property law to prevent the importation of goods placed on the market in another Member State with the holder's consent.[43] Again, a Belgian charge on the import of diamonds was held illegal even though no diamonds are produced in that state and, hence, the charge did not serve to protect a domestic enterprise.[44] The Court held that any charges imposed on imports or exports, even *de minimis* fees designed to cover part of legitimate general administrative costs, are invalid unless shown to constitute a fee for a public service performed exclusively for the benefit of the taxpayer or a part of the general internal taxation system.[45] These rulings, it is argued, rest upon the Court's view that the Treaty provisions expressing the free-movement-of-goods principle not only proscribe protectionism, but embody a policy of integration which supersedes state legislation that would hinder the establishment of a single, unified market. On this view, any legislation that would tend to fragment the Community-wide market is, if not *per se* invalid, at least subject to careful judicial scrutiny.[46]

Some Americans argue that, in contrast with this view of the Community case law, the decisions of the Supreme Court do not similarly restrict state power, and that they may be explained by the single principle of "anti-protectionism," the so-called "non-discrimination" principle, without recourse to other "federalist" values such as promoting a unified market and a more integrated economy. The Commerce Clause, it is argued, is a "free trade charter" on an interstate level, but on an intrastate level the states are free to maintain a regulated, "non-free" trading policy. The non-discrimination principle is a way of reconciling the two competing policies. Once the Court crosses the threshold of non-discrimination as the sole criterion of validity, it runs the risk—so goes the argument—of fastening upon the states an economic philosophy of *laissez-faire* that lacks constitutional warrant. During the first third of the current century, the Court did, indeed, attempt to impose such a philosophy on both state and federal governments under now discredited doctrines of "substantive due process."[47] The unhappy consequences of that effort, it is suggested, are likely to keep the Court from making a similar effort under the Commerce Clause.

The accuracy of these differing characterizations of European and American case law is difficult to assess. To begin with, the relative paucity of European cases that raise the issue is itself an obstacle to determining whether, or to what extent, the Court of Justice is prepared to invalidate non-protectionist legislation that impedes the development of an integrated market. Of the cases cited in support of the claim that the Court applies an "integration" principle, those involving import and export license cases may be explained without recourse to such a principle since there was at least a risk that the licence requirements might come to be administered in a way that would serve to protect the domestic market. The industrial property cases cannot be explained by the non-discrimination principle, but the history of the case law in that field suggests that the Court's concern in those cases may have been the distortion of competition as much as the free movement of goods. The strongest support for the claim that the Court has embraced a principle of integration comes from the Belgian diamond case and the cases invalidating minor cost-related charges on imports and exports. But though the rulings in these cases do seem to depend upon such a principle, the cases are plainly too few in number to permit a judgment about the depth of the Court's commitment to that principle and the circumstances in which it will be invoked.

In the United States, there is no paucity of cases, but equivalent difficulties are encountered in confidently describing the restrictions to which the states are subject under the Commerce Clause. In a series of cases involving transportation, the Court has clearly gone beyond the non-discrimination principle, invalidating legislation that was not protectionist but that interfered with movement across state boundaries. The state interests served by the invalidated legislation, the Court held, must yield to the national interest in an integrated transportation network. A similar principle has yet to be applied with respect to regulations affecting the movement of goods, but dicta in a number of the Court's opinions—including several of the most recent—indicate that the integration principle is in some measure applicable in that context.[48]

An interesting test of the attitudes of the two courts is presented by recent legislation, enacted in Denmark[49] and in several American states, prohibiting the marketing of beverages in non-returnable bottles. The effect of such legislation, apparently, is substantially to increase the transport costs of bottlers, thereby disadvantaging those who are at a distance from the market served. Moreover, the capital costs of complying with the legislation may impede entry into the market by bottlers whose primary business is conducted in a state that does not impose the restriction. The legislation has not, however, been enacted in pursuance of a protectionist policy, but as a means of reducing litter. The question is nicely posed, therefore, whether, or under what circumstances, legislation may be enacted that fragments the "common market" in pursuance of legitimate state objectives. Neither the Supreme Court nor the Court of Justice has yet had occasion to pass judgment upon the legislation. The Oregon Court of Appeals, however, did sustain that state's statute against a challenge based upon the Commerce Clause[50] and the industry did not seek review by the U.S. Supreme Court, apparently in the belief that it would reach the same result.[51]

In evaluating the reluctance of the Supreme Court to invalidate state legislation in such cases, it is worth recalling that the Court is not the only agency of government empowered to act. Congress may, under the Commerce Clause, limit state power to enact legislation that it thought to interfere unduly with an integrated national market. In the Community, similarly, the Council has power to restrict the authority of the Member States to enact such legislation if it can be shown that the legislation distorts the condition of competition.[52] The Council may, moreover, be able to invoke its authority to harmonize national laws.[53]

2. The Method

Whether or not one concludes that the two courts apply substantially the same or different principles, it is clear that the methods they employ for determining the limits of state power are quite similar. In the past, the Supreme Court attempted to evolve diverse mechanical formulas for this purpose. The modern Supreme Court has rejected this approach and now seeks, instead, to balance the legitimate interests of the states and the national interest in free trade among the states. State legislation that in terms restricts imports or exports is presumptively invalid and will be upheld only if it is supported by a compelling state interest. The few cases in which restrictions on imports have been upheld involved measures necessary to protect against virulent diseases. Restrictions on exports have been upheld only when necessary to protect the quality of exported goods. The validity of legislation that does not directly restrict imports or exports, but that has a disparate effect upon them, is judged by determining whether it is supported by a legitimate state interest and, if so, whether the state interest could be served by means that would impose a lesser burden on interstate commerce.

In the Community, a similar balancing process is prescribed by the Treaty itself (Article 36) and it occurs in three stages. When the Court of Justice is faced with a state restriction on exports or imports, it will uphold it if it finds that it is justified on grounds of public health, security, or other important public policy, providing, however, that such a measure does not constitute "arbitrary discrimination or disguised restriction on trade" between the states. In applying this provision, the Court has established the so-called "principle of proportionality" parallel to the American "less restrictive alternative" principle, which it employs to determine whether the state interest, however legitimate, could be achieved by a measure less damaging to free trade than the one adopted. However, the Court does not engage in balancing when passing judgment upon the legality of state charges equivalent to customs duties or of discriminatory taxes since all such charges and taxes, with the narrow exceptions mentioned above, are held invalid.

Of course, as Professor Blasi writes in chapter III of *Courts and Free Markets,* to say that "the appropriate standard is a balancing test tells very little about the pattern of results that will be generated by applying the standard. Everything turns on what factors are placed on the scale, how they are characterized for purposes of evaluation, and how they are weighed and ordered in the analysis." Professor Blasi's and Schermer's discussions of these issues (see chapter III of *Courts and Free Markets* for Professor Schermer's discussion) are not easily summarized, but a few comments may be useful. As might be expected, neither court recognizes a state interest in protecting local buyers and sellers from competition with buyers and sellers from other states. On the contrary, the courts' belief that such an interest underlies legislation is virtually certain to lead to its invalidation. Thus, the Supreme Court recently struck down a North Carolina statute imposing labelling requirements on fruit allegedly for the purpose of consumer protection, but in reality to discourage competition from out-of-state fruit.[54] Similarly, the Court of Justice did not hesitate to declare illegal, as applied to products imported from other Member States, a German law prohibiting the sale of certain types of liqueur with less than a fixed minimum alcohol content.[55] The Court concluded that the law was passed not to reduce the spread of alcoholism, as alleged by the German government, but to exclude competing imported liqueurs. As a result of this ruling, German industry is likely to press the national parliament to modify the legislation in order to remove the restriction altogether so that local production may not be hampered in competing with the imports.

Balancing occurs only when legislation is plausibly supported by legitimate interests. In the United States, the Court has, not surprisingly, given substantial weight to the state interest in the health and safety of its residents, to protecting plants and animals from disease, and to environmental protection. The Court has also been highly respectful of the state interest in maintaining the stability of markets, upholding price regulation and compulsory marketing arrangements designed to promote that interest. Similar results have been reached by the Court of Justice, though that Court has held price regulations to be illegal restrictions on imports if they deprive foreign producers of a natural competitive advantage.

An informed balancing process will often require complex technological data and elaborate market analyses. In the United States, the data gathering takes place before the trial court, state or federal, since no new facts are admissible on appeal. In the absence of an institutional mechanism for informing the court systematically of the "legislative facts," the burden is upon the parties to do so. The limited resources of one or both of the parties or their limited stake in the litigation will often affect the adequacy of the record developed by them. Thus in the Oregon non-returnable bottle litigation, the plaintiff attacking the state law was a well-endowed national trade association representing the entire industry concerned, while the state had to rely on its minuscule legal staff and a volunteer academic expert. In such uneven contests, the balance may at times be redressed by the appearance of interest groups as interveners or "friends of the Court." On the whole, however, it may fairly be said that American courts have not adequately solved the problem of informing themselves regarding the complex determinations which are necessitated by the balancing process required by contemporary Commerce Clause doctrine. Although the courts generally have the authority to appoint impartial experts and charge the costs to the parties, they do not commonly do so.

In the Community, the state trial courts which carry the burden of assembling the data for the balancing process may be in the same quandary as their American counterparts. Their task, however, is alleviated somewhat when they refer the questions of Community law to the Court of Justice. That Court will have before it the referring tribunal's file, but it will also receive the "observations" by the Commission's expert staff and, very likely, statements by one or more Member governments. Moreover, the Court will have the benefit of the independent submissions by its Advocate General, who at times has drawn on data outside the record of the case. Last, the Court has the authority to commission independent experts, although thus far it has not invoked it. In its "preliminary ruling" procedure, however, the Court of Justice provides only more or less general guidance, so that the referring court must complete the process by deciding the case, often an excessive burden for a provincial trial court unfamiliar with the Community law system.

B. Central Power "Consent" to State-Imposed Burdens on Commerce

A question has arisen in both systems whether the central authorities may authorize the states to take action burdening interstate commerce. On first sight, the two systems appear to differ in their answers to that question. The Supreme Court's sweeping decision in the 1946 *Prudential* case sustains Congress's power to authorize the states to enact legislation that, absent Congressional authorization, would be invalid under the Commerce Clause.[56] Congress, the Court reasoned, has plenary power over interstate commerce; it may burden or prohibit such commerce as well as promote it. Its choice among policies is unfettered, subject only to the restrictions placed upon its authority by other constitutional provisions.

The Court's decision in *Prudential* is especially striking because the state statute at issue imposed a tax that in terms discriminated against out-of-state insurance firms. Critics of the decision acknowledge that Congress should be able to authorize some state legislation that would otherwise be invalid under the Commerce Clause, but they maintain that Congress should not be permitted to consent to discriminatory legislation. The Commerce Clause, they argue, should not be read as merely a "neutral" grant of power, but as containing certain minimal substantive principles of free trade, including at least a principle prohibiting consent to protective measures that are in terms discriminatory. Whatever the underlying merits of the dispute, there is not the slightest indication that the Court is considering a modification of the position it adopted in *Prudential.*[57]

In the Community, on the other hand, the Court of Justice in principle would strike down a Council law purporting to introduce, or authorize the states to introduce, a trade barrier prohibited by the Treaty. As an exception, the Court did uphold such a measure where the alternative would have been a more serious trade disruption (the imposition of "the monetary compensatory amounts" on agricultural trade) or where it was dictated by the general interests of the Community (a state charge for veterinary inspection of imports if the inspection is undertaken pursuant to a Community directive or an international agreement).[58] In any case, it is clear that the Court will scrutinize any such measure quite rigorously for its purpose.

It has been suggested that one reason for the difference between the two systems is the fact that whereas the Commerce Clause extends a general grant of power to Congress to *regulate* commerce, the Treaty *prohibits* Member States from interfering with commerce. In other words, the fact that the Treaty prohibits tariffs and quotas does not lead to a concomitant competence in the hands of the Community institutions. The Council and the Community institutions generally cannot go back on the customs union and cannot reintroduce tariffs and quotas in intra-Community trade. The United States Constitution, it is pointed out in this context, expressly permits Congress to consent to state-imposed tariff barriers,[59] whereas the Treaty envisages no similar competence in the Council after the lapse of the "transitional period."

Perhaps a more compelling explanation for the difference may be found in the different levels of integration of the two systems as manifested in their respective institutional frameworks. Unlike the Congress, the Council currently acts more as a diplomatic conference, in which states pursue discrete national interests, than as a common institution which decides in the common interest, if necessary by majority vote. Since negotiations continue until unanimity emerges, the decision often reflects the lowest common denominator of national positions at the lowest level of integration policy. The bargaining process is fraught with a distinct risk that states may accept a Treaty violation by one of their own as a quid pro quo or in the expectation that their own similar infringement may also receive the blessing of the Council. Such compromises would lead to a gradual disintegration of the Common Market. It is therefore essential for the Court to check any serious deviation from a rigorous and uniform application of the free trade rules throughout the Community. In the United States, the risk of disintegration of the national market, at this stage of the federation at any rate, is minimal. Since, moreover, the Congress may act by simple majority, the tendency towards the lowest common denominator may be less compelling, even though alliances between regional and special interests on a quid-pro-quo basis are quite common.

Although the Court of Justice has, for these reasons, refused to go as far as the Supreme Court in permitting central authorities to consent to state legislation prohibited by the constitutive document, careful scrutiny reveals that the Council is not deprived of all flexibility in responding to the pressure of local problems. Pursuant to a variety of "safeguard" provisions, the Council or the Commission may authorize deviations and exceptions from the common rules, including reimposition of trade barriers on a selective, non-uniform basis. Although the broadest of such authorizations (Article 226) expired at the end of the transitional period, Articles 115, 103, and 108 have been used to authorize restrictive measures, often benefiting a single Member State.

The argument has been advanced with some passion that the Court and the other Community institutions should be more tolerant of protective measures in order to take into account not only the grave threats to local enterprise from foreign competition, but also the diversity in levels of development and in other conditions in different parts of the continent and even the different working pace of the national governments. Italy, for instance, has been brought before the Court of Justice for noncompliance with Community law more frequently than other Members because, more often than not, bureaucratic procedure or a government crisis delayed the necessary repeal of illegal legislation. Most would agree, however, that at this early stage of integration a strict and uniform enforcement of the irreducible core of the customs union rules is vital, although some believe that in exceptional circumstances, even in that area, competing values, such as the protection of the environment, might call for bending a specific trade rule. The issue of whether there should be strict and uniform enforcement of trade rules becomes more controversial when the Community action begins to reach important economic policy, as for instance when the Court interprets the prohibition of restrictions in Article 30 as a limitation on state domestic price controls, or when the Council enacts environmental or consumer protection legislation, or regional policy measures that by definition are designed to benefit certain regions over others. The diversity of the Community territory, which will be substantially magnified with the accession of Portugal and Spain, in many respects demands local or regional rather than Community solutions. Such diversity is also the underpinning for the hotly-debated concept of a "Europe at two speeds," which contemplates a different rhythm in the integration process for different groups of Member States.

C. Preemption

1. The Concept

At the outset, it is important to note a difference in the terminology of Americans and Europeans. In the United States, the term "pre-emption" refers exclusively to whether a federal statute has the effect of precluding legislation by the states that is otherwise within their constitutional authority. Europeans employ the term in the same way but, in addition, may also use it in discussing whether the Treaty directly limits the competence of Member States to enact legislation. In this essay, we have confined our use of the term in accordance with the American practice.

So defined, "pre-emption" raises only issues of statutory interpretation. Since legislation enacted by the central authorities is supreme, the sole question in pre-emption cases is whether the central legislation should be interpreted to preclude enactment of the challenged state law. Often, the answer to that question will be free of doubt, either because the central legislation contains express language permitting or prohibiting action by the states or because state law is in direct conflict with central legislation: for instance, by requiring conduct that is forbidden by the latter. As Professor Cohen suggests in his paper on this topic (chapter VI in *Courts and Free Markets*), such situations do not produce court decisions. Courts become involved when the issue is less plain, when the central legislature has not made its intention clear and it is logically possible to comply simultaneously with both central and state legislation.

The question of the pre-emptive effect of central legislation may arise in a variety of settings. There may be the question, for example, whether a state may forbid an activity that central authorities have licensed or whether it may impose regulations stricter than those imposed by central legislation. Moreover, the challenge to the state legislation may rest upon its particular features, or it may rest on the ground that the central legislation "occupies the field," i.e. that it precludes any state legislation touching upon the general subject-matter. Whatever the issue, the courts are, in all such cases, required to decide without the benefit of a clear legislative direction. For if the legislature had clearly expressed its intention, that intention would by hypothesis dispose of the case.

Of the two papers on this topic, Professor Waelbroeck's (chapter VI in *Courts and Free Markets*) is much broader in that it ranges across the entire field of the Community legislative activities, while Professor Cohen's is confined to the core area of interstate commerce. It would have been impractical for Cohen to deal with the massive Supreme Court case law on pre-emption in labour, trademark, environmental, and antitrust law, which is dealt with by scholars specializing in these disciplines.

The two papers disclose a significant difference in the practices of the Supreme Court and the Court of Justice with respect to the pre-emption doctrine. When the Supreme Court is asked to rule that a state law is illegal because it burdens interstate commerce, it prefers to rest its decision on the pre-exemption ground, that is to rely on a violation of a federal statute, if one exists, rather than on the constitutional ground of a violation of the Commerce Clause. The Court of Justice, on the other hand, is prone to rely on both the Community legislation and the relevant provision of the Treaty.

Several explanations for the difference have been suggested. First, since the integration process in Europe is still very much in the formative stage, the Court of Justice, when it feels confident of the result in a case, does not want to decide only on the narrow "statutory" ground, but prefers to reach the "constitutional" question in order to build the new constitutional law framework for the Community. Its position is similar to the Supreme Court's attitude during the Marshall era. With so many constitutional issues undecided, Chief Justice Marshall often seized the opportunity to engage in a general "pro-federalist" discussion of the new constitutional law, even when the case might have been decided on narrower grounds. In *Gibbons* v. *Ogden,*[60] for example, he wrote a lengthy essay on his preferred view of the Commerce Clause before deciding the case on the pre-emption ground. With federal power firmly established, however, the modern Supreme Court favours the flexibility of basing its decision on a particular federal statute rather than establishing a constitutional principle that is likely to be understood as having broader applicability.

Second, the Court of Justice may be more comfortable in reaching the "constitutional" question because the Treaty expressly sets forth substantive values as well as notions of jurisdiction and power. In contrast, the Commerce Clause is in terms only a grant of power to Congress. The restrictions on state power that the Court has imposed in reliance upon it depend upon substantive values that the Court must itself read into the Clause. The Court thus lacks a frame of reference comparable to that which the Treaty provides for the Court of Justice.

Finally, the attitude of the Court of Justice may be in part explained by a procedural characteristic. If the national judge raises both the pre-emption and the Treaty ground in the questions he addresses to the Court under Article 177, the Court may feel encouraged to deal with both, even though it would have the authority to confine itself to the pre-emption ground.

2. The Method

It is generally agreed by American scholars that the Supreme Court cases cannot be explained and reconciled on the basis of general standards or criteria that permit a consistent application of the pre-emption doctrine. Waelbroeck finds a comparable "inconsistency" in the Court of Justice case law, which oscillates between what he labels the "conceptualist-federalist" and the "pragmatic" approaches.

In theory, under American law the Supreme Court searches for "the intent of Congress" to ascertain whether state legislation has been pre-empted. As suggested above, however, the only cases that reach the Courts are those in which Congress has not clearly expressed an intention. In practice, therefore, the Court is required to rely upon its own judgment as to whether, or to what extent, an intelligent legislature would have wished to permit state legislation touching upon the subject-matter of the federal legislation. The details of the particular state and federal statutes at issue are, inevitably, of central importance, but it is plain that the Court is also influenced by extrinsic considerations, such as whether the subject-matter is one traditionally regulated by the states and whether the challenged legislation trenches upon constitutionally protected interests.

It has been suggested that the "inconsistencies" Waelbroeck finds in the European cases are only apparent because there are at least three groups of different situations, each requiring a different approach. In the first group, involving the crucial objective of preserving the "direct applicability" of Council regulations, the Court of Justice has taken the most intolerant view and has in principle opposed any state legislative or regulatory action that purported to add to, implement, or interpret a central regulation and that might dilute its direct applicability. For the same reason, the Court has come out in the strongest terms against the practice, initially followed particularly in Italy, of "transforming" Community regulations into state law. In the second group, raising questions of pre-emption of *general* state legislation, such as domestic price control law, by a *specific* Council rule (a regulation regarding the common marketing organization for an agricultural commodity) the Court has currently been more permissive and pragmatic, and the case law is reminiscent of the American approach. Finally, where a state has sought to intervene by a *specific* measure in a sector ruled by a *specific* Council rule the Court is apt to find pre-emption.

In the Court of Justice, as in the Supreme Court, a variety of factors and considerations that are theoretically extraneous to the pre-emption issue have exerted an important, if not always a controlling influence. The Court of Justice has, for example, considered the fairness of the state legislation that was claimed to be pre-empted and its impact on the efficiency of production. Institutional and procedural factors also play a part. The fact that, in contrast with the situation in the United States, the Community must rely on state authorities, for instance on state customs officials, to administer Council legislation militates for a stricter enforcement of pre-emption in the interest of uniformity and equal treatment.[61] Similarly, when the Court is asked to rule whether a Council regulation reserves its implementation for the Commission and thus pre-empts any state implementing action, the Court will incline towards finding pre-emption because Commission action would presumably be more likely to conform to Community policy and also because a state measure (unlike a Commission decision) would not be subject to direct judicial review by the Court of Justice at the initiative of an individual plaintiff. On the other hand, where there is no Council regulation (and thus no Community policy) but the Court of Justice is urged to find preclusion of state law by the Treaty itself (the "pure Commerce Clause" case in the United States), the Court may be concerned about creating a legal vacuum if the state law is held void.

The division of responsibility between the state courts and the Court of Justice under Article 177 may pose problems particularly in those cases where the Court has employed the pragmatic approach to pre-emption. Thus, in the agricultural price control cases following (and departing from) *Galli*,[62] the Court defined the limits of state law in general terms[63] (as it is expected to do under Article 177) and the state court had to carry the burden of applying the broad "preliminary ruling" to the state measure in the context of the specific facts of the case. The state court was thus required to explore not only the policies behind the state legislation, but also those underlying the complex Community agricultural policy, a burden that is hardly tolerable for what is often a low-level court, even if that court is in possession of the submissions made before the Court of Justice. From this viewpoint, it would be more satisfactory for the cases in this category to be brought before the Court by the Commission or by a Member government for a direct review and decision under Article 169 or 170.

V. The Free Movement of Persons

Law and practice on the two sides of the Atlantic differ more with regard to the movement of persons than they do with respect to the movement of goods. From the very beginning of their history, Americans (and, for that matter, resident aliens as well) have been free to move and resettle, without legal barriers, throughout the expanse of the United States, and they have done so with abandon, assisted by the cultural and linguistic homogeneity of the society. Neither the same legal freedom nor the same practical conditions for mobility have existed historically in Europe. The common national citizenship envisaged in the original Constitution and reinforced by the Fourteenth Amendment has had a pervasive influence on safeguarding the freedom of movement. There is no equivalent Community citizenship. The right of movement within the Community, so far as it exists, is not an incident of membership in a single political community, but of Treaty provisions and Council regulations designed to further the limited objectives of the Community.

Among the first purposes of those who drafted the Treaty was to facilitate the movement of labour and entrepreneurs as "factors of production." Their objective was, in brief, similar to that which they had in establishing the customs union and in including other provisions designed to facilitate the free movement of goods: that is, to gain the economic advantages of a large, free market in which the factors of production might be employed in accordance with the theory of comparative advantage. In the United States, the Constitution does not mention movement of persons, apparently because the framers thought it unnecessary to include a provision on the subject in view of the history and practice among the states. Despite these differences, judicial doctrines show some tendency towards convergence under the influence of contemporary notions of human rights.

A. Entry

In the few cases in which the Supreme Court has had to deal with the issue of free movement from one state to another, it has had no difficulty finding that, as against the states, individuals have an unlimited "right to travel" for any purpose whatsoever.[64] Without the benefit of an express constitutional provision, the Court has grounded this right, variously, on several provisions of the Constitution and at times has simply found it within the interstices of the Constitution. On the other hand, a Member State citizen has a Treaty right to enter another state only to get a job, to receive or to supply a service on a temporary basis, or to engage in self-employed economic pursuits. However, the Court of Justice has elevated this right to the status of "a fundamental right" which can be invoked not only against state action, but against private restraints as well. Moreover, the Council has broadened the right of entry to include the worker's family, as well as the right to remain in the host country for any purpose whatsoever after a certain minimum period of employment. Suggestions to extend the right of entry beyond strictly economic purposes, at least to students and possibly to retired persons, on the basis of Article 235 are at present under consideration.

In the Community, the Treaty specifically authorizes exclusion of persons otherwise entitled to entry for reasons of public health, safety, and public policy. Although the Court of Justice has refused to follow the Commission's proposal to "federalize" the concept of "public policy," it has drawn on principles common to the laws of the Member States and on the European Human Rights Convention, to which all Member States are parties, to limit severely the discretion of the states to exclude or deport Community nationals. In some measure, these decisions obviously do "federalize" the concept of public policy, but a full-blown Community law definition of public policy is likely to emerge only after further progress in the integration process. In the United States there is no counterpart to the power to exclude for reasons of public policy. The states simply are not permitted to deny entry to travellers from other states, except perhaps to prevent the spread of contagious disease.

B. Post-entry Rights

When a United States citizen moves from his state of residence to another state and establishes a physical presence with intention to remain there, he automatically becomes a "resident" and a citizen of that state, entitled to the full panoply of a citizen's rights. The state is not allowed to impose any conditions (such as a certain duration of in-state residence) as a prerequisite for the acquisition of the citizenship, though it may condition some state-provided benefits upon satisfaction of durational residence requirements.

In contrast, a citizen of a Member State does not change his national citizenship when he crosses a national frontier in pursuit of his Treaty rights. The "host" state must issue him a "resident permit," and his position is in a sense parallel to that of an American who travels from his home state to another without wishing to change his residence (and his state citizenship) and thus becomes a "non-resident" in that state.

The position of the non-resident is in many respects more favourable in the Community than in the United States. Article IV, Section 2 of the Constitution broadly states that "[the] Citizens of each State shall be entitled to all Privileges and Immunities of Citizens in the several States," but the Supreme Court has consistently refused to interpret the provision literally, and it has over the years served a rather limited function. As traditionally interpreted, the provision undoubtedly guarantees non-residents equality with citizens in respect of the right to contract, to own property, and to engage in the common occupations of life, but it does not restrict the power of the states to discriminate in favour of their citizens in many other ways.

The text of the Treaty confers a right of equal treatment on citizens of other Member States only in respect of the incidents of employment, but here again the Council and the Court have extended it both vertically and horizontally. In the vertical dimension, the right has been elevated to the level of a "fundamental right" which they can invoke directly against discriminatory action not only by a state, but by private individuals or associations as well. Although there is no clear authority on the point, it would appear that in the United States a private employer may legally refuse to hire an individual on the basis of the latter's citizenship. His counterpart in Europe, on the other hand, can no longer do so without exposing himself to an action in a state court for violation of Community law. Nor can a private association with an economic purpose bar a citizen of another Member State on the ground of his citizenship. Except where the supply of services is involved, the Court of

Justice has gone to the limits of its jurisdiction to eliminate discrimination based on citizenship or residence.

Horizontally, the right has been broadened by the Council to include equal treatment not only regarding salary and working conditions, but also access to housing and participation in union activities. The Court of Justice, stressing the humane objectives of the Treaty, has extended the coverage beyond economic concerns to include children's access to education, educational grants, and the benefits of general social legislation for the handicapped and large families. Elaborate Community legislation provides for a co-ordination of the state social security system to ensure that workers who move from one state to another are not impaired in their pension, unemployment benefits, and other rights. In the process of interpreting this legislation, the Court of Justice has evolved what may be termed a detailed code of social benefits for migrant Community workers. According to a Commission proposal, these workers would also be given the right to vote in local elections—an important extension from the economic into the political rights sphere. Although this proposal has little chance of adoption as a Community measure, national legislation to the same effect is under consideration in several parliaments.

Although both systems confer substantial rights to equal treatment, neither accords non-citizens full equality. In the Community, the states are free to restrict public employment to their citizens and the Court is expected to interpret the scope of this restriction in the near future. In the United States, the case law has not unequivocally recognized state power to bar non-residents from public employment, but the decisions point quite clearly in this direction. Indeed, the Supreme Court cases suggest that the states enjoy considerable freedom to favour their own citizens as against non-residents when it comes to awarding public contracts, expending public funds, or disposing of state-owned resources. Such state legislation denying equal treatment to citizens of other Member States would be clearly contrary to Community law. Perhaps because state subsidies of private enterprise are more common in Europe than in the United States, Community control over discriminatory conferral of such subsidies appears on the face of it, if not necessarily in practice, stricter than in the United States.[65]

In both systems access to licensed professions presents particular problems, in that non-discriminatory requirements of local diplomas and other qualifications constitute often insurmountable obstacles to outsiders. In the United States, the difficulty is alleviated somewhat, but by no means resolved, by state-to-state arrangements for reciprocal recognition of certain professional qualifications. To meet the problem in the

Community, the Treaty calls for the elaboration of Community-wide education and training standards and for recognition throughout the Community of diplomas obtained in compliance with such standards. Council directives to that effect have concentrated thus far on the medical and nursing professions. Other directives harmonize state regulations of the insurance and banking industries to facilitate interstate business. No such effort by the central government exists in the United States, but the diversity is mitigated in some fields by the harmonizing work of nation-wide private professional organizations.

The majority of foreign workers in the Community come from nonmember European states such as Turkey, Portugal, Spain, and Yugoslavia.[66] Although these workers cannot claim any Treaty benefits with respect to entry and access to employment, which are strictly controlled by state governments, once they are allowed to enter and are established inside the Community in conformity with the applicable state law, the state authorities, obviously responding to the contemporary emphasis on the protection of basic rights, tend to extend to them some, if not most, of the Community law benefits. The movement in this direction is more pronounced in the United States, where aliens who are admitted and given resident status under the federal immigration laws are entitled to many of the civil, economic, and social rights that states accord to American citizens.

VI. Legitimacy and Legitimation: Concluding Observations on the Role of the Judiciary

In a celebrated statement, Justice Holmes once opined:

> I do not think the United States would come to an end if we [the Supreme Court] lost our power to declare an Act of Congress void. I do think the Union would be imperiled if we could not make that declaration as to the laws of the several States. For one in my place sees how often a local policy prevails with those who are not trained to national views and how often action is taken that embodies what the Commerce Clause was meant to end.[67]

Holmes's statement might be made with equal force about the Community. In both systems, the courts have served most importantly to check centrifugal tendencies.

With the exception of a forty-year period beginning in 1895, the Supreme Court has only rarely invalidated acts of Congress on the ground that they encroached upon the power of the states. And even during that period, the Court's efforts to stem the growth of federal power were spasmodic and far from fully effective. In the main, the Court has supported and legitimated the extension of federal power. The role of the Court of Justice, during its much shorter history, has been similar. Over the course of a quarter-century, the Court has yet to hold that the Council has impermissibly encroached upon the power of the Member States. Its opinions, like those of the Supreme Court, tend to provide doctrinal support for extension of central power. Indeed, the Court has even attempted to arrest centrifugal tendencies in the Council.

The crucial importance of the Supreme Court in barring parochial state action, as reflected in Holmes's statement, is also paralleled by the experience of the Community. The Treaty is far more explicit than the Constitution in defining the limits of state power, but the Court of Justice has played no less vital a role than the Supreme Court in elaborating those limits and in enforcing them. As Justice Stewart writes in his foreword to *Courts and Free Markets,*

> It is, of course, an open question whether the central political institutions of the two systems might, in the absence of judicial review, have summoned the will to curb protectionist policies adopted by the states. Yet, even if one supposes that they might have done so, it is difficult to imagine that they could effectively have coped with the myriad local enactments that, though perhaps of minuscule effect when viewed individually, constitute in the aggregate a serious impediment to the maintenance of a common market.

Because of the unique institutional structure of the Community, the role of the Court of Justice in dealing with issues of "federalism" may be both more vital and more difficult than that of the Supreme Court. For one thing, the Court of Justice carries a heavier burden in upholding the legitimacy of the system because the Council, as the legislator, is not perceived to carry political authority comparable to that of the popularly elected Congress, particularly when it comes to expansion of Community power by Council action. Illustratively, the British government appeared unwilling and unable, because of the unyielding opposition of the unions, to comply with a Council regulation making mandatory the installation in trucks of devices to record speed, mileage, and rest stops. When the specially extended deadline lapsed, the Commission sued and the Court held the United Kingdom in violation of Community law.[68] The British drivers then were persuaded to vote to refrain from action against the installation and the government was in a position to comply.

Although, as this illustration suggests, the Court may at times have certain advantages over the Council in achieving compliance with Community law, it seems true nevertheless that the position of the Court, especially in contrast with that of the United States Supreme Court, is weakened by the fact that its rulings often do not rest upon a political consensus. Because of the existence of broad-ranging federal legislation, the issues before the Supreme Court most frequently concern the conformity of state action with an act of Congress. In the Community, on the other hand, except in the agricultural sector, the Court of Justice is frequently required to rely directly on the "Treaty-constitution." Without the benefit of the political consensus that would be embodied in a Council act, the Court's task is more demanding, and it may even raise the question of its legitimacy.

Again, there is no question about the legal power of the Supreme Court to have its decision enforced through federal instrumentalities, including ultimately the armed forces, although enforcement against a state government may of course pose political difficulties. In the Community, by contrast, final judgments of the Court of Justice against individuals and companies must be enforced by state authorities in the same manner as judgments of the local courts and there is no provision for a forcible execution of judgment rendered against a Member State. Open defiance of such a judgment—such as the refusal of the French government to remove illegal restrictions on the import of lamb, as mandated by the Court—presents a political issue that can be resolved only in the Council.[69] However, the French case appears to be an isolated instance.

The Court of Justice has not been faced thus far with truly important "political" issues and it has succeeded in rendering the most far-reaching rulings in relatively trivial controversies, those least likely to generate opposition because of their immediate consequences. Nevertheless, it has been accused of pressing legal integration beyond the political consensus and attempting to turn the Community into "a government by judges."[70] It is said in the Court of Justice's defence that the criticism is due to the bewilderment of the Member governments accustomed to acting unilaterally in the fulfilment of their international obligations and finding themselves restrained by the discipline imposed by the Treaty law as judicially interpreted. The Court, as the institution most independent of the state governments, has the primary duty—it is argued—to defend the Treaty and to support the "weaker" institutions, the Commission and the European Parliament, against the state governments. The Commission, although theoretically independent of the state governments, has become timid and hesitates to use its powers of legislative initiative without obtaining a prior *placet* from the governments; and the Council has strayed from the Treaty as a result of the "unconstitutional"

Luxembourg agreement banning majority voting. There is, however, at present no indication that the uncompromisingly "pro-integrationist" posture of the Court is about to give way to a more state-oriented policy, as occurred in the Supreme Court when Chief Justice Taney took over from Marshall.

Notes

1. The European Economic Community is part of a system, commonly referred to as "the European Community," consisting of three international organizations, established by three separate treaties, but sharing the principal institutions: Treaty Establishing the European Coal and Steel Community (ECSC), 18 April 1951, 261 U.N.T.S. 140, [1973] Gr. Brit. T.S. No. 2 (Cmd. 5189) at 7; Treaty Establishing the European Atomic Energy Community (EURATOM), 25 March 1957, 298 U.N.T.S. 11, [1973] G. Brit. T.S. No. 1, Part II (Cmd. 5179 II) at 1; Treaty Establishing the European Economic Community (EEC), 25 March 1957, 298 U.N.T.S. 1969, [1973] Gr. Brit. T.S. No. 1 (Cmd. 5179) at 162. For a list of other relevant treaties, see E. Stein, P. Hay, M. Waelbroeck, *Documents for European Community Law and Institutions in Perspective* iii (1976). Unlike the ECSC and EURATOM Treaties, which are limited to special economic sectors, the EEC Treaty embraces the entire economy.

2. Carreau, "Droit communautaire et droits nationaux: concurrence ou primauté," 14 *Rev Trim. d.e.* 381 at 403 (1978).

3. The ECSC has a modest power to tax the production of coal and steel within its territory. Art. 49 of the ECSC Treaty. The EEC derives a part of its resources from revenues of the value-added taxes of the Member States.

4. Update: Spain and Portugal acceded on Jan. 1, 1986; Austria, Finland, and Sweden on Jan. 1, 1995. In 1998, negotiations for accession began with 10 post-Communist European States and Cyprus.

5. Pescatore, "L' executif communautaire: justification du quadripartisme institué par les Traités de Paris et de Rome," [1978] *Cah. dr. eur.* 387.

6. P. S. R. F. Mathijsen, *A Guide to European Community Law* 184 n. 48 (2nd ed. 1975).

7. Art. 10 of the "Merger Treaty," Treaty Establishing a Single Council and a Single Commission of the European Communities, 8 April 1965, [1967] J.O. 152/2 at 4–5, [1973] Gr. Brit. T.S. No. 1 (Cmd. 5179) at 279.

8. The size of the staff reflects the heavy linguistic requirements. Only about a quarter of the above figure represents the "category A" professional-level personnel.

9. Some 400 such groups operate in Brussels.

10. See L. N. Brown and F. G. Jacobs, *The Court of Justice of the European Communities* 4–5 (1977).

11. 5 U.S. (1 Cranch) 137 (1803).

12. Ibid. at 177.

13. Art. VI, Sec. 2.
14. See *Cooper* v. *Aaron,* 358 U.S. 1 (1958).
15. Art. VI, Sec. 2.
16. Art. III, Sec. 2.
17. Stein and Vining, "Citizen Access to Judicial Review of Administrative Action in a Transnational and Federal Context," 70 *Am. Jour. Int. L.* 219 (1976). Republished *infra* at 161ff.
18. Arts. 174, 176.
19. Art. 171. See also Arts. 169–70.
20. Fourteen cases were brought by the Commission against Member States in the first five months of 1980.
21. Case 26/62, *N.V. Algemene Transport—en Expeditie Onderneming van Gend & Loos* v. *Nederlandse Administratie der Belastingen,* [1963] ECR 1.
22. Case 6/64, *Flaminio Costa* v. *ENEL,* (1964) ECR 585.
23. Case 106/77, *Amministrazione delle Finanze dello Stato* v. *Simmenthal SpA,* [1978] ECR 629.
24. Case 26/62, n. 21 above, at 12.
25. *McCulloch* v. *Maryland,* 17 U.S. (4 Wheat.) 316 (1819); *United States* v. *Curtiss-Wright Export Corp.,* 299 U.S. 304 (1936).
26. *Ministre de l'Intérieur c. Sieur Cohn Bendit (Daniel), Conseil d'État* No. 11604, 22 December 1978. Excerpt in [1979] *Cah.dr.eur.* 265.
27. Case 26/62, n. 20 above, at 12.
28. "In the absence of express provisions as to the compatibility of a national regulation . . . with the market set up by [Council] Regulation . . . , it is necessary to seek the solution . . . in the light of the objects and the purposes of the Regulation within the framework of the principles laid down by the Treaty itself." Case 190/73, *Officir van Justitie* v. *J. W. J. van Haaster,* [1974] ECR 1123 at 1133.
29. 17 U.S. (4 Wheat.) 316 (1819).
30. Ibid. at 407.
31. U.S. Const. Art. I, Sec. 8, Cl. 18.
32. See the "Dialectics of Law-Making" section below. See also Sasse and Yourow, Chap. II, sections III. A–F, in *Courts and Free Markets—Perspectives from the United States and Europe* (1982).
33. *Gibbons* v. *Ogden,* 22 U.S. (9 Wheat.) 1 at 195 (1824).
34. Case 22/70, *Commission of the European Communities* v. *Council of the European Communities,* [1971] ECR 263. Update: The materials in the essay entitled "Uniformity and Diversity in a Divided-Power System: The United States' Experience" in Part 2 of the current collection update the case law on this subject.
35. *National League of Cities* v. *Usery,* 420 U.S. 833 (1976); *Oregon* v. *Mitchell,* 400 U.S. 112 (1970).
36. Update: *National League of Cities* v. *Usery,* the more important of the two cases cited *supra* in n. 35, was overruled by a divided court in *Garcia* v. *San Antonio Metropolitan Transit Authority,* 469 U.S. 528 (1985). Nevertheless,

during the past decade decisions of the Supreme Court manifest a renewed interest in protecting the constitutional autonomy of the states. In *United States* v. *Lopez,* 115 S.Ct. 1624 (1995), the Supreme Court, by a 5 to 4 majority, struck down a federal statute forbidding possession of firearms in local school zones as lacking the nexus to interstate commerce required under the interstate commerce clause of the federal constitution. In *New York* v. *United States,* 112 S.Ct. 2408 (1992), the Court found a provision of the Federal Low-Level Radioactive Waste Policy Act to be objectionable because it essentially directed state legislatures either to enact federally prescribed methods for disposing of privately generated low-level radioactive waste or to take title to it. *Federalism, Politics, Accountability, and the Spending Clause,* 107 HARV. L. REV. 1419, 1423 (1994). *New York* v. *United States* was reaffirmed, and arguably extended, in *Prinz* v. *United States,* 117 S.Ct. 2365 (1997), which invalidated a federal statute requiring state and local police to conduct background investigations of prospective handgun purchasers. Taken together, the two decisions stand for the proposition that Congress may neither require the states to legislate nor require state bureaucracies to enforce federal law without the state's consent. The Court's concern with limiting the reach of federal legislative power is also reflected in *City of Boerne* v. *Flores,* 117 S.Ct. 2157 (1997), which rejected an interpretation of the Fourteenth Amendment that would have permitted Congress to establish standards for determining the validity of state legislation more restrictive than those adopted by the Supreme Court.

37. In Case 113/77, *NTN Toyo Bearing Company* v. *Council of the European Communities,* the Court explained: "The Council, having adopted a general regulation with a view to implementing one of the objectives laid down in Article 113 of the Treaty, cannot derogate from the rules thus laid down in applying those rules to specific cases without interfering with the legislative system of the Community and destroying the equality before the law of those to whom the law applies." [1979] ECR 1185 at 1209.

38. U.S. Const. Art. I, Sec. 8, Cl. 1.

39. Case 8/73, *Hauptzollamt Bremerhaven* v. *Massey-Ferguson GmbH,* [1973] ECR 897.

40. European Foundation, Commission Report to the European Council, 1975 *Bull. E.C.* Supp. 5. The Danish government takes the position that Art. 235, as interpreted at Denmark's accession to the Community, can be applied only in the fields covered by the Treaty, thus excluding education. The government points to the provision in the Danish constitution providing for the possibility of transferring certain powers to international organizations, such as the Community, but only in properly specified sectors. However, the government apparently is not opposed to close co-operation in education or other areas not specified in the Treaty, but only by extra-Community methods not involving Community institutions. "Europe," (n.s.) No. 2933, 21 June 1980 at 7, and No. 2938, 28 June 1980 at 10.

41. In June 1980, seven Members signed a Convention laying down uniform conflict-of-laws rules applicable to contracts.

41a. See on the "democratic deficit" *infra* at 335ff.

42. Case 68/76, *Commission of the European Communities* v. *France,* [1977] ECR 515 at 530, citing Joint Cases 51 to 54, *International Fruit Company NV* v. *Produktshap voor Groenten en Fruit,* [1971] ECR 1107.

43. See the cases discussed by Schermers, Chap. III, section III. F.5, in *Courts and Free Markets.*

44. Joined Cases 2 and 3/69, *Sociaal Fonds voor de Diamantarbeiders* v. *SA Brachfeld and Sons and Chougol Diamond Co.,* [1969] ECR 211.

45. See Schermers and Wägenbaur, Chaps. III and V, *passim,* in *Courts and Free Markets.*

46. Update: In Keck & Mithoward, joined Cases C-267 and C-268/91, [1993] ECR I-6097, by reinterpreting the EEC Treaty text the Court removed a large group of national non-discriminatory regulatory measures from the scope of the prohibition of non-tariff barriers. For subsequent case law, see Walter van Gerven in 2 *Colum. Jour. Eur. L.* 217 (1996).

47. See, e.g. *Lochner* v. *New York,* 198 U.S. 45 (1905); *Adkins* v. *Children's Hosp.,* 261 U.S. 525 (1923).

48. See, e.g. *H. P. Hood & Sons* v. *DuMond,* 336 U.S. 525 (1949); *Pike* v. *Bruce Church, Inc.,* 397 U.S. 137 (1970).

49. Written Question No. 1287/77 and Commission answer in [1979] O.J. 214/5, 27 August 1979.

50. *American Can Co.* v. *Oregon Liquor Control Comm'n,* 517 P. 2d 691 (Ore. App. 1973).

51. Update: In the Case 302/86, *Commission* v. *Denmark,* [1988] ECR 4627, the Court upheld the validity of the Danish legislation with the exception of a feature concerning directly foreign imports that the Court viewed as a limitation on such imports "disproportionate to the objective" of environmental protection. In *Minnesota* v. *Clover Leaf Creamery Company,* 449 U.S. 456 (1981), the United States Supreme Court upheld a state law prohibiting the sale of milk in plastic non-returnable, non-refillable containers.

52. Treaty Art. 101.

53. Treaty Art. 100.

54. *Hunt* v. *Washington State Apple Advertising Comm'n,* 432 U.S. 333 (1977).

55. Case 120/78, *Rewe-Zentral AG* v. *Bundesmonopolverwaltung für Branntwein,* [1979] ECR 649. See also the cases noted *supra* in note 46.

56. *Prudential Insurance Co.* v. *Benjamin,* 328 U.S. 408 (1946).

57. Update: In *Metropolitan Life Insurance Co.* v. *Ward,* 470 U.S. 869 (1985), the Court held that a state statute discriminating against out-of-state insurance companies, although exempted from the reach of the commerce clause by an act of Congress, was nevertheless unconstitutional as contrary to the equal protection clause of the federal Constitution. The full implications of this decision for the principles stated in the text are unclear.

58. See cases discussed by Waelbroeck, Chap. V, section IV.B, in *Courts and Free Markets.*

59. Art. I, Sec. 10, Cl. 2.

60. 22 U.S. (9 Wheat.) 1 (1824).

61. *E.g.* Case 118/76, *Balkan-Import-Export GmbH* v. *Hauptzollamt Berlin-Packhof,* [1977] ECR 1177.

62. For a discussion of the Galli and the following cases, see Waelbroeck, Chap. V, text at nn. 33ff, in *Courts and Free Markets.*

63. Thus in Case 65/75, *Riccardo Tasca,* [1976] ECR 291, the Court held (at 309) that the unilateral price fixing by a Member State was incompatible with a Council regulation on a market organization "once it jeopardizes the objectives and the functioning of this organization and in particular its system of prices."

64. The extent to which Congress may restrict interstate travel is an open question in the Supreme Court. Congress has, on occasion, imposed such restrictions, for example by prohibiting interstate travel to avoid prosecution or to avoid testifying in a crucial case or in aid of racketeering enterprises, but the question of their validity has not yet reached the Court.

65. The Treaty (Arts. 92–94) declares *any* state subsidy which distorts competition by favouring certain undertakings or the production of certain goods as incompatible with the common market but lists a series of important exceptions. See Schermers, Chap. III, part VII, text at nn. 115ff, in *Courts and Free Markets.* The enforcement of the anti-subsidy provisions has proved very difficult. Cf. Blasi, Chap. III, text at n. 113, in *Courts and Free Markets.*

66. In 1977, 8,162,000 third-country nationals were living in the Community while 2,629,000 Member-State nationals were registered in another Member State. Written Question No. 312/79, [1980] O.J. C 74/3–4.

67. O. W. Holmes, *Collected Legal Papers* 295–96 (1920).

68. Case 128/78, *Commission of the European Communities* v. *United Kingdom,* [1979] ECR 419.

69. Case 232/78, *Commission of the European Communities* v. *French Republic,* [1980] ECR 2729. Update: According to the Maastricht Treaty on the European Union of 1992, if a Member State fails to comply with a judgment of the Court of Justice, the Court—on proposal by the Commission—may impose a lump sum or penalty payments upon the delinquent Member State (Art. 171(2)).

70. See on this Wägenbaur, Chap. V, n. 4, in *Courts and Free Markets;* R. Lecourt, *L'Europe des juges* (1976); C. J. Hamson in Court of Justice of the Eur. Communities, *Judicial and Academic Conference, 27–8, September 1976, Reports* at II 10–15 (1976); see also Casper in *Proceedings of the 72nd Annual Meeting of American Society of Int'l Law,* April 1978 at 175. Such sporadic criticism is in no way comparable to the persistent vituperations of the newspapers which denounced the Marshall Court as an instrument of the central government. There was even much sentiment in Congress favouring impeachment of Marshall and his fellow Federalist judges. G. Gunther, *Cases and Materials on Constitutional Law* 12–14 (9th ed. 1975).

Citizen Access to Judicial Review of Administrative Action in a Transnational and Federal Context

In this variant of an across-the-Atlantic comparison my colleague Joseph Vining provided the expertise in American law. The essay was prepared for a conference in London, organized by Professor F. G. Jacobs of the University of London (now Advocate General of the Court of Justice of the European Communities), and it was published in a collection edited by him under the title European Law and the Individual. *I used it as a basis for talks I gave at a number of universities throughout the United Kingdom during my appointment as visiting Ford Foundation Professor at the Institute for Advanced Legal Studies in London.*

The subject, again an aspect of judicial methodology raising issues of the rule of law as well as the separation of powers and federalism, attracted me for several reasons.

First, individual access to judicial remedy against public power is at play, along with the corresponding principle that a state is not above the law. This is particularly important in the Community, considering the complaints about "the democratic deficit" in the working of its institutions (see the essay entitled "Panel Statement on 'Democracy without "a People" ' " in Part 2).

Second, an important aspect of federalism is posed by the question as to what extent the central judiciary in a divided-power system should insist that the individual complainants seek a remedy in a component-state court, if such a court is available.

Finally, on the European side, I was struck by the contrast between the liberal posture of the Court of Justice on individual "indirect" access to judicial review of member state action for conformity with Community law as described earlier in this book, as against its narrow, strictly textual reading of the complainant's standing for judicial review of actions by the organs of the Community itself. In the latter instance the Court denied standing even in the face of a complainant's claim that no other legal remedy existed either under national or Community law.

Reprinted from 70 AMERICAN JOURNAL OF INTERNATIONAL LAW 219–41 (1976). With G. Joseph Vining. Reproduced with permission,

In his gracious introduction to the Italian version of this collection, Professor (and former Advocate General of the European Court of Justice) Francesco Capotorti gently questions my criticism of the Court for clinging so closely to the text. It is for the reader to take sides in this friendly disagreement.

The historic record in the United States shows a gradual widening of the access to judicial review of administrative action. More recent developments have taken the form of a continuing search for workable limitations that will avoid exposing agencies to suit by any citizen but will not slip back to the restrictive private law basis for a right to judicial review. The search has involved a turn to constitutional considerations, as well as refinements in interpretation of statutory materials and the Court's own doctrine, and has begun to pull constitutional and administrative law closer together than they stood in 1976.

In our conclusion we presaged a loosening of the Community Court's restrictive posture, not unlike the evolution in the U.S. federal law. The more recent European cases confirm such tendency primarily when the Court is asked to review decisions taken by the Community organs in quasi-judicial proceedings relating to competition, antidumping, and state subsidies. In his 1991 opinion on an antidumping case (Case 358/89, Extramet Industrie SA v. Council, [1991] ECR I-2501, 2519, 2525), the respected Advocate General Francis G. Jacobs called for a liberal construction of the access provisions "in light of the way the Community has developed," avoiding, of course, opening the court to "an unlimited class of applicants."

Evidently, there is a commonality on the basic issue in the European and American systems; if there are common elements in the solutions, we found no evidence of any conscious transference from one system to the other. This would confirm what Judge Pescatore had to say on the subject of transference as quoted in the introduction to the essay in Part 2 entitled "Excerpt from Courts and Free Markets—Perspectives from the United States and Europe.*" However, further empirical research on this point might be warranted.*

Since 1993, direct actions for judicial review by natural and legal persons against decisions by the Community organs are heard before a newly created Court of First Instance with the possibility of appeal to the Court of Justice. As a result, the burden of the Court of Justice is lessened in some measure, a factor relevant to the argumentation in this essay.

The Individual Citizen in International Law

In an international legal order dominated by states, the individual citizen is generally viewed as lacking international legal personality. It is true with little exception that an individual cannot appear in an international forum, political or judicial, to press his rights. Despite the dramatically increased emphasis upon international protection of basic human rights, individuals have been given access to international dispute-settlement machinery in only a few isolated instances within the United Nations system, and on a regional level pursuant to the European Convention on Human Rights.[1]

The Paris Treaty establishing the European Coal and Steel Community (ECSC) and the Rome Treaties establishing the European Atomic Energy Community (EURATOM) and the European Economic Community (EEC, the Common Market) are the only international agreements providing for a judicial tribunal of general compulsory jurisdiction open not only to member states and Community institutions but individual citizens as well. The purpose of this essay is to explore the case law of the Court of Justice of the Communities and the considerations that may have motivated that Court in its effort to define limits on access by individuals seeking judicial review of acts of Community institutions and to inquire whether experience with judicial review of administrative action in a federation may be relevant to the evolution of transnational European administrative law.

Three Cases

A convenient way of introducing the subject is to present three little dramas in contemporary costume, drawn from three different milieux:

(1) The Federal Comptroller of Currency, an agency supervising federal banks in the United States, issued a regulation allowing federal banks to expand their activities into the business of selling data processing services. A trade association of companies also engaged in selling data processing services and claiming loss of profit and customers sued the Comptroller to obtain review and annulment of the regulation. The data processing companies relied on a federal statute which prohibited banks from engaging in any activity other than the performance of bank services. In 1970 the Supreme Court of the United States upheld their standing to sue.[2]

(2) In the nineteen sixties, the Parliament of the German Federal Republic appropriated funds to the individual German States (Länder) for the purpose of subsidizing construction of wine vaults by German wine producers and thus increasing their competitive position in the Common Market by improving the quality of their wine. The Land in question allocated the subsidies to wine producers but refused the application of a company engaged in wine marketing. The company sued for review and annulment of the Land decisions granting the subsidies to producers,

alleging illegal denial of an equal opportunity to compete. Its business consisted of entering into long-term contracts with wine producers for the annual purchase of quantities of wine at a minimum price, storing the wine, and ultimately marketing it. As a result of the subsidies, the producers were now able to market wine directly to consumers at a cheaper price than competing retailers who like the plaintiff company did not have access to the subsidy. The Federal Administrative Court upheld the plaintiff company's standing to institute judicial review.[3]

(3) In 1968, the Commission of the European Communities decided to grant substantial subsidies from Community funds to three Italian sugar refineries to enlarge their production. The award was conditioned upon enlargement by the Italian Government of the production quotas allotted to the three refineries within the Italian quota fixed by the Community. The plaintiffs, competing sugar refinery enterprises who did not get any subsidies, sued in the Court of Justice of the Communities for review and annulment of the Commission's decisions, alleging unlawful distortion of competition in violation of the articles of the Treaty on subsidies, because their own production quotas were to be reduced to make possible the required enlargement of the quotas of the three subsidized competitors. The Court denied standing to sue on the ground that the plaintiffs failed to demonstrate a "direct and individual concern."[4]

Thus in the United States private plaintiffs claiming consequential harm have been given standing to contest a general regulation. In Germany they have been permitted to contest decisions addressed to third parties. But in analogous situations in the European Economic Community (EEC) they have been denied standing to sue. Two of the three milieux are more or less mature federations in which citizens are directly subject to federal and state laws. The third is different—a hybrid, "a new legal order in international law."[5] It is a treaty-based international organization, but is distinctive among such organizations in its broad impact upon the rights and obligations of individual citizens.

To what extent does or should this distinction make a difference? Should or will the experience of the Community follow that of mature political federations? Or should we approach each sui generis and see nothing remarkable in current differences in treatment of apparently similar problems?

The Federation and the Community: Some Dissimilarities

The comparative method, in law or in any other discipline, has its problems. Above all there is a danger of losing sight of controlling dissimilarities behind the smokescreen of superficial likeness. It may help to avoid pitfalls if we review some of the relevant similarities and differences between the European Economic Community and a federal system as exemplified by the United States.

At the core of our inquiry is the position of the individual before governmental authority in an increasingly complex and technology-based society, which now exists on both sides of the Atlantic. On one hand government regulation steadily widens, and on the other individuals and groups demand ever greater recognition and participation in governmental processes. In the United States as in the Community, governmental authority is divided among separate hierarchies of institutions exercising normative powers. The United States has states with different constitutions, a federal government, fifty state judiciaries, and a federal judiciary. But in the United States, the power of the federation dwarfs the states' power. In the Community the balance goes the other way. In the United States there is little question about the basic legitimacy of the governmental institutions, even though today the Watergate cloud is still hovering over them, while in the Communities the institutions are brittle and as yet have little grass roots participation. Moreover, Community lawmaking is in the hands of an executive. There is no popularly based legislature. In the American federation, federal agencies and federal courts execute federal legislation (with some important exceptions such as federal grant programs where implementation is left in considerable part to the states). But in the Community, member states carry the bulk of the responsibility for implementing Community law: state officials issue import licenses and collect customs duties; state parliaments transform major directives into national law; and state courts decide controversies involving Community law, albeit after preliminary ruling on Community law questions by the Court of Justice.[6] This broad decentralization and delicate symbiotic relationship between national and Community institutions at the political as well as the judicial levels, to which there is no real analogy in the United States, is a feature of crucial importance in evaluating the case law on standing before the Court of Justice. The Community is a body at the borderline between the federal and the international and in international law the very notion of an individual having independent standing to sue before an international tribunal is little short of revolutionary.

The Standing Question: What the Court of Justice Said

With these differences in mind, let us turn to the similarities between the American federation and the Community bearing directly upon the standing question. In each the formal source of law determining the requirements of standing can be found in principle in a single normative provision: in Article 173 of the EEC Treaty[7] and in section 10 of the federal Administrative Procedure Act.[8] In addition, however, federal statutes often provide specifically for judicial review of specified types of administrative action. Similarly, in the Community certain regulations, such as Regulation 17 implementing the Treaty rules of competition, might have the effect of broadening individual access to judicial review.[9]

Article 173 sets no limitations whatsoever upon the standing of member states to contest *any* normative act of the Commission or the Council, nor for that matter upon the standing of the Commission to contest acts of the Council and vice versa. The much discussed second paragraph of that Article provides that

> [a]ny natural or legal person may . . . institute proceedings against a decision addressed to that person or against a decision which, although in the form of a regulation or a decision addressed to another person, is of direct and individual concern to the former.

The posture of the Court of Justice with regard to this provision was set in two groups of early cases in which the question of individual standing was raised for the first time: Cases 16–17/62 and 19–22/62 in which associations of producers and associations of traders respectively sued for annulment of Council regulations,[10] and the *Plaumann* Case 25/62,[11] in which a German importer of citrus fruit sought to contest a Commission decision addressed to the German Government refusing to authorize a reduction of the common external tariff on certain fruit imports from third states. The Court denied standing in both instances and adopted a strict reading of the requirement of "direct and individual concern." It did so despite an express recognition of the principle in the *Plaumann* case that provisions for access to legal remedy should never be narrowly construed.[12]

Judging by what the Court *said,* the factor that influenced it most was the difference between the language in the second paragraph of Article 173 and the corresponding provision in the earlier Treaty Establishing the Coal and Steel Community.[13] That latter provision, which expressly grants standing to contest acts of general application on the ground of *détournement de pouvoir* (misuse of powers, abuse of discretion) affecting a plaintiff, had been given a rather liberal interpretation by the Court. The Court concluded from the differences between the two treaties that the authors of the EEC Treaty deliberately intended to restrict access of individuals to the Court, presumably because of the much broader power to issue general regulations granted to the EEC institutions and the much wider range of persons affected by the EEC Treaty. "It is not for the Court to pass upon the merits of such system," the Court stated, "since the latter clearly stems from the text under scrutiny."

The formula that the Court evolved in the early cases for the application of the second paragraph of Article 173 may be summarized as follows:

1. An act is a "regulation"—as opposed to a "decision in the form of a regulation"[14]—if, by its "legal nature," it applies to categories of persons treated theoretically. Private persons may not contest such a general regulation under any circumstances.[15]
2. "Decisions" may be contested but persons other than those to whom a decision was addressed must show not only a *direct* concern but also an *individual* concern. They can claim an individual concern only if the decision affects them because of factors peculiar to them or by reason of circumstances "in which they are differentiated from all other persons and by virtue of these factors distinguishes them individually just as in the case of the persons addressed."[16]

Professor Waelbroeck has called the second part of this formula "not enlightening," which is a resounding understatement. The real question, he wrote, is to know just what the characteristics or fact situations are that "individualize" a person.[17] It is nevertheless this formula or its variant that the Court has repeated in every case and applied to deny standing to all the "natural or legal persons" who thus far have come before it as plaintiffs,[18] with the exception of three cases. Let us consider this triad in some detail since it may be easier to divine the Court's criteria from cases where standing was granted than from the much more numerous cases where it was denied.

The Triad Where Standing Was Allowed

In the *Toepfer* case,[19] the German Government import agency posted a zero levy on the import of corn for a specific date as a result of a Commission error. Seizing this opportunity, plaintiffs, large grain wholesale enterprises, applied for import licenses on the zero-levy basis. When the error was discovered, German and Commission officials consulted and agreed on a course of action. The German Government invoked its safeguard power under a Council regulation which enabled the German agency to reject the requested licences. The Commission, pursuant to the same regulation, issued a decision directed to the German Government and "authorizing" its safeguard measure retroactively. It was this Commission decision that the plaintiffs sought to have annulled. The Court held that the plaintiffs had standing. They were concerned "directly" because the Commission decision was "directly applicable" to them;[20] *there was no need for any further action by the German Government.* The plaintiffs were also concerned "individually" because the number and identity of the parties affected by the Commission's act ("no less than 27 companies") were determinable at the time the decision was adopted.

In the *Bock* case,[21] as in the *Toepfer* case, the Commission responded to a request from the German Government and addressed a decision to that government authorizing it to reject already pending applications for import licences, including one by the plaintiff. In this case also the Court granted standing: The plaintiff was concerned directly (even though the formal rejection of the licences required an act of the German Government and *in theory,* it was argued, that government might have decided not to use the authorization to reject). The plaintiff was also concerned individually, because, as in *Toepfer,* his licence application was already pending at the time of the Commission decision and "the number and identity of importers thus affected was certain and determinable."[22]

Finally, in the *International Fruit* case,[23] the Commission, as part of a safeguard system designed to ensure stability of the apple market, was given authority to consider the total quantity of apples for which import licences were requested and to decide what percentage, if any, of that quantity should be admitted. In that context, the Commission issued a "regulation" limiting the percentage and preventing acceptance of the applications for import licences filed during a specified past period with the Dutch Government. Plaintiffs whose applications were among those rejected were given standing to sue for annulment of the regulation which, the Court said, was in effect a bundle of individual decisions.[24] Plaintiffs were concerned directly because after the Commission had acted the member governments had no intervening power, no discretion whether or not to accept or reject that action. The plaintiffs were also concerned individually because the Commission based its regulation upon applications already filed. Hence the number of the parties concerned was determined at the time of the adoption of the regulation even though the Commission, acting upon the aggregate quantity of apples for which import licences were requested as reported by the Dutch Government, had no knowledge of the identity or even of the number of the parties affected.

The Court of Justice in Search of a Rationale

The manner in which the Court and the Advocates General have employed the prerequisite of "direct concern" manifests an intense interest in maintaining the delicate balance between member state and Community power, and we shall turn to this shortly. But the three cases where standing was allowed, seen against the background of all the cases where standing was denied, demonstrate the difficulties the Court and the Advocates General have encountered in drawing a line between what is and what is not of direct concern. Is the presence or absence of administrative discretion on the part of the member state under the challenged Community act the determining factor? And in which situations is such discretion present? In the *Toepfer* case where a Commission decision granted the requested authorization to the German Government the Court found a direct effect upon the plaintiff, although the Advocate General disagreed. In theory the German Government still had discretion whether or not to make use of the Commission's authorization but this did not seem to bother the Court.[25] Yet in the *Eridania* case denying standing, one of the three dramas at the beginning of this article, the most remote possibility that the Italian Government might not make use of an authorization, which in fact it had recommended and to which it was financially committed, was enough for the Court to deny direct effect.[26] In the *Alcan* case[27] where the Commission in a decision addressed to a government refused an authorization, the Court found no direct effect on the plaintiff although the refusal eliminated any discretion on the part of the addressee government. (The Advocate General found a scintilla of discretion in the possibility that the government might appeal the decision to the Court!)[28]

The Court has struggled in a similar way with the second prerequisite, that of "individual concern." In the *Eridania* case, with which we began, the Court denied individual (as well as direct) effect, contrary to the advice from the Advocate General, to Italian sugar producers who were affected by a Commission decision granting subsidies to their competitors. But there were only twenty-five sugar producers affected. In another case, the *Zuckerfabrik Watenstedt,* not more than 30 raw sugar producers in the entire Community were *in fact* directly affected by a Council regulation and there was no real chance of new producers being added in view of the depressed conditions in the sugar market and the size of the necessary investment.[29] Such "*de facto* individualization" satisfied the Advocate General but not the Court. Again, in *Getreide-Import,* despite the *Toepfer* ruling, a German importer-plaintiff was held not to be "individually" concerned by the Commission's decision fixing a price on imports for a specific date, although he was ultimately the only one to request an import licence on that date.[30] It would seem that in the Court's view, the plaintiffs can be considered "individually" affected only if they are members of a group of persons whose identity and number are fixed and, in addition, if the challenged act has a retroactive effect on their *legal* position, that is, if the act affects their "vested rights." But it is not the unfairness or the actual harm in retroactive lawmaking that moves the Court to grant standing. In two more recent cases where a retroactive effect clearly existed, the Court found no standing.[31]

We might note that in the *Glucoseries* case, the Court, after reciting the *Plaumann* formula, proceeded to inquire into the "general economic scope" and "purpose" of the Commission's act.[32] The preoccupation with the "purpose" of the challenged act may suggest one reason why the Court may have granted standing in *Toepfer* and *Bock,* two of the three Community cases where standing was allowed. In *Toepfer* some evidence suggested a collusion between national and Commission officials to erase an administrative error through means not entirely compatible with good administration,[33] and in *Bock* an improper delay and perhaps arbitrary recourse to a protective measure. It is significant that in both cases the Court ultimately annulled the contested act in proceedings on the merits. In the *International Fruit* case, the third case of the triad, the Court may have been concerned, in granting standing, that the Commission should not be in the position of precluding judicial review of its act by labelling it "regulation" rather than "decision."[34] This somewhat speculative line of analysis would suggest that in reality the Court may be inclined to look beyond jurisdictional arguments and grant standing where it senses an element of irregular administration.

This possibility aside, it is fair to say in summary that with respect to "direct concern," the Court of Justice has sought to give content to the requirement by invoking a Community interest in preserving the discretion of member governments; but the distinctions the Court has made on this basis are so illogical that one may question whether there is yet a workable or meaningful doctrine of "directness." As for the "individual concern" prerequisite, the Court seems to require that a plaintiff show something in the nature of an exclusive legal right analogous to a "vested right," something similar in its impact, as we shall see, to the original common law standing test in American federal law.

Elements of Legal Policy

One may well wonder what considerations have induced the Court to reject even the modicum of flexibility suggested by its own Advocate

General,[35] particularly if we recall, by way of a contrast, the Court's imaginative and teleological approaches to other institutional questions.[36]

(1) We have already mentioned the political concern with respect to member governments. A real likelihood of the exercise of member state discretion in implementation does appear to be relevant to the technical definition of a "direct" concern in the Community act being challenged. But Advocate General Gand went so far as to invoke "diplomatic courtesy" dictating that state discretion and state "sovereignty" not be impaired,[37] language reminiscent of the International Court of Justice which umpires international disputes among states.

While prudence is obviously in order for a freshly established judicial tribunal in a body politic where states play a crucial part, the method by which the Court has sought to limit its jurisdiction is, as we have suggested, open to question. Moreover, can the Court seriously assert respect for states' rights and sovereignty when a plaintiff, claiming present harm, is offering to show that the contested Community act is illegal and thus can not serve as a legal basis for further state action?

(2) Another and perhaps more compelling consideration was articulated by Advocate General Lagrange: Since the Treaty is largely a "*traité cadre*" or framework law which normally must be implemented by general regulations, the possibility of even a partial annulment of such a regulation poses "an extreme danger" to the system, if, as is frequently the case, the regulation represents a laborious compromise reached in the Council pursuant to the unanimity rule or practice.[38] The solution, he suggests, lies in increasing the role of the European Parliamentary Assembly in the legislative process so that there is less danger of paralysis if the compromise is annulled. In the present circumstances, it may also be recognized that it is difficult to brand a Council regulation unanimously adopted by representatives of the member states as "illegal" even where it appears to be inconsistent with the Treaty: it would be to a degree a modification of the basic law albeit in disregard of the amending procedure. These considerations, however, would hardly apply to standing with respect to Council regulations of lesser stature, routine regulations of the Commission, or to Commission decisions addressed to other persons (particularly to private parties).

The Court may also have had in mind another argument advanced by Commission jurists with respect to Council regulations which the Commission is required to implement. Even where a plaintiff feels directly injured by a general regulation which he considers illegal, he should be denied standing, it is said, until the regulation is actually applied to him by a Commission decision addressed to him, at which time he would have standing to contest the decision.[39] Apart from making rational business planning impossible, the argument does not take into account a potentially serious or even irreparable harm that might result from the delay.

It has been suggested that the Court ought to develop more nuanced criteria of standing depending upon whether the act is predominantly "legislative" or purely "administrative," such as a Commission decision addressed to a government[40] and responding to its request for a special exemption from a general rule.[41]

(3) The political considerations are no doubt buttressed by the inherent aversion of administrators everywhere (including the United States) to judicial control. Attorneys appearing in defense of the Council and the Commission have been uncompromising and consistent in their opposition to plaintiff standing. The Court of Justice is not a federal court, and even the Supreme Court of the United States would hesitate to rule in a controversial matter against both the Congress and the Executive. In very few instances has the Court of Justice ventured substantially beyond the Commission's position in important systemic questions. The opposition of the Commission and Council makes it difficult to do so on the standing issue. While the Commission has invariably urged liberal, purpose-oriented interpretations in defining the scope of its own power or the power of the Communities generally, it has taken the narrowest and the most mechanistic position in the standing-to-sue cases where the question was one of potentially curbing its own power.[42] However, at this stage of development, the opposition of Community attorneys to a more liberal interpretation may be due as much to the customary bureaucratic aversion to any deviation from an established policy line as to a strong attachment to principle.

(4) The Court has said that it cannot modify the Treaty. In one case the plaintiff contended that, if recourse to Article 173 were denied to him because of a narrow interpretation of the text, he would be deprived of all judicial safeguards both under Community law and under national law, which would be contrary to the basic principles governing all member countries.[43] The Court responded that these considerations could not "be allowed to override the clearly restrictive wording of Article 173, which, it is the Court's task to apply."[44] Yet at least in the case of an individual contesting a decision addressed to a third party, the question involved—the interpretation of the words "direct and individual concern"—is hardly a matter of Treaty modification.[45]

Of course in many, though not in all cases, the plaintiff would in fact have recourse to national courts, and, via the procedure of Article 177, to the Court of Justice, which then would have an opportunity to pass upon the validity of a decision or regulation in a "preliminary ruling," with a binding effect upon national courts. This procedure involves substantial cost and delay.[46] Nevertheless, from the very outset the Court has interpreted access to national courts for the purpose of enforcing individual rights derives from Community law in a most liberal way, far beyond what may have been the intent of the authors of the Treaty. The Court has clearly preferred to enhance its jurisdiction, and the protection of individuals, through this avenue which is particularly appropriate to the symbiotic Community system, rather than by opening up the individual's direct access pursuant to Article 173. In this, the Court has succeeded beyond any expectation, considering the many cases referred to it by national courts from the member states. Because of the political problems which a member state or a Community institution faces in initiating an action against an institution or a state before the Court, the Article 177 procedure has become the most frequently employed course for enforcing Community law. More recently, the Court has also given a more liberal interpretation to the Treaty provisions allowing private persons to sue the Community for damages caused by an act of a Community institution.[47] The question for the future will be whether these procedures are sufficient.

(5) It is interesting to speculate whether the Court has been influenced in this field by the laws of the member states.

The Court's records show that the Advocates General, if not the Court itself, have at least had in mind the relevant national laws and practices. But there has been no unanimity of opinion. M. Lagrange, the distinguished first Advocate General from the French Conseil d'Etat, was prepared to discount the fact that "the legal situation within the Community is undoubtedly less favorable [to the plaintiff] than that which has been reached for a greater or lesser length of time by some of the Member States, but it is similar to that known in other States."[48] His counterpart, the able Mr. Roemer, coming from private corporate law practice in Germany, appeared troubled, in 1968 at any rate, by the Court's formalistic approach as compared with rules applied by the German Federal Administrative Court, and particularly by the possible constitutional implications of leaving a citizen without any remedy.[49] The current German and Italian Advocates General appear to take somewhat different views on the relevance of national administrative law solutions to analogous Community cases.[50]

In any event, although the Court has not hesitated in other contexts to canvass national laws for "general principles" that may be common to them, we cannot find any evidence that the Court may be getting ready to soften its strict posture in this area to reflect some of the more liberal trends in national laws. The Court's present position is reminiscent of the earlier German standing requirement that plaintiff show infringement of "subjective public *right*" rather than the more flexible formula evolved by German doctrine holding "legally protected *interest*" sufficient. Obviously the liberal French jurisprudence has also had little impact.[51]

(6) One factor which may explain the apparent absence of effective pragmatic pressures on the Court to grant broader access is the still relatively limited scope of the Community regulatory power, confined essentially to customs union, movement of factors of production, and competition. Some of the economic and noneconomic forces and interests such as environmental and consumer protection, which have had such impact on the liberalization of the American rule, operates thus far, if at all, at the national level and are only beginning to be reached by Community power.

(7) Finally, although the Court has been reticent on the subject, an important concern may be the possibility of multiplicity of suits should citizen access to the Court be defined in broad terms. We shall return to this problem after a discussion of the American experience.

Standing in U.S. Federal Courts: The Common Law Test and Its Demise

The Community Court's difficulties in applying its current interpretation of Article 173 are similar to those experienced by American federal courts in the decades before 1970. American doctrine has not been troubled by a basic distinction between "decisions" and "regulations." Both have long been judicially reviewable "administrative action."[52] But, as we have seen, in specific circumstances "regulations" can be viewed in Community law as a "bundle of individual decisions,"[53] and it is likely that the classification of Community action as a "regulation" or not for purposes of the first part of the second paragraph of Article 173 will follow and simply express the resolution of the real problems of standing, which have to do with the "individuality" and "directness" of the plaintiff's stake in the case. Here the parallels between American and Community developments are striking.

A concern that the judiciary not undermine the sense of responsibility within administrative agencies for the legality of their programs, or interfere with the process of interest group accommodation carried on by agencies in the development of a program, has led to doctrines in American federal administrative law designed to allow postponement of judicial review where discretionary agency steps are still to be taken before enforcement of an agency decision or regulation. These, the doctrines of "finality" and "ripeness," are now treated separately from the law of standing. Whether that part of the Community standing test that focuses on member state discretion is meant to take into account similar concerns is difficult to know, in view of the way the "directness" prerequisite has been administered. It is quite clear, however, that access to judicial review under the American doctrines of "finality" and "ripeness" does not turn simply on whether or not there is discretion. A showing of discretionary implementation is only the beginning of an analysis of the relative costs and benefits of delaying judicial review. The argument that a plaintiff has too indirect and attenuated a concern with administrative action if it does not fix rights or obligations, an argument still made by government attorneys, has been labeled by the Supreme Court as having "the hollow ring of another era."[54]

With regard to "individuality," the basic rule of standing in the United States until the late nineteen sixties was the common law test, under which the plaintiff could invoke the jurisdiction of a court only if he could point to a *private legal right* that would be violated by a named government official if that official failed to show that his action was authorized—a test which still obtains in many of the states today and which resembles the formula now employed in the Court of Justice. It was only in 1970 that the U.S. Supreme Court expressly "discredited" this test and turned to the Administrative Procedure Act for a definition of standing.[55] However, the formula drawn from the Act to replace the so-called "private legal right" test did not burst upon American jurisprudence full blown. There is a history which merits a brief account, for it indicates that we may be dealing with underlying currents of thought and concept that are likely to have an impact on societies functioning in a comparable frame of reference.

The attack upon and demise of the "legal right" test had two main historical roots. One involved "economic" interests and the other "noneconomic." On the economic side, it has been a rule of the common law that no person has a "right" to be free of competition. When a person came into court and complained that he had suffered injury through the increased competition of someone else made possible by an allegedly illegal government act or subsidy, the classic response was that he had no standing to seek an injunction against the illegal act hurting him because he had not shown the invasion of a legal right of his "own." For instance, in 1938 competing private utilities were held to have no standing to challenge the legality under the National Industrial Recovery Act of a program of public work grants to municipalities for construction of electric distribution systems. In reading this case one immediately thinks of *Eridania.* The U.S. Supreme Court held that a person injured by government action can not challenge that action in court unless the injury resulted in the violation of a legal right,[56] which the Court later defined as "one of property, one arising out of contract, one protected against tortious invasion, or one founded on a statute which confers a privilege."[57]

There was never a self-evident logic to a position that because a business had no right to be free of competition it had no right to be free of illegally created competition, and as government was seen to intervene more and more into the market and affect and determine the relative advantages of the players in the market, business interests became more and more determined to gain access to the courts to review the legality of administrative actions affecting them in this most important way. One response by the courts was to view the specific standing provisions often written into statutes creating the regulating agencies and often couched in vague terms—conferring standing for instance on "aggrieved" persons—as congressionally mandated exceptions to the courts' own self-imposed and restrictive requirement of a legal right.[58] Much more threatening to the conceptual integrity of the legal right test, however, was the conclusion that if a person or group of persons could show that they were in some sense the intended beneficiary of the establishment of an administrative regulatory scheme or any part of it, they could be viewed as having "quasi-property" rights in the common law sense, and standing followed when government officials administered the scheme in such a way as to deny the benefit. This was a transparent circumvention of the legal right test, for such persons as the private utilities operating around the territory of the Tennessee Valley Authority, and claiming to be the beneficiaries of that authority's limited geographical jurisdiction, had no private legal rights under the common law of property and none granted them by the statute. Nor was their standing arguably mandated specifically by Congress. Their quasi-property rights were recognized solely for the purpose of standing to challenge the administrative action.[59] This search for and discovery of "beneficiaries" of the regulatory scheme was extended into a number of fields beyond those of economic competition. The concept recalls the "legally protected interest" test in German administrative law which, as we have mentioned earlier, German doctrine constructed as a more flexible alternative to the rigid standing requirement that the plaintiff must show a "subjective public right."[60]

The second major thrust against the common law test concerned noneconomic values. It is usually impossible to claim any private or exclusive right to the beauty, health, safety, or recreational opportunities so widely regulated by modern administrative bodies. The money loss resulting from a bureaucratically dictated change in relative economic advantage was at least discrete and theoretically measurable, like other private harms which the common law traditionally considered and sometimes prevented. A noneconomic loss often did not resemble a loss of "property" in any way. Yet it might be of even greater importance to an individual; and as the growth of legislation and regulation established causal connections between noneconomic losses and official action, lower federal courts began to give remedies to individuals against such action when it was illegal. Consumers of television were granted standing to challenge the licensing of particular television stations[61] and consumers of food were granted standing to challenge the legality of adding color to oleomargarine.[62] Frequently the courts claimed to be interpreting the general language contained in specific statutory standing provisons in various licensing acts, provisions which most observers would have originally thought were included for the benefit of persons and groups, such as manufacturers of food or chemicals or television licensees, economically associated with the regulatory scheme in question and subject to administrative sanctions. These cases in the lower courts go back to the 1940's and 50's, but appeared in great numbers during the 1960's and were ultimately cited with approval in the 1970 decisions of the Supreme Court which brought about the major change.

The New Test

Technically, the change was effected by holding that the Administrative Procedure Act, which had been enacted more than a quarter of a century earlier, was a source of standing independent of both the common law and the special standing provisions incorporated into the various acts setting up administrative agencies. The Act applies to all agencies unless they are specifically excepted, and provides that any person is entitled to judicial review of agency action if he "suffers legal wrong or is adversely affected or aggrieved within the meaning of a relevant statute." Even though the term "legal wrong" was used in the statutory language, the Court declared that the legal right test of the common law, under which, it will be remembered, the plaintiff stated a cause of action only if he showed a private legal right invaded by a government official acting under the color of law, was discredited. The Court used the word "discredited" and was unanimous in this regard. The Court then went on to construct a new formula for the standing of private parties in challenges to administrative action, namely that the party must be "injured in fact" and must show that "the interest he is seeking to protect"—to quote the language which the Court has since repeated in subsequent cases—is "arguably within the zone of interests protected or regulated by the statute in question," the "statute in question" being the statute setting up the administrative agency and providing substantive standards for judging the legality of its actions. A French lawyer reading the language of this formula might immediately think of his own "*interêt à agir,*" the rather liberal standing test developed by the Conseil d'Etat.[63]

Applying the new test, the U.S. Supreme Court granted standing to a trade association of independent data processing companies, and later to a travel agency, to challenge the legality of regulations issued by the Comptroller of the Currency which permitted federal banks to compete with them by expanding into the fields of data processing and travel services.[64] The Court made clear that it was not relying on any evidence that Congress had intended to make data processors or travel agents specific beneficiaries of bank regulation.[65] Two years later, the Court seemed to imply that it would hear the challenge of the Sierra Club, a conservationist group, to actions by federal officials of dubious legality which had permitted Disney Enterprises to begin the development of a wilderness area in a national forest in California, providing that the club showed that it spoke on behalf of members who were injured, whether in economic or noneconomic fashion, in their use of the wilderness area.[66] Then, in 1973, the Court did grant standing to a group of law students who used a national park and who challenged a railroad rate regulation that might have the effect of polluting the park.[67] In none of these cases could a claim to a personal legal right be made out, nor were there specific provisions in the statutes governing the agencies in question for judicial review of the agency decision at the request of the plaintiffs.

One cannot doubt that the conceptual and pragmatic pressures that led to these results would have succeeded in finding some other mode of expression if the language of the Administrative Procedure Act had not been at hand ready for use.[68] Had the judiciary truly conceived itself as limited to the protection of private rights except in those instances where the legislature expressly instructed it to go beyond that role, a quite reasonable interpretation of the standing language of the Act was available. As we have noted, many of the special standing statutes providing for judicial review of certain agency actions in specified circumstances use the term of art "aggrieved" to designate those persons who may seek redress, and it was open to the Court to conclude that the language of the Administrative Procedure Act which suggested a ground of standing other than "legal wrong," or invasion of private and personal legal right, was meant to do no more than refer to those situations where specific statutory standing was given to individuals by such statutes. But the Court did not do so, and held instead that standing emanated from the

Administrative Procedure Act itself. Although grounded in legislative language—as the formula for standing in the Court of Justice is grounded in Article 173—the decision to hear challenges to the legality of administrative action in a larger number of situations was clearly a matter of *judicial* choice.

It is, however, far easier to see what American courts have put behind them than to see what lies ahead. Lower federal courts have found the new standing formula difficult to administer without opening their doors to all litigants who have demonstrated a personal concern for the values affected by the challenged action sufficiently strong to support the costs of litigation.[69] Explicit approval of such a result would not be incompatible with existing jurisprudence,[70] and, as we shall note below, might cause relatively few practical difficulties. But there are indications that the Supreme Court is not prepared to go so far. In constitutional judicial review of congressional action, litigants have sought to use developments in the review of administrative decisions to establish the standing of persons in their capacity as "citizens" to enforce the Constitution. In its most recent decisions, the Court has explicitly rejected the concept of the "public action"[71] and while, as we have noted, review of acts of Congress involves considerations different from those governing the review of administrative action and has proceeded on doctrinely separate routes, the Court used language in justifying its limitation on constitutional standing that may apply to both the administrative and the constitutional areas.[72] Ironically, the difficulties in charting the reach of the new American administrative law standing formula and in determining whether a constitutional challenge is more than a "public action" are now discussed in terms of whether the plaintiff's injury or interest is sufficiently "individual" and "direct,"[73] the very terms mandated by Article 173 for equivalent discussions in the Community. But all we can say with assurance is that the questions of "directness" and "individuality" are not to be answered in the United States according to whether or not a private and established right is at stake in the case.

Concluding Observations: How Relevant Is Federal Experience?

What has happened in the United States is a reflection of and indeed now a principal symbol of a significant change in the conception of the role of a judiciary in a modern administrative state. Courts are no longer to be viewed as restricted to the settlement of private disputes and protecting vested private rights against government intrusion. The very notion of a self-sustaining sphere of private rights into which government action "intrudes" is now difficult to grasp. And with the growth of government it has been increasingly widely perceived that leaving government activities outside that sphere to take care of themselves may well mean leaving individual government officials essentially unchecked. Neither bureaucratic processes nor the legislature itself is in fact capable of policing the activities of government agencies on a day to day basis. Not even the U.S. Congress with its massive staff of experts can attend to details or tend to them in time. The burden of inertia is such that relegating a challenger to a legislative remedy is itself a decision on the merits.

In sum, we think the American courts and Bar have at last acknowledged that they and their processes play an integral part in the business of government. Of course, in a pluralistic democratic society it is the elected legislature that in principle has power and responsibility to determine the hierarchy of common values and resolve conflicts among them. But no society pursuing a multitude of public values of different weight and importance through a multitude of largely independent implementing agencies can do without courts and still hope to achieve a satisfactory realization of its goals. The Supreme Court now speaks of "private attorneys general," a phrase which appeared as early as 1943 in the American judicial vocabulary.[74] Responding to their initiative, American courts are holding in check and inquiring into the legality of challenged agency action on behalf of interests of a broader and more general concern than the private interests in contract and property traditionally protected.

The Rome Treaty has made the Court of Justice an important part of its mechanism for achieving its goals. In a body without an elected legislature, where law is made by national and transnational executives through processes shielded from the glare of publicity, the judicial role is if anything even more essential than in a mature federation. As a single tribunal serving the entire expanse of the Community, the Court may understandably be concerned with judicial economy and avoidance of cranky proceedings and multiplicity of suits. Both these dangers have troubled American courts. The burden of merely being required to respond to an argument on the merits and the potential for harassment resulting from a broadened test of standing are no doubt among the factors making the exploration of the boundaries of the new American formula a rather cautious one, particularly in the noneconomic area. But the State of Michigan and several other American states are experimenting with environmental protection legislation that permits extremely broad access to courts, and the experience to date is that no large scale multiplicity of suits is developing. Rather the impact has been on the attitudes of the administrators and on proceedings before them.[75] If in fact a great number of suits, perhaps of an identical nature, are brought with a shift from a "private right" basis for standing to the new formula, and given the cost of litigation that is dubious, then the problem can be handled through consolidation and class action procedures.[76] Whether a suit is cranky or not seems to us a matter for the merits. If it is frivolous, it can be disposed of far more rapidly by getting to the merits than by litigating the question of standing.

It has clearly been a wise judicial policy for the Court of Justice to encourage private plaintiffs to bring their complaints before their own national tribunal, despite the additional risks, cost, and delay which this may entail. But as the scope of the Community regulatory powers broadens to include other fields and affect other values, economic and non-economic—health and safety, environment, consumer protection, energy conservation—the Court may well feel called upon to broaden direct access by private complainants. If it does, we suggest that it will act not only to protect private interests but also to advance the common interest in effective enforcement of Community legality and broader participation of citizens in Community administration.[77]

Notes

The substance of this article was presented at the workshop organized by the Institute of Advanced Legal Studies in London, July 1–4, 1975.

1. International civil servants may press their service-connected grievances before administrative tribunals established by the United Nations and the specialized agencies. M. B. AKEHURST, THE LAW GOVERNING EMPLOYMENT IN INTERNATIONAL ORGANIZATIONS (1967); BYUNG CHUL KOH, THE UNITED NATIONS ADMINISTRATIVE TRIBUNAL (1966). If the state concerned consents, an individual may complain against it to a committee of experts under the UN sponsored Convention on the Elimination of All Forms of Racial Discrimination. Schwelb, *The International Convention on the Elimination of All Forms of Racial Discrimination,* 15 INT'L & COMP. L.Q. 996 (1966). Pursuant to procedures evolved in UN General Assembly Committees and in certain other UN bodies, individuals may file petitions and even may be heard in person. Individuals may complain directly to the European Commission of Human Rights if the state against which the complaint was lodged recognizes such jurisdiction, but only the states contracting parties and the Commission have access to the European Court of Human Rights. European Convention for the Protection of Human Rights and Fundamental Freedoms, Arts. 25 and 48, 213 UNTS 221 (1955).

2. Association of Data Processing Service Organizations, Inc. v. Camp, 397 U.S. 150 (1970).

3. Judgment of Aug. 30, 1968, 30 BVerwGE 191.

4. Cases 10 and 18/68, Società "Eridania" Zuccherifici Nazionali *et al.* v. Commission of the European Communities, 15 RECUEIL DE LA JURISPRUDENCE DE LA COUR DE JUSTICE DES COMMUNAUTÉS EUROPÉENNES (REC.) 459 (1969).

5. The Court of Justice of the Communities in Case 26/62, N.V. Algemene Transport–en Expeditie Andernemung van Gend en Loos v. Nederlandse Tariefcommissie, 9 REC. 1 (1963); [1963] EUROPEAN COURT REPORTS (ECR) 1 at 12; [1963] COMMON MARKET LAW REPORTS (C.M.L.R.) 105; COMMERCE CLEARING HOUSE, Chicago, COMMON MARKET REPORTER (CCH COMM. MKT. REP.) ¶8008.

6. Art. 177 of the EEC Treaty.

7. The corresponding articles in the other Community treaties are Article 33 of the ECSC Treaty and Article 146 of the Euratom Treaty.

8. 5 U.S.C. §702 (Supp. V, 1965–1969). This discussion is limited to judicial review of acts of federal administrative agencies which have both rulemaking and decisionmaking authority. We do not address the special problem of judicial review of congressional acts for constitutionality.

9. Daig in H. VON DER GROEBEN, H. VON BOECKH, J. THIESING, 2 KOMMENTAR ZUM EWG-VERTRAG 209 at 234 (2nd ed. 1974); Peters in 3 C.M.L. REV. 233 at 241 (1965).

10. Cases 16/62 and 17/62, Confédération Nationale des Producteurs de Fruits et Légumes *et al.* v. Council, 8 REC. 901 (1962); [1962] ECR 471; [1963] C.M.L.R. 160; CCH COMM. MKT. REP. ¶8005 at 7186. Cases 19/62–22/62, Fédération Nationale de la Boucherie en Gros, etc. v. Council, 8 REC. 943 (1962); [1962] ECR 491; [1963] C.M.L.R. 160; CCH COMM. MKT. REP. ¶8006.

11. Case 25/62, Plaumann & Co. v. Commission, 9 REC. 197 (1963); [1963] ECR 95; [1964] C.M.L.R. 29; CCH COMM. MKT. REP. ¶8013 at 7274.

12. In the above cases the attorneys for the defendant Council and Commission urged an even more restrictive interpretation that would have denied any association capacity to sue as much under any circumstances despite the specific Treaty language to the contrary ("any . . . legal person") and that would not recognize a government as a "person" within the meaning of the second paragraph of Article 173. The Court rejected these assertions and on this issue followed the conclusions of its Advocates General.

13. Article 33 of the ECSC Treaty reads: ". . . Undertakings or the associations referred to in Article 48 may, under the same conditions, institute proceedings against decisions or recommendations concerning them which are individual in character or against general decisions or recommendations which they consider to involve a misuse of powers *(détournement de pouvoir)* affecting them *(à leur égard—ihnen gegenüber)*." Compare the above language "decisions . . . concerning them" with the requirement of "direct and individual concern" in the corresponding EEC Art. 173(2) *supra.* There is considerable literature comparing the ECSC and the EEC Treaties on this issue and commenting on the case law. *See e.g.* G. BEBR, JUDICIAL CONTROL OF THE EUROPEAN COMMUNITIES 68–77 (1962); A. TIZZANO, LA CORTE DI GIUSTIZIA DELLE COMMUNITÀ EUROPEE 396–415 (1967) and also in R. QUADRI, R. MONACO, A. TRABUCCHI, 3 TRATTATO ISTITUTIVO DELLA COMMUNITÀ ECONOMICA EUROPEA, COMMENTARIO 1277–85 (1965); Daig in KOMMENTAR *supra* note 9, at 222–36; C. H. ULE, EMPFIEHLT ES SICH, DIE BESTIMMUNGEN DES EUROPÄISCHEN GEMEINSCHAFTRECHTS ÜBER DEN RECHTSSCHUTZ ZU ÄNDERN UND ZU ERGÄNZEN?, GUTACHTEN FÜR DEN 46. DEUTSCHEN JURISTENTAG

13–32 (1966); Bebr, *Recours en annulation et en carrence* in W. J. GANSHOF VAN DER MEERSCH (ed.), LES NOVELLES, DROIT DES COMMUNAUTÉS EUROPÉENNES 309–19 (1969) with bibliography at 309; Rasquin et Chevallier, *L'article 173, alinéa 2 du Traité C.E.E., 2* REV. TRIM. DR. EUR. 31 (1966); Barav, *Direct and Individual Concern: An Almost Insurmountable Barrier to the Admissibility of Individual Appeal to the EEC Court,* 11 C.M.L. REV. 191 (1974).

14. According to Article 189, a "regulation" is "directly applicable" by national courts and other authorities throughout the Community territory.

15. Cases 16/62 and 17/62, Confédération Nationale, *supra* note 10. The Court added in Confédération Nationale that it would look beyond the official designation of the act as a "regulation":

> Consequently, in order to determine in doubtful cases whether one is concerned with a decision or a regulation, it is necessary to ascertain whether the measure in question is of individual concern to specific individuals. In these circumstances, if a measure entitled by its author a regulation contains provisions which are capable of being not only of direct but also of individual concern to certain natural or legal persons, it must be admitted, without prejudice to the question whether that measure considered in its entirety can be correctly called a regulation, that in any case those provisions do not have the character of a regulation and may therefore be impugned by those persons under the terms of the second paragraph of Article 173.

[1962] ECR at 478–79. In support of a more liberal interpretation, see A. TIZZANO, *supra* note 13, at 404–11. *But see* Bebr, *Recours en annulation et en carrence, supra* note 13, at 318. On the above cases, see note by Cartou in [1962] SIREY JURISPRUDENCE 126.

16. Case 25/62, Plaumann, *supra* note 11, [1963] ECR at 107. Since the plaintiff in this case was not concerned "individually," the Court found it unnecessary to deal with the question of "direct" concern.

17. Waelbroeck, *Les compétences de la Cour de Justice* (II), [1971] REV. CRITIQUE DE JURISPRUDENCE BELGE 513 at 530.

18. The cases in which this paragraph was applied or discussed are: Cases 16 & 17/62, Confédération Nationale des Producteurs de Fruits et Légumes *et al.* v. Council, 8 REC. 901 (1962); [1962] ECR 471; [1963] C.M.L.R. 160; CCH COMM. MKT. REP. ¶8005. Cases 19–22/62, Fédération Nationale de la Boucherie en Gros et du Commerce en Gros des Viandes *et al.* v. Council, 8 REC. 943 (1962); [1962] ECR 491; [1963] C.M.L.R. 160; CCH COMM. MKT. REP. ¶8006. Cases 31 & 33/62, Milchwerke Heinz Wöhrmann & Sohn KG et Alfons Lütticke GmbH v. Commission, 8 REC. 965 (1962); [1962] ECR 501; [1963] C.M.L.R. 152; CCH COMM. MKT. REP. ¶8007. Case 25/62 Plaumann & Co. v. Commission, 9 REC. 197 (1963); [1963] ECR 95; [1964] C.M.L.R. 29; CCH COMM. MKT. REP. ¶8013. Case 1/64, Glucoseries Réunies v. Commission, 10 REC. 811 (1964); [1964] ECR 413; [1964] C.M.L.R. 596; CCH COMM. MKT. REP. ¶8024. Case 38/64, Getreide-Import

Gesellschaft v. Commission, 11 Rec. 263 (1965); [1965] ECR 204; [1965] C.M.L.R. 276; CCH Comm. Mkt. Rep. ¶8033. Case 40/64, Marcello Sgarlata *et al.* v. Commission, 11 Rec. 279; (1965); [1965] ECR 215; [1966] C.M.L.R. 314; CCH Comm. Mkt. Rep. ¶8034. Cases 106 & 107/63, Alfred Toepfer et Getreide-Import Gesellschaft v. Commission, 11 Rec. 525 (1965); [1965] ECR 405; [1966] C.M.L.R. 111; CCH Comm. Mkt. Rep. ¶8031. Case 30/67, Industria Molitoria Imolese *et al.* v. Council, 14 Rec. 171 (1968); [1968] ECR 115; CCH Comm. Mkt. Rep. ¶8060. Case 6/68, Zuckerfabrik Watenstedt GmbH v. Council, 14 Rec. 595 (1968); [1968] ECR 409; [1969] C.M.L.R. 26; CCH Comm. Mkt. Rep. ¶8063. Cases 10 & 18/68, Società "Eridania" Zuccherifici Nazionali *et al.* v. Commission, 15 Rec. 459 (1969); CCH Comm. Mkt. Rep. ¶8099. Cases 63 & 64/69, La Compagnie française commerciale et financière, SA v. Commission, 16 Rec. 205 (1970); [1970] C.M.L.R. 369; CCH Comm. Mkt. Rep. ¶8090, ¶8091. Case 65/69, La Compagnie d'approvisionnement, de transport et de credit, SA v. Commission, 16 Rec. 229 (1970); [1970] C.M.L.R. 369; CCH Comm. Mkt. Rep. ¶8092. Case 69/69, SA Alcan Aluminium Raeren *et al.* v. Commission, 16 Rec. 385 (1970); [1970] C.M.L.R. 337; CCH Comm. Mkt. Rep. ¶8110. Case 15/70, Amedeo Chevalley v. Commission, 16 Rec. 975 (1970); CCH Comm. Mkt. Rep. ¶8115. Cases 41–44/70, NV International Fruit Co. *et al.* v. Commission, 17 Rec. 411 (1971); CCH Comm. Mkt. Rep. ¶8142. Case 15/71, Firma C. Mackprang, Jr. v. Commission, 17 Rec. 797 (1971); [1972] C.M.L.R. 52; CCH Comm. Mkt. Rep. ¶8155. Case 62/70, Werner A. Bock v. Commission, 17 Rec. 897 (1972); [1972] C.M.L.R. 160; CCH Comm. Mkt. Rep. ¶8150. Case 42/71, Nordgetreide GmbH & Co. KG v. Commission, 18 Rec. 105 (1972); [1973] C.M.L.R. 368; CCH Comm. Mkt. Rep. ¶8174. Cases 9 & 11/71, Compagnie d'approvisionnement, de transport et de credit SA et Grands Moulins de Paris SA v. Commission, 18 Rec. 391 (1972); [1973] C.M.L.R. 529; CCH Comm. Mkt. Rep. ¶8177. Case 96/71, R. & V. Haegeman v. Commission, 18 Rec. 1005 (1972); [1973] C.M.L.R. 365; CCH Comm. Mkt. Rep. ¶8181. Case 134/73, Holtz & Willemsen GmbH v. Council, [1974] ECR 1; [1975] C.M.L.R. 91; CCH Comm. Mkt. Rep. ¶8255. Case 175/73, Union Syndicale *et al.* v. Council, [1974] ECR 917; [1975] C.M.L.R. 131. Case 18/74, Syndicat Général du Personnel des Organismes Européens v. Commission, [1974] ECR 933; [1975] C.M.L.R. 144. Cases 44, 46 & 49/74, Marie-Louise Acton *et al.* v. Commission, [1975] ECR 383. Case 72/74, Union Syndicale *et al.* v. Council, [1975] ECR 401.

19. Cases 106/63 and 107/63, Alfred Toepfer v. Commission, *supra* note 18.

20. The Court equated "direct concern" with the important Community concept of "direct applicability" and this raises some interesting problems which are beyond the scope of this article. The former is a procedural prerequisite for action before the Community Court; the latter goes to the merit of an individual's claim against a member state enforceable in a national court. For comments see Fromont in [1966] Rec. Dalloz-Sirey, Jurisprudence 58; Peters in 3 C.M.L. Rev. 233 (1965).

21. Case 62/70, Werner A. Bock v. Commission, *supra* note 18. For a comment, see Verougstraete, 8 Cahier de droit eur. 666 (1972).

22. The Commission "was in a position to know that the decisions would affect only the interests and legal status of these importers. Under these circumstances the importers are set apart from all other persons in a manner similar to the addressee" (CCH COMM. MKT. REP. at 7720).

23. Cases 41/70–44/70, N.V. International Fruit Company *et al.* v. Commission, *supra* note 18. For a comment, see V.C. in 99 JOURNAL DE DROIT INTERNATIONAL 687, 693 (1972).

24. Subsequently, the Court dismissed the case on the merits.

25. The Court said that the Commission decisions modifying or abolishing safeguard measures are "directly applicable" because Article 22 of the regulation under which the Commission acted provided that the Commission's decision shall take effect immediately and therefore "[i]t would be illogical to say that a decision to retain protective measures had a different effect. . . ." Alfred Toepfer v. Commission, *supra* note 18, [1965] ECR at 411.

26. Cases 10 and 18/68, Eridania, *supra* note 18. *See also* Adv. Gen. Roemer in Case 1/64, Glucoseries Réunies v. Commission, and in Case 26/62, Plaumann & Co. v. Commission, and also in Cases 106/63 and 107/63, Alfred Toepfer v. Commission, *supra* note 18.

27. Case 69/69, SA Alcan Aluminium Rearen *et al.* v. Commission, *supra* note 18. *See also* Case 25/62, Plaumann & Co. v. Commission, *supra* note 18; *cf.* Adv. Gen. Gand in Case 38/64, Getreide Import v. Commission, *supra* note 18.

28. Advocate General Gand relied here on the views of his colleague Roemer in *Plaumann.* In the *Alcan* case Advocate General Gand pressed the argument that if the Commission's decision had granted the requested authorization to the government the decision would not have direct effect on the plaintiff; consequently, the actual decision in this case refusing the authorization must be equally without direct effect on him, apparently in the interest of symmetry. Case 69/69, Alcan, *supra* note 18, CCH COMM. MKT. REP. at 7256. Daig distinguishes the decisions in which the Commission addresses an order, prohibition, or authorization to a member state. Daig in KOMMENTAR, *supra* note 9, at 232–33.

29. Case 6/68, Zuckerfabrik Watenstedt v. Council, *supra* note 18. *See also* Case 1/64, Glucoseries Réunies v. Commission, *supra* note 18, where both the Advocate General and the Court found no individual concern.

30. Case 38/64, Getreide-Import Gesellschaft v. Commission, *supra* note 18. For comments on this case, see Mailänder, *Privater Rechtsschutz im Recht der Europäischen Wirtschaftsgemeinschaft,* [1965] BETRIEB 1312; ULE, *supra* note 13 at 17–19. The Court attempted to distinguish the case from Toepfer on the ground that, unlike the Toepfer situation, the Commission did not know of the plaintiff's application at the time of its decision. Bebr feels that factual difference might explain the two different holdings "at least partially." Bebr, *Recours en annulation et en carrence, supra* note 13, at 315. *See also* Case 30/57, Industria Molitoria Imolese v. Council, *supra* note 18.

31. In Case 69/69, Alcan v. Commission, *supra* note 18, the Court found no direct concern and remained silent on the issue of individual concern although Advocate General Gand held individual concern to be present. In Case 64/69,

La Compagnie française v. Commission, *supra* note 18, the Court found no individual concern even though, according to the plaintiff, the contested provision of the Commission regulation applied to a group of specified enterprises (including the plaintiff) since these enterprises were positively known and identifiable even before the contested provision was issued. The Court stated: "The fact that a transitional rule concerns only certain situations created prior to a date which it sets and which are therefore often determined even before the rule goes into effect does not prevent such a rule from being an integral part" of and sharing the general character of a regulation. Thus retroactivity alone is not enough "unless there is a misuse of discretionary power." CCH COMM. MKT. REP. at 8323.

32. Case 1/64, Glucoseries Réunies v. Commission, *supra* note 18.

33. Kovar in 93 JOURNAL DE DROIT INTERNATIONAL 707, at 711–12 (1966).

34. In his opinions in the International Fruit case, Advocate General Roemer stated: "[I]t is extremely doubtful that we are actually dealing with a regulation in the sense of the definitions that were so often given in previous decisions of the Court" (CCH COMM. MKT. REP. at 7635). *But see* Case 64/69 La Compagnie française, *supra* note 18. In that case, denying that a provision in a regulation was of individual concern to the plaintiff, the Court said: "Unless there is a misuse of discretionary power, such a provision shares in the general legal nature" of the regulation (CCH COMM. MKT. REP. at 8323).

35. *E.g.* Advocate General Roemer in Case 6/68, Zuckerfabrik Watenstedt v. Commission, *supra* note 18. It is, however, difficult to reconcile Mr. Roemer's own position in this and in the *Glucoseries* case 1/64, *supra* note 18, unless one concludes that the lapse of four years and the intervening experience with the system led him to change his mind.

36. *See* Stein, *Review of Europäisches Gemeinschaftsrecht by Hans Peter Ipsen* in 22 AM. J. COMP. L. 156 (1974).

37. Case 69/69, Alcan, *supra* note 18, CCH COMM. MKT. REP. at 7256.

38. M. Lagrange very likely had in mind the type of Council regulation comparable in substance if not in form to an act of Parliament which, according to the French conception of separation of powers, could not be made subject to judicial review.

39. In that case, the Court could also consider the legality of the Council regulation; if it found that the regulation infringed the Treaty, it would annul the decision, holding the underlying regulation inapplicable pursuant to Article 184.

40. It is, in any case, doubtful that the Court would want to adhere to its present narrow interpretation of "individual concern" should a private party contest a decision addressed not to a member state but to another private party, as is likely to occur particularly in the field of competition. *E.g.*, a Commission decision addressed to parties to a restrictive agreement which exempts the agreement from the Treaty prohibition and third parties (competitors) feel aggrieved by the decision. P. J. G. KAPTEYN and P. VERLOREN VAN THEMAAT, INTRODUCTION TO THE LAW OF THE EUROPEAN COMMUNITIES AFTER THE ACCESSION OF NEW MEMBER STATES at 169 (1973).

41. A. W. GREEN, POLITICAL INTEGRATION BY JURISPRUDENCE—THE WORK OF

THE COURT OF JUSTICE OF THE EUROPEAN COMMUNITIES IN EUROPEAN POLITICAL INTEGRATION 111 (1969).

42. Some of the Commission's extreme positions were criticized by the Advocates General. We were able to find only one case in which the Commission's counsel, having first taken a rather untenable position against standing on one of the two requirements, reversed himself in the course of the proceeding. Case 38/64, Getreide-Import Ges. v. Commission, *supra* note 18, Opinion, [1965] ECR at 211.

43. Kovar criticizes such potential "denial of justice," *supra* note 33, at 710.

44. The Advocate General buttressed this view by adding that:

> [t]his argument can only avail if the applicants first prove that the Treaty gives private individuals concerned a guarantee of direct and complete legal protection, for it clearly cannot fall within the powers of the Court of Justice to amend the Treaty on this point.

Case 40/64, Sgarlata *et al.* v. Commission, *supra* note 18, Opinion, [1965] ECR at 235.

45. In defining the reach of Article 173(2) the Court must have had in mind the long-range consequences in national legal systems if it ignored the principle underlying national constitutions that, in a system of power relationships based on law, an affected citizen must presumptively have some remedy against illegal official action. The German Federal Constitutional Court has ruled that at this stage of integration it retains power to review a Community act for compatibility with the Federal Constitution if it is claimed that the act violates a basic right protected by the Constitution. Decision of May 29, 1974, 37 BVerfGE 271 (1974).

46. Since, according to Article 177, only the court of last instance is *required* to refer the Community law questions to the Court of Justice, it may take years before the case reaches the highest national court. ULE (*supra* note 13, at 19–20, 22) considers this route "a difficult and prolonged detour." He suggests *(de lege ferenda)* a modification of Article 173(2) that would omit the requirement of direct and individual concern and allow standing to contest a decision addressed to another if the plaintiff's "legally protected interests" are affected. Thus the Treaty would conform to German administrative law which allows standing in case of impairment of a right as well as a legally protected interest. Ule cites J. H. Kaiser, Mailänder, and possibly Badura as supporting this suggestion. He cites Zweigert, Lagrange, Mathijsen, Catalano, and Ehle as urging replacement of the requirement of "direct and individual" or (Daig) of "individual" so as to broaden access to the Court. Zweigert, *Empfiehlt es sich, Bestimmungen über den Rechtsschutz zu ändern?* HAUPTREFERAT, ZEHN JAHRE RECHTSSPRECHUNG DES GERICHTSHOFS DER EUROPÄISCHEN GEMEINSCHAFTEN 580–97 (1965). *Rapport fait au nom de la Commission juridique sur la protection juridique des personnes privées dans les Communautés européennes,* Rap. M. A. Deringer, PARL. EUR. Doc. 39, 3 May 1967.

47. *Cf.* Case 25/62, Plaumann & Co. v. Commission, *supra* note 18, with Case

4/69, Alfons Lütticke GmbH v. Commission, 17 Rec. 325 (1971), CCH Comm. Mkt. Rep. ¶8136. *See also* Case 5/71, Aktien-Zuckerfabrik Schöppenstedt v. Council, 17 Rec. 975 (1971), CCH Comm. Mkt. Rep. ¶8153; Gilsdorf, *Die Haftung der Gemeinschaft aus normativem Handeln auf dem Hintergrund der Rechtssprechung des Europäischen Gerichtshofs,* 10 Europarecht 73 (1975).

48. Cases 19/62–22/62, Fédération Nationale v. Council, *supra* note 18, [1962] ECR at 486.

49. Case 6/68, Zuckerfabrik Watenstedt v. Council, *supra* note 18, [1968] ECR at 418; Cases 10 & 18/68, Società "Eridania" v. Commission, *supra* note 18, CCH Comm. Mkt. Rep. at 8431–34.

50. Case 175/73, Union Syndicale *et al.* v. Council, *supra* note 18, [1974] ECR at 930 (Opinion by Mr. Reischl); Case 18/74, Syndicat Général du Personnel des Organismes Européens v. Commission, *supra* note 18, [1974] ECR at 948 (Opinion by Mr. Trabucchi).

51. The German courts and the doctrine have mitigated the rigor of the language of the statute requiring that plaintiff be injured "in his rights." §42(2) Verwaltungsgerichtsordnung of Jan. 21, 1960. *See also infra,* text at note 60.

52. *See, e.g.,* CBS v. United States, 316 U.S. 407 (1942); Administrative Procedure Act, 5 U.S.C. §551(13), 7 U.S.C. §§702, 704, 706 (Supp. V, 1965–1969).

53. *Supra* text at note 24.

54. Marine Terminal v. Rederiaktiebolaget Transatlantic, 400 U.S. 62, 71 (1970); *see* Vining, *Direct Judicial Review and the Doctrine of Ripeness in Administrative Law,* 69 Mich. L. Rev. 1443 (1971).

55. *Supra* note 8.

56. Alabama Power Co. v. Ickes, 302 U.S. 464, 479 (1938).

57. Tennessee Electric Power Co. v. TVA, 306 U.S. 118, 137–38 (1939).

58. *See, e.g.,* Associated Industries v. Ickes, 134 F.2d 694 (2d Cir. 1943), *vacated as moot,* 320 U.S. 707 (1943).

59. *See, e.g.,* Hardin v. Kentucky Utilities, 390 U.S. 1 (1968).

60. *See supra* text at note 51. *See also* Ule *supra* note 13, at 21–22. Fromont believes, referring to the *Toepfer* case, that the Court of Justice in fact adopted the "subjective public right" test without saying so in so many words. Fromont, *L'influence du droit français et du droit allemand sur les conditions de recevabilité du recours en annulation devant la Cour de Justice des Communautés européennes,* 2 Rev. trim. dr. eur. 47, at 63 (1966). *See also* Fromont, *Der Rechtsschutz gegen Massnahmen der Verwaltung im Europa der Sechs,* 4 Europarecht 202 (1969).

61. Office of Communication of United Church of Christ v. F.C.C., 359 F.2d 994 (D.C. Cir. 1966).

62. Reade v. Ewing, 205 F.2d 630 (2d Cir. 1953).

63. Commissaire du gouvernement Mosset stated in his well-known conclusions that standing to institute judicial review of administrative action will be given if the contested decision "injures the plaintiff materially or morally" and if the consequences of the decision affect plaintiff in his capacity as a member of a "defined or limited category." C.E. 26 Oct. 1956, Association Générale des

administrateurs civils, R.D.P., 1956, 1309, *cited* in Fromont, *L'influence du droit . . . , supra* note 60, at 56.

64. The principal case was Association of Data Processing Service Organizations, Inc. v. Camp, 397 U.S. 150 (1970), described *supra* at note 2. *See also* Barlow v. Collins, 397 U.S. 159 (1970); Arnold Tours, Inc. v. Camp, 408 F.2d 1147, 1151 (1st Cir. 1969), *vacated* 397 U.S. 315 (1970), *reaffirmed* 428 F.2d 359 (1st Cir. 1970), *reversed* 400 U.S. 45 (1970).

65. Arnold Tours, Inc. v. Camp, *supra* note 64. Update: *See also* Clarke v. Securities Industry Assn., 479 U.S. 388 (1987).

66. Sierra Club v. Morton, 405 U.S. 727 (1972).

67. United States v. S.C.R.A.P., 412 U.S. 669 (1973).

68. The Court commented at the time and has emphasized since that rules of standing are developed by the Court "for its own governance." Data Processing Service Organizations, Inc. v. Camp, *supra* note 2, 397 U.S. at 154; Warth v. Seldin, 95 S. Ct. 2197, 2205, 2215 (1975). The Court had never required a statutory basis for its legal right test. In essence the Court shifted the judicial presumptions within which legislatures must work. Legislative materials are now searched for a specific intent to deny standing rather than a specific intent to grant it.

69. *See, e.g.,* Coalition for the Environment v. Volpe, 504 F.2d 156 (8th Cir. 1974); Diggs v. Schultz, 470 F.2d 461 (D.C. Cir. 1972), *cert. den.* 411 U.S. 931 (1973); Ballerina Pen Co. v. Kunzig, 433 F.2d 1204 (D.C. Cir. 1970).

70. *See, e.g.,* Jaffe, *The Citizen as Litigant in Public Actions: The Non-Hohfeldian or Ideological Plaintiff,* 116 U. PA. L. REV. 1033 (1968); SAX, DEFENDING THE ENVIRONMENT (1970).

71. *See, e.g.,* Warth v. Seldin, *supra* note 68; United States v. Richardson, 418 U.S., 166 (1974). Update: *See* Valley Forge Christian College v. Americans United for Separation of Church and State, 454 U.S. 464 (1982).

72. In addition, in one case following the announcement of the new formula three members of the Court turned again to a special standing statute using the term "aggrieved" to justify hearing the challenge of a white resident of a housing project to the legality of the housing agency's alleged exclusion of black applicants. The Justices did, however, concur in the majority decision to grant standing, which was based on general principles rather than any specific permission by the legislature. Trafficante v. Metropolitan Life Ins. Co., 409 U.S. 205 (1972).

73. *See, e.g.,* Linda R. S. v. Richard D., 410 U.S. 614 (1973); Sierra Club v. Morton, *supra* note 66.

74. Associated Industries v. Ickes, *supra* note 58. *See also* F.C.C. v. Sanders Bros. Radio Station, 309 U.S. 470 (1940); Association of Data Processing Service Organizations, Inc. v. Camp, *supra* note 2.

75. Sax and Dimento, *Environmental Citizen Suits: Three Years' Experience under the Michigan Environmental Protection Act,* 4 ECOLOGY L. Q. 1 (1974).

76. *See* Abbott Laboratories v. Gardner, 387 U.S. 136, 155 (1967). Although the Court of Justice has made full use of the consolidation procedures, most recently it has defined the standing to sue of associations so as to cause numerous

separate actions to be filed by individual association members instead of a single action by the association itself. Case 18/74, Syndicat Général du Personnel des Organismes Européens v. Commission, *supra* note 18. *See* Cases 44, 46 & 49/74, Marie-Louise Acton *et al.* v. Commission, and Case 72/74, Union Syndicale *et al.* v. Council, *supra* note 18. The Court held, with the support of the Advocate General, that although an association has a general capacity to appear in court as a "legal person," and may also participate as an intervenor, it cannot sue for annulment in its own name unless it can show that it was aggrieved in its own functional rights (*e.g.*, violation of its contract with the public agency) or upon an express "mandate" from the aggrieved members.

77. Update: Since the completion of this essay, the Court of Justice has broadened somewhat the access of individuals according to Art. 173(2) (now Art. 173(4)). *See e.g.*, Case 75/84, Metro SB-Grossmärkte GmbH & Co. KG v. Commission [No. 2], [1986] ECR 3021 *(competition);* Case 264/82, Timex Corporation v. Council and Commission, [1985] ECR 849 *(antidumping);* Case T-3/93, Société Anonyme à Participation Ouvrière Compagnie Nationale Air France v. Commission, Judgment of the Court of First Instance, Mar. 24, 1994, [1994] ECR II-121 *(merger control);* Case 358/89, Extramet Industrie SA v. Council, [1991] ECR I-2501, with an interesting discussion by the Advocate General Francis Jacobs *(antidumping);* Case 191/82, EEC Seed Crushers' and Oil Processors' Federation (Fediol) v. Commission, [1983] ECR 2913 *(countervailing duties);* Case 169/84, Compagnie française de l'azote (Cofaz) SA and Others v. Commission, [1986] ECR 291 *(state subsidy);* Case 11/82, A. E. Piraiki-Patraiki and Others v. Commission, [1985] ECR 207 *(protective measures);* Case 294/83, Parti écologiste "Les Verts" v. European Parliament, [1986] ECR 1339 *(European parliament group standing on budget expenditure for elections);* also 309/89, Codorniu SA v. Council, [1994] ECR I-1853 *(discrimination).*

For developments in the United States, *see* Clarke v. Securities Industries Association, 479 U.S. 388 (1987) *(interpretation of congressional intent);* Allen v. Wright, 468 U.S. 737 (1984) *(the definition of causation);* Lujan v. Defenders of Wildlife, 497 U.S. 871 (1990) *(the definition of injury).*

Towards a European Foreign Policy? The European Foreign Affairs System from the Perspective of the United States Constitution with Excerpts from *External Relations of the European Community: Structure and Process*

For anyone who like myself grew up in Europe, the world beyond frontiers intruded into private destinies in ways unfathomable to most Americans. For this, if for no other reason, foreign affairs have been from the

---

With the exception noted below, this text is reprinted from my article "European and U.S. Foreign Affairs Systems Compared," in Mauro Cappelleti, Monica Seccombe, and Joseph Weiler (eds.), Integration through Law: Europe and the American Federal Experience, vol. 1, Methods, Tools and Institutions, bk. 3, Forces and Potential for European Identity 3–82 (in collaboration with Louis Henkin) (Berlin, New York, Walter de Gruyter, 1986). Reprinted by permission. I am indebted to Professor Louis Henkin of Columbia University Law School for his invaluable advice. I also appreciate greatly the assistance of Mr. Hermann da Fonseca-Wollheim, Deputy Head of the Commission of the EC, Washington, D.C., and Mr. Per Lachmann. Chief Legal Advisor on Common Market Law, Ministry of Foreign Affairs, Copenhagen, Denmark, visiting scholar, University of Michigan Law School.

While preparing "European and U.S. Foreign Affairs Systems Compared," I received helpful comments from Dr. C.-D. Ehlermann, Director General, Legal Service of the Commission of the EC, and from Mr. J. Bourgeois of his staff; from Professor H. G. Schermers of Leiden University, the Netherlands; and from the participants in the conference held at the European University Institute, Florence, Italy, in December 1981. Herbert Glaser, Philippe Jambrun, Jeffrey Lehman, Jacqueline Letzler-Kuster, Paul van Leeuwen, Mitri Najjar, and Yves Quintin, students at the University Law School, assisted me in the research. However, I alone am responsible for the opinions expressed in that article.

I completed the final draft of "European and U.S. Foreign Affairs Systems Compared" at the Max-Planck Institut für ausländisches öffentliches Recht und Völkerrecht in Heidelberg, with the support of the Alexander von Humboldt Stiftung, which is gratefully acknowledged.

The material on pp. 223–25, 227–31, 234–36, 238–42, and 245 contains excerpts from my lectures delivered to the Academy of European Law in Fiesole and published in Academy of European Law (ed.), Collected Courses of the Academy of European Law, vol. 1, book 1, 111–88, pp. 151–56, 161–62, 164–68, 171–77, and 179.

outset a natural area of my concern, and they have become the center of my professional interest.

Foreign affairs, or "external relations," of the European Community impressed me as the most absorbing aspect of Community study, since it reveals a cubistlike perspective of both the internal and external scaffolding of the complex process that is the Community. The growing role of the Community in international fora and the mostly benign, but at times adversarial, relationship with the United States have added a pragmatic incentive.

In 1979 Professor Mauro Cappelletti, then at the University of Florence, invited me to provide a foreign affairs dimension for an ambitious joint European-American project on methods of integration, centered at the European University Institute in Fiesole. I was glad to accept, particularly since my friend of long standing, Professor Louis Henkin of the Columbia University Law School, agreed on a common effort. Henkin, with his Foreign Affairs and the Constitution (*now in a second edition as* Foreign Affairs and United States Constitution [*Oxford, Clarendon, 1996*]), *pioneered a new discipline in American constitutional law.*

The Cappelletti-Seccombe-Weiler project resulted in a multivolume collection of comparative studies ranging from political theory, institutions, factors of production, and economic policy to company law, private international law, protection of consumers and the environment, and basic human rights. Our piece was included in the part entitled Forces and Potential for a European Identity, *and it forms the first item in this chapter. It brings out the differences and the similarities in the structure of the foreign affairs establishment and the foreign policy process in the U.S. and the European systems. The comparison yields interesting insights in the area of foreign trade and related policies; it becomes problematic because of the systemic differences when it extends to foreign political, security, and defense policies.*

Our essay is complemented by excerpts from my lectures delivered in 1990 at the opening session of the Academy of European Law in Fiesole and published in the collected Courses of the Academy of European Law. *I used the ideas in teaching as a Jean Monnet Professor at the European University Institute, at the College of Europe in Bruges, and at the University of Michigan, as well as in my talks in Germany, Spain, the Netherlands, Japan, and China.*

The next essay appeared as an editorial in the Common Market Law Review. *It raises the question that has occupied me for some time: in the face of economic globalization, as the line between domestic and foreign concerns becomes increasingly blurred within modern states, does the historically based sharp distinction in the ways and means for managing domestic and foreign policies still serve its purpose? The problem acquires an additional dimension in Europe. The protofederal "constitutional" system is encrusted with confederal or consociational elements that enable the national governments to control collectively policy and lawmaking in the Community institutions. Moreover—and this is in strong contrast to the U.S. Constitution—although the member states have transferred to the Community powers in vital domestic sectors and foreign trade policy, they have refused to do so with respect to other aspects of foreign relations, thus accentuating the division between domestic and foreign affairs. As I mentioned in the introduction to the second essay in Part 2 ("Excerpt from* Courts and Free Markets—Perspectives from the United States and Europe"*) the second "pillar" of the European Union embraces "common foreign and security policy." As was its predecessor, the "European Political Cooperation," described in some detail within this chapter, it remains based on intergovernmental cooperation outside the Community discipline and the Community Court's authority. The Amsterdam Treaty of 1997 failed to "communitize" the common foreign and security policy, but it did set out for the first time a decisional structure for cooperation in that policy. Thus although the member governments singing in a choir may still use different songbooks, they now have at least a common tuning fork (Gerard Meehan).*

I have several more specific observations. First, with one exception, the Court of Justice has maintained generally its initial activist, "broad constructionist" attitude despite the turnover in its membership (there has been no Taney Court to follow the Marshall Court) although, with the dramatic increase in Community legislation, there has been much less need for the Court to fill in the gaps. Only in the foreign affairs field did the Court clip the wings of its early, broad, implied powers doctrine, the aspect of its jurisprudence most criticized by the "strict constructionists." It has consistently refused to review in any context the compatibility of Community's and member states' measures with GATT agreements, leaving it to diplomats to cope with the problems. And the Court ruled, contrary to the Commission's claim, that the conclusion of the World Trade Organization Agreements was not within the exclusive treaty power of the Community and that the member states must join as parties.

Second, in the text that follows I took a somewhat pessimistic view of the chances for a European common currency, the "Euro." In fact, ever since the idea was first advanced, I could not believe that its time had come. I am still astonished that at the present stage of integration the member states would abandon, as the German journalist Josef Joffe put it, the power to mint money and the power to regulate its quantity as well as its price at home (the interest rate) and abroad (the foreign exchange rate);

that they would transfer the control over these essential instrumentalities of national policy to a European Central Bank, a body presumably insulated from the normal political process and modeled after the German Bundesbank, which in turn was modeled after the American Federal Reserve Bank; and that they would take this unprecedented step without conferring on the Community institutions the authority to determine the budgetary, tax, and social policies that are linked inextricably with monetary policy decisions. Yet all that is precisely what the members pledged themselves to do in the Maastricht Treaty of 1992. In fact, it appears that a "Euro club" of some eleven of the fifteen members will be in place even before the end of the millennium.

Third, at this writing the United States has joined the world and become a party, albeit with heavy reservations, to most of the human rights treaties listed in this chapter as languishing in the Senate. However, the president in making a treaty, and the Senate in consenting to it, has assumed unilateral authority (as to any treaty) to declare the treaty non-self-executing in the domestic legal order, a posture adopted also by the Community Council when concluding the WTO agreements on behalf of the Community. Such lack of concern for a treaty as an act under international law does not advance the rule of law in the international system. Henkin opines that behind the practice in the United States may lurk the ideological resistance to lawmaking by treaty, at least in the eminently domestic human rights matters.

I. Introduction

A. Purpose of the Study

This study will describe the constitutional and institutional arrangements for the conduct of foreign relations in the United States and in the Europe of the Ten, identifying the differences and their consequences. It will consider what features of the United States system and experience were important in achieving a unified, national posture in foreign affairs and it will explore whether, despite the crucial differences, the federal experience may offer helpful insights to European decision-makers. Consideration will be given to the trends affecting the institutions of the European Community and the European Political Cooperation mechanism which militate for or against Europe speaking with a single voice in the international arena.

This introductory part will set forth definitions of the basic concepts and the pattern for analysis employed in the study, and it will highlight the salient differences between the foreign affairs structures in the United States and in the Europe of the Ten.

B. The "Foreign Affairs Powers": A Definition and a Pattern for Analysis

States, the classic "persons" in international law, wield the full panoply of foreign affairs powers. International organizations may also have an "international personality" and possess certain foreign affairs powers. Federal states and international organizations are archetypes of divided power systems. We are concerned with the scope and modalities of foreign affairs powers in two divided power systems, a federal state and the Community, a *sui generis* divided power system (a "new legal order in international law"[1]), placed on a continuum somewhere between a traditional inter-governmental organization and a federal state, exercising more extensive foreign affairs powers than any other international organization.

1. States: Foreign Affairs Powers

In the international political system, the government of a state has the following principal capacities, rights and duties: (a) to communicate with other governments (and other "persons" in international law) through a variety of formal and informal means ("diplomacy," active and passive right of legation); (b) to determine national policies affecting other states (authority within the territory and maritime and air space, foreign economic policy, security and defense policy, communication and transportation, regulation of aliens, or of nationals abroad); (c) to make treaties and participate in the formation of customary international law and to participate in international organizations; (d) to carry out obligations under international law and agreements, and to pursue remedies for violations of obligations by others; and to extend diplomatic protection and advance international claims on behalf of its nationals and to respond to international claims.[2]

2. International Organizations

Pursuant to different theories, international organizations have: (a) only such "personality," capacity, rights and duties in the international system as are specifically attributed in their charter; (b) all such powers as are needed to achieve the charter purposes as determined by the appropriate interpretation of the charter; (c) certain "inherent" powers, not necessarily derived from the charter but recognized by international law as applicable to international organizations generally.[3]

3. Divided Power Systems: Allocation of Powers

In divided power systems all powers are allocated between the composite entity and its component parts. The allocation is grounded in the constitutive documents which may take the form of a constitution or a treaty. As a treaty-based system becomes more intimately integrated, important questions arise whether the provisions relating to the allocation of powers are to be interpreted in accordance with international institutional law or in a constitutional mode, germane to internal public law.

In divided power systems, two principles of allocation of powers may be examined: (a) allocation between the central authority and the component units; and (b) allocation between the institutions of the central authority (in a federation: legislative, executive, judiciary; in the Community: inter-governmental law-and-policy-making, executive, judiciary, parliament).[4]

The allocations vary over time. Tension may develop, due either to power competition or disagreement on the merit of an action, either between the central authority and the component units (problems of "federalism"); or, between the institutions of the central authority itself (problems of "separation of powers," "checks and balances").

Allocation apart, there may be limitations on the government's exercise of power in foreign relations because some powers are in principle withheld by the constitution or charter or because general limitations on delegated authority exist, for instance the limitations embodied in a "Bill of Rights" or based on general principles for the protection of human rights.

4. Foreign Affairs Powers and Foreign Policy

Effective foreign policy postulates a communications network assuring a flow of information, establishing and reviewing objectives on a hierarchic scale of priorities, strategic planning of action and implementation through diplomacy and through foreign economic, financial, cultural, and military instrumentalities. In modern pluralist systems, the process is "democratized" with parliamentary bodies, political parties and cultural-scientific-special interest groups claiming greater voice. In particular, even where the component states as such are excluded from any *participation* in foreign policy process, they may *impinge* on the process. Moreover, foreign affairs cannot be separated from domestic affairs: above all in economic life, they are inseparably mixed.[5]

C. United States and European Systems Contrasted: The Relevance of a Comparison

Despite basic systemic and contextual differences, comparison in certain "internal" fields (*e.g.*, interstate commerce in the United States and free movement of goods within the EEC) has clearly proved of interest to both Americans and Europeans.[6] However, in the foreign affairs field the institutional differences are even more pronounced so as to raise the question whether a comparison can be meaningful.

1. Some Differences

a) Unitary Authority v. Divided Power

With respect to foreign affairs the United States is, in effect, a unitary state with exclusive federal foreign affairs power, a national diplomatic establishment and a national army. Under the United States Constitution, the component states are excluded from participation in foreign affairs but their activities and laws often impinge on federal policy and activities.[7] In the Community, on the other hand, there is a complex division of foreign affairs powers between the Member States and the Community institutions. The Member States remain sovereign nation-states, they retain full control of their armies, defense policies and foreign "political" policies (subject to an extra-Community consultative mechanism, the European Political Cooperation).[8] In the economic and monetary fields, the Members share their authority with the Community. However, even in the areas within the exclusive power of the Community, the Member States, unlike the American states, *participate* in the policy-making as a result of their role in the central Community organ, the Council of Ministers.

The foreign affairs power of the Federal Government in the United States has been exclusive of the states since its inception by virtue first of the Articles of Confederation and then of the Constitution. The President and the Congress have been the primary actors and whatever constitutional controversy there has been has related to allocation between President and Congress, not between federal and state authority. "Federalism," on the whole, has not been an issue in foreign relations. In general, any controversy between states of the Union about the foreign policy of the United States has centered on the content of the policy, *e.g.*

free trade or protectionism, rather than on its constitutional underpinning, although the arguments have sometimes been dressed in a constitutional mode. In comparison with "domestic" constitutional law, the changes in foreign relations constitutional law have not been radical. The courts have not played a crucial role in foreign affairs law, and scholars, accustomed to dealing principally in case law, have neglected the field.[9]

Allocation of power within the Community generally continues to evolve. The Community foreign affairs power, too, has been subject to evolution, since the Community itself is conceived as a *dynamic* progression. The Community institutions are expected to assume new powers as economic and political integration advances. As a result, the "federalism" issue—the tension between Member States ("assembled in the Council of Ministers")[10] and the Community (represented by the independent executive Commission)—has been at the center of the foreign relations debate, and the Court of Justice has performed the task of umpire. In contrast with the United States, the case law of the Court of Justice is essential and legal literature is more than abundant. The Community's "parliamentary" organ, the European Parliament, on the other hand, has played but a limited advisory role, although, particularly since it has been chosen by direct election, it has been increasingly vocal in demanding more meaningful participation in foreign affairs.

b) *Relations among Constituent States*

In the United States, relations among the states of the Union are "internal" relations and they are governed exclusively by "domestic" (principally constitutional and federal) law.[11] In the Community, major sectors of relations among Member States are not governed by Community law, but continue to be determined by international law or appropriate Member State Law.

c) *Citizenship*

In the United States, the Constitution itself provided the foundation for a single national citizenship and federal control of immigration. Federal citizenship is primary, state citizenship is of minor importance and of none in foreign affairs. A citizen of the United States is ipso facto citizen of the state of his domicile.[12]

In Europe, however, there is no Community citizenship,[13] only Member State citizenship, and each state retains its own alien control regime, subject only to the Treaty rights of Member State nationals to move freely within the Community for specific economic purposes. By a special agreement the Benelux countries maintain a common control over aliens.

2. The Relevance of a Comparison

Considering these vital differences, one may ask whether a comparison may be useful only for highlighting and better comprehending the characteristics of each system, or whether the federal experience and method may also be relevant for the European decision-makers. The question is particularly appropriate in view of the different methods employed by American federalism in domestic and foreign affairs. In the domestic field states continue to have considerable scope in pursuing their domestic policies but no such suppleness and flexibility exist in dealing with foreign nations.

Pescatore rightly rejects any effort to attribute any specific foreign relations power to the Community by analogy with the powers of a nation-state, unitary or federal; he is nevertheless convinced that "federalist interpretation of the European Treaties is particularly fruitful; . . . it is really in the thought, in the methods and in the historical experience of federalism that the future builders of Europe should seek their inspiration, much more than in the domain of international relations."[14]

II. The Formal Allocation of Powers in the United States and in the European Community

A. The Impact of Foreign Affairs Concerns on the Allocation of Powers in Both Systems

"Foreign affairs" played an important role at the inception of the American Republic and of the Community: both emerged from a war which loosened the established order and called for innovating structures. The necessity of presenting a united front to the rest of the world has had far-reaching implications for both. However, interesting as this juxtaposition may be, the egregious contextual differences call into question any facile comparison.

1. Post-Revolution America

In America, it was the 1776 War of Independence that severed the centralizing tie between the colonies and their mother country, Britain. Under the "Articles of Confederation and Perpetual Union" the foreign affairs powers were vested in "the United States, in Congress assembled" with each of the thirteen states wielding one vote; major foreign affairs issues were to be decided by a majority of nine of the thirteen votes.[15] There was no provision for an executive. Despite the decisive contextual differences, the analogy in institutional terms between "the United States, in Congress assembled," and the ten Member States of the Community, "assembled" in the EC Council of Ministers (and deciding in effect by consensus) is tempting, but the existence of the executive Commission, and its role in foreign affairs, bear testimony that in this respect the Community is more effectively organized than was the Confederation.

The inadequacies of the Confederation for coping with foreign affairs supplied a significant impulse for the federal Constitution. In the first place, the proceeding whereby Congress conducted diplomacy and negotiated treaties through its agents "suffered from the want of secrecy and dispatch"[16] so as to seriously impair the international position of the young republic. The efforts to build up the office of the Congress' secretary for foreign affairs from that of a glorified clerk met with only a qualified success due to Congress' jurisdictional jealousy.[17] One is reminded of the checkered history of the attempts—thus far similarly unsuccessful—to establish a permanent secretariat for the European Political Cooperation mechanism.[18] While confederate diplomatic activity lagged, contrary to specific prohibitions in the Articles individual states engaged in diplomatic negotiations with foreign nations, concluded agreements, outfitted their own armies and navies, imposed embargoes, engaged in war with the Indians and formed compacts with each other.[19] The Congress' lack of independent power to raise troops and impose taxes for their support resulted in the nation being forced to endure incursions on its territorial sovereignty.[20] The chaotic situation which undermined the credibility of the Confederation was compounded by the inability of the Congress to force recalcitrant states into compliance with treaties concluded by the Congress with European nations.[21] The lack of power in the Congress to regulate foreign commerce[22] made effective trade negotiations impossible, and when the British imposed an embargo on the crucial American trade in the West Indies, the Congress was in no position to retaliate. The young Republic was frustrated in its attempts to establish a "new international economic order" based on equitable commercial relations.[23]

The prominence of foreign relations concerns in the Constitutional Convention and in the subsequent ratification debates confirms the influence the external environment exerted toward a radical reshaping of the central government in the federal pattern.

2. Post-War Europe

In Europe, the upheaval caused by "the greatest civil war in history" loosened the traditional attachments to state sovereignty enough to allow for a modest transfer of power in pursuance of the Monnet model of progressive integration by sectors.[24] In 1951, the Community, in its first incarnation, became reality in the coal and steel sector because, at a critical moment, it offered an urgently needed solution for dealing with the defeated Germany.[25] The inexorable American pressure for German rearmament arising from the Korean War forced the temporary abandonment of Monnet's priority for integration in the economic and monetary sectors and brought forth, in the early 1950's, the abortive draft for the European Defense Community, with the concomitant European Political Community.[26] "I have never believed," wrote Monnet, "that we should tackle the problem of Europe via defense. Although this would no doubt be one task for the future federation, it seemed to me by no means the most powerful or compelling motive for unity. . . . [W]e were forced to take short cuts."[27]

It is illuminating for an understanding of the European Political Cooperation mechanism as it has developed since 1969 that, although the Defense Community had envisaged an integration of armed forces and military budgets and other steps toward a federal structure, the Political Community did not call for additional transfer of national powers; a common foreign policy was to evolve through coordination of national policies by the member states.[28] In 1954, the two schemes (both of which were of French origin, as was the European Coal and Steel Community) fell victim to a change of the French Government and its reversion to the policy of a "French Europe." As a result, instead of a European controlled army, France had to accept the most dreaded of alternatives, the reconstitution of a German national army in a "feebly coordinated structure" of a military alliance.[29] This marked the end of the attempt to create a European army as an instrument of a common foreign policy and defense.

With France having lost the initiative, it was left to Belgian and Dutch statesmen to restore the sectoral integration process on the basis of Monnet's priorities. The result was the European Economic Community and the Euratom Treaties. It is difficult to identify or to measure the weight of the discrete variables motivating a major historic movement but it is probably accurate to say that foreign affairs concerns played a less prominent role in the impulse toward these two treaties than was the case with the ECSC.[30] However, the Suez Canal imbroglio may have eased the passage of the Rome Treaties through national parliaments.[31]

Moreover, it is beyond question that particularly during the early history, the perceived threat from the East and American power in the West favored significantly the integration process.[32] Generally, the Community's foreign relations have developed to a great extent in response to outside pressures and demands.[33] In responding to these outside stimuli the Commission has often acted not only in the interest of Community foreign policy but also in furtherance of its own authority and of the integrity of the Community's independent personality.

B. The Allocation of Powers in the Constituent Documents

Unlike some modern national constitutions[34] neither the United States Constitution nor the Community Treaties allocate in bulk "power to conduct foreign relations." Instead, on their face they adopt the pattern of "enumerated powers" or "*compétence d'attribution*" by attributing specific powers to particular central authorities. More specifically, in the Constitution provisions scattered in three articles vest certain powers in Congress, others in the President (alone or jointly with the Senate),[35] and in one article states are expressly denied a role in the important aspects of foreign affairs.[36] The Constitution is silent on many other foreign affairs powers. Similarly, the Treaties contain attributions to the Commission and the Council of specific powers in a series of articles[37] but, in contrast with the Constitution, there is no express denial of a Member States' role in foreign affairs. However, the argument that the absence alone of such denial preserved Member State power has been rejected by the Court of Justice.[38] It is left to the central authorities to deal with the "silences and gaps" in the constitutive instrument.

1. Specific Attributions of Foreign Affairs Powers—An Overview

a) In the United States Constitution

As mentioned earlier,[39] the dissatisfaction with making war and conducting diplomacy by the collective "United States, in Congress assembled," was a major impetus for the decision to convene the Constitutional Convention and seek a "more perfect union." The same painful experience impelled the Founders to create the office of President and vest it with "executive powers." The sparse clauses in the Constitution pertaining to his role in foreign affairs (shared in some instances by the Senate) provide:

Article II:

Section 2. 1. The President shall be commander-in-chief of the army and navy of the United States, and of the militia of the several States, when called into the actual service of the United States. . . .

2. He shall have power, by and with the advice and consent of the Senate, to make treaties, provided two thirds of the senators present concur; and he shall nominate, and by and with the advice and consent of the Senate, shall appoint ambassadors, other public ministers and consuls. . . .

3. The President shall have power to fill up all vacancies that may happen during the recess of the Senate, by granting commissions which shall expire at the end of their next session.

Section 3. . . . [H]e shall receive ambassadors and other public ministers; he shall take care that the laws be faithfully executed, and shall commission all the officers of the United States.[40]

However, on the face of the Constitution at any rate, the principal policy powers in foreign (as in domestic) affairs were assigned to Congress. Article I, section 8 provides in pertinent part:

The Congress shall have the power

1. To lay and collect taxes, duties, imposts, and excises, to pay the debts and provide for the common defense and general welfare of the United States. . . .

   . . .

3. To regulate commerce with foreign nations. . . .
4. To establish an uniform rule of naturalization. . . .

   . . .

10. To define and punish piracies and felonies committed on the high seas, and offenses against the law of nations;
11. To declare war, grant letters of marque and reprisal, and make rules concerning captures on land and water;
12. To raise and support armies, but no appropriation of money to that use shall be for a longer term than two years;
13. To provide and maintain a navy. . . .

    . . .

18. To make all laws which shall be necessary and proper for carrying into execution the foregoing powers, and all other powers vested by this Constitution in the government of the United States, or any department or officer thereof.

There is, as I have already suggested, more to foreign affairs than can be accounted for by the laconic allocations of the Constitution. Although Congress' enumerated grants are much more generous—since they include "all legislative powers," war power, the power of the purse and regulation of commerce—powers not expressly delegated in the Constitution have largely flowed to the President who has become the predominant actor in foreign affairs. The President and Congress share the *total* and *exclusive* foreign affairs power of the United States but the distribution between them corresponds only in some measure to the classic separation of legislative from executive functions in domestic affairs. The competition for power between the two branches has constituted "the dominant, least-tractable constitutional issue of American foreign relations."[41]

b) In the EEC Treaty

The specific attributions of foreign affairs powers to the Community center on foreign commercial policy which is implemented through "autonomous" Community acts, international agreements and interaction with international organizations. Except perhaps for the power to enact common commercial policy there are no general grants such as we encountered in the Constitution.

The attributed powers are shared between the independent Commission, "the conscience of the Community," and the "Member States assembled in Council," with the Council holding the preponderant authority of final decision. In specified instances, (but not, for example, in the important tariff and trade negotiations) the European Parliament must be consulted, but its opinions are advisory only and its budgetary power is very limited. The traditional structure of three separate and equal branches—the executive, legislative and judicial—obviously has no application in the foreign affairs area any more than in the domestic affairs.

The Commission is given the exclusive right of initiative which, with respect to "autonomous acts," such as modifications of the Common Customs Tariff, it exercises by making a formal proposal to the Council; the Council cannot act without such proposal and cannot modify it except by a unanimous vote.[42] However, in the process of making commercial agreements the Commission can only recommend opening the negotiations but it alone negotiates under the direction of the Council which in turn "concludes" the resulting agreement.[43]

Outside the commercial policy chapter, the Treaty part dealing with general and final provisions is headed by article 210 which affirms the Community's "legal personality."[44] Other provisions lay down the general treaty-making procedure;[45] authorize the Community to enter into agreements of "association" of an undetermined content with third countries or international bodies;[46] direct the Commission to enter into appropriate relationships with specified international organizations;[47] and regulate the conditions of accession to Community membership of "any European State" which may apply.[48]

In the United States, where the monopoly in foreign affairs of the Federal Government has been accepted from the inception, the courts were left with the task of inventing a plausible doctrine.[49] In Europe, although the Commission with the Council are called upon in the first instance to draw a line between the Member State and Community foreign affairs powers, the complex and controversial task of fashioning a coherent doctrine from the handful of Treaty attributions fell to the Court of Justice.

2. Methodology of Constituent Documents — Interpretation

a) Gaps in the United States Constitution and How They Are Filled

In the United States, no explanation of the lacunae and no interpretive method for filling them have been universally accepted, but under all the doctrines, foreign affairs remain exclusively federal.[50] Henkin lists several attempts to fill the missing powers by traditional methods of constitutional interpretation and construction:

> Traditional interpreters of the Constitution have attempted to find the missing powers by traditional doctrines of constitutional construction. Foreign affairs powers expressly granted have been held to imply others: for example, the power to make treaties implies the power to terminate or break them. And some powers taken together have been found to "result" in others: for example, the power to appoint ambassadors and the power to receive foreign ambassadors "result" in the power to do other things involved in maintaining relations with a foreign country. Foreign affairs powers . . . have been spun also from general grants of power and from designations read as grants, for example, the power of Congress to do what is "necessary and proper" to carry out other powers (Art. I, sec. 8), or the provision vesting in the President "the executive Power" (Art. II, sec. 1). Additional powers for the federal government might be inferred from their express denial to the States.[51]

Neither these methods nor the extrapolation from "the Constitution as a whole," while serving their purpose in specific instances, have been accepted as sufficient and exclusive. In 1889, in the *Chinese Exclusion Case,*[52] the Supreme Court embraced a more radical interpretation, when it held that in addition to the enumerated powers and their derivatives, the Constitution vests in the Federal Government powers inherent in the United States as an independent and sovereign state.[53] But it did not explain where in the Constitution one can find such a grant and how it can be justified in the face of the Tenth Amendment which lays down the rule of "enumerated powers," namely that powers not delegated to the Federal Government are reserved to the states.[54] Finally, in the celebrated *Curtiss-Wright* case,[55] decided in 1936, the Court concluded that the federal foreign affairs powers do not depend on the Constitution (or on the Constitution alone) but are inherent in the national "external sovereignty." Although some of these powers are mentioned in the Constitution, they—unlike federal domestic powers—are not reserved to the states if not enumerated. Instead one must look to international law and practice to determine their full array.[56] Thus, the status of the United States as a subject of international law (its "international personality") determines not only the scope and reach of its inherent foreign affairs powers in relation to other nations but also—and this is the remarkable implication of Justice Sutherland's doctrine—the allocation of all these powers to the federal authorities to the exclusion of the states. One is reminded in this context of the ambiguous reference by the Court of Justice to "the international personality" of the Community as a source of its "capacity" in international relations.[57]

Justice Sutherland supported his doctrine by a historical argument. The thirteen American colonies, he argued, upon independence became a sovereign nation, the "external sovereignty" passing directly from the Crown not to the colonies severally but to them "in their collective and corporate capacity as the United States of America." Powers of "internal sovereignty," however, remained in the individual states. Even before the Declaration of Independence the Continental Congress exercised the power of war and peace, and thereafter foreign affairs powers were assumed by the Confederation as the "sole possessor of external sovereignty" and subsequently under the Constitution they passed to the Federal Government.[58] Yet in contrast to this view of history, there is evidence that after the Declaration of Independence at least some of the former colonies considered themselves sovereign states and even under the Articles of Confederation it is not entirely clear whether "the United States, in Congress assembled" were a sovereign state rather than a league of states in Vattel's sense, acting together through the agency of the Congress.[59] Justice Sutherland's historical perception by no means goes unchallenged[60] but it has received considerable support.[61] The *Curtiss-Wright* opinion has been cited with approval in later cases and has never been rejected by the Supreme Court. However, subsequent cases discreetly avoid specific reference to Sutherland's "extra-Constitutional underpinning"[62] and the courts usually appear satisfied with inferring the federal power from the explicit or implied powers of the President or Congress.

The sharp distinction between the limitations on domestic and foreign affairs power which is at the core of the *Curtiss-Wright* doctrine has lost most of its practical cogency after the mid-1930's, as a result of the dramatic expansion of the Federal Government's domestic powers, particularly under the broad construction of the Commerce Clause.[63] Although the Supreme Court continues to pay lip-service to the theory of enumerated powers, its decisions since 1937 in practical effect sanction virtually plenary Congressional authority in the domestic economic sphere and nearly plenary authority beyond that sphere.[64] Subject to a few thus far isolated exceptions in the domestic area, the Constitution "has largely ceased to limit powers delegated to the Federal Government in domestic as in foreign affairs and federalism, as a limitation on national power, survives only by grace of the Federal Government and the political forces it reflects."[65] Thus the limitations on the Federal Government's powers in the foreign as in the domestic fields are generally determined not on the basis of the Tenth Amendment but by reference to specific prohibitions in the Constitution, particularly the Bill of Rights or implied prohibitions derived from the fundamental nature of the governmental structure established by the Constitution. However, despite the removal of the "federalism" issue as the ground for constitutional controversy, tension in foreign affairs continues because of the contest for power and disagreement over policy between the legislative and executive branches of the Federal Government itself.

b) Gaps in the Community Treaties and How They Are Filled

In sharp contrast with the situation in the United States, there can be no dispute over the continuing "external sovereignty" of the Member States of the Community, considering their exclusive power over their respective armies and national defense and foreign policies; only in the foreign economic sphere where the Members share their powers with the Community does the "federalism" issue of power allocation arise. In that sphere the Court of Justice was asked – not unlike the American Supreme Court in a comparable situation—to rule whether the Community had the authority to exercise specific foreign affairs powers which were not expressly listed among its "enumerated powers."

Early in its history, when faced with the question of the limitations on the Community power in the *domestic* economic field, the Court of Justice applied the traditional implied powers doctrine according to which international treaty norms "imply those norms without which the first mentioned norms make no sense or could not be applied in a reasonable and useful manner."[66] Subsequently it broadened the formula by adding the teleological concept of "*effet utile*" and the more elaborate articulation looking to "the spirit, general scheme and the wording of the Treaty" *(esprit, économie, texte).*[67] It was primarily the last mentioned interpretive device on which the Court relied in the landmark *ERTA* case[68] to reach a remarkable conclusion that would do away for all practical purposes with the "enumerated powers" principle as applied to foreign affairs. The Community foreign affairs power, the Court held, does not depend on the limited specific Treaty attributions but may be found in the general provisions as viewed in the over-all Treaty system. Thus, the Community has the power to enter into international agreements with third countries on any matter which falls within its internal competence if such agreement is necessary for the achievement of a Community objective.[69] As in the United States, the need for the Member States to speak with a single voice in international economic relations has been held to require a broad Community power.

To buttress its novel doctrine, the Court referred to the "international personality" of the Community which it found emplanted in article 210.[70] It interpreted the article to mean that "in its external relations the Community enjoys the capacity to establish contractual [*i.e.* treaty] links with third countries over the whole field of objectives defined" in the Treaty part on "Principles" and in its general and final provisions.[71] If the Court meant to say that the Community may derive foreign affairs powers from its status as a person in international law it would have—*mutatis mutandis*—applied to the Community the Supreme Court's rationale in the *Chinese Exclusion Case,* if not in the *Curtiss-Wright* case.[72] It is more likely, however, that the *ERTA* Court had in mind simply buttressing its broad systemic construction of the Treaty and rejecting the fanciful doctrine that only states—and not international organizations or groupings—can possess an international personality,[73] and that in particular the Community itself, being devoid of any functional personality, is nothing more than an agency, "a common organ in the hands of States."[74] "This theoretical construction," observed extra-judicially one of the judges who participated in the *ERTA* case, "expresses quite realistically the attitude taken in practice by some Member States who tend to consider the Community as a convenient tool for furthering their interest in some respect, but who at the same time would reserve the possibility of resuming at will their own prerogatives whenever it fits their national interests."[75]

It deserves particular attention that the *ERTA* Court went out of the way to declare (in what may be viewed as a dictum) that the "necessary and proper" powers provision in article 235 of the EEC Treaty applied not only to domestic powers but to foreign affairs powers as well.[76] In fact, the Council has invoked the article as a supplementary authority when enacting certain regulations concerning foreign commerce[77] and as an exclusive source in concluding treaties dealing with objectives not specifically included among the objectives enumerated in the Treaty such as the protection of the environment.[78]

In domestic affairs, the Court of Justice, without specifically rejecting the "enumerated powers" doctrine, has also employed the teleological, system-conditioned formula discussed above, to reduce legal restraints on the Community law-maker in the economic field to a minimum—and in this respect the situation is not dissimilar to the virtually unfettered powers pursuant to the Commerce Clause of the United States Congress after 1937. There are of course important political constraints on Congress. The political constraints on the Community institutions have been formidable indeed, particularly in the last few years when the Community has been prevented by Member States "assembled in the Council" from progressing even in areas clearly within its exclusive powers.[79]

In foreign affairs, as we have seen, the Court of Justice begins its Treaty analysis with the same teleological formula but ends with the controversial "internal/external parallelism" doctrine which in effect lifts the "enumerated powers" restraints. Thus—as in the United States—the ways of identifying "constitutional limitations" differ in domestic and foreign affairs. Unlike in the United States, however, where the "federalism" issue has ceased to be a limiting factor, the power allocation between the Member States and the Community (represented by the Commission) has been the principal cause of tension.

It should not come as a surprise that Community power—like American federal power—is limited by specific prohibitions in the Treaty; by the basic institutional structure;[80] and, last but not least, by norms protecting fundamental human rights, written and unwritten,[81] which the Court derives from the general principles common to the national legal orders of the Members and from the European Convention on Human Rights since all Members have ratified it.

III. The Reality of Foreign Affairs Powers

This part will investigate the nature and the actual working of the mechanisms for the exercise of the foreign affairs powers in both the United States and the European systems, illustrating the institutional tensions rooted in the constituent documents. In respect of each of the foreign affairs powers, as defined earlier, the first section examines the provisions which have been made for the division of powers, both between the central authority and the constituent states, and between the institutions of the central authority, concentrating primarily on the manner in which the centralized authority executes its functions. The second part focuses on the foreign affairs powers retained by the Member States, and in particular on one important device, the European Political Cooperation mechanism, through which the Member States seek to coordinate the exercise of certain non-delegated powers outside the Community framework.

A. The Division of Powers and Arrangements for the Exercise of the Foreign Affairs Powers

1. Communication and Diplomacy

a) In the United States

From the beginning, the President has been the "sole organ of the nation in its external relations, and its sole representative with foreign nations."[82] He directs a huge "foreign affairs establishment" in Washington which is linked to more than a hundred American diplomatic missions abroad and maintains contact with a host of local foreign embassies. The President has a near-monopoly of information and expert advice although professional staffs of the Congressional Committees dealing with foreign affairs have recently been "the fastest growing bureaucracy" on the Capitol.[83] The President, with Senate consent, appoints American ambassadors and receives foreign ambassadors;[84] in addition, that he has the power to appoint personal representatives for foreign assignments without Senate's concurrence is now firmly established, although this was challenged in the Senate in the early yers.[85] In fact, the President has often appointed members of Congress to United States negotiating teams[86] as a means of "coopting" them and marshalling congressional support for his policies. On the other hand, Congress by legislation has at times purported to impose Congressional representation on the President.[87] Moreover, Congress has acquired substantial control over the foreign service by detailed legislation on the number, qualifications, and organization of the personnel[88] and it has also vested foreign affairs functions in administrative agencies which have enjoyed considerable independence of the President, such as the International Trade Commission.[89]

b) *In the Community*

In the Community, there is no "sole organ" to do business with the outside world even though the Commission aspires to this function and, despite its collective character, is perhaps best organized for it. The Commission has its own expert "foreign establishment" in Brussels, centered in the Directorates General for External Relations (DG I) and for Development (DG VIII), and comprising other specialized units dealing with the customs union, financing, agricultural exports, international environment, etc. Outside its headquarters, the Commission maintains over sixty "delegations," missions, and press and information offices in foreign capitals and at the seat of major international organizations, where they enjoy diplomatic or functional immunities. The delegations at the major world centers perform tasks of information and liaison similar to traditional diplomatic functions. The other missions have predominantly technical duties and assignments under cooperative agreements between the Community and the host states.[90] In Brussels, more than one hundred foreign missions are accredited to the Community[91] (not to the Commission) and provide the Commission with the information and the opportunity for day-to-day contacts.

The Treaty is silent on the active or passive right of legation, although some authors point to a provision in the supplementary protocol on privileges and immunities which assumes the presence of third-party missions at the seat of the Community.[92] Others would rely on the Community's "inherent powers" or its "international personality" as the appropriate source of the right of legation.[93] The more convincing approach is to imply the necessary Community power from its power to enter into treaties; and the Commission's authority from its role in treaty negotiations, its general executive authority to provide for its own organization,[94] and, last but not least, at this juncture, from the ample reservoir of "subsequent practice," a legitimate index of interpretation.

The division of powers and functions between the Commission and the Council has proved particularly controversial, because of the sensitivities and idiosyncrasies of the Member Governments with respect to diplomatic contacts and representation. The Member Governments keep an eagle's eye on, and tight control over, the Commission's activities. The Commissioners are appointed by "common agreement" of the ten Governments.[95] Although the Commission appoints its employees, their number and status are governed by Council regulations and the budget requires concurrence by the Council. The Commission seeks the Council's consent before opening a permanent delegation abroad and the accreditation of a foreign state representative to the Community is considered to require unanimous agreement in the Council. Thus France in 1964 blocked the establishment of relations with Taiwan and delayed the acceptance of a representative from Fiji because he had criticized French nuclear tests.[96] The complex procedure for "establishing relations" with a foreign government and accreditation of its ambassador involves both the Commission and the Council through the Committee of Permanent Representatives. Until 1966, following diplomatic usage, the foreign representative presented his credentials in a formal champagne ceremony to the President of the Commission exclusively but, after an outburst of the Gaullist Government's outrage at such pretension, the ceremony was dropped and since then the credentials are submitted to the President of the Council as well as to the Commission's President.[97]

In foreign capitals, the Commission's missions parallel the national embassies of the Member States. Moreover, as a part of the European Political Cooperation scheme, heads of these embassies meet in groups chaired by the ambassador whose state holds the rotating "Presidency" of the Council, to discuss political issues of common interest.[98] The line dividing the respective competences of the Commission's delegations and the national embassies is to follow the division between Community and national jurisdictions. It takes little imagination to fathom the problems of coordination and friction to which I shall return.[99]

2. Power to "Make" and to "Implement" Foreign Policy by "Autonomous Acts"

Foreign policy is made and implemented[100] by "autonomous" (unilateral) acts, such as declarations, resolutions, instructions to representatives, assertions of claims, appropriation of funds and legislation; and by "conventional acts," that is, international agreements, bilateral or multilateral.

a) In the United States

i) The President's Ascendancy in Formulating Policy

From the inception tension has existed between the President and Congress over which institution should be supreme in formulating foreign policy, but over the years the President has gained the ascendancy. Because of the President's exclusive charge of relations with other nations and his control of the channels of communications, and because Congress was not always in session, successive Presidents began to make not only small decisions in daily intercourse but larger policy determinations as well. For instance, by implication from the power to appoint and receive ambassadors, the President asserted, against some early opposition by Congress, the exclusive power to recognize or not to recognize new states, governments or foreign annexations of territory.[101] As a result, the President is now able to set prospective policy committing the United States to future action, for example, in influential doctrines such as the Monroe, Open-Door, Truman, or Nixon doctrines, while the legislative branch has been relegated to merely adopting "sense of Congress resolutions," which have no legal effect and often have little political impact.[102]

Although it is the Congress that provides for defense and declares war,[103] the President has independent powers as a Commander-in-Chief,[104] including the controversial right to send troops abroad. This right, although established by repeated exercise, has been limited by the War Powers Resolution of 1973.[105]

ii) Congress' Role in Formulating Policy

Congress' power to regulate foreign commerce[106] has been a crucial instrument of American foreign policy and it has grown, incident to "the explosion" of the power to regulate interstate commerce. The commerce power supports virtually any federal legislation relating to foreign relations including trade, shipping, aviation, communications, trade marks, and travel abroad.[107] In the vital field of trade, Congress provided for a federal tariff structure[108] and related customs law as well as extensive protective legislation on antidumping, countervailing duties, economic sanctions, etc.[109] "Statutory" tariff rates, set by Congress, are modified pursuant to bilateral or multilateral agreements negotiated by the President upon Congressional authorization periodically extended under elaborate safeguards.[110] The extensive federal international finance and banking legislation is based on the commerce and "money" power,[111] foreign aid is supported by the "spending power,"[112] and the power of Congress to regulate gambling and narcotics trade is founded on its power to tax.[113]

Congressional legislation regulating entry, status and exclusion of aliens and immigration, originally based on the commerce power, was later justified on the power "inherent in sovereignty" or on the "foreign affairs" power, the latter supporting also statutes governing the conduct of Americans abroad.[114]

Only relatively recently did the Congress undertake to legislate on two foreign affairs issues that until then had been within the exclusive province of the Department of State and the courts: the rules governing "acts of state" and sovereign immunity of foreign governments.[115]

The Congress has delegated extensive powers to the President, thus contributing to the growth of his authority. In many instances, however, the Congress has subjected the delegation to elaborate devices designed to scrutinize and recoup the delegated authority. The favorite instrumentality has been the so-called legislative veto.[116]

In international trade legislation the Congress has mandated complex administrative procedures of a quasi-judicial character, involving several executive departments and independent agencies, with a recourse to judicial review. Some view this trend as an excessive "judicialization" of a field where at least the major problems affecting national economy may call for high level governmental decisions and a flexible approach rather than formalized adversary procedures.[117]

b) In the Community

As we have seen, the foreign affairs powers of the Community lie primarily in the field of external economic relations, with the Member States determining policy in other areas. The Community institutions, invoking article 103 and the "necessary and proper" clause, article 235, have taken a few hesitant steps toward an economic and monetary union, which—if it should ever become a reality—would have far-reaching foreign affairs implications.[118]

In the foreign trade area, the Community institutions were not granted the broad power "to regulate foreign commerce." However, not unlike the Congress, the Council, drawing on articles 28 and 235, has been able to reenact annually a consolidated Common Customs Tariff (CCT),[119] modify it,[120] and adopt customs related regulations on customs valuation[121] and rules of origin.[122] Other regulations based primarily on article 113 deal with import monitoring systems, goods from state-trading countries, consolidation of the remaining quantitative import restrictions, general preferences for less developed countries and others.[123] The autonomous protective measures enacted by the Council include a regulation against dumping and subsidies.[124] In legislation on agricultural export subsidies, fisheries, and food assistance the Council has relied on its broad Treaty power to fashion common agricultural policy.[125] The Council has delegated substantial implementing functions to the Commission, but invariably has insisted on surrounding it by "management committees" composed of national officials through which the Member Governments have exerted an even tighter control over the Commission's activities than Congress exercises over the President and over the International Trade Commission under the trade legislation. Comparing the scope of the delegated power in the two systems, Bourgeois casts an envious eye at the relatively wide powers granted by Congress to the President to take speedy protective measures. On the other hand he notes (again by comparison with American procedures) the "deficit in legal protection" of individuals injured by Community protective measures, due to the excessively restrictive interpretation of individual access to the Court of Justice.[126]

In addition to the power delegated to it by the Council, the Commission possesses limited autonomous authority. In the exercise of that authority, the Commission determines grants of aid to victims of catastrophes and the opening of a delegation or mission in third countries. Nevertheless, the Commission in fact always seeks prior opinion or agreement from the Council. The Commission's role in certain foreign affairs matters (*e.g.* food aid, aid to non-associated developing countries) has become enmeshed in the dispute between the Council and the Parliament over the responsibility for the implementation of the Community budget.[127]

In contrast with the United States federal power, the Member States retain full authority over citizenship, immigration, and the status of nationals of third countries on Community territory. A suggestion has come from the Members of the European Parliament that certain aspects of the treatment of third country nationals, such as the granting of the right of asylum and the status of alien family members of Community workers, need to be treated in the Community or European Political Cooperation context.[128]

3. Treaty-Making Power

a) In the United States

The unhappy experience with the Confederate Congress undertaking to negotiate treaties and its inability to enforce them against the states[129] motivated the treaty provisions in the Constitution. Thus it is the President who makes treaties but only with "the advice and consent" of two-thirds of the Senators present.[130] The states are expressly barred from treaty-making and from entering, without the consent of Congress, into "any agreement or compact with another state, or a foreign power."[131] Treaties, along with the Constitution and federal legislation, are given the normative status of "supreme law of the land." This means that state courts must give effect to treaties, even if inconsistent with state law, and, in addition, cases arising from treaties are placed within the power of the federal judiciary.[132] These provisions, although clearly a radical break with the Confederate system, have left many questions for later answers.

i) Treaty-Making Process

The Founders did not wish to make treaty-making unduly easy and—in what has proved to be a vain hope—did not expect the need for many treaties. The House of Representatives was excluded from the procedure because its fluctuating, short-term, large membership would not allow it to act with expertise, speed, or secrecy.[133] On the other hand, the Senate, at that time "a cozy club of twenty-six members," representing particularly state interests and not elected by popular vote, proved more acceptable. Nevertheless, the proposal that the Senate should act by simple majority was defeated, albeit by a single vote.[134]

The "advice" function of the Senate, which was intended to enlist senatorial participation in ongoing negotiations, began to "slip" as early as 1794.[135] Gradually, but quite early, the function was virtually abandoned. The President has refrained from consulting the Senate on terms of a treaty before or during the negotiations and the Senate, itself preferring to "pass judgment" rather than to advise, has responded by insisting on changes in the finished texts of agreements as a part of its "consent" function.[136] The restrictions, conditions and understandings that the Senate sought to impose upon already signed and often delicately balanced treaties, such as the Versailles Settlement, SALT I, the Panama Canal Treaty or the British Tax Treaty, have caused acute difficulties with the treaty partners. Although the Senate may not be exactly a "graveyard" for treaties it may be termed, with a touch of poetic license and some exaggeration, their mortuary, considering the host of important treaties gathering dust in the Senate Foreign Relations Committee.[137]

Franck and Weisband give a vivid description of the President's efforts to deal with "senatorial obstructionism" by two devices: by "cooption"—that is by appointing Senators to treaty negotiating delegations and drawing on both Houses for key foreign policy appointments in the Administration; and by "circumvention."[138] The latter tactic involves by-passing Senate opposition by means of an executive agreement concluded by the President alone, or by seeking an approval by simple majorities of both Houses for an executive agreement negotiated (or to be negotiated) by the President. Neither device is mentioned in the Constitution but both have been sanctioned by extensive practice.[139]

The employment of executive agreements by the President alone has been responsible for a great deal of friction in the uneasy partnership between the two branches of government.[140]

Despite the congenital deficiencies of the system, there is broad support for the role of the Senate as a necessary "brake" on the "imperial Presidency," and any remedy is invariably sought in improved consultation procedures which would restore and perhaps institutionalize some of the Senate's "advice" function.

ii) Limitations on Treaty-Making Power

Although it is not obvious that the Founders intended to subject treaties to any constitutional limitations and no treaty has ever been held unconstitutional, the treaty-makers have always assumed, and the Supreme Court has made it clear, that such limitations exist.[141] These limitations, however, have different effects than, and they are determined through a different method than that employed in respect of, the limitations on domestic powers of the Federal Government.

(a) *Separation of powers.* In the first place, limitations derived from the separation of powers between the legislative and executive branches can hardly apply in the traditional way since a treaty may legislate as well as create international obligations although the House is excluded from the process.[142]

(b) *Federalism and the Tenth Amendment.* The federalism argument, that would allow treaty power only in matters already delegated to the Federal Government for legislative regulation, was put to rest in 1920 in the landmark case of *Missouri v. Holland.*[143] The treaty power, according to Justice Holmes who wrote the opinion in this case, was delegated to the federal treaty-makers in addition to, and independently of, the delegations to Congress, and since the treaty power was so delegated, whatever is within it was not reserved to the states by the tenth amendment or by "some invisible radiation" from its terms. Thus many matters clearly "reserved to the states" as regards domestic legislation (such as inheritance and access to local occupations) may and have been the subject of international treaties. However, "the Constitution probably protects some few states' rights, activities, and properties against any federal invasion, even by treaty."[144] In *Geofroy v. Riggs*[145] the Supreme Court held,

> [i]t would not be contended that [the treaty power] extends so far as to authorize what the Constitution forbids, or a change in the character of the government or in that of one of the States, or a cession of any portion of the territory of the latter, without its consent. . . .

> But with these exceptions, it is not perceived that there is any limit to the questions which can be adjusted touching any matter which is properly the subject of negotiations with a foreign country.[146]

(c) *The Bill of Rights.* The most important if not the only real constitutional limitations on the treaty power can clearly be found in the Bill of Rights which prohibits impairment of individual rights by federal authorities.[147]

In the past a much debated question was what the Court had meant in seeming to confine the treaty power to matters "properly the subject of negotiations with a foreign country." The often repeated assertions that the treaty power is barred from "domestic matters" or "matters not of international concern"[148] or "not pertaining to the conduct of international relations" can mean only—although authoritative case law is conspicuously absent—that a treaty must be a bona fide agreement between the United States and another state.[149]

iii) Self-Executing and Non-Self-Executing Treaties

Although the "supremacy clause" was included in the Constitution primarily to assure treaty compliance by states[150] it was interpreted by Chief Justice Marshall to mean also that treaties may add to, and change, domestic law automatically and directly upon ratification, without any "transformation" by an act of Congress:[151]

> A treaty is in its nature a contract between two nations, not a legislative act. It does not generally effect, of itself, the object to be accomplished, especially so far as its operation is infra-territorial; but is carried into execution by the sovereign power of the respective parties to the instrument.
>
> In the United States a different principle is established. Our Constitution declares a treaty to be the law of the land. It is, consequently, to be regarded in courts of justice as equivalent to an act of the legislature, whenever it operates of itself without the aid of any legislative provision.
>
> But when the terms of the stipulation import a contract, when either of the parties engages to perform a particular act, the treaty addresses itself to the political, not the judicial department; and the legislature must execute the contract before it can become a rule for the Court.[152]

Whether a treaty is self-executing or non-self-executing is ultimately a matter of judicial interpretation in a "case or controversy." The courts, however, will accord "great weight" to the interpretation offered by the Department of State, but they will not consider themselves bound by it.[153] The courts have as a rule applied the historic method of interpretation to determine intent on the basis of the text, context and legislative history of the treaty. Yet, unless legislative implementation is specifically provided for or clearly implied, the search for subjective intent is often illusory since the question in fact was not considered by the negotiators. Only more recently, perhaps under the impact of the many multilateral treaties, have the courts inclined toward the objective purpose-oriented method, but they have failed to develop consistent objective criteria by which to decide whether a treaty is to be considered self-executing.[154] It is accepted, however, that a treaty that entails expenditure of funds by the United States or imposes criminal sanctions cannot be executed without an act of Congress; but a treaty apparently can serve as "authorization" legislation supporting subsequent appropriation of funds by Congress.[155] On the other hand, the courts have generally attributed self-executing effect to treaties of friendship, commerce and navigation, often without even discerning the issue.[156]

iv) Some Unanswered Questions

(a) *Congress' obligation to implement a treaty.* Among the problems unresolved by the courts is the question whether Congress is constitutionally obligated to implement a non-self-executing treaty. Congress has accepted the obligation to carry out treaty commitments, although it has not always given the President all he said the treaty called for.[157]

(b) *Conflict between a treaty and federal statute.* Another question on which the Constitution is silent is how to resolve a conflict between a treaty and a federal statute. The Supreme Court has ruled that although a self-executing treaty supersedes any conflicting state law or constitution, it supersedes only a *prior* inconsistent federal statute (if the two cannot be reconciled), but it is itself superseded as "law of the land" by a subsequent federal statute if Congress clearly intended to legislate against it.[158] Thus although the Congress may legislate against a treaty—and the courts enforce the legislation—internationally the United States remains obligated and in default until the treaty is terminated. This situation, which contrasts with the earlier view of a treaty as a "higher law,"[159] is surely not conducive to reliable partnership or consistent with the modern conception of the effect to be given to international law in domestic legal orders.

(c) *Limitations on Presidential power to conclude executive agreements.* Although the Supreme Court has upheld, in a few instances, the President's independent power to enter into executive agreements and has also given them effect to modify state law, the limits of this power and the effect on federal law remain largely undefined.[160]

(d) *Procedures for termination of treaties.* There is no conclusive answer to the question of who can terminate a treaty although a Court of Appeals recently upheld, and the Supreme Court affirmed, the President's decision to end the Mutual Defense Treaty with Taiwan without reference to the Senate or to the Congress.[161]

v) Attacks on the Existing Procedures

The Supreme Court's broad interpretation of the treaty power was at least in some measure responsible for the periodic campaigns in and outside the Congress to impose limitations on the treaty process. In the early 1950's a coalition of Mid-Western Republicans and Southern Democrats in the Senate, disturbed by the United Nations human rights program that they regarded as an attempt at imposed "social engineering" unrelated to international concerns of the United States, launched a massive effort to amend the Constitution. In its extreme form, the Bricker Amendment,[162] although not purporting to limit the federal power to make treaties, would have eliminated the self-executing feature and made all treaties non-self-executing. It would also have barred Congress from implementing treaties by laws which were not within the power of Congress apart from the treaty. This, it was assumed, would prevent the implementation of the human rights and other treaties in the United States.

Although the amendment in a diluted form passed the Senate after a long and acrimonious debate, it was not pressed further.[163] Yet the great constitutional free-for-all has contributed to the Executive Branch's reluctance to sign and urge Senate approval of human rights treaties; and when it has attempted to promote such treaties, it has met with stony silence in the Senate.[164] More recently, disturbed by the Presidential use of executive agreements particularly concerning foreign military bases, Congress has had before it numerous bills to limit or regulate executive agreements. Congress succeeded only in adopting a law requiring the Executive Branch to notify the appropriate Congressional committees within a set deadline of any executive agreements it had concluded.[165] Responding to the continuing pressure from the Congress, the Department of State agreed to extend the notification duty to consultation on the form, although not on the substance, of the proposed agreement.[166]

b) In the Community

Most of the landmark cases decided by the Court of Justice in the foreign affairs area concern the treaty-making authority. In its earliest years the Community was understandably absorbed with the demanding internal task of building the common market, but because the Community was born into an interdependent world economy it was from the outset compelled to deal with third countries and the proliferating international organizations. By the nature of things, the treaty power was the principal instrument for the Community to replace bilateral relationships between its Members and third countries and to create new relationships. After an initial phase during which it reacted to the most insistent outside pressures, the Community has sought to evolve a more comprehensive foreign commercial policy within which to place its treaty-making activities. The Community was virtually thrust into the GATT negotiations as it progressively assumed responsibility for the Common Customs Tariff. Other European states, concerned with the economic and political impact of the emerging new "trade block," insisted on negotiating special "associations" aiming at eventual admission to full membership (Greece and Turkey) or creating industrial free trade areas comprising their and the Community's territories (the European Free Trade Association (EFTA) states). Mediterranean and North African countries, historically within the Member States' orbit, demanded preferential arrangements, and the original Treaty-based tie with former African colonies was expanded into a novel type of treaty partnership—Yaoundé and Lomé Conventions—ultimately including some sixty African, Caribbean and Pacific states. The Community has concluded arrangements with almost all the industrialized and third-world states in a bewildering variety of commercial, "association," and "economic cooperation" agreements, dealing with questions of trade, economic development, science and technology, environment, transport, fisheries, food aid, etc. The Community has also established links with a great number of global and regional organizations. Only Japan, and the Soviet Union with most of its allies, remain outside this elaborate treaty-network, bearing evidence of the Community's position as the world's largest trader.[167]

i) Treaty-Making Process: Who "Makes" Treaties?

(a) *The Community procedure.* According to the Treaty provisions[168] the Commission negotiates international agreements under a "mandate" from the Council. The Council, after consulting the European Parliament where the Treaty requires it to do so, "concludes" the agreement. Case law and ample practice, often inspired by accepted international treaty-making procedures, have filled in some of the gaps.

(i) *The Commission's role: Negotiating under the Council's direction.* In principle, the Commission—like the President in the United

States—is responsible for handling the negotiations.[169] Although not necessarily required to do so, the Commission does not institute formal negotiations without obtaining an authorization from the Council, and at times it even seeks Council concurrence for exploratory talks.[170] The Commission makes recommendations and the Council issues directives or "mandates" to it at the outset and in the course of the negotiations which the Commission must follow.[171] The Commission's recommendations do not have the status of formal proposals as in the internal lawmaking procedure and they can be freely changed or disregarded by the Council. In addition, a Council-appointed committee composed of officials from national ministries sits with the Commission negotiator and looks over his shoulders during the negotiations, but its members do not speak. This pattern, prescribed for commercial agreements,[172] has in practice been adopted for other negotiations as well.

As a rule the Council's directives allow the Commission only limited discretion and require references to the Council, where consensus is often elusive. The consequent delays irritate the Commission's partners in the negotiations. One is reminded of the position of an American negotiating team which, in important commercial negotiations, must keep close contact not only with the office of the Representative for Trade Negotiations, the Department of Commerce and the Department of State in Washington which issue the negotiating instructions, but also at times directly with the White House and the appropriate Congressional committees.[173]

The Council directives cannot be kept secret and the publicity handicaps the Commission's negotiating posture. When the negotiation results in an agreed text the Council, if it approves, authorizes a specific official to sign the agreement, subject to final "conclusion." It is after the signature that the European Parliament is consulted.

(ii) *The European Parliament's role: Consultation by the Council prior to "conclusion."* In response to increasingly insistent criticism by the deputies, the Council agreed, first in 1964 with respect to "association" agreements and in 1973 with respect to commercial agreements, to provide information and an opportunity for the Parliament to hold a debate on a proposed negotiation before it is started, to have the Commission advise the appropriate committee of the Parliament on a confidential basis of the substance of the agreement before it is signed, and last, but not least, to make available to the Parliament the text before it is finally "concluded."[174] It is said, however, that the procedure has not increased the Parliament's input to any appreciable degree, and suggestions have been advanced that the Parliament be given formal power to approve or reject an agreement, in line with the corresponding powers of the national parliaments.[175] It is probably correct to say that without such formal power of "consent" the power of "advice" will remain largely illusory.[176]

(iii) *Conclusion of a treaty and the Council's role.* An agreement becomes internationally binding upon the Community when the Council "concludes" it either by a "regulation," or by a decision *sui generis,* and the instruments of ratification are exchanged with the other party.[177] According to the Treaty, a weighted majority suffices when the Council votes on commercial agreements while unanimity is required for agreements concluded under articles 238 or 235—a distinction of little practical import as long as the consensus requirement prevails.[178]

In comparison with the American system, the Council performs the Senate's original function of "advice" on ongoing negotiations (albeit with a mandatory effect), the Senate's "consent" role, as well as the President's function of "making" the treaty. Paradoxically, in the United States, the House of Representatives, initially the only popularly elected chamber, is entirely excluded from treaty-making, although it has a part in implementation of treaties and an equal voice in authorizing the President to conclude executive agreements especially on tariffs and trade. In Europe the European Parliament may at least give advice and clamors for additional influence.

(b) *Mixed agreements and areas of Member State competence.* It will come as a surprise to an American lawyer that in a variety of instances an agreement is concluded by both the Community and by the Member States in their individual capacities. This form referred to as "mixed agreements," although viewed by some as of a doubtful constitutional validity, has become established practice and has received the implicit blessing of the Court.[179] Mixed agreements developed when circumstances called for an agreement to include subjects which fell outside the treaty-making power of the Community and could not conveniently be dealt with separately, but they have also been employed where the Community alone should have been the party.[180] In fact, there has been a rapid increase in the number of mixed agreements and they have been extended to cover a variety of subjects with the result that they may be considered to be more important than agreements concluded by the Community alone.[181]

* * *

The important *United Nations Law of the Sea Convention* is an example.[182] Some subjects of the Convention, conservation and management of fishing resources for instance, are clearly within the current competence of the Community, some are still within the competence of the Member States or within a shared competence, and some of these may later be taken over by the Community. During the negotiations for this Convention, Third States were concerned that some Member States of the Community might decide to stay out of the Convention system and yet might "get a free ride." In other words, if the Community as such accedes, those of its members who do not become parties in their own name might obtain the treaty benefits through the Community without assuming corresponding obligations. This, at any rate, was the argument. The dilemma that stumped the diplomats in Vienna negotiating the convention on treaties of international organizations[183] is compounded here by the uncertainty inherent in the "mixity": What rights and obligations does a Third State, party to a mixed agreement, acquire with respect to the Community on one hand and the Member States on the other hand—now and in the future evolution of the Community?

As a solution, a special Annex was added to the Law of the Sea Convention which provides in the first place that the Community may become a party only if a majority of the Members accede. Moreover, the Community is required, on signing the Convention, to deposit a declaration that specifies the allocation of competences between the Community and its Members as it exists at the time, and the Community is further required in the future to notify all the other parties to the Convention of any change in the allocation of competences. A failure to provide this information makes the Community as an international person together with its Members liable jointly and severally for whatever damage this failure to inform may bring about. The Community has in fact deposited such a declaration although it has not acceded to the Convention thus far. The Community has not been happy with this solution since it challenges its position that the division of competences is internal Community business[184] and reduces flexibility in its progressive evolution.

The Community obtained a better bargain during the negotiations for the *Ozone Layer Convention.*[185] In particular, its accession is no longer conditional on the adherence by any Member State, and in case one or more Member States adheres, it is for the Community itself to decide on the respective responsibilities for the performance.[186]

The *Lomé Convention,*[187] a complex mixed agreement, although generally referring to the "parties" or to "the Community," in several instances mentions the "Member States" alone or along with the Community.[188]

The prevailing view seems to be that a mixed agreement that does not distinguish, expressly or by implication, between the rights and obligations of the Community and the Member States imposes obligations on both the Community and its Members under all its provisions.[189]

"Mixity" has added an element of uncertainty if not outright irritation to the negotiating process and any lawyer of some imagination may conjure up a host of potential problems relating particularly to performance. Yet to my knowledge no such difficulties have materialized thus far and some view the mixed agreements as an innovative "confederate" foreign affairs instrument.[190]

* * *

Although the practice has not been consistent, in principle the Commission alone conducts the negotiations for bilateral "mixed agreements," but in multilateral treaty negotiations or international conferences there are either eleven delegations (ten Members and the Commission), or a "two-headed" delegation of the Commission and the "Presidency" of the Council, or a single combined delegation with the Commission representative more often than not acting as the spokesman on Community matters.[191]

ii) The Reach of, and "Limitations" on, the Community Power—ERTA *and Its Progeny*[192]

In contrast to the United States, the issue in Europe has been the division between the "delegated" Community power and the broad "reserved" powers of its Members.

As we have seen, the Treaty expressly authorizes the Community only to enter into tariff and trade and "association" agreements (articles 113, 238) and to establish working relationships with international organizations (articles 229 to 231). However, contrary to the prevailing learned opinion, and to the consternation of some Member Governments, the Court of Justice rejected the principle of enumerated powers in favor of the doctrine that Community treaty power should be coextensive with its internal powers (internal/external parallelism).[193]

(a) *Internal and external parallelism: Implied Powers.* The main issues in this connection have been whether it is possible for the Community in support of its given internal functions to take measures in the international arena for which no explicit powers exist, and the extent to which the internal functions must actually have been already undertaken before the external competence may be said to arise. Once external competence has been established, the problem has been to determine whether it is exclusive or concurrent with the competence of the Member States.

In the *ERTA* case[194] the Court was asked by the Commission to rule that the Commission alone had the power to negotiate a multinational road transport agreement within the United Nations Economic Commission for Europe. The Court answered that although the Treaty part on transportation does not expressly confer such power on the Community, its "internal" authority to frame a common policy in the field of transport carries with it treaty power in that field and that a regulation previously adopted by the Council on the same subject covering internal transport "necessarily vested in the Community power to enter into any agreements with third countries relating to the subject-matter governed by that regulation to the exclusion of any concurrent powers of the Member States."[195] Thus although declaring the Community's exclusive power the Court left open the question whether its treaty-making authority is in principle merely potential and inchoate, and must be first activated by a "common rule" to be adopted by the institutions within the internal sphere (such as a regulation) and if so, what sort of a rule would have that effect. Similarly, in the *Kramer* case,[196] the Court found that despite the absence of a specific Treaty grant in the fisheries area, the Community had the authority to enter into a convention on conservation of ocean fishing resources because of its power under the Treaty to frame a common agricultural policy and given the existence of a Council regulation on fisheries conservation in Member States' maritime waters.[197] Not until its *Opinion 1/76*[198] has the Court made it clear that the Community treaty power is not necessarily dependent on a prior internal measure but may flow "by implication" directly from the Treaty provision creating the internal competence, "in so far as the participation of the Community in the international agreement is . . . necessary for the attainment of one of the objectives of the Community."[199]

(b) *Express treaty-making powers: The field of commercial policy.* In the foreign commercial policy field, where the Community is given expressly the power to make common policy and specifically to negotiate tariff and trade agreements, the principal issues have been to identify the subjects falling within the category of foreign commercial policy and to determine whether the Community treaty-making power is "exclusive," "shared," or concurrent with the powers of the Member States.

The European Court has adopted an expansive approach in delineating the areas of Community competence. For instance, the Court had no difficulty in finding that an "understanding" on export credit standards negotiated in the Organization for Economic Cooperation and Development (OECD) fell within the scope of commercial policy and thus within the Community's treaty power which is not dependent on prior exercise of an internal power[200] and excludes any parallel power on the part of the

Members. Most recently, the Court recognized, against the Council's opposition, that the Community's commercial-policy treaty power extends beyond the classic agreements designed to liberalize international trade: it embraces also the modern commodity agreements (specifically the International Agreement on Natural Rubber under negotiation in the United Nations Conference on Trade and Development), despite their essentially regulatory features and complex objectives that impinge upon the development policies and general economic policies which are within the national competence of the Member States.[201]

* * *

(bb) *Express treaty-making powers: Article 238—a "legal Lohengrin."*[202]

(i) *The discord.* Consider the ambivalent first paragraph of this Article:

> The Community may conclude with a third State, a union of States or an international organization agreements establishing an association involving reciprocal rights and obligations, common action and special procedures . . .

The text highlights the structural components but it resonates in silence on the substance. What sort of "reciprocal rights and obligations," what "action," what "special" procedures? Since the documents of the legislative history of the EEC Treaty have not been published (they are reported to be quite skimpy and unrevealing) we have no clue as to the origin of this Lohengrin.[203]

The textual interpretation does not help and the contextual method points, as we shall see, in different directions. No wonder that the principal actors disagreed from the very outset on how to fill the silence. As could be expected, the Council and some, if not all the Member States—ever protective of national dominance over foreign affairs—insisted on the narrowest possible interpretation which would shear the text of most of its practical function.[204] By contrast the Commission, the European Parliament and the majority of writers saw in it a significant independent source of Community treaty power.[205]

The discord over the interpretation was submerged by the Community's practice of negotiating Article 238 agreements in the form of "mixed agreements" in which the Community was joined by the Member States as parties,[206] but it surfaced full blown in 1986 when the Court of Justice was asked in the *Demirel* case[207] to interpret the Association

Agreement between the Community and Turkey.[208] This was a mixed agreement concluded with the aim of "the approximation of the economic and legal systems and indeed political ones"[209] in anticipation of the ultimate admission of Turkey to full membership.

(ii) *The* Demirel *case.* A major question in the *Demirel* case (which was raised in the form of a challenge to the Court's jurisdiction[210]) was whether the Community had the power according to Article 238, to undertake obligations contemplating a step-by-step introduction of the free access for Turkish workers to the Community independently of the Member States. It was widely assumed, and the British and German Governments argued, that since the Member States retained control over access of third-country nationals to the Community territory and market, only they could be considered parties to those clauses of the mixed agreement. The EEC Treaty—so went the argument—does not confer any power on the Community either to legislate or to enter into international agreements on this subject and Article 238 does not confer on the Community the power to conclude association agreements on matters outside the recognized treaty-making powers "but expressly requires in such case that the procedure under Article 236 [amending the EEC Treaty] be used."[211] It was to obviate this difficulty, so went the argument, that the form of a mixed agreement was chosen by the parties and the implementation of the agreement was entrusted to the Joint Council of Association which may act only with the consent of all the Member States. According to this view the only addition to the Community treaty-power deriving from Article 238 would be the authority to enter into more enduring relationships with third states or organizations marked by institutional structures, such as a joint association council, a joint parliamentary body and a dispute settlement mechanism. This interpretation—it is generally agreed—had been adopted in actual practice, since all association agreements exceeding the scope of Article 113 were negotiated in the mixed form.[212]

In the Commission's view, on the other hand, the concept of association has a very wide scope. More specifically, Article 238 is a valid and sufficient legal basis for the Community to include rules on free movement of third-country workers in association agreements such as that with Turkey, intended to pave the way to future accession:

> In order to be distinct from agreements confined to trade or certain sectors [such as textiles, etc.], all association agreements must include areas, such as that of freedom of movement for workers, which are part of the single internal market, but in regard to which the Community does not in any event already have external compe-

> tence, whether expressly, for example under Article 113, or impliedly [e.g. under the ERTA doctrine].[213]

According to the Commission, the argument that the EEC Treaty concerns only freedom of movement *between* the Member States and that the Community cannot claim more extensive powers in its external dealings than it has within the Community fails to take account of the fact that the purpose of Article 238 is not to deduce an external competence from an existing internal one but to accord a specific external competence. The very position of that Article, grouped with other structural provisions dealing with "necessary powers" (Article 235), Treaty amendment (Article 236) and enlargement (Article 237), shows that it confers "a general power." This contextual interpretation is confirmed—so goes the Commission's argument—by the strictest possible procedural requirement of unanimous decision in the Council after consulting and, since the Single Europe Act, after approval by the European Parliament.[214]

In a pungent single paragraph, the Court embraced the tenor of the Commission's position:

> Since the agreement in question is an association agreement creating special, privileged links with a non-member country which must, at least to a certain extent, take part in the Community system, Article 238 must necessarily empower the Community to guarantee commitments toward non-member countries *in all the fields covered by the Treaty.* Since freedom of movement for workers is, by virtue of Article 48 et seq. of the EEC Treaty, one of the fields covered by the Treaty, it follows that commitments regarding freedom of movement fall within the powers conferred on the Community by Article 238.[215]

Clearly, the Court has gone some considerable distance toward dispelling the mysteries of Article 238. It identified the Article as a source of power "in all the fields covered by the Treaty" which implies not only the four freedoms but also the entire gamut of objectives listed in Article 3 of the EEC Treaty, with the increments evolved in practice and confirmed in the Single European Act. In all these fields, an association agreement may regulate rights and obligations of nationals of the third-country party, even if the Community had no comparable power with respect to Member States' nationals inside the Community. Interestingly, even some of the writers who supported a broad view of the association concept would not include in it the access of non-Member nationals to the Community territory since entry and residence of aliens is commonly ranked in importance with prime security and defence interests of national governments.[216]

(iii) *The open questions.* Several questions remain unresolved. The Advocate General, although supporting the broad construction adopted by the Court, concluded with some emphasis that it was confined to agreements "concluded with a view to accession."[217] That would exclude Article 238 agreements with Third World countries aimed primarily at development assistance and any other agreements concluded without an anticipation of membership in the Community. Although the issue before the Court originated in the agreement contemplating Turkish accession, the Court's ruling does not contain any such limitation. It would apply presumably to any association agreement that creates "special, privileged links" and that takes part "at least to a certain extent" in the Community system.

Another question to which there is no complete answer relates to the implementation of an association agreement. The Commission argued that where the Community's external competence is based on Article 238, "if necessary" the Community itself may execute it internally, drawing on Article 235.[218] The Court did not pass upon this assertion but it did state that its jurisdiction to interpret the Agreement with Turkey (and by implication the Community power to negotiate it) "cannot be called into question" because of the fact that in the field of the freedom of movement, "as Community law now stands," the agreement is to be implemented internally by the Member States or by the Joint Association Council and not by the Community institutions.[219] By implication—it may be argued—the Court rejected a possible claim that the external treaty power, based on Article 238, carried with it as a corollary an internal implementing power, that is the idea of an external/internal parallelism, opposite to the internal/external doctrine of the *ERTA* case and its progeny. Yet the Court did not expressly exclude the possible reliance by the Community on Article 235. At any rate, if, as the law now stands, the Community does not have the power itself to execute the agreements, the Member States are committed to the Community by virtue of Article 228(2) of the EEC Treaty to do so.[220]

(iv) *The prospects.* Only the future will provide the answer to what is perhaps the most interesting question: what will be the impact of the Court's ruling on the Community's practice? In the past, as I adumbrated earlier, all Article 238 agreements except those dealing exclusively with trade subjects were concluded in the mixed form, with the Member States joining as parties. This practice, it was argued, implied the acceptance of the narrow interpretation of Article 238. The Commission, however, sought to explain the choice of the mixed form for the

Turkish agreement by the legal uncertainty as to the scope of the Community external powers due to the absence of case-law at the time of its conclusion and by the limited need for such powers prior to the completion of the customs union. At the later stage, the Commission opined, the practice was continued for "political reasons" because of "established usage"; moreover financial commitments of the Member States and certain aspects of economic and technical cooperation fell traditionally within the jurisdiction of the Member States, and the decisions of the Council of Association potentially could exceed "normal" Community powers.[221]

I shall describe below the refusal by the Member States in the Council to draw upon the ample reservoir of the Community treaty power offered by the Court in the form of the *ERTA/Opinion 1/76* doctrine. Will the Council be more likely to follow the Court's lead, accept the broad definition of the treaty power under Article 238, and abandon the insistence on the mixed form for association agreements? Will it require "mixity" only when financial commitments of Member States (or also technical and economic cooperation) are involved?[222] The issue is timely in view of the ongoing negotiations with the European Free Trade Association states for the "European economic space," and the proposed new association arrangements with the Eastern European countries. Two procedural factors distinguish the treaty power under Article 238 from the implied power based on the *ERTA* doctrine: the unquestioned requirement of unanimity in the Council and the need for approval by the European Parliament. The first of these prerequisites should assuage the fear of the national governments of being forced into an agreement by a majority fiat. The second requirement entails delay and further complication which might make recourse to Article 238 less desirable. At any rate, there still remains the pervasive reluctance by the national governments to allow their independent international status as treaty makers to be whittled down beyond the express terms of the Treaty.

* * *

(c) *Exclusive, shared or concurrent powers?—Pre-emption.* At this juncture, due to the consistent case law of the Court of Justice, the principle of internal/external parallelism is no longer in question, and it is accepted by all the Member Governments. The controversy centers, however, on the bold assertions of the exclusive character of the Community power within the orbit of its competence, to the preclusion of the Member States. In reality, the Court has been more prudent and pragmatic in this respect, balancing the institutional interests of the Community against the concerns of third states and taking into account the practical need for effective action, as well as the political sensibilities of the Member Governments bent on protecting their own foreign affairs power. The Court's practice is reminiscent of the method used by the United States Supreme Court in the *domestic* sphere when it is asked to rule whether a state law is "pre-empted" by an act of Congress. In the absence of clear evidence of "the intent of Congress," the Court in effect must "rely upon its own judgment as to whether, or to what extent, an intelligent legislature would have wished to permit state legislation touching upon the subject-matter of the federal legislation."[223] In particular, the Supreme Court will consider whether the law is non-discriminatory and reflects a legitimate state objective which is consistent with the federal objective.[224]

Thus in the *ERTA* case, although the Court of Justice solemnly proclaimed that the Community alone was competent particularly in view of the "pre-emptive" Council Regulation, the Court nevertheless let the Member States continue the negotiations that they had been carrying on for a number of years, because "[a]t that stage of the negotiations, to have suggested to the third countries concerned that there was now a new distribution of powers within the Community might well have jeopardized the successful outcome."[225]

In *Kramer*[226] the Court again found exclusive Community power over maritime fisheries conservation policy, but it held that the Dutch Government's conservation measures were not "precluded" by prior Community law as long as the Council was unable to agree on what the common policy should be. Yet in other cases the Court disallowed Irish and British "conservation" measures on the ground that they were discriminatory or were enacted in disregard of the agreed consultation procedures.[227]

In what is perhaps the most striking compromise, (the logic of which has been criticized), in the *International Natural Rubber Agreement* case the Court ruled that although the Agreement was within the Community's exclusive commercial treaty power, nevertheless the Member States were entitled to join as parties, since the anticipated expenses would not necessarily be borne by the Community budget and the Member States might be called upon to assume the burden of financing the proposed buffer stock which the Court considered an "essential feature" of the Agreement.[228] In fact, by a later mutual accommodation between the Commission and the Council all commodity agreements are now dealt with as "mixed agreements."[229]

In the *International Natural Rubber Agreement* case, the Court made it clear that if the funding were to be provided from the Community budget rather than from Member State funds "no problem would arise as regards the exclusive powers of the Community to conclude the agreement."[230] One may assume that if the Community enters into an agreement which falls within its treaty power and provides for financial expenditure to come from the Community budget, then the budgetary authorities, that is the Council with the European Parliament, are obligated not only under international law but also under Community law to make the necessary entry into the budget without further Community legislation.[231] The analogous question in the United States has no truly authoritative answer from the Supreme Court, but beginning in 1796 Congress has consistently appropriated funds to meet treaty commitments, considering itself morally obligated.[232]

In the commercial policy field, the Court appears to be more insistent than in other areas on enforcing Community pre-emption with respect to both "autonomous" and "conventional" acts.[233] Waelbroeck calls the Court's approach in that field "conceptualist-federalist," as compared with the more lenient, "pragmatic" approach to pre-emption now employed internally in the area of the common agricultural policy.[234]

(d) *General "constitutional" limitations and judicial review.* In *Opinion 1/76,* where the question before the Court concerned the position of the Community in setting up an international organization by international agreement, the Court held the proposed agreement incompatible with the Treaty because the structure of the international organization it envisaged would "call in question the power of the institutions of the Community and, moreover, alter in a manner inconsistent with the Treaty the relationship between Member States within the context of the Community."[235] One is reminded of the warning by the Supreme Court in *Geofroy v. Riggs*[236] that a treaty purporting to "change the character of the government" would be held unconstitutional[237] although the Supreme Court thus far has had no occasion to hold a treaty unconstitutional on this or any other ground.

In a later opinion, arising under the Euratom Treaty, the Court again manifested its concern lest the adhesion to the proposed international convention on nuclear safety impair the internal distribution of powers between the Community and its Members.[238] A more significant aspect of this opinion is the ruling that even though the Treaty expressly preserves the Member States' authority to regulate access to nuclear materials by national public safety and health regulations, the Community is not thereby prevented from entering international commitments on the same subject.[239]

The two opinions just discussed illustrate the exercise by the Court of its "preventive" jurisdiction (EEC Treaty article 228(1)) that enables it to rule on the compatibility of an "envisaged" Community agreement with the Treaty before the agreement comes into force. However, the Court has extended its power of "constitutional review" to agreements already in force, even though the Treaty does not specifically sanction such extension. When asked to interpret the Community Association Agreement with Greece, the Court held that as soon as such an agreement enters into force its provisions become "an integral part of Community law" and that as an act of one of the Community institutions the agreement becomes subject to the Court's jurisdiction.[240]

It appears, therefore, that the "constitutionality" of an agreement (or perhaps more specifically of the Community act concluding the agreement) may be tested through the entire gamut of procedures available for contesting the validity of any Community act.[241] Thus a Community agreement, like a treaty concluded by the United States, may be held invalid internally while continuing in force as an international obligation, although thus far in neither system has a treaty actually in force been held "unconstitutional."[242] In reality, it is unlikely that in the United States a treaty which passed the barrier of a vigilant, conservative Senate could be successfully challenged in the courts, and the same applies to a Community agreement approved by a consensus of the Member States in the Council.

* * *

(dd) *More on review of mixed agreements:* Demirel. By definition, as we have seen, a mixed agreement is a "bundle" of discrete undertakings assumed by the Community and—separately and individually—by the Member States. In a series of cases the Court proceeded to interpret mixed agreements and their effects without inquiring into its jurisdiction to do so.[243] It tacitly assumed that it had undisputed jurisdiction since the provisions which it was asked to interpret evidently fell within the Community power.[244]

In the *Demirel* case,[245] however, the German and British Governments took the position that since the provisions in the Turkish agreement regarding the access of Turkish workers to the Community had been included by the Member States in the exercise of their own powers, they were beyond the Court's interpretative jurisdiction. We noted that the Court disagreed and held that the clauses in question fell within the Community's own treaty power under Article 238: "Thus the question whether the Court has jurisdiction to rule on the interpretation of a provision in a mixed agreement containing a commitment which only the Member States could enter into in the sphere of their own does not arise."[246] In the Court's view, the mixed agreement is an act of the Community institutions, just as any agreement concluded by the Community, and as such it is "an integral part of the Community legal system."[247] Consequently, it is for the Court to decide with finality which of the undertakings fall within the treaty-power of the Community and to interpret (and apply) them as such. The Court found it unnecessary to rule on its authority with respect to the "commitments which only the Member States could enter into." However, since it has recognized the division of the undertakings and powers, the obvious implication is that it would lack jurisdiction with respect to the Member States' "commitments." These, one would assume, would be interpreted and applied as bilateral international law obligations between the third country party to the agreement and each individual Member State, in accordance with the processes of general international law.

Still on the issue of competence, the Court held that it lacked jurisdiction to pass upon the claim that the German legislation was contrary to Article 8 of the European Convention on Human Rights because — the Court opined — "there is at present no provision of Community law defining the conditions in which Member States must permit the family reunification of Turkish workers lawfully settled in the Community."[248] Yet it is part of the "*jurisprudence constante*"[249] that Community acts must be interpreted in the light of the general principles on the protection of fundamental rights drawn, *inter alia,* from the European Convention to which all the Member States are parties. If — as the Court held — the EEC-Turkish Agreement is an act of the Community, and "the commitments regarding freedom of movement fall within"[250] the Community treaty power, is the Court not bound to interpret these commitments in the light of those general principles? If the Court had accepted the jurisdiction to do so, it may have concluded that — as suggested by the French Government — the case-law of the European Court of Human Rights would not support the claim of violation by the German legislation of a basic right.[251]

An author perceived a risk "that the European Court becomes [as a result of its ruling in *Demirel*] a sort of appeals court above the national jurisdiction."[252] Clearly, the Court has ascribed to itself a rather broad discretionary authority, considering the uncertainties inherent in the division or competences between the Member States and the Community which are compounded as they shift in the course of time. The assertion of the Community's competence and the Court's jurisdiction in the face of the opposition by two leading Member States, based on a traditional national security interest, may give rise to some questions regarding the observance of the "subsidiarity principle"[253] as the yardstick of the division of competences between the Community and its members. I see, however, no evidence that it will rekindle the notorious "Kompetenz—Kompetenz" controversy and the dire warnings of a "government by judges."

Yet the much vaunted advantage of the mixed agreements, that of eschewing the controversy over the division of powers, is put in question in *Demirel.* In fact, the case illustrates still another pitfall of the mixed agreements which might contribute to a dampening of the national governments' love affair with this form.

(e) *Extra-legal and political constraints.* Owing primarily to outside pressures, treaty-making has been a growth area even during the current period of relative stagnation in other Community activities. However, after *ERTA,* some Member Governments have opposed certain "internal" legislation in the Council on the ground that its adoption may give rise to Community treaty power on the same subject matter. Moreover, there is evidence that, except for agreements falling squarely within the area of commercial policy, the Council has been reluctant to rely on Community powers as declared in the *ERTA* case and in *Opinion 1/76,* preferring instead to invoke the less controversial "necessary and proper" clause of article 235, either exclusively (as in the environmental protection agreements), or in conjunction with article 113 (as in the agreement of cooperation with Canada) or article 43 (as in the United Nations Relief and Works Agency Conventions).[254] Moreover, as to the form in which Community agreements are concluded, apart from the many agreements in the basic commercial policy field which the Community has concluded alone, the Council has clearly favored "mixed agreements" in which the Community is joined by the Member States as parties. Thus the practice confirms the acute sensitivity of the Member Governments when it comes to recognizing the foreign affairs powers of the Community.

iii) Effects of Agreements Concluded by the Community[255]

The lapidary text in article 228(2),[256] that agreements concluded by the Community are "*binding*" both on its *institutions and on the Member States,* is the only clue the Treaty offers with respect to the effect of such agreements in international law, in Community law or Member State law. The silence is even more resounding if compared with the explicit statement in the United States Constitution that treaties are "supreme law of the land" and binding on the states.[257]

* * *

(a) *Effect in international law: no exit in Vienna.*[258] The Court of Justice, as we shall see, has filled in the lacunae to some degree as regards the effects in Community law and in Member States' law but not in international law. The question then is whether the paragraph in question encapsulates only an internal rule of the Community or whether it purports also to affect the rights and obligations of third countries.

The problem emerged in the course of the preparation of the Vienna Convention on the Law of Treaties between States and International Organizations or between International Organizations.[259] The International Law Commission (ILC) which provided a draft of the Convention attempted to tackle this issue in the famous Article 36b that was to apply to international organizations generally, not just to the Community. This was the Article on which the ILC—and the Vienna Conference itself—spent more time than on any other. Yet in the end the Conference ended up by dropping it altogether, as the diplomats could not agree on a generally acceptable formula.[260] They abandoned the Article on the ground that the law of international organizations had not yet crystallized so as to allow this problem to be codified. Although the EEC was not the exclusive reason—the issue was also raised, for instance, in connection with the Headquarters Agreement between the United Nations and the United States—the principal concern, articulated particularly by the Eastern European delegations, was with the Community. As a result, the Convention does not contain a specific rule on the subject[261] and the issue would be governed by an appropriate stipulation in a given treaty or, in the absence of such a stipulation, by the internal rules of the organization itself, that is, in our case by Article 228(2). This brings us back to the implications of this provision and, as one may imagine, "learned opinion" is divided on its reach.[262]

Some writers take the view that Article 228(2) deals only with the effects of agreements in the Community legal system and that third states, party to agreements with the Community, acquire international legal rights only as against the Community and not also against the Member States. This posture would be consistent with a mature federal system because a third state, party to a treaty for instance with the United States, in principle acquires treaty rights only against the United States and not against its component states. The important difference between a "mature federation" and the Community is that in the Community, the Member States—unlike the states of the American Union—have preserved their full international personality.

One writer points to the Court's language in *Kupferberg* as possibly supporting the contrary view to the effect that direct obligations arise between the Member States and the third state.[263] At any rate, whether or not one concludes that Article 228(2), a an exclusively internal rule, binds the Member States only vis-à-vis the Community, with the Community alone answering the non-Member State, the Member States would still be held subsidiarily liable under general international law for obligations undertaken by the Community.[264]

* * *

(b) *Conflict between Community international agreements and acts of the Community or of the Member States.* As we have seen, the Court of Justice has taken the view that an international agreement is *an act of one of the institutions* of the Community and as such is open to review in the regular manner before the Court of Justice. However, although the Court has upheld the superiority of the constitutive Treaty over Community agreements with third states, it does view such agreements as a special category of Community acts, partaking of the "higher" rank of international law, and, because of that, superior to both prior and subsequent ordinary Community acts, including Council regulations.[265] Whether or not this significant holding can be derived from positive Treaty law, it is a reasonable application of an evolving modern constitutional practice that recognizes the necessity of granting international commitments superior recognition in domestic law, in the interest of a more stable world order.[266] Regrettably, the United States Supreme Court, without a compelling constitutional reason, has established the contrary rule that in the internal legal order a treaty prevails only over a prior, but not over a subsequent, act of Congress.[267] In any event, in the Community, any act of the institutions that violates a Community agreement with a third state may be brought directly or indirectly before the Court and annulled or declared invalid.[268]

Since international agreements concluded by the Community form an integral part of Community law as soon as they come into force, any violation of such an agreement by *a Member State* constitutes a violation of Community law and may be branded as such in a declaratory judgment of the Court of Justice, in an action instituted by the Commission or another Member State[269] in accordance with the normal rules for judicial review. The Member State violation may also in certain circumstances be brought indirectly before the Court of Justice by means of the preliminary ruling procedure initiated by a private party before a Member State tribunal.[270] In the United States there is some authority in support of the Federal Government's judicial remedy against a state that violates a treaty,[271] but it is very sparse. Generally, a private party must raise the issue in the course of private litigation, and since that may not happen, the foreign state, party to the treaty, may find itself without a remedy in the American domestic legal order.[272]

Perhaps the most effective remedy against violations of Community agreements was fashioned in the landmark *International Fruit* case,[273] where the Court extended the concept of the "direct applicability" (or self-execution) of provisions of the constituent Treaty to include Community agreements with third states. At the same time, the Court reserved to itself the final authority to determine whether such an agreement is "directly applicable," and can produce "direct effects," that is whether an individual can derive directly from the agreement a right which Member State courts must enforce, without any implementing action by either the Community institutions or Member States.[274] It is of obvious importance for the uniform application of a Community agreement throughout Community territory (and it accords with the federal pattern) that the Court of Justice's determination bind Member State courts regardless of their national constitutional practices governing the effects of treaties in their internal legal order. To decide whether an agreement is directly applicable and has direct effects, the Court examines "the spirit, general scheme and text" of the agreement in question. This is the same purpose-oriented interpretive formula that the Court employs in deciding which parts of the constitutive Treaty itself are "directly applicable." This test, on its face at any rate, is more liberal than the method generally followed by American courts in deciding the "federal question" whether a treaty accords rights to an individual for which he or she has a direct judicial remedy.[275] Yet in *International Fruit,* the Court of Justice held several GATT articles not to be directly applicable, contrary to the view adopted by American lower courts and doctrine.[276]

Should the Court interpret Community agreements in the same liberal spirit as it has the provisions of the constitutive Treaty itself,[277] individual recourse to the judiciary would prove the most effective of the varied means available for enforcing Community agreements in the Community legal order.[278] It has been suggested, however, that such liberal enforcement of Community agreements may be against Community interests unless a reciprocal treatment in the courts of the Community's partners, parties to such agreements, is assured. In fact, the judgment in the *Polydor* case, rendered in 1982, is a clear signal that the Court will interpret Community agreements with third countries less liberally than it has done with regard to similar, if not identical, provisions of the EEC Treaty although the later *Kupferberg* case pointed in the other direction.[279]

* * *

In the *Demirel* case with which I dealt earlier in another context,[280] the Court formulated the direct applicability test in the following terms:

> A provision in an agreement concluded by the Community with non-member countries must be regarded as being directly applicable when, regard being had to its wording and the purpose and nature of the agreement itself, the provision contains a clear and precise obligation which is not subject, in its implementation or effects, to the adoption of any subsequent measure.[281]

This is essentially the same interpretative definition developed in the internal Community context but it may lead to quite a different result when applied externally. In this vein Advocate General Darmon observed:

> Whereas under Community law it is automatically assumed that the Contracting Parties intended to confer rights on individuals by means of the [constituent] Treaties[282] and the only requirement for direct applicability is that the rules in question be precise and complete, no such intention may be presumed for the applicability of an international agreement.[283]

Applying the above test the Court found that the relevant provisions in the Turkish Agreement and Protocols "essentially serve to set out a programme and are not sufficiently precise and unconditional to be capable of governing directly the movement of workers."[284]

Finally, in the *Sevince* case[285] the Court extended the application of this test to the decisions rendered by the Council of Association established by the same EEC-Turkish Association Agreement. The Court upheld its jurisdiction to review these decisions which it found directly applicable but not covering "the situation" of the Turkish workers.[286]

In summary, the Court undertakes a two-prong inquiry into the purpose and nature of the agreement (rather than the subjective intent of the parties as suggested by Mr. Darmon), and the finite character of the provision in question. This formula preserves the appearance of logical consistency between the internal and external sphere of the Community legal order. At the same time, it allows the Court considerable discretion to take into account a range of economic and political concerns such as the choice between the diplomatic and judicial route for the settlement of controversies arising under a given international agreement.

Based on the pronouncements of the Court, the principles governing the effects in Community law and in the national legal orders of an agreement concluded by the Community with a non-Member State may be stated as follows:

First: such an agreement must be compatible with the constituent EEC Treaty and it is subject to "constitutional review" before the Court of Justice both before and after its final conclusion.

Second: such an agreement concluded by the Community with a third state prevails over conflicting Community legislation (such as a Council regulation).

Third: the Court of Justice decides whether such an agreement is directly applicable, or more precisely, whether a right based on it can be invoked by an individual in a national court—and such a decision binds all national courts in the Community.

Fourth: in case of a conflict, such an agreement prevails over national law, including national constitutions, of the Member States.

These then are the principles derived from the cases discussed. Jacques Bourgeois, however, has drawn a fine overlay of doubt across these principles.[287] There is, in fact, a legitimate question concerning the extent to which these principles will actually be applied in practice. The Court has never invalidated a Community law as contrary to a Community agreement with a third state, nor has it ever declared a legal act of a Member State incompatible with such an agreement.[288] However, in one instance it did hold a *proposed* Community agreement incompatible with the EEC Treaty.[289] There are, as we have seen, several byways for the Court to elude these delicate problems of enforcing Community obligations toward third states, and the Court has travelled them all.

Inside the Community system, genuine "separation of power" issues have arisen between the judiciary and the political institutions: to what extent should the Court enforce a Community agreement against its own institutions, a Member State or its nationals by a judicial decision, if this were to impair the chances of the Community to obtain a balanced negotiated settlement with a third state. In an international forum, such as GATT, the Community may be able to assert, among other defences, the lack of reciprocity on the part of the third state, a claim which the Court has been unwilling thus far to consider[290] and which is in fact hardly suitable for judicial determination.

According to the EEC Treaty the Commission has the mandate to see to the compliance with Community law and that includes Community international agreements. Is the Commission bound to bring a Member State accused of a violation of such an agreement before the Court under Article 169? It has apparently done so only in a single case.[291]

Demaret observes that the very commencement of an Article 169 proceeding against a Member State for a violation of GATT would necessarily engender "great visibility" for such a violation and thereby weaken the position of the Community in the international arena.[292]

One can sympathize with the Commission's reluctance to haul a Member State before the Court since it may have to defend the Community in an international forum. Bourgeois points out that this sort of judicial action by the central executive branch would go beyond the procedure in federal states (and that includes the United States).[293] Demaret suggests as an alternative that the Community establish a formal internal procedure, not open to publicity, by which the Commission and the Council would supervise the compliance by the Member States with the Community's international obligations.[294]

There are, of course, weighty countervailing considerations against excluding this category of controversies from judicial settlement. In the first place, adjudication is perhaps the most authoritative method of dispute settlement and assures good faith performance by the Community of its international obligations. The Community's own experience confirms that there can be no effective enforcement of the rule of law without individual initiative before the courts of law. Moreover, and perhaps more importantly, denying direct applicability to international agreements means that individuals are deprived of access to the judiciary, a serious matter in a modern legal order.

At any rate, the nuanced interpretations employed by the Court make one wonder about the prospects in practice of a forceful judicial application of the constitutional principles declared by the Court. It is, however, too early in Community history to draw any reliable conclusions.

* * *

Provisions in the Community agreements that are not "directly applicable" may be implemented either by Community legislation or by the Member States under Community direction. Bourgeois believes that Member States are obligated to enact the necessary implementing measures by virtue of article 228(2).[295]

(c) *Community succession to multilateral treaty obligations of the Member States.* Another significant conclusion in *International Fruit,* illustrating the integration dynamics, bears upon the problem of "succession" by the Community to the rights and obligations of a multilateral treaty to which the Member States are party, even if the Community itself does not become a party. The Court stated:

> [I]n so far as under the EEC Treaty the Community has assumed the powers previously exercised by Member States in the area governed by the General Agreement [on Tariffs and Trade] the provisions of that agreement have the effect of binding the Community.[296]

To that extent the Community has "replaced the Members."[297]

As a general proposition, Member States are required by Treaty article 234 to bring their international treaty commitments antedating the Community in line with their obligations under the constitutive Treaty through whatever means are available in international intercourse.

4. Power to Protect Citizens Abroad and to Advance International Claims—International Responsibility

a) In the United States

Diplomatic protection and international responsibility are within the exclusive domain of the Federal Government in the United States. The Federal Government alone bears the responsibility for any action by federal or state authorities that violates an international law right of another state or of an individual under modern human rights law.[298]

The Department of State deals with other Governments in these matters. If negotiations do not produce a settlement of a claim, the United States may have recourse to political dispute settlement procedures or international adjudication and ultimately to means of self-help, such as retorsion or retaliation.

If a settlement is reached, it is incorporated in an agreement concluded either by the President alone in the form of an executive agreement, or by the President with the Senate in the form of a treaty. The settlement would provide for payment of an individual claim or more generally for lump-sum payment for a series of related claims, or for international arbitration. The Congress may prescribe conditions for the settlement, and it has established the International Claims Commission, a federal agency charged with distributing to American claimants funds received from lump-sum settlements. In the absence of Congressional opposition, the courts have consistently upheld broad Presidential powers to deal with international claims, even where a settlement was challenged on the ground that it was inadequate and not agreed to by the individual claimant and unless compensated by the United States, would deprive the claimant of property without due process of law.[299]

Aliens in the United States depend for their protection primarily on the judiciary. Since the Bill of Rights in principle protects aliens equally with citizens, it generally satisfies the standard required by the law on international responsibility for treatment of aliens.[300]

b) In the Community

There is no "hard law," but there is a great deal of academic discourse about the position of the Community in this field—a question that must be determined by interpretation of the constituent Treaty and customary international law, taking into account the *sui generis* character of the Community.[301] Several reasons support the position that the Community has the power to press international claims and may be held internationally responsible, not unlike the United States Government. First, despite the pervasive role of the Member States in the Community's life, its institutions have a sufficient degree of autonomy in the areas of its competence, including foreign affairs. Second, the Community is capable of providing relief through its law-making and judicial system, and it has its own financial resources, budgetary procedures and limited borrowing powers to offer material reparation. Third, its international personality has been widely recognized by other states and international organizations. Fourth, particularly because of its control of the import and export regimes, the Community is capable of imposing economic measures of retorsion or retaliation where its rights or interests are disregarded.[302] Finally, by virtue of Community law, Community institutions (as well as the Member States in Community matters) are bound to respect international obligations even more firmly than is the Federal Government in the United States.[303]

Accordingly, if a third state violates an agreement it has concluded with the Community, the Community is in a position to demand relief and reparation, both in its own interest and on behalf of a Community citizen concerned. Similarly, in a non-contractual setting, the Community may bring a claim against a third state responsible under customary international law for sub-standard treatment of a Community official, agent or enterprise.[304]

Conversely, the Community may be held internationally responsible by a third state if its institutions or a Member State act against a commitment undertaken by the Community in an international agreement or if the Community institutions treat a third-state national below the international law standard. In the latter case the individual alien is required to exhaust "domestic remedies" under Community law before an international claim may be pressed against the Community. It would presumably be the Commission, acting under a Council mandate, that would conduct the necessary negotiations on behalf of the Community.

If an agreement with a third state fails to provide a dispute settlement procedure, the Community and the third state may resort to the generally available diplomatic and judicial settlement procedures.[305] However, since only states have access to the International Court of Justice or the Permanent Court of Arbitration, a special arbitration tribunal would have to be agreed upon by the parties for adjudication of the dispute. In practice, the burden of satisfying a claim of the third state may ultimately fall upon the Member States. Moreover, Member States could probably be held directly responsible if Community institutions are unable to provide due satisfaction or, of course, if the Community should cease to exist.[306]

* * *

By its very nature "mixity" adds elements of uncertainty and unpredictability in the realm of international responsibility. Unless a mixed agreement provides unambiguously for a distinction between the Community's and the Member States' rights and obligations, a breach on the part of the Community or the Member States causes joint responsibility. Conversely, the Community can press an international claim against the third state, party to the agreement, regardless of the nature of the obligation breached by that party.[307]

* * *

B. Arrangements for the Coordination of Non-Attributed Powers: "Political" Foreign Policy—European Political Cooperation (EPC) and Its Interaction with the Community

As we have seen, whereas in the United States the totality of foreign affairs powers has been delegated to the Federal Government, in Europe it is only in limited fields that powers have been attributed to the Community. Thus, while the Community has far-reaching powers in the area of external economic relations, areas such as defense and "political" foreign policy remain within the competence of the Member States. The way in which the non-attributed powers are exercised, however, has important implications for the common venture, and it is therefore in the interest of both the Community as a whole and of each of the Member States to coordinate policies even outside the Community framework. A major attempt to meet this need in the "political" foreign policy field has resulted in the development of a new mechanism, known as European Political Cooperation.[308]

1. The EPC: Its Origins, Structure and Scope

The European Political Cooperation (EPC) mechanism began to evolve in 1969. It is as elusive in its mode of operation as in its actual impact on European foreign policies and it must be understood in the light of its antecedents.

a) Origins and Foundation of the EPC

i) The antecedents of the EPC

After his return to the Presidency in 1958, General de Gaulle, no longer hopeful of a membership in the "nuclear power club," concluded that France could recapture its world power status within more intimate forms of cooperation among European sovereign states. But he remained emphatically opposed to the pattern of integration: "supranationality" was an illusion which would only solidify the division of Europe and strengthen its dependence on the United States. It was in this context that the French Government launched its proposals for a new consultative framework outside the Community institutions.[309]

The major French proposal, the "Fouchet plan" of 1961, called for a "Union of *States*" (in contrast with the "union among the *peoples*" in the EEC Treaty Preamble) which would cover common foreign and defense policies, and beyond that, extend cooperation to science, culture, and human rights. Under the plan, the Heads of Government and Foreign Ministers of the Six would meet regularly in a "Council," and a "European Political Commission" of senior national diplomats, with its seat in Paris (rather than Brussels), would prepare the Council's work.

The Dutch and the Belgians perceived the proposal as a time bomb aimed at NATO and at the foundations of the Community, and they interpreted de Gaulle's opposition to British membership in the Community as further evidence of a design to establish a Franco-German "directorate" without the institutional protection for the smaller members that is offered in the Community. In December 1961, the European Parliament prepared a counterproposal designed to mitigate what were considered the pernicious aspects of the Fouchet Plan.[310] The acrimonious negotiations ended in a deadlock. During the ensuing period of dissension, France embarked on a boycott of the still fragile Community institutions and withdrew from the NATO military structures.[311]

ii) The Foundation of the EPC

The year 1969 marks a turning point and the "birth year" of the EPC. That year the recently installed Pompidou Government lifted the bar on British membership in the Community. In an atmosphere of a revived "European euphoria" a summit meeting of the Six at the Hague directed the Foreign Ministers to study the best way of achieving "political unification, within the context of enlargement," in order to make Europe capable of assuming its world-wide responsibilities. At the same time, the Heads of Government called for a series of concrete measures to advance the Community toward an economic and monetary union.[312]

The Ministers responded a year later by approving, in Luxembourg, the "Davignon Report"[313] which serves as a foundation for the EPC. The report reverts to the method of governmental cooperation in foreign policy and may be read as implicitly rejecting the idea that a "political Community" could emerge through the integration process.[314] In the post-Gaullist climate the concept of "cooperation," rejected less than a decade earlier, received unanimous acceptance—not as a substitute for the integration process[315] but as a complementary, parallel, but separate process in the foreign affairs area. The two processes were to be transformed "before the end of the present decade . . . into a European Union" that would encompass "the whole complex of relations [between the Member States]."[316] In contrast with this undefined ultimate goal, the immediate modest objectives of the cooperation were stated to be, better mutual understanding by the Governments of the "great international problems" through exchanges of information and consultation; harmonization of views; coordination of positions; and, "where it appears possible and desirable, common actions."[317]

There was no normative instrument—only communiqués and "reports" reflecting political undertakings by the Heads of State or Government—no legal obligation of any sort. However, the engagement to consult was extended somewhat in 1973 to include seeking "common policies on practical problems," and on these questions "each State undertakes as a general rule not to take up final positions without prior consultation with its partners."[318] The consultation practice was "codified" and the commitment to consult was reaffirmed in somewhat greater detail in 1981.[319]

b) The Organizational Structure of the EPC

Unlike an international organization, the EPC does not have any institutions of its own since it is entirely in the hands of national officials acting for their respective Governments. This—it is said—is appropriate and necessary in a field that demands the highest degree of mutual trust and respect for the confidentiality of "state secrets."[320] At French insistence, the EPC structures were to be hermetically separated from Community institutions in order to avoid contamination with the insidious Brussels atmosphere of "supranationalism" and "atlanticism."[321] The Community staff also inclined initially toward a separation because it eyed the EPC with a jaundiced eye as still another French device directed against Community power but, as we shall see, in practice this separation has proved difficult to maintain.

i) The High-Level, Policy-Making Fora

At the head of the actual EPC mechanism is the "*European Council,*" an institutionalized summit of the ten Heads of State or Government accompanied by Foreign Ministers that was to convene initially at least three times a year.[322] As a "common roof," this Council is expected to coordinate the work of the EPC and the Communities.

The principal forum is the formal *Conference of the Foreign Affairs Ministers* meeting on EPC matters. Originally scheduled to take place at least once each six months in the capital of the Council President-in-Office, the meetings have in fact been much more frequent.

In 1973, the French Foreign Minister, M. Jobert, pressed the separateness from the Community to a point of forcing the Ministers to meet in EPC in Copenhagen in the morning, and to assemble the same afternoon in Brussels as a Community Council to deal with Community business. With the change in personnel and atmosphere, however, the EPC ministerial meetings now often take place back to back with the Community Council in Brussels or Luxembourg.

In 1974, the pretended separation was diluted somewhat further at the high level by still another common forum, the "*informal*" *meetings of Foreign Affairs Ministers* to discuss both EPC and EC affairs ("meetings *à la Gymnich*").

ii) Advisory Bodies, Back-up Services and Mechanisms for the Exchange of Information

The heads of the political departments in the Ministries of Foreign Affairs meet once a month as a *Political Committee* to prepare ministerial meetings and steer the groups of experts, and more often during the sessions of the U.N. General Assembly and of the Councils. The Committee's function is comparable to the role of the Brussels Committee of Permanent Representatives which prepares the work for the Community Council.

Within each Ministry of Foreign Affairs, a "*European correspondent*" coordinates the EPC work under the supervision of the Political Director. These diplomats constitute a "*group of European correspondents*"[323] which takes care of the procedural and organizational matters and prepares papers for the higher-level meetings.

Also under the direction of the Political Committee are the varied "*groups of experts,*" drawn from Foreign Affairs Ministries and organized according to regions (Africa, Asia, Mediterranean, Middle East, Latin America);[324] international fora (U.N., Conference on Security and Cooperation in Europe (CSCE)); subject matter (U.N.-disarmament); or function (chiefs of protocol, chiefs of communications).[325] Practical considerations forced the creation of the "Group for Coordination of the Arab-European Dialogue," common to the Community and EPC.

Another quasi-institutional element consists of the organized *cooperation of the Ambassadors* of the Member States posted in third states and at the seats of international organizations. They consult daily if necessary, as in time of a crisis (*e.g.* in Teheran or at the U.N.). Occasionally, the Political Committee asks the Ambassadors for a common report on a specific subject but such reports are said to reflect the lowest common denominator.[326] The Ambassador of the Member State holding the Presidency of the Council acts as a spokesman in any demarche or outside contacts. When a Minister receives an important third country visitor or himself returns from a visit to a third country, he provides a briefing, which has now become institutionalized, for the resident Ambassadors of the other members.[327]

A special coded *telex system* ("COREU," "*correspondence européenne*") facilitates continuing contacts, with some 5000 messages exchanged annually.

iii) Administration of the EPC

Since there is no permanent secretariat,[328] the *Presidency*, that is the Foreign Minister of the country holding the office of the President in the Community Council of Ministers, with whatever special staff of his own he may have available, is responsible for preparing all the meetings, drafting most of the declarations, reports and conclusions, even responses to questions to be answered in the European Parliament during his term of office. With the increasing business, the burden of the Presidency has become extremely heavy particularly for the smaller Members. During the busy periods the Presidency must organize a multitude of consultation meetings and act as spokesman in a variety of fora.[329] Building upon evolving custom, the Foreign Ministers agreed in 1981 that "the Presidency will be assisted by a small team of officials seconded from preceding and succeeding Presidencies" and assigned to the staff of their Embassies in the Presidency capital; as a further means to alleviate his burden the President may delegate certain tasks to his successor or predecessor.[330]

c) The Scope of the EPC

i) The General Scope

In principle, EPC embraces foreign policies of Member States with respect to third states. By this definition, foreign policy problems *between* the Members, such as the Northern Ireland question (or earlier, the status of Algeria), are excluded.[331] More recently, voices have been heard in and outside the European Parliament in support of bringing the Irish question within the EPC, particularly in the context of the violations of basic rights.[332] Also excluded are the economic and monetary aspects of foreign affairs that are within the jurisdiction of the Community—a jurisdiction that cannot be impaired by EPC. Finally, entire geographic regions and certain important aspects of foreign affairs have eluded the EPC process in practice.

ii) Particular Exclusions from the EPC Scope

(a) *Private and reserved domains.* In deference to certain Members' special interests, particular areas, namely East Berlin, the Maghreb and (until the Chad affair) "francophone" Africa, have been viewed politically as "private domains." Similarly, France and the United Kingdom generally are not prepared to consult on their vote in the U.N. Security Council.

(b) *Special relationships: East-West, EFTA and the U.S.A.* Political East-West relations were exclusively bilateral until the establishment of the common position at the Conference on Security and Cooperation in Europe (CSCE). This was the first successful EPC inroad which was broadened after the Afghanistan affair.

No need has been felt for special political consultations among the Ten on political relations with the EFTA countries. Although the procedural aspects of relations with the United States (the incidence and form of advance consultations) have been considered by the EPC,[333] substantive issues had only rarely been the subject of multilateral deliberations before the Iranian hostage and Afghanistan affairs.

(c) *Defense.* Defense policy is the farthest reaching exclusion, considering its vital role in foreign policy. Ireland and France, a nonmember and a "half-member" of NATO, have been insistent on keeping the NATO and EPC fora separate.[334]

2. Coordination and Interaction with the Community[335]

Although the necessity for coordination between the economic decision-making in the Community and the EPC procedures has been recognized from the outset, only a limited progress has been made in establishing a working relationship between the two systems.

a) Interaction at the Highest Levels

As indicated above, at the highest level the same individuals, the Heads of State or Government in the European Council and the Foreign Ministers, play two roles—one in Community matters and one in EPC—thus assuring a degree of awareness if not coordination. However, different and separate staffs do the preparatory work through different procedures: in the Community, formalized decision-making, initiated by the Commission's proposals, culminates in proposals by the Committee of Permanent Representatives to the Council of Ministers; in the EPC the small national staff in the capital of the Council's President-in-Office, backed up by the committees of national diplomats, prepares the political files through the consensual consultation process.

From an institutional point of view, responsibilities within the two frameworks remain strictly divided. Although the Ministers are no longer obliged to hold the respective meetings at separate times, they maintain the distinction scrupulously. As Bonvicini reports, the degree of the rigidity in the allocation of questions on the agenda depends on the incumbent President's inclination and his ability to persuade his colleagues.[336]

b) The Commission's Participation

The most important step toward coordination has been the admission of the Community Commission to regular participation in EPC work.[337] The President of the Commission and the commissioner responsible for external affairs now participate regularly in the European Council and in the EPC Conference of Foreign Ministers. They speak but do not vote, and their particular role is undefined. This development represented a radical change in the attitudes of both sides. It was due to the greater flexibility of the French President as much as to the positive experience with the Commission's role in the preparation for the CSCE and the realization that Community instrumentalities are useful, if concrete results are to be achieved in foreign policy. For the Commission itself this new activity posed a problem of internal organization and coordination.[338]

At the working level, since 1975 the Commission staff has participated without any restrictions in the meetings of the Political Committee.[339] Although Community officials take part in most of the EPC groups of experts touching upon Community affairs, until recently they were not allowed to take part in the European Correspondents' Group and thus could not participate in the preparation of the Political Committee's meetings nor, perhaps more importantly, in the follow-up of any decisions taken. The Commission is still denied a direct connection with the COREU telex network, but it receives daily copies of the messages from the Belgian Foreign Affairs Ministry.[340]

The participation of the Commission personnel, "still sporadic and superficial, even if growing" is based on custom and express or tacit invitation. In 1981, the Foreign Ministers agreed that "[w]ithin the framework of the established rules and procedures the Ten attach importance to the Commission of the European Communities being fully associated with Political Cooperation at all levels."[341] Unlike its important role in the Community, the Commission does not have the authority to initiate action.

It is interesting that the Political Committee has emerged as a competing actor not so much for the Commission, as may have been expected, but for the Committee of Permanent Representatives who until the arrival of EPC had the exclusive role of backing up the work of the Ministers and filtering the activities of the Commission. There is no satisfactory working relationship between these two important bodies; the fact that both are staffed predominantly from the same national Foreign Affairs Ministries does not seem to prevent a degree of jealousy and friction.

c) The Interaction between the European Parliament and the EPC

Under the Community Treaties, the European Parliament has "political" control over the Commission, including the theoretical authority to dismiss the Commission by a vote of no-confidence. It has no such power with respect to EPC, and its functions, broadly defined in the EPC documents,[342] are entirely advisory. This condition appears unpalatable to the deputies who have criticized both the separation of the two systems and the scarcity of information made available to them.[343]

Although the Parliament has routinely adopted resolutions on current international political problems,[344] the impact has been indifferent and its link with the EPC perfunctory: The Foreign Minister of the "Presidency" state meets periodically with the Parliament's Political Committee in more or less desultory "colloquia"; and the President-in-Office makes annual reports and answers Parliamentary questions (the number of which has risen substantially since the direct parliamentary elections). The answers require a consensus of the ten Governments, and no information is published on EPC consultations unless and until a consensus is reached. It is not surprising that the answers have been a source of frustration for the Parliamentarians, since any information supplied has invariably already entered the public domain and decisions have already been taken by the Governments.

3. Activities, Accomplishments and Limitations of the EPC

a) Internal Process: Exchange of Information, Consultation and Harmonization of Positions

A basic function of the network of national diplomats has been the exchange and pooling of information. The "club atmosphere," it is said, encourages openness and reduces surprises; and the absence of transnational institutions eliminates jurisdictional friction and doctrinal disputes. The working of the Communities has drawn into the European arena large sectors of national bureaucracies in the economic, environmental, scientific and social bureaus. Because of the EPC, this process of "Europeanization" has now reached deeply into the national foreign service establishments, and is producing, the argument continues, a "European reflex" among them that is bringing about a basic change in their outlook.[345] By the same token, the exclusive character of the "club" has added fuel to the charges of elitism and of a lack of genuine democratic control over European institutions. There is also the danger that a consensus reached on a confidential basis among the diplomats may not survive when exposed to the winds of national politics.

Unlike the Community Treaties, the documents establishing the EPC[346] set no concrete objectives, programs of action or deadlines. The hope, however, if not the expectation, is that the consultation process will mature into a customary rule, the breach of which will appear increasingly costly and that it will lead to a definition of common basic conceptions and common planning.[347] Thus far, the EPC has selected the consultation topics — within the arbitrary limits discussed above — episodically, in reaction to international developments, rather than on the basis of overall planning.

The consultation and consensus process has its own costs in efficiency and timeliness, as shown in the Afghan affair and in the Iranian hostage situation.[348] There are physical limitations on the diplomats' capacity to travel to the innumerable meetings and on the number of tasks that can be handled by the "Presidency."[349] Moreover, the much vaunted informality and flexibility of the process is beginning to show signs of bureaucratization. To mitigate the danger of undue delays, the Foreign Ministers agreed in 1981 that the Political Committee, or, if necessary, the Ministers, will convene within forty-eight hours at the request of three Member States.[350]

Although there is no objective way of measuring the impact of the process, there has been a gradual movement toward common positions on Rhodesia, Namibia, Cyprus, human rights violations and, surprisingly, on the Middle East.[351]

b) External Process: "Declaratory" Diplomacy and Common Positions in International Fora

Once a consensus is reached it may take the shape of a declaration following a meeting of the Ministers or the Heads of State or Government; a demarche with a third state; a mandate to the President-in-Office to undertake a diplomatic mission; or an agreement on a common position to be taken at an international conference or in an international organization, or even on a common guidance for nationals (*e.g.* the code of conduct for national business enterprises working in South Africa).

i) Recognition

Efforts to coordinate and synchronize national acts of recognition of new states or governments—and thus to initiate something akin to a "common recognition"—have proved unsuccessful thus far even with respect to Bangladesh, not to speak of Angola or Mozambique.[352] The European Council has made it clear that "in the present state of European integration, international rules on recognition remain applicable in their entirety and such recognition still lies within the exclusive competence of each State." Thus, although the establishment by Spain of diplomatic relations with Israel is not a prerequisite for Spain's accession to membership in the Community, it "could only facilitate the harmonization of the foreign policies of the Nine [all of whom maintain such relations], which would be in keeping with the objectives of European political cooperation."[353]

ii) International Conferences and Missions

The common position which the Nine were able to maintain over a period of four years at the thirty-five states' Conference on Security and Cooperation in Europe (CSCE) in Helsinki catapulted the Nine into a position of leadership in the Atlantic Alliance group. With the U.S. occupied elsewhere, the Nine became the principal spokesman for that group in relation to the Warsaw Pact and the non-aligned groups. Commission officials formed a part of the negotiating team which was led by the "Presidency of the day."[354] The solidarity of the Member States persevered through the Belgrade and Madrid sessions as well. This appears to be one demonstrable accomplishment of the EPC.

On the Arab-Israeli conflict the Member States have reached a significant measure of agreement since 1973, despite initial dramatic differences. Having agreed on a common platform, the Ministers sent the President-in-Office on two exploratory missions that, however, have not produced any noticeable impact. The "Euro-Arab dialogue," initiated by the European Summit in 1973 on a French proposal, led to the establishment of an EPC coordination group which reports both to the EPC Political Committee and to the Committee of the Permanent Representatives of the Community Council. In the General Commission of the dialogue, composed of European and Arab delegations at the Ambassadorial level, the Chairman of the EPC coordinating group speaks on political aspects, while a Commission official deals with economic and technical matters.[355] Thus far, however, this laboriously constructed structure has failed to show tangible results.

iii) The U.N. General Assembly

Several months prior to a U.N. General Assembly session the EPC working-group on the United Nations begins to study the agenda items for the benefit of the Political Committee. That Committee meets in New York at the opening of the session. During the three months' session, the permanent representatives to the United Nations, delegates and staff of the Ten meet at the call of the "Presidency" as many as 200 times. The President-in-Office states the common views of the Ten in the general debate.[356]

While the number of subjects covered by the consultations had grown, the percentage of identical voting had remained more or less stable since 1974 at the 80% to 84% level. The statistics, however, do not tell the whole story because the voting has diverged on important resolutions.[357] It has been suggested that despite the divergences, the Ten have acquired in the United Nations a "reputation of a coherent and effective group"[358] but the progression towards common voting seems to have reached a plateau.

Suggestions have come from Belgian Socialist Parliamentarians that Members of the European Parliament be appointed to national delegations of the United Nations. This would conform to a consistent United States practice of including Members of the Senate or House of Representatives foreign affairs committees in United States delegations to the United Nations General Assembly.[359]

c) "Common Action": Positive and Negative

Since the EPC system has no instrumentalities for implementing a common position, it must rely on Member States who hold a wide arsenal of such means, and on the Community with its budget and commercial and economic development policies powers.

Occasionally, when the Commission contemplates specific action, it requests an opinion on political aspects directly from the Political Committee or from one of the EPC groups, and at times an EPC group takes up the political implications of a Community activity at its own initiative.[360] Paradoxically, however, neither the important agreement between the Community and the People's Republic of China nor the (now deadlocked) negotiations between the Community and COMECON have appeared on the EPC agenda.[361]

i) Positive Action

When in 1975 the existence of the freshly established democratic institutions in Portugal was in danger following the "Revolution of Carnations," the European Council declared its political support of "a pluralist democracy" in that country, but it was the Community's European Investment Bank that provided special credit from the Community budget, and the Commission that opened economic negotiations with the Portuguese Government.[362] Similar interaction between the EPC and the Community led to substantial economic assistance, from both the Community and national budgets, to Indochina refugees in 1979 and, a year later, to the supply to Poland of critical agricultural commodities at favorable prices.

ii) Negative Action: The Sanctions

Imposition of economic sanctions against a third state has posed particular problems of interaction between the EPC, the Community and the Member States. Clearly, the EPC is concerned in view of the exclusively political objective; however, the means invariably fall within the commercial policy which is the exclusive domain of the Community. Yet EEC Treaty article 224 does contemplate that the Member States may act individually in the event of "serious international tension constituting threat of war" or in order to carry out obligations they have accepted for the purpose of maintaining peace and international security, and it calls for consultations if the sanctions may affect the functioning of the Common Market.[363]

(a) When the United Nations Security Council imposed an economic embargo against *Rhodesia* there were consultations within the EPC but the response came exclusively from the individual Member States. Several years later, when the question of compliance with the embargo was raised in the European Parliament, the Council of Ministers took the view that such measures, because of their political objective, were outside the common commercial policy sphere and within the national competence under article 224; although the Community "as a separate entity is not responsible for applying these decisions," nevertheless its regulations must be applied with due consideration to international commitments.[364]

(b) In the *Iranian hostage* case, the resolution on sanctions against Iran was vetoed in the United Nations Security Council by the Soviet Union, but the Foreign Ministers agreed, again in the context of the EPC, to seek necessary legislation in the national Parliaments that would enable the Member States to impose sanctions in accordance with the defeated United Nations resolution.[365] "We ha[d] to resort," reported a Dutch diplomat, "to Articles 224 and 225 because the opportunity to base the operations of the Community on Article 113 has been lost."[366]

(c) Following the Soviet invasion of *Afghanistan,* the EPC Conference of Ministers issued an anodyne declaration reflecting the previously publicized national policy statements, but in this case the Community became directly involved in support of President Carter's wheat embargo. The Commission, with the Council's approval, acted to prevent Community wheat exports replacing American deliveries.[367]

(d) A breakthrough of sorts for Community power occurred in connection with the sanctions against the Soviet Union after the declaration of martial law in *Poland.* In a regulation based specifically on article 113, the Council of Ministers noted that the "interests of the Community" required reduction in the imports from the Soviet Union and imposed a series of minor restrictions on such imports. In a companion regulation the Council exempted Greece from this measure, allegedly because the current state of incomplete integration of that country into the customs union called for special protection of its commerce.[368]

(e) Finally, in response to Argentina's "invasion" of the *Falkland*

Islands, "discussions" and "a decision" in EPC culminated in the adoption by the Council of a regulation, also based on article 113, imposing a general embargo on Argentinian imports into the Community. Problems had arisen, however, when it came to extending the embargo beyond the initial period.[369]

iii) The Division of Functions and the "Federalist" Tension

It is characteristic of the basic differences between the European and American systems that whereas in the former the imposition of sanctions raised the ubiquitous problem of State power against Community power, in the latter the controversy arose exclusively at the federal level, between the President and Congress, or between the Federal Government and individuals contesting the validity of federal action under federal law and the Constitution.[370]

European scholars and practitioners disagree on a variety of issues concerning sanctions, some real, others imaginary. Subject to one dissenting voice, however, it is widely agreed that, in contrast with its position in GATT, the Community has not "replaced" the Member States in the United Nations and thus is not bound as such by a Security Council resolution.[371] Beyond that, the ambiguity of articles 224 and 225 allows for a wide range of interpretations regarding the impact of these articles on Community commercial policy power and generally its role in this context. On the one hand, the bureaucrats see in article 113 a convenient way for bypassing national parliaments and obtaining quick action, but on the other hand, they conjure up a myriad of contingencies which in their conception call for preserving exclusive national powers.[372] However, in the light of the Council action in the Polish and Falkland Islands situations, the Community power to impose economic sanctions appears now established in practice, without necessarily precluding the power of a Member State to protect its essential interests as contemplated in article 224.[373]

IV. Concluding Observations

The contemporary European system for conducting foreign affairs is unprecedented, unparalleled, and hybrid. In this system foreign affairs are conducted neither strictly by states, nor by the central authority alone (as in federal states generally); rather, some affairs are conducted by individual states alone; some by the states in consultation with each other within the European Political Cooperation mechanism; some by the Community as an entity; and some by the Community together with or in parallel to the states. The European system is in flux, with the Community in some contexts replacing the Member States, in others appearing as an additional person in the international arena. Although the scope of Community foreign affairs is growing, foreign policy is still largely determined by the Member States within as well as outside the Community institutions. Because the Council works like a conference of states, Community foreign policy represents the sum of particular national interests of the Member States rather than a common interest.

A. On the Value of the Comparison

1. The Significant Variables to the Comparison

While *prima facie* Europe before the Community might be compared to the thirteen American states before the Union, the contextual reality is wholly different. Moreover, the American states moved to complete union for foreign policy purposes in one step, with individual states withdrawing completely from foreign affairs. Europe has not moved in one step to such a union and, as of today, its gradual movement is not headed towards the type of union in which the states would disappear as international persons. In the 1980's, surely, Europe is in a situation very different from that of the United States, whether in 1787 or since. States of Europe continue to have international personality, and to act on the international scene largely like other states, although in some areas they have given the Community powers to act.

In relation to its constituent states, the foreign affairs system of the United States is essentially as originally created by the Constitution. Important developments since 1789 were in the allocation of authority within the Federal Government, and not between the Federal Government and the states. In Europe, on the other hand, there is a continuing tension between the Member States and the Community. The precise allocation of foreign affairs power between the Community and the Member States is determined in the context of that tension, and it is articulated through interpretation of the constituent Treaty, with different perspectives by different Member States as well as by the Community institutions, and with the Court of Justice acting as ultimate umpire. Because of the reluctance of the Member State Governments, the Community political institutions have not been prepared to take full advantage of the Community foreign affairs power as defined liberally by the Court.

The continued existence of the states of Europe as major, if not predominant, international actors is perhaps the principal feature that raises serious question about the comparability with the United States system at both the political and constitutional levels. Nevertheless, on the assumption that the Europeans will wish to pursue the integration process, United States example and experience may serve to suggest particular devices by which democratic entities retaining substantial domestic independence can reduce their international sovereignty in pursuit of a more effective common role on the international scene.

2. Ways in Which the American Experience Can Be Used to Provide Guidelines for Community Development

a) As a Source of Ideas for Developing European Legal Doctrines

The experience of the United States, a country with democratic values and institutions kindred to those of Europe, may offer useful principles and techniques, whether by interpretation or formal amendment, as regards, for example:

"filling in the gaps" in the attributions of foreign affairs powers to central authorities;

determining limitations on the foreign affairs powers of the central authorities, to be derived from specific prohibitions in the constitutive document, from the basic character of the central institutional system, and above all, from principles of concern for individual human rights;

rights and remedies for individuals;

the role of the judiciary;

the supremacy of central authorities in foreign affairs and procedures for making it effective against the states;

the use of the pre-emption doctrine to determine whether, in a particular case, central foreign affairs power excludes state power;

the status of international agreements in "internal" law and remedies for enforcing them in that law (including the concept and import of "directly applicable and effective" treaties);

claims by central authorities against third states for violation of international law and response to third states' claims of such violations by central authorities;

assuring compliance by central authorities with international law on treatment of aliens by extending to them the protection of basic human rights available to citizens; and assuring compliance by central authorities with international law by extending central power to foreign affairs issues such as the "act of state" and sovereign immunity of foreign states, and generally removing such issues from power of individual states.

Within the sphere of its competence, that is essentially in economic affairs, the Community has already evolved its own variants of a number of these techniques. In some respects, such as the weight according to international agreements in its internal legal order, the Community doctrine, if not its practice, represents a clear advance over the American rule. Also, the judiciary in the Community has played a more decisive role in foreign affairs than American courts. While the United States Supreme Court has had only occasionally to confirm the legitimacy of federal action or to strike down interference by individual states, the Court of Justice has been called upon to employ its independent power for the purpose of enforcing Community authority to replace the Member States in the international arena. Yet American practice, extending as it does over more than two centuries, may be helpful, especially because of its longer historical perspective and the amplitude of the material.

b) As a Model for Possible Allocations of Powers within the Central Institutions

The United States experience may be particularly relevant in suggesting allocations of power within the central institutions, again taking into account the differences in those institutions and in the role of the component states in the two systems. The United States experience is especially suggestive as regards:

the distribution of authority between President and Congress with respect to the daily conduct of international relations, and representation of the United States in informal international intercourse as well as international bodies and activities;

extensive delegation of authority by Congress to the President, with devices (*e.g.*, the legislative veto) designed to supervise the uses of delegated authority or to terminate the delegation;

improving the expertise and facilities of Congressional committees dealing with foreign affairs; and

accepting a treaty with a third state as a sufficient basis for appropriation by Congress of the funds necessary for implementation of the treaty.

c) *As a Cautionary Tale*

However, the United States example can also suggest features which Europe should avoid. In fact, the United States, despite the Federal Government's monopoly of foreign affairs powers, often does not "speak with one voice" and experiences chronic deficiencies in evolving sustained foreign policy. This is due in part to the "Presidential system" in which the President is often unable to rely on the required majority support in the Senate; in part to the power competition and faulty coordination among Executive Departments and between them and the White House foreign relations contingent; and also to frequent lapses in communication between the Executive and Congress. Features to be particularly avoided include:

delay and frustration such as occur in the Senate for treaties laboriously negotiated by the Executive;
uncertainty as to the scope of the President's sole authority, especially his independent power to enter into executive agreements;
subjecting international law and treaties to "repeal" by Congressional legislation;
the "case or controversy" requirement that bars courts from giving opinions for institutional guidance;
obstacles to access to courts in the form of technical requirements of standing, and the uncertain and controversial doctrine rendering certain "political questions" nonjusticiable; and
"overjudicialization" and complexity of administrative procedures particularly in international trade matters.

B. Prospects for Europe

The American experience will become more interesting for the Europeans if and when the Community Council begins to act as a genuine Community organ rather than as a diplomatic conference of the Member States. The Council would have to honor the principle of majority voting as required in the Treaty and recognize the political, administrative and managerial functions of the Commission.[374] The Commission in turn would have to assert with greater vigor its role as an important, if not the leading, institution in foreign affairs. Finally, in Europe as in the United States, it is hard to find a policy issue that is not both "domestic" and "international" in its implications. The European Parliament will have to be given a more compelling voice in both domestic and foreign policy, not only to strengthen democracy in the Community but also to assure broad political support for common action.

A cardinal fact of American constitutional history has been the massive accretion of Presidential power in the twentieth century. Because of his control over the foreign affairs establishment and the military, he has become truly the "sole organ" capable of responding effectively to the needs of a centralized foreign policy. At this juncture, there is no evidence that an organ equipped with centralized diplomacy and other requisite instrumentalities will emerge in Europe in the foreseeable future. Although fully centralized foreign affairs power has never been seriously questioned in the United States, the same degree of centralization may not prove necessary or even desirable for Europe. The European Political Cooperation mechanism does not point in the direction of centralization. It remains to be seen how, in the longer run, this mechanism can be brought into an organic relationship with the Community if the essential character and dynamics of the integration process are to be preserved.[375]

Notes

1. Case 26/62, Van Gend en Loos v. Nederlandse Administratie der Belastingen, [1963] ECR 1, 12.

2. *See, e.g.,* Pescatore, *Les relations extérieures des Communautés européennes,* [1961] II REC. DES COURS ACAD DR. INT. 1, 19–20.

3. E. STEIN, P. HAY & M. WAELBROECK, EUROPEAN COMMUNITY LAW AND INSTITUTIONS IN PERSPECTIVE 927–29 (Indianapolis/New York, Bobbs-Merrill, 1976).

4. Is the foreign relations power "executive," "legislative," or "federative"? *See,* Q. WRIGHT, THE CONTROL OF AMERICAN FOREIGN RELATIONS 134 ff (New York, MacMillan, 1922).

5. In seeking to identify the variables that enhance or inhibit integration in foreign affairs the paradigms evolved by the various doctrines (functionalist, neo-functionalist, federalist, security-Community, etc.) may be helpful. For a discussion and further references *see* Elazar & Greilsammer, *The Federal Democracy: The U.S.A. and Europe Compared—A Political Science Perspective,* in INTEGRATION THROUGH LAW, vol. 1, METHODS, TOOLS AND INSTITUTIONS, Bk. 1, at § II.A.3.b (M. Cappelletti, M. Seccombe, & J. Weiler eds., Berlin/New York, Walter de Gruyter, 1986) [hereinafter cited as INTEGRATION THROUGH LAW].

6. *See, e.g.,* Stein & Sandalow, *On the Two Systems: An Overview,* in COURTS AND FREE MARKETS: PERSPECTIVES FROM THE UNITED STATES AND EUROPE 3, 3–4 (T. Sandalow & E. Stein eds., Oxford/New York, Clarendon Press, 1982) [hereinafter cited as COURTS AND FREE MARKETS].

7. In foreign affairs, states are "deaf and dumb" according to King, as quoted in 1 FARRAND, THE RECORDS OF THE FEDERAL CONVENTION OF 1787, at 323

(New Haven, Yale U.P., 1937). *See* L. HENKIN, FOREIGN AFFAIRS AND CONSTITUTION 336 n.71 (New York, Foundation Press, 1972). Update: A second edition of Henkin's treatise appeared under the title FOREIGN AFFAIRS AND THE UNITED STATES CONSTITUTION (Oxford, Clarendon Press, 1996).

8. For discussion of the European Political Cooperation mechanism, *see infra* notes 308–73 and accompanying text.

9. L. HENKIN, *supra* note 7, at 5–6. More recently, scholarly output has been increasing because of the increased number of litigations with foreign affairs aspects.

10. I have used the phrase "assembled in the Council of Ministers" to stress the intergovernmental nature of the Council. "The Representatives of the Member States meeting in the Council" are, of course, an entirely different matter. *See* P.S.R.F. MATHIJSEN, A GUIDE TO EUROPEAN COMMUNITY LAW § 5–12, at 243–44 (2nd ed., London/New York, Sweet & Maxwell/M. Bender, 1975). *Cf.* the phrase "United States, in Congress assembled" in the Articles of Confederation, *e.g.* in Art. V: "In determining questions in the United States, in Congress assembled, each State shall have one vote."

11. The Supreme Court occasionally draws on customary international law in deciding disputes between states, especially in matters analogous to international disputes, *e.g.*, boundaries. *See, e.g.*, Arkansas v. Tennessee, 246 U.S. 158, 170 (1918) and 310 U.S. 563, 570 (1940).

12. Congressional power over naturalization is exclusive of the individual states. The Constitutional foundation was solidified by the post-Civil War fourteenth amendment which provided in sec. 1: "All persons born or naturalized in the United States, and subject to the jurisdiction thereof, are citizens of the United States and of the state wherein they reside." Under the Articles of Confederation, "the free inhabitants" of each state (not including paupers, vagabonds and fugitives from justice) were "entitled to all privileges and immunities of free citizens in the several States" (Art. IV), but it was left to each state individually to prescribe the terms upon which it would admit foreigners to citizenship. Thus, a lax policy of naturalization in one state could frustrate the stricter policies of the other states. According to Roger Sherman, the Constitution gave Congress the powers to establish a uniform rule of naturalization (art. I, sec. 8, cl. 4), in order "to prevent particular States receiving citizens, and forcing them upon others." Quoted in E. DUMBAULD, THE CONSTITUTION OF THE UNITED STATES 139 (Norman, Okla., U. Okla. P., 1964).

13. Update: The Maastricht Treaty (arts. 8–8e), as amended by the Amsterdam Treaty (art. 2, Part II, EC), establishes "a Citizenship of the Union" to complement national citizenship and specifies the rights and duties of the Union's citizens including the right of free movement and residence within the Union, the right to vote and run in municipal elections and the elections for the European Parliament in the state of their residence, to petition the European Parliament and the Ombudsman, etc.

14. Pescatore, *supra* note 2, at 21.

15. M. JENSEN, THE ARTICLES OF CONFEDERATION–AN INTERPRETATION OF THE

SOCIAL CONSTITUTIONAL HISTORY OF THE AMERICAN REVOLUTION 1774–1781, at 143–45 (Madison, Wis., U. Wis. P., 1940).

16. THE FEDERALIST No. 64, at 393 (J. Jay) (C. C. Rossiter ed., New York, The New American Library, 1961). The Congress was not in continuous session, it was rent by bitter disagreements; absenteeism often caused lack of a quorum and it was frequently embroiled in trivialities. E. DUMBAULD, *supra* note 12, at 32–33.

17. On the first secretary, Robert R. Livingston, *see* L.S. KAPLAN, COLONIES INTO NATION: AMERICAN DIPLOMACY 1763–1801, at 151 (New York, MacMillan, 1972); on John Jay's tenure, *see id.* at 155.

18. *See infra* text accompanying note 329.

19. W.P. MURPHY, THE TRIUMPH OF NATIONALISM 38 (Chicago, Quadrangle Books, 1967); F.W. MARKS, INDEPENDENCE ON TRIAL 3–4 (Baton Rouge, La. State U.P., 1973); Van Tyne, *Sovereignty in the American Revolution: A Historical Study,* 12 AM. HIST. REV. 529, 540–41 (1907).

20. F.W. MARKS, *supra* note 19, at 15, 47. Under the Articles, the Congress had only the power to agree upon the number of troops to be raised but the men were recruited by the states, although at Continental expense.

21. T. BAILEY, A DIPLOMATIC HISTORY OF THE AMERICAN PEOPLE, ch. 5 (8th ed., New York, Appleton-Century-Crofts (Meredith), 1969).

22. *See* Art. VI as read with Art. IX of the Articles of Confederation.

23. F.W. MARKS, *supra* note 19, at 54–56, 68. *See also, generally,* P.A. VARG, FOREIGN POLICIES OF THE FOUNDING FATHERS 51–53 (Lansing, Mich., Mich. State U.P., 1963).

24. For further discussion of the process of integration after World War II, *see* Elazar & Greilsammer, *supra* note 5, at § II.A.3.b.

25. J. MONNET, MEMOIRS 288–317, 340 (New York, Doubleday & Co., 1978).

26. The European Defense Community Treaty, Paris, 27 May 1952, CMD. No. 9127 (London, H.M.S.O., 1952); J. LEGARET & E. MARTIN-DUMESNIL, LA COMMUNAUTÉ EUROPÉENNE DE DÉFENSE — ETUDE ANALYTIQUE DU TRAITÉ DU 27 MAI 1952 (Paris, Lib. J. Vrin, 1953); Ad hoc Assembly, Draft Treaty embodying the Statute of the European Community presented to the Assembly by the Constitutional Committee, Doc. 12, 2nd Part, Paris, 26 Feb. 1953.

27. J. MONNET, *supra* note 25, at 338, 343.

28. *Id.* at 394.

29. *Id.* at 395, 398.

30. The important *Spaak Report* which served as a foundation for the two treaties devotes a single page — on "unification of the commercial policy" — out of a total of 135 pp. to a foreign affairs subject. COMITÉ INTERGOUVERNEMENTAL CRÉÉ PAR LA CONFÉRENCE DE MESSINE, RAPPORT DES CHEFS DE DÉLÉGATION AUX MINISTRES DES AFFAIRES ETRANGÈRES 75 (Brussels, Secrétariat, 21 Apr. 1956).

31. Monnet quotes Armand as suggesting "that we erect a statue to Nasser, the federator of Europe. It was a joke." J. MONNET, *supra* note 25, at 422.

32. The intensity of American power — and its impact — has varied. For instance, Secretary Dulles' pressure in support of the European Defense

Community is said to have contributed to its defeat in France, but Secretary Kissinger's counterproductive "Year of Europe" campaign may have stimulated the debate over "European identity."

33. *See infra* note 167 and accompanying text.

34. *See, e.g.,* GRUNDGESETZ (GG) art. 32 (W. Ger.). *See also id.* art. 59.

35. U.S. CONST. art. I, § 8, cls. 1–5, 10–16; art. II, § 2, cls. 1–2, § 3; art. VI, § 2. On judicial power, *see* art. III, § 2, cls. 1–2; § 3, cl. 1.

36. U.S. CONST. art. 1, § 10 provides:

> 1. No State shall enter into any treaty, alliance, or confederation; grant letters of marque and reprisal. . . .
> 2. No State shall, without the consent of the Congress, lay any imposts or duties on imports or exports, except what may be absolutely necessary for executing its inspection laws: and the net produce of all duties and imposts, laid by any State on imports or exports, shall be for the use of the treasury of the United States; and all such laws shall be subject to the revision and control of the Congress.
> 3. No State shall, without the consent of Congress, lay any duty of tonnage, keep troops, or ships of war in time of peace, enter into any agreement or compact with another State, or with a foreign power, or engage in war, unless actually invaded, or in such imminent danger as will not admit of delay.

See also art. I, § 9, cls. 5 & 6.

37. EEC Treaty arts. 28, 111–14, 228–31, 237–38.

38. *See infra* text accompanying note 239.

39. *See supra* notes 15–23 and accompanying text.

40. Art. II, cls. 1 & 2, § 3. *See* E.S. CORWIN, THE PRESIDENT'S CONTROL OF FOREIGN RELATIONS 3 (Princeton, Princeton U.P., 1917).

41. L. HENKIN, *supra* note 7, at 90.

42. EEC Treaty arts. 28, 113(1)–(2) & 149.

43. EEC Treaty arts. 111 and 112: tariff negotiations and harmonization of national policies during the transitional period; arts. 113 and 114: negotiation and conclusion of tariff and trade agreements with third countries. *See also* art. 115: protective measures against deflections of trade; art. 116: Member States to proceed "only by common action" within international organizations.

44. Discussed *infra* text accompanying note 79.

45. Art. 228 provides:

> 1. Where this Treaty provides for the conclusion of agreements between the Community and one or more States or an international organisation, such agreements shall be negotiated by the Commission. Subject to the powers vested in the Commission in this field, such agreements shall be concluded by the Council, after consulting the Assembly where required by this Treaty.
>
> The Council, the Commission or a Member State may obtain before-

hand the opinion of the Court of Justice as to whether an agreement envisaged is compatible with the provisions of this Treaty. Where the opinion of the Court of Justice is adverse, the agreement may enter into force only in accordance with Article 236.

2. Agreements concluded under these conditions shall be binding on the institutions of the Community and on Member States.

Update: As amended, this article now provides procedures for provisional application and for suspension of treaties concluded by the Community. It details the voting formulas in the Council, codifies the role of the Commission and specifies the role of the European Parliament whose assent is now required for enumerated categories of treaties.

46. Art. 238 provides:

> The Community may conclude with a third State, a union of States or an international organisation agreements establishing an association involving reciprocal rights and obligations, common action and special procedures.
>
> These agreements shall be concluded by the Council, acting unanimously after consulting the Assembly.
>
> Where such agreements call for amendments to this Treaty, these amendments shall first be adopted in accordance with the procedure laid down in Article 236.

47. EEC Treaty arts. 229, 230, 231. Part Four on association of the overseas countries and territories is of limited importance today.

48. EEC Treaty art. 237.

49. *See infra* text accompanying notes 50–65. Those who reject *Curtiss-Wright* (*see infra* note 55) would say that the federal monopoly is on the face of the Constitution, the missing powers being there but hidden in other clauses and the exclusion of the states complete in art. I, § 10.

50. L. HENKIN, *supra* note 7, at 16. For this section, and throughout this essay, I rely heavily on his classic study.

51. *Id.* at 17.

52. 130 U.S. 581 (1889).

53. *Id.* at 603–4.

54. The tenth amendment came into force two years after the Constitution and is commonly considered to be one of the "Bill of Rights" amendments (the first ten amendments).

55. United States v. Curtiss-Wright Export Corp., 299 U.S. 304 (1936). The question was whether the Congress had the authority to delegate to the President broad discretionary power to impose an arms embargo on countries embroiled in the Chaco war.

56. *See* L. HENKIN's lucid summary, *supra* note 7, at 22–23.

57. Discussed *infra* text accompanying notes 70–75.

58. United States v. Curtiss-Wright Export Corp., 299 U.S. 304, 316–18 (1936).

59. For references in support of this view, *see* Morris, *The Forging of the Union Reconsidered: A Historical Refutation of State Sovereignty over Seabeds,* 74 COLUM. L. REV. 1056, 1066 (1974).

60. Levitan, *The Foreign Relations Power: An Analysis of Mr. Justice Sutherland's Theory,* 55 YALE L.J. 467, 478 (1946).

61. L. HENKIN, *supra* note 7, lists the authorities at 289–91 n.10. He concludes that there is perhaps no disagreement that under the Articles of Confederation the states retained no external sovereignty but it is not agreed whether the states had sovereignty before the Articles; whether under the Articles they could have gained (or regained) sovereignty at will; and whether the sovereignty passed directly from the United States under the Articles, to the United States under the Constitution. *Id.* at 291. Also, Sutherland's view need not depend on whether the Constitution was a compact among the states or among the peoples of the states. *Id.* at 289 n.8. For an effort to show that "challenging his history does not necessarily destroy" Sutherland's doctrine, *see id.* at 23–24.

62. *See* Justice Jackson's concurring opinion in Youngstown Sheet & Tube Co. v. Sawyer, 343 U.S. 579, 635–36 n.2 (1952) referring to Sutherland's discussion as a "dictum." For the support and criticism (prior to *Curtiss-Wright*) of the "general theory of sovereign powers which would vest in the national government all [foreign affairs] powers not expressly prohibited" by the constitutional document *see* Q. WRIGHT, *supra* note 4, at 131.

63. *See* Sandalow, *The Expansion of Federal Legislative Authority;* Linde, *Transportation and State Laws under the United States Constitution: The Evolution of Judicial Doctrine*; and Blasi, *Constitutional Limitations on the Power of States to Regulate the Movement of Goods in Interstate Commerce,* in COURTS AND FREE MARKETS, *supra* note 6, at 49, 139 & 174, respectively.

64. *See* Stein & Sandalow, *supra* note 6, at 18.

65. L. HENKIN, *supra* note 7, at 26. The two cases indicating the exceptions are Oregon v. Mitchell, 400 U.S. 112 (1970) and National League of Cities v. Usery, 426 U.S. 833 (1976), *overruled,* Garcia v. San Antonio Metropolitan Transit Authority *et al.,* 105 S. Ct. 1005 (1985). Update: See *supra* p. 157, note 36.

66. *See e.g.,* Case 8/55, Fédération Charbonnière de Belgique v. High Authority, [1954–56] ECR 245; Case 20/59, Italy v. High Authority, [1960] ECR 325; Case 25/59, The Netherlands v. High Authority, [1960] ECR 355. *See also, generally,* Ganshof van der Meersch, *L'ordre juridique des Communautés Européennes et le droit international,* [1975] V REC. DES COURS ACAD. DR. INT. 1; Sasse & Yourow, *The Growth of Legislative Power of the European Communities,* in COURTS AND FREE MARKETS, *supra* note 6, at 92, 94.

67. Stein & Sandalow, *supra* note 6, at 16 ff, emphasizing the analogy to Justice Marshall's approach in McCulloch v. Maryland, 17 U.S. (4 Wheat.) 316 (1819).

68. Case 22/70, Commission v. Council, [1971] ECR 263 *[ERTA]* (the case involved the European Road Transport Agreement, referred to as ERTA). *See infra* text accompanying note 194.

69. Also discussed *infra* text accompanying notes 193–99. EEC Treaty art.

4(1) ("Each institution shall act within the limits of the powers conferred on it by this Treaty") is often cited as a basis for the "enumerated powers" principle. But, as Pescatore points out, this provision "lays down the idea of 'separation of powers' [between the Community institutions], but says nothing about the question of the power relationships between the Community and its Member States." P. PESCATORE, THE LAW OF INTEGRATION 37 n.19 (Leiden, Sijthoff, 1974). Update: *See also infra* text at, and cases in, notes 179, 194–201, 207, 216, and more recently Opinion 2/91 (*Re* ILO Convention 170), [1993] ECR-I-1061 denying the Community's exclusive competence. In Opinion 1/94 (*Re* the WTO Agreements), [1994] ECR I-5267, the Court affirmed the Community's exclusive foreign commercial policy power as including World Trade Organization agreements on EURATOM and coal and steel products, on agriculture and sanitary and phytosanitary measures and technical barriers to trade; but it held—contrary to the position of the Commission—that the exclusive competence covered only cross-border aspects of the important agreement on services (involving no movement of persons), that it did not cover international agreements in the field of transport nor the Agreement on Trade Related Measures of Intellectual Property (except for a section dealing with border measures). The principal reasons for the restrictive interpretation appear to be the existence of chapters in the EC Treaty covering services, movement of persons, transport and intellectual property, as well as the fact that the existing Community legislation covered only parts of these sectors. According to Opinion 2/92 (*Re* OECD National Treatment Instrument), 1995, [1996] ECR I-521, exclusive competence in the absence of *any* internal legislation applies *only* to situations where the conclusion of an international agreement is necessary to achieve a treaty objective which could not be attained by the adoption of internal measures. Thus, in practical terms, there might be only a few instances where the implied exclusive competence could be invoked. *See* F.G. Jacobs, *The Completion of the Internal Market v. the Incomplete Common Commercial Policy,* in THE LEGAL REGULATION OF THE EUROPEAN COMMUNITY'S EXTERNAL RELATIONS AFTER COMPLETION OF THE INTERNAL MARKET 3 (S.V. KONSTANDINIDIS ed., Dartmouth, Aldershot, 1996).

70. EEC Treaty art. 210: "The Community shall have legal personality."

71. Case 22/70, *ERTA,* [1971] ECR 263, 274; and Joined Cases 3, 4 & 6/76, Cornelis Kramer and Others, [1976] ECR 1279, 1308.

72. *See supra* notes 52 and 55. Most writers agree that in the passage quoted *supra,* text accompanying note 71, the Court purports to say that "international personality" provides the general capacity to enter into international agreements but that any specific treaty-power must be found in the Treaty. Kovar, *L'affaire de l'A.E.T.R. devant la Cour de justice des Communautés européenes et la compétence internationale de la C.E.E.,* 17 A.F.D.I. 386, 391 (1971); Ganshof van der Meersch, *Les relations extérieures de la C.E.E. dans le domaine des politiques communes et l'arrêt de la Cour de Justice du 31 mars 1971,* 8 C.D.E. 127, 137 ff (1972). But some question the need for or logic of the passages as so interpreted.

I was able to find only one writer who interprets the ECJ case law to mean the

Community may fill the lacunae in the Treaty grants of foreign relations powers directly from public international law, *i.e.,* Bleckmann, who argues that the Court, "in the *Kramer* case, expressed an opinion which we might indeed generalize: the Community, in the limits of its competence for agriculture, traffic *[sic]* and so on, might execute all competences which public international law attributes to States . . ."; and, more generally, that, contrary to the prevailing opinion in literature, "certain competences might be directly deduced from public international law" (a proposition reminiscent of the *Curtiss-Wright* rationale adjusted to the partially integrated nature of the Community). Bleckmann, *The Competence of the E.E.C.,* in DIVISION OF POWERS BETWEEN THE EUROPEAN COMMUNITIES AND THEIR MEMBER STATES IN THE FIELD OF EXTERNAL RELATIONS 3, 13–14 (C.W. Timmermans & E.L.M. Völker eds., Deventer (N.L.), Kluwer, 1981) [hereinafter cited as DIVISION OF POWERS]. *See also* Bleckmann, *Zur Verbindlichkeit des allgemeinen Völkerrechts für internationale Organisationen,* 37 ZAÖRV 107 (1977). In *Kramer* (also discussed *infra* text accompanying note 196)—a progeny of *ERTA* applying the "internal/external parallelism" doctrine—at issue was the power of the EC to enter into international commitments for the conservation of fishing resources of the sea. Having determined that the pre-condition (existence of "internal" powers *re* conservation measures) was satisfied and holding that the Council in fact had such power, the Court had to decide whether this power was limited to the fishing zones of the Member States or if it extended to also allow regulation of high sea fishing by fishermen from the Member States. The Court found, on the basis of art. 102 of the Act of Accession as well as art. 1 of Council Reg. (EEC) No. 2142/70 (JO No. L 236, 27 Oct. 1970, p.5; [1970] OJ (spec. Eng. ed.) at 707) and "the very nature of things," that "the rule-making authority of the Community *ratione materiae* also extends—in so far as the Member States have similar authority under public international law—to fishing on the high seas." Joined Cases 3, 4, & 6/76, *Kramer,* [1976] ECR 1279, 1309.

73. *See especially* Quadri, *La personalité internationale de la Communauté,* in LES RELATIONS EXTÉRIEURES DE LA COMMUNAUTÉ EUROPÉENNE UNIFIÉE 41, 41–42, 47 (M. Melchior ed., Univ. of Liège, Institut d'Etudes Juridiques Européennes, 1969) and sources cited therein at 41 & 42 n.2.

74. A. GIARDINA, COMUNITÀ EUROPEE E STATI TERZI 115, 160, 167 (Naples, Jovene, 1964).

75. Pescatore, in DIVISION OF POWERS, *supra* note 72, at 69, 75. In the United States, the states could not "regain" anything that the Federal Government has except by constitutional amendment, and the amendment process is not within the exclusive control of the states since an amendment usually requires prior approval of two-thirds of both Houses of Congress.

76. Case 22/70, *ERTA,* [1971] ECR 263, 283.

77. *See, e.g.,* Council Reg. (EEC) No. 802/68 of 27 June 1968, on the Common Definition of the Concept of the Origin of Goods, JO No. L 148, 20 June 1969, p. 1 ([1968–69] II OJ (spec. Eng. ed.) at 165) and Council Reg. (EEC) No. 1318/71 of 21 June 1971 amending Reg. (EEC) No. 802/68, OJ No. L 139, 25 June 1971, p. 6 (referring to EEC Treaty arts. 111, 113, 155, 227 & 235).

78. Mastellone, *The External Relations of the E.E.C. in the Field of Environmental Protection,* 30 I.C.L.Q. 104, 111 ff (1981). U.S. CONST. art. I, § 8, cl. 18 empowers Congress to "make all laws which shall be necessary and proper for carrying into execution for foregoing powers, and all other powers vested by this Constitution in the government of the United States," whereas EEC Treaty art. 235 authorizes powers necessary "to attain, in the course of the operation of the common market, one of the objectives of the Community." Thus in the United States, in theory, an implied power can be derived only from a power enumerated in the Constitution, whereas in the Community it must be related to one of its "objectives," obviously a broader concept than "powers." Yet early in its history, Chief Justice Marshall's Supreme Court turned "powers" into "objectives" to reach a broad definition of federal legislative powers. *See* McCulloch v. Maryland, 17 U.S. (4 Wheat.) 316 (1819) and comment by Sandalow, *supra* note 63, at 59. As in *ERTA,* in *McCulloch* Marshall upheld federal power without relying solely on the "necessary and proper" clause, but he nevertheless expatiated on it at length. As for foreign affairs powers, it may be argued under *Curtiss-Wright* that Congress can carry out all powers of the United States inherent in its sovereignty.

79. *See, generally,* Krislov, Ehlermann & Weiler, *Political Organs and the Decision-Making Process in the United States and the European Communities, supra* INTEGRATION THROUGH LAW, Bk. 2.

80. *See infra* text accompanying notes 235–42, 254.

81. *See, e.g.,* right to equal pay for men and women in EEC Treaty art. 119 and Case 43/75, Defrenne v. Sabena, [1976] ECR 455; and Case 44/79, Hauer v. Land Rheinland-Pfalz, [1979] ECR 3727.

82. John Marshall's statement in the House of Representatives, 10 ANNALS OF CONG. 613 (1800), *reprinted in* 18 U.S. (5 Wheat.) Appendix at 26 n.1 (1820).

83. Rovine, *Congressional-Executive Relations and United States Foreign Policy,* 17 WILLAMETTE L. REV. 41, 48 (1980). *See also* Weiss Fagen, *U.S. Foreign Policy and Human Rights: The Role of Congress,* in PARLIAMENTARY CONTROL OVER FOREIGN POLICY: LEGAL ESSAYS 111 (A. Cassese ed., Alphen a/d Rijn/ Germantown, Md., Sijthoff & Noordhoff, 1980); Kohl, *Congressional Foreign Affairs Committees in the United States of America,* in PARLIAMENTARY FOREIGN AFFAIRS COMMITTEES: THE NATIONAL SETTING 285 (A. Cassese ed., Padua/New York, CEDAM/Oceana Pubs., 1982).

84. U.S. CONST. art. II, § 2, cl. 2 and art. II, § 3. The Senate consents to or rejects the appointment; it probably cannot consent with conditions. E.S. CORWIN, THE PRESIDENT: OFFICE AND POWERS 1787–1957, at 78 (New York, N.Y.U.P., 1957).

85. H.M. WRISTON, EXECUTIVE AGENTS IN AMERICAN FOREIGN RELATIONS (Baltimore, Johns Hopkins Press, 1929).

86. This despite the apparent prohibition in U.S. CONST. art. I, § 6, cl. 2.

87. *See, e.g.,* Trade Act of 1974, ch. VI, § 161(a), Pub. L. No. 93–618, 88 Stat. 2008, 19 U.S.C. § 2211(a) (1975). In the Community the Council often "imposes" its representatives on the Commission. *See infra* text accompanying notes 171 & 191.

88. To what extent can Congress impose duties on an executive officer? Kendall v. United States, 37 U.S. (12 Pet.) 524, 610 (1838).

89. Formerly called the Tariff Commission. *See* the Trade Act of 1974, §171(a), 19 U.S.C. § 2231(a).

90. 12 J. Mégret, J.V. Louis, D. Vignes, M. Waelbroeck, J. Deworst & P. Brückner, Le Droit de la Communauté économique européenne, Commentaire du Traité et de textes pris pour son application 6–8 (Brussels, Institut d'études Européennes, Ed. de l'Univ. de Bruxelles, 1970–) [hereinafter cited as Brussels Commentary]; G. Sjöstedt, The External Role of the European Community 107 (Westmead, U.K., Saxonhouse, 1977).

91. Bull. EC 1–1981, point 2.2.35. The Protocol on the Privileges and Immunities of the European Communities of 8 Apr. 1965, art. 17 provides that the "Member State in whose territory the Communities have their seat shall accord the customary diplomatic immunities and privileges to missions of third countries accredited to the Communities." The Protocol, along with the Merger Treaty, became part of Belgian domestic law. *See* Salmon, *Les représentations et missions permanentes auprès de la CEE et de l'Euratom,* in 1 Les Missions permanentes auprès des organisations internationales 561, 718 ff (M. Virally, P. Gerbet & J. Salmon eds., Brussels, Bruylant, 1971).

92. Protocol on the Privileges and Immunities of the European Communities of 8 Apr. 1965, art. 17. *See supra* note 91.

93. *See* authors listed in Salmon, *supra* note 91, at 718 n.1.

94. EEC Treaty arts. 155 & 228. *See* Sauvignon, *Les Communautés européennes et le droit de legation actif,* [1978] R.M.C. 176, 180. *See generally,* 2 H.G. Schermers, International Institutional Law 733 (Leiden, Sijthoff, 1972); 12 Brussels Commentary, *supra* note 90, at 8.

95. Update: The nominee for the Presidency must be approved by the European Parliament and the members of the Commission are nominated by the member states in "common accord" with that nominee. The President and the other members of the Commission must be approved as a body by the European Parliament. After such approval the President and the Commission members as a body are appointed by common accord of the member governments. Amsterdam Treaty of 1997, art. 2 (40).

96. 12 Brussels Commentary, *supra* note 90, at 10–11.

97. The new procedure was included in the "Luxembourg Compromise" following the French boycott of the Community. Bull. EC 3–1966, at pp. 8–9.

98. *See infra* notes 326–27 and accompanying text.

99. *See infra* text accompanying notes 335–43.

100. There can be no meaningful distinction between making and implementing foreign policy.

101. In the early 20th century Congress pretended to some part in the recognition of new states. 1 G. Hackworth, Digest of International Law 162–63 (Washington, Dep't. of State Pubs., U.S. Gov't Print. Off., 1960); L. Henkin, *supra* note 7, at 82, & 335 n.65.

102. *See, e.g.,* 26 Cong. Rec. 2001–2 (1894) (a resolution of the House of

Representatives condemning a U.S. minister for illegally aiding in overthrowing the government of the Hawaiian Islands); S. Res. 327, 69th Cong., 2nd Sess., 68 CONG. REC. 2233 (1927) (favoring arbitration of an oil dispute with Mexico); H.J. Res. 1145, 78 Stat. 384 (1964) (Gulf of Tonkin Resolution).

103. U.S. CONST. art. I, § 8, cls. 1, 11–14.

104. U.S. CONST. art. II, § 2, cl. 1.

105. In the War Powers Resolution of 1973 the Congress denied that the President had authority to commit U.S. forces into hostilities on his own authority unless there had been an attack on the U.S. or its armed forces. The Resolution requires the President to consult with Congress "in every possible instance" before introducing U.S. forces into hostilities. The President must terminate hostilities within 60 days unless Congress authorizes him to continue, and Congress may direct him to terminate hostilities at any time by concurrent resolution (not subject to the President's veto). Pub. L. No. 93–148, 87 Stat. 555 (codified at 50 U.S.C. § 1541–48 (1975 & Supp. IV 1980) (H.R.J. Res. 542, adopted over a Presidential veto on 7 Nov. 1973)). The Constitutionality of this Resolution has been questioned. *See generally* A. VAN W. THOMAS & A.J. THOMAS, JR., THE WAR-MAKING POWERS OF THE PRESIDENT — CONSTITUTIONAL AND INTERNATIONAL LAW ASPECTS (Dallas, SMU Press, 1982); W.T. REVELEY, III, WAR POWERS OF THE PRESIDENT AND CONGRESS — WHO HOLDS THE ARROWS AND OLIVE BRANCH? (Charlottesville, U.P. of Va., 1981). In view of the broad language in the *Chadha* case, *infra* note 116, the "legislative veto" feature of the Resolution must probably be considered unconstitutional unless the war power is viewed as particularly "legislative." Although President Washington alone proclaimed neutrality, thereafter Congress asserted this authority. The President can occupy territory but annexation can be done only by Congress or a treaty approved by the Senate. Hawaii and Texas became states by an agreement concluded by the President and approved by both Houses of Congress. Update: The President does not have a concurrent war power, Dellums v. Bush, 152 F. Supp. 1141 (D.D.C. 1990). The President has no right to act contrary to a Congressional enactment; he could not fight the Gulf War without Congressional approval on the ground that it was *authorized* by the U.N. Security Council, but may have been able to do so had the Council adopted a *decision* commanding the U.S. to do so. L. Henkin, *Foreign Affairs and the Constitution,* 66 FOREIGN AFFAIRS 284 (1987–88); L. Henkin, *Congress, the President and the United Nations,* 3 PACE YEARBOOK OF INT'L LAW 1 (1991).

106. U.S. CONST. art. I, § 8, cl. 3.

107. Patent and copyright legislation is based on a specific grant in art. I, § 8, cl. 8. Trademarks are regulated under the commerce power, art. I, § 8, cl. 3.

108. *See* U.S. CONST. art. I, § 8, cl. 1.

109. *See, e.g.,* Tariff Act of 1930, ch. 497, 46 Stat. 590 (1930) (codified *as amended* at 19 U.S.C. §§ 1202–1677 (g) (1976 & Supp. IV. 1980)). Customs Simplification Act of 1956, ch. 887, § 2(a), 70 Stat. 943, 19 U.S.C. § 1401(a) (1976 & Supp. IV 1980) (adding new § 402 to the Tariff Act of 1930), *as amended by* Pub. L. No. 96–39, title II, § 201(a), 93 Stat. 194 (1979), and Pub. L. No. 96–490, § 2, 94

Stat. 2556 (1980) (Valuation). International Emergency Economic Powers Act, Pub. L. No. 95–223, title II, § 202, 91 Stat. 1626, 50 U.S.C. §§ 1701–1706 (1976 & Supp. IV, 1980). Trade Agreements Act of 1979, Pub. L. No. 96–39, 93 Stat. 144, 19 U.S.C. §§ 1671–1677(g) (1976 & Supp. IV, 1980) (Countervailing and Antidumping Duties).

110. The Tariff Act of 1930 sets the tariff structure and rates which are amended from time to time. The tariff schedules of the U.S. show in one column the "most-favored-nation" ("proclaimed" or "modified") rates and in the other the "statutory rates." A column marked "LDDC" states the rates for least developed developing countries. *See* Tariff Schedule of the United States, Annotated 1111 (Wash. D.C., U.S. Int'l Trade Comm'n Pubs., 1981). Update: In several cases the Congress has provided that when an agreement, negotiated by the President pursuant to Congressional authorization, is brought before Congress for approval, it will not be subject to any amendments and must be either approved in full or rejected. This "fast track" procedure has been viewed as essential with respect to World Trade Organization agreements, and the North American Free Trade Agreement.

111. U.S. Const. § 8, cl. 2: "To borrow money on the credit of the United States."

112. U.S. Const. art. I, § 8, cl. 1.

113. U.S. Const. art. I, § 8, cl. 1.

114. *See* L. Henkin, *supra* note 7, at 74–76. On the power to extradite aliens or U.S. citizens, *see id.* at 326 n.40. U.S. Const. art. I, § 8, cl. 4 gives Congress the power "[t]o establish an uniform rule of naturalization." The "necessary and proper clause" has also played a significant role in Congressional action affecting foreign affairs. L. Henkin, *supra* note 7, at 78.

115. The Supreme Court has "federalized" the "act of state" doctrine and possibly other rules of customary international law as well, in Banco Nacional de Cuba v. Sabbatino, 376 U.S. 398 (1964) (although some believe that the act of state doctrine has always been viewed as federal); but Congress reduced the scope of the doctrine as laid down by the Court in the "Sabbatino Amendment" to the Foreign Assistance Act of 1964, 78 Stat. 1013 (*as amended* and codified in 22 U.S.C. § 2370e). The Foreign Sovereign Immunities Act was adopted on 21 Oct. 1976, Pub. L. No. 94–583, 90 Stat. 2891, 28 U.S.C. §§ 1602–11 (1976).

As contemplated in EEC Treaty art. 220, the Member States concluded treaties among themselves "federalizing" (*i.e.* turning into Community law) rules on jurisdiction and recognition of their national courts' judgments, on recognition of companies and on Community patent. Presumably, in an advanced state of integration, this process could be employed to provide Community law rules on issues pertaining to foreign affairs, such as the two issues mentioned above, extradition, etc.

116. An agreement negotiated by the President pursuant to a delegated authority must be brought before the Congress and the President is authorized to conclude it unless, within a set period of time, both Houses of Congress, and in some instances either House alone, disapprove it. However, in a sweeping opin-

ion the Supreme Court held a section of the Immigration and Nationality Act authorizing "one-House veto" unconstitutional because a veto by the House of Representatives is essentially legislative and thus subject to the constitutional requirements of passage by a majority of both Houses and presentation to the President. Immigration & Naturalization Serv. v. Chadha, 103 S. Ct. 2764 (1983). In other instances the President may use a delegated authority only if he makes an express finding of a special national interest (*e.g.,* supplying foreign aid or arms to countries violating human rights, exporting nuclear materials to states unwilling to accept safeguards). T.M. FRANCK & E. WEISBAND, FOREIGN POLICY BY CONGRESS 83–115 (Oxford/New York, O.U.P., 1979).

117. Ehrenhaft, *The "Judicialization" of Trade Law,* 56 NOTRE DAME L. REV., 595 (1981).

118. *See generally* 6 BRUSSELS COMMENTARY, *supra* note 90, at 29 ff. Update: In the 1992 Maastricht Treaty on the European Union the member states agreed on an economic and monetary union, including a common currency, and set a time table for achieving it.

119. 1 H. SMIT & P.E. HERZOG, THE LAW OF THE E.E.C., A COMMENTARY 2–112 (New York, M. Bender, 1976). The CCT shows two columns of rates: "autonomous" and "conventional." *See, e.g.,* Council Reg. (EEC) No. 3000/79 of 20 Dec. 1979, OJ No. L 342, 31 Dec. 1979, p.1.

120. 1 H. SMIT & P.E. HERZOG, *supra* note 119, at 2–113.

121. Council Reg. (EEC) No. 1224/80 of 28 May 1980, OJ No. L 134, 31 May 1980, p.1. *See generally* Snyder, *Customs Valuation in the European Economic Community,* 11 GA. J. INT'L & COMP. L. 79 (1981).

122. Council Reg. (EEC) No. 802/68 of 27 June 1968, JO No. L 148, 20 June 1969, p.1. ([1968–69] II OJ (spec. Eng. ed) at 165), *amended by* Council Reg. (EEC) No. 1318/71 of 21 June 1971, JO No. L 139, 25 June 1971, p 6 ([1971] OJ (spec. Eng. ed.) at 394) and the Act of Accession, Annex I, point I (1).

123. 6 BRUSSELS COMMENTARY, *supra* note 90, at 396 ff and 12 *id.* at 178–79; 3 H. SMIT & P.E. HERZOG, *supra* note 119, at 3–671 ff.

124. Council Reg. (EEC) No. 459/68 on Protection against Practices of Dumping, Premiums and Subsidies by Non-Member States, JO No. L 931, 17 Apr. 1968, p.1 ([1968–69] II OJ (spec. Eng. ed.) at 80), as amended by Council Reg. (EEC) No. 2011/73, OJ No. L 206, 27 July 1973, p.3; Council Reg. (EEC) No. 3017/79 on Protection against Dumped and Subsidized Exports, OJ No. L 339, 31 Dec. 1979, p.1.

125. EEC Treaty arts. 38–47; 12 BRUSSELS COMMENTARY, *supra* note 90, at 179–80.

126. *See* Bourgeois, *The Common Commercial Policy—Scope and Nature of the Powers,* in PROTECTIONISM AND THE EUROPEAN COMMUNITY 1 (E.L. Völker ed., Deventer (NL), Kluwer, 1983). *See* in this connection Case 307/81, Alusuisse Italia SpA. v. Council and Commission, [1982] ECR 3463. *See also supra* text accompanying note 117.

127. *See* Ehlermann, *Conflict in Implementation of Community Law,* in 3 F.I.D.E., REPORTS OF THE NINTH CONGRESS, LONDON, 25–27 SEPT. 1980, at pp.

3.1, 3.10–11, 3.14–15 (London, Sweet & Maxwell, 1980). L'AIDE ALIMENTAIRE DE LA CEE DANS LE NOUVEAU CONTEXTE DES STRATÉGIES ALIMENTAIRES 97–99 (P. Richard ed., Brussells, Prométhée & Agence Europe, 1983); Peter van den Bossche, The Nature of the European Community Food Aid to Developing Countries (Doctorate thesis, European University Institute, Florence, 1983).

128. *See Migrant Workers,* No. 3212 (NS) EUROPE, 23 Sept. 1981, at 16 (Eng. ed., Brussels, Agence Internationale d'Information pour la Presse). "The rules regarding freedom of movement for nationals of the Member States also apply, in part, to members of their families who are not nationals of a Member State. The relevant Community regulations provide that Member States shall provide such persons with all possible facilities in obtaining the necessary visas." Answer by Commissioner Narjes to Written Question No. 2161/80, OJ No. C 165, 6 July 1981, p.18. Update: See *supra* note 13 on a "citizenship of the Union." On common treatment of aliens, citizens of third states, see *supra,* introduction to the essay entitled *Excerpt from* Courts and Free Markets—Perspectives from the United States and Europe, in Part 2 of this collection.

129. *See supra* text accompanying note 21; *see also* T. BAILEY, *supra* note 21, at 52–66.

130. U.S. CONST. art II, § 2, cl. 2.

131. *See* U.S. CONST. art. I, § 10, cl. 1; "No State shall enter into any treaty, alliance, or confederation. . . ."; and cl. 3: "No State shall, without the consent of Congress . . . enter into any agreement or compact with another State, or with a foreign power. . . ." There is no authoritative determination of the distinction between a "treaty" and an "agreement or compact." In Virginia v. Tennessee, 148 U.S. 503, 519 (1893), involving an interstate (not foreign) compact, the Court held that despite the constitutional language, agreements or compacts require consent of Congress only when they "tend to the increase of political power in the States, which may encroach upon or interfere with the just supremacy of the United States." Whether by so narrowing the constitutional requirement, or because consent was assumed, state and local authorities have in fact entered into agreements and arrangements with foreign counterparts (such as Canadian Provinces or towns) without seeking consent of Congress on such matters as coordination of roads, police cooperation and border control. According to COUNCIL OF STATE GOVERNMENTS, INTERSTATE COMPACTS, 1783–1977 (A Revised Compilation) (Kentucky, Lexington, 1977) (updated), Congress consented or was asked to consent only to 10 compacts with foreign authorities, dealing with an international bridge, a port authority, forest fire prevention, lake basins, tax on fuel in busses, motor vehicle registration, and interpleader (8 with Canadian, one with Mexican and one generally with foreign authorities); in two instances the Congress reserved its decision on foreign participation in an interstate compact and in one case it expressly disapproved it. The Council of State Governments lists 177 interstate compacts. *See generally,* L. HENKIN, *supra* note 7, at 229–34; L. DIMARZO, COMPONENT UNITS OF FEDERAL STATES AND INTERNATIONAL AGREEMENTS 38–42, 82–84, 100–1 *et passim* (Alphen a/d Rijn, Sijthoff & Noordhoff, 1980); Engdahl, *Characterization of Interstate Arrangements: When*

Is a Compact Not a Compact?, 64 MICH. L. REV. 63 (1965); P.T. HARDY, INTERSTATE COMPACTS—THE TIES THAT BIND (Georgia, Univ. of Georgia, Institute of Government, 1982).

Several states of the Union have maintained trade offices in foreign countries with a view to promoting exports of their products.

If Denmark wished to conclude an agreement with Norway on a matter clearly within the treaty power of the Community but of local interest only, could it do so with the consent of the Commission or the Council, without engaging the Community treaty-making machinery?

132. U.S. CONST. art. VI, § 2; art. III, § 2, cl. 1.

133. L. HENKIN, *supra* note 7, at 373 n.4.

134. L. HENKIN, *supra* note 7, at 374, *quoting* 2 FARRAND, *supra* note 7, at 532–54. The two-thirds majority corresponds roughly to the nine of the thirteen states whose consent was required under Art. IX of the Articles of Confederation.

135. In a widely told story, President Washington actually went to the Senate in 1789 expecting yes-or-no answers on a proposed treaty with Creek Indians, but the Senate referred the matter to a committee; the President, stalking out, muttered that he was damned if he would ever go there again—and he did not—but he continued to seek Senatorial advice by less direct means. The Jay Treaty of 1794 was the first treaty on which the Senate's "advice" in advance was not sought. T.M. FRANCK & E. WEISBAND, *supra* note 116, at 135–36. *See also* Franck & Weisband, *Advice and Consent,* N.Y. Times, 28 Feb. 1978, at M35 (commenting on the efforts by individual senators to negotiate with the Panamanian Government on the Canal Treaty).

136. Some 167 treaties were modified and 104 more rejected of the 1046 treaties submitted up to 1944. T.M. FRANCK & E. WEISBAND, *supra* note 116, at 136–37.

137. All currently unapproved treaties can be found at SENATE COMM. ON FOREIGN RELATIONS, LEGISLATIVE CALENDAR No. 3, 97th Cong., 2nd Sess. 7 (1982). *See, e.g.,* the Convention on the Prevention and Punishment of the Crime of Genocide, signed on behalf of the United States on 11 Dec. 1948 (EX. O, 81–1, 16 June 1949); the International Convention on the Elimination of All Forms of Racial Discrimination, signed on behalf of the United States on 23 Sept. 1966 (EX. C, 95–2, 23 Feb. 1978); the International Covenant on Economic, Social and Cultural Rights, signed on behalf of the United States on 5 Oct. 1977 (EX. D, 95–2, 23 Feb. 1978); the International Covenant on Civil and Political Rights, signed on behalf of the United States on 5 Oct. 1977 (EX. E, 95–2, 23 Feb. 1978); the American Convention on Human Rights, signed on behalf of the United States on 1 June 1977 (EX. F, 95–2, 23 Feb. 1978); and Convention No. 105 Concerning Abolition of Forced Labor adopted by the International Labor Organisation at its 40th session at Geneva, 25 June 1957 (EX. K, 88–1, 22 July 1963). Update: The above Conventions, except the International Covenant on Economic, Social and Cultural Rights and the American Convention on Human Rights, have now been ratified by the United States, although with many reservations, understandings and declarations. In addition,

the United States is a party to the Inter-American Convention on Political Rights of Women, Convention against Torture and Other Cruel and Inhuman and Degrading Treatment or Punishment. U.S. Dept. of State, Treaties in Force, June 1996, *passim.*

138. T.M. FRANCK & E. WEISBAND, *supra* note 116, at 138–45.

139. *See supra* note 105, last sentence. There is considerable support for the proposition that whatever the President can do by a treaty with the consent of two-thirds of the Senate he can also do by an executive agreement with the approval of the majority of both Houses. In principle, however, the Department of State would not agree with this proposition.

140. *See infra* text accompanying note 165.

141. Reid v. Covert, 354 U.S. 1, 16–17 (1957).

142. L. HENKIN, *supra* note 7, at 148–51, 159–60, discusses the arguments in support of limitations on the treaty power based on separation of powers. There is little reality today in these arguments. The Circuit Court of Appeals for the District of Columbia recently held that the Constitution does not prohibit the transfer of U.S. property to Panama through the self-executing Panama Canal Zone Treaty, and the Supreme Court denied certiorari. Edwards v. Carter, 580 F.2d 1055 (D.C. Cir.), *cert. denied,* 436 U.S. 907 (1978). *See* Comment, *Constitutional Law—Treaty Power—Disposal of United States Territories—Panama Canal Treaties,* 1979 WIS. L. REV. 837.

143. 252 U.S. 416 (1920). *See infra* notes 193, 227.

144. L. HENKIN, *supra* note 7, at 147.

145. 133 U.S. 258 (1890).

146. *Id.* at 267.

147. For other prohibitions in the Constitution *see* art. I, § 9. *See generally* L. H. TRIBE, AMERICAN CONSTITUTIONAL LAW (Mineola, Foundation Press, 1978–79).

148. *See, e.g.,* the statement by Charles Evans Hughes (formerly Secretary of State and later Chief Justice of the Supreme Court) in 23 PROC. AM. SOC'Y INT'L L. 194–96 (1929).

149. Henkin, *International Concern and the Treaty Power of the United States,* 63 AJIL 272, 276–77 (1969). This view has now been accepted in the revised draft RESTATEMENT OF FOREIGN RELATIONS LAW § 304 (Tent. Draft No. 1; Philadelphia, A.L.I., 1 Apr. 1980); *see id.,* Reporter's Note 2, at 88.

150. *See supra* text accompanying note 129.

151. Even a self-executing treaty, however, may not become "law of the land" binding individuals until it is proclaimed by the President so as to give notice to the persons concerned. Haver v. Yaker, 76 U.S. (9 Wall.) 32, 34–35 (1869).

152. Foster v. Neilson, 27 U.S. (2 Pet.) 253, 313–14 (1829).

153. Factor v. Laubenheimer, 290 U.S. 276, 295 (1933).

154. *See generally,* Evans, *Self-Executing Treaties in the United States of America,* 1953 BRIT. Y.B. INT'L L. 178; *see* cases collected in draft RESTATEMENT, *supra* note 149, § 131 at 55–57. *See,* in this context, *infra* note 279, last paragraph.

155. L. HENKIN, *supra* note 7, at 159 n. 98, with a list of authorities.

156. *See, e.g.,* Asakura v. City of Seattle, 265 U.S. 332 (1924). For an analysis of the more recent case law *see* J.S. Hilboldt, The Enforcement of Treaty Rights by American Courts and the Self-Executing Treaty Doctrine (unpublished research paper, Univ. of Michigan, 1981). Update: The President in making a treaty, and the Senate in consenting to it, have assumed authority (as to any treaty) to declare a treaty non-self-executing, *e.g.,* with respect to the Covenant on Civil and Political Rights, the Genocide Convention and the Convention against Torture. For a criticism of this position, see L. Henkin, FOREIGN AFFAIRS AND THE UNITED STATES CONSTITUTION, 201–3 (2nd ed., Oxford, Clarendon, 1996).

157. L. HENKIN, *supra* note 7, at 162.

158. *See, e.g.,* Whitney v. Robertson, 124 U.S. 190, 194 (1888).

159. Both Jay and Jefferson (at least initially) assumed that a treaty as "higher law" in the natural law sense would prevail not only over pre-existing but also over later federal law. Jay in THE FEDERALIST NO. 64, *supra* note 16, at 394, and Jefferson in 2 J. STORY, COMMENTARIES ON THE CONSTITUTION OF THE UNITED STATES § 1841, at 609 n.1 (M.M. Bigelow ed., 5th ed., Boston, Little, Brown & Co., 1891). The U.S. Supreme Court has chosen a different rule. *See* E. STEIN, P. HAY & M. WAELBROECK, *supra* note 3, at 106–8.

160. United States v. Pink, 315 U.S. 203 (1942); United States v. Belmont, 301 U.S. 324 (1937); Dames & Moore v. Regan, 453 U.S. 654 (1981). *But see* United States v. Guy W. Capps, Inc., 204 F.2d 655 (4th Cir. 1953), *aff'd,* 348 U.S. 296 (1955) (on other grounds). Update: For an interesting exchange, see B. Ackerman & D. Golove, *Is NAFTA Constitutional?* 108 HARVARD L.R. 799 (1995) and L.H. Tribe, *Taking Text and Structure Seriously: Reflections on Free-Form Method in Constitutional Interpretation, ibid* at 1221.

161. Goldwater v. Carter, 617 F.2d 697 (D.C. Cir. 1979), *aff'd per curiam,* 444 U.S. 996 (1979). *See* Pappas, *The Constitutional Allocation of Competence in the Termination of Treaties,* 13 N.Y.U. J. INT'L L. & POL. 473 (1981); Glennon, *Treaty Process Reform: Saving Constitutionalism without Destroying Diplomacy,* 52 CIN. L. REV. 84 (1983).

162. S.J. Res. 1, 83rd Cong. 1st Sess., 99 Cong. Rec. 6773 (1953).

163. *See* the Bricker Hearings before the Senate Subcommittee on the Judiciary, listed in L. HENKIN, *supra* note 7, at 384 n.35, 394 n. 69. *See also* W.W. BISHOP, JR., INTERNATIONAL LAW, CASES AND MATERIALS 110–12 (3rd ed., Boston/Toronto, Little, Brown & Co., 1971).

164. Update: See *supra* note 137. Of the 140 conventions on uniform labor standards adopted by the ILO, the U.S. has ratified only 7, as compared, for example, with 96 accepted by France, and 68 accepted by the U.K. INTERNATIONAL LABOR OFFICE, INTERNATIONAL LABOR CONVENTIONS CHART OF RATIFICATIONS (Geneva, 1975).

165. The Case-Zablocki Act, Pub. L. No. 92–403, 86 Stat. 619, 1 U.S.C. § 112b (1972), *as amended by* Pub. L. No. 95–5, § 5, 91 Stat. 224 (1977), and Pub. L. No. 95–426, title VII, § 708, 92 Stat. 993 (1978).

166. Franck and Weisband believe that "for the first time in this century, a

procedure has been established for getting advice of the Senate Foreign Relations Committee, before and during negotiations," on the form of the agreement. T.M. FRANCK & E. WEISBAND, *supra* note 116, at 151. *See also supra* text accompanying notes 135–37.

167. The Soviet Union refuses to "recognize" the Community. *See,* however, the Convention on Future Multilateral Cooperation in the North-East Atlantic Fisheries, art. 20 (OJ No. L 227, 12 Aug. 1981, p. 22, at p. 27), which opened the Convention for signature by 12 states including the Soviet Union, and by the EEC. The Convention was "approved" by Council Dec. 81/608 of 13 July 1981, OJ No. L 227, 12 Aug. 1981, p. 21. Of course, joining with the EEC in a multilateral treaty does not by itself imply recognition. *See generally* Wellenstein, *The Relations of the European Communities with Eastern Europe,* in ESSAYS IN EUROPEAN LAW AND INTEGRATION 197–208 (D. O'Keeffe & H.G. Schermers eds., Deventer (NL), Kluwer, 1982). The problem with Japan is simply one of economic considerations. *See generally* K.J. TWITCHETT, EUROPE AND THE WORLD—THE EXTERNAL RELATIONS OF THE COMMON MARKET (London, Europa Pub., 1976); W.J. FELD, THE EUROPEAN COMMUNITY IN WORLD AFFAIRS (New York, Alfred Pub. Co., 1976). Update: After 1988, the Community has negotiated an extensive network of agreements with the states of the former Soviet Union and other Central and Eastern European states. Ten Central-Eastern European states have applied for membership in the European Union. The Community and its members have become original members of the World Trade Organization, a successor to GATT.

For a classification of the various types of agreements concluded by the Community, according to their legal basis, form and content *see* C. FLAESCH-MOUGIN, LES ACCORDS EXTERNES DE LA COMMUNAUTÉ ÉCONOMIQUE EUROPÉENNE—ESSAI D'UNE TYPOLOGIE (Brussels, Ed. de l'Univ. de Bruxelles, 1979).

168. Essentially EEC Treaty arts. 113, 114, 228–31, 238. *See supra* notes 42–43, 45–47. Update: See in particular on the new text of the crucial article 228 *supra,* note 44.

169. For exceptions, particularly where the Community treaty power is contested or in international organizations, *see* 12 BRUSSELS COMMENTARY, *supra* note 90, at 32. As a rule, the negotiations on behalf of the Commission are conducted by an official of the DG for External Relations but other departments have been drawn into the process. *Id.* at 33. *See generally* Mégret, *Conclusion, formes et effets des accords internationaux passés par la CEE,* 1965 R.M.C. 19; Melchior, *La procédure de conclusion des accords externes de la CEE,* 2 REV. BELGE DR. INT. 187 (1966); C. FLAESCH-MOUGIN, *supra* note 167, at 72–75.

170. EEC Treaty art. 113 does, but the general art. 228 does not, require such prior authorization. The Commission embarked on exploratory talks with Egypt without checking with the Council and that brought the wrath of the Council on its head. On the readiness of the U.S. Department of State to consult with the Senate on the form of the proposed agreement, *see supra* text accompanying note 166.

171. These Council acts are prepared by COREPER with the Commission's collaboration. On the negotiations generally, *see* U. AYBERK, LE MÉCANISME DE

LA PRISE DES DÉCISIONS COMMUNAUTAIRES EN MATIÈRE DE RELATIONS INTERNATIONALES 341 ff (Brussels, Bruylant, 1978); Bot, *Negotiating Community Agreements: Procedure and Practice,* 7 C.M.L. REV. 286 (1970).

172. EEC Treaty art. 113(3).

173. *See generally* Winham, *Robert Strauss, the MTN, and the Control of Faction,* 14 J. WORLD TRADE L. 377 (1980).

174. 12 BRUSSELS COMMENTARY, *supra* note 90, at 42–44 (discussing the "Luns" and "Luns-Westerterp" procedures).

175. It is questionable whether this could be done under the "necessary and proper" power, art. 235, as suggested by Seeler, *Das direkt gewählte Europäische Parlament—ein neues Parlament,* 15 EUR 201, 210 (1980). A Treaty amendment would probably be necessary to grant the Parliament such legal power. However, the Parliament could be given such authority in practice by a political understanding with the Council.

176. Discussion with Professor Joseph Weiler, E.U.I., Florence. In the present state of the Community decision-making it is difficult enough to obtain the consensus of the ten Governments; obviously, a requirement of Parliamentary "consent" would add to the complexity of the process. *See generally* Weiler, *The European Parliament and Foreign Affairs: External Relations of the European Economic Community,* in PARLIAMENTARY CONTROL OVER FOREIGN POLICY, *supra* note 83, at 151. Update: Significantly, the assent of the European Parliament is now required with respect to accession and association agreements as well as agreements establishing "a specific institutional framework," having important budgetary implications, and others, as specified in (80) art. 228(3), of the Maastricht Treaty on the European Union.

177. Raux & Flaesch-Mougin, *Les accords externes de la C.E.E.,* 11 R.T.D.E. 227, 246–47 (1975). Past practice shows no consistency in the choice between a regulation and a decision. Bebr suggests that "at present" the Council acts by regulation. Bebr, *Agreements Concluded by the Community and Their Possible Direct Effect,* 20 C.M.L. REV. 35, 39 (1983).

178. The voting requirements with respect to agreements concluded under other Treaty articles in application of the internal/external parallelisms rule would presumably be determined by the article in question.

In the less formal "short" procedure, the Council directs the President to authorize signing the agreement and the signature constitutes the conclusion binding the Community. On the form of conclusion, *see* Raux & Flaesch-Mougin, *supra* note 177, at 245–51; Raux & Perrot, *Les accords externes de la C.E.E.,* 12 R.T.D.E. 295, 311–13 (1976); Raux, *Les accords externes de la C.E.E.,* 15 R.T.D.E. 664, 666 (1979).

179. *See especially* Opinion 1/78, given pursuant to Art. 228(1) EEC, (International Agreement on Natural Rubber), [1979] ECR 2871, discussed *infra* text accompanying note 201. On this subject, *see generally* 12 BRUSSELS COMMENTARY, *supra* note 90, at 49–52.

180. *See* Costonis, *The Association with Nigeria,* in L'ASSOCIATION À LA COMMUNAUTÉ ECONOMIQUE EUROPÉENNE 215, 298 (Brussels, Institut d'Etudes Européennes, Presses Univ. de Bruxelles, 1970).

181. *See generally* Mixed Agreements (D. O'Keeffe & H.G. Schermers eds., Deventer (NL), Kluwer, 1983), and *especially* Ehlermann, *Mixed Agreements: A List of Problems, id.* at 1.

182. The text with notes 182–90 is drawn from my *External Relations of the European Community: Structure and Process,* in Academy of European Law (ed.), *Collected Courses of the Academy of European Law,* vol. 1, bk. 1, 161–62 (the Netherlands, Kluwer Academic Publishers, 1991).

The United Nations Law of the Sea Convention was concluded on 10 December 1982. Update: In force 16 November 1994, text in A/CONF.62/122 and Corr. 1 to 11. The text of the Community declaration on signature, in Multilateral Treaties Deposited with the Secretary General, Status as of 31 December 1988, XXI.6, 759–60, U.N. 1989.

183. *Infra* text at note 260.

184. The Court of Justice took this position in Ruling 1/78, [1978] ECR 2151, at 2180.

185. Vienna Convention for the Protection of the Ozone Layer, signed 22 March 1985, US Senate Treaty Doc. 99–9, 99th Cong. 1st Sess., 1985, 26 *ILM* 1529. Cmed. 9652, in force 22 September 1988.

186. See Arts. 1(6), 13, 14. See also Art. 15 on the voting rights. The Community has the number of votes equal to the number of its Member States but cannot cast them if the Members vote, and vice versa. See generally, Lang. "The Ozone Layer Convention: A New Solution to the Question of Community Participation in 'Mixed' International Agreements." 23 *CML Rev.* (1986) 157; Close, "Subordination Clauses in Mixed Agreements," 34(2) *ICLQ* (1985) 382. See also Declaration in the Annex to Council Decision of 22 October 1990 concerning the conclusion, on behalf of the European Economic Community, of the United Nations Convention against Illicit Traffic in Narcotic Drugs and Psychotropic Substances, 1990 OJ L 326, 24 November 1990, p. 56–57.

187. Fourth (Lomé) African Caribbean and Pacific States–EEC Convention of 15 Dec. 1989, 29 ILM (1990) 783.

188. E.g., Arts. 148, 152, 272. Update: The Agreement establishing the World Trade Organization is "a mixed agreement" (see *supra* note 69) concluded by both the Community and its members.

189. Gaja in D. O'Keeffe and H.G. Schermers (eds.), *Mixed Agreements* (1983), at n. 8, citing Krück, Deuses, Beutler *et al.,* and Bleckman (with some question).

190. Weiler, "The External Legal Relations of Non-Unitary Actors: Mixity and the Federal Principle," in O'Keefe and Schermers, *ibid.* 74ff.

191. *See infra* text accompanying note 354, on representation in the EPC system. EEC Treaty art. 116 provides: "Member States shall, in respect of all matters of particular interest to the common market, proceed within the framework of international organizations of an economic character only by common action. . . ." For obvious reasons, the Commission has been down-playing the importance of this provision, and the Court ignored it in *ERTA;* but the Council has relied on it in several instances, as in the International Energy Agency and

earlier commodity agreements negotiations. 12 BRUSSELS COMMENTARY, *supra* note 90, at 52.

192. The extensive literature is listed *inter alia* in Pescatore, *External Relations in the Case-Law of the Court of Justice of the European Communities,* 16 C.M.L. REV. 615, 615–16 n.1 (1979).

193. *See supra* text accompanying note 69. It has been said that the internal/external parallelism principle is the "exact reverse" of the rule of Missouri v. Holland, 252 U.S. 416 (1920), where the Supreme Court held on the basis of the "necessary and proper" clause that "internal" legislative powers of Congress are coextensive with the federal treaty power. Riesenfeld in 1978 PROC. AM. SOC'Y INT'L L. 185. *But see infra* note 227. *See also supra* text accompanying note 143.

194. Case 22/70, *ERTA,* [1971] ECR 263. For references to comments on this case, *see* Pescatore, *supra* note 192, at 619 n.6. Update: *But see* Opinion 1/94, *supra,* note 69.

195. Case 22/70, *ERTA,* [1971] ECR 263, 275, 276.

196. Joined Cases 3, 4 & 6/76, *Kramer,* [1976] ECR 1279. For references to comments, *see also* Pescatore, *supra* note 192, at 620 n. 8.

197. In addition to the regulation mentioned above the Court referred to art. 102 of the Act of Accession of the United Kingdom, Denmark and Ireland. Joined Cases 3, 4 & 6/76, *Kramer,* [1976] ECR 1279, 1309.

198. Opinion 1/76, given pursuant to Art. 228(1) EEC, (Draft Agreement establishing a European laying-up fund for inland waterway vessels), [1977] ECR 741. For comments, *see* Groux, *Le parallélisme des compétences internes et externes de la Communauté économique européenne,* 14 C.D.E. 3 (1978); Philip, *A propos de l'avis 1/76 de la Cour de justice des Communautés européennes,* 1978 R.M.C. 55.

199. Opinion 1/76, [1977] ECR 741, 755. Ruling 1/78, delivered pursuant to Art. 103 EAEC, (Draft Convention of the International Atomic Energy Agency on the Physical Protection of Nuclear Materials, Facilities and Transports), [1978] ECR 2151, may perhaps also be interpreted to support the above cited position, even though the Euratom Treaty provisions differ from those of the EEC.

200. Opinion 1/75, given pursuant to Art. 228(1) of the EEC Treaty, (Understanding on a Local Cost Standard), [1975] ECR 1355.

> A commercial policy is in fact made up by the combination and interaction of internal and external measures, without priority being taken by one over the others. Sometimes agreements are concluded in execution of a policy fixed in advance, sometimes that policy is defined by the agreements themselves.

Id. at 1363. Maas, *The External Powers of the E.E.C. with Regard to Commercial Policy: Comment on Opinion 1/75,* 13 C.M.L. REV. 379 (1976).

201. Opinion 1/78, (International Agreement on Natural Rubber), [1979] ECR 2871. For comments *see* Brückner, *Quelques observations au sujet de l'avis 1/78 ('caoutchouc') de la Cour de Justice,* 1980 R.M.C. 4; Steenbergen, *La notion*

de politique commerciale commune après l'avis 1/78 de la Cour de Justice, 16 C.D.E. 54 (1980). The Court pointed to the clauses in the agreement "concerning technological assistance, research programmes, the maintenance of fair conditions of labour in the rubber industry and consultations relating to national tax policies which may have an effect on the price of rubber." [1979] ECR 2871, 2916.

202. The text with notes 202–22 is drawn from my *External Relations of the European Community: Structure and Process,* in Academy of European Law (ed.), *Collected Courses of the Academy of European Law,* vol. 1, bk. 1, 151–55 (the Netherlands, Kluwer Academic Publishers, 1991).

For citations to the literature and helpful comments on Art. 238, see Vedder in E. Grabitz (ed.), *Kommentar zum EWG-Vertrag,* Art. 238 (1967).

203. Vedder, ibid, n.4, citing Seidl-Hohenveldern, states that in formulating Art. 238 the drafters had in mind the later EFTA States of which Britain was already "associated" with the ECSC.

204. Meesen, "Das Abkommen von Lomé als gemischter Vertrag." 15 *EuR* (1980) 36, 38–40.

205. Hailbronner, "Die Freizügigkeit türkischer Staatsangehöriger nach dem Assoziations-Abkommen EWG-Türkei," 19 *EuR* 54 (1984) 58–59; Nolte, "Freizügigkeit nach dem Assoziationsvertrag EWG-Türkei: Auslegungskompetenz, unmittelbare Anwendbarkeit und Familiennachzug," 47 *ZaÖRV* (1987) 755, 759. The early position of the European Parliament was not quite uniform. EP Doc. 122/61–62 (Report Birkelbach) 2; EP Doc. 175/69 (Report Bersani) 4. See also Krück, "Die Freizügigkeit der Arbeitnehmer nach dem Assoziierungsabkommen EWG-Türkei," 19 *EuR* (1984) 289, 297–299.

206. See *supra* text at notes 179, 180.

207. Case 12/86, *Meryem Demirel v. Stadt Schwäbisch Gmünd,* [1987] ECR 3719. For comments see Neuwahl, "Freedom of Movement for Workers under the EEC-Treaty Association Agreement." 13 *ELR* (1988) 360; Vedder, "Ausländernecht für türkische Arbeitnehmer—die Demirel-Entscheidung des EuGII, das Bundesverfassungsgericht und die Folgen," 23 *EuR* (1988) 50; Vedder, in 1 *European Journal of International Law (EJIL)* (1990) 375; Nolte, "Freedom of Movement for Workers and the EEC Turkish Association Agreement," 25 *CML Rev.* (1988) 403.

208. Agreement establishing an Association between the EEC and Turkey, signed 12 September 1963, OJ L 217, 29 December 1964, with Additional and Financial Protocols of 23 November 1970 and Interim Agreement of 30 June 1973. Texts in EEC, *Collection of the Agreements Concluded by the European Community,* Vol. 3, (1978) 539–717.

209. Opinion of the Advocate General Darmon, in 12/86, *Demirel,* para. 14.

210. For the jurisdictional problem in this case, see *infra,* text at note 244.

211. See Art. 238(3). U.K. in 12/86, *Demirel, supra* note 207. Report for the Hearing, II 4(a). See also Germany, ibid. II 1. France and Greece did not comment on the issue of jurisdiction in their observations.

212. See *infra* sec. iv.

213. Commission in 12/86, *Demirel,* Report for the Hearing, II 6.

214. Ibid.

215. 12/86 *Demirel,* Judgment para. 9, emphasis added. The Advocate General buttressed the Commission's argument by pointing to the need for a uniform application of all subjects of the association agreements and to the fact that rules for free access of third-country workers may affect the free movement within the Community of workers who are nationals of the Member States. Conclusions, para. 14.

216. Hailbronner, *supra* note 105, at 60. Update: The Court followed its *Demirel* ruling in Case C-192/89, S.Z. Sevince v. Staatssecretaris van Justitie, [1990] ECR 3461 and in Case C-237/91, Kazim Kus v. Landeshauptstadt Wiesbaden, [1992] ECR 6781; Case C-58/93, Yousfi v. Belgian State, [1994] ECR I-1353; Case C-126/95, A. Hallouzi-Choho v. Bestuur, [1996] ECR-I-4807.

217. 12/86, Opinion of Advocate General Darmon.

218. Report for the Hearing, II 6(a).

219. Case 12/86, Judgment para. 10.

220. Vedder, Ausländerrecht 50.

221. Report for the Hearing, II 6(a). The Court did not comment on the Commission's explanation but by implication it rejected the claim that "subsequent practice" of the parties has established the narrow interpretation of Article 238.

222. According to Opinion 1/78, *supra* note 201, a financial commitment by national governments would trigger "mixity" for an agreement which is otherwise covered by article 113. There is nothing in art. 238 that *specifically* excludes financial obligations assumed by the Member States in an association agreement. Update: See also on this issue Opinion 1/94, Re the WTO Agreement [1994] ECR-I-5267.

223. Stein & Sandalow, *supra* note 6, at 35. In the Community, the preemption concept appears to be used also in discussing whether the Treaty directly limits the competence of Member States to enact legislation. *Id.* at 33.

224. *See generally* Cohen, *Congressional Power to Define State Power to Regulate Commerce: Consent and Pre-Emption,* in COURTS AND FREE MARKETS, *supra* note 6, at 523.

225. [1971] ECR 263, 282. *See also supra* text accompanying note 194. However, the Members must continue to act "in the interest and on behalf of the Community." Case 22/70, *ERTA,* [1971] ECR 263, 282 at para. 90. When the Court held an agreement incompatible with the Treaty in Opinion 1/76, (inland waterway vessels), [1977] ECR 741, Switzerland was the only non-member party affected.

226. Joined Cases 3, 4 & 6/76, [1976] ECR 1279. *See supra* text accompanying note 196.

227. Case 61/77, Commission v. Ireland, [1978] ECR 417; Case 804/79, Commission v. U.K., [1981] ECR 1045. *See also* Case 181/80, Procureur Général près la Cour d'Appel de Pau and Others v. Arbelaiz-Emazabel, [1981] ECR 2961.

> It is fairly universally accepted that the Community has exclusive external authority with regard to fisheries. The debate has been rather as to whether the Member States are also excluded from internal competence, that is,

> whether internal and external fisheries policy is so inter-linked that the exclusivity of the one must be reflected in the other.

J. Usher, European Community Law and National Law 66–67 (London, Allen & Unwin, 1981). In this light the issue resembles Missouri v. Holland, 252 U.S. 416 (1920) (discussed *supra* at note 143). There a lower federal court held a Congressional act for the protection of migratory birds unconstitutional on the ground that the Congress impinged on the "states' rights." The Federal Government then entered into a treaty with Canada on the same subject and the Supreme Court upheld the act of Congress on the basis of the "necessary and proper" clause in the Constitution as necessary to implement the treaty. It may thus be said that the President with the Senate could do what Congress alone (at that time) perhaps could not constitutionally do. Thus, it could be said that in the fisheries situation in Europe, the internal/external rule is not applied as "the exact reverse" of the American constitutional practice (*see supra* text accompanying note 193), but in conformity with it.

228. For a criticism, *see, e.g.,* Steenbergen, *supra* note 201, at 67; and Barav, *The Division of External Relations Power between the EEC and the Member States in the Case-Law of the Court of Justice,* in Division of Powers, *supra* note 72, at 29, 51. *But see* the response by Pescatore, *id.* at 69, 71.

229. In 1981 the Council decided on a proposal from the Commission that "all international commodity agreements will be signed simultaneously by the Community and the Member States which will be parties to such agreements. The negotiations will be conducted by a single delegation; as a general rule the Community's position will be expressed by the Commission representative." Bull. EC 3–1981, p. 55, point 2.2.17. The arrangement has given rise to difficulties in UNCTAD which have not been resolved as yet. Ehlermann, *supra* note 181, at 8.

230. Opinion 1/78, [1979] ECR 2871, 2917–18.

231. On this assumption, could the Commission seek to enforce the obligation against the other institutions in an action before the Court? What would be the European Parliament's authority over this item of the budget?

232. *See supra* text accompanying note 157.

233. *See* Waelbroeck, *The Emergent Doctrine of Community Pre-Emption—Consent and Re-Delegation,* in Courts and Free Markets, *supra* note 6, at 548, 553–54, and the case law cited therein.

234. *Id.* at 551, 555 ff. *See also* Louis, *Quelques réflexions sur la répartition des compétences entre la Communauté européenne et ses états membres,* [1979] II Rev. d'intégration européenne/J. Eur. Integration 355.

235. Opinion 1/76, (inland waterway vessels), [1977] ECR 741, 757.

236. 133 U.S. 258 (1890). *See supra* text accompanying note 145.

237. *See supra* text accompanying note 146. Perhaps the Court had in mind a different type of a change, *e.g.,* from a republican form of government to a monarchy?

238. Ruling 1/78, [1978] ECR 2151. The Court made it clear, however, that

the matter of the distribution of powers between the Community and the Member States was an internal Community question of no concern to the third parties, and need not be spelled out in the convention "particularly as it may change in the course of time." *Id.* at 2180. Note, however, that according to Ehlermann "third countries insist increasingly that the Community and its Member States explain and define the internal distribution of powers." *Supra* note 181, at 8.

239. *Id.* at 2172–73.

240. Case 181/73, Haegeman v. Belgium, [1974] ECR 449, 460 [*Haegeman II*]. Louis and Brückner seem to suggest that the Court's ruling has made art. 228(2) superfluous but that the article "gives third states a complete security." 12 Brussels Commentary, *supra* note 90, at 62–63. In a similar vein, *see* Pescatore *Les Communautés en tant que personnes de droit international,* in Les Nouvelles, Droit des Communautés européennes 107, 119 (W. Ganshof van der Meersch ed., Brussels, Maison F. Larcier, 1969) [hereinafter cited as Les Nouvelles]. What, in this context, would be the status of a "mixed agreement"? Would only the part within the Community competence become "an integral part of Community law"? *See also infra* note 265. Update: See *supra,* ii, bb.

241. EEC Treaty arts. 173, 175, 177, 184. 12 Brussels Commentary, *supra* note 90, at 184–86. Case 181/73, *Haegeman II,* [1974] ECR 449, involved art. 177 jurisdiction. *See also* Opinion 1/76, [1977] ECR 741, 760. para. 18. However, in *Opinion 1/75* the Court declared that

> the question whether the conclusion of a given agreement is within the power of the Community and whether, in a given case, such power has been exercised in conformity with the provisions of the Treaty is, in principle, a question which may be submitted to the Court of Justice, either directly, under Article 169 or Article 173 of the Treaty, or in accordance with the preliminary procedure.

[1975] ECR 1355, 1361. *See also supra* note 200. On the effects of an "annulment" of a Community agreement, *see* Barav, *supra* note 228, at 32, with further references.

242. The legal basis for the absolute "supremacy" in the Community legal order of the constitutive Treaty over its agreements with third states is apparently derived from the "preventive" control in arts. 228(1) & 238, and from the nature of the Community's treaty power as derived from, and limited by, the EEC Treaty. 12 Brussels Commentary, *supra* note 90, at 181–82.

243. The text with notes 243–53 is drawn from my *External Relations of the European Community: Structure and Process,* in Academy of European Law (ed.), *Collected Courses of the Academy of European Law,* vol. 1, bk. 1, 164–66 (the Netherlands, Kluwer Academic Publishers, 1991).

Case 181/73 *Haegeman,* [1974] ECR 449, Case 87/75 *Bresciani,* [1976] ECR 129, Case 17/81 *Pabst,* [1982] ECR 1331, Case 65/77 *Razanatsimbe,* [1977] ECR 2229, the last cited by the Commission in *Demirel, infra,* text at note 244.

244. Hailbronner, "Die Freizügigkeit türkischer Staatsangehöriger nach dem Associations-Abkommen EWG/Türkei," *EuR* (1984) 54, 63.

245. Case 12/86, *supra* note 207. Update: On subsequent cases following the *Demirel* precedent, see *supra* ii, bb.

246. Case 12/86, para. 10.

247. Case 12/86, para. 7, citing *Haegeman.*

248. Case 12/86, para. 28.

249. Case 44/79, *Hauer v. Land Rheinland-Pfalz,* [1979] ECR 3727, para. 15.

250. Ibid., para. 9.

251. Case 12/86, Report for the Hearing, II Written Observations, Government of the French Republic, para. 3, refers to the *Abdulaziz* case, Judgment of 28 May 1985. The above point was suggested to me by my colleague Professor J. Weiler. See in this context Case 60–61/84, *Cinéthèque S.A. v. Fédération Nationale des Cinémas,* [1985] ECR 2605, paras. 25 and 26.

252. Neuwahl, *supra* note 207 at 364.

253. Jacqué and Weiler, "On the Road to European Union—A New Judicial Architecture: An Agenda for the Intergovernmental Conference," 27 *CML Rev.* (1990) 185, 202.

254. J. Bourgeois, a member of the EC Commission's legal staff dealing with foreign affairs, was able to cite only a single agreement "justified by an implicit but clear reference to *Opinion 1/76,*" *i.e.,* the European Convention for the protection of animals kept for farming purposes, based on arts. 43 (common agricultural policy) and 100 (harmonization of laws), EEC Council Dec. of 19 June 1978, OJ No. L. 323, 17 Nov. 1978, p. 12. He suggests that the Community's numerous international agreements on fisheries conservation (*see also supra* notes 72, 227) may also be regarded as based on art. 43 in conformity with the *Opinion 1/76* doctrine, although the Council had previously adopted limited provisions that may be regarded as "common rules" in the *ERTA* sense. Bourgeois states:

> [The] Community has initiated early in 1980 an agreement on international passenger transport by road which ought to be concluded in the course of 1980 by a decision based on *Article 75* [Commission proposal in 1982, OJ No. C 31, 8 Feb. 1982, p.1]. Relying on Article 84(2) the Council set up information on the activities of third countries in the area of maritime transport (Decision of 19 September 1978, OJ No. L 258 of 21. 9. 78, p. 35). Articles 43 and 100 are the legal bases of the Council Decision of 18 July 1977 on the acceptance of Codex alimentarius standards for sugar.
>
> *Article 235* has been relied upon together with *Art. 113* for the EEC/Canada Agreement (OJ No. L 260 of 1976, p.1) and the additional protocol to the EEC/Portugal Agreement (OJ No. L 274 of 1978, p.8). The Council concluded the EEC/ASEAN Agreement on the same bases (OJ No. L 144 of 1980, p.1). The Commission proposes to conclude the Agreement with Brazil also on those bases (OJ No. C 169 of 9. 7. 80, p.3). Article 235 is the (sole) legal basis on which the Council relied to conclude agreements in the

field of environmental protection: Bonn Convention of 1976 (OJ No. L 240 of 1977, p.35). Barcelona Convention of 1976 (OJ No. L 240 of 1977, p.1), Paris Convention of 1974 (OJ No. L 194 of 1975, p.5).

DIVISION OF POWERS, *supra* note 72, at 109 n.4. *Article 235* has been relied upon together with *art. 43* for the conclusion of the Convention between the EEC and the United Nations Relief and Works Agency for Palestine Refugees (UNRWA), Concerning Aid to Refugees in the Countries of the Near-East. *See* Council Dec. 80/444/EEC of 21 Apr. 1980, OJ No. L 108, 26 Apr. 1980, p.5; Council Dec. 81/1071/EEC of 21 Dec. 1981, OJ No. L 392, 31 Dec. 1981, p.3; Council Dec. 82/879/EEC of 21 Dec. 1982, OJ No. L 371, 30 Dec. 1982, p.42; Council Dec. 83/518/EEC of 17 Oct. 1983, OJ No. L 293, 25 Oct. 1983, p.17.

See also the Convention on Conservation of Wild Animals and Natural Environment of Europe, approved by Council Decision of 3 Dec. 1981, OJ No. L 38, 10 Feb. 1982, p.1. The Convention is based on art. 235, although the decision preamble mentions the Community action program on the environment and Council Directive 79/409, concerning conservation of wild birds.

On earlier efforts to apply the *ERTA* doctrine, *see* C. FLAESCH-MOUGIN, *supra* note 167, 175–77.

255. On this topic *see especially* 12 BRUSSELS COMMENTARY, *supra* note 90, at 62–63, 181–97; H. KRÜCK, VÖLKERRECHTLICHE VERTRÄGE IM RECHT DER EUROPÄISCHEN GEMEINSCHAFTEN (Berlin/Heidelberg/New York, Springer, 1977); O. JACOT-GUILLARMOD, DROIT COMMUNAUTAIRE ET DROIT INTERNATIONAL PUBLIC (Geneva, Georg-Librairie de l'Université, 1979); Bleckmann, *Der gemischte Vertrag im Europarecht,* 11 EuR 301 (1976); Pescatore, *supra* note 240, at 107; Meessen, *The Application of Rules of Public International Law within Community Law,* 13 C.M.L. REV. 485, 497 (1976); White, *Effects of International Treaties within the Community Order,* 1 EUR. L. REV. 102 (1976).

256. Update: This is now para. 7 in the amended text of art. 228. *See supra* note 45. *Cf.* the preliminary draft art. 36 *bis* (with a commentary) of the International Law Commission, *Question of Treaties Concluded between States and International Organizations or between Two or More International Organizations,* [1978] II Y.B. INT'L L. COMM'N, Part Two, at 123.

257. U.S. CONST. art. VI, § 2. *See supra* text accompanying note 132.

258. The text with notes 258–64 is drawn from my *External Relations of the European Community: Structure and Process* in Academy of European Law (ed.), *Collected Courses of the Academy of European Law,* vol. 1, bk. 1, 167–68 (the Netherlands, Kluwer Academic Publishers, 1991).

259. UN Doc. A/Conf. 129/15 of 20 March 1986, 25 ILM (1986) 543, Cm. 244.

260. E. Klein and M. Pechstein, *Das Vertragsrecht Internationaler Organisationen* (1985) 34–60; Zemanek, "The United Nations Conference on the Law of Treaties between States and International Organizations or between International Organizations: The Unrecorded History of Its 'General Agreement' " in K.-H. Böckstiegel *et al.* (eds), *Law of Nations, Festschrift für Ignaz Seidl-Hohenveldern,* 665, 674–675 (1978, C. Heyman, Köln); Gaja, "A 'New' Vienna Conven-

tion for Treaties between States and International Organizations or between International Organizations: A Critical Commentary," 58 *BYBIL* (1987) 253.

261. See in this context Article 74 of the Convention providing that its provisions shall not prejudge any question with regard to the establishment of obligations and rights for states members of an international organization under a treaty to which that organization is a party.

262. See citations for both sides in Pernice, "Völkerrechtverträge internationaler Organisationen etc.," 48 *ZaÖRV* (1982) 229, 238, n. 42. See also Vedder in E. Grabitz (ed.), *Kommentar zum EWG-Vertrag,* Art. 228, No. 42, 54 (May 1986); J.V. Louis and P. Brückner, *Relations Extérieurs,* J. Mégret et al. (eds.), 12 *Le droit de la Communauté Economique Européenne,* 62, 63 (1980); H. Von der Groeben *et al., Handbuch des Europäischen Rechts,* IA 76 (Art. 228, 1985).

263. Manin, "L'Article 228, paragraph 2 du Traité C.E.E.," in P.-E. Teitgen (ed.), *Études de droit des Communautés européennes,* (1984), 289, 302–304.

264. See comments by the EEC delegate in Conference Participants' Comments, Provisions A/CONF.129/C1/SR.25 at 6.

265. Joined Cases 21 to 24/72, International Fruit Co. NV v. Produktschap voor Groenten en Fruit, [1972] ECR 1219 [*International Fruit*]; Case 9/73, Schlüter v. Hauptzollamt Lörrach, [1973] ECR 1135. *See also* Case 40/72, Schröder v. Federal Republic of Germany, [1973] ECR 125; Case 112/80, Firma Anton Dürbeck v. Hauptzollamt Frankfurt am Main-Flughafen, [1981] ECR 1095; Case 181/80, *Arbelaiz-Emazabel,* [1981] ECR 2961; Joined Cases 180 & 266/80, Crujeiras Tome v. Procureur de la République, and Procureur de la République v. Yurrita, [1981] ECR 2997. One commentator believes that a "mixed agreement" concluded jointly by the Community and the Member States on their behalf also binds both the Community institutions and the Members in its entirety, unless it provides that certain provisions bind specific parties only. Moreover, in this view, a mixed agreement has the same rank of superiority over national law as does an agreement concluded by the Community alone. Bleckmann, *supra* note 255, at 303. *But see* Lachmann, *EF's Forhold Til Tredjelande,* in KARNOVS EF SAMLING 1028 n.20 (O. Due, O. Lando & W. von Eyben eds., 2nd ed., Copenhagen, Karnovs Forlag, 1979).

266. Such a rule is recognized in the Netherlands, Luxembourg, Belgium, France, and Greece. In the Netherlands, the courts are expressly barred from reviewing treaties for constitutionality. Pescatore believes that since in the Community legal order the Court affirmed the supremacy of Community law over Member State law (including Member States' Constitutions) "it would be inconceivable" not to apply the same rule to the relationship between Community law and international law. Cited in 12 BRUSSELS COMMENTARY, *supra* note 90, at 182.

267. *See supra* text accompanying note 158. In contrast with the Continental system, in the U.S. treaty-making and law-making are not effectively in the same hands. This fact may perhaps be advanced in explanation of the Supreme Court's posture. *See infra* note 370.

268. EEC Treaty arts. 169, 173, 175, 177, 184. The Commission, the Council, or a Member State, and if they can show "direct and individual concern," "any natural or legal person" (regardless of their nationality) may institute a direct

action before the Court, but a third state party to the agreement cannot, unless it could qualify as a legal person with a "direct and individual concern." An act of the institutions that violates a Community agreement may also be referred to the Court by a Member State tribunal in accordance with art. 177. *See infra* text accompanying notes 273–79, 295. *And see* Case 40/72, Schröder v. F.R. Germany, [1973] ECR 125.

269. EEC Treaty arts. 169, 170, 171. Again, the third state would most likely not itself have standing.

270. EEC Treaty art. 177. *See, e.g.,* Case 181/73, *Haegeman II,* [1974] ECR 449. As to the circumstances in which such challenges can be raised in Member State courts, *see infra* notes 273–79 and accompanying text.

271. L. HENKIN, *supra* note 7, at 167.

272. *See* the position of the Department of State in its note to the Japanese Government in E. STEIN, P. HAY & M. WAELBROECK, *supra* note 3, at 1071. The challenge by a private party assumes of course that the treaty grants private rights to individuals.

273. Joined Cases 21 to 24/72, [1972] ECR 1219. *See also, e.g.* Case 181/73, *Haegeman II,* [1974] ECR 449 (Association with Greece); Case 87/75, Bresciani v. Amministrazione Italiana, [1976] ECR 129 (Yaoundé Convention); Case 65/77, Razanatsimba, [1977] ECR 2229 (Lomé Convention); Case 52/77, Cayrol v. Rivoira, [1977] ECR 2261 (commercial agreement with Spain).

274. The individual will sue in the appropriate Member State court that will be expected to refer this "preliminary question" to the Court of Justice pursuant to art. 177.

275. *See supra* text accompanying note 154.

276. I agree with Ganshof van der Meersch that the teleological test employed by the Court is *mutatis mutandis* compatible with the rules on treaty interpretation in the Vienna Convention on the Law of Treaties of 1969. Cited in O. JACOT-GUILLARMOD, *supra* notes 212, at 116. It should be kept in mind, however, that the non-availability of legislative history materials of the Community Treaties and the special nature of integration dynamics necessarily influence the interpretation. In 1972 in *International Fruit* the ECJ found that GATT provisions cannot be considered directly applicable and to have direct effects because of the indeterminacy of the obligations, flexibility and the many derogations, and it has not since departed from that view (Case 266/81, Società Italiana per l'Oleodotto Transalpino (SIOT) v. Ministero delle Finanze dello Stato, [1983] ECR 731; Joined Cases 267–269/81, Amministrazione delle Finanze dello Stato v. Società Petrolifera Italiana SpA & Others, [1983] ECR 801; Joined Cases 290 & 291/81, Compagnia Singer SpA v. Amministrazione delle Finanze dello Stato, [1983] ECR 847). This is also the view taken by German courts but it is contrary to the Italian and United States doctrine. *See* Joined Cases 21 to 24/72, [1972] 1219, 1237–38 (opinion of Mayras, A.G.). For the American cases and view, *see* Jackson, *The GATT in United States Domestic Law,* 66 MICH. L. REV. 249 (1967). Update: The Case 280/93, [1994] ECR I-4973, extended the ruling in the International Fruit Company by holding that the Court is precluded from taking provisions of GATT into consideration in assessing the lawfulness of

a regulation, not only in a proceeding instituted by an individual in a national court and referred to it under article 177, but also in an action brought by a Member State under article 173 of the EEC Treaty.

277. *See* cases cited *supra* note 225. The holding on GATT has been criticized. *See* Pescatore, *supra* note 192, at 637 n. 42.

278. Individual action in national courts with a reference to the ECJ under art. 177 has been by far the most frequently invoked and the most effective means of enforcing the Treaty and the Community legislation against violations by Member States. In one case, involving the Multifiber Agreement concluded by the Community, this enforcement process proved ineffective because the French *Conseil d'Etat* improperly refused to refer the question of direct applicability to the Court of Justice and itself ruled that the agreement was not directly applicable. C.E. (F), Judgment of 12 Oct. 1979, Syndicat des importateurs de vêtements et de produits artisanaux, [1979] Rec. Leb. 373; 15 R.T.D.E. 730 (1979).

279. *See* Case 270/80, Polydor Ltd. and RSO Records Inc. v. Harlequin Record Shops Ltd. and Simons Records Ltd., [1982] ECR 329. The Free Trade Association Agreement (FTAA) with Portugal contains a prohibition of measures equivalent to quantitative restrictions in terms essentially identical with EEC Treaty arts. 30 and 36. The same prohibitions appear in the other six FTAA's with the other EFTA countries, and practically in the same terms in many other agreements. In *Polydor,* an English owner of a copyright protected by English law sought to prevent importations from Portugal into England by a third party of gramaphone records lawfully manufactured and marketed in Portugal by his licensee. The ECJ has consistently held that similar attempts to prevent importation *from one Member State to another* constitute measures equivalent to quantitative restrictions (a partitioning of the "single market") prohibited by art. 30 in conjunction with art. 36. In *Polydor* it held that despite the identity of the language, the restriction on imports from Portugal was not prohibited by the FTAA because its provisions do

> not have the same purpose as the EEC Treaty inasmuch as the latter . . . seeks to create a single market reproducing as closely as possible the conditions of a domestic market. . . . In the present case such a distinction is all the more necessary inasmuch as the instruments which the Community has at its disposal in order to achieve the uniform application of Community law and the progressive abolition of legislative disparities within the common market have no equivalent in the context of the relations between the Community and Portugal.

280. The text with notes 280–94 is drawn from my *External Relations of the European Community: Structure and Process,* in Academy of European Law (ed.), *Collected Courses of the Academy of European Law,* vol. 1, bk. 1, 174–77 (the Netherlands, Kluwer Academic Publishers, 1991).

Supra note 207.

281. Case 12/86, para. 14. With the same outcome, *Regina v. Secretary of State for Home Dept. ex parte Unal Narin*, English Court of Appeal, 2 CMLR (1990) 233.

282. The Advocate General obviously had in mind *Van Gend and Loos* and its progeny.

283. Case 12/86, Opinion of Mr. Advocate General Darmon, para. 18.

284. Ibid. para. 23.

285. Case 192/89, *S.Z. Sevince v. Staatssecretaries van Justitie*, [1990] ECR I-3461. This case became available after completion of the manuscript of these lectures.

286. The Court found direct applicability despite the "essentially programmatic character of the relevant provisions in the Turkish agreement" (ibid. para. 21) and despite the text of the two decisions contemplating that the Contracting Parties will take measures to execute the decisions (para. 23).

287. Bourgeois, "Effects of International Agreements on European Community Law: Are the Dice Cast?" 82 *Mich.L.Rev.* (1984) 1250; also in *The Art of Governance, Festschrift for E. Stein* (1984) 112.

288. Frowein, "The Competence of the European Community in the Field of External Relations," in J. Schwarze (ed.), *The External Relations of the European Community, in Particular EC-US Relations* (1989) 29, 34 feels "it is not clear whether Community agreements should have priority over Community law in general although Judge Pescatore has stated that this should be the rule."

289. Opinion 1/76. *Supra* note 198.

290. In *Kupferberg* the Court stated that "the fact that the courts of one of the parties consider that certain of the stipulations in the agreement are of direct application whereas the courts of the other party do not recognize such direct application is not in itself such as to constitute a lack of reciprocity in the implementation of the agreement." Case 104/81, [1982] ECR 3664.

291. Joint Cases 194 and 241/85, *Commission v. Greece*, [1988] ECR 1037, concerning a violation of the Lomé Convention.

292. Demaret, "La politique commerciale: perspectives d'évolution et faiblesses présentes," in J. Schwarze and H.G. Schermers (eds.) *Structure and Dimensions of European Community Policy* (1988) 69 at 103–104.

293. Ibid. However, in the U.S. the concept of self-executing treaties enabling individuals to press their rights derived from violations of commercial treaties of the United States is firmly established, thus making it unnecessary in principle for the federal government to intervene. On GATT application in the U.S., see Jackson, "The Genese Agreement on Tariffs and Trade in the United States Domestic Law," 66 *Mich.L.Rev.* (1967) 249; Hudec, "The Legal Status of GATT in the Domestic Law of the United States," in M. Hilf, F.G. Jacobs, E.-U. Petersmann (eds.), *The European Community and GATT* (1986) 187.

294. Ibid.

295. Update: Now art. 218(7). Bourgeois, *Some Comments on the Practice*, in DIVISION OF POWERS, *supra* note 72, at 97, 107.

296. [1972] ECR 1219, 1227.

297. Case 38/75, Douaneagent der NV Nederlandse Spoorwegen v. Inspecteur der invoerrechten en accijnzen, [1975] ECR 1439, 1450. This case reached the same conclusion with respect to Community succession to the Brussels Nomenclature Convention of 1950. The question of "succession" has also been raised in relation to the European Convention on Human Rights, to which the ECJ has referred as one source for determining the common standards of fundamental human rights that the Community institutions must observe. *See* most recently, Case 44/79, *Hauer,* [1979] ECR 3727, 3745.

298. *See* Foreign Relations Law of the United States, Restatement (Second) of the Law §§ 164 ff (St. Paul, Minn., ALI Pubs., 1965).

299. *See, e.g.,* United States v. Pink, 315 U.S. 203 (1942); Dames & Moore v. Regan, 453 U.S. 654 (1981).

300. *See generally* L. Henkin, *supra* note 7, at 251–70.

301. *See* authorities cited in 12 Brussels Commentary, *supra* note 90, at 15–19. *But see* Bothe, *Die Stellung der Europäischen Gemeinschaft im Völkerrecht,* 37 ZaöRV 122 (1977) and authorities cited therein. On the special problems arising from "mixed agreements," *see* Ehlermann, *supra* note 181, at 20.

302. *See, e.g.,* retaliatory action by the Community against the U.S., Council Decision of 4–5 June 1962, [1962] JO No. 1518, p.62, *reproduced in* E. Stein & P. Hay, Law and Institutions in the Atlantic Area 384–85 (Indianapolis, Bobbs-Merril, 1967). On the EC power to impose sanctions *see infra* notes 368–69 and accompanying text.

303. *See supra* text accompanying note 265.

304. Bleckmann, *The Personal Jurisdiction of the European Community,* 17 C.M.L. Rev. 467 (1980). Where the Community advances a claim on behalf of an official or an enterprise, it would no doubt coordinate its action with the Member State of the claimant's nationality. The Community's power to bring an international claim is frequently explained or buttressed by a reference to the opinion of the International Court of Justice on the Reparation for Injuries Suffered in the Service of the United Nations, 1949 I.C.J. Rep. 174.

305. Hilf, *Europäische Gemeinschaften und internationale Streitbeilegung,* in Völkerrecht als Rechtsordnung, Internationale Gerichtsbarkeit, Menschenrechte 387 (R. Bernhardt, W.K. Geck, G. Jaenicke, H. Steinberger eds., Berlin/Heidelberg/New York, Springer, 1983).

306. Particular problems in this context may arise from "mixed agreements," discussed *supra,* text accompanying notes 179–81, 191.

307. This paragraph is drawn from my *External Relations of the European Community: Structure and Process,* in Academy of European Law (ed.), *Collected Courses of the Academy of European Law,* vol. 1, bk. 1, 179 (the Netherlands, Kluwer Academic Publishers, 1991).

D. O'Keeffe and H.G. Schermers (eds.), *Mixed Agreements* 137 (1983). See also Balenkjian, *ibid.* 150.

308. In addition to the works cited *infra* notes 309–71, *see generally* P. de Schoutheete, La Coopération politique européenne (with bibliography at

227–31) (Paris/Brussels, Fernand Nathan/Ed. Labor, 1980); J. MONNET, *supra* note 25; THE UNITED STATES AND WESTERN EUROPE—POLITICAL, ECONOMIC AND STRATEGIC PERSPECTIVES (W.F. Hanrieder ed., Cambridge, Winthrop Publishers, Inc., 1974) (particularly Hoffmann, *Toward a Common European Foreign Policy?* at 79); W. Wessels, The European Political Cooperation—Model or Nuisance for a New Institutional Equilibrium (mimeo, prepared for "Symposium on: The Community Institutions at the Beginning of the 1980's—In Search of a New Balance," Semaine de Bruges, 1980, College of Europe, Bruges, Belgium, 1980); DIE EUROPÄISCHE POLITISCHE ZUSAMMENARBEIT—LEISTUNGSVERMÖGEN UND STRUKTUR DER EPZ (R. Rummel & W. Wessels eds., Bonn, Europa Union, 1978); AUF DEM WEG ZUR EUROPÄISCHEN UNION—DISKUSSIONSBEITRÄGE ZUM TINDEMANS—BERICHT (H. Schneider & W. Wessels eds., Bonn, Europa Union, 1977); Dolan & Caporaso, *The External Relations of the European Community,* 440 ANNALS AM. ACAD. POL. & SOC. SCI. 135 (1978); von der Gablentz, *Luxembourg Revisited or the Importance of European Political Cooperation,* 16 C.M.L. REV. 685 (1979).

309. Wood, *Foreign Policy and Defense in the European Community,* 18 VA. J. INT'L L. 389, 399 ff (1978); Stein & Carreau, *Law and Peaceful Change in a Subsystem: "Withdrawal" of France from the North Atlantic Treaty Organization,* 62 AJIL 577 (1968).

310. For the text of the Fouchet Plan and the Recommendations of the European Parliament, *see* Council of Europe, Consultative Assembly, Political Committee, Doc. No. AS/Pol (13) 69 and AS/Pol (13) 77.

311. P. DE SCHOUTHEETE, *supra* note 308, at 18–26; and Wood, *supra* note 309, at 405.

312. EUROPEAN POLITICAL COOPERATION (EPC) 23–24 (3rd ed., Press and Information Office of the Federal Government, Public Document, Bonn, 1978) [hereinafter cited as EPC Docs.].

313. BULL. EC 11–1970, at p. 9. (The Davignon Report was adopted by the Foreign Ministers of the Six as the *Luxembourg Report of 27 Oct. 1970. See* EPC Docs., *supra* note 312, at 26.)

314. H. da Fonseca-Wollheim, Dix ans de Coopération politique européenne 1 (mimeo, EC Commission, 1981). (Also translated into German: *Zehn Jahre Europäische Politische Zusammenarbeit,* 1981 INTEGRATION 47 (No.2, Institut für Europäische Politik, Bonn) [hereinafter *EPZ*]; and into English: Ten Years of European Political Cooperation (mimeo, EC Commission, 1981). The English text became available only after the completion of the present study.)

315. Some feel that the EPC offers in fact a competing alternative method preferable to the "mistaken" Community pattern. However, the *Hague Communiqué* reaffirmed the support for the Community as a nucleus of European unity. EPC Docs., *supra* note 312, at 22.

316. Paris Summit, 1972. *Id.* at 38.

317. *Luxembourg Report, 1970. Id.* at 29.

318. *Copenhagen Report, 1973. Id.* at 58–59.

319. Part 1 of the *Report on European Political Cooperation* approved by the

Foreign Ministers in London on 13 Oct. 1981. The Report provides more specific procedural guidelines for the cooperation process. *Report on European Political Cooperation,* EUROPE, Docs. No. 1174, 17 Oct. 1981; BULL. EC, SUPP. 3/81, at pp. 14–17 [hereinafter cited as *London Report, 1981*]. *See also infra* note 332.

320. H. KRAMER & R. RUMMEL, GEMEINSCHAFTSBILDUNG WESTEUROPAS IN DER AUSSENPOLITIK, ZUR TRAGFÄHIGKEIT DER EUROPÄISCHEN POLITISCHEN ZUSAMMENARBEIT (EPZ) 20 (Baden-Baden, Nomos, 1978).

321. Wallace & Allen, *Political Cooperation: Procedure as a Substitute for Policy,* in POLICY-MAKING IN THE EUROPEAN COMMUNITIES 227, 230 (H. Wallace, W. Wallace & C. Webb eds., London, John Wiley & Sons, 1977).

322. Paris Summit, 1974. EPC Docs., *supra* note 312, at 90. *See generally* on the machinery, *Luxembourg Report, 1970,* and *Copenhagen Report, 1973. Id.* at 26 ff, 51 ff.

323. The name recalls the American "Committees of Correspondence" that organized the American Revolution.

324. Only North America and the EFTA states are not covered.

325. There were 12 such groups when this study was written. The "Group of High Officials of Ministries of Justice" deals with judicial cooperation under EPC.

326. H. da Fonseca-Wollheim, Dix ans de CPE, *supra* note 314, at 5.

327. This adds a new function for Ambassadors sheared of their traditional importance because of the innumerable direct contacts among the Ministers.

328. Update: A secretariat of the EPC headed by a Secretary General with the seat in Brussels was established by the Single European Act of 1986. The Amsterdam Treaty of 1997 provided that the Secretary General of the Council shall be the High Representative for the common foreign and security policy.

329. *E.g.,* in the seven U.N. General Assembly Committees.

330. *London Report, 1981, supra* note 319, at para. 10. *See also* H. da Fonseca-Wollheim, Dix ans de CPE, *supra* note 314, at 6.

331. Etienne, *Community Integration: The External Environment,* 18 J.C.M. STUD. 289, 290 (1980). It has been suggested that one reason for such exclusion was to avoid adverse repercussions on inter-Member relations.

332. *See European Parliament,* No. 3147 (NS) EUROPE, 27 May 1981, at 4; Written Question No. 1042/80 by Mr. Ansart to the EPC Foreign Ministers meeting, OJ No. C 60, 19 Mar. 1981, p.1. In their 1981 Report, the Foreign Ministers agreed "to maintain the flexible and pragmatic approach which has made it possible to discuss in Political Cooperation certain important foreign policy questions bearing on the political aspects of security." *London Report, 1981, supra* note 319, at Part I.

333. Document on the European Identity, Copenhagen, 14 Dec. 1973, in EPC Docs., *supra* note 312, at 72 ff; Press Statement after the 14th EPC Ministerial Meeting, Bonn, 11 June 1974, *id.* at 86 (the *Gymnich* formula for consultation). Detailed consultations with the United States and other allies have taken place in CSCE.

334. United Kingdom and Denmark, and in part the Federal Republic as well, take the same position to protect NATO. Commissioner Tugendhat argued that since it is difficult to draw a dividing line between industrial policy and defense issues such as equipment procurement, cooperation should not be left exclusively to NATO. "If the commitment to political cooperation were strengthened, it would inevitably spill over into the security field." *Mr. Tugendhat says that there is a Community side to Europe's Defence Problems,* No. 3140 (NS) EUROPE, 16 May 1981, at 3. Other issues not dealt with by EPC are the Law of the Sea negotiations (coordinated within the Community framework), UNESCO items (dealt with in Ministries of Culture), and anti-terrorism measures ("TREVI") (coordinated by Ministries of the Interior and police experts). On "judicial cooperation" *see* H. da Fonseca-Wollheim, Dix ans de CPE, *supra* note 314, at 8–9. *See* Resolution on the European judicial area (extradition) adopted by the European Parliament on 9 July 1982, OJ No. C 238, 13 Sept. 1982, pp. 83–85.

335. *See especially* Bonvicini, *The Problem of Coordination between Political Cooperation and Community Activities,* 12 LO SPETTATORE INTERNAZIONALE 55 (1977).

336. *Id.* at 58–59.

337. *The Luxembourg Report of 1970* provided that should the work of the Ministers affect activities of the Communities, "the Commission will be invited to make known its views." EPC Docs., *supra* note 312, at 31. The *Copenhagen Report of 1973* noted with satisfaction the expanded practice. *Id.* at 53.

338. General responsibility was given to the Commission President and the General Secretariat who are given support by the Commissioner responsible for external relations and his staff. Bonvicini, *supra* note 335, at 60.

339. H. da Fonseca-Wollheim, Dix ans de CPE, *supra* note 314, at 15 (and also in *EPZ* at 52); Bonvicini, *supra* note 335, at 60. According to Bonvicini, at a low level there is practically no coordination; correspondents, ambassadors, and experts employed by the ad hoc groups work independently with practically no support from Community officials. *Id.* at 64. The accuracy of the reference to ad hoc groups is questioned by H. da Fonseca-Wollheim, letter to Eric Stein (4 Dec. 1981).

340. The Commission receives political information from the EPC groups which the economic officials on the COREPER staff may not have because of the separation between the political and economic sections within some of the national ministries. H. da Fonseca-Wollheim, Dix ans de CPE, *supra* note 314, at 15–16, (also in *EPZ* at 52); Bonvicini, *supra* note 335, at 61–62.

341. *London Report of 1981, supra* note 319, at para. 12.

342. *See supra* note 312, at 31, 47, 58, 91, 93. A link between the EPC and the European Parliament was envisaged already in the *Luxembourg Report of 27 Oct. 1970,* in the form of a biannual colloquy between the Ministers and the Political Commission of the Parliament to discuss questions within the EPC ambit. On the other hand the Commission was to be invited "to make known its views" only "should the work of the Ministers affect the activities of the European Communities." EPC Docs., *supra* note 312, at 31.

343. *See, e.g.,* Blumenfeld, *Report on EPC,* 1977–78, E.P. WORKING DOCS., Doc. 427/77 (containing language of the Resolution of the European Parliament of 19 Jan. 1978 on EPC). The separation is "artificial . . . comic division . . . more a pretense than a reality," *per* Patijn (EMP), E. Parl. Debates, Sitting of Tuesday, 9 July 1974, OJ Annex, No. 179, p. 89; "utterly false," "fiction," *per* Lord Chelwood (EMP), *id.* at 92. *But see contra* Maigaard (EMP), (Danish Socialist People's Party), insisting on keeping the fiction alive to avoid freezing the Iron Curtain and to preserve the limits of Denmark's commitment as defined in the national referendum. *Id.* at 93. *See generally* the report drawn up on behalf of the Political Affairs Committee, REPORT ON EUROPEAN POLITICAL CO-OPERATION AND THE ROLE OF THE EUROPEAN PARLIAMENT (Rapporteur: Lady Elles) 1981–1982, E.P. WORKING DOCS., Doc. 1–335/81, 30 June 1981 [hereinafter the *Elles Report*]. *See also London Report of 1981, supra* note 319, at para 11.

344. *See generally* Gaja, *The European Parliament and Foreign Affairs: Political Cooperation among the Nine,* in PARLIAMENTARY CONTROL OVER FOREIGN POLICY, *supra* note 83, at 191, 198 ff.

345. P. DE SCHOUTHEETE, *supra* note 308, at 50–53, 118. Schoutheete suggests, at 118, that in the Communities after 1965–66 the movement has been in the direction of "renationalization" of common policies. In his view, the EPC has contributed to a movement in the opposite direction.

346. Collected in EPC Docs., *supra* note 312.

347. Simonet in P. DE SCHOUTHEETE, *supra* note 308, at 49. The progressive enlargement bringing in new members has not made this harmonization any easier.

348. After the Soviet entry into Afghanistan on 27 Dec. 1979, it took the Ministers until 15 Jan. 1980 to formulate a common declaration, long after the national governments had stated their positions and the U.N. General Assembly had taken up the matter. *Id.* at 128.

349. *See supra* text accompanying note 329; P. DE SCHOUTHEETE, *supra* note 308, at 127.

350. *London Report of 1981, supra* note 319, at para. 13. The Political Committee is said to constitute a bottle neck. Unlike in the Community, however, where about one third of the personnel works on interpreting and translating in the seven languages, EPC documents are prepared and discussions held in French or English without translation. P. DE SCHOUTHEETE, *supra* note 308, at 49.

351. P. DE SCHOUTHEETE, *supra* note 308, at 48.

352. McGeehan & Warnecke, *Europe's Foreign Policies: Economics, Politics or Both?* 17 ORBIS 1251, 1268 (1974); Wallace, *British External Relations and the European Community: The Changing Context of Foreign Policy-Making,* 12 J.C.M. STUD. 28, 45 (1973); P. DE SCHOUTHEETE, *supra* note 308, at 90.

353. Written Question No. 489/80, OJ No. C 251, 29 Sept. 1980, p. 12. *See* similarly with respect to the level of Member State diplomatic representation, Written Question No. 2047/82, OJ No. C 104, 18 Apr. 1983, p. 21.

354. Aldo Moro signed the final act in his position as Prime Minister of Italy and, expressly, also as President of the Council of the Communities.

355. P. de Schoutheete, *supra* note 308, at 82; Allen, *The Euro-Arab Dialogue,* 16 J.C.M. Stud. 323, 330 (1978).

356. In 1979 a representative of the "Presidency" spoke 82 times to explain the votes of the Nine. P. de Schoutheete, *supra* note 308, at 73.

357. In the 1980 Assembly, there were "three-way split" votes (yes/no/abstention) on decolonization, apartheid, UNCTAD, and legal aspects of the New International Economic Order. Certain progress has been noted in the disappearance of yes-votes by a Member State on resolutions openly critical of another Member. H. da Fonseca–Wollheim, Dix ans de CPE, *supra* note 314, at 28 (also in *EPZ* at 58). P. de Schoutheete, *supra* note 308, at 73, offers a more encouraging view of the statistics: in 1978 the Nine voted the same way on two-thirds of resolutions whereas in 1973 the number did not exceed 50%. In the 37th session of the General Assembly (1982) the Ten shared a common position on 270 resolutions (including "Consensuses"), 72% of the total. On resolutions which were put to a vote the Ten voted together on only 41% of the cases. Written Question No. 2125/82, OJ No. C 125, 9 May 1983, p.20. *See also* Written Question No. 687/75, OJ No. C 139, 21 June 1976, pp. 6–8 (on the general activities in New York). For a more detailed analysis and statistics, *see* B. Lindemann, EG-Staaten und Vereinte Nationen, particularly at 143, 145 (Munich/Vienna, R. Oldenbourg Verlag, 1978); Hurwitz, *The EEC in the United Nations: The Voting Behavior of Eight Countries, 1948–1973,* 12 J.C.M. Stud. 224 (1975); Hansen, *Die Europäische Politische Zusammenarbeit bei den Vereinten Nationen,* 30 Europa-Archiv 493 (1975).

358. P. de Schoutheete, *supra* note 308, at 73.

359. *Elles Report, supra* note 343, at 23.

360. Examples are the Community negotiations with the Andean Group after the military coup in Bolivia, the association agreement with Cyprus, the compatibility with foreign policy objectives of Member States of proposed Community assistance to certain third states. H. da Fonseca–Wollheim, Dix ans de CPE, *supra* note 314, at 26 (also in *EPZ,* at 56–57).

361. *Id.* at 26–27 (in *EPZ* at 57).

362. *Id.* at 22–23 (in *EPZ* at 55). It is said this common action was in fact an ex post facto "Europeanization" of an undertaking by the German Government about which there had been no agreement at the outset and that this was also the case with the French "initiative" in Zaire in 1977 and 1978. De Montbrial, *Gedanken über das politische Europa,* 36 Europa-Archiv 217, 221 (1981).

363. Art. 225 adds that if the individual Member State measures distort competition the Commission with the Member State concerned shall examine how these measures can be adjusted to Treaty rules.

364. Written Question 526/75 to the Council, OJ No. C 89, 16 Apr. 1976, p. 6. The Commission agreed that Member States could act under art. 224 but it pointed to U.N. Charter Article 48(2) which obligates the UN members to carry out Security Council decisions "directly and through their action in the appropriate international agencies of which they are members"; because "the Community as such has never been approached by the Security Council [regarding compliance with the embargo] the Commission sees no need to consider the

feasibility of applying in its common commercial policy the sanctions," nor did it see any need for consultation. *See* Commission's Answer to Question 527/75, OJ No. C 89, 16 Apr. 1976, p.8. *See generally* P.J. KUYPER, THE IMPLEMENTATION OF INTERNATIONAL SANCTIONS: THE NETHERLANDS AND RHODESIA (Alphen a/d Rijn, Sijthoff & Noordhoff, 1978); *see also* Kuyper, *Sanctions against Rhodesia. The EEC and the Implementation of General International Legal Rules,* 12 C.M.L. REV. 231 (1975). In 1977, the U.N. Security Council adopted an arms embargo against the Republic of South Africa. The chairman of the EPC Conference of Foreign Ministers declared the Nine "are resolved to apply the arms embargo." BULL. EC 11–1977, point 3.2.6. Under art. 223(1)b any Member State may act to protect its security interests with respect to arms trade and the arms embargo was apparently handled by the Member States under this provision.

365. BULL. EC 4–1980, point 1.2.7.

366. Gosses in DIVISION OF POWERS, *supra* note 72, at 127. The Commissioner concerned claimed that "the Commission shares responsibility for the implementation of whatever measures are agreed at the political level." BULL. EC 4–1980, point 1.2.5. For detailed discussion of the sanctions against Iran, *see* Petersmann, *Internationale Wirtschaftssanktionen als Problem des Völkerrechts und des Europarechts,* 1981 ZVGLRWISS 22, 22–26; and Schröder, *infra* note 369. *See generally* Nicolaysen, *Autonome Handelspolitik der EWG,* in STAATSRECHT—VÖLKERRECHT—EUROPARECHT. FESTSCHRIFT FÜR H.-J. SCHLOCHAUER ZUM 75. GEBURTSTAG, 855, 869 ff (I. von Münch ed., Berlin/New York, Walter de Gruyter, 1981). *See also* DIVISION OF POWERS, *supra* note 72, at 140–42.

367. BULL. EC 1–1980, points 1.1.3, 4, 8 & 2.1.36. The Council also called for examination of other trade measures, including export credit restrictions.

368. Council Regs. (EEC) Nos. 596/82 & 597/82 of 15 March 1982, OJ No. L 72, 16 Mar. 1982, pp. 15–19. Denmark initially opposed Community action, ostensibly on the legal ground that sanctions were beyond Community power. Eventually it abandoned its opposition but the Council greatly reduced the Commission's list of items to be affected by the sanctions. The Regulations were expected to have minimal practical impact and they were viewed as little more than an indication of displeasure with the Soviet role in Poland. *See, EEC Proposes Cuts in Soviet Imports,* Int'l Herald Trib., 26 Feb. 1982, at 2. The exemption of Greece by a special regulation, obviously motivated by the political stance of the Greek Government rather than by serious economic considerations, illustrates the difficulty in Council decision-making under the unanimity practice. The lesson from the Afghanistan affair may have contributed to the willingness of the governments to employ Community action rather than to rely on individual national measures. In that case some governments, to the irritation of others, proved unable (or unwilling) to obtain parliamentary approval for the necessary measures.

On 23 June 1982, in an answer to a question by Mr. Ephremidis criticizing by implication Council action against the Soviet Union, the Council stated:

> In establishing the common commercial policy the Council can legitimately take account of a range of factors attributable to the state of

> relations with one or other country or group of countries. In the present case, the Council considered that the interests of the Community required that imports from the USSR should be reduced. It therefore adopted, on the basis of Article 113 of the Treaty, the commercial policy measures which are the subject of Council Regulations (EEC) No. 596/82 and (EEC) No. 597/82. Article 113 of the Treaty permits the Council to adopt decisions by a qualified majority. . . .

OJ No. C 188, 22 July 1982, p.10. In fact the first mentioned regulation was adopted despite the negative vote of Greece which, however, did not interpose a "vital interest" claim. The Council position in this response can hardly be reconciled with its answer on the embargo against Rhodesia, summarized *supra* in text accompanying note 364.

369. Council Regulation (EEC) No. 877/82 of 16 Apr. 1982, OJ No. L 102, 16 Apr. 1982, p.1, and corresponding Decision of the representatives of the Governments of the Member States of the European Coal and Steel Community meeting within the Council of the same day, *id.* at p.3, were adopted unanimously. In addition to the discussions and decision in the EPC, the preamble of the regulation refers also to a U.N. Security Council resolution on the "invasion" and to consultations under art. 224 as well as to art. 113. Products in transit or to be imported in execution of existing contracts were exempted. The embargo was limited in time but it was extended twice, first by Council Regulation (EEC) No. 1254/82 of 18 May 1982, OJ No. L 136, 18 May 1982, p.1, and Decision of the representatives of the Member States of the European Coal and Steel Community meeting within the Council of the same day, *id.* at p.2; and then, without any time limit, by Council Regulation (EEC) No. 1254/82 of 24 May 1982, OJ No. L 146, 25 May 1982, p.1, and Decision of the representatives of the Member States of the European Coal and Steel Community meeting within the Council of the same date, *id.* at p.2. There was, however, no unanimity in support of the extension. Italy and Ireland declared that for political reasons they would not observe the embargo and would limit themselves to taking measures against trade diversion caused by their non-observance; and Denmark was prepared to cooperate subject to approval (subsequently obtained) by its Parliament. Yet the above measures extending the embargo do not provide any exceptions for the three dissenting Member States. This anomaly obviously raises serious questions which have not been officially answered. After Argentinian surrender, the regulations and decisions imposing the embargo were repealed by Council Regulation (EEC) No. 1577/82 of 21 June 1982, OJ No. L 177, 22 June 1982, p.1, and Decision of the representatives of the Member States of the European Coal and Steel Community meeting within the Council of 21 June 1982, *id.* at p.2. *See* Bruha, *Handelsembargo gegen Argentinien durch EWG–Verordnung?,* 98 DVBt 674 (1982). Bruha concludes that the embargo regulations based on art. 113 were illegal: because they were motivated exclusively by foreign-policy and security reasons they could not be viewed as legitimate commercial policy measures. He believes that, despite the initial unanimous support, the new embargo practice based on art. 113 cannot be viewed as representing "either political or

legal consensus." *Id.* at 682. There is, however, substantial earlier authority in support of Community jurisdiction to impose sanctions on the basis of art. 113: Petersmann, *supra* note 366, at 25–26; Schröder, *Wirtschaftssanktionen der Europäischen Gemeinschaften gegenüber Drittstaaten, dargestellt am Beispiel des Iran-Embargos,* 23 GERMAN Y.B. INT'L L. 111 (1980) (Schröder appears to believe that art. 113 may be employed if all Member States agree); also by implication probably Everling, *Das europäische Gemeinschaftsrecht im Spannungsfeld von Politik und Wirtschaft,* in EUROPÄISCHE GERICHTSBARKEIT UND NATIONALE VERFASSUNGSGERICHTSBARKEIT, FESTSCHRIFT FÜR HANS KUTSCHER 155, 171 (G. Grewe, H. Rupp & H. Schneider eds., Baden–Baden, Nomos, 1981). *See also* Meng, *infra* note 373; Kuyper, *Community Sanctions against Argentina: Lawfulness under Community and International Law,* in ESSAYS IN EUROPEAN LAW AND INTEGRATION, *supra* note 167, at 141; and *see generally* Dupuy, *Observations sur la pratique récente des "sanctions" de l'illicite,* 87 REV. GÉN. DR. INT. PUB. 506, 532–33 (1983).

370. In the Rhodesian case the President was able to implement the U.N. Security Council resolution by drawing upon the United Nations Participation Act, an Act of Congress adopted in implementation of the U.N. Charter. However, the Congress revoked the President's authority, thus placing the U.S. in violation of the U.N. Charter, and a court action against this Congressional measure proved unsuccessful. Diggs v. Schultz, 470 F.2d 461 (D.C. Cir. 1972), *cert. denied,* 411 U.S. 931 (1973). The President's authority to apply sanctions against Southern Rhodesia was restored by Congress in Pub. L. No. 95–12, 95th Cong., 91 Stat. 22, 18 Mar. 1977. Reid, *Congressional Power to Abrogate Domestic Effect of U.N. Treaty Commitment,* 13 COLUM. J. TRANSNAT'L L. 155 (1974). *See generally supra* text accompanying note 267. In the Iranian case, companies with claims against the Iranian Government pending before American courts challenged the President's power to apply sanctions in a way that would interfere with the judicial proceedings and contested his power to conclude an agreement with Iran whereby the claims were to be referred to international arbitration. The Supreme Court upheld the President's power. Dames & Moore v. Regan, 453 U.S. 654 (1981).

371. The lone voice is O. JACOT–GUILLARMOD, *supra* note 255, at 191. *See generally* P.J. KUYPER, *supra* note 364, at 192; Meier, *Zur Kompetenz der EG–Mitgliedstaaten zur Durchführung von Sanktionsbeschlüssen des Sicherheitsrats der Vereinten Nationen,* 25 RIW/AWD 247, 250 (1979).

372. Per Lachmann of the Danish Foreign Ministry worries about the following questions: If art. 113 is held to apply, would it be possible for Member States individually to discontinue the sanctions? What would happen if new sanctions or amendments were proposed in the U.N. Security Council? Would the Community then be exclusively competent to determine the vote and what about U.K. and French veto rights? *See* DIVISION OF POWERS, *supra* note 72, at 141. Interestingly, even the members of the legal staff of the Commission disagreed among themselves. *Id.* at 140–42. On the discontinuance of the sanctions against Argentina, *see supra* note 369.

373. *See* in this sense C.-D. Ehlermann, The Scope of Article 113 of the EEC Treaty (paper presented at the European University Institute in February 1982); and Meng, *Die Kompetenz der EWG zur Verhängung von Wirtschaftssanktionen gegen Drittländer,* 42 ZaöRV 780 (1982).

374. However, a modification of Council practice along the above lines will not suffice to alter the fundamentally inadequate process of the bureaucratic decision-making in the Community. Everling, *supra* note 369, at 168.

375. The "Solemn Declaration on European Union," adopted on 19 June 1983 by the Heads of State or Government "meeting within the European Council," became available after the completion of this study. It does not purport to bring about any substantive change in the relationship between the Community and the EPC; it calls, however, *inter alia,* for a better coordination of the two processes within the "European Union," full Commission association with the work of EPC and the inclusion of political and economic aspects of security within the EPC scope. For the text of the Declaration with a commentary, *see* Neville–Jones, *The Genscher/Colombo Proposals on European Union,* 20 C.M.L. Rev. 657 (1983); *see also* Bull. EC 6–1983, at p.24. *See also* the Draft Treaty Establishing the European Union and the Resolution of the European Parliament concerning the Draft, OJ No. C 77, 19 March 1984, p. 33; Bull. EC 2–1984, at p.7; Bull. EC 9–1983, at p.7.

Foreign Policy at Maastricht: "Non in Commotione Dominus"

Guest Editorial

The arch-conservative Joseph de Maistre, speaking "in language reminiscent of Burke, Herder and Chateaubriand," held that "all legitimate operations, of whatever kind, always proceed by insensible steps . . . Non in commotione Dominus."[1] The Twelve at Maastricht may be said to have taken "an insensible step" toward a common foreign policy, but they failed to accept full Community discipline in the area of foreign affairs.

There have been several such steps since the inception of the integration process more than forty years ago: for the first twenty years there was no foreign policy forum for the Member States. The European Political Cooperation, originally a purely political improvisation of the nineteen seventies, was given a treaty basis in the Single European Act of 1987 in the form of a broad obligation of the Member States to consult. The Maastricht Treaty has finally brought the "common foreign and security policy" within the orbit of the Community Council, albeit under a special regime. On the basis of guidelines from the heads of state or government assembled in the European Council, the Ministers take all decisions by a unanimous vote except in matters which by unanimous agreement they designate as subject to a special, qualified majority vote. A "political committee" of national diplomats parallels the Commission, the role of the European Parliament is little more than marginal and judicial control is excluded.

The general assumption has been that foreign policy merits special treatment in both the national and transnational contexts. My question is: to what extent is this a valid assumption today?

It may be argued that the traditional view of foreign policy as a

---

Reprinted from 29 Common Market Law Review 663–68 (1992).

"reserved domain" of executive power and expert diplomats is an arcane relic of the era of foreign relations dominated by dynastic concerns and "crown privilege" in its various manifestations. This is how Philip Allott describes diplomacy as practiced in a "statally organized" international society:

> Diplomacy is a dismal charade, with its panoply and protocol, its rituals and formalities, its treaties and communiqués and *bouts de papier,* its sound-bites and photo-calls of conniving politicians, its diplomatic emotions which are said to be warming or cooling, its tiffs and reconciliations, its infantile world of enemies and friends. . . . From time to time the drama bursts the bounds of the gilded conference-chambers and the electronic chattering, and the people of the world are swept into some new collective fantasy or some new unnatural disaster contrived by the monarchs and the presidents, the ministers and the ambassadors and the undersecretaries, as they choose the future of the human race.[2]

On the substance of the foreign policy making process, Allott comments:

> Policy-making thus comes to be a system acting in two modes—*advantage seeking; equilibrium-seeking.* Foreign and defence policies come to be either a calculation of the circumstances in which an advantage in well-being of one society may be gained at the expense of another, or else a calculation of the willing and acting needed to avoid or neutralize the possible effect of one society on another through matching perceived power with perceived power. And international relations become the fortuitous aggregation of such unilateral calculations. So it is that unwilled wars may occur.[3]

One may not share fully this jaundiced perception of diplomacy. Yet—paradoxically—in Europe, diplomats and politicians of the Member States play their games not only against the so-called third states but also, at least on some occasions, against each other, as demonstrated most recently in the early phases of the Yugoslav imbroglio.

Although foreign policy involves additional variables that are not present in the domestic arena, there is a legitimate question as to the extent to which the traditional treatment of foreign affairs is still justified in the light of contemporary realities:

1. With the decreasing long-term importance of military power, economic power has become the true power determinant; and

economic foreign policy is today the most important branch of foreign policy. In the European Community foreign commercial policy has been under Community discipline from the very inception and, with the prospect of the Economic and Monetary Union, the Community writ will presumably extend to most if not all foreign economic policy. Will the unnatural and inherently unstable separation of foreign economic and political policy be continued?

2. Both the scope and instrumentalities of foreign policy have undergone important mutations.

Foreign policy today embraces not only diplomacy but economic, social, cultural and environmental concerns and—last but not least—protection of basic human rights. As a result, foreign policy impacts domestic affairs substantially and directly, and it is no longer within the exclusive domain of national foreign affairs establishments. At the executive branch level, ministries of finance, economics, agriculture, labour, culture, environment and others demand participation. The executive is no longer the sole receptacle of vital information. Parliaments and special interests insist on being heard.

In the international arena marked by a globalized economy and a widening consensus on a free market and democracy, bilateral discourse is largely replaced by "parliamentary diplomacy," with the participation no longer limited to diplomats.

Allott again:

> Statal interacting has increased so much in volume and complexity that it is difficult any longer to disentangle the strands of calculating self-interest, and as economic interaction has overwhelmed in volume and almost in significance the interacting foreign and defence policies of governments. Governments are being swept up into self-socializing by the flood of their own activity. It seems possible now to say that through diplomacy and international relations, slowly and laboriously and ironically, it is being learned, first, that interest can be reciprocal and, then, that there can be a universal interest which transcends particular interests, and that there can be a particular interest which may be served by the universal interest—in short, the lessons of a society socializing itself.[4]

If this is the true picture of the late twentieth-century world, what is it that keeps the Member States from bringing foreign policy fully within the Community system, with such adjustments, to be sure, required by the factors germane to foreign affairs. Even if one disagrees with Allott and perceives the "outside world" as still indifferent, if not hostile, and aggressively competitive, why not face it jointly with the benefit of the full instrumentation of the Community?

I suggest the following restraining factors as influencing the reluctant posture of the Member States:

The residue of the traditional perception of foreign policy mentioned earlier;
Considerations of national pride and prestige of a "sovereign state" in the international arena;
Vested interests of the national bureaucracy;
The discrete treatment of foreign affairs powers in national constitutional practices motivated in part by the historic concept mentioned earlier. The conduct of foreign affairs is still left essentially to executive branches with relatively limited parliamentary input and little, if any, judicial control—a situation hardly compatible with both the importance of foreign affairs and the idea of a modern democratic state.

I have eschewed thus far—the reader may have noticed with some surprise—any reference to defence policy. Jean Monnet, looking back to the abortive proposals for the European Defence Community of the 1950s, wrote in his memoirs:

> I had never believed that we should tackle the problem of Europe via defence. Although this would no doubt be one task for the future federation, it seemed to me by no means the most powerful or compelling motive for unity. But if circumstances were to accelerate or reverse the course of events—well, then, that would be another matter . . . We were forced to take short cuts.[5]

A federation is not in place as yet, there are no true European political parties or European public opinion. Defence, it is said, is "the bedrock of national existence and it is the last element of sovereignty that a nation is prepared to abandon." The two European nuclear powers continue to insist on unrestricted control over their nuclear forces. The roles of NATO, of the United States forces and of the German forces outside the NATO area are far from clear. The Western European Union is still little more than a shell.

The Maastricht Treaty contemplates "the eventual framing of a common defence policy, which might in time lead to a common defence." It makes the Western European Union "an integral part of the development of the Union" and calls on it and the Council to adopt "the necessary practical arrangements." Bilateral and NATO cooperation is safeguarded and further progress is envisaged "having in view the date of 1998."

Some, if not all the considerations I listed in support of full Community discipline for foreign policy apply to defence as well. German Foreign Minister Hans-Dietrich Genscher declared in Berlin "that he did not see why a Europe that is to have a single currency should not have a common defence policy."[6] There can hardly be a credible "European Union" without a defence policy. Yet until the many new elements in the European scene are clarified, it is difficult to argue that the Maastricht treatment of defense policy is inadequate.

Notes

1. Cited in I. Berlin, *The Crooked Timber of Humanity* (1991), pp. 131–132.
2. P. Allott, *Eunomia: New Order for a New World* (1990), p. 270.
3. Ibid. at p. 271.
4. Ibid. at p. 273.
5. J. Monnet, *Memoirs* (1978), pp. 338, 343.
6. *Europe,* April 2, 1992, No. 5702 (n.s.) p. 5.

Uniformity and Diversity in a Divided-Power System: The United States' Experience

A pervasive problem of contemporary federalism is to reconcile the values of diversity and local autonomy with the needs for centralization and uniformity endemic to a modern state. In this essay, originally prepared for a conference at the Max Planck Institute for Foreign and International Private Law in Hamburg, I sketch the ways in which the complex, multijurisdictional American system, spanning a continent, has coped with this challenge. In contrast with the other items in this part of the collection, this paper (and the essay in Part 2 entitled "Panel Statement on 'Democracy without "a People" ' ") does not provide a comparative dimension. Yet several comparative observations from this side of the Atlantic come to mind.

The outright chaotic situation in American company law that I briefly describe here is a telling example of the high tolerance of diversity, at a substantial cost in efficiency and other values. It invites a comparison with the European situation I describe in the book Harmonization of European Company Laws—National Reform and Transnational Coordination *(1971) excerpted in Part 1 of this collection.*

Again, as I think about the manifold actions in American public institutions and private organizations leading to uniformity, I have the impression that private, voluntary groupings play a more important role in the United States than in Europe. This may be testimony to the particularity of the American civil society, marked by an infinite number of private associations in all walks of life and noted already by de Tocqueville.

One of the more powerful tools for uniformity in America is the authority of the Congress, upheld by the Supreme Court of the United States, to

---

Reprinted from 61 WASHINGTON LAW REVIEW 1081–1102 (1986). Reprinted with permission. I wish to acknowledge the generous advice I have received from my colleagues of the University of Michigan Law Faculty, particularly the detailed comments by Professors Chambers, Conard, Pierce and Dean Sandalow, and by Professors Friedman of the Stanford Law School and Juenger of the University of California at Davis Law School. Dr. Mathias Reimann assisted me ably in the research. I completed this article during my stay as a fellow at the Wissenschaftskolleg zu Berlin—Institute for Advanced Study Berlin. An earlier version served as a basis for a paper delivered at the Max Planck Institute for Foreign and International Private Law in Hamburg, Federal Republic of Germany, and was translated into German for publication in the Rabels Zeitschrift fur ausländisches und internationales Privatrecht.

offer funds to state governments in return for their acceptance of federal rules and standards, the famous "carrot and stick" technique. A comparable device does not exist in the European Community's armory as a "constitutionally" sanctioned instrumentality.

Finally, and perhaps most importantly, in this essay I outline a taxonomy of forces that have worked for uniformity in the United States. They range from demands for nationwide guarantees of freedom and equality to profit maximization and bureaucratic centralization. These forces, I suggest, operate in Europe and, for that matter, in other pluralistic societies, and they form the source of the challenge I mentioned at the beginning of this introduction.

The closing decade of the century has seen the rise of a reaction against the centralizing and unifying tendency on both sides of the Atlantic. In the United States it is manifested by moves to reduce the central government and transfer certain public functions (such as welfare) to the component states. And the U.S. Supreme Court has struck down as unconstitutional several congressional acts purporting to impose new obligations on the states.

In Europe, both the Maastricht Treaty of 1992 and the 1997 Treaty of Amsterdam have marked an expansion of the central powers in the European Union. However, the debate surrounding the 1992 Maastricht Treaty on the European Union revealed public skepticism about delegating new powers to Brussels authorities. This has led to the adoption, in the same treaty, of the principles of "subsidiarity" and "proportionality," according to which the Community shall act (in areas outside its exclusive powers) only if the objective can not be sufficiently achieved by the member states and, in any case, its action must not go beyond "what is necessary" to achieve the objective. In the same vein, the Court of Justice, although maintaining intact its constitutional jurisprudence, has reduced in some measure the Community's (and its own) control over member states' regulatory activity. Another mark of the pressure for decentralization is the introduction, also in the Maastricht Treaty, of a new consultation organ, a committee of representatives of regional and local bodies that, although quite active, has been thus far without noticeable influence. I touch upon these aspects in the Part 2 essay mentioned earlier in this introduction.

Ted Stein and I became friends during his term as visiting professor in Ann Arbor. He was immersed in the United States-Iranian arbitration and I worked on problems of integration of states in divided-power systems. We had long talks. The general idea of this essay goes back to that time. The last time I saw Ted was at a conference in Florence. I still see him deeply moved, contemplating the church of Santa Croce and the sea of Florentine roofs bathed in the scintillating light of the Tuscan morning. It was with a sense of grave personal loss that I dedicated this essay to his memory.

I. The Problem

Tension between harmony and disharmony, uniformity and diversity, central power and local power, legislature and judiciary, executive and legislature—is endemic to a divided-power system such as the United States federation. Even while constructing a more centralized order to replace a disintegrating confederation, the drafters of the American Constitution worried about preserving regional diversity.[1] In the new federation, private law was to remain in principle within the preserve of the states, subject to specified powers delegated to the federal authorities and general constitutional restrictions. The states were to retain the complete hierarchy of state courts, with the full federal judiciary added. Although common law has provided a vital underpinning for essential uniformity, the process of administering common law has allowed for substantial diversity. The concern for diversity has remained a part of the public discourse in America even though the forces of the industrial, post-industrial, and "post-material" revolutions have worked mightily against diversity and for uniformity and a uniform rule.

The modest purpose of this paper is to inquire, in a specific contemporary context, why, by whom, and through what process a uniform rule is accepted or imposed in place of diverse rules. The first, methodological part of the paper offers a pattern for an analysis; the second part applies the pattern and illustrates the working of the process in the field of family law. I have chosen family law because in that field there has traditionally been concern for regional differences and because there has been an instructive interplay between regional and central powers.

It may not come as a surprise that the inquiry will lead us to issues at the heart of the federal process. Moreover, the institutional analysis will bring us to the threshold of societal problems arising out of cultural heterogeneity and caused by value conflicts of private against public good and equality against individual achievement.[2]

II. Toward Uniformity—A Process

A. The Three Faces of Uniformity

When I speak of uniformity I have generally in mind not only the situation of identical norms but also a situation in which norms are diverse but lead to essentially identical results. As is the case with many concepts, "legal" uniformity has different meanings in different contexts.

There is, in the first place, the uniformity within each component state of the Union, ultimately promoted by the state's supreme court—a concept essentially similar to the uniformity in a unitary state. However, this aspect of uniformity is complicated in the American federation by the existence of two complete hierarchies of courts, federal and state. Until 1938, federal courts were free to make their own determination about common law. A party in a controversy with a citizen of another state who considered the federal law more favorable to his side could bring it before a federal court, which would apply federal common law, rather than before a state court, which would apply potentially different and less favorable state common law. Uniformity thus prevailed within the federal system at the price of diversity within the same state, since federal and state courts within the same state could apply different law to the same facts.[3] Since 1938, however, by a decision of the United States Supreme Court, "[t]here [has been] no federal general common law,"[4] so that both the federal and state courts in a state must apply the same substantive state law: the uniformity within the state is victorious at the price of uniformity in the application of common law by the federal courts. Yet, subsequently a subtle development has led to the reemergence of federal common law in a new reincarnation, where federal interest in a uniform rule demands special recognition.[5]

There is, in the second place, the uniformity within the system of federal law based on federal statutes (Acts of Congress) and rulings of the federal executive and of federal agencies implementing federal statutes. The problem here, for instance, is to ensure that in the application of the federal income tax law, a citizen of Michigan is taxed not more nor less than a citizen of California.

Last but not least, there is uniformity, or—perhaps more accurately—the lack of uniformity between the states (and sometimes even within the states). The bulk of all law in the United States is still the law of the fifty states, which varies often quite egregiously from state to state. The vast majority of judicial cases are decided by state courts under these divergent state laws, and, in the absence of a federal question, there is no judicial super-authority—such as one encounters in unitary states—which would wield the power to review decisions of state supreme courts for uniformity. Although not compelled to do so by the rule of precedent, state courts do look at sister states' court decisions, except in matters of particularly local concern.

The diversity of results in various state courts is aggravated by each state's liberty to apply its own rules even to events that occur in other states. Neither the Supreme Court, nor for that matter Congress, has been prepared to bring order into the confused field of interstate conflict of laws, which by definition would seem to call for uniform rules.[6]

To illustrate the complexity of the system, Professor Conard suggests that if, for instance, an American attorney is to give reliable advice to a national corporation doing business throughout the American "common market," he should have in his library the fifty sets of state corporate laws, the forty-nine sets of state securities laws, the fifty sets of state courts decisions, not to speak of the extensive federal materials governing corporate securities.[7]

On first sight—and perhaps on the second as well—the picture is one of unmitigated chaos. Are there any ordering forces and instrumentalities that work to reduce the "chaos" in the interest of uniformity?

B. Uniformity through Voluntary Process

In what I would call a "voluntary" process, a "lead" state, responding to pressures for a change, may initiate a trend in state legislatures toward similar if not identical solutions.[8] Again, states may enter into interstate agreements or "compacts," with (but often without) the consent of Congress. Such agreements have harmonizing effects on the laws of the participating states.[9]

The movement toward uniformity is abetted by the public or private institutions offering uniform or model acts for consideration by state legislatures. Foremost among the public institutions is the venerable Conference of Commissioners on Uniform State Laws established in 1892 by the legislatures of all the states of the Union. Its triumph (shared with the American Law Institute) has been the acceptance by every state of the Uniform Commercial Code, thus bringing about a substantial uniformity in commercial law in the United States; but the majority of the currently recommended acts in other fields have been adopted by less than ten states, and quite a few by none.[10]

The uniform laws are often substantially modified in the process of adoption and, after adoption, divergent interpretations by state courts may further dilute the uniformity. However, the influence of the Commissioners' work cannot be measured solely in terms of formal adoptions. Their activities have been particularly helpful to smaller states that lack expert staff and adequate facilities to engage in studies and to draft legislation.[11]

Various private organizations have furthered the trend towards uniformity. The voluntary national association of lawyers, the American Bar Association (ABA), often operates in conjunction with the

Conference of Commissioners. While the ABA generally supports the work of the Conference, it also supplements the uniform laws with its own model acts and "minimum standards," with varying success in the legislative halls. In addition, the model codes and "restatements" of the law prepared by the American Law Institute, another voluntary institution, have exerted considerable impact, particularly on the judiciary, in a number of fields. A myriad of professional organizations (for example, accountants, brokers, state government officials), insurance companies, and testing laboratories have been an important force in overcoming—outside the prescriptive process—some of the glaring inconveniences of diversity.

Finally, the codes of federal rules of civil and criminal procedure and evidence, promulgated by the United States Supreme Court under a congressional mandate for use in federal courts, have also served as models for state legislation. About one half of the states have adopted part or all of the Federal Rules of Civil Procedure, so that lawyers in many states work, in effect, with a largely equivalent set of procedural rules. At times, states have built their own regulatory system in the image of national legislation such as the National Labor Relations Act. A somewhat analogous radiation effect upon state administrative rules and procedures can be traced to the lively intercourse between state and federal officials, particularly as a result of state administration of federal programs, the new patterns of federal-state co-decisionmaking, and the mobility between state and federal bureaucracies.[12]

C. Uniformity through Federal Power (compulsory process)

1. The National Rule

Not surprisingly, federal power has provided the most powerful impetus toward uniformity, resulting in a uniform national rule, uniformity's most radical manifestation. A national rule may take one of several forms: an act of Congress; an executive order or a federal agency rule, both of which result from a delegation by Congress; or—last but not least—of a judgment of the United States Supreme Court interpreting federal statutory law or the Constitution.[13]

Federal power is circumscribed by the text of the Constitution, by tradition, and above all by important political restraints. Nevertheless, since the late 1930's, owing to the broad construction of federal power by the "New Deal" Supreme Court, the Congress has been able, for all practical purposes, to exercise plenary legislative power in the economic field at any rate, not unlike the legislature in a unitary state. This has meant a dramatic proliferation of uniform national rules. In areas where Congress may feel barred by the Constitution or by politics from legislating uniform rules, it has employed extensively the device of making federal funds available to states on condition that they accept a more or less stringently defined policy.

Keep in mind that federal law "rests upon a substructure of state law,"[14] in that "[i]t builds upon legal relationships established by the states, altering or supplanting them only so far as necessary for [its] special purpose."[15] Even where federal power is exclusive, as for instance in federal tax laws, in the social security system, or in foreign relations, state law and state authority often impinge on its operations. Federal statutes often contain words and embody concepts the meaning of which is defined by state law. Where divergence among state law definitions impairs the uniform application of the federal rule, as in federal income tax law, Congress steps in and provides its own uniform definition.[16] Where state and federal jurisdictions are concurrent, as in economic regulation (for example, in environmental law or labor law), the two systems interact intimately. Finally, even where state power is "exclusive," federal power has increasingly intruded, as will be demonstrated in the example of family law.[17]

2. The Role of Federal Judiciary

a. Uniformity and Conflicts between the Courts

As I have suggested earlier, state courts decide the overwhelming majority of cases, and it is the responsibility of the respective state supreme courts to maintain uniformity within each state by resolving conflicts between decisions of the lower courts of the same state. State courts have to share judicial power with federal courts in only an "infinitesimally small" fraction of cases that raise federal questions.[18]

In the federal system, ninety-four federal district courts are supervised by thirteen circuit courts of appeal with the United States Supreme Court at the apex of the pyramid. The problem of maintaining uniformity has been greatly magnified by the enormous growth in the appellate dockets. The rapid increase in the number of judges required to cope with the overload has made it more difficult within each appellate court to avoid internal conflicts between the panels.[19] More importantly, since no federal court of appeal is bound to respect the decisions of another, conflicts among these courts occur. Although the Supreme Court takes into consideration the existence of such conflicts in accepting cases for review[20] it does not review a sufficient number of cases to resolve all such conflicts "or indeed even a small fraction of [them]."[21] As a result, the "non-constitutional" areas of federal law, such as the important cases that come out of federal administrative agencies, are generally left by the Supreme Court to the courts of appeal.[22] These courts talk about the need of uniformity and they stress a policy of avoiding conflicts,[23] but one experienced critic has charged them with a lack of "institutional responsibility" about avoiding conflicts because they know that their decisions will not be reviewed.[24] This leads to "forum shopping" among federal courts and uneven enforcement of federal law in different parts of the country.

There is currently a wide-ranging national debate on whether or not the Supreme Court has the time and will to resolve the divergence in interpretation. There are controversial proposals to establish a new National Court of Appeals with the jurisdiction to resolve inter-circuit conflicts.[25] Opponents of these proposals contend that the persistence of the divergent interpretations over a period of time will enable the Supreme Court to deal with issues "more wisely at a later date,"[26] and that elimination of regional influence in divergent interpretations would be undesirable.[27]

Whatever may be the merits of the National Court of Appeals proposal, it is not likely to be accepted by the Congress in the foreseeable future. In the meantime, much depends on the willingness of the courts of appeals to pay attention to the courts in other circuits. As Judge Lay expressed it:

> Although we are not bound by another circuit's decision, we adhere to the policy that a sister circuit's reasoned decision deserves great weight and precedential value. As an appellate court, we strive to maintain uniformity in the law among circuits, wherever reasoned analysis will allow, thus avoiding unnecessary burdens on the Supreme Court docket. Unless our 11 courts of appeals are thus willing to promote a cohesive network of national law, needless division and confusion will encourage further splintering and the formation of otherwise unnecessary additional tiers in the framework of our national court system.[28]

b. Preserving Uniformity of National Rules

The United States Supreme Court performs another influential function by protecting the integrity of the uniform rules in the Constitution against the other federal branches of government, and, more importantly, by defending the Constitution and federal law against state intrusions. Although the Court often exalts national uniformity, this goal appears to be more an inspiration to silver-tongued rhetoric than a decisive variable. For instance, in wielding the power of constitutional review under the clause that gives Congress the authority to regulate interstate commerce, the Court is concerned more with economic unity of the nation, rather than with normative uniformity. At this stage of its history, at any rate, the Court is tolerant of diverse state legislation unless the legislation is motivated by a more or less explicit protectionist purpose to discriminate against goods or services from other states. Where, however, national transportation systems are hampered by state regulation of train lengths, truck sizes, mudguard requirements, etc., the Court imposes strictest uniformity and strikes down deviant state laws.[29]

The Court also imposes rigorous restrictions on state power when it comes to applying a uniform rule for the protection of individual rights derived from the Bill of Rights of the Constitution. This is the process of "constitutionalization" of traditional areas of state law, as manifested, for example, in criminal procedure and family law. The scope of this "constitutionalizing" process is unprecedented in other systems.

When faced with an allegation of a conflict between a federal statute and state law, the Court manipulates the doctrine of "preemption"—a finely-tuned instrument for determining whether Congress "intended" to preclude the exercise of state power on a given subject or in an entire field. After attempting without success to construct a generally applicable preemption standard, the Court now openly resorts to balancing the respective state and federal interests. In areas where in the Court's judgment uniform national policy is needed—as for instance in labor relations, in the interest of preserving industrial peace—the Court generally holds that the federal statute "preempts" the state law.[30]

In the process of deciding whether to lay down a constitutional rule or whether a federal statute has preempted the field, the Court sometimes considers trends in state legislation.[31] Occasionally, the Court even subordinates uniformity as a value to the utility of social or economic experimentation, with one or more states serving as laboratories.[32]

After the Second World War and through the earlier years of the Burger Court, the controlling emphasis was on preserving and expanding national rules as against the diverse state rules. Recent developments in fields as varied as criminal procedure and corporate securities may signal a slowing down of this trend.[33] It would be interesting to observe whether such a trend from uniformity toward greater diversity, if it indeed materializes, could be correlated with the cyclical oscillation between liberalism and conservatism which Schlesinger discerns in American history.[34]

D. Forces for Legal Uniformity: The Five Syndromes

It would exceed the scope of this study to attempt an economic and social analysis of the advantages and disadvantages of diversity and uniformity, important as such an effort would be in providing an appropriately broad context for a normative inquiry. I trust, however, that some, if not most of the relevant variables can be found, at least implicitly, in the text that follows. It must suffice here to enumerate, in neutral terms and on the basis of little more than intuition, the principal syndromes that unleash forces which pull towards legal uniformity:

1. *The freedom and equality syndrome:* Social and economic change that has created a demand for national guarantees of freedom and equality, and for uniform policy in many areas of life.[35]
2. *The "dollars-and-cents" syndrome:*
   (a) Profit-maximization of *private* interest groups through improved standards, increased efficiency, simplification and systematization, etc.
   (b) Budgetary concerns of *public* institutions.
3. *The bureaucratic centralization syndrome:* The expanding role of the central government in the life of the nation.
4. *The effective law enforcement syndrome:* The need for effective enforcement in inter-state situations, and the need for preventing subversion of local policies and "forum shopping," which creates a drive to "patch up the holes" in the federal system.
5. *The Cartesian syndrome:* Theoretical concern for comprehensiveness and structural harmony.

The forces for social and economic change of the first syndrome may initially cause the prevailing uniformity to be undermined, only to be replaced, after a period of fragmentation and diversity, by a new uniformity. In contrast with continental Europe, the Cartesian syndrome is the weakest of the five in the United States, where common law mentality and innate pragmatism place little value on systematization as such. It may be present, however, along with the other syndromes, in the minds of the reporters on uniform state laws, drawn predominately from among law professors.

The five syndromes do not operate in isolation but interact actively in most instances when a uniform rule emerges. For example, the first four syndromes are discernible in the growth of uniform national rules intruding into the state-law-governed relationship between corporate management, shareholders, and investors: the 1930's scandal of massive fraud causing widespread financial disasters and nationwide indignation; the failure of the states to act, with the consequent radical intervention by Congress; and the persistent reach for more power by the supervising bureaucracy imposed by the Congress.

The revolution in transport and communication (first syndrome) and the consequent dramatic growth of nationwide commerce demanding uniformity (second syndrome) are reflected in the important "voluntary" uniformization of commercial law. However, a threat of federal imposition had loomed in the background and it may have contributed to the success of the voluntary process.[36] The interplay of the fourth, "gap filling" syndrome with the first two, is illustrated by the two acts of Congress described in the next section, which were designed to deal with "child-snatching" and with absent fathers owing family support in interstate situations beyond the reach of enforcement by individual states.[37]

The syndromes also operate transnationally—with greater or lesser intensity—on the global and regional levels and lead to uniform rules or principles in treaties and resolutions or declarations by international groups and organizations. Their influence upon the United States, while increasing in the last decades, is substantially less pervasive than it is upon smaller countries with less power and more dependent economies. Thus, for instance, the United States has not accepted the bulk of the widely ratified conventions of the International Labor Organization that have been motivated by both social concerns over working conditions (first syndrome) and considerations of international economic competition (second syndrome). Nor has the United States adhered to the principal United Nations covenants purporting to provide uniform world rules on fundamental human rights (first syndrome).[37a] Needless to say, the process toward uniformity at the international level, although propelled largely by identical syndromes, is much more onerous than in the domestic arena.

III. The Working of the Process: Toward Uniformity in Family Law?

Ever since Montesquieu, and surely since Max Weber, there has been little doubt about the interaction between law and society. If there is any field in which one would expect a particularly intimate link between legal norms and local culture, it is family law. In the United States, that law has been left within the preserve of the states. As late as 1956 the

Supreme Court declaimed: "[T]here is no federal law of domestic relations, which is primarily a matter of state concern. . . ."[38] State legislation varied greatly, though reflecting, on the whole, traditional family values.

A dramatic change in the society over the last thirty years has brought about a radical turn from diversity to a degree of uniformity. World War II, new technology, massive movements to cities, changes in the composition of the urban population, increased mobility—all of these factors contributed to the breakdown in the consensus over the traditional concepts of marriage, family, and sexual morality. There has been a new emphasis on a pluralistic society and varied styles of life. Personal relations are seen less in moralistic traditional terms, and more in terms of personal growth and satisfaction; and psychiatric expertise has been given a major role. Minority and women's groups have entered the political process and there has been a change in the perception of the role of the government. "[I]t seems no exaggeration," wrote Dean Sandalow, "to say that the United States has, during the past decade, experienced a revolution, a momentous alteration in the aggregation of attitudes and practices that defined a traditional societal stance toward the family."[39]

A. Uniformity by State Action: Marriages and Divorce

In 1963, 66.31% of all terminated marriages ended by death and 33.69% by divorce. By 1979 only 42.79% terminated by death, while 57.23% ended by divorce. In 1930 there were six marriages to every divorce; in 1981 the ratio was two to one.[40]

Most Americans in the twentieth century no longer believed that divorce should be available only when one of the parties had committed some marital sin, such as adultery or "cruel treatment," yet nearly all state laws still required proof of fault. Unhappy couples regularly engaged in collusion to obtain divorces both partners wanted; and the courts winked at the practices. The underpinnings of the traditional concept of divorce for fault had been eroded. The time for reform was ripe and the reform objective clear. Desire for simplification and greater coherence provided additional impulses for change in the law. At the end of the 1960's California started the trend toward no-fault divorce.[41]

In 1965 the Ford Foundation and the federal government provided funds for a study, sponsored by the State Commissioners on Uniform Laws with the advice of the American Bar Association. In 1970, the Uniform Marriage and Divorce Act,[42] incorporating no-fault divorce and a greatly reduced list of prohibited marriages, saw the light of day, and by 1983 it had been adopted in full or as amended in seven states. By 1984, however, all the other states had already removed the fault features except for South Dakota which continued to adhere to fault-based divorce.[43] The introduction of no-fault also advanced uniformity in the granting of divorces by eliminating judicial discretion inherent in the determination of fault of one side against the other. Thus substantial uniformity on a vital issue was achieved in two decades without federal intervention. Uniformity or similarity in substantive divorce law has reduced the problem of "migratory" or "tourist" divorces, which had subverted state autonomy in local affairs — the object of federalism — and which had caused unacceptable discrimination and legal uncertainty.[44]

The Uniform Marriage and Divorce Act extended the no-fault notion to the treatment of property upon dissolution of the marriage and most states incorporated in their legislation modifying the divorce law a provision for "equitable distribution" between the divorced spouses. This approach was further articulated in the innovative 1983 Uniform Marital Property Act ("Property Act"), which takes into account the rapidly growing number of two-worker households, and responds to the new militancy of women's groups.[45] Under the Property Act, married couples own jointly all property acquired by the effort of either or both of them during the course of the marriage. This regime parallels the marital sharing under the community property systems that have been historically the law in eight states. The Property Act, which is also supposed to stem the migration of well-to-do couples to the southwestern community property states, has already been adopted (with some changes) in Wisconsin and is under consideration in several other states.[46] A recent empirical study suggests, however, that — contrary to universal expectations — the "equitable distribution" rule in a no-fault divorce leaves the woman in a worse position than under the old law.[47] Under the old law "the levers of fault and consent gave them some power to bargain for a better financial settlement. . . . It is now obvious that equality cannot be achieved by legislative fiat in a society in which men and women are differently situated."[48]

B. Uniformity by State and Federal Action: Enter the Congress

Two problems have risen to the level of national concern: custody of children, and support of mother and children. Both problems have been aggravated by the mercurial mobility of the population, by the ease of disappearing and assuming a new identity elsewhere, and by the discontinuity of federalism. In both cases the perceived crisis elicited responses at both the state and federal levels.

1. "Child Snatching" across State Lines

Thousands of children are shifted from state to state every year while their parents battle over their custody in the courts of several states. Child snatching is rampant, and it was abetted by the absence of statutory law, competing jurisdiction of the state courts, and the cavalier treatment of custody awards received in sister states.[49] Each state saw itself free to provide for the custody of a child physically within its borders and did not consider itself bound by the custody decrees of another state. Children have been the innocent victims of the "family law chaos."

The public debate over the legal remedy resulted in the 1968 Uniform Child Custody Jurisdiction Act, which proved to be the first true success of the State Commissioners on Uniform Laws in the family law field. After a slow start, this Act has become the law in all states.[50] The Act's jurisdictional provisions, although favoring strongly the child's "home state,"[51] maintain some flexibility—at a certain price of stability and certainty—in order to ensure the best interests of children. A noteworthy feature is the law's reliance on the direct cooperation between the courts of the different states.

Despite the progress of state legislation and practice, the pressure of aroused public opinion led Congress to step in with the Parental Kidnapping Prevention Act of 1980.[52] This statute provides a nationwide rule that seeks to eliminate the jurisdictional uncertainty left under the Uniform Act by awarding exclusive jurisdiction to the "home state," and it compels each state to recognize as binding custody decrees previously entered by the court of another state. There is now some possibility of a conflict between the greater flexibility of the widely adopted Uniform Act and the federal statute; however, the latter must prevail by virtue of the supremacy clause of the Federal Constitution.[53]

2. The Child Non-Support Scandal

In 1981, twenty-eight percent of the mothers who were owed child support payments from absent fathers received nothing, while half did not get the full amounts ordered by the court. Some two million children were entitled under court orders to support that they were not receiving. In 1983, federal and state governments spent more than $690 million to collect over $2 billion worth of child support.[54]

Clearly, love was not enough to motivate absent parents to pay child support; and the states faced special problems when the parents moved from state to state. The states were able to arrest men within their own territory who persistently refused to pay, but had no power to arrest a person in another state. Similarly, states had begun passing laws that permitted courts to direct local employers to deduct child support from a nonpayer's wages, but when the parent had moved to another state, the original state had no power to order an out-of-state employer to make deductions.

The Commissions on Uniform State Laws have been concerned with this problem since early in this century. The Uniform Reciprocal Enforcement of Support Act, adopted after several revisions in 1968, leaves it to the state legislatures to define family support duties and is concerned solely with enforcement of these duties where the "obligor" is in a state different from the "obligee." All states have accepted the Act with various amendments,[55] another resounding success of the "voluntary process." In reality, however, the state measures "only slightly improved the chances for collection."[56]

Because of the explosive rise in welfare cost for aid to dependent children, Congress has been concerned with the problems of support enforcement since 1967. Finally, in the 1984 election year, when women voters loomed particularly important, the President, although dedicated to the "new federalism," signed, with enthusiasm, the "radical" Child Support Enforcement Amendments of 1984, after they were adopted unanimously by both houses of Congress.[57] According to this Act, states are required at the risk of losing vital federal funds, to enact far-reaching enforcement legislation, including mandatory withholding from the delinquent parent's wages if support payments are in arrears, holding the employer liable for the arrears he failed to withhold, imposing liens for such arrears, expediting judicial proceedings, facilitating establishing paternity, etc. Only the State of Wisconsin is exempted in order to allow it to continue experimenting with its own system. This unprecedented federal intervention, no longer confined to federally aided welfare cases, was motivated by commitment to women and compassion for children as well as by a concern about growing expenditures of public welfare funds.

C. A Federal Constitution for the Family? The Supreme Court Speaks

By the mid-1960's, "[the] Supreme Court Justices could no longer suppress conscious awareness of familial or social conflict with the easy aplomb of their predecessors."[58] Social changes brought the allocations of competence between the state and federal power (and between the legislature and the judiciary) into conflict, leaving "the Court with a substantial degree of freedom to decide whether they should be resolved by the adoption of a constitutional—and, therefore, [uniform] national—rule or whether they should be left for resolution by the states."[59]

In today's climate, it is difficult for example to conceive that in 1966, sixteen states still maintained on their books statutes outlawing and punishing interracial marriage.[60] When a couple, sentenced in Virginia under such a statute to one year's imprisonment, appealed to the Supreme Court, the unanimous Court reversed, striking down the statute on the ground that it violated the equal protection and due process clauses of the fourteenth amendment to the federal Constitution. Clearly, the Court could not allow for this type of "diversity"; here was an example of the imposition of a uniform national standard of civil liberties.

An even more striking example is provided by a case that originated in the State of Connecticut. A physician was convicted in the state court for prescribing a contraceptive device to married persons. Under a statute imposed by a Catholic majority in the Connecticut legislature this was illegal. The United States Supreme Court invalidated the statute as violating the right of marital privacy which—although not mentioned in the Constitution—is within the "penumbras, formed by emanations" from the "specific guarantees in the Bill of Rights . . . that help give them life and substance."[61]

The greatly expanded right of privacy subsequently became an important component of the "new constitutional doctrine to adjudicate relations both within the family and between the family unit and outsiders."[62] In reviewing state (as well as federal) legislation, the Court has manipulated its formulas of standards for judicial review to balance, on a case by case basis, the interests of the state, of legitimate and illegitimate children, parents and teachers, husbands and wives, women and men. And, the Court has invoked the Due Process (both procedural and substantive) and Equal Protection Clauses to invalidate legislation that did not conform to its vision of contemporary society. It is, as Dean Sandalow points out, a striking testimony of the Court's inattention to the issues of federalism, that no reasons are given in the opinions why, in an area traditionally within the policy power of the states, they should now be foreclosed by a national rule.[63]

In 1971, the Court, for the first time in its history, held a classification on the basis of sex unconstitutional.[64] In subsequent cases striking down both federal and state statutes, the Court has established the "presumptive invalidity of governmental discrimination on the basis of sex,"[65] though with some exceptions, to be sure. In the words of the Court, "[n]o longer is the female destined solely for the home and the rearing of the family, and only the male for the marketplace and the world of ideas."[66]

In the 1968–1977 decade, fourteen cases "have rather suddenly focused legal concern upon a group which had previously received no attention"[67]—illegitimate children. The Court caused "a turn-about in the status" of these children by invalidating during that period ten of the fourteen statutes involved in these cases.[68]

Of all the Supreme Court's excursions into family matters once regulated solely by the states, "perhaps the most egregious instance with the most far-reaching social consequences"[69] is the decision in *Roe v. Wade,* where the Burger Court (with two dissents) laid down in detailed, statute-like fashion the parameters of legality of abortion, and in the process invalidated legislation in some forty-odd states.[70]

Only a year before, the House of Delegates of the American Bar Association had approved, over some opposition, the Uniform Abortion Act, which was adopted earlier by the Conference of Commissioners on Uniform State Laws.[71] This Act reflected a more liberal trend in state laws and court decisions, but it was so drafted as to allow the states considerable discretion to prohibit or regulate abortion as local attitudes might dictate. Actually, some one-third of the states had, since the late 1950's, significantly liberalized their abortion laws,[72] and during 1970 four states practically abolished restrictions.[73] Individual freedom to decide for abortion thus became an accident of residence.

Yet the Court, motivated perhaps by the concern for "back room" abortions of the poor in the more restrictive states, decided to end the nationwide debate by imposing a detailed uniform rule. Unlike the situation in the Connecticut contraceptive case, even a semblance of a national consensus had not evolved at the time. However, there was some prospect that the political process could work out a tolerable accommodation of strongly held competing views. The Court's intervention did not terminate the debate, but on the contrary it sharply exacerbated the emotionally charged controversy. In addition to the usual criticisms of the Justices—that they were "legislating" on issues of policy, and that they were operating on the basis of limited data—the Court was also blamed in this case for failing to see the significance of the ongoing debate in other institutions. As an "implicit accommodation" to the anti-abortionists, Congress proceeded to limit severely the use of federal funds for abortions and the deeply divided Court upheld the measure.[74] After *Roe,* the Court has nonetheless consistently continued to uphold the basic principle that a woman has a fundamental right to make the "highly personal choice" whether or not to terminate pregnancy, and it has tightened still further the restrictions on the states, thus reducing the states' opportunities for dealing with local discontent. By 1983, however, the Court's liberal-conservative alliance over the abortion issue showed some signs of wear; three Justices rejected the basic premises of *Roe* and were perhaps even willing to overrule it.[75]

IV. Some Summary Thoughts

If one projects the developments in family law against the grid of the forces for uniformity outlined earlier, it becomes readily apparent that all five syndromes are involved, albeit in varying degree. The first syndrome (social and economic change) is a pervasive force and it is propelled by influential women's groups and other special interests. The financial concerns (second syndrome) of private individuals (single parent families, women and children left without support), private welfare agencies and public authorities (state welfare departments and the federal treasury) motivate, at least in part, most of the state and federal legislation. Both acts of Congress mentioned above reflect also the third and fourth syndromes; they illustrate the expansion of the central government and at the same time they seek to mitigate specific glaring flaws of federalism. As for the fifth syndrome, academics and some members of the bar who provide the principal brain power in drafting uniform laws are at times concerned with the need for systematization of a particularly fragmented field of law.

There is no national "family policy," but the trend is toward national, more or less uniform solutions. Ideas move quickly across the country, reform groups operate nationally, and national academic circles and national law schools exert considerable influence.

In the last two decades the Conference on Uniform State Laws has scored some significant successes by having its uniform laws widely adopted in state legislatures. The Conference has been encouraged by Congress.[76] However, when an issue emerges as a national problem and political forces are effectively mobilized, the federal government does not hesitate to act. The Congress has shied away from direct substantive legislation except to fill the gaps arising in the federal system and where federal competence was clear. However, under successive administrations, including the current one, the Congress has been employing freely the "carrot" technique by offering states federal funds in return for their acceptance of federal policies on a variety of subjects that have impinged directly or indirectly on family law and relations.[77]

Although the vast majority of court cases are decided in state courts under still more or less divergent state laws, the process of "constitutionalization" has gone some considerable distance toward imposing uniformity. The process also offers an insight into the interaction between law and society. Thus, when it came to removing criminality from interracial marriages or discrimination against illegitimate children, statutory law lagged behind a widely held, changed attitude in the society, but it proved difficult to activate change through legislation because of strongly entrenched forces. The Supreme Court's ruling imposed uniformity more in keeping with general attitudes despite striking local variations. In the use-of-contraceptive situation, the Court's ruling helped to crystallize a clear trend toward a new consensus. On the issue of abortion, however, the Court imposed a uniform norm in the face of persistent, strongly-held differences; political and legal difficulties persist.

In family law, as in some other fields of law, constitutional law as declared by the United States Supreme Court serves as "the means by which effect is given to ideas that from time to time are held to be fundamental in defining the limits and distribution of governmental power in our society."[78] A uniform rule imposed upon the states and reducing their role in response to social change often has had as its consequence an advancement of individual freedom.

Notes

1. *See, e.g.,* THE FEDERALIST NO. 10, at 22–23 (J. Madison) (R. Fairfield ed. 1961); THE FEDERALIST NO. 56, at 365–70 (J. Madison or A. Hamilton) (1976).

2. Smelser & Halpern, *The Historical Triangulation of Family, Economy and Education.* 84 AM. J. SOC. S288, S300–01 (Supp. 1978).

3. Swift v. Tyson, 41 U.S. (16 Pet.) 1 (1842).

4. Erie v. Tompkins, 304 U.S. 64, 78 (1938).

5. Friendly, *In Praise of Erie—and of the New Federal Common Law,* 39 N.Y.U. L. REV. 383 (1964). *See generally* E. SCOLES & P. HAY, CONFLICT OF LAWS 133–48 (1982).

6. E. SCOLES & P. HAY, *supra* note 5, *passim;* Juenger, *Conflict of Laws: A Critique of Interest Analysis,* 32 AM. J. COMP. L. I (1984); Kay, *Theory into Practice: Choice of Law in the Courts,* 34 MERCER L. REV. 521 (1983).

7. A. CONARD, CORPORATIONS IN PERSPECTIVE 49 (1976). The State of Delaware has no securities act. *Id.* at 19.

8. G. STEINER, THE FUTILITY OF FAMILY POLICY 56 (1981) (Colorado on legalizing abortion). On the process generally, see Friedman & Teubner in 1 INTEGRATION THROUGH LAW—EUROPE AND THE AMERICAN FEDERAL EXPERIENCE (M. Cappelletti, M. Seccombe, J. Weiler eds., 1986).

9. L. DIMARZO, COMPONENT UNITS OF FEDERAL STATES AND INTERNATIONAL AGREEMENTS (1980).

10. 1983 HANDBOOK NAT'L CONF. COMMR'S ON UNIF. ST. LAWS & PROC. ANN. CONF. MEETING 470–75 [hereinafter (year) HANDBOOK UNIF. ST. LAWS].

11. The beneficial effects of the "voluntary process" at its best are illustrated

by the unification, for all practical purposes, of the law of commercial transactions in goods (as distinguished from services), resulting from the universal adoption of the Uniform Commercial Code. There have been systemic benefits incidental to the primary business purpose: in interpreting the Uniform Code, state courts are more inclined to consider decisions of other states, and they frequently give greater weight to the original text of the Code than to deviations in their own state enactment; courses on commercial law in law schools, which form the attitudes of the bar, emphasize uniformity of interpretation; the attraction of the Code is illustrated by the fact that although federal common law governs contracts with the United States, the Supreme Court has "incorporated" the relevant Code provisions into federal law (*see* United States v. Kimbell Foods, Inc., 440 U.S. 715 (1979)); last but not least, Congress, which enacted the Code for the Virgin Islands, the District of Columbia, and Guam, has found it unnecessary to enter the commercial arena with broad legislation as contrasted with its role in consumer protection. Divergent state courts' interpretations appear to be limited to a few areas where litigation abounds; when substantial consensus emerges the Commissioners draft appropriate amendments to the Code for adoption by the Code states. Many of the above ideas were suggested to me by my colleague Professor J.J. White.

12. The interaction between federal and state authorities has contributed to the improvement of state governments.

13. For a discussion of the Supreme Court's role, *see infra* notes 18–34 and accompanying text.

14. Sandalow, *Federalism and Social Change,* 43 LAW & CONTEMP. PROBS. 29, 29 (1980).

15. P. BATOR, P. MISHKIN, D. SHAPIRO & H. WECHSLER, HART AND WECHSLER'S THE FEDERAL COURTS AND THE FEDERAL SYSTEM 471 (2d ed. 1973) [hereinafter P. BATOR].

16. *E.g.,* I.R.C. § 2518 (CCH 1985) (disclaimers).

17. *See infra* notes 52–75 and accompanying text.

18. R. STERN & E. GRESSMAN, SUPREME COURT PRACTICE 262 (5th ed. 1978) (quoting from Brennan, *State Court Decisions and the Supreme Court,* 31 PENN. BAR ASS'N Q. 393, 395–96 (1960)).

19. Marcus, *Conflicts among Circuits and Transfers within the Federal Judicial System,* 93 YALE L.J. 677, 689 (1984).

20. At present there are only a few classes of cases that can be appealed to the Supreme Court as matter of right, rather than by application for the discretionary "writ of certiorari." *See* R. STERN & E. GRESSMAN, *supra* note 18, at 317 & *passim; id.* at 262–73; SUP. CT. R.P. 19(b) (listing inter-circuit conflicts as one of the possible reasons for granting a review); *see also* Bailey v. Weinberger, 419 U.S. 953 (1974) (White, Douglas, and Stewart, JJ., dissenting); Harlan, *Manning the Dikes,* 13 REC. A. B. CITY N.Y. 541, 550 (1958); *generally* P. BATOR, *supra* note 15, at 631. Some doubts have been raised as to how much weight the Court gives in practice to the existence of conflicts among lower courts. A 1963 analysis of 3500 Supreme Court cases from the 1947 through 1958 terms named

three "cues" as exerting major influence in the selection of cases for review: first, the favoring of the grant by the federal government; second, a conflict among lower courts; and third, the presence of a civil liberty issue. Tanenhaus, Schick, Muraskin & Rosen, *The Supreme Court's Certiorari Jurisdiction: Cue Theory,* in JUDICIAL DECISION-MAKING 111 (G. Schubert ed. 1963). However, a 1972 study based only on cases from the 1958 term, rejected the second and third cues and found that only the fact that the federal government favored the review could be shown to have significant impact. Ulmer, Hintze & Kirklosky, *The Decision to Grant or Deny Certiorari: Further Consideration of Cue Theory,* 6 L. & SOC'Y REV. 637 (1972).

21. Note, *Securing Uniformity in National Law: A Proposal for National Stare Decisis in the Courts of Appeals,* 87 YALE L.J. 1219, 1223 (1978).

22. *Id.*

23. Marcus, *supra* note 19, at 687.

24. Griswold, *Rationing Justice—The Supreme Court's Caseload and What the Court Does Not Do,* 60 CORNELL L. REV. 335, 341–42 (1975).

25. Chief Justice Burger and Justices Blackmun and White favored the idea. *See* Brown Transport Corp. v. Atcon, 439 U.S. 1014 (1978). The recently established United States Courts of Appeals for the Federal Circuit (replacing the United States Court of Customs and Appeals) was given exclusive jurisdiction to receive appeals in patent infringement matters and this eliminated inter-circuit conflicts in that field. 28 U.S.C. § 1294 (1982). A similar solution in the federal tax field was blocked by the opposition of the tax bar.

26. See Justice Stevens' opinion on denial of certiorari in McCray v. New York, 461 U.S. 961, 962 (1983). However, *McCray* did not concern a conflict of decisions within the federal system. In Justice Stevens' judgment, "it is a sound exercise of discretion for the Court to allow the various States to serve as laboratories in which the issue receives further study before it is addressed by this Court." *Id.* at 963.

27. Marcus, *supra* note 19, at 690 (citing the Commission on Revision of the Federal Court Appellate System, Structure and Internal Procedures: Recommendations for Change, 67 F.R.D. 195, 235 (1975) (Hruska Commission)).

28. Aldens, Inc. v. Miller, 610 F.2d 538, 541 (1979). As stated above, there are now 13 courts of appeals.

29. See articles by Stein & Sandalow, Linde, Blasi, Rosberg, and Conard in COURTS AND FREE MARKETS—PERSPECTIVES FROM THE UNITED STATES AND EUROPE 26–27, 140–221, 276–384 (T. Sandalow & E. Stein ed. 1982).

30. *See, e.g.,* Brotherhood of R.R. Trainmen v. Jacksonville Terminal Co., 394 U.S. 369 (1969). *But cf.* Brown v. Hotel & Restaurant Employees & Bartenders, 468 U.S. 491 (1984).

31. Santosky v. Kramer, 455 U.S. 745, 769 (1982) (considering the law in "a majority of the States").

32. Johnson v. Louisiana, 406 U.S. 356, 377 (1972) (Powell, J., concurring). *But see* New State Ice Co. v. Liebmann, 285 U.S. 262, 310–11 (1932) (Brandeis, J., dissenting) (a "pre-New Deal" decision describing the Court's holding to

mean that a state business regulation cannot be saved from condemnation by calling it "experimental"); *see also* Truax v. Corrigan, 257 U.S. 312, 344 (1921) (Holmes, J., dissenting). In *Truax,* Justice Holmes observed that:

> There is nothing that I more deprecate than the use of the Fourteenth Amendment beyond the absolute compulsion of its words to prevent the making of social experiments that an important part of the community desires, in the insulated chambers afforded by the several states, even though the experiments may seem futile or even noxious to me and to those whose judgment I most respect.

Id.

33. In criminal procedure, *see, e.g.,* United States v. Leon, 468 U.S. 897 (1984); New York v. Quarles, 467 U.S. 649 (1984). Responding to voices for a stricter enforcement of "law and order," the Court has been grafting substantial exception on its earlier constitutional rulings that imposed strict restraints upon law enforcement authorities. Constitutional Law Conference in 53 U.S.L.W. 2187, 2189–91 (Oct. 16, 1984) (comments of Professor Yale Kamisar); 54 U.S.L.W. 2196, 2202 (Oct. 15, 1985) (comments of Professor Lawrence Tribe). Professor Tribe observed that compared with the United States Supreme Court's "sharp and visible turn to the right" in the 1983–84 term, the Court "this past term" appeared to be moving back toward the "constitutional mainstream." *Id.* at 2202. Professor Conard also sees a "sharp rightward turn taken [by the Supreme Court] during the 1970's in the Court's approaches to [corporate] securities law." Conard, *Tender Offer Fraud: The Secret Meaning of Subsection 14(e),* 40 Bus. Law. 87, 96, 97–99, 101 (1984). In the area of corporate securities law, the Court's tendency to restrict the reach of a uniform national rule (and even to disregard the interpretations by the competent administrative agency) reflects "the widespread suspicion that regulation has reached the point of diminishing returns, where further expansion is unlikely to confer economic benefits that exceed its costs." *Id.* at 98. The Court's tendency in this area also reflects the possible negative effects of the volume of litigation, and the reluctance to interfere with commercial expectation in a "traditional area of state law." *Id.* at 101. *See, e.g.,* Santa Fe Indus. v. Green, 430 U.S. 462 (1977); Blue Chip Stamps v. Manor Drug Stores, 421 U.S. 723 (1975); *see also* Hazen, *Corporate Chartering and the Securities Markets: Shareholder Suffrage, Corporate Responsibility and Managerial Accountability,* 1978 Wis. L. Rev. 391, 415 & *passim.* At the same time, according to Professor Buxbaum, federal courts currently do not hesitate to strike down state securities regulations as contrary to the Federal Constitution or congressional legislation—thus upholding a uniform rule. He sees the "preemptive slaughter of state securities regulation law spreading to state corporation law." Buxbaum, *Federalism and Company Law in Festschrift in Honor of Eric Stein,* 82 Mich. L. Rev. 1163, 1165–66 (1984).

34. Schlesinger, *Tides of American Politics,* 29 Yale Rev. 217–30 (1939).

35. Professor Allen speaks of the "pervasive unease [after World War II]

about threats to individual liberty" and of the "danger of systems of criminal justice being employed as instrumentalities of tyranny." Allen, *American Criminal Procedure: Why the Dominance of Judge-Made Law?* in POLICE PRACTICES AND THE LAW, ESSAYS FROM THE MICHIGAN LAW REVIEW 1, 2 (F. Allen ed. 1982).

36. Dunham, *A History of the National Conference of Commissioners on Uniform State Laws,* 30 LAW & CONTEMP. PROBS. 233, 241 (1965).

37. *See infra* notes 52, 53, 57 and accompanying text.

37a. Update: See *supra* p. 277, note 137.

38. De Sylva v. Ballantine, 351 U.S. 570, 580 (1956).

39. Sandalow, *supra* note 14, at 29–30. For a critical view, see Riga, *The Supreme Court, Marriage and the Family· Tradition or Transition?* 1979 JURIST 325 (1979).

40. UNIF. MARITAL PROPERTY ACT, in 1983 HANDBOOK UNIF. ST. LAWS, *supra* note 10, at 135 (prefatory note).

41. *Id.*

42. 1970 HANDBOOK UNIF. ST. LAWS, *supra* note 10, at 180–222.

43. 1970 UNIF. MARRIAGE AND DIVORCE ACT, in HANDBOOK UNIF. ST. LAWS, *supra* note 10, at 176–79 (Commissioner's prefatory note); *see also* Letter from Professor William J. Pierce, Executive Director of the National Conference on Uniform State Laws, to Professor Eric Stein (Dec. 7, 1984) (on file with Washington Law Review) [hereinafter the Pierce letter]. Interestingly, when the National Conference of Commissioners was formed in 1892, marriage and divorce were named as one of the two major subjects appropriate for uniform laws. Yet it was not until 1970 that agreement was reached on a measure combining marriage and divorce. In the intervening years some dozen model statutes were approved dealing with the various aspects of one or the other; but none of them received substantial acceptance by the states. *Id.* at 176.

44. *See* UNIF. DIVORCE RECOGNITION ACT, in 1947 HANDBOOK UNIF. ST. LAWS, at 174–76 (Commissioner's prefatory note). For the text, see 9 U.L.A. 644 (master ed. 1947). It can be argued, on the other hand, that the migratory divorce used to provide an escape valve from state rules that hampered divorce unreasonably.

45. 1983 HANDBOOK UNIF. ST. LAWS, *supra* note 10, at 135. The drafters report that the Act was "a response to the twenty-year-long challenge of the President's Commission on the Status of Women issued in 1963. . . ." *Id.* at 9. Also relevant are provisions in the Uniform Probate Code of 1969 adopted in 15 states. *Id.* at 6.

46. The drafters point out that:

> [f]orty-one traditional common law jurisdictions now use some form of property division as a principal means of resolving economic dilemmas on dissolution of marriage. Adding the eight community property jurisdictions in which such a division is an inherent aspect of spousal property rights yields a total of 49. The one state missing . . . is Mississippi.

Id at 5. *See generally* Cheadle, *The Development of Sharing Principles in Common Law Marital Property States,* 28 UCLA L. REV. 1269 (1981); Younger,

Marital Regimes: A Story of Compromise and Demoralization, together with Criticism and Suggestions for Reform, 67 CORNELL L. REV. 45 (1981).

47. L. WEITZMAN, THE DIVORCE REVOLUTION—THE UNEXPECTED SOCIAL AND ECONOMIC CONSEQUENCES FOR WOMEN AND CHILDREN IN AMERICA 362, 365 (1985).

48. *Id.*

49. R. LEFLAR, AMERICAN CONFLICTS LAW 93–94 (3d ed. 1977). In this section I rely substantially on Foster, *Child Custody Jurisdiction: UCCJA and PKPA,* 27 N.Y.L. SCH. L. REV. 297 (1981). See the extensive sources cited therein, particularly Bodenheimer, *Interstate Custody: Initial Jurisdiction and Continuing Jurisdiction under the UCCJA,* 14 FAM. L.Q. 203 (1981). The author was reporter for the Act and also played an important role in drafting the Hague Convention on the Civil Aspects of International Child Abduction Act. *See* Bodenheimer, *The Hague Draft Convention on International Child Abduction,* 14 FAM. L.Q. 99 (1980).

50. UNIF. CHILD CUSTODY JURISDICTION ACT, 9 U.L.A. 116 (master ed. 1979); Table of Jurisdictions Listing Uniform Acts Adopted, U.L.A. DIRECTORY OF UNIFORM ACTS AND CODES 8 (master ed. pamphlet 1986). *See also* the Pierce Leter, *supra* note 43.

51. "Home state" means the state in which the child immediately before the time involved lived with both or one of the parents for at least six months. A similar definition was adopted in the federal legislation referred to in the text immediately below. *See* Foster, *supra* note 49, at 301 (giving the legislative texts).

52. Pub. L. No. 96–611, 94 Stat. 3566 (1980), (codified at 28 U.S.C. § 1738A).

53. The Parental Kidnapping Prevention Act "needlessly disturbs [the Uniform Act's] cooperative system by mandating exclusive continuing jurisdiction of the original home state, unless a technical home state chooses to defer to a state having closer connection with the pertinent facts and the child's welfare." *Foster, supra* note 49, at 342. However, Professor William J. Pierce, Executive Director of the National Conference of the Commissioners on Uniform State Laws, rates the possibility of a conflict between the federal and state legislation as minimal. The Pierce letter, *supra* note 43.

54. *House Adopts Bill to Enforce Child Support,* N.Y. Times, Aug. 9, 1984, at A12, col. I; *Reagan Signs Bill Forcing Payments for Child Support,* N.Y. Times, Aug. 17, 1984, at 1, col. 1; S. REP. NO. 387, 98th Cong., 2d Sess., *reprinted in* 1984 U.S. CODE CONG. & ADMIN. NEWS 2397, 2408, 2416 [hereinafter cited as S. REP. NO. 387].

55. UNIF. RECIPROCAL ENFORCEMENT OF SUPPORT ACT (REVISED), in 1968 HANDBOOK UNIF. ST. LAWS, *supra* note 10, at 225–37. The older Uniform Civil Liability Support Act shows five adoptions.

56. G. STEINER, *supra* note 8, at 115.

57. The Child Support Enforcement Amendments, Pub. L. No. 98–378, 98 Stat. 1305 (1984). The legislation was designed to strengthen radically the pro-

gram instituted by the 1967 amendments to the Social Security Act. The Senate Committee on Finance concluded as far back as in 1972 that the program needed to be strengthened. S. REP. No. 387, *supra* note 54, at 2402.

58. Burt, *The Constitution of the Family*, 1979 SUP. CT. REV. 329, 347.

59. Sandalow, *supra* note 14, at 31.

60 Loving v. Virginia, 388 U.S. 1, 6 (1966).

61. Griswold v. Connecticut, 381 U.S. 479, 484 (1965) (opinion for the Court by Douglas, J.). Two Justices dissented.

62. Burt, *supra* note 58, at 329. *See, e.g.*, Zablocki v. Redhail, 434 U.S. 374 (1978).

63. Sandalow, *supra* note 14, at 30, 33.

64. Reed v. Reed, 404 U.S. 71 (1971) (invalidating an Idaho statute imposing a preference of a male over a female applicant for an appointment as an administrator of an estate).

65. Sandalow, *supra* note 14, at 32. For the cases in which the Court rejected or sustained the gender classification, see *id.* at 32–38. The proposed Equal Rights Amendment to the Federal Constitution, pressed with great vigor by women's groups, has failed to receive the required number of ratifications by state legislatures.

66. ORR V. ORR, 440 U.S. 268, 280 (1978) (citing Stanton v. Stanton, 421 U.S. 7, 10, 14–15 (1975)). In *Orr,* the Court struck down an Alabama statute imposing alimony obligation on husbands but not on wives, on the ground that such a law violated the Equal Protection Clause of the Fourteenth Amendment.

67. Stenger, *The Supreme Court and Illegitimacy: 1968–1977,* 11 FAM. L.Q. 365, 400 (1978).

68. *Id.* The majority of the Court was not prepared to hold that a classification based on illegitimacy or gender was "inherently suspect" (as in race or alienage) for the purpose of the equal protection clause; such classification would call for the strictest standard of judicial review. The Court has thus kept its hands free for case-by-case adjudication. On gender discrimination, *see, e.g.*, Michael M. v. Superior Court, 450 U.S. 464 (1981). *See generally* H. KRAUSE, ILLEGITIMACY: LAW AND SOCIAL POLICY (1971).

To help the states to adjust their law to the new constitutional situation, the National Conference of Commissioners on Uniform State Laws approved the Uniform Parentage Act of 1973. The Act was adopted in seven states (including California). 1973 HANDBOOK UNIF. ST. LAWS, *supra* note 10, at 335.

69. Burt, *supra* note 58, at 388.

70. Roe v. Wade, 410 U.S. 113 (1973). The decision decreed a total decriminalization of abortion during the first trimester of pregnancy and limited decriminalization thereafter. G. STEINER, *supra* note 8, at 52. *See also* Regan, *Rewriting* Roe v. Wade, 77 MICH. L. REV. 1569 (1979).

71. For the text, which was based largely on New York legislation, see Roe v. Wade, 410 U.S. 113, 146 (1973).

72. *Id.* at 140.

73. *Id.* at 140 n. 37.

74. Harris v. McRae, 448 U.S. 297 (1980). *See also* G. Steiner, *supra* note 8, at 54.

75. City of Akron v. Akron Center for Reproductive Health, Inc., 462 U.S. 416 n.7 (1983).

76. In addition to the Uniform Acts mentioned in the text, see also the currently recommended acts. Uniform Parentage Act, 9A U.L.A. 579 (1973); Uniform Adoption Act, 9 U.L.A. 11 (1971); Civil Liability for Support Act, 9 U.L.A. 171 (1953).

77. Sandalow, *The Expansion of Federal Legislative Authority,* in T. Sandalow & E. Stein, *supra* note 29, at 83–84. On the many federal activities with an impact on the family, see, *e.g.,* welfare laws, family planning legislation, housing authority laws, etc.; Federal Protection of Children against Sexual Exploitation Act of 1977, Pub. L. No. 95–225, 92 Stat. 8 (1978) (codified as amended at 18 U.S.C. §§ 2251–2253 (1982); U.S. Comm'n on Civil Rights, Federal Response to Domestic Violence (1982).

78. Sandalow, *Judicial Protection of Minorities,* 75 Mich. L. Rev. 1162, 1184 (1977).

Panel Statement on "Democracy without 'a People' "

In the introduction to the immediately preceding essay on "Uniformity and Diversity" I allude to the public skepticism regarding the growing powers of the Brussels institutions. In this essay I comment on a particular strain of this criticism, the widely discussed "democratic deficit" in the working of the European Union.

Like the "Uniformity and Diversity" essay, the piece here lacks a transatlantic dimension. While the former is grounded on the American side of "the bridge," this text has its footing in Europe. Yet the reader will readily note that issues such as lack of citizen participation and accountability of public power loom large in any modern democracy, including the United States.

The material in this essay—concise as it is—should, nevertheless, be helpful in updating the description of the Union lawmaking process offered in the previous essays and in supplying information on some of the changes brought about by the Maastricht and Amsterdam Treaties amending the constituent treaties.

I spoke from the text that follows as a member of a panel at the New York International Law Week in November 1998 and at the International Conference of the European Community Studies Association in Pittsburgh, June 1999. The material was to serve as a basis for a fully documented study of the problems, the possible remedies, and, more generally, the future of the Union.

I want to speak briefly about the criticism directed at the European Union not only by the usual Euroskeptics and Cassandras but also by presumably objective, friendly observers. The core of the criticism is the insufficient citizen participation in, and control over, policy that has resulted from moving political authority from the national to the supranational Community level.

The various strains of this criticism are subsumed under the heading of "democratic deficit," a series of discrete but related concepts such as lack of popular representation, lack of legitimacy and transparency, lack of accountability, and distance between the decision-making institutions and the citizens.

The public debate over this issue gained in intensity in the early

1990s; as it expanded to include the more general issue of the Union's future shape, other concepts such as solidarity and identity came to the fore.

The time allotted to me is obviously not enough even to scratch the surface of these complex issues, so I shall put before you two general propositions followed by two avenues for exploration.

The first general proposition ends with a query rather than an answer: When a group of democratic states creates an international structure and endows it with lawmaking powers, how much democracy must it build in and in what form? There have been complaints about the lack of transparency and fair representation of states in international institutions and pressures for private group participation particularly in environmental and trade decision making, but I know of no debate on a "democratic deficit" in an international structure except in Europe. This is so because there exists no international body with extensive, directly effective powers comparable to the "supranational" European Union. Thus, we do not get an answer from international law, although some argue that current trends indicate a broadening acceptance of the idea of democracy, signaling an emergent general principle of international law [Thomas M. Franck, "The Emerging Right to Democratic Governance," 86 AJIL 46 (1992)]. It would be a general principle in any case, with no specific institutional arrangements prescribed, so we do not find an answer to our question here.

My second general proposition suggests that for our purpose the democracy requirement must be viewed in the broader context of a democratic liberal state. When a group of modern liberal democratic nation-states organize what they call "a Community," they are bound to build in three components:

a. democracy (I shall offer a "European" definition later)
b. constitutionalism (rule of law and protection of basic individual rights)
c. respect for civil society and market economy.

Taking up the last point first, in the European Union area, the public-private boundary is drawn generally so as to allow ample space for an active civil society and a private sector of the economy. The Union's single market and its monetary, economic, and social policies are based on social market economy principles.

The second component, constitutionalism (rule of law and protection of basic rights), has been in place in the Union, with some gaps generally no wider than in the legal orders of the member states. Drawing on the innovative provisions in the constituent treaties and on elements in national legal systems, and guided by its own vision of the Community, the European Court of Justice has developed an original design based on "direct effect" of Community law in member state legal orders, its supremacy, and the principle of judicial review. In the application of Community law, citizens' rights, including basic human rights, are protected not only against the Community institutions but against their own governments as well.

The German Constitutional Court and courts in some other member states have experienced difficulties in reconciling the supremacy of Community law with what they conceived—in their traditional positivist way—as the mandates of their national constitutions. After some four decades, they still hesitate to accept the existential shift from international to constitutional discourse (Federal Constitutional Court 2 BvR 2134/92–2 BvR 2159/92). However, direct confrontation has been avoided thus far, and a sensible restrain is the obvious approach. It is, I believe, a mistake to speak about a crisis calling for a new Union constitutional supercourt. Despite the criticism directed at the Court of Justice, the basic scaffolding of Community rule of law is beyond question. This—I feel strongly—is of immense importance since it provides the Union with a measure of legitimacy. David Hume, in his time, considered that "our government" had "ultimately no other object or purpose but the distribution of justice," with the support of the judiciary (David Hume, *Essay V on the Origin of Government,* in Thomas Hill and Thomas Hoge Grose [eds.], David Hume, *The Philosophical Work,* 113–14, [Aalen: Scientia Verlag, 1964]). And most recently, an American political scientist has written that in the West, the "impartial judge" came before modern democracy (Fareed Zakaria, "The Rise of Illiberal Democracy," For. Aff., Nov./Dec. 1997, 22 at 27).

Of course there is ample room for improvement of the rule-of-law component: for example, the division of competencies between the Union and its members must be defined more clearly; the hierarchy of normative acts should be clarified; and administrative procedures should be improved.

Finally, the third component—democracy and its deficit: Here we confront three elements, the idea and practice of democracy, the nation-state, and the international system—all three interacting with each other and all three subject to profound mutation in the course of history.

Direct democracy in Athens, in the Renaissance city-states, in the Canton of Bern became impractical and obsolete with the rise of large states. The idea of democracy was saved by the invention of representative government, but an Athenian would hardly accept it as democratic. Today in Europe, modern democracy appears in a great variety of systems in which the voice of an individual citizen is heard in varying ways and degrees. It ranges from the "omnipotent" Parliament in Westminster to the republican-presidential system in France, the consensual pattern in Switzerland, the strong regionalism in Spain, and the federal variants in Germany, Austria and Belgium.

In contemporary Europe the democratic idea has surely become a general principle of the law of the region and particularly in the European Union itself, where it was written into the preamble of the Union Treaty and made into a prerequisite of membership.

It is not surprising that the builders of the new Community would look to their own systems for a specification of the general principle. Thus—as an example of European thinking—a German constitutional scholar would break it down into five more specific principles common to the constitutions of all the Union members: the people as the source of all government power; majority rule; accountability of all public institutions; separation of powers; and an independent judiciary (Karl Doehring, "Demokratiedefizit in der Europäischen Union," DVBl, 1997, No. 19, 19 at 19–20). But how does one apply these principles to the European Union?

Taking up again the last item first, an independent judiciary is the cornerstone of the rule of law that prevails in the Union. The fact that the judges of the European Court are appointed by "common accord" of the member governments has not been a reason to question their independence, although perhaps confirmation by the European Parliament would be desirable. Separation of powers between the legislative and the executive is blurred considerably in some member states such as Britain and France; and the concept may not fit the Union institutions as presently structured. There is no "government" or "legislature" in the conventional sense. I shall deal with the other principles on the list later, either expressly or by implication.

Any attempt to apply literally the national models of democracy runs into two problems. To start with, as I suggested in my first proposition, by superimposing a new layer of normative activity upon the national system, one creates a new situation for democratic representation and accountability. Even within a nation-state federation, superimposing a central power on component states unavoidably modulates the voice of an individual citizen, no matter what the representation arrangements.

And, second, modern democracy has developed within the nation-state which, however, has changed greatly from its original post-Westphalian form: its traditional "external sovereignty" has been diminished by an increasing need for international action on basic domestic problems and by the new international actors such as the many international regimes and even individuals under the new human rights system;

and its "internal sovereignty" is undermined by public and private networks often working across national frontiers. Some go so far as to conclude that representative democracy in reality no longer exists (J. M. Guéhenno, La fin de la démocratie, [Paris: Flammarion, 1993]), and that it has been replaced by a polyarchy of bureaucracy and organized interests in a modern administrative state, with massive bureaucracies, "independent" administrative agencies, and central banks.

In any event, it is vital—in thinking about how to remedy the "democratic deficit"—to recognize that the Union must develop an original version of representative democracy as it has already succeeded in designing its own original version of a rule of law.

What is the result if these general thoughts are applied to the institutions and processes of the Union and, more specifically, to its principal pillar, the European Community?

In the Community, the executive Commission ("the conscience and motor" of the Community), appointed by the governments but presumed to be independent, proposes legislation and policy, and the Council of Ministers, composed of Ministers in national governments, "disposes," originally with mere advice from the European Parliament. The European Council, comprised of the heads of member states or governments, provides general political direction. Formally, the Ministers as such in the Council are controlled by, and accountable to, their respective national parliaments. This, and the approval by these parliaments of any transfer of national powers to the Community, would appear to offer one avenue toward satisfying the representation and accountability requirement. But the reality has been different. In the first place, in foreign affairs the role of national parliaments has been notoriously limited. Moreover, there have been serious problems with the timely flow of information to and from the parliaments. Again, final decisions are made in the give-and-take negotiations of the Council meeting behind closed doors. Last, since the Council in many instances decides by a qualified majority, a Minister may be outvoted, whatever may have been his or her national mandate. A more recent complication, if one can put it that way, is the substantially increased role of the European Parliament in lawmaking, to which I shall return promptly.

To enhance the control over their respective Ministers, most of the national parliaments have established special committees to deal with Union affairs—but only some, such as the Danish, British, and the German Committees, seem to be positioned to influence, if not control, their respective Ministers.

One obvious way of reducing the democratic deficit is to lift the veil of secrecy of the proceedings in the Commission, but above all in the

Council with its pyramid of committees, which has been dubbed "the Kremlin of the West." To make things more difficult, a vast majority of decisions are made in committees of bureaucrats and only rubber-stamped by the Council. In a sense the conflicting and collusive interaction between the Union officials and national bureaucrats in practically all fields of public affairs is at the base of Union action. Secrecy frustrates accountability and feeds the tendency to shift the balance from the legislative to executive branches within the member states. A suggestion has been made to place the entire process on the Internet. Transparency is essential to inform not only the national parliaments but the electorate as well, thus helping to form an all-European debate and opinion. Comparable problems of transparency exist in the modern administrative state.

There is substantial room for improvement here but for reasons I enumerated earlier, I do not believe the approach through national parliaments of the member states will ever provide an exclusive remedy for the democratic deficit.

The other obvious avenue is through the European Parliament. Here, history is revealing. In 1950, the European Coal and Steel Community was conceived as a technocrat regime: the so-called Common Assembly was added by Jean Monnet as an afterthought at the urging of the Dutch and others. It was composed of delegates from the national parliaments, and it had a purely advisory function. President George Washington has told us that the power to "advise" is meaningless without the power to "consent." He went up to the U.S. Senate once for "advice" on a proposed treaty and vowed never to come back. And he kept his vow.

Today the European Parliament is an altogether different artifact. It is directly elected by universal suffrage within each member state, albeit under different electoral systems, although here also, a unification is anticipated.

The Parliament now has a significant voice on the Union budget; its assent is needed for major "constitutional" and foreign affairs decisions; and it has about an equal voice with the Council in lawmaking, although still in specified areas only.

The European Parliament must be consulted on the appointment of the President of the Commission; it approves the President and the Commission members before they are appointed by the member governments; and it may dismiss the Commission by a vote of censure. Former Commission President Jacques Delors made the intriguing suggestion that the President of the Commission should be elected directly by the people—this would certainly liven up all-Union politics. Or the President could be elected by the European Parliament.

The European Parliament appoints an ombudsman who receives citizen complaints of mismanagement in the Union system, and it may set up its own committees of inquiry. It does not have, but should be given, the powers to subpoena witnesses. Recently it grilled the President-designate of the new European Central Bank for several hours.

So the European Parliament is elected to represent the distinct peoples of the Union; it shares in budgetary and legislative powers and holds the executive Commission accountable. In March 1999, when an inquiry instituted by the European Parliament brought forth serious charges of fraud and mismanagement, the entire Commission resigned. Yet the European Parliament's powers are still limited if one insists on a comparison with national parliaments. Thus, it has no taxing power nor does it have the formal power of legislative initiative, which is reserved to the Commission; its legislative competencies are still limited, and more importantly, except for the legislative codecision, it has no authority over the Council or any of its members. To meet this last problem, some would want to turn the Council into an upper chamber of the European Parliament in the image of the original U.S. Senate or the German *Bundesrat* whose members are appointed by the governments of the component states of the federation.

Those who still see the member states as the "masters" of the Union (whatever this may mean) [see Jochen Abr. Frowein, "Legitimation und Wirkung des Rechts der Europäischen Union/Gemeinschaft" in Müller-Graff (ed.), Perspektiven des Rechts in der Europäischen Union, 105, 123–24 (Heidelberg: C.F. Müller Verlag, 1998)] would seek the improvement of representation and accountability through national parliaments only. This is likely to be the inclination of the "realists" and "intergovernmentalists." On the other hand, those (including myself) who view the Union as a multilevel governance regime with the member states wielding major influence in a complex process see no contradiction in pursuing both the national and the European Parliament avenues. There is obviously a dialectic tension here. However, I find utterly unconvincing the attitude of those who oppose the approach through the European Parliament because they question its representative status and are against a further expansion of its powers on the ground that it cannot speak for "the European people": they argue that there is no European people (demos), only "the peoples" in the different member states; there are no European-wide political parties, no European public debate or opinion. [These arguments are explored by J.H.H. Weiler *i.a.* in

"European Constitutionalism and Its Discontent" (with Joel P. Trachtman), 17 Nw. J. Int'l L. & Bus. 354 at 377 (No. 2/3, 1996/97).]

One simple answer to this argument is that while there may be no "European people," the Union is not a nation-state. The European Court of Justice calls it "a new legal order," and the German Constitutional Court sees it as a "Staatenverbund," an association of states. Here again it is vital to break the tie between the democratic institutions in a nation-state and the unique conceit of the Union that calls for its own idiosyncratic solution.

It is of course quite legitimate to point to the important cultural differences that divide the peoples of the Union, although we have learned that these differences have a way of turning into exclusionary, xenophobic nationalism with catastrophic results. For better or worse, worldwide economy and technology have worked toward reducing these differences. But it is right to say, I believe, that democracy and legitimacy postulate a certain community of a common good and common expectations of the people that bridges the cultural differences to the extent necessary to sustain the common institutions as their powers increase [Neil MacCormick, "Democracy, Subsidiarity and Citizenship in the 'European Commonwealth,' " 16 Law and Philosophy 331, 339 and passim].

The Maastricht and Amsterdam Treaties, amending the original Community Treaties, contain rudiments of institutional arrangements designed to advance this general purpose. They provide for Union citizenship superimposed on national citizenship, Unionwide political parties, and closer cooperation between national parliaments and the European Parliament. An advisory regional organ is established to bring subnational voice into the Union process. The common currency is in effect the first undertaking in which all Union people are called to participate. The "subsidiarity principle" was incorporated with the view to confining Union action to instances where the member states cannot act effectively. Of course, the proof of the pudding will be in the implementation of these provisions.

Actually, some Unionwide parties now exist, albeit in an embryonic form. The interplay between these emerging all-Union political parties, the political "groups" organized in the European Parliament on the traditional right-left pattern, and the corresponding parties in the national parliaments promises to help politicize the working of the Union and reduce its image as a technocratic monster in the eyes of its citizens.

Although cable TV makes cross-boundary broadcasting possible, genuine all-Union mass media outlets do not exist, and the different languages are a problem. All-Union issues should be aired in the electoral campaigns for the European Parliament rather than matters of domestic politics as has been the practice thus far.

As the powers of the European Parliament increase, so do lobbying and general public interest. Current Union activities, such as the massive exchange of students and standardization of health and safety regulations, have promoted the same objective. In 1998, two hundred thousand students (5 percent of the EU student population) studied in another member state (N.Y.T., Dec. 24, 1998, A10). A wealth of proposals for further action is on the table that I have no chance to discuss here.

The historic basis of national identity *within* the member states appears to be shifting from ethnicity and cultural heritage to respect for constitutional order and democratic tradition. Elements of what might emerge as a "European identity" are in place, but as it evolves, it will be different from, and will coexist with, the discrete identities of the peoples in the individual member states. That, at any rate, is the hopeful vision [Ulrich R. Haltern, "Europäischer Kulturkampf: Zur Wahrung 'nationaler Identität' im Unions-Vertrag," 37 Der Staat 591, 608–609 (1998)].

My conclusion is that although much remains to be done, the Union today has the potential to develop its own system of democracy as it did in the rule-of-law area.

The respected Judge Mancini of the European Court of Justice recently launched an impassioned call for turning the Union into a European federal state as the only possible way of eliminating the democratic deficit [G. Federico Mancini, "Europe: The Case for Statehood," 4 Eur.L.Rev. 29 (No. 1, Mar. 1998)]. Professor Weiler, who has done seminal writing on the subject, opposes the idea with equal vigor. He sees a European "global superstate" with all the vices of a major nation-state, including its own brand of exclusionary nationalism and excessive aggregation of central power. He clearly prefers a unique Community within the Union, and I am inclined to agree [J.H.H. Weiler, "Europe: The Case Against the Case for Statehood," *ibid.* 43]. I only wonder whether the Union, despite its uniqueness, will be able to resist the centrifugal or, on the contrary, the centripetal forces and avoid the historic fate of loose confederal-type structures that invariably either break up or turn into centralized states of one shape or another (American Confederation, German Bund, Belgium, Switzerland, Tito's Yugoslavia).

I personally believe that the secret of the success of the European integration enterprise has been in the phased, consensual movement toward an "ever closer union among the peoples of Europe" — as the constituent treaties put it — with the ultimate shape of the "union" remaining undefined. With the Union occupied by enlargement to the east and the necessary institutional adjustments, the reform of major policies, and the introduction of a common currency, I wonder whether this is the time for seeking more democracy by radical proposals such as the adoption of a formal Union constitution or the scheme for taking the procedure for further integration out of the hands of the national governments.

Thinking about the future is important, but what is now needed to reduce the democratic deficit is the enactment of the incremental reform measures along the lines I have suggested here.

PART 3

Europe's Burden of History

History against Free Speech: German Law in European and American Perspective

This part of the book signals a drastic change of focus from the lofty structures of the emerging "new Europe" to the baneful heritage of Nazism and Communism. The piece on war-time, postfascist Italy mentioned in the introductory chapter to this collection is not included.

I wrote most of the first piece in this part as a 1984–85 fellow at the multidisciplinary and "multinational" Institute for Advanced Studies in Berlin. It appeared in the Festschrift for the late Professor Wilhelm Karl Geck of Saarbrücken; it is an expanded version of the text published earlier in the Michigan Law Review.

Several factors made me pursue the dark subject of denial of the Holocaust, the notorious "Auschwitz lie."

During my Berlin stay, stories exploring one aspect or another of the Holocaust appeared in the press and on television with astonishing regularity, and the subject was raised by Germans of all walks of life in daily conversation. After some three decades of silence, the Germans had begun to face their past in public and private discourse.

As a concomitant, German historians, some with a political ax to grind, were locked in the Historikerstreit, *an impassioned academic quarrel about the position of the Nazi episode and the Holocaust in German historiography. "Nationalists" were ranged against the partisans of the modern "constitutional patriotism." I met and later corresponded with some of the protagonists. Extracts from the correspondence reproduced in this chapter illustrate the emotion-laden dispute.*

At the time a bill was winding its way through the German Federal Parliament that was designed among other things to facilitate prosecution of public statements of the "Auschwitz lie." Until then, the prosecution

---

The essay "History against Free Speech: German Law in European and American Perspective," is reprinted from Wilfried Friedler and Georg Ress (eds.), VERFASSUNGSRECHT UND VÖLKERRECHT, 831–84 (Cologne, Carl Heymans Verl., 1989), copyright © 1988 Eric Stein. Some materials of this article were used earlier in Stein, "History against Free Speech: The New German Law against the 'Auschwitz'—and Other—'Lies' " 85 MICHIGAN LAW REVIEW 277 (1986).

The correspondence that appears on pp. 410–16 is reprinted from 87 MICHIGAN LAW REVIEW 1026–32 (1989). Reprinted with permission.

had to rely on general provisions of the criminal code banning race hate incitement. Although the courts had a difficult time drawing a line between a serious breach-of-the-peace crime and a criminal libel in a wide variety of factual situations, the Federal Constitutional Court showed no hesitation in upholding the constitutionality of the sentences. However, a new sharp controversy erupted in the Parliament when a clause in the bill was interpreted as equating the Holocaust with other instances of mass violence, thus disputing its "uniqueness" in history.

For an outside observer, the parliamentary proceedings, echoed in the press, provided a singular insight into the national political process. The unpublished decisions of lower courts, which I obtained by approaching individual tribunals, offered tantalizing clues to the motivation of the "deniers" within contemporary German society. I might mention here that in 1994, the Federal Parliament, responding to an increase in racist incidents, adopted still another law making the dissemination of the "Auschwitz lie" a separate crime subject to imprisonment for five years. The Swiss followed the German lead after a referendum of the same year.

Finally, another factor that I had encountered already in the Department of State during the debate on the proposed UN Covenant of Basic Civil and Political Rights drew me to this subject. Of all the comparisons I have attempted between Europe and the United States, the one here, centering on the treatment of freedom of expression, has revealed the widest chasm ever. Why is it that the United States today stands virtually alone on the world scene, subordinating other values such as individual and group integrity to, as the Supreme Court of Canada has put it, "the abstract panegyrics to the value of open expression"? (Canadian Human Rights Commission v. Taylor, [1990] 3 S.C.R. 892, 922). The question relates to the more general idea of "American exceptionalism," which has intrigued me for a long time. I touch upon it in this essay, and I ruminate about it in my book Czecho/Slovakia: Ethnic Conflict, Constitutional Fissure, Negotiated Breakup, *which is excerpted in the last item of this part.*

To conclude, a "methodological" observation. A judge judging and a scholar writing are expected to detach themselves from their own and their community's value scale in the interest of the integrity and logic of the "law," whether it is perceived as a web of rules or a process. Yet the law is not a system closed to life, particularly when it comes to balancing one basic value against another under broadly formulated legal texts. I thought in this context of the German judges, some raised in the nationalist tradition, and of the American judges in the Skokie case I mention in this essay, where the disjunction between the personal values and the declared law was particularly wrenching. And I myself faced the problem of an "objective" observer.

I. Introduction

Although the Western-type pluralist democracies share their basic values they differ in the order of importance attributed to these values. The freedom of expression offers a telling example.

Each society determines the position of freedom of expression in relation to other freedoms according to its own history, institutions, sense of security, and tolerance of dissent. As I shall show in the concluding section of this essay, although in the United States the reach of freedom of expression has not been static, the contemporary Supreme Court speaks of this freedom in almost absolute terms and attributes to it a commanding priority over the other competing liberties.[1]

In the Federal Republic of Germany, on the other hand, the Basic Law *(Grundgesetz)* guarantees freedom of opinion and speech but makes it expressly subject to limitations defined by "the general laws, the provisions of law for the protection of youth, and by the right to inviolability of personal honour."[2] The experience with the abuse of freedoms that contributed to the demise of the Weimar Republic and the suppression of these freedoms by the National Socialist regime left a deep imprint upon the Basic Law and subsequent legislation:[3] the democratic, pluralist system with an elaborate bill of rights, established by the Basic Law in abhorrence of the totalitarian past, was to be secured against those who would invoke the protection of basic rights as a cover for attacking the constitutional order;[4] and all Germans were given the right of resistance—in the absence of other remedies—against anyone who attempted to overthrow that order.[5] The doctrine evolved by the Federal Constitutional Court postulates a community employing the law in the defense of the Basic Law's political values: free speech claims must be weighed against the values of human dignity and personal honor that are grounded in the Basic Law itself.[6]

The Criminal Code, a prime example of the "general laws" by which certain basic freedoms may be limited, contains far-reaching provisions outlawing political organizations and activities hostile to the Basic Law—including public speech and writings—which would hardly stand up to constitutional scrutiny in American courts. The postwar resurgence of neo-Nazi activities has led to legislative reforms designed to strengthen these provisions still further. Left-extremist terrorism and propaganda, abetted by the uneasy propinquity of the totalitarian empire, have also served as the ground for legal countermeasures.

The latest reform of the Criminal Code, the law of June 13, 1985,[7] first proposed in 1982 in the face of a rise of neo-Nazi incidents,[8] was motivated primarily by the perceived need to facilitate prosecution of an increasingly employed propaganda theme, the so-called "Auschwitz lie"—the claim that the extermination of European Jews by the National Socialist regime never took place, that such reports were a deliberate lie.

This theme has become an aspect of multifarious efforts to revise the history of the National Socialist regime in the service of diverse and often contradictory ideologies: antisemitism of the neo-Nazi hue, anti-communism of the extreme conservative right, anti-Zionism, German nationalism and varied nationalisms in the Eastern European countries, libertarian pacifism, and Marxism of the extreme left.[9]

A French scholar who has surveyed the proliferation of tracts, "scholarly" and outright propaganda books, brochures, mimeographed pamphlets, video-cassettes, and periodicals with or without scholarly pretensions, suggests that it would be an exaggeration to speak of "a vast international enterprise," although "undoubtedly" the center for the collection and distribution of all this literature is located in California.[10] Only in France have the "revisionists" obtained access to respectable press and managed to entangle academic historians in a "debate."[11] More or less obscure individuals or groups are active in Canada, the United States, the United Kingdom, Australia, Switzerland, and Sweden, as well as in the German Federal Republic.[12]

An American observer would expect the central issue in the public debate to be the conflict between the constitutionally protected values of individual freedom of expression on the one hand and public security and personal honor on the other. This however, has not been the case. To the contrary, the constitutional issue has played a marginal role in the legislative process, and it has been resolved by the courts with obvious ease in favor of the constitutionality of the previous legislation on the same general subject. There is every reason to believe that the 1985 law will also be upheld, even though, as we shall see, it potentially restricts freedom of speech still further. Moreover, it has been widely assumed (albeit with some dissent) that law and the courts have a significant role in protecting against the infamous and the ignorant who propagate the "Auschwitz lie." The core issue in public discourse has been the scope and the modalities of this contribution.

In this essay I propose, first, to outline the state of the German legislation before the enactment of the 1985 law; second, to illustrate the travail of the courts in applying that legislation; third, to identify the principal legal and political issues that have emerged in the wide-ranging debate surrounding the genesis of the 1985 law and in the lawmaking process itself; and fourth, to consider early reactions to the law and its implications in the broader context of contemporary Germany. Finally, for purposes of comparison, I discuss the way the problem is dealt with by the European Commission of Human Rights and in the United States.

II. The Criminal Code

Three provisions of the German Criminal Code[13] are crucial to this inquiry. The first two, articles 130 and 131, fall within the group of serious crimes against "public peace."

A. Attack on Human Dignity by Incitement to Hate: Article 130

Article 130 replaced a provision of the Criminal Code of the German Empire which penalized breach of the peace (public order) by incitement to class hatred.[14] Its antecedent was a proposal offered in 1950 by the Social Democratic group in Parliament in response to a series of antisemitic incidents including increased circulation of antisemitic tracts. An earlier version of the governmental bill was opposed on constitutional and policy grounds, and it was put aside until a new wave of desecration of synagogues and cemeteries in 1959 had brought about a radical change in the legislative atmosphere. The outcome of the notorious *Nieland* case in Hamburg was the last straw, which helped to sweep away all arguments that new legislation was neither necessary nor desirable.[15]

In that case Nieland, a Hamburg businessman, distributed two thousand copies of a brochure primarily among federal politicians. The brochure stated that "international Jewry" ("the devils of the earth") was responsible for the two World Wars (financing Hitler), for planning the third, and for spreading the "monstrous lie of a butchery of the six million Jews by the Germans under Hitler." All Jews, it said, must be removed from positions of influence since it was "almost impossible" to look into the Jewish hearts in order to determine which ones belong to "international Jewry." The defendant was charged under the then-existing provision of the Criminal Code prohibiting dissemination of writings hostile to the Basic Law.[16] In addition, a Jewish member of the Hamburg state legislature filed a petition for prosecution of a criminal libel ("insult") under article 185.[17]

The trial court refused to institute the proceeding on the ground that it was not possible to disprove the defendant's allegation that his target was "not Jews in general" but only the "clique" of "international Jewry." The private petition was also rejected because there was no evidence that the petitioner was a member of the "closely circumscribed circle of Jews (international Jewry)."[18] The state appeals court rejected the Chief Prosecutor's urgent complaint without explanation.[19]

Although it was beyond the Federal Supreme Court's power to order the opening of the prosecution, that court did approve, in a separate proceeding, the seizure of the remaining copies of the brochure—and in an elaborate opinion it reached conclusions diametrically opposite those of the Hamburg courts. It found that the tract was contrary to the prohibition against writings designed to impair the existence of the Republic and to suppress democratic freedoms by undermining basic constitutional principles.[20] The reasoning, if not the decision, of the Hamburg judiciary is said to have evoked "much astonishment, even disgust."[21] The mayor of the city of Hamburg is reported to have traveled to Bonn to appeal to Chancellor Adenauer, and it was the latter's intervention that led to the prompt adoption of the new article 130 on May 20, 1960, by a unanimous Parliament.[22]

The motivating idea behind article 130 was the feeling that although the courts in most cases were able to impose punishment under the prevailing law (and that they should have done so in the *Nieland* case), the law did not "strike at the core of the evil . . . , that is, the attack on humanity, human dignity, and general public peace."[23] Thus, rather than aiming at the protection of private individual or group honor, which is assured by the criminal libel ("insult") provisions, the new criminal provision is motivated by the public interest in safeguarding public peace.[24]

Article 130 introduces the concept of human dignity which is also enshrined in the Basic Law of the Republic.[25] It prohibits attacks against human dignity "apt to breach the public peace," committed in the form of acts of "particular gravity"[26] against "parts of the population."[27] The proscribed acts consist of (1) incitement to hatred ("stirring up enmity in an invasive manner, beyond mere rejection or contempt"); (2) provocation to violent or arbitrary acts (that is, acts of violence or lawlessness against personal freedom);[28] and (3) insult, ridicule, and defamation (not just "mere expression of disrespect" or "disparaging assertions whose truth or untruth cannot be proven").[29]

When requested to elucidate the concept of "attack on human dignity," the Justice Ministry's spokesman drew an analogy with the established doctrine on degrading treatment of subordinates in the Military Criminal Law *(Wehrstrafgesetz):* article 130 would reach "not any expression of disrespect," but only an attack "*on the core area of* [*the victim's*] *personality,*" a denial of the victim's "right to life as an equal in the community," or his treatment as "an inferior being excluded from the protection of the constitution."[30]

One writer questions the analogy between degrading treatment of a soldier, which envisages a personal confrontation, and the attack on human dignity; he believes that such an attack can exist only in cases of incitement to violence or lawlessness, but he "would not hesitate for a moment" to brand statements such as "Jews are inferior beings *(Untermenschen)*" as an attack on human dignity; because of the "unavoidable connection with the cruel persecution of Jews . . . it is nothing less than an endorsement of the call for a revival of the terrible extermination . . . ."[31]

B. Race-Hatred Writings: Article 131

Article 131, also within the category of crimes against public peace, is said to be "almost without parallel in foreign legislations."[32] Its reach was substantially broadened in 1973.[33] The clause that concerns us here makes punishable the production or dissemination of writings "which incite to racial hatred."[34] Reports on contemporary events or history are protected by an express exclusion.[35] As in the previous article, it is "the inner peace of the society" that is protected;[36] the clause in question is directed "primarily at the incitement of hatred against Jews."[37]

C. Insult: Article 185

The third of the triad, article 185, has been a part of the Criminal Code from its inception. It makes punishable an offense against personal honor, "insult."[38] Proof of the truth is no defense "when the insult arises from the manner in which the assertion was made or disseminated or the circumstances in which it was made."[39] Until the modification brought about by the 1985 law, prosecution could be instituted only on the basis of a petition "by the person insulted."[40]

In the period between the coming into force of the Criminal Code in 1871 and the fateful year of 1945, the German Supreme Court *(Reichsgericht)* consistently refused to apply this article to insults against Jews as a group[41] — although it gave the benefit of its protection to such groups as "Germans living in Prussian provinces, large landowners, all Christian clerics, German officers, and Prussian troops who fought in Belgium and Northern France."[42] It has been said that during that period the courts were quite ready to extend group protection to the "pillars of the throne and the altar," while denying it to the Jews on the basis of an "often suspect argumentation."[43] A more charitable interpretation would point to the avid desire of many German Jews to shed the characteristics that would mark them as a group and to be assimilated as rapidly as possible.

The "hopefully unconscious onesidedness"[44] of the Supreme Court vanished, as we shall see, after 1945.[45]

In summary, the principal instrumentalities in the criminal-law armory against the spreading of the "Auschwitz lie" consist of the prohibitions against attacks on human dignity by incitement to hatred (article 130) and against dissemination of writings instigating hatred (article 131), both conceived as serious offenses against the public peace, and finally, the less weighty offense of insult, protecting primarily a private good which—until the 1985 reform—required a private petition.

III. On the Constitutional Question

The Federal Constitutional Court, the only tribunal that may declare a federal law unconstitutional, was faced with a challenge to the constitutionality of article 130 and 131 in a case in which a defendant, a member of the "Action Front of the National Socialists (ANS)," was convicted for taking part in an event organized by this group in the center of Hamburg.[46] The group was dressed in Nazi-type black clothing with Nazi paraphernalia, and it marched in military formation with Nazi salutes. Three members of the group carried signs which read: "I, a donkey, still believe that Jews were 'gassed' in German concentration camps. I, a donkey, believe the 'gassing' lies and want to pay, pay, pay to Israel. I, a donkey, still believe the propaganda lies of the victors.' " The courts below found the defendant guilty of an attack on human dignity in conjunction with incitement to race hatred.

In a preliminary proceeding, the screening committee of the Constitutional Court refused to accept the defendant's complaint of unconstitutionality on the ground that it had no prospect of success, since the "interpretation and application of articles 130 and 131 by the competent courts did not disclose any violation of basic freedoms."[47] The court also rejected the "due process" claim that the courts had disregarded the complainant's offers of evidence:

> The complainant, who does not deal even with the numerous generally accessible sources about the mass destruction of the Jews, not to speak of trying to reach an independent opinion through a thorough consideration, is not impaired either in this right to a hearing nor to an effective protection of law *when the courts judge this mass destruction to be commonly known* and consider irrelevant the mere offering of the names of individual witnesses.[48]

If other courts had harbored any doubt about the constitutional issue they would have been required by the prevailing law to refer the question to the Federal Constitutional Court. There is no record of any such referral. The Federal Supreme Court, the highest tribunal in civil and criminal matters, entertained no such doubt. In a case involving a prosecution for criminal insult based on a leaflet branding the murder of millions of Jews as a "Zionist swindle," the Court gave short shrift to the defense argument:

> [N]o one who denies the historic fact of the murder of the Jews in the "Third Reich" can invoke the guarantee of freedom of opinion (Art. 5, para. 1 GG). Even in a confrontation on a question that concerns substantially the public as is the case here, no one has a protected interest to publicize untrue allegations. The documents about the destruction of millions of Jews are overwhelming.[49]

The lower tribunals have taken essentially the same view of the alleged constitutional conflict, to the extent they have given it any attention at all.[50]

IV. The Law in the Courts, 1960–1985

Most of the courts and prosecutors have tried to do their best in coping with a law that contains some novel concepts unrelated to established criminal law doctrine, formulated in vague language, motivated by a traumatic collective experience, and saturated with political considerations of the day. In carrying the burden of protecting the democratic system of the young Republic, the judiciary has received relatively little assistance from the scholarly community, which would normally analyze and classify the legislative and case material with a view to helping develop an acceptable doctrine. The burden of providing a rational framework and guidance for the lower courts has rested heavily on the Federal Supreme Court.

A. Case Categories: The Issues

Depending upon the Code provisions applied, the cases penalizing the "Auschwitz lie" may be grouped in three basic categories: (1) attacks on human dignity (article 130), alone or in conjunction with race-hatred incitement (article 131) or—if private petition is lodged—insult (article 185); (2) incitement to race hatred (article 131), alone or in conjunction with article 130 or 185; (3) insult (article 185), alone or in conjunction with article 189 (disparaging the memory of the dead) or articles 130 or 131.

The principal problem facing the courts has been to determine whether a given fact situation fell within the ambit of the serious crime of article 130. Where a private party lodged a petition, the court, in reality, could turn to the less weighty alternative of an insult under article 185. This has been a crucial determination because in some courts, at any rate, a conviction under article 130 may carry a sentence of one year's imprisonment, as against six months or merely a fine for an insult.[51] Yet the line between the two fact situations is drawn, as we shall see, largely by the judges' intuitive reactions, with only a few somewhat more general criteria emerging. With some exceptions, the trial courts have been reluctant to follow the "attack on human dignity" route, and their judgments of acquittal on this count have been subject to frequent reversal by the state courts of appeal and, even more consistently, by the Federal Supreme Court.

The following are the issues with which the courts have had to grapple:

(1) What is an attack on human dignity?
(2) When is an act apt to breach public peace? The courts have not entered into the discussion of "objective" or "subjective" public peace that one encounters in other contexts.
(3) What constitutes incitement to race hatred?
(4) Are Jews "a race"?
(5) Is the court required to admit evidence designed to disprove the existence of the extermination camps?

Some specific issues have arisen in prosecutions for "insult" under article 185:

(1) Are Jews as a group protected against "insult"?
(2) Which acts involving "the Auschwitz lie" are capable of causing injury?
(3) Who is a legitimate petitioner?

B. On Judicial Notice

In German as in common law, courts may take notice of generally known facts without the need of formal proof.[52] German courts do not seem to agree whether judicial notice may or must be taken of the extermination of Jews or whether appropriate evidence must be placed on the record to prove the falsity of "the lie."

Although the Federal Supreme Court held in 1976 that the essential facts of the Jewish persecution were "generally" and even "publicly known," it suggested that such facts must be introduced in the trial and that "this can be done expediently by hearing a historian as an expert witness."[53]

In a later case the High Court spoke of the "historical fact of the murder of the Jew in the 'Third Reich,' " without, however, any reference to the problem of proof.[54] It was on this statement that the appeals court in Bochum relied when it refused to entertain any evidence designed to prove the "Auschwitz lie." The court assumed as true the defense allegation that a French professor, Robert Faurisson "after a thorough working through the 'gas chambers' complex," and an American Professor Butz, "after five years' research of all sources available to him," had reached the conclusion that the mass murders of Jews had not taken place; but this fact, the court held, represented only the research results of the two witnesses and did not upset "historically secure and thus generally accepted knowledge."[55] On similar grounds of irrelevancy the court upheld the refusal to hear witnesses claiming personal knowledge of the nonexistence of the camps, to obtain expert opinions on when the camps were built (it was alleged that they were constructed after the war), and to hear a photographic expert who would prove that the purported photographs of the camps were recent falsifications.[56]

In another case, the court in Frankfurt emphatically proclaimed the existence of the extermination measures to be an "established" and "historically proven" "historical fact" which "does not need any proof" and that no evidence need be admitted on this issue. Nevertheless, "manifest historical facts were merely introduced into the proceedings by means of Professor Broszat's opinion."[57] Reflecting perhaps the observation by the Federal Supreme Court in the earlier case, the court evidently preferred to accept an authoritative confirmation of the facts which it felt mandated to take as proven.

C. The Case Law

In this area of the law, consideration of the facts of the cases, in more or less detail, is vital for a meaningful analysis of the judicial posture.[58] The stories behind the cases reveal a good deal about certain dark corners of life in contemporary Germany.

1. The Federal Supreme Court on Articles 130 and 131

In 1981, the Federal Supreme Court had before it an appeal from the court of Braunschweig.[59] In that case the defendant was charged with distributing a brochure denying that "Hitler's gas chambers" had existed and that the "genocide" of the Jews had taken place, and claiming that such "six-million lies" and "horror tales" of essentially Zionist origin had brought about a gigantic political and financial swindle, principally for the benefit of the State of Israel. Also included was a picture of a gallows with a person beneath it, and a text to the effect that on this gallows people were tortured and blackmailed by their Jewish accusers to give false evidence and were murdered "in an assembly line" manner. The defendant was convicted and fined for disseminating writings that incited to race hatred (article 131). He was, however, acquitted of the more serious charge of attacking human dignity by incitement to hatred under article 130. The trial court concluded that although the brochure could be seen as an attack on the honor of the Jews as a population group, it was not an attack against human dignity; it was not apt to disturb public peace because it could not be assumed that the circle of persons to whom the brochure was sent could feel threatened in their sense of security.

The Federal Supreme Court reversed; it affirmed the conviction under article 131 but disagreed with the trial court's refusal to apply article 130. In the context of article 131, the Supreme Court came to grips with the issue of whether Jews could be considered a "race" for the purpose of this provision. It dismissed as irrelevant the defense argument that there could not be a crime of incitement to race hatred since the Jews did not form a race in a biological-anthropological sense. "The concept of race hatred," the Court declared,

> falls within the conceptual world of racial ideology. This is not based on a scientifically grounded, clearly delimited race concept. Rather it proceeds from merely an approximate anthropological classification of humanity into human races, that is, according to common hereditary, predominantly physical characteristics, as a starting point for a theory pursuant to which biological diversity of the "races" is supposed to be the cause of their relative superiority or inferiority and corresponding different value. The emotionally heightened hostility of the provocation directed against the Jews is one of the phenomena of the incitement to race hatred which the lawmaker wanted to include in article 131.[60]

In reversing the acquittal under article 130 the Supreme Court confirmed that an attack against human dignity exists only if "it is directed against the unrenounceable *(unverzichtbar)* and nonincidental *(unaus-*

bleibbar) core of a personality of another, against him as a human being, and only if it denies his value." This language clearly recalls the rationale offered by the government spokesman for the new article 130 and mentioned earlier as part of its legislative history.[61]

Contrary to the court below, however, the Supreme Court found that there was such an attack in this case, because the brochure "was apt to provoke an emotional, hostile stance toward the Jews." The distributor appeared to identify himself with the fundamental National Socialist outlook

> which classifies the Jewish fellow citizen as a member of an inferior "race," that branded him formally by forcing him to wear the Jewish star, deprived him of all rights, and treated him no longer as a fellow human being. In such cases involving similar allegations, the Supreme Court has approved the findings that writings which aim at stirring up hostile feelings against the Jews in general and against the Jews living in Germany in particular constituted attacks against human dignity.[62]

The High Court thus rejected the notion of the court below that it is the sense of security of the brochure's addressees (rather than their potential response to the incitement) that should be the yardstick in finding a breach of the public peace. The same Court had made it clear in an earlier case that article 130 does not require proof of an actual breach of public peace:

> It suffices that there are justified grounds for the apprehension that the attack will shatter confidence in legal security, even if it is only on the part of the population group against which the attack is directed. That this is true of an antisemitic smear tract destined for distribution needs no further explanation in light of the historical experience.[63]

In an observation bearing upon general methods of interpretation, the Court found that the trial tribunal should not have limited its evaluation to the contents of the printed text "along with the generally known facts," but was obligated to include "also other circumstances that are significant for the facts of the case"; the reasoning of the contested judgment did not make clear that the defendant's "eventual identification with the National Socialist ideology" was taken into account.[64]

2. Lower Courts on Articles 130 and 131

a) *Teachers in Trouble*

In the nature of things, only a small fraction of litigated cases reaches the high federal tribunal. But a broad range of activities has been prosecuted—all the way from a teacher's casual remark in a classroom to a "one-man propaganda machine" spouting open letters, thousands of postcards, periodic publications, placards, etc. The "Auschwitz lie" has appeared also in a variety of versions, ranging from a simple "I am a donkey—I still believe the lies about the extermination camps," to greatly embroidered pronouncements of elaborate offensiveness.

A court in Goslar made the following findings of fact. A middle-aged teacher (a family man with several children) in a vocational school discussed in his class an impending class excursion that was to include a visit to the Dachau concentration camp. In this context, the teacher observed that there were no concentration camps or killings of Jews in the Third Reich: there were only work camps in which Jews lived peacefully with their families. When several students mentioned films about the extermination of Jews the defendant observed that they were American-made; he had at his home documentary evidence which anyone was welcome to inspect. At the end of the class he asked that his statements not be passed on because they were prohibited "and he has a family to support." When the story began to make the rounds in the school, the editor of the student paper obtained a written statement from four students confirming that the controversial assertion had been made. When the defendant learned about it he assembled the entire class with the exception of "the four"; in response to his plea for help, all students present signed a paper denying that he had made the allegations attributed to him and that he had ever questioned the existence and inhumanity of the camps. With this paper in hand the defendant then visited the parents of the four "dissidents" and threatened them with court action and other "difficulties" (hinting at possible trouble with the immigration authorities in the case of one family of Portuguese nationality). A few days later, when the teacher's approach to the parents became known, the entire class signed another statement revoking, in effect, the earlier paper and confirming the allegations against the defendant.

A Hamburg Jew, whose wife, mother, and brother died in the concentration camps, and the Hamburg Jewish community filed a petition of criminal insult. In the proceedings the defendant denied making the contested statements and claimed that his efforts to stimulate a balanced class discussion were intentionally distorted by the students in revenge for poor grades he had given in a physics test.

After hearing some twenty witnesses the court found the defendant (who was without prior criminal record), guilty of an attack against human dignity (article 130), in conjunction with insult (article 185) and disparagement of the memory of the dead (article 189); it imposed a suspended sentence of six months' imprisonment.[65] In an elaborate, carefully reasoned opinion (which incidentally provides some insight into the teacher-student relationship in a newly multi-ethnic community), the court followed the interpretation of the attack-on-human-dignity concept and the breach-of-public-peace prerequisite as given by the Federal Supreme Court.[66]

Another teacher's trouble was the subject of a case before a court in Schleswig.[67] A letter to the editor, published in a periodical for which the defendant was responsible, noted a news story that a history teacher was fired because he branded the "destruction of six million Jews" a lie: "Thus, once more," the letter stated, "one who opposes Jewish propaganda is silenced while Jews (!) are trained as teachers for German children." In an editorial annotation to the letter the defendant signaled that he approved of its contents.

The trial court found that although the contents of the letter fell within the scope of article 130 the charge must be dismissed on the grounds that the editor could not be held criminally responsible for the contents of a letter addressed to him and published as such. The appeals court reversed. The letter to the editor, the court reasoned, incited hatred against the Jews in that it denied their ability to teach German children and pretended that the destruction of the Jews was a lie based on Jewish propaganda. The aim was to make Jews, as a part of the population, contemptible and inferior by attacking the human dignity of each individual Jew, "in its indispensable personality core."[68] The letter was apt to disturb public peace by potentially shaking the sense of security of the attacked group or by provoking the "incited" group to insults.[69] The defendant was liable for publishing such a letter.[70]

Another case, drawn also from a school setting, is one of a number that came out of the aftermath of the showing of the television film *Holocaust.* It concerns a youngster who at the age of six had been enrolled by his parents (born in 1918 and 1920) in the Viking Youth, a right-wing organization, and was brought up in a right-wing atmosphere. A high school graduate, age nineteen, he and his teenage girlfriend appeared as responsible editors for a student periodical that was distributed in an edition of ten thousand copies in local and other schools. In a story directed particularly at young people and commenting on *Holocaust* ("a horror show of the worst Hollywood make"), the National Socialist terror and murders were characterized as falsifications: "renowned historians" including the "famous American Professor Butz with his book on *The Hoax of the [Twentieth] Century*" had provided the "breakthrough." Other books and documentations were cited to disprove the "monstrous lying provocations." The "gas chambers" were mock-ups built under the direction of the American military, and camp inmates died of illness and undernourishment owing to war conditions.

The juvenile court in Cologne held both defendants guilty of violating articles 130 and 131.[71] The young man was sentenced to a fine (ninety "daily rates" of fifteen marks), while his friend, who had withdrawn from the co-editorship, got away with a warning and forty days of service for the public good. The court noted that, in addition to the usual allegation of the "Auschwitz lie," Jews, particularly American Jews, were pictured as "inventors of the legend." Although such allegations were quoted as the opinions of others, they were approved without reservation.

The state appeals court affirmed.[72] In embracing the trial tribunal's analysis, the court stressed that even the "revelations" in the form of extensive citations from historical literature may tend to stir hostility against the Jews, and in this case young readers were exhorted "to protect themselves" against "the lies." The potential for disturbance of public peace existed from the sole fact that the story had appeared in a high school student paper and was addressed—combined with a direct challenge—to young people still in a state of intellectual development. Here also the court rejected the argument, paradoxically advanced by the defense, that since Jews were not a race in a biological-anthropological sense there could be no race-hatred incitement.[73]

b) Pamphleteers: The Trend

The "run of the mill" cases deal typically with production and dissemination of "Auschwitz lie" variants by means of brochures, placards, periodicals, open letters to public officials and mass media, or books. More often than not the defendant, young or old, is a hardened extremist with a prior record of neo-Nazi activity.[74]

It is difficult to discern a consistent pattern in the judgments of the various courts, and the sentences differ from one court to another. The indeterminate language of article 130 allows for substantial judicial discretion. The varied degrees of offensiveness in the language employed necessarily involve a subjective evaluation and make comparisons difficult. A court passing upon the text of two leaflets distributed by the same defendant would explain a lower sentence in one case on the ground that the text was "less embellished" and thus of "lower intensity" than in the other.[75] Courts, particularly those at the trial level, incline to the view that a "simple" denial of mass extermination, which is not accompanied by a "specific or at least incidental charge" against the "Zionists" for originating the "gassing lie," would not constitute an attack on human dignity.[76] Even where such a charge was made against "Zionists and other professional liars" a lower court acquitted a defendant, publisher of a periodical, of a charge of incitement to race hatred, since the Jews were not attacked for belonging to a certain race but rather were merely accused of ignominious behavior ("peddling a lie"). The appeals court rejected this reasoning and reversed the acquittal.[77]

Another trial court acquitted a defendant of an article 130 charge where the "Auschwitz lie" was a minor component in a book which called for an elaborate scheme of an "Aryan Europe" based on the "Führer principle." This court viewed the contents as not exceeding the bounds of legitimate criticism of a democratic state, but the judgment of acquittal was reversed, in this instance by the Federal Supreme Court itself.[78] Finally, as mentioned earlier, the highly controversial refusal by the Hamburg courts to prosecute was justified on the ground that the defendant's target was not "Jews in general" *but only* "the clique of international Jewry."[79]

The apparent inclination of the lower courts to avoid convictions under articles 130 and 131 is perhaps even stronger in cases where a private party lodges a petition. In that situation the courts, if they do not acquit, may opt for a conviction under article 185 for an insult, at times limiting the penalty to a fine.[80] On the other hand, to add to the diversity, some sentences for an insult under that article match in severity, or even exceed, those imposed for the more serious offense against human dignity.

In general, the Federal Supreme Court and—with some interesting exceptions[81]—the state appeals courts have often tended to reverse judgments of acquittal because they have taken a more serious view of the "Auschwitz lie" than the trial courts. One can only speculate about the reasons behind this pattern of judicial interaction. For one thing, trial judges are generally of a younger generation, without oppressive memories and—understandably—without a sense of personal guilt. Lacking extensive experience, they may feel less confident in handing down convictions for a distinctly political crime. Perhaps they also are more in tune with local attitudes than the higher-level judiciary, and are less responsive to the national policy that has reflected both the recent historical experience and a sensitivity to international considerations.[82]

3. The "Insult" Alternative

The trials and tribulations in the application of the insult article 185, prior to its modification by the 1985 law, are illustrated in two cases.

a) The case of the "Sons and Daughters of Deportees from France"

This case arose out of a 1980 demonstration in Cologne of mostly French Jews, the "Sons and Daughters of Deportees from France," at the occasion of a Nazi war criminal trial held in that city. The defendant distributed to the participants, journalists, and bystanders several copies of a leaflet which he himself had produced. Under the heading "Incitement to Hatred" the leaflet declared that, contrary to the opinions of federal judges and prosecutors and contrary to the presentation in the film *Holocaust,* there had been no mass destruction of Jews through gassing, as witnessed by the statements of varied historians, first and foremost by the "Jewish historian" J. G. Burg. The reverse side of the leaflet contained a report on the earlier "I am a donkey" demonstration in Hamburg,[83] *without,* however, any mention of the banners carried in that demonstration in which Israel was blamed for the "gassing lies." Burg, the report continued, supported the Hamburg demonstration, but a criminal proceeding was instituted against the participants upon complaint by the Hamburg Jewish community.

The trial court interpreted the defendant's leaflet as purporting to brand those who believed in the mass destruction stories as liars, prevaricators, and falsifiers of history and to attribute to the Jews at least a part of the responsibility for the "gassing lie." It found the defendant guilty of an attack on human dignity—incitement to hatred—according to article 130 and sentenced him to imprisonment for a year and three months. The *Landgericht* reduced the penalty to ten months, but the state appeals court in Celle reversed the conviction.[84]

In the appeals court's perception, the leaflet attributed the belief in the holocaust only to the German federal authorities ("the Jewish historian Burg" holding the opposite view) but not to the Jewish population in the Federal Republic (the participants in the Cologne demonstration being predominantly French Jews not covered by article 130): "it cannot, without more, be concluded that the leaflet flatly accused the local Jewish population of originating the 'gassing lie.' " There could be no finding of an attack on humanity where the denial of the mass destruction was not accompanied by qualifying characteristics, "that is, by particularly offensive and inhuman invectives such as a charge that the Jews themselves were the perpetrators of the 'gassing lie.' "[85] Because of the absence of such characteristics, which delimit article 130 from article 185, the appeals court quashed the sentence and remanded the case to the *Landgericht* with the directive to determine whether the facts warranted a conviction for an insult pursuant to the latter article, provided the requisite petition was filed by an authorized person.

In the proceeding on remand the defendant was in fact convicted of an insult and sentenced to a fine (eighty-five "daily rates" of fifteen marks). However, on a new appeal by the defendant the appeals court rendered a judgment of acquittal of the insult conviction on the ground that "upon further inquiry by the Senate [chamber]" it transpired that the petitioner was not a Jew.[86] Only "full Jews" *(Volljuden)* or "Jewish mixed breeds" *(jüdische Mischlinge)* "who were persecuted in the Third Reich or who would have been persecuted had they been living at that time" were entitled to file the petition; although the petitioner sympathized with the Jewish participants in the demonstration he was not offended by the statements in the leaflet because they were not directed against him as a "non-Jew."

Some of the inferences drawn by the court are curious. Thus, according to the court's interpretation of the leaflet, the belief in the existence of the holocaust could not be imputed to the Jews ("the Jewish historian Burg" did not believe in it). And, even accepting the court's assumption that the French Jews deported to Germany by the National Socialists and returning there were not protected by article 185, there was no evidence to support the court's belief that the leaflet with a text commonly distributed elsewhere in Germany was directed exclusively at them (even though the demonstration was "predominantly" by the French deportees).[87]

Nevertheless, the court's refusal to consider the distribution of this particular leaflet a serious crime against the public order is not, as we have seen, out of line with lower jurisdictions elsewhere, as the text omitted the usual charge against Jews of having originated "the lie" and contained no other aggravating statements. In dismissing the case for the absence of a legitimate complainant, the Celle court relied on a judgment of the Federal Supreme Court in the second of the two principal cases in this field, which is discussed in the next section.

b) The Federal Supreme Court and the Nuremberg Racial Laws

In this case[88] the defendant posted a leaflet on a public wall declaring that the claim of the murder of millions of Jews in the Third Reich was a

Zionist swindle that "could not be accepted." According to the line of decisions described above there may have been a basis for prosecution under article 130, as the text went beyond the "simple" denial of the "gassing lie." However, the proceeding was instituted upon private petition under articles 823 and 1604 of the Civil Code in conjunction with article 185, rather than under article 130. The *Landgericht* in Mainz prohibited the posting of the offensive statements,[89] but the appeals court in Koblenz reversed and dismissed the complaint.[90]

The Federal Supreme Court reinstated the prohibition in a broad-ranging opinion that dealt with four issues: (1) Was the prohibition compatible with the Basic Law? (2) Were the statements capable of causing personal injury? (3) Did "the Jews" constitute a group that was delimited with sufficient clarity to allow prosecution for an insult? (4) Was the complainant personally injured and therefore entitled to file a complaint?

The court's view on the *first* issue has been described earlier, in the context of the judicial posture toward constitutional questions.[91]

Dealing jointly with the *second* and *third* issues, the High Court attempted to draw a line between a mere falsification of history and an injurious invective. No one can claim personal injury, the court reasoned, from a mere presentation of a false version of history, even if it is expressed in strong words causing shock and indignation. There are other means for seeking historically secured truth than a recourse to the courts. The statement in the leaflet, however, was not directed toward a specific understanding of history. Denying the fact of the racial murder of the Jew amounted to disavowing their "inhuman" and "unique" fate which

> gives every one of them a claim to recognition and respect, above all on the part of the citizens of the land burdened by the past . . . The very historical fact that humans were segregated according to their origin under the so-called Nuremberg laws and were robbed of their individuality with a view to their extermination, gives the Jews living in the Federal Republic a special personal relationship with their fellow citizens; in this relationship the past is present even today. They are entitled, as a component of their personal self-image, to be viewed as a part of a group, singled out by fate, to which all others owe a particular moral responsibility, and that is an aspect of their honor. The respect of this self-image constitutes for every one of them one of the guarantees against a repetition of discrimination and a basis for their life in the Federal Republic. Whoever attempts to deny these events deprives each

> and every one of them of the personal worth to which they are entitled. For the affected person such denial means a continuation of the discrimination against the group of people to which he belongs, and simultaneously a direct discrimination against his own person.[92]

With these words, in striking contrast to the pre-1945 case law,[93] the court confirmed that, despite its restrictive approach to other collectivities, the Jewish citizens of the Federal Republic have become, "at least since the special legislation of the National Socialist State . . . a sharply demarcated group."[94]

It has been suggested that the High Court, in addition to recognizing the Jews as a group, has created a new personal right to the recognition of past persecution of the group, which belongs to every Jewish citizen of the Republic whether or not he himself actually suffered persecution; and the question was raised at the time whether such a right could be claimed by members of other groups such as minorities, refugees, and German expellees from Eastern Europe. We shall see that the 1985 law, as interpreted by its legislative history, appears to supply an affirmative answer at least in regard to the German expellees.[95]

It was the *fourth* issue, the petitioner's standing, that had determined the disposal of the case by the appeals court below. That court dismissed the complaint because the petitioner was not a Jew and did not fall within the circle of the persons "insulted." With this the Supreme Court disagreed. It reached the opposite conclusion on the basis of a scrutiny of a page-long list of the Nuremberg laws. According to these laws the complainant would be classified as a *Mischling* of the second degree because he had one Jewish grandfather; he thus would still have been subject to substantial discrimination. As long as the past of the "horrible events" is still present, it is not possible to separate individuals from their group. "This may happen only when these events become merely a part of the historical process. In the Federal Republic such distance does not yet exist."[96]

It is, to say the least, somewhat bizarre to see the Supreme Court "apply," albeit for this benign purpose, the infamous laws that it had excoriated earlier in the very same judgment. It was, as we have seen, the appeals court of Celle that subsequently carried this argument to its logical conclusion: it acquitted a defendant of a charge of an insult because the petitioner was neither a "full Jew" nor a "*Mischling*."[97] It is therefore not surprising that—as we shall see—in the final phase of the legislative process leading to the adoption of the 1985 law, the Celle case was invoked in support of the provision that did away with the requirement of the private petition and thus authorized ex officio prosecution for an insult.

V. How the New Law Came to Pass

A. The Original Version: A New Crime

In September 1982, just two days before its demise, the minority Social Democratic government of Chancellor Helmut Schmidt submitted a proposal for a new law. As in the case of the 1960 reform, the reason given was that "the number of right-extremist, especially neo-Nazi activities most recently has increased substantially," and there was "a gap" in the law that needed to be filled for effective prosecution.[98] In fact, according to the official statistics the number of reported illegal acts of this type reached a new peak in 1981, with threats of violence rising by fifty-four percent. The number of violent crimes decreased somewhat, due possibly to "resolute prosecution and other governmental countermeasures."[99]

The government bill envisaged three modifications of the existing law. The first two did not bear upon our problem; they proved noncontroversial and were included in the final text.[100] The third change would have introduced a new crime of rewarding, approving, denying, or minimizing the National Socialist genocide in public statements or publications. The then Minister of Justice justified this proposal by the need to provide criminal sanctions for such statements which, although eschewing direct hate attacks against the Jews, denied or "minimized" their mass extermination "in the guise of apparent objectivity and often with reference to alleged 'proofs.' " It was not enough that such acts could be prosecuted for insults of individual honor on a private petition in accordance with the ruling by the Federal Supreme Court; the current provisions on crimes against the public peace needed to be expanded to comprise such acts since they endangered "the constitutionally guaranteed peaceful coexistence of all citizens and the protection of human rights." The new version was to be limited exclusively to denying the National Socialist genocide.[101]

When the new center-right coalition between the Christian Democratic Union/Christian Social Union (CDU/CSU) and the Free Democratic Party (FDP) took over the government in the fall of 1982, the new Federal Minister of Justice Engelhard pressed the bill of his predecessor in the Bundesrat, but that body disapproved it. This prompted the Social Democratic Party (SPD) group, this time as a part of the opposition, to resubmit the bill.[102]

After all pending bills had lapsed with the dissolution of the ninth

Bundestag, the new government presented the same bill once more to the Bundesrat in April 1983,[103] but that chamber reaffirmed its negative posture.[104] In January 1984, it was the Social Democratic group that again took the initiative by resubmitting an identical bill.[105] The Bundestag gave the bill its first reading on April 12, 1984, a day after the government transmitted the same text to that body.[106] Annexed to the government bill was a statement of the Bundesrat opposing the government's proposal on several grounds: it did not take into account the views of the administrations of justice of the *Länder,* it was vague and constitutionally questionable, and it would turn courts into propaganda fora. In its response, which was also attached, the government suggested that a denial of other actions "comparable" to the National Socialist genocide might be included in a new article 131.[107] The Bundestag referred the bill to its Legal Committee. Thereafter it disappeared "in the Bermuda Triangle" of the government coalition,[108] to be resurrected in 1985 by the Social Democrats. That group placed it on the Bundestag's agenda with the request that the law be adopted before the eighth of May of that year, the fortieth anniversary date of the final defeat of National Socialist Germany in 1945.

The Social Democrats and the FDP Minister of Justice Engelhard were the protagonists of the bill in the ensuing public debate. With both the government and the opposition (albeit in reversed roles) offering the same bill, one might have expected clear sailing. Only the stance of the Bundesrat and the brief response by the government foreshadowed the future imbroglio.

B. The Public Controversy and a "New" Idea

The thrust of the criticism of the bill in the legal literature and in the press of the day was directed against the idea of establishing a new crime. Those who agreed that a gap in the law needed to be filled to cope with the serious wrong urged that, instead of creating a new crime, the "public peace" articles 130 and 131 should be clarified to include unmistakably the "Auschwitz lie."[109] On the other hand, others felt that only "justifiable facts" should be covered and questioned the practicality and effectiveness of the proposed text.[110]

Early in February 1985, the bill became entangled in a squabble within the governing coalition over internal security policy. At a Berlin conference of legal experts "a deal" was reached according to which the CDU/CSU would support the proposed legislation in exchange for the FDP liberals accepting, first, a stiffening of an anti-demonstration law strongly desired by the Christian Democrats and, second, a broadening of the proposed new crime to cover the denial not only of the National Socialist genocide but "any genocide," including the violent expulsion of the German population from Eastern Europe after 1945. The Bavarian CSU was said to have insisted on the second condition. For one reason or another, however—the FDP was said to have backed away from the bargain—the deal promptly collapsed.[111]

During the often-adjourned, ten-week deliberation in the Legal Committee of the Bundestag, opposition to the bill mounted. "The [government] proposal is harmful in its core. Therefore it will be withdrawn," declared Mr. Dregger, the leader of the CDU/CSU Bundestag group; he added the Chancellor Kohl and his group almost unanimously agreed.[112] The head of the CSU, Bavarian Prime Minister Strauss, speaking in Tel Aviv, said that no new law was needed; the opposition Greens Party and even the Bavarian branch of the liberal FDP agreed.[113] On the other hand, the German Federation of Judges, the spokesmen for German Jewish groups, and the apparently unanimous Social Democrats voiced their support for the original text and opposed with particular emphasis the extension of criminal sanctions to the denial of other acts of violence (such as the expulsion of Germans) on the ground that it had a "ring of the loathsome setting-off-against mentality."[114]

It was at the insistence of the Social Democrats that a date was finally agreed upon for plenary consideration in the Bundestag. At this stage Minister Engelhard indicated to the press that although his party would "under no circumstances" deviate from the principle of an automatic prosecution of the "Auschwitz lie," it would accept a compromise, according to which prosecution would be instituted ex officio for an "insult," without the prerequisite of a private petition. In that case the idea of a change in the substantive criminal law could be dropped.[115] A day before the date set for the Bundestag consideration there was still no agreement within the government coalition.

C. The Report of the Legal Committee: A Compromise

In March 1985, the Social Democrats forced a round of debate on the floor of the Bundestag, before the Legal Committee was able to agree on a report; but they did not succeed in having the House formally set a deadline for the committee report.[116] When this report, accompanied by a new government proposal, was finally distributed at the end of April, it confirmed that the coalition majority had embraced in essence the Engelhard compromise idea described in the preceding section.[117]

According to the committee majority, the need for a new crime provision that motivated the original government proposal had been met in the meantime by the decision of the Federal Supreme Court sanctioning prosecution for an "insult" pursuant to the current Criminal Code provisions;[118] but since the offended Jewish citizen could not be expected to defend himself personally against the insult, possibly having to prove that he was Jewish, the requirement of a private petition should be removed. However, this dispensation should benefit a person insulted as a member of a group persecuted not only by the National Socialists but also by any "other violent and arbitrary dominance" *(Gewalt- und Willkürherrschaft)*, a phrase drawn from another article of the Criminal Code.[119] This, in the majority view, was not an attempt "to compare the incomparable"; nor did it evidence a failure to recognize "the historical uniqueness of the mass murder perpetrated in an organized and technological manner."[120]

The Social Democratic member of the committee considered the recourse to the "insult" provision inadequate and believed that a special crime provision was still necessary, because the denial of the mass murder meant "whitewashing the National Socialist regime and thus an attack on public peace" through impairment of the "basic consensus of our society." Moreover, since the National Socialist genocide was a unique event, any equation with other violence, such as the crime of the expulsion of the Germans, must be avoided. In any case, there was no need for criminal sanctions against denial of such other crimes, because no one denied their existence; they are, in contrast with the National Socialist genocide which is a generally known fact and needs no proof, not "justiciable."[121] The member of the opposition Greens Party viewed criminal law as an improper means for combatting neo-Nazism; nevertheless, he supported the elimination of the private petition. Both opposition groups submitted their views in the form of specific legislative proposals.[122]

D. The Bundestag Acts

The emotional debate on the floor of the Bundestag had distinctly partisan overtones.[123] Speakers from all four parties vied with each other in passionate professions of their abhorrence of neo-Nazism, and they all conceded that the menace must be met primarily in public discourse, in the school, and in the family circle. Beyond this there was sharp disagreement. Virtually identical arguments were employed and the same positions taken as in the Legal Committee.

The Social Democrats taunted the government for opposing its own original proposal and accused it of procrastination and lack of seriousness and sensitivity. With two exceptions, the FDP liberals, led by Minister Engelhard, stood solidly behind the government;[124] they sought to emphasize their attachment to freedom of opinion and to justify their grudging acceptance of the restriction on that freedom. The CDU/CSU also closed ranks behind the government, but the "young" CDU Representative Lowack refused to believe that there had been an increase in neo-Nazi activities and warned that the House was being diverted by "a bogey" from more important problems.[125] The Christian Democratic rapporteur provoked a sharp skirmish with the Social Democrats over their alleged opposition, in 1959, to special protection for Jews in criminal legislation.[126]

The spokesman for the Greens disclosed that a substantial minority of the group supported the original proposal for a special crime, but a majority would settle for the "insult" compromise; the entire group, however, was opposed to the juxtaposition of the National Socialist persecution with other instances of violence: with such a provision "no law is better than this law" (quoting the chairman of the Berlin Jewish Community).[127]

In fact, this juxtaposition caused the most acrimonious exchange in the chamber. The only dissenter in the government coalition ranks, a member of the FDP, declared:

> I am concerned with the political and moral core of this change [from the original government bill]. The words "or other violent and arbitrary dominance" signify at least indirectly the political intent which [former Federal President] Theodor Heuss branded as a "ghastly setting-off" and which he bluntly rejected as the "behavior of the morally empty."[128]

On the other hand, the Christian Democratic leader Dregger was moved to interject: "Crimes are crimes by whomever and against whomever committed."[129]

Chancellor Kohl's speech at Bergen-Belsen, his "promise" to Israel, the appeals from the Israeli Parliament, and the positions of the Federation of German Judges and of Jewish groups were invoked in support of the original bill and against the "juxtaposition." Even the controversial "Bitburg visit"[30] and the much-discussed reunion of former SS men were brought into the debate. The fateful date of May 8, 1945, was repeatedly mentioned. Both sides signaled a sensitivity to the reaction abroad.[131]

When it came to voting, the two uncontested items in the government's proposal[132] were accepted without opposition. The alternative proposals by the Social Democrats and the Greens[133] were defeated by the coalition majority.[134] On the third reading, the entire law as recommended by the Legal Committee was adopted on a voice vote "by a large majority with a number of abstentions."[135] It was published on June 13, 1985, and came into effect on August 1, 1985.[136]

E. The New Law

The essence of the new law is the elimination of the private petition requirement for insult, if (a) the act is committed by disseminating or by making publicly accessible a writing, or in an assembly or in broadcasting;[137] (b) the insulted party is a member of a group that was persecuted "under the National Socialist or another violent and arbitrary dominance"; and (c) this group is (at the time of the act) a part of the population of the Federal Republic.[138]

According to the Legal Committee, the insulted party, a member of the group ("e.g., the Jews or the Silesians") must *himself* have been persecuted *because* of his membership in the group:

> It is not enough that the group as such was persecuted, rather the insulted party must himself have been exposed to persecution, and that is assumed to be so in the case of the Jews who lived within the reach of the power of the National Socialist regime and were subjected to the racial legislation.[139]

The Committee minority questioned the prerequisite of personal persecution on two grounds: first, because the provision will lose any meaning at the latest when there are no longer any directly affected persons alive in the Federal Republic; and second, because the courts may be misled "unintentionally" to believe that the legislator intended to "overrule" the Federal Supreme Court and require a showing of personal persecution not only under the new law but also in cases instituted by a private petition under the current law.[140] Indeed, as indicated earlier, the Supreme Court had recognized the standing of a Jew living in the Federal Republic to file a petition regardless of whether he was personally persecuted or even born after the demise of the National Socialist regime.[141] Vogelgesang believes, however, that what appears to be "a step back" will have limited practical effect, since a person who did not suffer personal persecution may find it emotionally less difficult to file a petition and thus need not be freed from that burden.[142]

Still according to the new law, the insulted party who is not interested in a criminal prosecution is given the procedural right to oppose it, but this cannot stop the prosecution with respect to other insulted parties.[143] One may wonder how—in the absence of a private complainant—the courts will interpret the provision regarding the right of opposition to the criminal proceedings.[144] A more serious question remains: Although the burden of proving Jewish origin is lifted from any private party, it will presumably still be necessary for the prosecutor to prove that there are Jewish injured parties, and for the courts to determine the fact. Will the courts continue to perform the theater of the absurd by employing the Nuremberg racial laws as a yardstick?

The Federal Supreme Court has fashioned a rationale of a special and unique relationship between German Jews and their fellow citizens. It would be interesting to see whether and how the Court will construe a similar rationale with respect to other groups whose members were persecuted under "another violent and arbitrary dominance."

By avoiding a change in substantive criminal law and by tinkering instead with procedure, the legislature conjured up a hybrid: A norm originally designed to protect a private good is injected with a new public interest, not as strong as the avoidance of a breach of public peace but strong enough to turn the offense into an *Offizialdelikt*; yet the person who suffered impairment of the protected private good is given the personal right to stop the ex officio prosecution. Moreover, the essentially private-good protection under this provision is granted to offensive utterances made in public only.

It could nevertheless be argued, if one accepts the underlying analysis of the political and legal context, that this pragmatic patching-up has met the need of the day. It is a temporary expedient: when the last Jew who lived in Germany during the National Socialist regime (or the last Silesian who was expelled from Silesia) dies, things will revert to the original state as far as the criminality of the "Auschwitz" or other "lies" is concerned.

VI. A Summary and Two Perceptions

A. The New Law: Pro and Con

The attitudes toward the new law have ranged from total rejection to isolated instances of warm embrace.

1. The Law Is Bad on Grounds of Principle and Practicality

Voices opposing "crimes of opinion" *(Gesinnungsdelikte)* on constitutional grounds are on one end of the spectrum. There is no legal duty to tell the truth except where the law so specifies; morality and legality are two different categories, and any opinion, regardless of its moral color, must be free as long as it does not impair in actual fact the freedom of others.[145] Vagueness of terminology exacerbates the problem.[146] "To declare history a protected legal good means to open the door to government despotism under the guise of judicial truth-finding."[147]

Contrary to the official government position, the need for new legislation was questioned particularly in certain CDU/CSU circles, and the concern was expressed that the law might lead to a "stream of hardly bearable procedures."[148] Although the courts have generally accepted the genocide of the Jews as a historical fact, what, if any, evidentiary procedures will be required to prove "other" acts "of violent and arbitrary dominance"?

The experience with the earlier legislation shows, the argument continues, that its application at the prosecution, trial, and sentencing stages has posed serious problems of effectiveness, practicality, and consistency; almost without exception the defendants, young and old, remain convinced if not strengthened in their conviction of the truth of their allegations; individual as well as general deterrence purposes fail, and there is a danger of a "backlash"; the lie is forbidden but liars remain.[149] The judicial process is not equipped to carry the burden of education that is incumbent upon the family, the school, and political discourse, all of which have failed in this area. On the contrary, the courts have become a forum for neo-Nazi propaganda that helps make new heroes and martyrs for the movement.[150]

2. The Law Does Not Go Far Enough

At the opposite end of the spectrum are those who deplore the "trivialization" and "privatization" of the crime of the "Auschwitz lie": instead of reducing it to a mere "insult" the provisions dealing with the serious crimes of breach of the public peace should have been modified or a new special crime should have been added, as was contemplated in the original government and SPD bills. The Social Democrats, the executive director of the Association of German Judges, and the Jewish groups have taken this view (although the idea of a modified insult provision is said to have originated earlier in the Central Council of Jews). At any rate, court proceedings are important to help educate the ignorant, particularly the immature young, and to flag the new danger of neo-Nazism.[151]

3. The Law Would Be Good but for the "Set-off"

In the "Auschwitz lie" cases, the courts have been reluctant to find the necessary prerequisites (breach of the public peace, aggravating factors) for finding the serious crimes against human dignity or incitement to race hatred, so that there was a danger—and actual instances—of widely criticized acquittals. The Federal Supreme Court approved the "insult" route; thus, to make it possible to prosecute for an insult, without the requirement of a private petition, is the proper solution to the problem, particularly because it relieves the offended party from the burden of proof, including the showing that he is a Jew. What makes the law unacceptable, however, is the extension of the provision to "lies" about acts of "dominance" other than the National Socialist genocide—such as the expulsion of German nationals from Eastern Europe after 1945, brought about as a result of, and in revenge for, the aggression and atrocities committed by the National Socialists against the local populations:

> It may indeed . . . be a testimony to the deplorable spiritual state of the nation and a declaration of the bankruptcy of its public educational institutions that the act of denying historical truth must be made subject to a penalty. But that is the effect of a decade-long cover-up, minimizing the terrible crimes and balancing them against others.
>
> Who actually denies the crimes of expulsion? And what have they in common with the factory-type extermination of millions of human beings by the National Socialists? What else lurks behind this demand than the terrible mentality of those Germans who, in the manner of children caught at mischief, point to "the others" who were "no angels either."
>
> . . . The inability to acknowledge without any ifs, ands, or buts that a unique crime was committed by Germans and to feel ashamed of it will also bring a revenge in the future.[152]

This was, after some oscillation, the position of the Greens Party.[153]

4. The Law Is Good

To the extent that a vote on a compromise provides evidence of the view of the political parties, the entire government coalition (with only two dissents) favored the law as adopted. One official of the executive branch who welcomed the law added that he would have wanted it stiffened to prohibit "Auschwitz lie" statements made in private as well as in public (as is the case with ordinary insult) and to increase the penalty.[154] He defended the juxtaposition with other acts of "dominance" on the ground that other articles in the Criminal Code, although enacted with National Socialist actions in mind, are formulated in general terms and do not stipulate a special treatment for such actions.[155]

A less technical and more eloquent defense comes from a commentator in the conservative *Frankfurter Allgemeine Zeitung*.[156] In this clamorous and emotional quarrel no responsible person has suggested that the guilt of the National Socialists for the Jewish mass extermination could be annulled by the reference to the postwar mass crimes against the Germans. Those politicians who were accused by the SPD of a "setting-off-against mentality" wanted to facilitate, not to avoid, the prosecution of the "Auschwitz lie," but they wanted to apply the new procedure to the postwar genocide of the Germans as well. For the first ten to fifteen years after the war many Germans wanted "to push aside" the crimes against the Jews. But this silence changed in the early sixties at the latest, due to the important "Auschwitz trial" in Frankfurt. "The destruction of Jews has penetrated everybody's consciousness and has remained there." The opposite has occurred with the crimes committed against the Germans. These were widely discussed in the first postwar years, but later on the Germans turned to the "new affluence" and no longer wanted to hear about what had happened in the East. In 1969 the government commissioned a study of the events in the East but, by a decision of the SPD-FDP government in 1974, the resulting massive documentation had been kept from the public until the present coalition government lifted the publication bar.[157] "But there is no way of making up the knowledge gap caused by this blackout maneuver." The dreadful atrocities were not placed on record in any court proceedings; the perpetrators were not prosecuted but on the contrary were specifically relieved of any legal accountability.[158] The mass murders such as the "intentional decimation [of Germans] in Yugoslavia" with clear genocidal characteristics must not fall into oblivion any less than the genocide of the Jews.

The basic argument advanced by this commentator reflects the position taken by some CDU/CSU participants in the Bundestag debate.[159] It may or may not be indicative of things to come that, even before the new law had become effective, a sociology professor in Mainz is reported to have invoked it against the exhibitors of a Soviet film which he claimed "minimized and played down" the acts of violence committed by the Red Army against thousands of German women in 1945.[160]

B. The Trend

At the outset of this essay I suggested that each society must decide for itself where to draw the line between freedom of expression and the demands of public order and security for its institutions and people. It is not surprising that coping with "the Auschwitz lie" has proved to be a particularly arduous task.

One may recall that another lie—that Germany had lost the First World War because of the "stab in the back" at home, rather than because of defeat on the battlefield—had served as an important rallying theme for the enemies of the Weimar Republic. The spreading of the "Auschwitz lie" is viewed by the authorities as a serious matter. An unofficial list compiled by a federal ministry in 1981 shows no less than thirty-two books elaborating the false allegations. As mentioned earlier, official statistics show a sustained rise in right-wing incidents and terrorism,[161] although the current government appears to view the threat from the left as more pressing.[162]

A public opinion survey commissioned by the Chancellor's office in 1979–1980 purported to find that thirteen percent of the electorate held on to the National Socialist ideology and a further thirty-seven percent felt threatened, lost, disoriented, powerless, in the grip of a *Kulturpessimismus* characterized by antipluralist, partly antidemocratic features, arrogating solely to the German nation, excluding all others, the "typically German" traits of loyalty, industry, and sense of duty.[163] However, both the method and the interpretation of the results of this survey have been questioned. Other tests have shown on the one hand an impressive growth of public support for democratic institutions (seventy-one percent in 1978), and on the other hand a rising perception of the National Socialist regime as criminal (from fifty-four percent in 1964 to seventy-one percent in 1978).[164] Still another survey prepared for the Ministry of the Interior in 1979 identified 4.4 percent of the entire population as showing "left-protest potential," while only 1.5 percent appeared oriented toward a "right-protest potential."[165]

The Minister of the Interior concluded in 1982, when the new law was first contemplated, that the right-extremist and neo-Nazi groups remained isolated and did not enjoy the backing of the population at large; they had no chance in elections. He pointed out, however, that more than half of the population had grown up after the Second World War and had had no first-hand experience of National Socialist rule: thus, political education and enlightenment must take on right-extremist ideas at an early time.[166]

There appears to be a consensus in the political arena that criminal law must continue to supplement the enlightenment process. The legislature evidently accepted the view expressed by the Federal Supreme Court in 1979 that "the past is still present," and that the past events have not become as yet "merely a part of the historical process."[167]

Between 1982 and 1985, however, owing principally to the shift of governmental power from the Social Democrats to the center-right coalition, a change occurred in the ideas on how to improve the criminal law tools for combatting "the Auschwitz lie." The original proposal of creating a special crime was abandoned in favor of facilitating prosecution for an "insult." The option of a prosecution for more serious crimes of breach of the peace under articles 130 or 131 remains, but we have noted the reluctance of at least some lower courts to hand down convictions for these political crimes. With the passage of time, as the past fades from memory, such reluctance is likely to increase, particularly in cases of a "simple" version of "the lie" eschewing other offensive adornment. The legislative history of the new law may provide additional encouragement to prosecutors to rely on the "insult" route.[168] That route, as we have seen, was opened by the Federal Supreme Court[169] and widened by the new law. That law, it should be kept in mind, at the same time extended the area of a potential restraint on freedom of expression by making punishable the denial of other "lies."

C. Two Perceptions

The lawmaking process—and the new law itself—was directly affected by the intense nationwide debate over the implications for Germany's present of her 1945 defeat, a debate anticipating the fortieth anniversary of Germany's surrender on May 8, 1985. The respected Swiss *Neue Zürcher Zeitung* concluded that overall the debate about the complex "mortgage" left by the Third Reich deserved respect because of its openness, intensity, and soberness.[170]

An American observer, on the other hand, saw in this debate "tendencies to rewrite and prettify the past" running "stronger than impulses to recollection and contrition"; themes of Germans as victims of Allied bombing and Red Army pillaging were being turned by a government spokesman from a "sense of victimization into a weapon of outrage."[171]

Like the debate surrounding it, the new law itself, with its controversial clause, may be subject to two perceptions. It may be viewed in the first place as an instance of fatuous compromise dictated by the politics of the day, such as occurs from time to time in any working democracy, but as a compromise which nonetheless contains positive features. The other perception would see the law as a symptom of darker currents in the stream of German society. The idea that the administered genocide was unique, an unparalleled crime, provided the rationale for earlier legislation and judicial decisions;[172] that idea has now been jettisoned by the legislator, and with it went—it can be argued—an important premise underlying the stance of postwar Germany toward its past.

It would be a mistake to exaggerate the importance of the legislation. With the profound changes in the postwar social structure, German democracy today appears secure—at any rate barring an economic collapse such as would threaten the stability of any society. The Holocaust is widely discussed in the mass media, and only a minuscule minority questions its reality as a historical fact. Yet the controversy in the Parliament and the adopting of the juxtaposition clause reveal an ambiguity regarding the way of dealing with the burden of history.

In an address delivered before the Bundestag on the fateful anniversary day, Federal President Richard von Weizsäcker stated: "Indeed, there is hardly a state which in its history always remained free of culpable entanglement in war and violence. But the genocide of the Jews is without precedent in history."[173] It is open to question whether this statement represents today a part of the national consensus.

History abounds with large-scale atrocities, some matching the Nazi genocide in number of victims if not in "modus operandi." It is axiomatic that as a general proposition "a crime is a crime," and any genocide must be recognized as such. The crucial need is for any people to recognize their responsibility for a crime committed in pursuance of a policy of their established government. As time and generations pass, governments, educators, and other opinion leaders, as well as individuals, face a dilemma: To allow the sense of responsibility to vanish from the collective memory would distort history and would harbor the danger of new excesses. To make people wallow in nightmares of guilt so as to impair the self-confidence of the young and their positive view of the future might bring about a destructive backlash against democratic institutions. The problem is one of a delicate balance; there is perhaps a modest role for law and the courts in helping to maintain it.

VII. The European Dimension: An Interlude

The "Auschwitz lie" issue has had repercussions beyond national judiciary. It has reached the European transnational institutions when the "deniers" sought relief in Strasbourg from their convictions in Belgian, Swedish as well as German courts. One example is the Mainz case, discussed earlier in this essay, in which the Federal Supreme Court upheld the standing of a complainant with a Jewish grandfather and reinstated the trial court's injunction against the repetition of the "Auschwitz lie" allegations.[174] After the Federal Constitutional Court had rejected his complaint the defendant filed an application with the European Commission of Human Rights in Strasbourg. He claimed that he was deprived by the German courts of his rights to free expression and fair hearing guaranteed by the European Convention for the Protection of Human Rights and Fundamental Freedoms.[175]

The Commission recognized that the complainant's right to free expression assured in the first paragraph of article 10 of the Convention had been interfered with. It concluded, however, that the interference met the requirements of the second paragraph of this article: it was "prescribed by law" (German legislation as interpreted by courts), it was neither arbitrary nor unreasonable (the pamphlets not only distorted historical facts but attacked the reputation of an "insultable" group described as liars and swindlers), it had a "legitimate purpose" (the protection of the reputation of others) and "it could also be considered as necessary in a democratic society." "Such a society rests on the principles of tolerance and broadmindedness which the pamphlets in question clearly failed to observe. The protection of these principles may be especially indicated vis-a-vis groups which have historically suffered from discrimination."[176]

The Commission held further that there had not been a violation of fair hearing requirements (article 6 (1)) by the refusal of the German courts to admit evidence regarding the denial of

> the historical fact of the assassination of millions of Jews as such. This historical fact is not only common knowledge established beyond doubt by overwhelming evidence of all kind, it was even admitted by the applicant himself . . . The Federal Court of Justice . . . clarified that objective criticism of historiography, including the assessment of the number of the assassinated Jews, was legally permitted. The facts of the applicant's case, however, did not involve any necessity to take evidence in this respect because it was the denial of the historical fact as such which was considered as defamatory.[177]

Unlike the offense of slander, the Commission observed, defamation under Article 185 was not susceptible to be disproved by evidence of truth.[178] For these reasons the Commission declared the complaint inadmissible as manifestly ill-founded.[179]

The outcome is not surprising since protection of the reputation of others is listed expressly as a legitimate exception to the right to freedom of expression in article 10, as it is—for that matter—in the German *Grundgesetz.*[180] It is, however, noteworthy that the Commission has adopted the view of the German Constitutional Court which had held that the guarantees of fair trial did not include the right to offer evidence concerning the existence of the Holocaust.[181]

The text of article 10 represents the consensus on the limits on freedom of expression among the Western European democracies, and the application of the article in the "Auschwitz lie" context must be taken as reflecting the Western European view on the issue.

In the earlier cases the Commission and the Court of Human Rights have upheld a broad, almost unlimited margin of discretion of the Member States, to restrict freedom of expression pursuant to the second paragraph of article 10.[182] The more recent case law suggests, however, that in the balancing process, freedom of speech is one of the preferred fundamental rights which in matters of political discourse at any rate must be given greater weight than the competing interests, including the protection of reputation.[183] It is in this context that the Commission posture on the Auschwitz issue is of some interest.

VIII. The American Landscape: A Postscript

The United States was one of the countries in which, as I mentioned earlier, the "Auschwitz lie" has been circulated by the neo-Nazis and other extremist groups. In contrast to the Federal Republic, however, there is little evidence of legal action against them on that specific issue. One, if not the principal reason is very likely the expansive scope of the freedom of expression as articulated by the United States Supreme Court over the last four decades, which makes the ultimate success of any such legal action highly problematic. Furthermore, there appears to be a tacit understanding that any legal procedure aimed at suppressing or punishing extremist speech or cognate communicative acts would only play into the extremist hands by providing a public forum for their propaganda.[184] "The famous American professor" whose book, as we have seen,[185] is invariably offered in evidence to support the "Auschwitz lie" claims, continues teaching engineering science at a well known American university, with little public attention paid to his fantasies.[186] Finally, again unlike in Germany, there is at present in the United States a striking dearth of legislation on which legal action could be based.

1. Civil Action in Libel—Group Defamation

I have been able to identify two instances of legal action, both in the Los Angeles County Superior Court. A survivor of the Auschwitz camp sued the Legion for Survival of Freedom and its subsidiaries, including the Institute for Historical Review and the Liberty Lobby, claiming that they reneged on an offer to pay $50,000 to any person who provided proof that millions of Jews had been gassed by the National Socialists. The plaintiff demanded the payment of the prize and damages. In a ruling on the motions of the parties, the court took "judicial notice of the fact that Jews were gassed to death at the Auschwitz Concentration Camp in Poland during 1944. This is a fact not reasonably subject to dispute, determinable by resort to sources of reasonably indisputable accuracy."[187] In a judgment rendered pursuant to a settlement reached by the parties the Court held the defendants liable for $150,000, reduced to $90,000, and that they shall "officially and formally apologize to the plaintiff" and to "all other survivors of Auschwitz for the pain, anguish and suffering he and all other Auschwitz survivors have sustained relating to the $50,000 reward offer for proof that 'Jews were gassed in gas chambers at Auschwitz.' "[188] The same plaintiff also sued a Swedish resident on the ground that he had been emotionally tortured by the defendant's assertion that the Holocaust was a fiction. The jury awarded the plaintiff $500,000 in compensatory damages and $4.75 million in punitive damages for libel and intentional infliction of emotional distress. The defendant did not answer the complaint and the court rendered a default judgment which the plaintiff hoped to enforce in Sweden.[189]

In neither case has there been an opportunity for a higher court to pass upon the constitutional implications. To the extent that the cases were based on a civil action for group defamation it is questionable that the judgments for the plaintiff would be upheld. Apart from the constitutional concerns, as in Germany, American courts have been traditionally reluctant to recognize a right of an individual member of a group to recover in civil action for defamation leveled at the group unless the group was distinct and small enough to allow an inference of an offense against him personally and individually.[190]

2. Criminal Action

One can still encounter some criminal state legislation designed to punish incitement to race hatred, dissemination of racist propaganda, and group defamation along the lines of the much more elaborate provisions of the German Criminal Code discussed earlier in this essay. Whatever federal statutory basis may have existed for prosecution of criminal libel, it has become obsolete.[191] The interest in this type of legislation rose significantly during the nineteen thirties and forties in the face of the systematic fascist campaign but, according to Arkes, in 1974 only four states had criminal group defamation statutes on their books, prosecutions have been rare and convictions even rarer.[192]

The first such state statute reached the United States Supreme Court in 1950. In *Beauharnais v. Illinois,* a case reminiscent of the German "pamphleteer" cases discussed earlier, Beauharnais, the president of the racist White Circle League, was convicted by the Illinois court for distributing in downtown Chicago leaflets defaming the Negro race and calling on white people to resist Truman's "infamous civil rights program."[193] The Supreme Court upheld the conviction under an Illinois Statute.

3. After Beauharnais

In *New York Times v. Sullivan* and its progeny,[194] however, the Supreme Court imposed severe strictures on the law of libel. These opinions, as well as subsequent holdings striking down criminal state statutes,[195] and the rulings of the state and federal courts in the *Skokie* case which I shall discuss promptly, have raised serious questions as to the continuing vitality of *Beauharnais.*

Nevertheless, in less than a year after *Sullivan,* the Supreme Court mentioned *Beauharnais* with approval, albeit against a vigorous dissent.[196] In the same year, *Beauharnais* was relied upon by an Illinois appellate court in *Chicago v. Lambert.*[197] The case arose out of a rock-throwing imbroglio, also in downtown Chicago, caused by American Nazi party members picketing a movie theater and distributing leaflets directed against Negroes and Jews. The placards and leaflets included, among other offensive statements, a reference to the "Auschwitz lie."[198]

The darkest shadow over *Beauharnais* was cast by the outcome of the *Skokie* controversy. The neo-Nazi party applied for a permit to march in their customary regalia through the village of Skokie, a Chicago suburb. Forty thousand of the seventy thousand inhabitants of Skokie are Jewish, seven thousand are survivors of the Holocaust or their descendants. The Skokie village council enacted a series of ordinances designed to block the Nazi marchers, including one that prohibited the "dissemination of any materials within the Village of Skokie which intentionally promotes and incites hatred against persons by reasons of their race, national origin, or religion. . ." When the permit to march was denied, the American Civil Liberties Union filed a suit on behalf of the neo-Nazis to assert their constitutional right to free expression. In the ensuing national controversy the Jewish community became divided and some 30,000 members of the American Civil Liberties Union resigned their membership. Ultimately the ordinances which were not withdrawn were struck down as unconstitutional by the Illinois state and lower federal courts. Most of the judges found *Beauharnais* no longer controlling. The United States Supreme Court refused to review the lower court judgment[199] but two justices, favoring a review, noted that "*Beauharnais* has never been overruled or formally limited in any way."[200] Ironically, in the end the neo-Nazis called off the march at

Skokie and instead a band of twenty five in brown shirts held a rally in a Chicago park.

4. After Skokie: The Academic Discourse

Historically, extremist speech has not been at the center of the free speech discourse but the drama of Skokie and, more recently, the publication of an innovative treatise have revived the issue. "Why, after all," asks Dean Bollinger, "should a free speech principle be extended to those who would use it to advocate the destruction of our liberty? . . . Here individuals were advocating an ideology the country had invested incalculable resources only a few decades ago to defeat; now it was being protected in its efforts to resurrect itself. Surely, many wondered, there is something disturbingly anomalous about that."[201] The opinions in the Skokie case make it unmistakably clear that the judges personally repudiated the Nazi ideas as "a collection of monstrous errors," yet the opinions convey "a strong sense of helplessness on the part of the judges."[202] Why such a disjunction between the personal views of the judges reflecting a wide community consensus on the one hand, and the perceived limits of legal coercion on the other?

In reality, neither the language of the free speech clause of the First Amendment[203] nor its history, nor for that matter—prior case law, unequivocally foreclose considerations of any claim to regulate extremist speech that defames religious or racial groups and advocates a violent regime.[204] Bollinger points out the flaws in the traditional theories underlying the protection of extremist speech:[205] The classic idea that democratic self-government cannot survive without unrestrained citizens' debate from which truth will necessarily emerge is questionable in an age where influential public opinion is subject to modern propaganda techniques and manipulation by mass communications. Nor can the Skokie result be justified by the requirement of untrammelled freedom for self-expression as an essential component of individual identity. Finally, the "fortress model," envisaging a set of nearly absolute rules against restraint on dissent—in the hope that they will keep judges from yielding to majority pressures and protect unpopular dissenters in time of crisis—can be viewed as unrealistic ("a Maginot line against the wrong threat") and is not supported by historical experience.[206] Instead, Bollinger offers a theory of tolerance that sees as the purposes of free speech "not only the 'protection' of a category of especially worthy human activity but also the choice to exercise extraordinary self-restraint toward behavior acknowledged to be bad but that can evoke feelings that lead us to behave in ways we must learn to temper and control."[207] Although he recognizes that injury suffered by offensive speech may not be outweighed by the traditional benefits of free speech he believes that, under this theory, the *Skokie* outcome—and presumably the dissemination of the "Auschwitz lie" claims—would be justified.

I can not do justice in the context of this postscript to Bollinger's appealing but still inchoate theory, nor am I able to explore the questions of the continuing vitality of the traditional free speech doctrines invoked to protect extremist speech in situations such as the *Skokie* case. Clearly, the resolution of that case would be quite different in the Federal Republic. To conclude this essay, however, I should like to speculate briefly about some of the factors in American society that may bear upon the difference between the two systems.

5. Vive la Différence?

Despite intermittent episodes of doubt and questioning, America has enjoyed a sense of security and national identity, linked primarily to the idea of limited constitutional government and individual rights. The uninterrupted continuity of democratic institutions has been marked by a gradually expanding range of participants in the political process in a society racially and ethnically diverse, and yet subject to compelling social, economic and political pressures for uniformity and centralized power. The environment of the third quarter of this century has proved particularly, if not uniquely, hospitable to individual rights, including the freedom of expression: relative economic stability, increased geographic and social mobility, continued opportunity for individual initiative and self-reliant entrepreneurship, combined with the emerging toleration of alternative lifestyles and new rights such as the constitutional right of privacy. A major if not the principal factor, however, was the civil rights movement, "the central moral enterprise of our time" that "has made rights solutions to social problems paradigmatic and has lent them powerful moral authority in popular and legal thought."[208] It was in this perhaps unparalleled setting that the individual right to free expression has been affirmed in unparalleled, absolutist terms as the dominant political right.

The German society, on the other hand, has been until recently at any rate, quite homogenous and the young democracy in the divided nation has not had the benefit of either a constitutional tradition or a comparable sense of security and identity; the prevailing "old" values have been loyalty, family, obedience to authority and patriotism (which—as we have seen—were invoked in the cases before the German courts), rather than individual freedoms and devotion to constitutional government. It was the latter values that the new "militant" *Grundgesetz* was to protect, even at the cost of abridging the free expression of those intent on undermining the new institutions. Moreover, the sense of responsibility for the recent past that still permeates the legal discourse in Germany arguably calls for the suppression of right-extremist speech lest its toleration be interpreted as concealed approval.

In the United States today, the neo-Nazis, and for that matter the entire right-extremist movement, may pose a challenge but can hardly be considered a threat to national security. A 1988 report indicates that although the membership of hate groups, overall, declined in recent years, the movement became more dangerous with certain elements resorting to open violence that resulted in a crackdown by federal authorities.[209] There are at least 67 hate organizations and some 50 periodicals of hate. A by-product of organized hate activity that, it is said, has increased disturbingly, is imitative behaviour of non-affiliated persons. Instances tracing this expanding effect include cross burning and the painting of swastikas and even arson and firebombing against minority group targets.[210] The rise of "skinhead" groups offers the neo-Nazis a new base of support among the youth.[211] The "Auschwitz lie" continues to be an important propaganda theme of the extremist groups.[212]

It may be useful to recall in this context that not so long ago, in the depression thirties and early forties, one third of American households was flooded by fascist hate-mongering literature seeking to exploit the economic distress and divisions in the society.[213] This, and the victorious advance of the totalitarian armies during the earlier war years created an atmosphere quite different from the sense of security existing today. At that time many feared for the security of the nation and some ethnic and religious minorities wondered about their own security in American society.

Against the background of today's broad national consensus, a critic of the unrestrained freedom for race-hate speech may say—in the words of Professor Strauss—that "our self-congratulation for allowing groups like the Nazis to march is empty and hypocritical."[214] It may or it may not be relevant that the United States stands alone on this issue against the position of other democracies and against the mandate of several international conventions, to which, alas, the United States is not a party.

The question has also been raised whether the American courts, in refusing to draw a line between race hate and permissible speech, underestimate the harm to the defamed groups, such as the Skokie Jews. Actually, in the *Skokie* case, the federal court of appeals appears to reason that since the Jews could stay at home and out-of-sight of the proposed march, it was unnecessary to take into account whatever suffering may have been in store for them.[215] Compare this stance — discounting of course the egregiously different context within which American and German courts function when dealing with the Holocaust — with the compassionate rationale offered by the German Federal Supreme Court in condemning group defamation.[216] The American society may be turning away from the "Americanization" and "melting pot" pattern to become a multicultural society. The discrete communities, particularly the Hispanics and Asians, are likely to advance new claims to protection not only against actual acts of discrimination that are proscribed by the equal protection clause of the Constitution but also against communicative acts against their ethnic integrity.

Finally, a more general, systemic question may be raised, based on the comparison with the German and other democratic legal orders: should courts be the institution to carry the full burden of drawing the line between permissible and prohibited speech under an ambiguous constitutional mandate or should the legislature play a larger role — and in particular, in a federal system, should state and municipal lawmaking bodies be relied upon? In the United States the question goes beyond the institutional concerns to the problem of fundamental values: "The debate between liberals and communitarians is latent in the problem of group vilification: forbidding localities to interfere with the public advocacy of group hatred affirms individual liberty, but denies the political community the opportunity to express through law the central commitment and ideals that unite its members."[217]

American society has benefited immensely from the emphasis on individual human rights. But "[t]hinking in terms of rights . . . encourages us to . . . think about what constrains us from doing what we want, not what obliges us to do what we ought."[218] In its extreme version, as manifested in the absolute free speech concept, the rights theory "using an entirely abstract method of discourse . . . has created a moral vacuum" and the question is how and by whom this vacuum will be filled.[219] What is one to think of a law that pleads inability to distinguish between neo-Nazis parading through Skokie and civil-rights advocates marching through white-racist neighbourhoods in the South?

Notes

I did a major part of the work on this essay as a fellow at the Wissenschaftskolleg zu Berlin — Institute for Advanced Study in Berlin, and I wish to express my appreciation for the support I received there. Several sections appeared earlier in the Michigan Law Review. All translations from German are my own, unless otherwise indicated.

1. See generally Section VII infra.

2. *Grundgesetz* [GG] art. 5 (2) (English translation from *The Basic Law of the Federal Republic of Germany* (Press and Information Office of the Government of the Federal Republic of Germany 1977)). On the concept of "general laws," see STARCK, *Herkunft und Entwicklung der Klausel "allgemeine Gesetze" als Schranke der Kommunikations-freiheiten im Artikel 5 Abs. 2 des Grundgesetzes,* in *Im Dienst an Recht und Staat 189* (H. Schneider & V. Götz eds. 1974). This approach is neither novel nor specifically German: it is comparable to other European constitutions. See e.g., *Denmark Const.* of 1953, art. 77, in 4 G. BLAUSTEIN, *Constitutions of the Countries of the World 24* (Feb. 1985); *Netherlands const.* art. 7 (amended 1983), in 11 *id.* at 4 (Jan. 1984); *Spain const.* art. 20 (1978), in 14 *id.* at 5 (Oct. 1979). See also European Convention for the Protection of Human Rights and Fundamental Freedoms, art. 10, discussed in the text at note 176 *infra.*

3. BUBNOFF, *Die strafrechtliche Bekämpfung rechts-extremistischer Aktivitäten,* 1982 *Zeitschrift für Rechtspolitik* 118, 120.

4. GG art. 18.

5. GG art. 20 (4); see also e.g., GG art. 9 (2) (prohibition of associations directed against the constitutional order); art. 21 (2) (unconstitutionality of political parties directed against the basic democratic order); art. 5 (3) (obligation of loyalty of university teachers toward the constitution). According to Steinberger, this form of a "militant" democracy which is capable of protecting itself is unique among modern democratic constitutions. H. STEINBERGER, *Konzeption und Grenzen freiheitlicher Demokratie* 8–9 (1974).

6. KOMMERS, *The Jurisprudence of Free Speech in the United States and the Federal Republic of Germany,* 53 S Cal. L. Rev 657, 693 (1980) (with citations to case law).

7. Einundzwanzigstes Strafrechtsänderungsgesetz, 1985, Bundesgesetzblatt [BGBl] I 1965.

8. See SCHMUDE, *Aufgaben und Grenzen des Strafrechts im Kampf gegen Neonazismus,* 1981 *Recht und Politik* 153, 154–55 (explanation of proposed legislation by Minister of Justice); see also text at notes 98–99 *infra.*

9. This section relies on Professor Pierre Vidal-Naquet of the École des Hautes Études en Sciences Sociales in Paris. See P. VIDAL-NAQUET, *Les juifs, La mémoire et le présent* 195–279 (1981); VIDAL-NAQUET, *Thèses sur le révisionnisme,* in *L'Allemagne nazie et le Genocide juif* 496, 501–6 (1985). The statement in the text is from *id.* at 502. See also his *Les Assassins de la Mémoire* (1987).

10. VIDAL-NAQUET, *Thèses sur le révisionnisme, supra* note 9, at 501.

11. See VIDAL-NAQUET, *Thèses sur le révisionnisme,* supra note 9, at 505; see also note 55 *infra.* In June 1985, the University of Nantes awarded a doctorate to Henri Roques, a 65-year-old agronomist, for a 371-page thesis that asserted there was no firm evidence to prove that the Nazis had gassed prisoners in concentration camps. The paper, which received special honors, provoked a storm of protests. The French government ordered that the doctorate be

withdrawn because of improprieties in the examining process, and that the head of the examining board be suspended. See MILLER, *Frenchman Assailed for Denying Nazi Crimes,* N.Y. Times, June 13, 1986, at 4, col. 1; *France Revokes Thesis That Denies Nazi Acts,* N.Y. Times, July 3, 1986, at 2, col. 2. In Germany, the doctorate of a seventy-year-old former judge of a Hamburg court was revoked in 1983 by the president of the University of Göttingen on the ground that the judge had authored a book entitled *The Auschwitz Myth—Legend or Reality,* in which he questioned the death of six million Jews. The Administrative Court of Braunschweig upheld the president's action. Der Tagesspiegel (Berlin), Jan. 31, 1986, at 7, col. I. A Swiss high school teacher and military judge in the Swiss army who questioned the existence of World War II Nazi gas chambers in public statements, news conferences, and right-wing newspapers edited by her husband has been formally barred from teaching history (but would be able to teach French). *Swiss Doubter of Nazi Camps Is Forbidden to Teach History,* N.Y. Times, Feb. 22, 1987, at 10, col. 3.

12. In Sweden, an Austrian-born Jehovah's Witness publishes a periodical and organizes summer trips to Auschwitz and to other localities in Poland to demonstrate that "nothing serious had taken place there." In Australia, it is the former secretary of the Victorian Council for Civil Liberties, in Italy a "small libertarian and Marxist group." VIDAL-NAQUET, *Thèses sur la révissionisme, supra* note 9, at 504–5. On the prosecution of the Holocaust-denier James Keegstra, ex-mayor and ex-teacher in Alberta, Canada, for promoting race-hatred, see R. v. Keegstra, Alta. Q.B. July 20, 1985 (appealed), D. BERCUSON and D. WERTHEIMER, *A Trust Betrayed—The Keegstra Affair* ((1985) and *Law Reform Commission of Canada Working Paper 50, Hate Propaganda* 4–5 (1986); Ernst Zundel, a post-war German immigrant who married the daughter of a Canadian fascist leader, was prosecuted for purveying "false news." Simon Wiesenthal Center, Response, Feb. 1988, p. 6. On the developments in United States, see text in Sections VIII *infra.*

13. Translation from the German original, *Strafgesetzbuch* [StGB], are my own. For an English translation of the entire Criminal Code as of April 1, 1961, see *The German Penal Code of 1871* (G. Mueller & T. Buergenthal trans. 1961).

14. See StGB art. 130 (1871). For an English translation, see *The Criminal Code of the German Empire* 221 (G. Drage trans. 1885).

15. For a detailed history, see G. KRONE, Die Volksverhetzung als Verbrechen gegen die Menschlichkeit 1–54 (dissertation, Johannes-Gutenberg-Universität Mainz, Law & Economics Dept., 1979); see also SCHAFHEUTLE, *Das sechste Strafrechtsänderungsgesetz,* 15 Juristenzeitung [JZ] 470, 470–72 (1960); P. PAEPCKE, Antisemitismus und Strafrecht 164 (dissertation, Albert-Ludwigs-Universität Freiburg i. Br., 1962). See generally COBLER, *Das Gesetz gegen die "Auschwitz-Lüge": Anmerkungen zu einem rechtspolitischen Ablasshandel,* 18 KRITISCHE JUSTIZ 159 (1985).

16. Article 93 made punishable by imprisonment the production, stocking, and dissemination of writings aimed at the impairment of the existence of the Federal Republic or the suppression of democratic freedoms. *Strafgesetzbuch* art. 93 (1953). Article 93 was abrogated by a later law.

17. The German term is *Beleidigung.* Article 185 of the Criminal Code is the last of the three provisions mentioned above. It is discussed in the text at notes 38–45 *infra.*

18. Decision of Nov. 26, 1958, Landgericht Hamburg, 14 JZ 176 (1959).

19. See 14 JZ 176–78 (1959) (complaint by the Chief Prosecutor against the decision below, Az. 14a Js 236/57; brief of the State Prosecutor General, Az. 2 OAR 801/58; decision of June 1, 1959, Hans. Oberlandesgericht [OLG] Hamburg, Ws 724/58).

20. Judgment of Feb. 28, 1959, 13 Bundesgerichtshof in Strafsachen [BGHSt] 32. The court applied the original article 93. See note 16 *supra.*

21. KÜSTER, *Anmerkung zum vorstehenden Beschluss des OLG Hamburg,* 14 JZ 178, 179 (1959).

22. See G. KRONE, *supra* note 15, at 32–33.

23. SCHAFHEUTLE, *supra* note 15, at 471. The author was an official of the Ministry of Justice which drafted the law.

24. On the concept of "public peace" in this context, see E. DREHER & H. TRÖNDLE, *Strafgesetzbuch und Nebengesetze,* art. 130, no. 2 (42d ed. 1985); see also N. ANDROULAKIS, *Die Sammelbeleidigung* 99–100 (1970). See also decision of Mar. 25, 1985, OLG Munich, 40 JZ 807, 807–8 (1985) (citations omitted):

> The protected good in Criminal Code art. 130 . . . is the public peace (unanimous view). But it is disputed whether the dignity of the individual is an added protected good. . . . A member of a religious community or of a part of the population, however, is not directly injured by an attack such as the incriminating statement in this case because he is not a carrier of the public peace, only the community organized in the state is the carrier.

25. See GG art. 1 (1): "The dignity of man shall be inviolable." Moreover, "[t]his inviolability of human dignity is not a mere programmatic statement but a 'directly effective norm of the objective (constitutional) law . . .' " Judgment of Feb. 28, 1959, 13 BGHSt 32, 35 (citing 1 H. v. MANGOLDT & F. KLEIN, *Das Bonner Grundgesetz* 147 (2d ed. 1955)).

26. SCHAFHEUTLE, *supra* note 15, at 473.

27. The enumeration of the protected groups contained in the earlier versions ("a national, racial, religious, or ethnic group") followed article 220a of the Criminal Code, implementing the Genocide Convention. G. KRONE, *supra* note 15, at 35. This formulation was replaced by the neutral "parts of the population" in response primarily to the concern expressed by the Central Council of the Jews in Germany lest the text create a *privilegium odiosum* for the Jews. The Jewish group ultimately approved the final text. *Id.* at 37; P. PAEPCKE, *supra* note 15, at 168 n.l.

On its face "parts of the population" could be read as including political, social, and economic groups, but such potentially unconstitutional application is precluded, it is said, by the requirement that the act must constitute an attack on human dignity. *Id.* at 164–65.

The first legislation against racial hatred was the Law of the State of Bavaria of March 13, 1946, 3 Bereinigte Sammlung des bayerischen Landesrechts 1802–1956, at 149 (1957). This law was expressly preempted by the new article 130. SCHAFHEUTLE, *supra* note 15, at 473. See in this context article 20 (2) of the United Nations International Covenant on Civil and Political Rights of 1966 (in force 1976), providing that "advocacy of national, racial or religious hatred that constitutes incitement to discrimination, hostility or violence shall be prohibited by law." 21 U.N. GAOR Supp. (No. 16), 52, U.N. Doc. A/6316 (1966), 999 U.N.T.S. 171, 178. See also article 4 of the Convention on the Elimination of All Forms of Racial Discrimination (in force 1969), requiring prohibition of advocacy of racial hatred and incitement of racial discrimination and violence. 660 U.N.T.S. 195, 218. There is no corresponding provision in the European Convention on Human Rights. But see Resolution of the Committee of Ministers of the Council of Europe on Measures to be Taken against Incitement to Racial, National, and Religious Hatred, Res. 68 (30) of Oct. 31, 1968, 1968 Y.B. Eur. Conv. on Hum. Rts. 94 (Eur. Commn. on Hum. Rts.); the model law defining the offense of incitement to hatred adopted by the Consultative Assembly of the Council of Europe, *Recommendation 453 on Measures to Be Taken against Incitement to Racial, National and Religious Hatred,* Eur. Consult. Assoc., 17th Sess. (Texts Adopted by the Assembly) (1966). See generally LERNER, *International Definitions of Incitement to Racial Hatred,* 14 N.Y.L.F. 49 (1968).

28. *Cf.* STGB arts. 234a, 241. [All STGB citations are to the current code, unless otherwise indicated.]

29. The statements in parentheses are by SCHAFHEUTLE, *supra* note 15, at 473. For definitions of the terms "insult," "ridicule," and "defamation," see E. DREHER & H. TRÖNDLE, *supra* note 24. art. 130, no. 7. It has been suggested that the constitutionally protected freedom of opinion precludes penalization of any of the above acts except those that incite to violence or lawlessness. N. ANDROULAKIS, *supra* note 24, at 96.

30. Dr. Schafheutle, Ministerialdirektor, before the 99th Session of the Legal Committee of the German Bundestag, Mar. 17, 1960, *quoted* in G. KRONE, *supra* note 15, at 51–53 (emphasis added), see also SCHAFHEUTLE, *supra* note 15, at 473: "Jews out" or "Negro half-breeds living in Germany should be gassed" would qualify as attacks under article 130.

31. N. ANDROULAKIS, *supra* note 24, at 96–97. The penalty for violating article 130 is imprisonment for three months to five years or a fine. See also STGB art. 47 (2) (amount of fines). Today more than 83% of all sentences rendered by German courts impose fines rather than imprisonment. See E. DREHER & H. TRÖNDLE, *supra* note 24, art. 40, no. 1.

32. E. DREHER & H. TRÖNDLE, *supra* note 24, art. 131, no. 1; see also A. SCHÖNKE & H. SCHRÖDER, *Strafgesetzbuch Kommentar,* art. 131, no. 1 (21st ed. 1982).

33. The concept of "race hatred" was taken from article 112 of the Law against Writings Endangering Youth of June 9, 1953. Judgment of Oct. 28, 1980, OLG Cologne, 34 *Neue Juristische Wochenschrift* [NJW] 1280, 1281 (1981).

34. Also included in the prohibition are writings which "describe cruel or

otherwise inhuman acts of violence against humans in a manner which glorifies or minimizes such acts of violence or represents the cruel or inhuman aspects of the occurrence in a manner offending human dignity." The forms of dissemination (including broadcasting) are defined in para. 1 (1)–(4) and in para. 2. A critical note is GEHRHARDT, *Die Beschränkung der Gesetzgebung auf das Unerlässliche*, 28 NJW 375 (1975).

35. STGB art. 131 (3). The penalty is imprisonment up to one year or a fine.

36. E. DREHER & H. TRÖNDLE, *supra* note 24, art. 131, no. 1.

37. *Id.* at art. 131, no. 6. Another commentary suggests, however, that in contrast to article 130 the incitement to race hatred need not be such as to potentially disturb public peace, and that races that do not form "a part of the internal population" are also protected. A. SCHÖNKE & H. SCHRÖDER, *supra* note 32, art. 131, no. 3. In the same commentary it is said, however, that the "legal good" protected is "ultimately here also public peace." *Id.* at art. 131, no. 1.

38. This offense is punishable by imprisonment of up to one year or by a fine, but when it is committed by a physical act *(Tätlichkeit)* the punishment is up to two years of imprisonment or a fine. See also STGB arts. 186 (damage to reputation consisting of factual statements insulting a third person), 187 (defamation), 187a (persons in political life), 189 (disparaging the memory of the dead).

39. StGB art. 192.

40. In case of the death of the offended person, the right of petition passes to his family—and if he or she died as a result of a "violent or arbitrary dominance" (Gewalt- und Willkürherrschaft), to which the insult is related, the requirement of a petition is dispensed with. STGB art. 194 (1)–(2).

41. See P. PAEPCKE, *supra* note 15, at 81–87, 92; N. ANDROULAKIS *supra* note 24, at 12–23 (citing the relevant case law). German law distinguishes between insult of a group and insult of individuals by statements directed against a group. See A. SCHÖNKE & H. SCHRÖDER, *supra* note 32, Vorbemerkungen 3–8 to arts. 185–200.

42. P. PAEPCKE, *supra* note 15, at 86.

43. N. ANDROULAKIS, *supra* note 24, at 32–33.

44. P. PAEPCKE, *supra* note 15, at 92.

45. See notes 88–97 *infra* and accompanying text. After the war, the Jewish population in the Federal Republic amounted to 30,000, down from the original 500,000 in the *Reich*. See Judgment of May 8, 1952, BGHSt, 5 NJW 1183, 1184 (1952).

46. Decision of Apr. 27, 1982, Bundesverfassungsgericht, Vorprüfungsausschuss, 35 NJW 1803 (1982).

47. *Id.*

48. *Id.* (emphasis added). It should be kept in mind that the decision was taken not by the complete *Senat* (chamber) but by a committee of three judges who probed into the merits only to the extent necessary for them to find the complaint "manifestly groundless" and thus inadmissible, not worthy of consideration by the full *Senat*. However, the brief language quoted above gives a good indication of what the outcome would have been in the full *Senat*.

49. Judgment of Sept. 18, 1979, 75 Bundesgerichtshof in Zivilsachen [BGHZ] 160, 161, 33 NJW 45, 45 (1980). The Court pointed out that the defendant himself admitted the murder of millions but questioned the figure of six million as being too high. But the "objective content" of his statement did not sustain such limitation. *Id.*

50. See, e.g., Judgment of July 23, 1980, Landgericht Bochum, No. 8 Ns 33 Js 287/79, at 22. [Copies of unpublished opinions cited in this essay are on file at *Michigan Law Review.*] The court stated that in addition to the inapplicability of GG art. 5, the defendant could not rely on the protection of freedom of science clause in GG art. 5 (3) (1). See also Judgment of Oct. 28, 1980, OLG Cologne, 1981 NJW 1280, 1281 (admitting that general criminal law must be interpreted in the light of, and in observance of, basic rights: "Whoever downright denies the historical fact of the destruction of the Jews may no longer claim the guarantee [of art. 5]—at any rate when the denial occurs in an injuring form.") (citations omitted). For the same reason this court approved that the defendant knew and intended all the factual elements of the crime. As another striking example, a 72-page appellate opinion of the Frankfurt Landgericht in five consolidated cases contains not a mention of the constitutional issue. Judgment of Mar. 25, 1981, Landgericht Frankfurt, No. 4 Ls 32/76 (Ns) (appeal from five judgments of the Amtsgericht-Schöffengericht Frankfurt).

51. See Judgment of Mar. 25, 1981, Landgericht Frankfurt, No. 4 Ls 32/76 (Ns); see also note 50 *supra.*

52. See *Strafprozeßordnung* (Code of Criminal Procedure) art. 244 (3) (2).

53. Judgment of Nov. 11, 1976, Bundesgerichtshof [BGH], No. 2 StR 508/76 (unpublished), *quoted* in Cobler, *supra* note 15, at 168. On the view of the screening committee of the Federal Constitutional Court, see text at note 48, *supra.*

54. Judgment of Sept. 18, 1979, 75 BGHZ 160, 161, 33 NJW 45, 45 (1980). For more on this case, see notes 88–97 *infra* and accompanying text.

55. Judgment of July 23, 1980, Landgericht Bochum, No. 8 Ns 33 Js 287/79, at 17, 19 (appeal from judgment of Jan. 17, 1980, Schöffengericht Witten), see also note 50 *supra* & note 74 *infra.* Robert Faurisson, Maître de Conférences (Lecturer) at the University of Lyon, has published and broadcast a number of statements asserting "the Auschwitz lie." He has been the subject of civil and criminal proceedings. See, e.g., Judgment of June 28, 1983, Cass. Crim., Fr., 1983 Bulletin des arrêts de la Cour de cassation, chambre criminelle 518, which affirmed the judgment of the Court of Appeal of Paris upholding Faurisson's conviction for group defamation and his sentence of three months' imprisonment (suspended), a fine of 5000 francs, and damages to the complainant. The court of appeal had reversed the conviction by the trial court for incitement to race hatred, and the Cour de cassation agreed. As of the fall 1985, A. R. Butz was Associate Professor of Engineering at Northwestern University. See A. R. Butz, *The Hoax of the Twentieth Century* (1976).

56. Judgment of July 23, 1980, Landgericht Bochum, No. 8, Ns 33 Js 287/79, at 17–79. See similarly Landgericht Nürnberg-Fürth, No. 8 Ns 344 Js 32 404/79, at 26–29 (photo copy).

57. Judgment of Mar. 25, 1981, Landgericht Frankfurt, No. 4 Ls 32/76 (Ns), at 43–44. Similarly Landgericht Nürnberg-Fürth No. KLS 91 Js 27 412/76, at 49–57 (photo copy), but expert witness "disproving" Nazi responsibility also admitted.

58. Unhappily, in this as in other areas not all cases of even the highest courts are published, and in most instances the published texts provide a bare minimum of facts.

59. Judgment of Jan. 14, 1981, BGHSt, 1981 *Neue Zeitschrift für Strafrecht* [NStZ] 258.

60. *Id.*

61. See text at note 30 *supra.*

62. 1981 NStZ 258 (citing judgment of Nov. 10, 1976, BGH, No. 2 StR 508/76; decision of Apr. 25, 1979, No. 3 StR 74/79 [S]; decision of Apr. 9, 1980, No. 3 StR 506/79 [S] (reversing, among others, acquittals for attacks on human dignity (incitement to hatred) in the judgment of May 23, 1978, Landgericht Nürnberg-Fürth, No. 1 KLs 91 Js 27 412/76, and judgment of May 18, 1979, Landgericht Nürnberg-Fürth, No. 1 KLs 91 Js 4500/78)).

63. Judgment of Apr. 21, 1961, 16 BGHSt 49, 56–57 (an antisemitic tract about a bankers' conspiracy in the United States held hostile to the Constitution and as inciting hatred (StGB arts. 93, 130)).

64. Judgment of Jan. 14, 1981, BGHSt, 1981 NStZ 258. The Supreme Court was clearly concerned lest history be omitted from the relevant context.

65. Judgment of Mar. 27, 1981, Amtsgericht Goslar, No. 6 Ls (O) 303 Js 3643/80. The original sentence of seven months was reduced by eliminating a conviction for duress against the parents. Decision of Sept. 21, 1981, Landgericht Braunschweig, No. 31 Ns 303 Js 3643/80. The judgment has become final.

66. See text at notes 55–58 *supra.* There are potential breaches of public peace when the entire population loses confidence in legal security, or the attacked group alone feels threatened, or when there is a strengthening of the tendency to violate the law on the part of the group which has inclinations toward violations of the law. The defendant's statements, the court held, were objectively apt to disturb public order by fueling the newly increased neo-Nazi tendencies and impairing the sense of security of the Jews in the Republic; the statements were made in "a large circle" of young persons by a teacher whose duty it was to educate them for democracy, with a potential for a "multiplying" effect; the defendant "knew that his statements do not correspond to the truth." Amtsgericht Goslar, No. 6 Ls (O) 303 Js 3643/80, at 13, 18.

67. Judgment of Dec. 14, 1977, OLG Schleswig, 32 *Monatsschrift für Deutsches Recht* [MDR] 333 (1978).

68. Citing judgment of Nov. 15, 1967, 21 BGHSt 371, 22 MDR 255 (1968).

69. OLG Schleswig, 32 MDR 333.

70. *Id.*

71. Judgment of Feb. 21, 1980, Amtsgericht Cologne, No. 652 (253) Ls 340/79 jug.–121 Js 145/79.

72. Judgment of Oct. 28, 1980, OLG Cologne, 34 NJW 1280 (1981). This judgment is final.

73. *Id.* at 1281. For the discussion of the constitutional issue in this opinion,

see note 50 *supra.* In May 1986, a Koblenz court found a 49-year-old high school teacher guilty of insult and incitement to hatred for making statements to students, e.g., that Auschwitz was "an American invention." The court sentenced him to one year's imprisonment, suspended on good behavior, and barred him from teaching for a period of three years. If the sentence becomes final the defendant may lose his status as a government official. The fact that state and local school supervisory authorities failed to intervene over a period of years in the face of mounting complaints was considered a mitigating circumstance. The court observed that "powerful protectors must have been at work," as the defendant is said to have threatened his supervisor with "his wide-ranging political connections." Frankfurter Allgemeine Zeitung, May 17, 1986, at 4, col. 6; see also judgment of July 23, 1984, Niedersächsischer Disziplinarhof (Disciplinary Tribunal of Lower Saxony), 39 NJW 1278 (1986) (affirming a salary reduction and ordering a demotion of a high school teacher *(Oberstudiendirektor)*).

74. As an example, the Landgericht Bochum upheld the conviction under article 130 of a tax accountant, born in 1920, for producing a brochure, entitled *Maidanek Forever?,* which advertised a book by J. G. Burg, a "Jew, [an] anti-Zionist writer" who "makes short shrift of the mass destruction lie" and "the Zionist million-size swindle." Extensive quotations from the book are given. Judgment of July 23, 1980, Landgericht Bochum, No. 8 Ns 33 Js 287/79. The sentence was for six months' imprisonment, suspended on good behavior. According to the brochure, Maidanek was "a model camp." "There were no doubt inconspicuous slips on the part of the personnel, but murders, and of this magnitude . . . ! Never!" *Id.* at 7–8. The defendant claimed that as a former SS man who was criminally prosecuted as such after the war, he was interested in clearing up the history; the Zionists wanted to bring about a new antisemitism in Germany by spreading the "Auschwitz lie" since that was necessary for the survival of the State of Israel; the Burg book was designed to bring about a reconciliation between the Jews and the Germans. The court noted that the quotations from the book are replete with offensive epithets and the Zionists are blamed for spreading "the lie" in order to get reparations. On the court's refusal to call professors and other witnesses or experts, see text at notes 55–56 *supra.* The court ordered the seizure of copies of the brochure. Some fifteen proceedings were previously instituted against the defendant, most of which were terminated because of the short statute of limitations.

See, similarly, judgment of Mar. 25, 1981, Landgericht Frankfurt, No. 4 Ls 32/76 (Ns). Defendant, born in 1914, son of a teacher, lost his father at the age of three, was brought up by a "national-conservative" grandfather, was unable to study beyond *Gymnasium* for financial reasons. He joined the National Socialist Party in 1933, served as a soldier in Russia, became an interpreter and journalist; since 1976 he had been living on support from relatives and political sympathizers and had devoted himself to two organizations (*Aktionsgemeinschaft Nationales Europa* and *Kampfbund Deutscher Soldaten*) which he had founded. *Id.* at 7–8. The "Auschwitz lie" was the principal theme in leaflets written in German and English, letters to broadcasting executives, to a general, etc. With his collaborators he started the "I am a donkey" campaign. With proceedings pending against him in two other courts, he was convicted in Frankfurt of eight separate cases of insult, two attacks on human dignity of Jews (including a charge of falsification of the Anne Frank diary), one disparagement of the memory of the dead, two cases of aggravated calumny, and one case of attempted duress. He received a "comprehensive sentence" of two years and eight months imprisonment. *Id.* at 3. The medical expert found him intelligent, spiritually alert, and responsible ("neither a paranoiac nor a sick fanatic") and related his "one-dimensional" insistence on the "Auschwitz lie" to his "emotionally grounded basic beliefs such as love of the fatherland, honor, loyalty, good character." *Id.* at 46. See also Landgericht Nürnberg-Fürth, No. 8 Ns 344 Js 32 404/79.

75. Judgment of Mar. 25, 1981, Landgericht Frankfurt, No. 4 Ls 32/76 (Ns).

76. Decision of Feb. 17, 1982, OLG Celle, 35 NJW 1545 (1982) (citing cases from courts in Frankfurt, Segeberg, Nürnberg-Fürth, Goslar, as well as prosecutors in Nuremberg).

77. Judgment of Feb. 3, 1981, OLG Hamm, 1981 NStZ 262. In the appeals court's view, the court below failed to distinguish between the true reason for the hatred and the means employed. Although under article 131 the feelings of hatred must be directed against others for the sole reason that they belong to a certain race, the characteristics attributed to them need not be present only in that race. *Id.* The court stressed that article 131 was designed to serve the struggle against the revival of racism and antisemitism in Germany, in view of the historical experience of the danger of "racially" motivated persecutions. This court and others have refused to draw the distinction urged by the defense between "the Jews" and the "Zionists."

78. Judgment of Aug. 24, 1977, BGH, No. 3 StR 229/77 (S). In this case the publisher of the German translation of a book entitled *Is Race Consciousness Reprehensible?,* originally published by a "Canadian scientific institute," was prosecuted for illegal activities against the state, defamation of the state, and violation of article 130. The book rejected democracy in favor of the "Führer principle," eulogized the Aryan race, minimized the Nazi crimes and euthanasia, and called for an Aryan Europe, a Federation of Aryan Nations, the removal of the nonwhites, reducing Jews to guest-people, and a prohibition, under the penalty of sterilization, of mixed marriages. The trial court (Landgericht Flensburg), pointing to passages where race separation is advocated as self-survival, and race-hatred and racist zealots are repudiated, acquitted on the ground that the contents did not exceed the bounds of legitimate criticism of the democratic state; although presenting "a presumptuous and overbearing valuation of the Aryan, [it does] not contain an attack on human dignity of the undervalued persons in the sense of [article 130]." *Id.* at 3. The Supreme Court vigorously disagreed with the legal interpretation, reversed, and remanded. Note also the reversal of acquittals on two counts for race-hatred incitement and two counts of insult by the Frankfurt *Landgericht.* Judgment of Mar. 25, 1981, Landgericht Frankfurt, No. 4 Ls 32/76 (Ns), at 2–3.

79. Decision of Nov. 26, 1958, Landgericht Hamburg, 14 JZ 176 (1969). Here the appeals court affirmed the refusal.

80. See e.g., Judgment of Mar. 25, 1981, Landgericht Frankfurt, No. 4 Ls 32/76 (Ns), at 17, 19, 68.

81. Decision of Feb. 17, 1982, OLG Celle, 35 NJW 1545 (1982); judgment of May 2, 1978, OLG Koblenz, 12 *Kritische Justiz* 193 (1979).

82. Due to the limited availability of trial court opinions, the above considerations are necessarily based on not more than a sample of cases.

83. See text at note 46 *supra.*

84. Decision of Feb. 17, 1982, OLG Celle, 35 NJW 1545 (1982).

85. The court cites unpublished judgments of other tribunals and distinguishes the case from judgment of Sept. 18, 1979, 75 BGHZ 160, 33 NJW 45 (1980). 35 NJW at 1546.

86. Decision of Jan. 30, 1985, OLG Celle, No. 1 Ss 126/84–10 Js 228/80 StA.

87. 35 NJW 1545 (1982).

88. For the final judgment, see 75 BGHZ 160, 33 NJW 45 (1980), see also text at note 49 *supra.* This case is relied upon in the judgment of Feb. 24, 1981, Landgericht Frankfurt (juvenile criminal chamber), No. 50 Js 29.138/79 Ns (confirming, with a modification, the sentence below). A juvenile with a record of persistent right-extremist activities, including a previous conviction, currently deputy chairman of the statewide "People's Socialist Movement of Germany" which wants the National Socialist Party restored, printed and distributed more than 1000 leaflets in which the "historical fact" (the court's words) of the mass extermination in gas chambers is denied; German and foreign professors are cited, and the allegation is made that thus far no witness has appeared to confirm a "gassing." The "provocative question" (the court's words) is posed: "What shall we do? We have no taste for lying." The Jewish Community of Frankfurt filed a petition. The court upheld the conviction but reduced the sentence from eight months to seven months and two weeks (suspended on good behavior) because the court below had mistakenly taken into account a previous conviction.

89. Judgment of Apr. 6, 1977, Landgericht Mainz, 11 *Kritische Justiz* 189 (1978). The defendant, a gardener, used the wall regularly for posting "radical-right" publications. *Id.* at 190.

90. Judgment of May 2, 1978, OLG Koblenz, 12 *Kritische Justiz* 193 (1979). This was a proceeding before the *Zivilsenat.* Here are court's principal arguments:

(1) The federal Supreme Court had held in a 1958 decision that the 30,000 Jews presently living in Germany and formerly persecuted by the Nazis formed a sufficiently defined group for the purposes of article 185. Decision of Feb. 28, 1958, 11 BGHSt 207; *see also* judgment of Apr. 21, 1961, 16 BGHSt 49, 57. Although the Supreme Court did not say so expressly, relatives of the persecuted persons were not included. The plaintiff, a student and the grandson of a Jewish grandfather who perished in Auschwitz, himself "not a Jew" and only a relative, did not belong to such a group. Moreover, the "arguments of the Supreme

Court are contradictory and thus do not persuade." 12 *Kritische Justiz* at 195.

(2) The defendant did not aim the insult expressly at the Jews and their relations but rather at all those, Jews and non-Jews, who denied the "Auschwitz lie"—and of these there were so many that they clearly could not be viewed as "a group."

(3) The very denial of the mass extermination by the defendant excluded any implication of his approval thereof.

(4) The question of the origin of "the lie" was left open in the leaflet—the beneficiaries of "the lie" were presumed to be "political or ideological groups," not necessarily Jews. The defendant rejected the charge of antisemitism and cheap-talk Goebbels propaganda; his purpose was to express his discontent with the official historiography and the postwar prevailing political conditions. The words "Zionist swindle" could not necessarily be attributed to all Jews ("not all Jews or Israelis are Zionists").

For a critical comment see Thomas Blanke in *Kritische Justiz*. BLANKE, *Anmerkung,* 12 *Kritische Justiz* 197 (1979). Blanke believes the above decision would be acceptable if it were based on a consistent liberal premise which, as a matter of principle, would exclude political controversy from the reach of the criminal judge. This, however, he feels has not been the case (citing NETTELBECK, *Meinungsäußerung und Tatsachenbehauptung: Ein Bericht über Einäugigkeit in der Zivilgerichtsbarkeit,* 11 *Kritische Justiz*. 135 (1978), because the protection of honor in both civil and criminal law has been manipulated in favor of the political right. BLANKE, *supra* at 198. He points out that if the Koblenz view were to be upheld, in the foreseeable future, when the last of the persecutees will have died, the Jews would again be exposed to "fascist incitement and pogrom campaigns." *Id.* at 199.

91. See text at note 49 *supra.*

92. Judgment of Sept. 18, 1979, 75 BGHZ 160, 161–663.

93. See text at notes 41–45 *supra.*

94. "The fate imposed upon them by National Socialism binds them into a unit which sets them off from the generality and its embodied in everyone who belongs to it." 75 BGHZ at 163 (with citation to earlier opinions).

95. Professor Edwin Deutsch sees here a new addition to private personal rights such as the right to one's own picture, own *Charakterbild* (against unauthorized psychological attempts), one's own life story. He is concerned about a possible extension of such "privatization." Is there a claim for damages for suffering? Can the right be attributed to other groups, such as minorities or refugees and expellees? He doubts it. DEUTSCH, *Anmerkung,* 33 NJW 1100 (1980); see also Judgment of May 8, 1952, BGH, 5 NJW 1183 (1952).

96. 75 BGHZ at 166. In a subsequent criminal proceeding the defendant was sentenced to one year's imprisonment under article 130. In a 1984 case, however, the Federal Supreme Court indicated that the principles enunciated in the above

opinion with respect to the denial of the mass murder of the Jews would not apply to the denial of other factual situations, such as the setting up of the Warsaw ghetto and the shooting of the inmates by the German occupation personnel. The court gave no reason for this observation. Judgment of Jan. 27, 1984, BGH, No. StR 866/83, at 4–5. In this case the Hamburg *Landgericht,* relying on the Federal Supreme Court's opinion in 75 BGHZ 160, *see* text at notes 88–96 *supra,* had held that a defense counsel who in his plea in another case had argued that the Warsaw ghetto was organized and the order to shoot was given by the Germans in an effort to stem a typhus epidemic, was guilty of an insult and of disparaging the memory of a decedent. The Federal Supreme Court quashed the conviction for the above and several other reasons and remanded for further proceedings. On remand the Hamburg court convicted the defendant again of the same crimes but increased the fine from 8100 to 8400 marks. Frankfurter Allgemeine Zeitung, Apr. 25, 1986, at 10, col. 5.

97. See text at note 86 *supra:* see also COBLER, *supra* note 15, at 166.

98. Bundesrat [BR] Drucksache [Dr.] 382/82, Sept. 29, 1982. This reason was recited in all subsequent proposals. It was as far back as 1979 that the Social Democratic Minister of Justice Hans-Jochen Vogel had called for stronger measures to deal with neo-Nazism and for closing legal loopholes. *The Week in Germany,* Nov. 28, 1979, at 5. See generally *Irrungen—Wirrungen: Der wechselhafte Gang des Gesetzgebungsverfahrens zum 21. Strafrechtsänderungsgesetz,* 1985 *Deutsche Richterzeitung* [DriZ] 225 [hereinafter *Der wechselhafte Gang*].

99. Sixty-six percent of all the right-extremist violations were of the neo-Nazi type; 936 cases (721 in 1980) involved smearing, pasting, and posting of placards; antisemitic tendencies were found in 323 violations, a rise from 263 in the previous year; there were 42 (49 in 1980) desecrations of Jewish cemeteries or places of worship. The membership in 73 right-extremist groups rose slightly from 19,800 to 20,300. The number of periodic publications rose from 85 to 98, although their circulation dropped by 1.2% to 324,000. *Verfassungsschutz* 1981, at 5, 21, 52 (Federal Minister of the Interior 1982). The Minister's report for 1982, at 5 (Federal Minister of the Interior 1983). An increase was also reported in left-extremist activities. *Verfassungsschutz* 1981, *supra,* at 6, 7. In the 1985 debate, Representative Lowack, a Christian Democrat, denied that there was an increase in neo-Nazi activity most recently or that there was a need for a new law. He nevertheless said he would vote for the new law as "a symbol of reconciliation." Bundestag [BT] 10 Wahlper., 135. Sitz., Apr. 25, 1985, at 10,086.

100. One of these modifications expanded the existing prohibition of the use and distribution of emblems of anti-constitutional organizations to include production, stocking, and import of such emblems. (There was at the time a sharp increase of imports of Nazi material from abroad.) The other change clarified the authority to confiscate left- and right-extremist writings even after the brief statute of limitations had precluded criminal prosecution. BR Dr. 382/82, Sept. 29, 1982, art. 1.

101. Art. 1 (4) in BR Dr. 382/82 would have added a new paragraph to article 140 of the Criminal Code. The punishment was to be imprisonment up to one

year or a fine. SCHMUDE, *supra* note 8, at 154–55. Article 131 does not apply, since a cruel and inhuman manner of description is not present, nor would article 130 cover such acts of mere denial. BR Dr. 382/82, at 12–14.

102. BT Dr. 9/2090, Nov. 10, 1982; *Der wechselhafte Gang, supra* note 98, at 227.

103. BR Dr. 158/83, Apr. 8, 1983.

104. *Der wechselhafte Gang, supra* note 98, at 227.

105. BR Dr. 10/891, Jan. 18, 1984.

106. BT 10. Wahlper., 67 Sitz., Apr. 12, 1984, at 4752–54; BT Dr. 10/1286, Apr. 11, 1984.

107. BR Dr. 10/1286 (annex 2–3).

108. Representative Schmidt (SPD) in BT 10. Wahlper., 67. Sitz., Apr. 12, 1984, at 4754.

109. BUBNOFF, *supra* note 3. A letter of the Evangelical Church addressed to the President of the Bundestag spoke of "an attack on our common existence." *Quoted* in BT 10. Wahlper., 135. Sitz., Apr. 25, 1985, at 10,080.

110. ESCHEN, *Das 21. Strafrechtsänderungsgesetz—eine stumpfe Waffe gegen den Rechtsradikalismus: Stellungnahme des Vorstandes des Republikanischen Anwaltsvereins zum Referentenentwurf eines 21. Strafrechtsänderungsgesetzes,* 16 *Zeitschrift für Rechtspolitik* 10 (1983) (statement of the board of the Association of Republican Attorneys); Münchner Merkur, *quoted* in *Der Tagesspiegel* (Berlin), Feb. 10, 1985, at 2, col. 5. By "justicable facts" are meant perhaps situations that are fit for adjudication by a court, presumably excluding disagreements over history.

111. Frankfurter Allgemeine Zeitung, Feb. 16, 1985, at 10, col. 2; Der Tagesspiegel, Feb. 20, 1985, at 8, col. 4; Der Tagesspiegel, Mar. 1, 1985, at 7, col. 1.

112. Der Tagesspiegel, Mar. 13, 1985, at 6, col. 3.

113. Der Tagesspiegel, Mar. 1, 1985, at 7, col. 1; Frankfurter Allgemeine Zeitung, Mar. 2, 1985, at 1, col. 1. In the same vein, see Badische Neueste Nachrichten (Karlsruhe), *quoted* in Der Tagesspiegel, Mar. 9, 1985, at 2, col. 5. For the criticism by the Bundesrat, *see* text at note 107 *supra.*

114. Chairman Leonardy of the *Deutscher Richterbund* (German Federation of Judges) on the Saar Radio, *quoted* in Der Tagesspiegel, Mar. 7, 1985, at 2, col. 3 (also quoting the deputy leader of the Social Democratic group in the Bundestag, former Justice Minister SCHMUDE); Der Tagesspiegel, Mar. 14, 1985, at 2. col. 2 (the chairman of the Jewish Community of Berlin); Der Tagesspiegel, Mar. 10, 1985, at 2, col. 5 (Central Council of Jews in Germany); Der Tagesspiegel, Mar. 16, 1985, at 2, col. 2.

115. Der Tagesspiegel, Mar. 14, 1985, at 2, col. 2. The Minister suggested in a later debate that this solution was considered under both of his Social Democratic predecessors. BT 10. Wahlper., 135. Sitz., Apr. 25, 1985, at 10,081–82. Deputy leader of the Social Democratic group Emmerlich declared to the press that the above idea was a "step in the direction" of the SPD demand for effective punishment of the "Auschwitz lie." Der Tagesspiegel, Mar. 14, 1985, at 2, col. 2.

116. BT 10. Wahlper., 12. Sitz., Mar. 14, 1985, at 9315–26. The SPD sought to have the House express a wish that the committee complete its work by April 25, 1985. *Id.* at 9326; Frankfurter Allgemeine Zeitung, Mar. 16, 1985, at 5, col. 4.

117. BT Dr. 10/3242, Apr. 24, 1985.

118. See notes 38–40, 88–97 *supra* and accompanying text.

119. See STGB art. 194 (2). The new text in fact amends article 194 (1) & (2).

120. BT Dr. 10/3242, Apr. 24, 1985, at 8–9.

121. *Id.* at 9. On "justiciable facts," see note 110 *supra.*

122. BT Dr. 10/3256, Apr. 24, 1985 (Social Democrats); BT Dr. 10/3255, 10/3260, Apr. 24, 1985 (Greens).

123. BT 10. Wahlper., 126. Sitz., Mar. 14, 1985, at 9315–26; 135. Sitz., Apr. 25, 1985, at 10,075–89; 136. Sitz., Apr. 26, 1985, at 10,122–24.

124. The FDP exceptions were Frau Dr. Hamm-Brücher, who voted for the SPD proposal, and Rep. Schäfer, who abstained. BT 10. Wahlper., 135. Sitz., at 10,086–89.

125. *Id.* at 10,086; Frankfurter Allgemeine Zeitung, Apr. 27, 1985, at 6, col. 4.

126. Frau Dr. Hellwig, BT 10. Wahlper., 135. Sitz., at 10,076–77. See also note 27 *supra.*

127. Rep. Mann (Greens Party), *id.* at 10,083.

128. *Id.* at 10,087 (Frau Dr. Hamm-Brücher).

129. BT 10. Wahlper., 126 Sitz., at 9321. Rep. Schmidt (SPD) claimed that the limitation to the genocide of Jews was not acceptable to the CDU group particularly because of the opposition of the expellees and Rep. Dregger, BT 10. Wahlper., 135. Sitz., at 10,081.

130. President Reagan's visit to a German military cemetery with, among others, graves of some *Waffen—SS* men. For the reference to Chancellor Kohl's speech, see BT 10 Wahlper., 135. Sitz., at 10,075–76, 10,078.

131. Rep. Schmidt (SPD), BT 10. Wahlper., 126 Sitz., at 9316; 135. Sitz., at 10,078–79; Minister Engelhard (FDP), BT 10. Wahlper., 126. Sitz., at 9320.

132. See note 100 *supra* and accompanying text.

133. See text at notes 121–22 *supra.*

134. BT 10. Wahlper., 135. Sitz., at 10,087–92. The SPD modifying proposal was defeated by 246 votes and 10 (nonvoting) Berlin Representatives (all of the CDU/CSU, all but 2 of the FPD, and 18 Greens) against 140 votes and 7 Berlin Representatives (all of the SPD and Dr. Hamm-Brücher, FDP), with 4 abstentions (3 Greens and one FDP). The proposal of the Greens was defeated by 229 and 9 Berlin Representatives against 156 votes and 8 Berlin Representatives, with three abstentions. See also Frankfurter Allgemeine Zeitung, Apr. 27, 1985, at 6, col. 4. The SPD text, BT Dr. 10/891, was also defeated by a majority vote. BT 10. Wahlper., 136 Sitz., at 10,122.

135. BT 10. Wahlper., 136 Sitz., at 10,124.

136. 1985 BGBl I 1965; see also 40 JZ (Gesetzgebungsdienst) 45 (1985).

137. According to the Legal Committee's report, an insult by a spoken word in private conversation is excluded (e.g., "beertable talk") but can be prose-

cuted on private petition as before, "since it only has meaning for the circle to which it was actually addressed." BT Dr. 10/3242, Apr. 24, 1985, at 10. This exclusion is criticized by Ministerialrat Vogelgesang who feels that the rationale for removing the prerequisite of a private complaint ("opening old wounds") applies equally to an insult in a private circle. VOGELGESANG, *Die Neuregelung zur sog. "Auschwitzlüge"—Beitrag Zur Bewältigung der Vergangenheit oder "widerliche Aufrechnung"?* 38 NJW 2386, 2388–89 (1985). "Making publicly accessible" does not require a public place, only a place that is accessible to an indeterminate number of persons who are not "personally linked" to the defendant. An "assembly" consists of any "significant number" of persons, and need not be open to the public. BT Dr. 10/3242, at 10.

138. Foreign groups are excluded. The term "group" is not defined. *Cf.* STGB art. 220a (implementing the United Nations Genocide Convention). The minority in the Legal Committee objected that the term could be interpreted as not encompassing resistance fighters or persecuted members of political parties. BT Dr. 10/342, at 10.

139. BT Dr. 10/3242, at 10.

140. *Id.*

141. Judgment of Sept. 18, 1979, 75 BGHZ 160, 33 NJW 45 (1980); see text at note 92 *supra;* see also judgment of May 8, 1952, BGH, 5 NJW 1183 (1952); Vogelgesang, *supra* note 137, at 2389.

142. Vogelgesang, *supra* note 137, at 2389. A new provision was also inserted into article 194 (2), which dispenses with the complaint requirement also when a deceased has lost his life as a victim of the Nazi or other violent dominance and the insult (disparagement of the memory of the deceased) is related to that fact. In that case the insult may be punished ex officio after the death of the victim. In other cases specified family members of the deceased have standing to lodge a petition. StGB art. 194 (2).

143. StGB art. 194 (2). The opposition is final and cannot be withdrawn.

144. It is clear from the cases discussed above that the statements of the "Auschwitz lie" are not directed at any particular person. In theory, at any rate, what will be the outcome if, in a prosecution instituted without a private complaint, one "insulted person . . . persecuted as a member of a group." StGB art. 94 (1), objects, but any other such "insulted person," or an organization of such persons, or for that matter the prosecutor himself insists that the proceeding should take its course?

145. KÖHLER, *Zur Frage der Strafbarkeit des Leugnens von Völkermordtaten,* 38 NJW 2389, 2390 (1985); Eschen, *supra* note 110, at 11.

146. OSTENDORF, *Im Streit: Die strafrechtliche Verfolgung der "Auschwitz-lüge,"* 38 NJW 1062, 1065 (1985) (pointing to GG art. 103).

147. COBLER, *supra* note 15, at 16; see also Leicht, *Die Lügner würden bleiben,* Süddeutsche Zeitung, Mar. 5, 1985, *reprinted* in 1985 DRIZ 199.

148. Frankfurter Allgemeine Zeitung, Apr. 27, 1985, at 12, col. 1.

149. LEICHT, *supra* note 147; Ostendorf, *supra* note 146, at 1063.

150. COBLER, *supra* note 15, at 167–68.

151. See MARQUA, *Dennoch: ein schlechter Kompromiss,* 1985 DRIZ 266; text at note 121 *supra.*

152. CORNELSEN, *Schreckliche Aufrechnung,* Frankfurter Rundschau, Apr. 18, 1985, *reprinted* in 1985 DRIZ 199.

153. See text at note 127 *supra;* see also JUNG, *Strafrechtliche Maßnahmen gegen die "Auschwitzlüge."* 26 *Juristische Schulung* 80 (1986). Although Prof. Dr. Jung sees some good in the "procedural solution," he believes that the inclusion of "other violent and arbitrary dominance" makes the principal purpose of the law "relative" and "could be (mis)understood in the sense of a 'setting-off-against mentality.' " He sees some difficulty with the requirement that the protected group must be part of the population at the time the criminal act occurred; and he regrets the loss of the prosecutor's discretion to deny public interest in the matter and refer it to the private complaint procedure. *Id.* at 80–81; see also BOEHLICH, *Wasch mir den Pelz, Titanic,* July 1985, at 26 (sharply critical of the new law).

154. VOGELGESANG, *supra* note 137, at 2388–89. The penalty for insult is imprisonment for up to one year (two years "if the insult is committed by a physical act") or a fine. StGB art. 185.

155. VOGELGESANG, *supra* note 137, at 2388 & n. 29. Vogelgesang lists StGB arts. 86, 86a, 90a, 130, 131, 140, 194 (2). Article 86, however, does mention specifically National Socialist organizations. It should be noted that before the new law article 194 (2) contained the general clause "violent and arbitrary dominance," to which the words "National Socialist or another" were added in the new law.

156. REISSMÜLLER, *Der Bertrug mit dem "Aufrechnen,"* Frankfurter Allgemeine Zeitung, June 18, 1985, at 1, col. 5.

157. See in this context *Dokumentation der Vertreibung der Deutschen aus Ostmitteleuropa* (4 vols.) (T. Schieder ed. 1953–57) (Federal Ministry for Expellees). The documents assembled and analyzed by a commission of historians deal with the forcible expulsion from the territories east of the Oder-Neisse line, Hungary, Rumania and Czechoslovakia. They suggest, for instance, that of the more than ten million Germans living east of the Oder-Neisse line in 1939, 2.15 million perished as a result of the war and the expulsion, 1.6 million of them in the process of expulsion. *Die Vertreibung der deutschen Bevölkerung aus den Gebieten östlich der Oder-Neisse* 158–59 (T. Schieder ed.) (Vol. I of *Dokumentation der Vertreibung der Deutschen aus Ost-Mitteleuropa*).

I received the following information from an official source after completion of this manuscript. "Dokumentation von an Deutschen begangenen Vertreibungsverbrechen" ("Documentation on Crimes Perpetrated against Germans in Connection with Their Expulsion") was prepared in 1974 for the information of the Federal Government; this documentation has been made available at the Federal Archives in Koblenz for use by scholars and publicists; beyond that, it is expected that the documentation will shortly become available in bookstores. This will in a certain way supplement the documentation prepared by T. Schieder, cited in the first paragraph of this footnote. Letter from G. Menke (Federal Ministry of the Interior) to Dr. R. Dolzer (Mar. 4, 1986).

158. See, e.g., the Czechoslovak Law 115, May 8, 1946, providing that acts occurring between 1938 and 1945, "designed to contribute to the struggle for regaining liberty by the Czechs and Slovaks or aimed at a just recompense for the acts of the occupants or their helpers, are not illegal even if they would be subject to penalty under the prevailing law." 1946 Sbírka zákonů a nařízení republiky Československé [Collection of Laws and Regulations of the Czechoslovak Republic] 922.

159. See especially text at note 129 *supra.*

160. Frankfurter Allgemeine Zeitung, July 5, 1985 at 5, col. 5.

161. See note 99 *supra.*

162. In his 1983 annual Report on the Protection of Constitution, the current Minister of the Interior, in contrast with his predecessors, deals with left-extremist activities ahead of right-extremist actions, devoting 94 pages to the first and 49 pages to the second category. *Verfassungsschutzbericht* 1983 (Federal Minister of the Interior 1984).

163. *Rechtsextremistische politische Einstellungen in der Bundesrepublik Deutschland,* in *Gewalt von rechts: Beiträge aus Wissenschaft und Publizistik* 207, 210, 218 (Federal Ministry of the Interior 1982) [hereinafter *Gewalt von rechts*] (poll by the Sozialwissenschaftliches Institut Nowak und Sörgel—SINUS). See in this context the medical profile of the defendant before the Frankfurt court, discussed at note 74 *supra.*

164. Reumann, *Studie über Rechtsextremismus—Fallen statt Fragen,* in *Gewalt von rechts, supra* note 163, at 221, 223–23 (reporting studies of the Institut für Demoskopie Allensbach).

165. *Infratest Wirtschaftsforschung GMBH, Politischer Protest in der Bundesrepublik Deutschland: Beiträge zur sozialempirischen Untersuchung des Extremismus* 19, 20 (1979). A 1987 poll conducted by the Allensbach Institute found eight percent " 'vehemently' antisemitic and an additional seven percent have 'a definite anti-Jewish attitude' " drawn in an above average way from older men above 60, people in the lower education and job strata, and rural population. Anti-Defamation League, New York, Press Release (undated).

166. Baum, *Vorwort,* in *Gewalt von rechts, supra* note 163, at 5, 5–6.

167. Judgment of Sept. 18, 1979, BGHZ 160, 166; see text at note 96 *supra.*

168. The suggestion that articles 130 and 131 be amended to remove any doubt of their applicability in this context, see Bubnoff, *supra* note 3, at 118–20, was not pursued.

169. 75 BGHZ 160, 161–63, see text at note 92 *supra.*

170. *Reprinted* in Frankfurter Allgemeine Zeitung, Apr. 27, 1985, at 2, col. 3.

171. Markham, *Bonn's President Seeking to Shift Guilt for Nazis from the Young.* Intl. Herald Tribune, June 26, 1985, at 9, col. 1 (referring particularly to the debate over President Reagan's visit to the Bitburg military cemetery).

172. In an opinion upholding the seizure of an antisemitic tract, the Federal Supreme Court held:

> When the legislature . . . expressly and especially protected the prohibition of arbitrary acts as a constitutional principle, it proceeded from the

> experience with the crimes of the National Socialist violent and arbitrary dominance. . . . But it is necessary to counteract even the beginnings of such occurrences, before new racial persecutions, in which violence and despotism appear under the guise of a law or an administrative act, again poison public life. Judgment of Feb. 28, 1959, 13 BGHSt 32, 37; see also 75 BGHZ 160, 161–63.

173. R. v. WEIZSÄCKER, *Zum 40. Jahrestag der Beendigung des Krieges in Europa und der Nationalsozialistischen Gewaltherrschaft 4* (Bundeszentrale für politische Bildung 1985). See in this context Vice-President Bush: "Our challenge today is to insist that time will not become the Nazis' friend . . . that time will not fade our sense of the specificity, of the uniqueness of the Holocaust . . . that time will not lead us to make the Holocaust into an abstraction." N.Y. Times, May 11, 1986, at E7, col. 1.

174. See text at note 89–96 *supra.*

175. *European Convention for the Protection of Human Rights, Collected Texts* 101 (Strasbourg 1978).

176. Application No. 9235/81, X. v. the Federal Republic of Germany, Decision of 16 July 1981 on the admissibility of the application, European Commission of Human Rights, 29 Decisions and Reports 194–204 (Dec. 1982). The above quotations are at 197–98.

177. *Ibid.* at 198–99.

178. *Ibid.* at 199.

179. In another case, a Belgian publisher was sentenced in Belgium to imprisonment and fine for publishing "A Letter to the Pope on Auschwitz" by L. Degrelle questioning the reality of the Holocaust and "relativising" Nazi atrocities. The sentence was based on a law barring persons who had been found guilty of endangering national security in wartime from *political* writing for the rest of their lives. Degrelle was condemned under this law. The defendant publisher claimed before the European Commission of Human Rights *i.a.* that the letter in question constituted a *historical* rather than political writing and that there were very few survivors of the atrocities. The Commission responded that the families continued to have the right to the protection of the memory of their parents and current events showed that anti-democratic ideologies similar to those that had inspired the atrocities have not disappeared in Europe. Relying on the second paragraph of Article 10 of the Convention, the Commission rejected the petition as manifestly ill-founded. Application No. 9777/82, T. v. Belgium, 14 July 1983, European Commission of Human Rights, 34 Decisions and Reports 158 (1983).

In the Decision on Application No. 11001/84 by Ditlieb Felderer against Sweden, 1 July 1985 (photo copy), the applicant (Austrian born Swedish journalist) was convicted by a Swedish court pursuant to the Freedom of Press Act for distributing publications with virulent antisemitic content including statements that the alleged killing of six million Jews was based on lies. The Commission of Human Rights declared his application, (based *i.a.* on art. 10 of the Convention) inadmissible, for reasons essentially similar to those stated in Decision on Application No. 9235/81, in the text above. On art. 10 as applied to distribution of race-hatred leaflets, see Applications No. 8348/78 and 8406/78, J. Glimmerveen and J. Hagenbeek v. the Netherlands, 11 Oct. 1979, 18 Decisions and Reports 187 (July 1980).

180. See text at note 2 *supra.* Although the protection of groups is not specifically mentioned in art. 10 (2) the Commission had no difficulty in assuming that group defamation was included See generally, J. A. FROWEIN and W. PEUKERT, *Europäische Menschenrechtskonvention,* EMRK KOMMENTAR, at 238–239 (1985).

181. See text at note 48 *supra.*

182. The Handyside Case, 24 Eur. Ct. H. R. (ser. A) (1976).

183. Lingens v. Austria, 103 Eur. Ct. H. R. 14 (ser. A) (1986). Compare this case with New York Times Co. v. Sullivan, 376 U.S. 254 (1964), note 194 *infra.*

184. Downs speaks of the "traditional 'quarantine policy' of the Anti-Defamation League and other major Jewish organizations . . . to ignore and avoid demonstration in the hope that it will pass away without causing disturbance and without attaining widespread publicity." D. A. DOWNS, *Nazis in Skokie* (1985) at 23. See discussion on the *The Utility of Suppression,* in F. SCHAUER, *Free Speech: A Philosophical Enquiry* 73–78 (1982).

185. See note 55 *supra.*

186. Only most recently has the "Holocaust revisionism" prompted a discussion among historians over how, or whether to respond. D. Lipstadt, a Holocaust scholar, was quoted as saying "you've got to expose these people rather than keep them under wraps" because of the danger of "relativizing" of the Nazi actions. BERNSTEIN, *Untwisting Revisionism on Holocaust,* N.Y. Times, June 21, 1988, p.11, col. 4.

187. Mel Mermelstein v. Institute for Historical Review et al., Superior Court of California, County of Los Angeles, C 356 542, Notice of Ruling, Oct. 19, 1981. The Court denied the defendants' request to take judicial notice.

188. *Ibid.,* Judgment of Aug. 5, 1985.

189. Mel Mermelstein v. Ditlieb Felderer (Docket no. C629224, filing date Dec. 17, 1986), reported in N.Y. Times, Jan. 18, 1986, p. 7, col. 4.

190. LEWIS, *The Individual Member's Rights to Recover for a Defamation Leveled at the Group,* 17 U. Miami L. Rev. 519 (1963); ARKES, *Civility and the Restriction on Speech: Rediscovering the Defamation of Groups,* 1974 The Supreme Court Review, 281, 283 (hereafter cited as Arkes); Nieman-Marcus v. Lait, 13 F.R.D. 311 (S.D.N.Y. 1952); on the earlier case law, see TANENHAUS, *Group Libel,* 35 Cornell Law Quarterly 261 (1950).

191. RIESMAN, *Democracy and Defamation: Control of Group Libel,* 62 Colum. L. Rev. 727, 745–50 (1942).

192. ARKES note 189 *supra* at 283–84, referring to Connecticut, Indiana, Massachusetts and West Virginia.

193. 343 U.S. 250 (1952). This was a five to four decision. The trial court refused to give a "clear and present danger charge" requested by the defendant

as well as evidence on the issue of truth. See also Chaplinsky v. New Hampshire, 315 U.S. 568 (1942), upholding a statute which prohibited offensive words in public places.

194. New York Times Co. v. Sullivan, 376 U.S. 254 (1964); on the "progeny" see LeBel, *Reforming the Tort of Defamation: An Accommodation of the Competing Interests within the Current Constitutional Framework,* 66 Neb.L.R. 249 (1987). See also Brandenburg v. Ohio, 395 U.S. 444 (1969).

195. Brandenburg v. Ohio, 395 U.S. 444 (1969).

196. Garrison v. Louisiana, 379 U.S. 64, 70 (1964).

197. 47 Ill. App. 2d 151 (1964).

198. "Here's some of the Things you Learn: . . . How to Hate Hitler and get people believing he killed six millions of us Jews even though we Jews are all over here living it upon dumb Christians." *Ibid* at 154. Ironically, the Illinois statute upheld in Beauharnais was repealed the same year by the Illinois legislature, although apparently not because of any question as to its legality. Arkes note 189 *supra,* at 287, note 20, at 326.

199. Collin v. Smith, 578 F. 2d 1197 (7th cir.), *cert. denied,* 439 U.S. 916 (1978); Village of Skokie v. National Socialist Party of America, 69 Ill. 2d 605, 373 N.E. 2d 21 (1978).

200. Smith v. Collin, 439 U.S. 916, 919 (1978). G. Gunther, *Constitutional Law* 1051–52 (11th ed. 1985). See generally L. C. Bollinger, *The Tolerant Society* 23–35 and *passim* (1986) (thereafter cited as Bollinger); A. Neier, *Defending My Enemy* (1979); Rosenfeld, *Extremist Speech and the Paradox of Tolerance,* 100 Harv. L.R. 1457 (1987).

201. Bollinger note 200 *supra,* at 15.

202. *Ibid.* at 28 and 29, with citations to the opinions.

203. "Congress shall make no law . . . abridging the freedom of speech or of the press. . ."

204. Bollinger, note 200 *supra,* at 88–89; Marshall, *On Learning to Love Vituperation,* 96 Yale L. J. 1687, 1696–97 (1987).

205. Bollinger, *ibid.* at 43–103.

206. *Ibid.* at 246. "The primary ingredient of this strategy is the idea that the people should be made to feel the suppression of speech is both unthinkable and unlikely to be successful and the judges should be led to think they have no choice but to protect the speech if the public should decide to suppress it." *Ibid.* at 100. See also Marshall note 204 *supra,* at 1697: "The story of important extremist speech is . . . that of the successful suppression of the Communist Party . . . , with judicial protection afforded only to inactive party members who were not shown to have spoken at all." Citing People v. Ruthenberg, 229 Mich. 315, 201 N.W. 358 (1924), *writ of error dismissed,* 273 U.S. 782 (1927). See also e.g. Dennis v. United States, 341 U.S. 494 (1951) upholding the conviction under a federal statute of Communist Party organizers by applying the "clear and present danger test" exception to the First Amendment protection. But see Blasi, *The Checking Value in First Amendment Theory,* 1977 Am. Bar Fdntn. Res. J. 521; Blasi, *The Teaching Function of the First Amendment,* 87 Colum. L. R. 387 (1987).

207. Bollinger, note 200 *supra,* at 120.

208. Schneider, *Rights Discourse and Neonatal Euthanasia,* 76 Cal. L. Rev. 151, 154 (1988).

209. *Hate Groups in America, A Record of Bigotry and Violence,* New Revised Edition, Anti-Defamation League of B'nai B'rith, New York, 1988 at 1.

210. *Ibid.*

211. *Neo-Nazi Activity Is Arising among U.S. Youth,* N.Y. Times, June 13, 1988, p. 10, col. 1–6.

212. *Holocaust "Revisionism": A Denial of History—An Update,* ADL Facts, Vol. 31, No. 1, Winter 1986, at 1, Anti-Defamation League of B'nai B'rith, New York.

213. Riesman, *Democracy and Defamation: Control of Group Libel,* 42 Colum. L.R. 727, 727 n. 6.

214. D.A. Strauss, *Why Be Tolerant?* 53 Chicago L.R. 1485, at 1504 (1986); for a Canadian criticism, see Lando, Book Review, 45 U. Toronto Fac. L. R. 187 (1987). For reference to the international conventions, see note 27 *supra.* See generally, Debate, *Freedom of Speech and Holocaust Denial,* 8 Cardozo L. R. 559–94 (1987).

215. 578 F. 2d 1197 (7th Cir.) at 1207 (1978). See also 69 Ill. 2d 605 at 618–19 (1978).

216. See quotation in the text at note 92 *supra.*

217. *Note—A Communitarian Defense of Group Libel Laws,* 101 Harv. L. Rev. 682, 683 (1988).

218. Schneider, *Rights Discourse and Neonatal Euthanasia,* 76 Cal. L. Rev. 151, 163 (1988). Sherry, *An Essay Concerning Toleration,* 71 Minn. L. R. 963 (1987), discussing Bollinger's theory.

219. Sherry, *ibid.* at 964 and *passim.*

On the "Auschwitz Lie"—Correspondence

In the November 1986 issue of the *Michigan Law Review,* Professor Eric Stein addressed the then-recent German legislation prohibiting the "Auschwitz lie."[1] The "Auschwitz lie" refers to contemporary attempts to deny the historical truth of the Holocaust. In an extended analysis of the 1985 legislation criminalizing such attempts to deny historical fact, Professor Stein revealed the contradictory impulses motivating restrictions on free speech. He reported that the most controversial aspect of the legislation was the question whether the criminalization of the denial of the Holocaust should be extended to cover the denial of other actions, such as the violent expulsion of Germans from Soviet-occupied East Germany—in other words, whether or not the Holocaust was a unique phenomenon. His examination of the legislative history and of decisions applying the predecessors of the 1985 Act suggested that the goals of the Act, the rules of standing it establishes, the ways in which it defines harm, and the time limits for its enforcement presented problematic issues for German constitutional scholars, for lawyers and judges, and for the German people as well.

In the time since his article was published, Professor Stein has corresponded with several European scholars on the issues raised by the 1985 legislation. That correspondence, though brief, highlights the contentious aspects of Professor Stein's analysis; it suggests that the issues of restricting "historical speech," promoting national consciousness, attributing collective guilt, and identifying the role of courts in punishing historical lies remain troublesome to German intellectuals. Excerpts from Professor Stein's correspondence follow.

Letter from Professor Herbert A. Strauss[2]

Your comprehensive study of the recent "Twenty-first Law Modifying the Criminal Law" passed by the Bundestag of the German Federal Republic on June 13, 1985, places the daily detail of the legal processes surrounding the treatment of the "Auschwitz lie" in German courts into a welcome perspective. Since I have been appointed director of the new "Center for Research on Antisemitism" at the Berlin Technical University in 1982, I have been following the debate surrounding this issue as closely as a layman would in my position. I am a historian of modern Germany, and of Jewish Zeitgeschichte [contemporary history].

Permit me some observations of a nonlegal nature on one or two of the issues reported by you on the general situation in Germany. At one point, you comment on the absurdity that lawyers and judges still apply law handed down from the Nazi period. Here, you point to a paradox that seems to me inherent in legal forms of thinking: German law commentaries still reproduce decisions seen as precedents that were handed down during the Third Reich, including some of the language then in use. Given this fact—I have hit on it when I had to look up a law book on associations—I seriously question whether a law, however well intentioned, is an effective vehicle in dealing with the political problems left behind by the criminal regime of the Third Reich, and by its survivals or revivals in contemporary political culture. Although I happen to have come to the conclusion, since working here, that the German constitution works and is accepted by the vast majority of Germans too young to have known the previous regime, I am equally convinced that the genocidal process that led to Auschwitz and the unique mass murder of the Jewish people has not been adequately integrated into a critical view of German history by intellectuals and public opinion alike. Since you completed your piece, the world had to witness a heated debate among German historians at whose core lay an attempt by the Berlin historian Ernst Nolte to relieve the burden of shame and responsibility felt by many liberal Germans about the Holocaust, and to point either to alleged Jewish actions—actions by Jews—and to the Soviet liquidation of the kulaks or the gulag concentration camps as "logical" or "historical" precedents of the Holocaust. It is unclear and precise information is lacking about how widely his views have been accepted: prominent historians had no difficulties proving his facts wrong, but establishment papers like the "Frankfurter Allgemeine Zeitung" have supported what they see as the underlying motive of his stance, to wit the perception that German youth can only reacquire a virile national consciousness if it sees the Nazi genocide as part of the "civil war" of the twentieth century, and thus as part of a universal historical process. This view is, of course, diametrically opposed to the positions taken by Bundespräsident Richard von Weizsäcker in the historic speech before the Bundestag delivered on May 8, 1985, and quoted by you. It would seem to me that even the best of laws making the "Auschwitz lie" offense an *Offizialdelikt* (subject to compulsory prosecution by the state attorneys) must, by the very nature of legal procedure and thinking, fail to speak to this most important juncture in German political culture.

Letter from Professor Dr. Ernst Nolte[3] (I)

Please accept my sincere thanks for your kind letter of June 4, 1987, and for sending me your article in the *Michigan Law Review.* You have chosen one of the most sensitive themes that exist in present-day Germany. The fullness of the examples and cases which you have found allows in any case a better-grounded judgment formation and makes the motives of the legislature more understandable. But I experience a great uneasiness about this law now, as I did before. It would be absurd to pass a law threatening punishment of whoever denies the existence of Napoleon; and it would be unbearable to decree by law that Napoleon won at Aspern (for one can have a different opinion about this, and generally it is assumed that there was a draw). The case of the German law reposes somewhere in the middle, but isn't it already quite questionable that only a German law is in question? The existence of gas chambers has been denied also by certain authors in England, France and the United States; does there exist a similar extraordinary law in those countries? Can a denial of a historical fact ever constitute an attack on human dignity of any person or any group? Is an Armenian really hurt in his human dignity when a Turk questions the existence of a genocide? Where should one draw the line between a simple expression of opinion and scientific research which obviously may err, and in fact must err, if new ways are to be explored? Could it consequently one day become punishable if somebody brings into connection Auschwitz and the Gulag Archipelago or cites the statement by Weizmann from the beginning of September, 1939? I therefore am inclined to think that the law was "bad," but your careful and balanced presentation makes it clear that those who consider it "good" are also able to offer weighty reasons.

My book will not be published in London but rather in Berlin and namely by Propyläen-Verlag under the title "The European Civil War, 1917–1945: National Socialism and Bolshevism." I had great difficulties with the publication that surely were connected with the "dispute of the historians." I am enclosing a copy (unfortunately a bad one) of an annotated biography which recently appeared in the periodical "Liberal."

Letter from Professor Dr. Ernst Nolte (II)

When a scholar answers another scholar's question that lends itself to scholarly treatment, he is basically always speaking to the public. A difficulty may arise only from the fact that he may not formulate his answer in his correspondence with only one colleague as carefully as he would in a publication. Nevertheless, rereading my letter of June 25 I have the impression that I, therein, raised several questions that might promote discussion. . . .

I write without having answered your kind letter which I found waiting for me in the beginning of October upon my return from a rather long vacation. This letter gave me a new cause for reflection. In short, and using a term I also used in the "Historikerstreit" (dispute of historians), I today am inclined to express my view as follows:

Every type of attribution of collective guilt, *i.e.,* of accusation against a group which is not constituted solely by free agreement of individuals, should be penalized. The penalty should be the most severe, if a group which experienced extreme suffering through genocidal intentions and measures (like "the Jews") is blamed for these very measures or rather for the alleged invention of such measures which, according to this thesis, in reality have not taken place ("group defamation").

No type of constraint of scientific inquiry and research is permissible, not even if the generally assumed numbers of victims of the "Holocaust" are drawn into question or even the fact of the intended and organized mass extinction by gassing is denied by arguments and findings. In that case, the majority of the "scientific community," insofar as it is competent, would have to refute the minority or the outsider conclusively through compelling arguments and incontestable factual proof. The fact cannot be denied that it would be hard to draw a sharp line between the "functionalists" and possible "scientific propagandists." This, however, may not be accepted as an argument for the prevention of free research. The "majority opinion" among scientific scholars must be formed in a scientific way, and every intervention of the judiciary power has to be rejected.

The "Historikerstreit" continues, and since my book has just been published, it might even gain new strength.

Letter from Helge Grabitz[4]

I want to thank you most sincerely for your interesting article about the "Auschwitz-lie" and for your friendly letter of June 4.

I was very impressed by your objective, balanced way of presenting the problems of Art. 194 of the Criminal Code and the complex questions connected with it.

I am of the view that "Auschwitz is unique" and for that reason the additional clause "or any other violent and arbitrary dominance" should have been eliminated; this addition is ahistorical and makes the holocaust, which is "an unparalleled crime," unjustifiably relative. What is more, the memory of the killed victims and the witnesses who today still live among us are offended by this juxtaposition: A grotesque result in view of the fact that this global insult is placed in the Criminal Code provision concerning the insult [defamation]. . . .

Letter from Professor Dr. Christian Meier [5]

I found your article highly interesting; a lot of what you gathered in it was new to me. I also consider your piece very useful. To the extent that you take specific positions, I agree with you entirely: especially at the end where you speak of the "delicate balance" that must be found, since on the one hand the memory of the Nationalist Socialist crimes must be kept alive while on the other hand, the self-consciousness of those who come after must not be made unbearable so as to cause a backlash. I am also persuaded by your estimate of a "modest contribution" that the courts may offer in this area.

You would certainly want to know in some detail where I stand on the issues raised. I shall articulate my position briefly. I consider the transformation of the "insult" into a crime to be prosecuted *ex officio* as necessary, of course only with respect to the victims of the National Socialist regime. The extension to other groups, particularly to the Germans expelled [from the areas which were given to Poland] was obviously an act of juxtaposition, whatever some others may say. One should not try a cover-up; every one can see it with open eyes. I see no reason for it, certainly not on the merit (no one would think of denying that terrible event), nor was it necessary (contrary to Vogelsang) from the viewpoint of the legal system. In my view, these reasons do not apply where the question clearly is one of a practical, urgent assistance to certain groups of victims who should be spared as much as possible the burden of instituting a criminal proceeding (and of all that is connected with it). Any juxtaposition strikes me as bad above all because—apart from the wretchedness of the attempts to set off the suffering of the German victims against the suffering of the Holocaust victims—in my judgment the criminal law measures against the "Auschwitz lie" can be justified only by the uniqueness of the German crimes during the National Socialist period. In principle I cannot approve of placing any historical fact under the protection of courts. And I must admit that I am particularly struck in my heart of hearts when the "right" holds it against me that one cannot tell "the truth" about Auschwitz without being hailed before a judge. I propose flatly to challenge any false allegations about the NS crimes, any attempts to deny, diminish or set them off against other crimes. But the reference to a judge causes me some embarrassment. I manage, however, to overcome that feeling as well, since there are sufficient grounds for the pertinent legislation and for the holdings of the Federal Supreme Court. All this—and I do not want to raise any doubt about it—is necessary. But it makes one feel uncomfortable.

I—and others—must put up with this uneasiness. It is not worth talking about in comparison with the suffering under the circumstances of those whom these provisions are designed to protect. But it also shows—and I want to offer my own personal experience as an example—that in principle it is not good for a democratic country to protect historical facts by criminal law. This therefore must remain an exception. It can find its justification only in the uniqueness of the NS crime.

It means, on the other hand: the safeguarding of the truth about the Holocaust must be left to historians, but also to politicians and even to the entire society. For the moment, this is not such a great problem since the liars, respectively the deniers, are in a minority. But it requires great vigilance and a lot of tact. The growing distance in time and the ever increasing progression of generations render difficult any recollection that should not be reduced to a ritual. What it means to be a German after 1945 is hardly clear—even to the majority of the Germans. There are evasions everywhere: they are understandable, one must admit. In my small volume, . . . I have enumerated several reasons why we Germans find ourselves in a "disproportionate" position in relation to all others as a result of the continuing worldwide remembrance of Auschwitz. It is unavoidable, but on the other hand, in the long run it could heavily burden the "delicate balance" described by you at the end of your piece. Why should children, and above all, the children's children of the perpetrators in such a bad world, be still made to feel responsible for the evil deeds of their parents and grandparents—why should they still be treated differently from those with whom they would rather like to feel equal? When one then hears reproaches from abroad—understandable as they may be from that viewpoint—that is not easy to bear.

Whatever errors were made at Bitburg, and there were many, the various conclusions drawn from them by American east coast newspapers were very unjust. (Parenthetically, Bitburg shows how even Federal Chancellor Kohl at that time entirely misjudged the dimensions of the event: After the act of conciliation in Verdun with President François Mitterand, he meant to do the same with Reagan: he obviously knew nothing about the difference between the First and Second World War. What then should the broad strata of the entire population think?

By the way, Helmut Kohl has learned his lesson since then (see my "40 Jahre nach Auschwitz," p. 69 n.26).)

In short, to conclude, here lie heavy burdens for the future which no court will be able to help alleviate. It will take a great deal of courage and tact and spiritual power, on the one hand not only to maintain alive the memory but also to take due account of the given reality of the worldwide remembrance of Auschwitz (which is also deeply anchored in Germany), and on the other hand to avoid injuring thereby the self-consciousness of the Germans living today.

Actually, one ought to be able to draw certain self-confidence from the forty years of a successful democracy and the almost thirty years of the appreciable public awareness of the full dimension of the crimes. For the one and the other are—despite the great deficiencies—without doubt significant positive items in the balance sheet of the Federal Republic. But then one sees again returning the signs of the old nationalism, the old bewilderment from the period immediately following 1945, the defense mechanisms arising from guilt feelings, innumerable repressions, and other factors designed to prevent many from facing the truth, the truth about the period from 1933 to 1945 and, on the positive side, the truth about the work of the Federal Republic in maintaining the memory.

Just now I am preparing a new, thoroughly revised edition of my book and the opening address for the session of historians in Bamberg in which I must deal with the "historians' dispute" of the last two years. Thus these lines should be sufficient for today.

Notes

1. Stein, *History against Free Speech: The New German Law against the "Auschwitz"—and Other—"Lies,"* 85 MICH. L. REV. 277 (1986).

2. Professor, Department of History (emeritus), City College of New York; Director, Center for Research on Antisemitism, Technical University, Berlin, Germany.

3. Faculty of History, Free University, Berlin. This letter and all the letters that follow are translated from the German by Professor Stein.

4. Senior Prosecuting Attorney.

5. Universität München, Institut für alte Geschichte.

Excerpts from *Czecho/Slovakia: Ethnic Conflict, Constitutional Fissure, Negotiated Breakup*

In this last item of Part 3 I describe my links to the late Czechoslovakia and the origins of my book on the post-Communist Czech-Slovak constitutional negotiations. For the book I drew mostly on primary sources including close to a hundred interviews. In addition to the constitutional issues, I sought to capture the evolving political and social scene as well as the personal stories of the principal players. The input of the international advisory group, of which I was a member, if not my own inclination, assured a strong comparative perspective with emphasis on American and West European legal orders.

I sought to provide as broad a context for the "case study" as I felt qualified to offer. Hence the introductory sections in the book on nationalism, sources of ethnic conflict, general criteria for a negotiation process, and theory of federalism. The questions raising some of these themes and the concluding part in which I suggest some responses are reproduced here.

A few words about the developments after the completion of the manuscript in early 1996. In November 1997, after some three years of financial stability and positive macroeconomic data, the minority government of the quarreling center-right coalition was forced to resign amid charges of financial irregularities in the prime minister's party. A sharp deterioration in the economy came as a surprise to the people, misled by the prime minister's boast that the travails of the transition were over. The legacy of an imperfect and incomplete privatization, a severe crisis in the banking and judiciary systems, abuse of the newly opened "economic space," the declining value of the currency, the expected rise in unemployment, and the attitude toward the Roma (gypsy) minority threw a shadow on the short-term future. However, the Parliament began to fill in the regulatory gaps by setting up a Securities Commission and debating a new banking law. The state's shares in the major banks were offered for sale and some austerity measures applied. President Havel, just back from the hospital

---

Reprinted from CZECHO/SLOVAKIA: ETHNIC CONFLICT, CONSTITUTIONAL FISSURE, NEGOTIATED BREAKUP, xix–xx, 1–3, 301–41 (Ann Arbor, University of Michigan Press, 1997).

after a serious illness, presided over the political development that took place in accordance with the established constitutional procedure. A Social Democrat minority government replaced the center-right coalition. The Czech Republic has been found qualified for inclusion in the "first wave" of the states to be admitted to NATO and the European Union.

As for Slovakia, the reader of this chapter will readily discern the clues for the reasons why the young republic was not included in the first contingent of candidate states.

Preface

I was born and raised in Czechoslovakia and graduated from the Charles University Law Faculty in Prague. On the raw morning of March 15, 1939, I awoke at the usual hour in the barracks of the 28th Prague Infantry Regiment where I was doing my military service. Looking out of the window, I saw the courtyard below teeming with gray uniforms and vehicles. The Czech officer on night duty did not bother to wake us before the arrival of the advance unit of the German army of occupation. I was directed to accompany a German noncommissioned officer with an escort on his search for concealed weapons in the barracks. Whenever we encountered a portrait of President Beneš, the Germans smashed it to smithereens. That was my last act of army duty. I was told to go home. I left the country not long thereafter for the United States, another legal training, another (the U.S.) army, and some nine fascinating years in the U.S. Department of State.

I revisited Prague 43 years later, in 1982—arriving by one of those baffling coincidences that defy explanation one day before the fiftieth reunion of my high school (gymnasium) class, which was attended by 15 of the 21 graduates. Their compelling stories took me through the Nazi occupation, the wartime, the brief return of the "second" democratic Republic in 1945–48, the Communist takeover of 1948, the Stalin-directed trials of leading Communists in the early 1950s, the "Prague spring" of 1968, and the subsequent re-Stalinization after the invasion by Warsaw Pact forces. Of all the gymnasium graduates, those who had chosen law had fared worst. The most talented one, because he came from a long established bourgeois family of lawyers, ended up as a lowly clerk in a government corporation after a stint at a construction site. Another found refuge in the transportation department of the Prague General Prosecutor's Office after returning, in 1945, from a concentration camp. One Law Faculty graduate, a convinced Communist since his adolescent days, became a successful documentary filmmaker but after 1968 was reduced to dubbing foreign films into Czech. Still another made a meager living as a "black market" purveyor of legal advice. A promising classics scholar was dismissed from his posts at the university and academy because of his kinship with the finance minister in the First Republic; his mother took him as a young boy to the funeral of the minister—the only connection with this relative. He ruined his eyesight working in a sandpit.

I returned again in 1985 and left with a firm determination never to come back to a country so grievously torn from its Western roots by a regime that, although it no longer relied on physical torture or faith in an ideology, reposed on a demoralizing combination of assured economic security (at the price of a low living standard) and pervasive surveillance. Although almost everyone criticized the government in private, there were few outward signs of dissent beyond reports of the courageous few, some 1,200 in number, who signed the Charter 77. That document, authored principally by Václav Havel in 1977, exhorted the Communist government to abide by its international obligations for the protection of human rights.

In the closing years of the Communist regime, a handful of American lawyers established contact with Czech and Slovak dissidents and provided them with a variety of support. Professor Herman Schwartz of the American University in Washington, D.C., went to Prague under the auspices of Helsinki Watch to monitor the criminal trial of Václav Havel and wrote a brief on his behalf.

In a startling turn of events, the same dissidents became leading actors in the government that emerged from the November 1989 revolution. It was not surprising for these leaders to suggest, building on the previous contacts, that the Americans provide assistance in the preparation of a new federal constitution by making available Western constitutional experiences from which the country had been cut off for 40 years. In response to this suggestion, a small international advisory group was organized and I was asked to become a member. This call—for better or for worse—made me return to Central Europe despite my earlier vow never to come back, and it was the origin of *Czecho/Slovakia: Ethnic Conflict, Constitutional Fissure, Negotiated Breakup.*

* * *

A Framework

1. The Questions

I have written this book in the twilight of my professional career. It is in one respect a record of an episode in the ageless learning process, a story of a lawyer's brush with contemporary nationalism, and his effort to grasp the elusive underpinning of that complex phenomenon. It centers on the clusters of people in former Czechoslovakia because of strong personal reasons — and also because I thought that the failed search for a constitutional framework in that country, one of the troubled "ethno-territorial"[1] groupings in Western and Eastern Europe, merited an inquiry.

I began writing on this subject in late 1990, about a year after the "negotiated revolution" of November 1989.[2] In a rare moment of their history, the Czechs and Slovaks were in a position to determine their future course freely and without outside dictation. It was my hope, if not expectation, that they would write a new federal constitution based on constitutionalism, democracy, and a free economy as vowed by Václav Havel, a leading dissenter from the old regime and the first post-Communist president of the country. By mid-1991, the common state was given a fifty-fifty chance by those privy to the constitutional negotiations. The prospect of its survival plunged when an apparent agreement reached in February 1992 was rejected in the Presidium of the Slovak National Council and it was further reduced by the outcome of the national elections of June 1992. The federation was terminated on December 31, 1992.

Czecho/Slovakia is idiosyncratic and more personal than is commonly expected from an academic study. It is written from a point of view determined largely by my experience. Without a point of view, the story would amount to a heap of unrelated happenings. Václav Havel's role is a thread running through the account. This might create a false impression of his actual influence on the course of events. In fact, the leader's clarion call faded into the voice of a Greek chorus at an early stage. Wherever possible I have the principal actors speak in their own words, but I make no pretense of "nonjudgmental" objectivity. For one thing, it is impossible to exhaust the mass of available sources so that the selection process, even with the best of intentions, is more or less arbitrary. Moreover, some of the crucial materials relating to the final phases of the negotiations are still sealed. Second, I do not delude myself into believing that I could completely transcend my biases, no matter how hard I tried. I have heard it said that a fact becomes history only when set in a chronological context. For that reason, subject to some exceptions, my study follows chronological order.

Within these parameters, the book should throw some light on a number of issues of more general import even though it cannot offer any complete answers:

- What is the source of ethnic conflicts? Is it, in the words of the American sociologist Donald L. Horowitz, "cultural differences," "ignorance or realistic divergence of interests"?[3] What is the impact of the structure and the individual actors on efforts to reach a settlement of such conflicts?
- What are the prospects for democratic multiethnic policies in an ethnically divided grouping? Why do territorially based ethnic groups choose secession or consensual separation even at the price of a substantial loss, and what makes for peaceful rather than violent separation? Is there anything new to be said about the immanent dilemma that has baffled international lawyers and diplomats, between assertions of self-determination up to secession on one hand and the integrity and "sovereignty" of states on the other? What, if any, is the role of the international community in the self-determination process and what forms for the expression of the wishes of "the peoples" are required or appropriate? Do differences in the perception of "sovereignty" or "international personality" matter?
- What institutional form offers the most promise to contain a specific ethnic conflict in given circumstances: a federation (the American or modern German variant), a "confederation," or a more complex arrangement with confederate and powersharing ("consociation") elements? Why do federations generally prosper in the West but wane not only in Africa and Asia but in Central-Eastern-Southern Europe as well? More specifically, does federalism fail in multiethnic societies in which the component units consist of different ethnic groups organized on a territorial basis? Would some of the multiethnic Western federations (Belgium, Canada) hold if exposed to a multilayered shock comparable to the 1988–91 revolutions and transformations?
- Is there a need for novel, more flexible regimes that would satisfy the demand of "a people" for self-determination, particularly in terms of participation in the international arena, and thus avoid a further fragmentation of the international system? Or is such a fragmentation a natural—and desirable—way toward a world (or

specifically Europe) of "regions" and more or less loose functional associations?

- What particular features characterize the interaction between constitution making and the political, economic, and societal transformation to a democratic, market economy system in an atmosphere of ethnic tension?
- Why are there such striking differences in attitudes toward the scope and the degree of flexibility of constitutional documents and the role of constitutions in a society?
- Can an ethnic conflict be bridged by constitution writing? In what way are post-Communist constitutional negotiations influenced by the institutions, the emergent political party system, special interest groups, the churches and religious organizations, the interests of the elites, personal ambitions of the leaders, mass media, public opinion, international developments, and legal experts? What are the respective roles of the executive and legislatures? How do these negotiations interact with the action on "quasi-constitutional issues" such as electoral legislation, status of central banks, and regulation of media?[4] What is the role of symbols such as the name of the country and its flag? What is the impact of legal training and thinking? Does "law" matter?
- Does an analysis of the tactics and strategies offer some insights for a methodology of negotiations?
- What is the impact on the negotiations of foreign consultation, foreign institutional models, and the comparative legal method? Can a foreign lawyer free himself from the bias of his cultural and educational background so as to be able to offer useful advice?

Notes

1. Robert J. Thompson and Joseph R. Rudolf Jr., "The Ebb and Flow of Ethnoterritorial Politics in the Western World," in J.R. Rudolf Jr. and R.J. Thompson (eds.), Ethnoterritorial Politics, Policy, and the Western World 1, 2 (Lynne Rienner Pub., Boulder and London, 1989), using "ethnoterritorial" to indicate "various political movements and conflicts that are derived from a group of people . . . having some identifiable geographic base within the boundaries of an existing political system."

2. President Havel prefers the term "negotiated revolution" to "velvet revolution," a term allegedly invented by Rita Klímová, the first ambassador to Washington of the now defunct Czech and Slovak Federative Republic. The revolutions in Hungary and Poland, for instance, were just as "velvety" as in former Czechoslovakia.

3. Donald L. Horowitz, Ethnic Groups in Conflict xii (University of California Press, Berkeley, Los Angeles, London, 1985). In this section I rely heavily on this important treatise.

4. Jon Elster, "Making Sense of Constitution-Making," 1 East Eur. Cons. Rev. 15, 17 (1992).

* * *

An Overview: Some Answers and Some Reflections at the End of the Day

1. Sources of Ethnic Conflict and Causes of Separation

In the opening pages of *Czecho/Slovakia,* I quoted Donald L. Horowitz's question about the source of ethnic conflicts: is it "cultural difference" or "ignorance or realistic divergence of interests?" I would conclude from the Czech and Slovak story that both cultural differences and ignorance are indeed the core of the conflict and the cause of the separation—along with significant subsidiary factors closely connected with, if not actually derived from, the cultural differences. I shall return to the divergence of interests promptly.

a. The Primary Cause

In the second chapter of *Czecho/Slovakia* I dealt with the relationship between the Czechs and Slovaks within the framework of three broad categories of environmental, historical, and social conditions. These conditions, I have suggested, formed the underpinning of the interests, real or perceived, of the two components of the Federation in their relationship with each other as well as with the federal state. The relative harmony or disharmony of these interests determined the position of the federal state on an imaginary continuum between an ideal symmetrical model and "a complete conflict potential" of the asymmetric model. My analysis disclosed significant similarities between the Czechs and the Slovaks, such as an almost identical language and similar living standards, but important differences as well, first and foremost a diverse history that exposed them to profoundly divergent influences. Both peoples experienced the evolution of the nationalist idea from the revival of folklore and the local language to the formulation of nationalist ideologies and a political movement.[1] In this development, however, due to the oppressive Hungarian regime, the Slovaks remained some half a century behind the Czechs, and this caused a distorted, almost colonial, type of relationship with the Czechs at the time of the formation of the first Czechoslovak Republic in 1918. The perception of the Czech dominance reinforced by the two-to-one Czech population majority, continued in some sectors of the Slovak society during subsequent decades, culminating in the fatal events of 1939 when German power destroyed the Republic and sponsored a separate Slovak state, and again after 1948 when a reunited Czechoslovakia became a part of the Soviet empire. The situation prevailing after the collapse of the Communist regime has been vividly described by a noted Slovak writer:

> A Czech with an average education knows nothing about Slovakia. He does not read Slovak literature, nor does he get around to Slovak papers. . . . Vacation outings to Slovakia are equally fruitless as regards getting to know the nation. . . . A Czech has the feeling of civilizational superiority and is not aware of the basic things that burden our life. The Slovak nation has an entirely different mentality . . . a different historical experience, it finds itself in an entirely different economic, political, and cultural situation. As long as the Czech citizen fails to take these matters into account, he will live together with an unknown nation without understanding its complexes. The Slovaks are a minority nation in the Republic, and are hypersensitive to Czech ignorance and nationalism. That is not the only one, but one of the principal reasons of the contemporary crisis.[2]

This statement illuminates the factors of ignorance, *ressentiment,* and "contempt" leading to the divergence of interests, even though in my judgment it overstates the weight of the actual differences in the conditions prevailing in 1989. However, the statement correctly recognizes the existence of other, albeit unspecified, factors, which I shall identify in the following section. I should signal that some of these factors, although often intertwined with the past, emerged only after the collapse of the Communist regime.

b. Subsidiary Factors

i. Structure and "Heroes"

Two structural barriers are readily identified as having contributed to the breakup. One was the inherent fault of a Federation composed of only two component units in which demands for parity ran sharply counter to the significant disparity in the size of their populations. The other was the Communist Constitution, which, although amended, remained in force and proved largely dysfunctional in the new setting.

Related but distinct were several subjective factors: the insistence on "continuity" and "constitutionality" of the process of change, the lack of understanding of federalism and the absence of the minimal trust required for its working, the lack of political experience of the actors, and the fatigue from the exhausting constitutional negotiations.[3]

However, perhaps the most important subsidiary factor was the massive structural change in the political system that began shortly after the first free elections in 1990 and was completed by the 1992 elections. The post-1989 federal political structure disintegrated and new power bases emerged in the two Republics with radically different constellations of political forces and leaders. Some of the political elites in both Republics, but notably in Slovakia, stirred and exploited nationalist feelings with a significant impact on the constitutional discourse. This development also had its roots in the "primary cause," the cultural differences.

What of the fascinating dichotomy between "the structure" and the individual actors and their acts of will? In Friedrich Nietzsche's world of disconnected individuals, it is the heroes or villains, rather than the structure, that determine the outcome.[4] Lev Tolstoy, on the other hand, passionately rejected "the heroic theory of history" in favor of "inexorable historic determinism."[5] Taking a different view on "what is meant by acts of will and their freedom," a gestalt psychologist wrote:

> In a functioning structure, acts of will are something better than arbitrary intrusions and coercions. They are vectors deriving by necessity from unresolved tensions that interfere with the equilibrium of the whole. These tensions call for appeasing of unsatisfied needs. As such they [the acts of will] are lawfully determined rather than "free" in the popular sense of arising as gratuitous acts from nowhere.[6]

The Czech-Slovak case confirms that, although the structure does not dictate outcome, individual actors, far from being freewheeling and unconstrained, act within the confines of the structure. They have real choices, real responsibilities. They may act in arbitrary, artless, or self-serving ways involving important political stakes, but they cannot ignore the historical-social realities any more than the constitutional framework. Constitutional issues, infused with politics of power and other interests, are significant. Even in Bosnia, where nationalist leadership has loomed so prominently, "to ascribe the courses of the war to unscrupulous leaders . . . is to ignore the historical and cultural sources of hatred."[7]

In a revolutionary period, individual personalities play a more significant role than in subsequent phases when conditions tend to stabilize and the hands of individuals become progressively tied by the structure.[8] If the first leaders in power after 1989 may have been in the position to restructure the state with a lasting effect, that opportunity evaporated quickly with the mutation of political forces and the rise of the institutions. In the last phase, two individuals, the Czech Republic Prime Minister, *homo economicus* (Adam Smith), and his Slovak counterpart, *homo sociologicus* (Emile Durkheim), articulating the new "vectors," sealed the breakup. "Of these, the former is supposed to be guided by instrumental rationality, while the behavior of the latter is dictated by social norms."[9]

I shall return to this theme in the concluding analysis of the constitutional negotiations.

ii. The Economic Component

In my judgment, economics and the divergence of economic interests, while present in the Czech and Slovak conflict—as they are in most ethnic clashes—did not play more than a secondary role in the breakup. Four sets of factors might be distinguished: first, the differences in the economic structures of the two Republics as they still existed in 1989; second, the divergent impact of post-1989 federal economic policies on the two economies; third, the results of the diverging economic policies in the two Republics, particularly after the 1992 elections; and last, but not least, the diverse perceptions and expectations of the economic impact of the dissolution of the state.

The Slovak economy underwent a radical modernization over the last decades under the Communist regime with living standards rising due to substantial (and often unwise) investments. According to the Czech-American economist, Professor Jan Švejnar, the basic macroeconomic data were quite similar in both Republics in 1989. With one important exception—the unemployment rate three times higher in Slovakia than in the Czech lands—these data have continued generally on a parallel course after 1989 and, surprisingly, also in the years following the breakup.[10] I am in no position to evaluate the economy-based reasons for the striking divergence in the unemployment figures. However, the most common explanation points to the structure of the Slovak economy and particularly to the fact that a major part of the arms industry and large Soviet style establishments were located in Slovakia, and they suffered disproportionately after 1989 from the loss of the eastern markets and the critical early decision of the federal government to terminate weapons production. These enterprises required large funds for conversion and were particularly difficult to restructure, with the result that the federal radical transformation policies had more severe social consequences in Slovakia particularly for the employment. This objective fact—the so-called Slovak "economic specificity"—had an understandable impact on Slovak voters, but it also lent itself readily to nationalist campaign exploitation with Prague being represented as the convenient enemy. In the same vein the Slovaks blamed centralist Prague—perhaps with some justification—for influencing the flow of foreign investment to the Czech part of the federation, to the prejudice of Slovakia.

The split of the common state, although enabling the Slovaks to frame their own economic policies, meant among other things the end of regular transfers of substantial resources from the Czech side to Slovakia. Owing to the intentional camouflage in the budget, it was virtually impossible to determine the size of these annual transfers, estimated by the Czechs at more than $800 million, an amount vigorously challenged by the Slovaks. This factor and the general economic cost-benefit issue of the split were barely explored in the media and in the campaign oratory. Citizens of both parts of the country agreed that separation would have negative economic consequences.[11] It is undisputed that the principal actors who decided on the dissolution were convinced that both economies would suffer, although for different reasons and to a different degree, with Slovakia carrying the heavier burden in the short run at any rate.[12] This expectation was confirmed by a drop of about one-third in the volume of trade between the newly independent states immediately following the split. However, the collapse of the Slovak economy predicted by some in the course of the constitutional negotiations did not materialize, and, two years after the dissolution, the gross national product in both Republics grew at the healthy rate of about 4 percent.

One would assume that the economic benefits from a larger state would have worked in favor of the continuation of a common state. As Ellen Comisso has pointed out, however, this condition is effective only when there is a commercial group able to capitalize on the advantages of a larger market and press for its preservation. No such group existed in the Czecho-Slovak state at the time of the dissolution decision. Moreover, the increasingly liberalized international economy has reduced the allure of the larger domestic market,[13] and there was also "the model" of a small successful economy (Austria and Switzerland). Finally, the issue was defused in part by the network of treaties between the two Republics designed to reduce, as much as possible, the negative economic impact of the separation, including a customs union, which has endured despite some frictions, and a monetary union, which collapsed after some six weeks.[14]

On the Czech side, economic considerations favoring a larger market obviously did not prevail over Prime Minister Klaus's determination to shield his concept of economic transformation from possible impairment by the Slovak divergent policies even at the price of a separation. Economists dominated the influential Civic Democratic Party[15] if not the Czech government. Like the Italian supporters of the Northern League, tired of carrying the poorer south, some Czechs welcomed the end of "subsidizing" their neighbors. This view reduced the perceived need for the common state, and, although it may not have influenced noticeably the final decision, it may have accounted in part for the passive attitude toward the impending split on the part of the Czech population at large.

The Slovak valuation of economic interests confirms—to paraphrase Adam Smith—that it is status in society that "is the end of half of the labors of human life" and that it prevails over economics. This conclusion applies as well to another possible economy-based "rival" of nationalism—class interest.[16] The Czech opposition on the left, presumably a primary advocate of such interest, toned down the unpopular class argument reminiscent of the old regime, even when it criticized the adverse social impact of the government reform, and ultimately, albeit reluctantly, it supported the termination of the common state. Nor was class rhetoric prominent in the public discourse in Slovakia, where populist nationalism ruled supreme, feebly challenged, and at times even seconded, by the reorganized, former Communist left.[17]

iii. The Media

In a thoughtful piece on "Nationalism and the Marketplace of Ideas," two American scholars suggest that during incipient democratization, when civil society is reviving but democratic institutions are not fully entrenched, the suddenly emerged openness of public debate often fosters nationalist myth-making and ethnic conflict because opportunistic governmental and nongovernmental elites exploit partial monopolies of supply, segmented demand, and the weakness of regulatory institutions. Moreover, journalists, public intellectuals, and public-interest watchdogs tend to perform poorly in the initial stages of the expansion of press freedom.[18]

The well-known Czech writer Jan Urban confirmed this perception. Speaking to a Slovak audience in 1993, he declared that if the journalists had acted as independent professionals the Czech-Slovak split would not have occurred: they copied the politicians, adding selected pieces of history to the statements of the ministers; they failed to distinguish facts from opinions and were unable to look beyond the confines of a single story. Urban's conclusion overstates the case, but with the memories of the First Republic freedoms faded, the concept of an independent, free press was in fact a novelty for which the journalists were not trained, and the general quality of reporting was low. The media discourse was uninformative and tended to magnify and sharpen the differences of views rather than explain them in a calm way. Above all, there was little effort to explore objectively the prospective consequences of the separation. The press was almost invariably in the service of a certain political orientation, did not seek to form independent public opinion, and was replete with inciting speculations of "who subsidizes whom." It helped to radicalize public opinion, which, even in Slovakia, was less nationalist than that of some of the elites.[19]

iv. External Influence

A distinction must be made between the "intervention" of outside forces into the internal processes on one hand, and on the other hand the impact of external events on the thinking and actions of the principal internal actors.

In the past, the fate of the Czechs and Slovaks was almost invariably determined by foreign powers. In fact, extraneous forces triggered even the 1989 revolution. However, the decision for the dissolution of the Federation was made without any intrusive intervention, in fact against friendly advice from other states, including the United States and members and institutions of the European Union, all of which uniformly favored the continuation of the common state.[20] Their bottom line interest was the preservation of peace and stability in an area of some geopolitical importance, and that concern appeared satisfied in the short run by the peaceful character of the separation. As for foreign private intervention, there is evidence that associations of Slovak emigrés, particularly in Canada, West Germany, and Australia, supported the militant nationalist circles in Slovakia.[21]

If there was no direct intervention from the outside world, world events had a noticeable influence on the thinking of the elites. With the collapse of Soviet dominion, "the eggs of Versailles and Brest Litowsk" resumed "hatching."[22] In a world of drastic change and uncertainty, with the Soviet-erected structures (the Warsaw Pact, COMECON) in liquidation, the prospect of joining the European Union and NATO was a lodestar of federal foreign policy supported by all mainstream movements and parties.[23] It was immensely important for the government, concerned about security, and for the people as a hopeful goal during the early travails of the transformation. Advanced democracies offered compelling political-economic alternatives to the Communist system. In Slovakia, the quick, in effect unconditional, recognition of the new, post-Communist states by the international community contradicted any assumption that world opinion was opposed to fragmentation.[24] If Croatia, Slovenia, and Moldova, why not Slovakia with its memory of "independent" statehood in 1939–45? The Slovak proposal for a "treaty" to replace a federal constitution was inspired by the compact for the establishment of the Commonwealth of Independent States of the former Soviet Union. A "union" between the two independent Republics, modeled after the Maastricht Treaty for a European Union, was the goal advanced ultimately by the Slovaks with the support of the Czech "moderates" and the left. Again, the idea of a "Europe of regions," which reemerged in the Western discourse over the Maastricht Treaty, was embraced by the Slovak Christian Democrats in support of an independent membership of the two Republics in the European integration structures.

2. On Eliminating Differences: A Taxonomy Applied

a. Neither Genocide nor Mass Population Transfer

One useful study offers a taxonomy of four methods for eliminating ethnic differences and resolving ethnic conflicts.[25] The first two, genocide and forced mass population transfers, did not come under consideration in the Czech-Slovak conflict. Both, I may say parenthetically, have been tolerated by the international community in the Serb-Croatian-Bosnian conflict, with some 3.5 to 5 million displaced since 1991.[26] Although some 300,000 Slovaks reside in the Czech Republic and a few thousand Czechs live in Slovakia, the only problem in this respect related to the Czech citizenship legislation as applied to Slovak residents. The fact that no measurable displacement of population was anticipated reduced the cost of the separation significantly. Yet a sort of "ethnic cleansing" occurred in Czecho-Slovakia, first by the German wartime deportation of the Jews and then, after 1945, by the expulsion of some 3 million Sudeten Germans and some thousands of Hungarians. For the

Czechs, at any rate, the split completed the process by the separation not only from the Slovaks but also from the Hungarian minority of some 600,000 in Slovakia.[27] The Czechs, it was said, are now "finally alone."

b. Integration/Assimilation/Multicultural Policy?

The question is whether integration and/or assimilation or multicultural policies might have succeeded in bridging the Czech-Slovak differences if given adequate time. T.G. Masaryk, president of the first Republic, said in the late 1920s:

> I think we need some twenty, thirty more years for safeguarding the Republic. Afterwards, I am not afraid for it any more. . . . At that time a new generation will be there, born in freedom. Surely, that generation won't let anyone take the freedom away.[28]

E.H. Carr, on the other hand, with the easy benefit of hindsight, disputed the viability of the First Republic from its very birth.[29] Yet, despite the controversial minority policy of the Czech-Slovak state and the Czech indifference toward Slovakia, economic, cultural, and professional interactions between the two people intensified over the years, and their mutual relations, although conflicting in some respects, were certainly closer than with any other country or community.[30] In that sense, an assimilation process was under way, but it was drastically shaken by the split even though a deeply divisive issue was eliminated by it. Another common state is nowhere on the horizon, but for the optimists, the prospective membership in the European Union is likely to advance "integration," albeit within a regional regime.[31]

c. Self-Determination/Separation

i. The Successor States in International Law

With the extinction of the Federation by a federal constitutional law, the two component Republics declared themselves independent successor states and the international community recognized them as such.[32] Except for some tactical maneuvers, neither side made a serious effort to force the other into a position of unilateral secession. The specific aspects of the solution relevant to the uncertain international law of succession of states may be summarized in a greatly simplified manner as follows:

The two Republics met the prerequisites of statehood, had to receive recognition by other states, and had to be admitted as new members to international organizations.[33]

They agreed to continue to observe their obligations toward other states under the bilateral and multilateral treaties concluded by the predecessor Federative Republic and to notify the respective parties and depositories.[34]

Each Republic alone determined who were its citizens, but a simplified procedure for changing citizenship was made available to citizens of one Republic living in the other. In contrast to the Czech Republic, Slovakia recognizes dual citizenship.

Federal immovable property was divided on the territorial principle, the movable on the two-to-one key, reflecting the size of the population, with a number of special provisions and agreements.

Special agreements determined the disposition of archives, taking into account their links to the institutions concerned and mutual access.[35]

The two Republics concluded with each other a dense network of treaties designed to establish a regime exceeding the traditional links between friendly states including a customs union.

The new relationship between the two Republics is a child of a compromise representing the remainder of the common interests as perceived by the political powers of the day: the Slovak side seeking to salvage the debris of their cherished dream of a "union" or "confederation," the Czech side interested in preserving the advantages of a common state, particularly a wider trading area, without institutional restraints. A pragmatic approach of this sort, eschewing "boilerplate normative responses" and tailor made for concrete circumstances, may offer an opportunity for dealing with other ethnic conflicts in which separation proves unavoidable.[36]

ii. On Self-Determination and Referendum

The ideological underpinning of the Slovak claim was the much discussed notion of self-determination, which the International Court of Justice has reaffirmed lately as "one of the essential principles of contemporary international law" with the important "*erga omnes*" (valid against everyone) character.[37] Whatever may be the disputed dimension of the concept of "peoples" entitled to self-determination,[38] the qualification of the Slovak people on that score was not at issue.[39] Even the often controversial problem of territory was not in question, since, subject to only a minimal adjustment, the administrative frontier between the two Republics in the expired Federation was accepted as the new international frontier. Nor was there at the time a problem in regard to another prerequisite, the observance of basic human rights in the nascent Republics.[40] Finally, a free expression of "the peoples" concerned is generally envisaged for the application of self-determination, but in the Czech-Slovak case no popular referendum was held. However, the dissolution decision was blessed by the Federal Parliament on recommendations from both Republic legislatures, with broad acquiescence of the population at large. No authoritative international voice was raised to question the legitimacy of the process.

Referendum is not a necessary condition for an expression of the right of self-determination under either general international practice or UN principles. "The minimum requirement seems to be the existence of some kind of representative procedures," which in the Czecho-Slovak case was clearly met.[41]

On the domestic scene, calls for a referendum resonated throughout the constitutional negotiations; it was available under the prevailing Constitution and demanded by a major part of the political representation in both Republics.[42] Some writers thought that "this is one of the rare cases where a referendum might have made it possible for a country to stay together."[43] There was indeed a lively internal controversy over whether the two "peoples" desired to achieve their right of self-determination in the form of independent states rather than in some variant of a continuing common state. Some on the Czech left argue that had the referendum been allowed and had it come out against the dissolution, the leadership—facing a complex and uncertain situation—could not have ignored popular opinion. However, the Federal Parliament failed to agree on questions to be submitted to the people. In fact, widespread dislike of the "Prague-centered" Federation in Slovakia and the lack of popular understanding and consensus in both Republics regarding the possible alternative forms of a common state would have made it difficult to compose meaningful questions for a referendum. In the end, Czech Prime Minister Klaus and his party opposed the referendum because it would delay the split and cause chaos in "the ungovernable state." The Slovak premier abandoned the idea in the face of this determined resistance, perhaps also bearing in mind the ambiguous state of Slovak public opinion with regard to a complete separation. There was indeed a possibility that the outcome of a popular vote would be inconclusive or even ignored by the elites. The final proposals for holding a referendum were rejected in the Federal Parliament.

In contrast to Czecho-Slovakia, which had no tradition of direct democracy, referendums proliferated during and after the collapse of Communism in Central, Eastern, and Southern Europe: "All in all, referendums in this part of the world have been much better at ripping apart than tying together."[44] In the West, they sanctioned the split of the Sweden-Norway Union in 1905, but they did not prove helpful in Canada[45] and have posed serious problems on the way to European integration. A referendum may be a helpful device for advancing legitimacy but it is a risky tool for dealing with complex constitutional arrangements, particularly in times of transition and disorientation.

I cannot deal here with the current outpouring of learned literature seeking to define a rational basis for self-determination claims. Suffice it to say that the Slovak demand might be justified under the theories stressing the right to territory,[46] under the "liberal theory of secession" (and its exceptions)[47] as well as pursuant to the doctrine postulating historical grievance, "discriminatory distribution," or the need to preserve the distinctive conception of a community.[48]

All domino theories are inherently suspect, but there is, for the time being, no danger of a domino effect of new claims for self-determination within one or both Republics. A movement for autonomy among the 1.3 million who claim Moravian nationality in the Czech Republic has been muted since independence; however, the extent of the eventual claims of the large Hungarian minority in Slovakia is unpredictable. Although other separatist movements, as in Belgium, Quebec, and most recently northern Italy, look to the Czech dénouement as a model,[49] it is difficult to say whether a "new virus" of peaceful separation is on the loose.

In one view, "excessive self-determination" works against democratization in nondemocratic countries and threatens democracy in countries that have already attained it.[50] Others offer "overwhelming" evidence that "democracy almost never works in societies that are highly divided along linguistic and cultural lines."[51] Current developments do not sustain any concern for the free institutions in the Czech Republic, but in the short run, at any rate, democracy in independent Slovakia appears less firm than within the late federal system.[52]

As I noted earlier, outside powers played no appreciable role in the Czecho-Slovak solution, nor did the United Nations provide "midwife" ministration as it did in the post–World War II decolonization wave of self-determination claims. In the absence of pervasive national interests of other states (oil in "Desert Storm") or international community concerns (breach of peace, humanitarian aid, protection of human rights or democracy), this was clearly not a case for outside "conflict management."

Although the Slovaks sought to invoke the right of self-determination as a revolutionary principle applicable extraconstitutionally, the Czechs balked and prevailed with their insistence on continuity and a constitutional route even when it came to the modalities of the dissolution.[53] Moreover—and this perhaps is the most valuable contribution to self-determination practice—the dissolution occurred without the slightest sign of a threat of force from either side.[54]

I have wondered why the Czecho-Slovak outcome was so different from the situation in former Yugoslavia and the Soviet Union. A major reason—Professor Petr Pitha suggested—was the fact that the Slovaks and the Czechs had never gone to battle against each other; there was no compulsion to revenge the blood spilled in such a conflict.[55] Another reason, identified by Ivan Gašparovič, chair of the Slovak Parliament, was the absence of any territorial dispute.[56] The humanist experience of Masaryk's First Republic may have had a role in taming militant nationalism in both parts of the Federation. For the last three centuries, the Czechs have been averse to taking up arms, and they were certainly not ready to fight for a common state that had lost its appeal for Czech leadership. Still in the Czech Republic, the elimination of most of the minority populations removed the most convenient motivation and target of extreme nationalism. In Slovakia, also, where a more pristine, "earlier stage" nationalism is seen as still prevailing, even the most aggressive nationalist rhetoric eschewed any implications of outright belligerent action. Finally, a major factor for the peaceful resolution of the conflict was the protodemocratic political environment in which the process took place.[57] This confirms the general thesis postulating a correlation between democratic regimes and peaceful behavior.[58]

d. Separation as an Alternative: Geopolitics and Legitimacy

Two scholars correctly conclude that the merits of separation as against integration had to be decided by political argument and pragmatic considerations such as feasibility and estimates about long-run efficacy. They suggest that there is no obvious moral hierarchy that would place separation over other alternatives such as integration.[59] However, if the international system is viewed as exclusively state based, fragmentation by separation would appear an inferior choice in principle. That system "relegates ethnic groups to the status of dependent variables or policy problems."[60] If, on the other hand, one perceives the international system in the process of change with individuals, groups, "regions," and a great variety of international regimes joining the "sovereign" states as actors ("subjects" or players) in the international arena, then the stance may be less negative. Fuming against the "stabilitarians" and mistaken prophets of the postnationalist world, some see less interstate conflict in a world of relatively homogenous nation-states than in a world of intrastate conflict between ethnic groups within multinational states. Even if a dozen or two new nations are added in the next few decades, "through peaceful or violent partition . . . the very inequality of power among states would prevent too great a degree of disorder."[61] This, the stabilitarians rejoin, would indeed increase the potential for global disorder, if the number of states of doubtful viability is raised dramatically and power vacuums result.[62]

As for the geopolitical impact of the Czech-Slovak separation, historic experience in Central Europe (for instance the Munich 1938 episode) suggests that one small larger state might not be necessarily less vulnerable than two small states. Two economically viable Republics coexisting peacefully may be preferable to a common state rent by ethnic conflict, even if arguably they might have done better economically together as a larger state.

As in the past, the policies of the West and of Russia will be the essential factor. Except for some voices in Slovakia, the "bridge role" between the East and West is generally rejected as a viable security option. The "buffer" idea behind the post–World War I Little Entente did not work either. Some see chaos in Russia overflowing to its neighbors; others—harking back to recent history—fear that Russia, unable or unwilling to cooperate with the West, might seek to "finlandize" the region under its own surveillance or, worse still, to restore its former empire, in which case—so goes the prophecy—it might attempt to establish a foothold in Slovakia. Disappointed with the Conference on Security and Cooperation in Europe and other European security schemes, the governments of both Republics are still looking toward a close association with the European Union and NATO although the depth of public support for NATO membership is uncertain. The Slovak government has been making a determined effort to build political and economic ties with its Eastern neighbors, including a free trade area with the Russian Federation. Both Republics are parties to the fledgling Central European Free Trade Agreement. The tension between Slovakia and Hungary over the status of the Hungarian minority in Slovakia is likely to continue despite the conclusion of a significant treaty. The controversy over the claims of the expelled Sudeten Germans has marred the Czech-German relations and some in the Czech Republic fear the growing German economic influence. The treatment of the thousands of Roma in the Czech Republic has been the subject of international concern.

Although at this juncture Central Europe—unlike Eastern and South Eastern Europe—appears relatively stable, the entire area experiences the aftermath of the disintegration of the Soviet empire, which is likely to have long-term destabilizing effects not unlike the breakup of other imperial structures in Europe's history. If nothing else, the pressure of substantial ethnic minorities in all states of the region is likely to contribute to the instability.[63]

One view heard particularly among the members of the first post-1989 government elite warns that the separation will eventually prove a heavy burden on those responsible for it and that the lack of a manifested consent of the people will undermine the legitimacy and the consciousness of the "stateness" of the two Republics. Unlike the states emerging from the former Yugoslavia or Soviet Union, the two Republics—the critics argue—are "unwanted children," like the post–World War I Republic of Austria in 1918; in Central Europe's environment, hostile to small states, they will be absorbed in one form or another by their powerful neighbors. Yet the newly independent Czech Republic seems to have slid smoothly into the shoes of the former Czechoslovakia with its tradition, history, and reputation, having appropriated its symbols, including the flag, the main state holiday, and the capital with its apparently irresistible lore. The Slovak "stateness" is viewed as a natural culmination of a historic process for assertion of national identity, although many Slovaks feel that full independence was neither a logical nor the most desirable option. Whatever it may be worth, in the fall of 1993, less than a year after independence, 60 percent of the Slovaks interviewed in an opinion poll indicated that they would vote against the separation, while only 23 percent would support it.[64]

Returning to the conceptual framework suggested earlier, one might conclude that on the continuum "symmetric-asymmetric systems," Czechoslovakia moved from the state of "latent secession" to separation. In other terms, the structure suffered from "tension-producing faults," which led to the split.

3. On Multiple Transformations

a. The Priorities

It has become a cliché in the literature on contemporary Central-Eastern Europe to expatiate upon the uniqueness of the simultaneous transformations at the societal, political, and economic levels. In fact, no precedent or theory exists for a transition from a Communist regime to a free market democracy. One scholar saw as the closest parallel natural or man-made disasters: floods, earthquakes, famines, or wars.[65] In contrast with unitary states such as Poland and Hungary, the political transformation in the Czecho-Slovak Federation was greatly complicated by still another "transformation" directed at the form of coexistence between the two peoples and ultimately by the painful process of dividing the state into two independent entities.

The necessary interaction between the political and economic transformation processes raised questions of priorities in the allocation of resources. Some writers, including Professor Bruce Ackerman, felt that in Eastern Europe political democracy and constitution writing should precede, and provide conditions for, the establishment of the free market, while others argued that a certain level of economic stability was an indispensable precondition for democracy. Judge Richard A. Posner, although disclaiming any expertise about European law and politics, had no doubt that the "priority for Eastern Europe" should be economic rather than political.[66] Jon Elster perceived a possible parallel with Latin American states but wisely warned that vital distinctions among the various countries could not be ignored in this context.[67] President Havel "did not agree with the view that the constitution is not the principal matter and that it can wait."[68] In the Czech-Slovak case, at any rate, the Slovaks saw to it that the fundamental constitutional issue defining the relation between the two peoples had to be tackled along with, if not before, economics.[69] As for some other Communist states, Bulgaria and Romania adopted their constitutions as early as in 1991, but Poland and Hungary, after years of transformation, in mid-1996 still do not have a new constitution in the formal sense, and the Ukrainian parliament adopted one as late as June 1996 only after the president threatened to call a popular referendum. In reality, these countries have enacted a veritable mass of constitutional laws amending the Communist constitutions, with the effect that in Hungary, for instance, almost all of the vital components of a new basic document have been in place for some time, with the post-Communist Constitutional Court undertaking to assure some coherence within the system. Even the Czecho-Slovak Federal Assembly adopted some 43 such constitutional laws before it went out of business. It follows that priority has never been a real issue: constitution-making has been pursued after the fall of the old regimes with vigor but, as an eminently political process, it has been subject in different countries to widely different forces and outcomes.

b. On Free Societies

A transformation from the atomized and passive to an active civil society postulates a certain constitutional and legal framework, but it cannot do without a change in individual behavior. As Ralf Dahrendorf told a Prague audience, the new civil society envisages "a broad scale of associations, organizations, and institutions independent of the government (at least of the central government) and fulfilling the real lives of real people."[70] Two American sociologists distinguish civil society from both the political society of parties, political organizations, and political publics (in particular parliaments) and an economic society composed of organizations of production and distribution (firms, cooperatives, etc.); political and economic societies generally arise from civil society.[71]

i. The Civil Society

"There is an enormous difference," wrote Ernest Gellner, "between longing for civil society . . . and being able to take it for granted," which was the condition at the time of the American Revolution. "The collapse of [the Marxist] system has left a moral vacuum. . . . The American Revolution by contrast . . . was not a collapse of a moral order. The moral order remained intact and the revolution was its expression, not its violation."[72] And Václav Havel, returning from his first voyage to the United States as Czech president, waxed enthusiastically over "the tremendously developed American civil society" with "millions of nonprofit organizations."[73] Clearly, at times a comparison enlightens by bringing into view not the similarities but the differences between the compared phenomena. Some American writers, however, take a less sanguine view of the current state of civil society in the United States.[74]

The Czechs have been known as inveterate joiners—a tradition revived with a vengeance after 1989. Over 50,000 associations functioned in the First Republic, but only 1,400 were counted in 1990–91, a testimony to the impact of the Communist regime. By 1994, in the Czech Republic alone there were more than 20,000 associations and clubs, about 3,000 foundations, 1,500 church organizations, 171 professional "chambers," and over 50 interest groups. The "economic society" counted some 55,000 companies.[75] A major part of the working population moved from the public to the private sector. Thousands became property owners through restitution of property confiscated by the Communists, and some six million became shareholders through privatization, a development toward a revival of the historically strong Czech middle class.

Unlike the Czechs, the Slovaks typically do not feel the need for association with others of the same persuasion except in religious organizations. Moreover, joining was risky under the old regime, and the distaste for it continues along with a fear of change and relapse to poverty, suspicion of authority, and a respect for power.[76] Privatization in Slovakia has been slower and was at times suspended. One Slovak view attributed the substantially higher unemployment in Slovakia in part to the inflexibility of the work force and a lack of entrepreneurial spirit among the people. Current statistics show a disproportionately smaller number of individual entrepreneurs and new small enterprises in Slovakia.[77]

Professor Robert Putnam has concluded, drawing on his study of differences between the societies of Italy's North and South, that good government and political-economic progress depended on the existence of a civil society marked by a traditional tendency to form small-scale associations.[78] I have asked myself whether the divergence between the Czech and Slovak societies might confirm this theorem. The newly independent Czech Republic continued to experience a stable, democratic government with favorable macroeconomic data including sizable economic growth, low unemployment and relatively moderate inflation, along with moderate social-economic tensions endemic to rapid post-Communist transformation.[79] In Slovakia, as I mentioned earlier, economic revival has paralleled and even somewhat surpassed the growth rate in the Czech Republic but the government and politics are a different story. In sharp contrast with the Czech Republic, where differentiation of political parties along the traditional West-European left-right spectrum was essentially completed even before the breakup, the scene in Slovakia has been dominated by the populist-nationalist movement of Vladimir Mečiar. Mečiar, dismissed twice before from the office of prime minister, nevertheless regained it for the third time in 1994. In that year's election his movement, supported widely in the rural areas, retained its plurality despite an unseemly conflict between Mečiar and the president of the Republic, the efforts to exclude the opposition from any participation, a series of scandals, and serious charges of abuse of governmental power. As for the civil society, the Slovak Parliament had adopted legislation making it substantially more costly for private nonprofit foundations to be recognized. The European Union and the United States took the unusual steps of expressing official concern about the state of democracy in the country. Slovakia was dropped at least for the time being from the first group of candidates for admission to NATO and the European Union.

Obviously, more empirical work on the region is called for, but the data appear to support Putnam's correlation between a civil society of vibrant private groupings and good government. Clearly, in the Czech-Slovak context, the degree of progress toward a civil society, or lack of it, has had an impact on the political and economic transformation process, but it was also reflected in the postures of the elites conducting the constitutional negotiations, in the tone of the public discourse and the political culture generally, and in the attitudes and votes of the people at large.

ii. The Political Society

As for the "political society," it was the political "movements" and parties that played a central role in the regime change generally and—as I stress throughout *Czecho/Slovakia*—in the constitutional negotiations in particular.[80] In some measure, these negotiations made more difficult the process of a differentiation of the parties along the traditional left-right spectrum. The rapid pace of regrouping and the lack of clarity of their programs impaired the role of the parties as instruments of integration of the political will of the people. They served as a natural vehicle for advancing not only party interests but individual ambitions as well.

As a result of the political fragmentation, the Slovak representation in the negotiations was not in a position to evolve a common strategy; it offered always a continuum of postures ranging from "mildly" federalist to extreme separatist. Only the "federal Slovaks," such as Federal Prime Minister Marián Čalfa, and whatever remained of the original Public against Violence stood for a strong Federation, and in the end they had little influence. The negotiations were complicated by the significant role played by the Christian Democratic Movement, which for a time was the strongest party in the Slovak National Council, and its founder-leader Dr. Ján Čarnogurský. Dr. Čarnogurský had in mind—and he said so at the outset—the independence of Slovakia not at once but in a number of years when both Republics would enter the European Union as separate members. In the negotiations, he and his colleagues supported any move that would loosen the Federation, so that at the time of accession to the European Union the separation would be a logical step since the structure of the common state, or what was left of it, would be too weak to ensure conformity with the European Union rules and discipline: thus, the two Republics would form a bloc of two votes in the Union councils. This stance was consistent with Dr. Čarnogurský's vision of a growing role of "regions" within the integrating Europe, but it appeared thoroughly disruptive to the Czech side.[81] The Slovak Party of the Democratic Left, although supporting a strong role for the Republics in line with nationalist aspirations, did not aim at the destruction of the Federation, but it was hampered by its Communist heritage. At times reluctant to take a clear stand, it sought to avoid a collision with the influential Mečiar's populist Movement for a Democratic Slovakia, which played the nationalist card for a confederation or "union."

On the Czech side, the breakup of the original majority Civic Forum and the emerging new factions and parties created divisions within the negotiating group, which, however, were gradually overcome by the ascending influence of the new "right wing" parties and their leaders, insisting on a "functional federation or nothing."

4. "Strategic Elements" of Constitutional Negotiations

At the beginning of *Czecho/Slovakia,* I referred to Howard Raiffa's empirically derived criteria, which, adjusted to the subject of the book, provide a convenient grid for an analysis of the negotiation issues, parties, strategies, and tactics.

a. The Time Dimension

The time factor was one of the strategic elements highlighted by Raiffa. Günther Winkler, an Austrian legal philosopher, has challenged the sacred canon that "at the beginning was the Word": neither the Word, nor Faust's existentialist "action," but Time was at the beginning of all things.[82] The importance of the time dimension for human affairs was brought out amply by the Czech-Slovak case. I stressed earlier the role of the time element in the potential assimilation or integration of the two societies. Whether or not an integration of the two peoples was feasible had more time been allowed for it remains a question.

In a less hypothetical context, time restraints haunted the constitutional negotiations of the 1990s from the outset. President Havel is blamed for the decision to limit the term of the first freely elected Federal Assembly (and of his presidency) to a mere two years, a period too short to allow for a consensus to have been reached on a new federal constitution.[83] There is some force in this argument, since the second elections after the lapse of this period marked the death knell of the state. Yet, even before the expiration of the first two-year term, with the swift disintegration of the ruling profederalist movements, the leadership in charge of the negotiations was losing its legitimacy and new elections confirming the realignment of political power appeared appropriate. Behind the decision on the shortened first term was no doubt the idea that the postrevolutionary euphoria offered the magic moment for achieving a constitutional consensus.

The succession of arbitrary deadlines for completing the constitution making both reflected and fed the growing impatience on both sides, with the media contributing to an atmosphere of irritation and peevishness. In the end, the fatal, short deadline for the dissolution of the state was set by the chafing Czech side with the grudging acquiescence of the Slovaks. This last time limit was employed to compel the opposition in both Republics, under the threat of an impending chaos, to abandon any delaying moves (such as proposals for a confederate scheme and a referendum) and support the termination of the state.

Finally, in the broadcast sense, the length of time required for the realization of the transformations in Central-Eastern Europe has imposed a severe test of patience on people suffering an abrupt deterioration of living standards against an uncertain promise of a better life in the future. It took the West generations (perhaps two centuries) to achieve a working model of democracy with a free market, an objective that the countries of Central-Eastern Europe have hoped to reach in one decade.

b. Issues and Parties

Vladimir Kusin has suggested a chronological scheme to analyze the process of disintegration of the "national-unitary" power structures in the former Soviet Union and Yugoslavia, as well as in Czechoslovakia, "the only multinational European [unitary] state formation remaining after the end of the First World War." He offers a three-phase perspective that I have found useful for thinking about the complex, multi–issue, Czech-Slovak negotiations in which both the main issues and the party constellations changed over the period of some three years.[84]

The first two phases at any rate were conducted under the spell of the "naive realism" described by two American scholars: "It is I who sees the things as they 'really' are (including history) so that other rational and fair people will share my responses, and any failure [on the part of the other party] to do so must be due to lack of information, ignorance, laziness, irrationality, unfairness or bias."[85] For the Czechs, indifferent and mostly ignorant of Slovak history and sensibilities, only a strong federation could successfully accomplish the multiple transformations, but for the Slovaks "self-determination," until now "unfairly denied," had to be finally realized now.

i. The "Reform" Phase

Issues: In this phase, the two basic issues were the transfer of powers from the center to the component Republics and "strengthening national symbolism" such as the change of the name from the "Czechoslovak" to the "Czech and Slovak" Federative Republic. The constitutional negotiations encompassed the entire spectrum of issues of federalism, constitutionalism, and democracy and led to the adoption in early 1991 of the Charter of Basic Rights and Freedoms and a host of other constitutional and "quasi-constitutional" legislation. The primary focus, however, was the devolution discourse.

The Czech side believed that a solution might be found in the form of "a moderate, enlightened, supranational centralism," a "functional federation," which would preserve a uniform economic and foreign policy, while the Slovaks signaled a growing, albeit not articulated, dissatisfaction. Nevertheless, the parties engaged in an essentially cooperative interaction: while seeking their own "payoffs" on the basic issues of power distribution and other aspects of the successive drafts of the federal constitution, they were prepared to cooperate in a solution that would preserve the federal state.

Parties: Nominally, there were three parties to the negotiations, the Federation and the two Republics, represented by spokespeople drawn in this phase primarily from the executive branches. However, all three legislatures became involved through their respective Constitutional Commissions working on various drafts of both the federal and Republic constitutions. With the governmental and parliamentary structure only slowly coming to life in late 1989 and early 1990, President Havel, armed with strong support and prestige, exerted during this brief phase a great, if not controlling, influence, along with the leaders of the two large movements victorious in the 1990 elections, which, however, had already begun the process of differentiation into conventional political parties. The discredited labor unions had scarcely begun to show signs of revival, and there were no other special interest groups pressing on the political leadership with a noticeable effect. This meant that in this protodemocratic system basic policy was made between the president and the organs of the political parties influenced by individual actors in crucial government positions. The three-party negotiation pattern quickly turned into a two-party face-off, with the Czech Republic representatives generally joining the "federals" in the defense of the federal scheme against Slovak pressure for change.

This phase ended with the adoption, under strong Slovak pressure, of the 1990 federal devolution law, which restored in effect the allocation of powers as it was originally made in the 1968 constitutional law, before the "recentralization" ordained in 1970 as an aspect of the Soviet imposed "normalization."

ii. The "Restructuring" Phase

Issues: In this phase, the Slovak side pressed beyond devolution and symbolism for a new contractual foundation of the state in the form of a "treaty" between the two "sovereign" Republics that would determine both the power allocation and the constitutional structure and would be embodied in the new constitution; the powers of the center would be limited to foreign affairs, defense, and the single market. The treaty would legally bind both Republics and would oblige the central legislature to incorporate it in the federal constitution. The hardest bargaining, however, centered on newly introduced issues regarding the legal nature of the treaty:

The treaty, the Slovaks proposed, should be binding under international law, in effect an extraconstitutional instrument. After the initial shock on the Czech side, which branded the proposal as unconstitutional and revolutionary, a compromise was reached, with the majority of the Czech spokesmen accepting the treaty idea and the Slovaks conceding that the treaty would be an internal rather than an international instrument. However, the question of the status of the treaty remained highly controversial.

The Slovaks insisted—and this appeared to be a point closest to their hearts—that the "sovereign" Republics must as such be the parties to the treaty, while the Czechs considered that absurd since the Republics were components of the Federation: only the Republic parliaments, acting on behalf of "the people," could be the contracting parties. This, in reality a largely symbolic issue, turned out to be a major reason, or at least a pretext, for the ultimate defeat of the draft treaty in the Slovak Parliament's Presidium.

The Slovaks demanded that the treaty be legally "binding" on the Federal Assembly, but the Czechs refused this claim as well as a constitutional amendment to that effect because it would impair the position of the Assembly as the highest constitutional organ. Although formulated in terms of a compromise, the Czech position, based on strict adherence to the 1960–68 Constitution, prevailed.[86]

Finally, the Slovaks claimed that the new constitution embodying the treaty, after adoption by the Federal Assembly, must be ratified by the two Republic parliaments, a demand that the Czechs reluctantly accepted, although they viewed it as an inappropriate "confederative element." They refused, however, to agree that any subsequent constitutional amendments would likewise be subject to such ratification.

As regards the issue of "international visibility," so close to Slovak hearts, a compromise solution recognized the treaty-making power of the Republics in the areas of their legislative competence, to be exercised "in harmony" with federal foreign policy (the modalities of assuring such harmony to be left to future legislation), as well as the authority of the Republics to send their own representatives abroad and receive foreign representatives.

Parallel to the Republic-to-Republic negotiations on the treaty, the Federal Assembly debated proposals for the core parts of the constitution that defined the three branches of the central government. The prevailing constitutional provisions for the protection of the Slovak minority and the guarantees of Czech and Slovak parity representation were to be retained or strengthened and consociational elements added to assure the participation of Slovak representatives in central decision making. The bill, based in part on President Havel's draft, failed in the Federal Assembly by four votes.

Parties: As regards the negotiating parties, this phase progressed in two distinct stages. First, the president assembled the representatives of the three executive branches and leaders of the two majority movements in no less than 18 meetings to deal with the treaty proposal. When this elaborate effort failed, due mainly to Czech intransigence, the negotiations were taken up by delegations of the two Republic parliaments, bringing in the opposition parties—a development that was viewed as "a catastrophe" by some and as the only possible alternative by others. The idea was that the Republic organs should shape the treaty content, relieving by the same token the president, whose influence on the negotiations faded rapidly. However, in what was supposed to be a Republic-to-Republic discourse, federal officials continued to loom large, if for no other reason because of the unique expertise of the federal establishment. The Czech Republic organs, although seeking with some hesitation to assert their own independent stance, found it difficult to extricate themselves from a position of serving as a "regional extension of federal organs and personalities."[87] Although the deputies of both the Czech and Slovak parliaments shared the feeling that federal parliamentarians looked down on them, the Slovaks identified federal "arrogance" with the Czechs. As both Republics proceeded to exercise their competences, enlarged by the new devolution law, frictions with federal organs occurred. The disintegration of the ruling profederalist movements in both

Republics into competing political groupings led by regional politicians changed the power interests and priorities on both sides. The rhetoric surrounding the negotiations fanned the rising Slovak nationalism, which in turn impacted the Slovak posture and evoked a negative response on the Czech side. The approach of national elections burdened the negotiations greatly. Against all odds, in February 1992 an agreement appeared to have been reached on a draft text of a treaty to be submitted to the Republic parliaments. The formal issues regarding the treaty seemed either resolved or intentionally left ambiguous, and a solution was found for the most vexing items of allocation of powers, including a single central bank, joint "protection of frontiers," and the division of foreign affairs powers. However, the Slovak Parliament Presidium rejected the draft. Thus, the Slovaks were the defectors at this critical juncture of "the game." It was likely that the Czech Parliament would have endorsed the agreement, although some observers on the Czech side doubt it.

iii. The "New Form of Coexistence" Phase

After the 1992 elections had sealed the radical restructuring of the political scene in the two Republics, a face-off persisted for a brief period between the Slovak demand, now formulated in terms of a "union" modeled vaguely on the Maastricht Treaty for the European Union, and a resolute Czech insistence on "a functional federation." The deadlock came to an abrupt end with the two leaders of the newly victorious parties quickly agreeing on the division of the common state into two successor states.

Issues: An entirely new phase, based on newly defined common interests, turned on the following two sets of issues:

The modalities of the separation, including
- the date of the split and budgetary implications for the period preceding it,
- the dismantling of the federal establishment,
- the constitutionality and legitimacy of the separation process, including a possible referendum and the role of the Federal Assembly and the Republic parliaments,
- the division of federal property and other rights and obligations of the Federation, and
- the stance toward the outside world.

The forms of the future coexistence of the two states. The Slovaks, eager to salvage as much as possible of the "union" scheme,

> pressed for a joint coordinating organ, but the Czechs were ready only for a dense network of bilateral international treaties between independent states. The Czechs prevailed, and some 40 such treaties or agreements were negotiated.

The negotiations at this stage proceeded with surprising speed under the Damoclean sword of the imminent date set for the split and in the new realization of the strong common interest in assuring an orderly, peaceful separation.

Parties: It is no exaggeration to say that in this episode the basic decisions were made essentially by two men, the prime ministers of the two Republics. Their decisions were blessed by their parties and coalition allies, by the Republic organs, and finally, after tumultuous debates, by the Federal Assembly. Both men first employed only small teams of close advisers, but, after the basic decisions had been made, the circle of participants broadened with the inclusion of many ministerial officials and experts who worked with considerable skill and efficiency on the maze of innumerable, overwhelming problems. There still was no evidence of special interest groups intruding in any significant way into the negotiations, although the top industrial management in Slovakia was said to be particularly close to Prime Minister Mečiar. The labor unions generally kept their distance from political involvement.[88] I may add, parenthetically, that after only a few months of Slovak independence most of his closest advisers in the negotiations turned against the Slovak prime minister in an unseemly squabble.

5. Forums and Tactics

All the tactical devices conjured up by Raiffa were employed.

The Slovak prime minister's ploy, of which he publicly boasted, to ask consistently for more than he knew he could expect and offer minimal concessions, built his home reputation as the only fighter who could stand up to the Czechs, but it provoked the charge of Slovak "extortion" and handicapped the moderates in the negotiations. Following this tactic, in an early encounter with newly appointed Czech Prime Minister Klaus, the Slovak premier demanded independent membership of the Slovak state in the United Nations, and Klaus promptly accepted, thus sealing the split. It was at this point that Klaus was able to make a showing that there was no longer any room for "splitting the difference." For a long time, perhaps until the final stage of the negotiations, Klaus believed, consistent with his economic view of the world and Mečiar's tactics, that the Slovaks, although engaging in a bargaining game, were not prepared to give up the financial benefits of the common state. Mečiar on the other hand might have labored under the misapprehension that the Czech side was so deeply wedded to the common state that in the end it would compromise to save it.[89] Thus, each leader may have misconceived the limits of the other's negotiating position. One is struck by the personal relationship between the two "strong men." Even at the height of the controversy, Mečiar professed his admiration of, and confidence in, Klaus as "the only trustworthy person" on the Czech side, while Klaus, although uncompromising on the merit of the issues, went out of his way to avoid any show of personal animosity.[90]

The negotiations in all three phases—excepting, of course, the proceedings in the parliaments—were conducted in secrecy. Although the final communiqués were mostly bland, considerable information became available. The expectation that secrecy would make it easier for the parties to make concessions did not materialize; it made it easier for the participants to "reinterpret" or deny any alleged agreement, and it played into the hands of demagogues.[91] This does not mean that secrecy would not have been appropriate in preparatory stages.

The Czech side appeared stronger not only because of its demographic and economic superiority but also because of the Czech-federal alliance and federal expertise, particularly in financial and other technical matters, confirming the Slovak underdog feeling. On the other hand, it was the Slovaks who had the initiative, but their way of gradually raising their claims contributed to the Czech inflexibility.

The effort to commit the participants to their negotiating positions by having them answer questionnaires or formally signing communiqués proved uniformly unsuccessful. This made it possible for the participants either to avoid any commitment or disavow any previously given or perceived agreement.

The "bulldozer" tactic by which negotiators concentrated in each session on issues that appeared tractable, "sweeping" the more controversial items out of the way to be considered in the future, worked to some degree in the initial stages only.

Appeals to common interest, rational principles, and fairness were made on both sides. The Slovaks insistently recalled the history of Czech broken promises of equality and autonomy. The "restructuring phase" was complicated by theoretical altercations regarding the meaning of "sovereignty," international subjectivity or personality, "confederation" versus federation, and national as against civic principles. The participants employed sometime questionable legal arguments and categories in support of their negotiating positions. Ignorance of modern legal thought and attachment to obsolete positivist ideas hampered the discourse.[92]

More or less veiled threats of unilateral action or retaliation were employed by both sides, more frequently, however, by Mečiar, who repeatedly feigned leaving the negotiations. He would walk out, "slamming the door," demand an apology, set preconditions to resuming negotiations, and make exuberant statements to strengthen his negotiating position. Klaus eschewed emotional reactions and pursued his main objective aggressively while generally willing to concede on nonessentials.

In the final phase, disregarding the agreement on the split, the Slovak side repeatedly attempted, in alliance with the Czech opposition, to resuscitate the idea of a "union" in open moves within the Federal Assembly as well as by employing an "anonymous" trial balloon and a mysterious document slipped into the negotiation files. The Czech coalition remained unified under Klaus's iron hand.

Both sides, although in reality agreed on the two new states as equal successors, maneuvered intermittently to pass the "black jack" of a secessionist to the other side.

6. The "Intervenor"

When Raiffa speaks of an "intervenor," "facilitator" or "mediator," Václav Havel's role in the negotiations comes naturally to mind. Yet the position of the last federal president bristled with paradoxes relating both to his private and political persona. One of his advisers, a high functionary in the Civic Forum, told me that, although not impartial, he was always reasonable. His performance—and his writings—disclose a deep ambiguity about power. As a product of the Czech bourgeoisie who enjoys the small pleasures of the "little Czech man," and as an artist at heart, he denies "any desire for power or love of it" and is horrified by its temptations.[93] Yet power holds a fascination for him, a gate to a great adventure in which a simple lad of the Czech folktale becomes a powerful king. Yet again, during a university ceremony at which he was given an honorary degree, he confessed expecting at any moment one of the familiar men from Kafka's "castle" to enter, wrench his freshly acquired diploma from his hand, and evict him from the aula as an imposter. Although he appears from the outside as the very "antipode" of Josef K., his sense of nonbelonging and self-doubt is, he suggests, the motor propelling him into the most unlikely exploits such as the presidency.[94] Yet again—and finally—this alienated modern intellectual believes strongly in a transcendental being as a measure of all human values and individual responsibility; any societal change in his view must come from within the individual.[95]

With great personal courage, he was able to confront the old regime and after its collapse to artfully articulate the ideals and ills of his evolving new society and of modern democracy in general. He emerged after 1989 with great prestige but with the sole experience of a dissident totally excluded from the public political process, confined to the world of samizdats, secret get-togethers of kindred souls, and seminars and theatrical happenings in private apartments, all under the ubiquitous eye of Big Brother, and in the end—a prison cell. He described this pitiful caricature of "public life" as "anti-" or "nonpolitical politics," which allowed him to preserve his personal integrity but did not prepare him for high office in a democracy.

His critics charged—and he vehemently denied—that he consciously continued to adhere to "nonpolitical politics" in his new environment because of his aversion, on moral grounds, to the normal give and take of the political process. Again, Havel's critics point to his public pronouncements evidencing a degree of diffidence toward traditional political parties, which he explained by the experience in the First Republic in which the ruling political parties, with their own presses, labor unions, cooperatives, and sports and educational facilities, exerted excessive influence over the life of the country. This posture, it is said with some justification, must have inspired the election slogan "parties are for partisans, the Civic Forum is for all."

There has been little comment on the way in which Havel orchestrated the first phase of the constitutional negotiations, starting with his meeting in a pub with Slovak Prime Minister Mečiar and extending over the many peregrinations "from castles to manors" in 1990 and early 1991. By definition, as a high federal official and as a Czech, he could not be disassociated from one of the parties to the negotiations. He is blamed, among other things, for having promised Mečiar in that meeting a new competence law in advance of, and separate from, the new constitution because, it is said, he could not conceive that a parliament, elected under the Communist regime, could frame a democratic constitution. With his influence at its peak, he may have been able to force an agreement on a full constitution at that time.[96] However, he was not given enough time to acquire the indispensable skills of working with the fragile, groping institutions that were the ultimate arbiters of the constitutional issues or to strike out on an extraconstitutional route. He never succeeded in forming a good working relationship with Alexander Dubček, the Slovak leader of the 1968 Communist reform movement, the kindly, but not very effective, chair of the Federal Assembly, or with its important committees. As his staff, Havel brought with him to "the Castle" people whom he met primarily as dissident journalists, artists, and musicians, who shared his beliefs and excelled in their dedication and enthusiasm rather than in competence in governmental affairs. Yet, if one listens to his first chancellor, persons with the needed background and training were simply not available, particularly if "the ruling circles" of the old regime were to be excluded. Havel remains fiercely loyal to his "old friends" and collaborators and promotes them to positions for which, at times, they are not suited.

When he first came into office, Havel was impressed by "the unusually extensive powers [of the president], almost as extensive as in the so-called presidential system," and he felt that in a new federal constitution "the power of the president could still be somewhat weakened." Not long thereafter, however, when in the course of his learning process he became aware of the increasing divisions in the Parliament and of the serious threat of an unresolvable deadlock due to the unworkability of the prevailing Communist Constitution, he proposed a series of legislative measures, including a bill for increasing his powers in specified situations. With one exception, all of these proposals failed of adoption. A former prominent deputy in the Federal Parliament and Havel's ardent supporter deplored the president's isolation and described the circumstances of the failure of his legislative initiative:

> Some of the advisers acted as if they did not know (or did not want to know) what they were really expected to defend in parliamentary committees. . . . The high distinction and learnedness of Professor Klokočka [a Czech emigré law professor at the University of Munich, consultant to the president] were for a number of deputies . . . unintelligible talk. Most of the deputies shunned his seminars on . . . the premises of the Parliament.[97]

When the negotiations under the president's patronage ran into the ground and the representatives of the two Republic parliaments took over, Havel continued to "intervene" at the margin. Concerned about the lack of progress in the talks between the parliamentarians, Havel proposed, in November 1991, that the Czech side accept the Slovak demands on the deadlocked formal issues relating to the parties and legal nature of the proposed treaty, but the Czech side almost unanimously recoiled against this suggestion with varied degrees of sincere or feigned horror.

Finally, when another series of his constitutional proposals was in dire distress in the Federal Parliament, he decided to appeal to the citizens over the heads of the deputies. He was encouraged to take this risky route by more than two million signatures (mostly Czech) on a petition urging the preservation of the common state. Some thousands of Prague citizens responded in a manifestation of the historic Wenceslas Square. It was perhaps at this point that the president had to decide whether to come out openly in support of the looser, "confederate" structure of the state demanded by the Slovak negotiators. Such a move would have brought Havel into a direct confrontation with the newly emerging Czech team led by Václav Klaus. Shortly after the first mass meeting, Havel declared that there was no need for further demonstrations, leaving behind a feeling of disappointment and — more importantly — an irritated Parliament, which then proceeded to defeat again his proposals for breaking the constitutional logjam. With the bulk of the Czech population more or less indifferent and the Slovaks generally distrustful of him, it is not at all clear what would have happened if Havel had decided to continue his campaign for popular support.

When the president ran for reelection in the summer of 1992, he was defeated in the Federal Assembly by the Slovak vote. His relationship with Slovakia was not an easy one. His original eight advisers included only one Slovak, who left after six months.[98] At the outset, Havel was no less unaware of the Slovak situation than any other Czech intellectual and no less surprised at the outburst of Slovak nationalist rhetoric during the early parliamentary debate on the new name for the Federation. On one of his visits to Bratislava, he was forcibly prevented from speaking by Slovak separatists. More importantly, he earned the undying hostility of Slovak Prime Minister Mečiar, first because he was said to have opposed Mečiar's appointment to a high federal office, then because of the alleged involvement of "the Castle" in Mečiar's "first" removal from the office of Slovak prime minister, and finally because in his preelection appeal he abjured the voters by clear implication from voting for Mečiar's new party, which nevertheless came out victorious in the elections. Mečiar, "who never forgets or forgives," tried to use Havel's office as a bargaining chip with Václav Klaus, by then his negotiating protagonist, but Klaus refused.

When in July 1992 Havel resigned the remainder of his term, he was accused of "having left the sinking ship," thereby hastening the breakup, because he had already accepted it as inevitable and wished to avoid being placed in a position that might compromise his chances for election to the presidency of the new Czech state. Yet under the circumstances his withdrawal a few weeks before the expiration of his term appeared understandable. This, many of his friends thought, marked the end of the politician and the rebirth of the artist. Yet, after another period of "summer meditations" in his country cottage, private citizen Havel plunged into frantic consultations with both the new coalition parties and the opposition on the left. He sought to facilitate the passage of the constitutional legislation on the termination of the state in the deadlocked Federal Parliament, at one point briefly suggesting an extra-constitutional action, this time not to save the common state but to end it quickly and peacefully. With that objective in mind, he ultimately abandoned his commitment to both the common state and a national referendum.

At the same time, he intervened actively and with limited success in the negotiations for a new Czech constitution, often airing the views of the opposition. Contrary to the position of Klaus's party, he advocated a direct election of the Czech president by the people in order to strengthen the authority of that office. His view did not prevail, but he carefully avoided an open confrontation. Having decided to run for the Czech presidency, he was well aware that Klaus's support was essential. In January 1993, he was in fact elected president of the new Czech Republic by a large majority of the Czech Parliament.

Although sincerely dedicated to the preservation of the common state, Havel was unable to sustain this objective in the capacity of "intervenor" or "facilitator," or for that matter as a member of one of the parties to the constitutional negotiations. This, however, is only one perspective from which to view his role. His is a moving story of a courageous struggle to preserve personal integrity under the old regime, of learning and adapting with some difficulty and mixed success to the post-Communist world, of living with internal conflicts, of coming to terms with his own limitations, and of making difficult judgments of "the reality" calling for often distasteful compromises.

In *Czecho/Slovakia* I speculated about a parallel with Lincoln, the consummate lawyer-politician. Bruce Ackerman has evoked George Washington's decision to lend his immense prestige to breaking the then existing confederate Constitution in order to save the Constitutional Convention from certain failure. Ackerman adds:

> If Mr. Havel had President Yeltsin's courage, he would have broken with the Communist Constitution and used his prestige to call a constitutional convention and a subsequent referendum, in which a national majority could have expressed its will.[99]

Ernest Gellner, a distinguished scholar with a Czech background, strongly disagreed, pointing to the fundamental differences in the relevant conditions.[100] I do not propose "to mock comparison" (Ackerman), and in fact I thrive on it, as evidenced in *Czecho/Slovakia.* But it is difficult to conjure up in Czecho-Slovakia a scenario comparable with President Yeltsin's troops storming the parliament building in October 1993. There may have been a magic moment, in the fall of 1990 at the latest, when Havel might have had enough influence to force an extra-constitutional way toward the adoption of a new constitution, such as the calling of a constitutional convention. In fact, Federal Prime Minister Čalfa, the astute, professional politician in a sea of amateurs, raised this alternative in one of the president's confabs but abandoned it promptly as unrealistic[101] since the Assembly never would have agreed to surrender its constitutional power. With the Federal Assembly functioning and the constitution-making process just gearing up, there was no apparent reason to foresee the eventual deadlock and to embark on a revolutionary route so foreign to the local tradition. Havel's prestige as seen from Bratislava or from the parliamentary couloirs in Prague might not have been as immense as it was perceived to be from New Haven. Apart from his lack of political experience, Havel's power position, in a civilized, protodemocratic environment stressing "continuity" and legality as against Communist arbitrariness, was not comparable to Boris Yeltsin's. However, the full story of his role as a statesman on the domestic and international scenes remains to be told.

Two separate but related questions will have to be addressed by historians: first, could Havel, in the face of prevailing reality, have done more to save the common state and would his effort have made a difference in the outcome; and, second, was the dissolution a preferred alternative to an uneasy coexistence of the two peoples?

If I were cornered with a demand to answer the first question, I would respond that it was not within Václav Havel's power to avert the breakup. The structure prevailed over the "hero" even though in the final phase the drama was played out by other heroes (or villains, depending on the beholder's view). As for the second question, I attempted in *Czecho/Slovakia* to recount as accurately as I could the factors militating for and against the breakup, including some estimate of the consequences of the dissolution for the two peoples and the international community. Beyond that I feel unable to go, although I am tempted to suggest that the dissolution was not in the interest of the Slovaks and perhaps—in the long run—of the Czechs as well. Both questions call for more empirical work and analytical thought; the second requires a particularly difficult cost-benefit analysis with a heavy dose of futuristic speculation.

According to Arthur M. Schlesinger Jr.: "There is no solution in the last chapter; there is no last chapter. The best the interpreter can do is to trace figures in the carpet, recognizing as he must that other interpreters will trace other figures."[102] In Alan Brinkley's words: "There's never a moment when a historical question is settled, about which over time there is not some debate."[103] This is evidenced by the generation of revisionist historians who have interpreted the American Civil War as an "avoidable conflict," heaping blame on Lincoln and others. I am quite composed to see my story—and my answers—"revised."

7. The Last Afterthought

Ross and Ward suggest that parties in conflict often attribute a stalemate to differences in basic values or incompatibility of basic interests: some conflicts do reflect such irreconcilable differences and have little chance of being resolved by negotiations until one party can impose its will on the other or until objective circumstances change in a way that creates a greater commonality of interest.

> Conflict resolution is not always a desirable goal—sometimes wrongs must be righted, structural changes accomplished, or power redistributed under circumstances where any germane resolution demands that the objectives and interests of one party to the dispute be compromised to a degree that it will deem unacceptable and resist as long as it has any means to do so. But . . . many and perhaps even most conflicts are far more tractable than they seem, . . . disputants are often constrained not by objective circumstances but by cognitive, perceptual and motivating biases, . . . that incompatibility in basic needs, interests, and values [is] often more apparent than real.[104]

Unlike the Serb, Croatian, and Muslim strife, the Czech-Slovak conflict, while much less tractable than it appeared to most observers, falls into the category in which the incompatibilities proved in fact susceptible to a negotiated solution, albeit by a dissolution of the common state.

Notes

1. However, the eighteenth-century Czech "*risorgimento*" contained a political element from the onset due to the memories of the long history of the Czech Kingdom and the role of the Czech nobility. Conversation with Professor P. Pitha.
2. Ladislav Mňačko in LN, June 27, 1992, pp. 1, 8.
3. Aleš Gerloch, "Československá federace: uzavřená minulost? [Czechoslovak Federation: Closed Past?]," in Vojtěch Šimíček (ed.), Česko-slovenské

vztahy a střední Evropa [Czecho-Slovak Relations and Central Europe] 71, 72 (Mezinár. politol. ústav právnické faculty Masarykovy university v Brně, Czech Rep., 1994); Aleš Gerloch, "Teorie federalismu a rozdělení Československa [Theory of Federalism and Division of Czechoslovakia]," 1995 POLITOLOGICKÁ REVUE 13 (June 1995).

4. Friedrich Nietzsche, Der Wille zur Macht, sec. 70 at 57, sec. 770 at 512–13 and *passim* (Alfred Kröner Verlag, Leipzig, 1930).

5. Isaiah Berlin, Russian Thinkers 41, 43 (Penguin Books, New York, 1979).

6. Rudolf Arnheim, "The Split and the Structure," 1992 MICHIGAN QUARTERLY REVIEW 195, 204. See, however, Gertrude Himmelfarb, On Looking into the Abyss: Untimely Thoughts on Culture and Society (A.A. Knopf, New York, 1994).

7. Misha Glenny, "Why the Balkans Are So Violent," N.Y. REV. OF BOOKS, Sept. 19, 1996, pp. 35, 39.

8. Conversation with Ján Budaj.

9. Jon Elster, The Cement of Society: A Study of Social Order 128 (Cambridge U. Press, Cambridge, New York, Port Chester, Melbourne, Sydney, 1989).

10. Jan Švejnar, "Economic Transformation in Central and Eastern Europe: The Task Still Ahead," in Economic Transformation — The Task Still Ahead — A Symposium, Jan Švejnar, Oleh Havrylyshyn, Sergei K. Dubinin 4–8 (Per Jacobsson Foundation, Washington, D.C., 1995). See also Eric Stein, Czecho/Slovakia: Ethnic Conflict, Constitutional Fissure, Negotiated Breakup chap. V, text at notes 59, 60 (U. Michigan Press, Ann Arbor, 1997).

11. Public opinion survey of mid-1992 in Sharon L. Wolchik, "The Politics of Transition and the Break-Up of Czechoslovakia," in Jiří Musil (ed.), The End of Czechoslovakia 235–36 (Central European U. Press, Budapest, London, New York, 1995).

12. Conversation with Docent Robert Holman, adviser to Czech Republic Prime Minister Klaus.

13. Ellen Comisso, "Federalism and Nationalism in Post-Socialist Eastern Europe," unpublished paper for a symposium on "Federalism for the New Europe," Benjamin Cardozo School of Law, New York, Sept. 10–12, 1992.

14. The monetary union was replaced by a payments treaty (text in 64/1993 Sb. [Czech]), providing a clearing system based on the European Currency Unit, which, however, was scheduled to end (as a result of the Czech notification) in October 1995.

15. Conversation with Jiří Weigel, adviser to the Czech Republic prime minister.

16. "To be sure, there are class realities, but ethnic realities are there as well. Increasingly they are the *dominant* realities." Daniel P. Moynihan, "Elitland" 4 PSYCHOLOGY TODAY 70 (no. 4, 1970).

17. Some suspected the left of actually favoring the split because of the turn to the right in the Czech lands perceived as a threat to the left's influence in a common state and in Slovakia as well.

18. Jack Snyder and Karen Ballentine, "Nationalism and the Marketplace of Ideas," 21 International Security 5, 24, and *passim* (no. 2, 1996).

19. *See generally* Jiří Pehe, "Czechoslovakia," RFE/RL RES. REP. Oct. 2, 1992, 34, 37.

20. Jacques Rupnik, "The International Context," in Jiří Musil (ed.), The End of Czechoslovakia, *supra,* note 9, 276.

21. Vladimir V. Kusin, "Czechs and Slovaks: The Road to the Current Debate," RFE/RL RES. REP., Oct. 5, 1990, 4, 5.

22. E.J. Hobsbawm, Nations and Nationalism since 1780: Programme, Myth, Reality 164 (2d ed., Cambridge U. Press, Cambridge, New York, Melbourne, 1992).

23. Regina Cowen Karp, Central and Eastern Europe: The Challenge of Transition 7 (SIPRI, Oxford U. Press, New York, 1993).

24. Germany led the move for recognition. See "Recognition of the Yugoslav Successor States," position paper of the German Foreign Ministry, Bonn, March 10, 1993, in Statements and Speeches, German Information Center, vol. 16, no. 10.

25. John McGary and Brendan O'Leary (eds.), The Politics of Ethnic Conflict Regulation: Case Studies of Protracted Ethnic Conflict 8–22 (Routledge, London, New York, 1993).

26. THE ECONOMIST, Aug. 19, 1995, p. 42.

27. Ondřej Neuman in LN, Aug. 2, 1996, p. 3. Apart from the Slovaks residing in the Czech Republic, only a few thousand Germans, Poles, Ukrainians, and Vietnamese remain, along with several hundred thousand gypsies (Roma), most of whom, however, do not claim Roma nationality. A prominent Czech Social Democrat speaks of "a principle of exclusion" and asks whom the new state will exclude in the next crisis ("Will [the Czechs] not rather get rid of the burdensome state?"). Miloš Zeman in RP, Oct. 17, 1992, p. 4. For a criticism of the Czech Government minority policy, see Ján Mlynárik, LN, Aug. 6, 1996, p. 11. See also Petr Pithart, "Paradoxy rozchodu: filosofická a právni hlediska a evropské paralely [Paradoxes of the Parting: Philosophic and Legal Views and European Parallels]," in Rüdiger, Kipke, Vodička (eds.), Rozloučeni's Československem [Parting with Czechoslovakia] 215, 220 (Český spisovatel, a.s. Praha, 1993).

28. Karel Čapek, Čtení o TGM [Reading about TGM] 18 (Melantrich, Praha, 1969).

29. Czecho/Slovakia, "A Framework," text at note 16.

30. Zdeněk Strmiska, "Quelques remarques sur 'Le divorce tchéco-slovaque,' " 26 REV. D'ÉTUDES COMPARATIVES EST OUEST 183, 193 (no. 2, 1995).

31. According to a public opinion poll taken in the Czech Republic three years after the breakup, more than half of the Czechs consider the relations between the Czechs and Slovaks as good; 43 percent would welcome more intensive relations, and 50 percent believe that cooperation with Slovakia should be parallel to that with other states. LN, Feb. 28, 1996, p. 3.

32. McGary and O'Leary speak of "Partition and/or secession (self-determina-

tion)" (*supra,* note 25, 11). There are no generally accepted categories: the principal distinction is between cases in which the original state continues to exist within its diminished territory after the "separation" and those instances where it ceases to exist. Based on a study by the U.S. Department of State, Williams lists the following cases of "separation": Greater Colombia (1829–31), Union of Norway and Sweden (1905), Austro-Hungarian Empire (1918), United Arab Republic (1961), Union of Iceland and Denmark (1944), and Federation of Mali (1961). Paul R. Williams, "The Treaty Obligations of the Successor States of the Former Soviet Union, Yugoslavia, and Czechoslovakia: Do They Continue in Force?" 23 DENVER JOURNAL OF INTERNATIONAL LAW AND POLITICS 1, 13–16 (1994); Michael P. Scharf, "Musical Chairs: The Dissolution of States and Membership in the United Nations," 28 CORNELL J'L OF INTERNATIONAL LAW 29, 66 (1995); Mahulena Hošková, "Die Selbstauflösung der ČSFR – Ausgewählte rechtliche Aspekte," 53/3 ZAÖRV 688, 715–31 (1993); Joelle de Morzellec, "Nástupnictví států: Příklad rozdělení České a Slovenské Federativní Republiky [Succession of States: The Example of Division of the Czech and Slovak Federative Republic]," 9/93 PRÁVNÍK 777 (1993); Vladimír Balaš, "Některé mezinárodní aspekty dělení státu [Some International Aspects of the Division of States]," 11/92 PRÁVNÍK 996 (1992).

33. The Czech and Slovak Federative Republic belonged to some 50 international organizations.

34. Some 2,000 bilateral and 800 multilateral treaties concluded by the Federal Republic were involved. See also Const. Law 4/1993 Sb. of the Czech National Council, adopted on Dec. 15, 1992, on measures connected with the extinction of the Czech and Slovak Federative Republic, arts. 4 and 5. Treaties not relating to the territory of the Czech Republic are excluded from these obligations. According to a Czech expert, rights and obligations deriving from international customary law are included; principles of the Vienna Convention on state succession in respect of treaties "received a strong endorsement." Václav Mikulka, State Succession in Respect of Treaties – Czech Republic (National Report) in my file. *See also,* for example, exchange of notes with the German Federal Republic on continuing observation of treaties "until both sides agree otherwise," BUNDESGESETZBLATT 1993, part II, p. 762.

See art. 153 of the new Constitution of the Slovak Republic. Dean Kenneth J. Vandevelde, who advised the Slovakian Ministry of Foreign Affairs on an assignment by the American Bar Association's Central and East European Law Initiative, reported in June 1994 that Slovakia was a party to about 3,300 treaties. Since a case by case consideration of each treaty would take some years, Slovakia declared that it will honor its obligations under all treaties. Having established this presumption, the Ministry of Foreign Affairs would then determine the advisability of pursuing modification or termination of particular treaties. A major problem would relate to the many reservations to multilateral treaties "Interim Report on Technical Assistance to Slovakia," June 24, 1994.

"The Vienna Convention on Succession of States in Respect of Treaties" (UN Doc. A/CONF/80/31 [1978]) is not in force.

35. *See,* for example, Treaty between the Government of the Czech Republic

and the Government of the Slovak Republic on the joint use of reserved information and archival materials from the Ministries of Interior in the field of internal order and security. Vladimír Mikule et al., Mezinárodní smlouvy mezi Českou a Slovenskou republikou [International Treaties between the Czech Republic and Slovak Republic] 317–21 (Codex Bohemia, Praha, 1995).

36. Gideon Gottlieb, Nation against State: A New Approach to Ethnic Conflicts and the Decline of Sovereignty 122, also 3–5 and *passim* (Council on Foreign Relations Press, New York, 1993).

37. East Timor (Portugal v. Australia), Judgment 30 June 1995, I.C.J. Reports 1995, p. 13, par. 29.

38. The UN Charter (art. 1) and the UN instruments on self-determination, including the Covenants of Human Rights, speak of the right of "peoples."

39. See Czecho/Slovakia 209.

40. Thomas M. Franck, "The Emerging Right to Democratic Governance," 86 AJIL 46 (1992). The Slovak Hungarian parties complained about the Slovak government minority policy during the proceeding for admission of Slovakia to the Council of Europe, but their complaint did not affect its outcome.

41. Markku Suksi, Bringing in the People: A Comparison of Constitutional Forms and Practices of the Referendum 247, 268–69 (Martinus Nijhoff Publishers, Dordrecht, Boston, London, 1993). *See generally* Robert J. Thompson, "Referendums and Ethnoterritorial Movements: The Policy Consequences and Political Ramifications," in Robert J. Thompson and Joseph R. Rudolph Jr. (eds.), Ethnoterritorial Politics, Policy, and the Western World 181 (Lynne Rienner Pub., Boulder and London, 1989).

42. See Czecho/Slovakia, chap. VII, 3e; XI, 4; XIII, 5c.

43. Henry E. Brady and Cynthia S. Kaplan, "Eastern Europe and Former Soviet Union," in David Butler and Austin Ranney (eds.), Referendums around the World: The Growing Use of Direct Democracy 212 (AEI Press, Washington, D.C., 1994).

44. Henry E. Brady and Cynthia S. Kaplan, *ibid.* at 215.

45. In the Swedish-Norwegian case, an overwhelming majority supported the dissolution of the union in a referendum, which was required by Sweden as a condition for the dissolution. The vote was 368,208 in support of the dissolution, 184 against. Karen Larsen, A History of Norway 491 (Princeton U. Press, Princeton, 1948). In the October 30, 1995, referendum, the Quebecois rejected independence by the slim margin of 50.6 to 49.4 percent. Fifteen years earlier the separatists lost 60 to 40 percent. N.Y. TIMES, Oct. 31, 1995, p. 1A. In early 1996, with the popular separatist Lucian Bouchard appointed provincial premier, the polls indicated that the support within Quebec for independence was even higher than in October 1995. N.Y. TIMES, Jan. 30, 1996, p. 4A. See also *infra,* note 49.

46. Lea Brilmayer, "Secession and Self-Determination: A Territorial Interpretation," 16 YALE J. INT'L L. 177 (no. 1, Winter 1991).

47. Harry Beran, "A Liberal Theory of Secession," XXXII POLITICAL STUDIES 21–31 (1984).

48. Allen Buchanan, "Toward a Theory of Secession," 101 ETHICS 322, 323 (January 1991); Allen Buchanan, Secession: The Morality of Political Divorce from Fort Sumter to Lithuania and Quebec (Westview Press, Boulder, San Francisco, Oxford, 1991). *See generally* Holly A. Osterland, "National Self-Determination and Secession: The Slovak Model," 25 CASE WESTERN RESERVE JOURNAL OF INTERNATIONAL LAW 655 (no. 3, Summer 1993).

49. Lionel Vandenbergh, head of the Flemish separatist movement: "Walloon friends, we have lived for 160 years together and we have not been happy. Let's now get a divorce before a notary, as did the Czechs and Slovaks." "Obava z čs. syndromu [Fear of the Czs. Syndrome]," HN, Oct. 20, 1992, p. 30. Former Czech Prime Minister Pithart "now finds himself being invited to Belgium and Quebec, to tell them how you make a velvet divorce." Timothy Garton Ash, "Journey to the Post-Communist East," N.Y. REVIEW OF BOOKS, June 23, 1994, 13, 17. The leader of the Italian Northern League, Umberto Bossi, suggested "a Czecho-Slovak solution" and the league organized a "Parliament of the North" and a "shadow government" for "Padania." N.Y. TIMES, May 12, 1996, p. 8; May 13, 1996, p. A5. In Quebec, the Prime Minister with an unblemished pro-independence record took the helm of the Provincial government after the referendum vote rejecting secession by the slimmest of margins. His strategy has been to "say as little [about the secession] as his radical supporters will allow" while seeking federal help for a recovery of the ailing Quebec Province economy, hoping for a referendum victory after 1999. THE ECONOMIST, June 15, 1996, p. 43. With one important exception, his design is similar to Ján Čarnogurský's plan for Slovakia to enjoy the advantages of a federation with the Czechs until both Republics join the European Union as independent states. The important difference was that Čarnogurský proclaimed his goal frankly and openly from the outset. When the Slovak Prime Minister Mečiar was asked in Strasbourg by Luciano Lorenzi of the Italian Lega Nord whether he had any suggestions regarding the independence of "Padania," he responded with unaccustomed self-restraint: "We have no advice to offer you," he said, but proceeded to enumerate the many difficulties requiring solution in cases of separation. In the case of Slovakia, he added, the benefits outweighed the disadvantages: two states that cooperate are better than a state in a disequilibrium. EUROPE, no. 6762 (n.s.), July 3, 1996, p. 4.

50. Amitai Etzioni, "The Evils of Self-Determination," 1992–93 FOREIGN POLICY 21.

51. The evidence listed includes Cyprus, Lebanon, Sri Lanka, Sudan, and "increasingly" India but curiously also the Soviet Union, Yugoslavia, and Czechoslovakia, where the absence of democracy had little, if any, connection with the cultural or ethnic differences. Michael Lind, "In Defense of Liberal Nationalism," 13 FOREIGN AFFAIRS 87, 95 (No. 3, 1994).

52. The U.S. government and the Parliament of the European Union expressed formally their concern about observances of democratic principles by the Mečiar government, and there was some criticism in the Council of Europe and among U.S. senators of the discrimination against the Roma by the Czech

government's application of the citizenship legislation. "Slovakia-Madness," THE ECONOMIST, Dec. 2, 1995, pp. 54–55; "Czech Government Eases Citizenship Restrictions," OPEN MEDIA RESEARCH INSTITUTE DAILY DIGEST II, no. 28, Feb. 8, 1996, p. 3.

53. *See* on this Jiří Boguszak and Luboš Tichý in LN, July 28, 1992, p. 8.

54. Even in the eventually peaceful dissolution of the Norway-Sweden Union in 1905 an armed conflict was a possibility. The last straw for its breakup was Norway's insistence on fully independent consular offices to represent its interests abroad, shades of the Slovak peremptory demand for their own representation abroad. The Czech side, during the negotiations, accepted separate treaty-making powers of the Republics and their own diplomatic representation within the federal foreign affairs framework. It rejected, however, separate membership in international organizations, arguing the concept of "indivisibility" of the international personality of the Federation. The Union of Norway and Sweden, which lasted 90 years, was a much looser association than the Czecho-Slovak Federation. Karen Larsen, *supra,* note 45, 484–87. It has been suggested that Norway's refusal to join the European Union might be "a consequence of Norway's relatively recent independence from Sweden." Christine Ingebritsen, "Norway and European Union," 7 ECSA NEWSLETTER 16 (no. 3, Fall 1994).

55. *See also* Sharon L. Wolchik, "The Politics of Ethnicity in Post-Communist Czechoslovakia," 8 EAST EUROPEAN POLITICS AND SOCIETIES 153, 174 (no. 1, 1994). The army was not an "independently functioning power factor." Vladimír Kusín in XXII LISTY 18, 20 (no. 2, 1992).

56. Conversation with I. Gašparovič. A minuscule territorial adjustment was approved by Slovakia but it was still before the Czech House in mid-1996.

57. Ted Robert Gurr and Barbara Harff, Ethnic Conflict in World Politics 85 (Westview Press, Boulder, San Francisco, Oxford, 1994).

58. Bruce Russet, "Politics and Alternative Security: Toward a More Democratic, Therefore More Peaceful, World," in Burns H. Weston (ed.), Alternative Security: Living without Nuclear Deterrence 107, 111 (Westview Press, Boulder, San Francisco, Oxford, 1990).

59. John McGary and Brendan O'Leary, *supra,* note 25, 6.

60. Cynthia H. Enloe, Ethnic Conflict and Political Development 7 (Little Brown and Co., Boston, 1972).

61. Michael Lind, "In Defense of Liberal Nationalism," 73 FOREIGN AFFAIRS 87, 89, 90–91 (no. 3, 1994). *See generally* Timothy Garton Ash, "Bosnia in Our Future," N.Y. REV. OF BOOKS, Dec. 21, 1995, p. 31.

62. Another writer offers a third alternative to separation and independence in the form of regimes not based on territoriality such as functional zones granting limited exercise of national rights beyond established frontiers, loose unions, and so on. Gideon Gottlieb, "Nations without States," 73 FOREIGN AFFAIRS 100 (no. 3, 1994).

63. An Oxford University scholar paints the following picture: "In every one of the new democracies, there are large national minorities. Even Poland, normally thought of as a homogeneous state, contains around 250,000 Germans,

while roughly the same number of Poles live in Lithuania. In every state bordering Hungary, except in Austria, there is a large Hungarian minority, amounting to two million in Rumanian Transylvania. Indeed, almost 30 percent of the Hungarian-speaking population of Central Europe live outside Hungary. Similarly, 1.8 million Albanians live in Kosovo, a region of Yugoslavia, while Bulgaria contains around one million Turkish-speaking Muslims, amounting to 10 percent of the population. The Baltic states contain large Russian minorities, and indeed there are 25 million Russians living outside Russia, while Bulgaria, the Czech Republic, Hungary, Rumania, and Slovakia contain large gypsy populations, and Hungary has a substantial Jewish minority. The internal divisions within the states formed from the former Yugoslavia are too painfully obvious to need recital." Vernon Bogdanor, "I. Overcoming the Twentieth Century: Democracy and Nationalism in Central and Eastern Europe," in Istwan Pogany (ed.), Human Rights in Eastern Europe 4 (Edward Elgar, Aldershot, England, 1995).

64. Sharon Fisher, "Slovakia: The First Year of Independence," RFE/RL Res. Rep., Jan. 7, 1994, 87, 91. This a posteriori expression of feelings does not say much about how the Slovaks might have voted in a referendum prior to the dissolution. *See* James F. Brown, Hopes and Shadows: Eastern Europe after Communism 63–66 ("Alone in the World") (Duke University Press, Durham, 1994).

65. Michael Mandelbaum, "Introduction," in Shafigul Islam and Michael Mandelbaum (eds.), Making Markets: Economic Transformation in Eastern Europe and Post-Soviet States 1 (Council on Foreign Relations, New York, 1993). *See generally* James F. Brown, *supra,* note 60; Georg Brunner, Politischer Systemwandel und Verfassungsreformen in Osteuropa (Verlag Josef Eul, Bergisch Gladbach–Köln, 1990). Christopher G.A. Bryant and Edmund Mokrzycki (eds.), The New Great Transformation? Change and Continuity in East-Central Europe (Routledge, London, New York, 1994). Robert A. Dahl, in Democracy and Its Critics (Yale U. Press, New Haven, London, 1989), sees two historical transformations toward democracy: the birth of democratic city states in ancient Greece and Rome; and the emergence of large-scale representative democracies in the eighteenth century, multiplied in the nineteenth and twentieth centuries. He asks whether the present marks the third democratic transformation.

66. Richard A. Posner, "Review of the Future of Liberal Revolution by Bruce Ackerman" (Yale U. Press, New Haven, 1992), in I E. Eur. Const. Rev. 35 at 37 (Fall 1992).

67. Jon Elster, "The Necessity and Impossibility of Simultaneous Economic and Political Reform," in Douglas Greenberg, Stanley N. Katz, Melanie Beth Oliviero, and Steven C. Wheatley (eds.), Constitutionalism and Democracy 267, 268 (Oxford U. Press, New York, Oxford, 1993).

68. "I felt on the contrary that we could not solve successfully any of the great problems with which our society was struggling, from the political to the economic to the social, without responding first to the question in what kind of a state do we want to live." Václav Havel, "Projev ve Federálním shromáždění, Praha, 3.12,

1991 [Address in the Federal Assembly, Prague, Dec. 3, 1991]," in Vážení občané—Projevy, červenec 1990—červenec 1992 [Esteemed Citizens—Addresses, July 1990–July 1992] 123 (LN, Praha, 1992).

69. Ilja Šetlik in LN, Sept. 3, 1993, p. 5.

70. Ralf Dahrendorf, in his lecture in Prague, in LN, March 15, 1994, p. 1.

71. Jean L. Cohen and Andrew Arato, Civil Society and Political Theory viii, ix (MIT Press, Cambridge, Mass., London, 1992). Michael Walzer points to the disagreement on what the concept of "civil society" includes and excludes. "It is enough to say," he writes, "that the civil society incorporates many of the associations and identities we value outside of, prior to, or in the shadow of state and citizenship." Michael Walzer (ed.), Toward a Global Civil Society 1 (Berghahn Books, Providence, Oxford, 1995).

72. Ernest Gellner, "Innocents Abroad: The Future of Liberal Revolution by Bruce Ackerman," New Republic, Nov. 30, 1992, 38, 39.

73. Havel complained that "at home" people confused the concept of civil society "with direct democracy" or "a chaotic rule of thousands of associations and civic initiatives." In America, the citizens voluntarily take over uncounted social, ecological, health, cultural, and education functions that can be better performed by them than by the state, in what can be described as "citizens' self-care" with millions of nonprofit organizations. It is a part of human self-realization because man is a social creature. LN, Oct. 10, 1994, p. 16.

74. Jean Bethke Elshtain, Democracy on Trial (Basic Books, New York, 1995). In the United States, participation in traditional voluntary associations declined between 25 and 30 percent, because, it is said, of television. Other data indicate, however, that the voluntary activity in other areas has risen substantially. Anthony Lewis, "An Atomized America," N.Y. Times, Dec. 18, 1995, p. A11; Frank Riessman, "America's Still a Nation of Joiners," N.Y. Times, Dec. 21, 1995, p. 28.

75. Sociologist Lubomir Brokl, quoted in Přítomnost, 4/1992, p. 2. LN, Aug. 1, 1994, p. 3. *See generally* Michael Walzer, "Political Actors and Political Roles in East-Central Europe," in Michael Waller and Martin Myant (eds.), Parties, Trade Unions and Society in East-Central Europe 21–35 (Frank Cass, Illford, Essex, Eng., Portland, Ore., 1994).

76. Petr Příhoda in LN, June 5, 1992, p. 8; conversations with M. Leško, Slovak editor in chief, Pravda.

77. Number of enterprises with up to 100 employees in 1991:

Cz. Sl. Fed. Rep. 12,975, employing 130,640
Czech Rep. 9,936, employing 99,181
Slovak Rep. 3,039, employing 31,459

Of these in the private sector:

Cz. Sl. Fed. Rep. 9,318, employing 62,014
Czech Rep. 7,390, employing 47,677
Slovak Rep. 1,928, employing 14,337

Number of small private entrepreneurs:

	March 31, 1991	December 31, 1992
Cz. Sl. Fed. Rep.	655,023	1,338,353
Czech Rep.	495,670	1,058,504
Slovak Rep.	159,353	279,849

Statistická ročenka [Annual of Statistics], Czech and Slovak Fed. Rep., p. 537 (SEVT, Praha, 1992). There are roughly twice as many people living in the Czech Republic than in Slovakia.

Another set of figures on the situation in the Czech Republic was made available by the Czech Bureau of Statistics:

	Business associations	Associations of natural and legal persons
1991	23,112	11,558
1993	60,376	28,446
1994	88,424	33,618

Pavel Machonin, Milan Tuček, "Genese nové struktury v České republice a její sociální aktéři [Genesis of the New Social Structure in the Czech Republic and Its Social Actors], in Vlasta Šafariková *et al.*, Transformace české společnosti 1989–1995 [Transformation of the Czech Society], (Doplněk, Brno, 1996), report (at 27) that the number of registered private entrepreneurs in the Czech Republic rose from 65,000 in 1989 to approximately one million in 1993. *See also* Jan Švejnar, *supra,* note 10, 5 and *passim*.

78. Robert D. Putnam with Robert Leonardi and Raffaella T. Nanetti, Making Democracy Work-Civic Traditions in Modern Italy (Princeton U. Press, Princeton, NJ, 1993).

79. In the 1996 election, the ruling right-of-center coalition lost its parliamentary majority in the face of an unexpected, dramatic rise of support for the left-oriented reconstructed Social Democratic party. A new minority government composed of the same coalition once again headed by Václav Klaus may find it more difficult to govern but there is no evidence that either the pluralist democracy or the basic economic reforms are in danger.

80. *See generally,* Michael Waller and Martin Myant (eds.), Parties, Trade Unions, and Society in East Central Europe (Frank Cass, Illford, Essex, Eng., Portland, Ore., 1994); Sten Berglund and Jan Åke Dellenbrant (eds.), The New Democracies in Eastern Europe: Party Systems and Political Cleavages (2d ed., Edward Elgar Publishing Ltd., Aldershot, Eng., Vermont, 1994); and Hans-Ulrich Derlien and George J. Szablowski (eds.), Regime Transition, Elites, and Bureaucracies in Eastern Europe, 6 GOVERNANCE, Special Issue (no. 3, July 1993).

81. If this were a society amenable to pragmatic solutions—which of course it is not—one might take a charitable view that over the years preceding the admission to the European Union, contrary to general expectation, the Federa-

tion would prove useful, if not indispensable. On the personality of Ján Čarnogurský, *see* Petr Nováček in MFD, May 27, 1992, p. 7. *See also* Čarnogurský's lecture at Oxford in PIATOK, Jan. 3, 1992, p. 12.

82. Günther Winkler, Zeit und Recht 569–70 (Springer Verlag, Wien, New York, 1995).

83. Havel strongly supported that decision in a speech of February 5, 1990. Václav Havel, Projevy [Addresses] 68 (Vyšehrad, Praha, 1990).

84. Vladimír V. Kusín, "O novém pojeti česko-slovenské vzájemnosti, [On a New Perception of the Czecho-Slovak Mutuality]," 22 LISTY 18, 19–20 (no. 2, 1992). The author is a former Czech emigré on the staff of the Radio Free Europe–Radio Liberty. He observes that Ireland separated from Great Britain in 1921.

85. Lee Ross and Andrew Ward, "Naive Realism: Implications for Social Conflict and Misunderstanding," unpublished, 1994. *See also,* by the same authors, "Naive Realism in Everyday Life: Implications for Social Conflict and Misunderstanding," in Kenneth Arrow et al. (eds.), Barriers to Conflict Resolution 103, 110–11 (W.W. Norton and Co., New York, London, 1995).

86. See Czecho/Slovakia, chap. IX, 2.

87. Kusín, *supra,* note 84, 18.

88. Martin Bútora and Zora Bútorová, "Slovakia: The Identity Challenges of the Newly Born States," 60 SOCIAL RESEARCH 705, 718–20 (no. 4, Winter 1993); Martin Myant, "Czech and Slovak Trade Unions," in Michael Waller and Martin Myant (eds.), *supra,* note 75, 59.

89. Jiří Weigel, economic adviser in the office of Czech Republic Prime Minister Klaus, asserted that there was no prior intent for a separation. I have noted, however, that as early as March 1991, Klaus made it clear that a breakup would be preferable to any constitutional arrangements that would endanger the reforms. When he perceived an actual threat (e.g., two banks of emission), he acted accordingly. LN, Mar. 13, 1991, p. 2.

90. While Mečiar "never loved" Klaus, he stressed that the Czech leader "has never criticized us, never offended, when we come to negotiations [presumably before Klaus became Czech prime minister], he is the only one to keep silent. We view it as a tactical variant for the future . . . ." SMENA, Jan. 29, 1992, p. 3.

91. Czech historian Jaroslav Valenta, XXIII LISTY 107, 108 (no. 4, 1993).

92. I dealt with the specific arguments in Czecho/Slovakia, particularly chap. VI, 4c, chap. VII, 3c, chap. IX, 1 and 2a–b, and chap. XV, 4, b, ii.

93. Marián Leško, "Mysleli sme, že nie je politik [We thought he was not a politician]," NOVÉ SLOVO BEZ RESPEKTU, Oct. 19, 1992, p. 24. *See also ibid.,* Oct. 26, 1992, p. 20; Nov. 2, 1992, p. 20; Nov. 16, 1992, p. 20; Nov. 23, 1992, p. 20; Nov. 30, 1992, p. 20. This is a "hatchet job" on Havel in which the author confronts Havel's rhetoric with his "deeds." What politician could fare well in such a confrontation? In 1995, Leško, by then editor in chief of the largest Slovak daily, told me with a sheepish smile that he had been carried away by a youthful enthusiasm and today would be "much softer" on Havel.

94. "Jerusalem, April 26, 1990," in Václav Havel, Projevy [Addresses] 100–103 (Vyšehrad, Praha, 1990).

95. *Ibid.* WASHINGTON, Feb. 21, 1990, 59, 60.
96. Conversation with V. Žák.
97. Heřman Chromý, "Politik Václav Havel," XXIV LISTY 11, 13 (no. 3, 1994).
98. Conversation with Milan Kňažko.
99. Bruce A. Ackerman, "1787 and 1993," NEW YORK TIMES, April 3, 1993, Op Ed, p. 23. *See generally* Bruce A. Ackerman, The Future of Liberal Revolution (Yale U. Press, New Haven, London, 1992).
100. Ernest Gellner, "Innocents Abroad: The Future Liberal Revolution by Bruce Ackerman," NEW REPUBLIC, Nov. 30, 1992, p. 38. *See* David Golove, "Liberal Revolution, Constitutionalism, and the Consolidation of Democracy: A Review of Bruce Ackerman's The Future of Liberal Revolution," 1993 WISC. L. R. 1591, 1595 (no. 6).
101. Czecho/Slovakia, chap. VII, 3c.
102. Arthur M. Schlesinger Jr., The Cycles of American History 3 (Houghton Mifflin, New York, 1986).
103. Quoted in James Atlas, "Ways to Look at the Past (or Did It Really Happen?)," N.Y. TIMES, Nov. 13, 1994, E3.
104. Lee Ross and Andrew Ward, "Naive Realism: Implications for Social Conflict and Misunderstanding" (unpublished).

Coda

Reminiscences of the Embryonic EEC

The following remarks were given by Professor Emeritus Eric Stein at a dinner in Villa Montalto, Florence, May 20, 1989, celebrating his seventy-fifth birthday.

I believe that this is the first time for me to meet most of you in my exalted position of emeritus. A few weeks ago I had an opportunity to explain the derivation of the word emeritus to our students, who of course are quite innocent of any knowledge of Latin. I told them the "e" in "emeritus" comes from the Latin "ex" which means "out" and "meritus" means "you deserve it," in other words, "you are out and you deserve it."

In a more serious vein, speaking of getting old, I want to confide to you that the rumors about old age bringing serenity, peace of mind and, above all, instant wisdom, are highly exaggerated. It is not easy to be wise, or even to pretend to know the truth in this complex world. Here is what W.B. Yeats said:

My temptation is quiet.
Here at life's end
Neither loose imagination
Nor the mill of the mind
Consuming its rag and bone
Can make the truth known.
Grant me an old man's frenzy . . .

Old age—I am told—brings an irresistible compulsion to look back to the past. Therefore, I shall impose on you a few personal reminiscences.

In the early 1950s—this was A.D., I hasten to say—when I was on the staff of the Department of State in Washington, I became increasingly intrigued by the dispatches we were receiving from our Embassy in Luxembourg about the brand new, rather bizarre structure coming to life there, something in the shape of a "supranational" administrative

Reprinted with permission from 34 LAW QUADRANGLE NOTES 19–21 (no. 1, fall 1989).

agency established to regulate two economic sectors—coal and steel—artificially severed from the national economies of six countries and saddled with an elaborate political and judicial instrumentarium. This was in the halcyon days of international institution building, and I was fortunate that my assignment in the State Department was the shining new United Nations.

There is in all of us a need for a myth, a mythology that would help us "to escape the two-dimensional, stale image of the world"; and for those of us who grew up without tradition or ritual, there is a compelling longing for a substitute. In my case it was the idea whose time appeared to have come after the Second World War—the idea, or myth, of a new international order under law. Again, there is in all of us—as Doctor Freud told us—a longing for returning in reality or in memory, to the locale of our childhood dreams and affections. To see my old Europe attempting to shed its old ways for a new art of governance was an appealing prospect. Consequently, the search for a myth and the desire to return have been the sources of some forty years of my professional effort. For better or for worse, the product of this effort bears the evidence of the source.

On the positive side, another episode from about the same period—the early 1960s—had a lasting impact on my thinking about the Community. Michel Gaudet, the brilliant first director general of the Legal Service of the Commission, let me have an office not far from his in Rue Beliard, and I spent some 10 months watching the Commission lawyers do what we tried to do in Washington and New York in 1946, 1947: to get the United Nations off the ground. I felt that without an experience in Brussels I would not understand the microcosm of the Community institutions. At that same time, the legal service was in the throes of preparing the Commission's position in what was to become the European counterpart to *Marbury vs. Madison,* the celebrated *Van Gend and Loos* case before the Community Court of Justice. The overarching issue was wrapped up in a trivial controversy over the customs duties on chemicals made of horse urine, imported from Germany to the Netherlands. The real issue was, Is the constituent treaty of the Community an ordinary treaty to be interpreted by the traditional canons of public international law or is it a quasi-constitution to be interpreted in the mode of a national constitution? There was a sharp division between those who, like myself, were accustomed to think in terms of the public international law and international organization and those led by Michel Gaudet himself, supported among others by Gerhard Bebr, who urged the quasi-federal, constitutional approach. I confess that, listening to the intramural debate, it took me some time before I was able to understand the historic implication of the controversy. As Jacques Bourgeois testified in one of his remarkable essays, this experience at Rue Beliard informed my basic classroom approach to the nature of Community law and the role of the Court of Justice.

The dispatches from Luxembourg I mentioned earlier reported the first judgments of the Court of Justice of the European Coal and Steel Community. Although I didn't find the subject matter particularly appealing, I wrote an article about them. The piece appeared in the *Columbia Law Review* in 1955, and it was the first article about the Court, as far as I know, to appear in the English language anywhere.

Here is another first. In 1960 we helped the Federal Bar Association to organize the Institute on Legal Aspects of the European Community in Washington, D.C. Several hundred American lawyers crowded into a large hotel hall to listen to a star-studded delegation headed by Jean Rey, then Commissioner in charge of External Relations, and including Fernand Spaak, Michel Gaudet, Pieter Verloren Van Themaat and Theodor Vogelaar. The mood at the time was strikingly similar to the current optimistic outlook about Europe. In my opening address, entitled "An American Lawyer Views the Community," I said, if you allow me to quote myself: "As far as I am aware—this [that is, the Institute] is the first undertaking of its kind in the United States, if not in the Western Hemisphere." I ended my talk with a clarion call for American lawyers to learn about "the new economic law" and for a new way of dialogue and cooperation with Europe.

Jean Rey, the amiable, irrepressible talker, succeeded the apostolic, austere, ceremonial Dr. Hallstein as President of the Commission. On one occasion, when my wife and I visited the Reys at their home in Liège, we found Mr. Rey in a state of a higher than usual exhilaration: The Council of Ministers had just agreed on the cereal prices in the context of the common agricultural policy. The price agreement, Mr. Rey waxed enthusiastically, meant that common currency and a monetary union were just around the corner. What was in fact around the corner, as we all know in retrospect, was the tricky monetary compensation amounts, and a common currency is today still a distant goal. This encounter has remained grafted in my mind as a warning, a telling illustration of the myth intruding upon the stark reality, an ever-present danger for all devoted "pro-Europeans."

To continue in the typically American vein of robust competitiveness—of being the first—the most important first, of course, was Michigan's teaching program on the Community, the first such program introduced in the United States, preceding even most European universities. Even today, there are more law students in Joseph Weiler's class than in comparable courses of many European law faculties. Our teaching program—and my own work—has been marked from the outset by an idiosyncratic, some might say parochial, orientation: It has stressed the American concern in the broadest, most benign, most cooperative sense of the word, and it has been consistently comparative, projecting the European story not only against the American federal experience, but also against the discrete disciplines of American public and private law. Alfred Conard, for instance, in his time, was the master of comparing European and American company law.

There were two milestones separated by two decades. In 1960 we brought together for the first time a transatlantic group, resulting in the two volumes on *The American Enterprise in the European Common Market—A Legal Profile.* Twenty years later, another group including some of the second and third generation of Community lawyers assembled in the enchanting quarters of the Villa Serbeloni in Bellagio to produce our book, *Courts and Free Markets—Perspectives from the United States and Europe.* Some of you here were present at Bellagio on Lake Como and remember those of our friends who no longer are living: Otto Kahn-Freund of Oxford, Justice Stewart of the United States Supreme Court, and Paul Leleux of the Commission of the European Community.

Our first conception in teaching Community law was the Community as a part of the broad Atlantic area. As the law of the Community mushroomed and the idea of equal partnership between Europe and America—the two pillars idea—came to the fore, our focus has necessarily narrowed. Finally, with Japan entering the scene, new perspectives have emerged in the complex, triangular relationship of cooperation and competition that needed to be addressed. No wonder that Joseph Weiler's two-term course, which he calls "Trading in and with Europe," devotes a major portion to such topics as the antidumping law and rules of origin. James Adams, an expert on European industrial organization, deals with competition policy in Europe, and of course John Jackson, the master of GATT, provides the global context, with Bruno Simma bringing in the fundamental concerns of humanity, the European mechanisms for assuring basic individual human rights.

The interesting question I would like to leave with you to ponder is what will be our classroom context in 1993, in 2000, in 2010? Can we indulge for once in the best case scenario in which the 1992 Community's magnetism will bring about the unification of Germany within free Europe from the Atlantic to the Urals? To bowdlerize Jean-Francois Revel, Euroeuphoria may perhaps be as dangerous as Europessimism.

Looking at this distinguished audience, ladies and gentlemen, it is difficult to ward off a feeling of sentimental nostalgia. My wife and I have been warm friends with three generations of Europeans with a Michigan connection. Moreover, the fourth generation, fresh from the graduation in Ann Arbor a few days ago, is in the wings.

As for my own plans and prospects, allow me to conclude by quoting, at the risk of appearing immodest, a letter written by Mr. J. Oliver Wendell Holmes in 1923, when he was 82 years old:

> I may work on for a year or two, but I cannot hope to add much to what I have done. I am too skeptical to think that it matters much, but too conscious of the mystery of the universe to say that it or anything else does not. I bow my head, I think serenely, and I say, [as I told someone the other day,] Cosmos, Now lettest thou thy ganglion dissolve in peace.

A Million Footnotes

Virginia Stein

Behind every successful academic there is a . . . million footnotes. I'll bet you thought I was going to say a good wife! That may be, but not necessarily so. So I propose to add a very few footnotes to the remarks Eric has just made—to give you my behind-the-scenes look at some of these career highlights.

Footnote Number One: That first article on the Coal and Steel Community was written in the course of our courtship in Washington. When other couples were out picnicking or spooning under the moon on Saturday nights—where were we? Sorting documents and checking the footnotes on this new institution. The next time I was confronted with that article was on our honeymoon in Geneva at a luncheon with the Coal and Steel Community's chief lawyer, Michel Gaudet, and his wife. It was the chief topic of the lunch conversation. Little did I know that this was to be the pattern of so much of our social life in the thirty-odd years to come. But I've absorbed by long exposure a lot of information about that Rome Treaty: Article 85—that's antitrust; Article 177—that's reference from national courts to the Luxembourg Court; and especially Article 173—"Standing to Sue." It took me a long time to understand the idea of "Standing to Sue." Apropos, have you heard about the 77-year-old lady in West Germany who asked a German court last fall to enjoin the Weather Bureau from using in its weather reports the expression "Altweibersommer," "Old Women's Summer" (our Indian Summer) because she found it offensive to her senior sex. She didn't get her injunction. The court denied her standing to sue.

Footnote Number Two: During all our research leaves from the Law School I have become intimately acquainted with practically every postal clerk in Western Europe—from Stockholm to Bari I've shipped back the manuscripts for all those books and articles authored by E. Stein.

Footnote Number Three: All this has not been without some risk to our health. In London we were fifty feet away from an IRA bomb explosion. Bloodied victims were rushed into our restaurant and we were evacuated on the run—unhappily, after we'd paid our check. In Rome we were within close earshot of a terrorist bomb attack on a U.S. Marine barracks and at a concert when another U.S. installation next door was bombed by Italian extremists. In Frankfurt we were taken off on the double from our Alitalia plane and held incommunicado, surrounded by gun-toting policemen for hours, due to a threat of a bomb on the plane.
Footnote Number Four: Our stays in Europe have produced a very important spin-off for me with a new career in art history. I turned all those hours I spent in museums on this old continent to good effect when I began to teach art history back home. Indeed, this by-product has enriched both our lives. I think by now Eric could certainly pass one of my exams on the Flemish Primitives and probably on Florentine art work, too! And finally:
Footnote Number Five: On all our sojourns in Europe we have enjoyed such boundless hospitality from all our friends—and so many of you are here tonight. It has added a great variety to our Arkansas-Czech cuisine—with a recipe for waterzooi from Belgium when it was one of the *Six,* for English trifle from London when it became one of the *Nine,* and most recently a great gaspacho from Spain when it made one of the *Twelve.*

As a part of the Law School family, I have been happy to have been a side-line witness to the building of the European Community here and the study of its law at Michigan.

This has been a wonderful reunion, and we are just delighted to see you all. Thank you so much for this great occasion.

Index

Abbreviations

AG	Advocate General
EC	European Community
ECJ	European Court of Justice
EEC	European Economic Community
EP	European Parliament
EPC	European Political Cooperation
EU	European Union

Academy of European Law, 192
Ackerman, Bruce, 438, 454
act of state doctrine, 274n. 115
Adams, James, 474
Adenauer, 352
Administrative Procedure Act, 175, 177–78
  section 10: 166
Afghanistan, 250, 257
Aktiengesetz (German corporation law), 96
Alcan case, 169
Algeria, 250
Allen, Francis A., 103
Allied Commission for Italy, 3
  Legal Subcommission, 3–4
Allied Military Tribunal, 4
Allott, Philip 305–7
American Bar Association, 100, 313–14, 320
  House of Delegates, 325
American Civil Liberties Union (ACLU), 384
American Civil War, 127, 456
American exceptionalism, 348, 386
American Journal of Comparative Law, 101
American Law Institute (ALI), 100, 313–14
American Revolution, 199, 439
American Union, 237
Amsterdam Treaty, 114, 193, 310, 335, 342
Angola, 254
Arab-Israeli conflict, 255
Argentina, 257–58
assimilation of laws, 106n. 23
Association of American Law Schools, 103
Auschwitz, 382–83, 411–12, 414–16
"Auschwitz lie," 347
  American cases, 382–85
  constitutional question, 354–55, 366
  European Commission of Human Rights, 380
  in France, 350, 394n. 55
  German cases, 355–57
  German Criminal Code, authority to prosecute, 354, 381

"Auschwitz lie" (*continued*)
judicial notice of Holocaust, 356–57
Law of 1985 (German)
origin, 368–69
perceptions of the law, 374–77
process of enactment, 370–73
text, 373–74
Nuremberg Laws "applied," 365–67
in Switzerland, 389–90n. 11
U.S.-German law compared, 385–88
Australia, 92, 350, 429
Austria, 338, 428, 437

balance of power, 113, 115, 180, 196
in EC, 19, 169
in UN, 5
in U.S., 204, 207, 216–17
Bangladesh, 254
Battaglia, 68
Beauharnais v. Illinois, 383–84
Bebr, Gerhard, 472
Belgium, 19–20, 28, 61, 69, 117, 338, 343, 353, 421, 434
Bellagio Conference and Papers, 8, 112, 114, 474
Beneš, 418
Bergen-Belsen, 372
Berkhouwer, 62, 64–65, 68
Berlin, Isaiah, 112
Bishop, William W., 10
Bitburg, 372, 415
Blaisse, 62, 64, 68
Blasi, 141
Bock case, 168, 170
Boerne v. Flores, 157–58n. 36
Bollinger, 385–86
Bonvicini, 251
Bosnia, 426
Bourgeois, Jacques, 215, 241–42, 473
Bricker Amendment, 220
Brinkley, Alan, 456
Britain. *See* United Kingdom
British Industrial Relations Act (1971), 92, 99
British Tax Treaty, 216
Broszat, 357
Bruns, 61, 69
Bulgaria, 6, 438
Bundesrat, 341, 368–69
See also Germany, Federal Parliament
Bundestag, 65, 369–71, 377, 380, 410–11
Legal Committee, 66, 371, 373
See also Germany, Federal Parliament
Burg, J.G., 364
Burger Court, 317, 325
Burke, 304
Butz, 357, 382

Čalfa, Marián, 441, 455
Cambridge University, 3
Canada, 92, 236, 350, 421, 429, 434
Quebec separatism, 434, 460n. 45, 461n. 49
Supreme Court of, 348
Capotorti, Francesco, 162
Cappelletti, Mauro, 192
Carboni, 69
Čarnogurský, Jan 441
Carr, E.H., 431
Cassese, Antonio, 10
Catholic Church, 92
Celle case, 364–68
Center for Research on Antisemitism, Berlin Technical University, 411
Central European Free Trade Agreement, 436
Cesare, Sig. de, 58
Chad, 250
Chamber of Industry and Commerce in the Federal Republic of Germany, 60
Charles University Law Faculty, 418
Charter 77: 419

Charter of Basic Rights and Freedoms in Czecho-Slovakia, 444
Chateaubriand, 304
Chicago v. Lambert, 384
Child Support Enforcement Amendments, 323
Chile, 97
Chinese Exclusion Case, 206, 208
citizenship, 149, 151, 198–99, 215, 264nn. 12, 13, 274n. 114, 342
  in Czech Republic, 430, 432
  EU citizenship in Maastricht Treaty, 115, 264n. 13, 342
Civil Rights Act of 1964: 132
civil society, 336, 428, 438–41
class action, 181
Cohen, 145–46
Cohen, Benjamin V., 6
Cohn-Bendit, Daniel, 32
Cold War, 5
College of Europe, 192
Colonna di Paliano, 68
Columbia University Law School, 192
COMECON, 256, 430
Comisso, Ellen, 427
Commerce Clause. *See* United States of America, Constitution
commerce, regulation of, 113, 128, 142–45, 174
commercial policy, 8, 221–22, 226–27, 283n. 200
  See also foreign affairs
Commission Bancaire (Belgian), 97
Commission des Operations de Bourse (French), 97
Commissioners on Uniform State Laws, 373
Commission of the European Communities, 17, 18, 118, 120
  appointments, functions, accountability, 339–41
  before the Court of Justice, 124, 127
  company laws, role in coordination of, 51–52, 55–61, 63–69, 71–73, 75, 114
  on "constitutional" cases, 35–37, 51
  in diplomacy and autonomous acts, 211–12, 215
  "direct effect," on expanding, 29–32
  in the *ERTA* case, 32–34
  in European Political Cooperation, 251–52, 304
  in foreign affairs, 200, 204–5
  generally, as a principal institution, 118
  in lawmaking, 119–21, 132–35, 142, 144
  Legal Service of, 17, 472–73
  standing to contest Commission decisions, 166–72
  on the supremacy of Community law, 24–25, 27
  in treaty making, 211, 221–23, 225, 227–31, 262
  in the *van Gend* case, 19–24, 472
  as a "weaker institution," 155, 164
  workers' rights, proposals on, 152–53
  WTO Agreements, on power to make, 193, 198
  See also foreign affairs
Commission v. Denmark, 159n. 51
Committee of the Permanent Representatives (COREPER). *See* Council of Ministers
common currency (Euro), 116, 193–94, 275n. 118, 342
Common Customs Tariff (CCT), 214, 221
common foreign and security policy (EU), 114, 193, 309
  See also European Political Cooperation; foreign affairs
Communism, 347
Community association agreements
  with Greece, 234
  with Turkey, 228, 235, 240

Community law. *See* Court of Justice of the European Communities
compact between states (U.S.), 276n. 131
company law, 10, 51, 95–98, 107n. 30, 135, 192, 309, 319
  financial disclosure, 54, 56, 58–59, 65–67, 69, 73
  transplants, 95–97
  U.S. Supreme Court on corporate securities laws, 330n. 33
  See also harmonization
comparative law, 89
  in constitutional negotiations, 422
  in legal research and education, 7–8, 101–4, 192
  method, 164
  transfer of rules from foreign systems, 90–101
    environmental and political factors in, 91, 93–95, 97
  use of comparative law, 99–101
  See also comparison of EC-U.S. systems
comparison of EC-U.S. systems
  citizenship, 149
  consent to impose trade restrictions, 142–45
  contextual and institutional differences, 116–18, 164–65
  on determining state power limits, method, 140–42
  EC-U.S. institutions, 118–21
  free movement of goods, Commerce Clause, 136–42
  free movement of persons, 113, 149–53
  interpretation of Treaty and Constitution, 129–30, 145–47
    lacunae, gap-filling, 205–9, 227, 237
  judicial review
    in EC, 124–28
    in U.S., 121–23, 127–28
  judicial review of administrative action, 162 (*see also* standing to sue, review of administrative action)
    in EC, 165–74
    in French law, 178
    in German Law, 174, 187n. 46, 188nn. 60, 63
    recent ECJ and U.S. cases, 190n. 77
    in U.S., 174–79
  legislative powers
    in economic matters, 135
    expansion by interpretation, 128–32
    in the movement of goods, 136–40
    states' rights, 132
  preemption, 145–49
  "principle of proportionality" (balancing interests), 140–42
  providing for public welfare, 117, 131, 140–41, 152
  rationale for comparison, 115–16
  role of the judiciary, 153–56
  state action, 126
  supremacy of Treaty and Constitution, 124, 236
  treaty-making, 215–23
  U.S.-Germany freedom of speech approach, 347–48, 382–88, 417
compliance with EC, U.S. federal law compared, 154–56
  See also comparison of EC-U.S. systems
Conard, Alfred F., 50, 313, 474
Conference of Commissioners on Uniform State Laws, 100, 313, 323, 325–26
  See also State Commissioners on Uniform State Laws
Conference of the Foreign Affairs Ministers, 248, 251, 257
Conference on Security and Cooperation in Europe (CSCE), 250–51, 255, 436

Conseil d'Etat (French), 32, 92, 112, 127, 173, 178
  Commissaires du Gouvernement, 17
Conseil National du Patronat Français (CPNF), 57
consociational, 193, 421
constitutionalism, 9, 10, 336
constitutionalization, 15, 317, 326
  See also Court of Justice of the European Communities
Consultative Commission of the Bar of the Six Countries of the EEC, 56
Council of Ministers, 17, 33, 52
  actions reviewed by ECJ, 154–55, 166, 171–72, 180
  in adopting the first directive on coordination of company laws, 55–57, 61, 69–75, 112
  authorizing trade barriers, 143–45
  budget, 133–34
  Committee of the Permanent Representatives (COREPER), 17, 70–71, 73–75, 119, 212, 248, 251
    Chairman, 72
    Group on Economic Questions, 71, 73
  composition, 118
  declaring WTO Agreements non-self-executing, 194
  "democratic deficit," reducing through accountability to national parliaments, 339
  deputies of, 73–75
  division of powers with Commission, 211–12
  European Parliament
    shares law-making with, 340
    as upper chamber of, 341, 473
  in European Political Cooperation, 251, 257–58, 262, 308
  in foreign affairs, 197–98, 200, 204, 340
  in foreign commerce, 214–15
  lack of transparency in, 340
  in lawmaking process, 119–21, 340
  legislative authority, 128, 131–32, 135–36
  Presidency of, 225
  regulations and directives, 148–53
  in the "second and third pillar," 114
  Secretariat of, 71–72
  standing before ECJ, 124, 127, 166
  in treaty-making, 221–23, 226–27, 231–33, 236, 238
  voting formula in, 52, 72, 114, 119, 134, 136, 144, 156, 171, 200, 213, 223, 231, 339
Court of First Instance (EC), 162
Court of Justice of the European Communities (ECJ)
  access of individuals to the Court for review of Community action, 161–74, 179–81
  action for damages, 40n. 14
  Amici curiae, 17
  in cases from 1983 to 1994: 190n. 77
  in commercial policy, 226–27
  on Community treaty power, 32–34
  in "constitutionalization" of constituent treaties, 15–18, 35, 336
  in *Demirel* and art. 238 cases, 227–31
  on "direct effect" principle, 18–20, 22–24, 35, 39n. 12
  on effects of Community agreements with third states, 236–42, 259, 261, 310, 337
  ERTA doctrine, 225–26
    progeny, other cases, 231–35
    See also *ERTA* case
  in the European judicial process, 16–18
  expanding "direct effect," 28–29, 31–32
  in foreign affairs, 193, 198, 202, 205, 207–9, 215, 220, 223, 225

Court of Justice of the European Communities (*continued*)
in free movement of goods cases, 137–41, 143–45
on free movement of workers, 29–30, 150–52
generally, 34–37, 50, 58
as judicial organ, 119, 121
judicial review
under art. 173: 124
under art. 177: 125–28
jurisdiction, 19–20
on legality of company law directive, 64–65, 73, 112–13
in Maastricht and Amsterdam Treaties, 114, 116
method of interpreting Community powers, 129–32, 134
on patents, trademarks, 135, 137–38
on preemption, 145–49
protecting basic rights, 26–28, 249, 337
role of judiciary, 153–55
on supremacy of Community law, 21, 24–26, 124 (*see also* supremacy of Community law)
on treaty-making power, 32
See also comparison of EC-U.S. systems, judicial review of administrative action; Germany, Federal Constitutional Court; Italy, Constitutional Court; standing to sue, review of administrative action
Croatia, 430
cultural differences, 91–92, 117, 149, 342, 421, 423–25, 430–37
Curtiss-Wright case, 206–8
Cyprus, 254
Czecho-Slovakia, 10–11
agreement on draft federal constitution, 447
The Castle, 451, 453
Charter 77: 419
Communist Constitution, 425, 452, 454
Communist regime, 418–19, 424, 439
constitutional negotiations, 417–18, 442–47
eliminating cultural differences, 430–37
ethnic conflict as a cause for separation, 423–30
external influences, 436–37
forums and tactics in negotiations, 448–50
Havel proposals, 446
Havel's role, 45, 456 (*see also* Havel)
international advisors, 419
issues for separation, 447–48
media, 428–29
1990 devolution law, 444
situation after 1996: 417
strategic elements in constitutional negotiations
reform, restructuring, new forms of coexistence, 442–47
successor states, 432
transformation, civil, political societies, 437–42
treaty power, 446
Czech Republic
Parliament, 417, 446–47, 452, 454
Securities Commission, 417
Czech-Slovak Federation, 10, 424–25
Charter on Basic Rights and Freedoms, 444
Federal Assembly (Parliament), 433, 438, 442, 445–48, 450–52, 454–55

Dachau, 360
Dahrendorf, Ralf, 439
Danzig case, 23
Darmon (AG), 240
Davignon Report, 247
decolonization, 6, 434
Defrenne case, 30, 35, 36

Dellum v. Bush, 273n. 105
Delors, Jacques, 340
Demaret, 242
Demirel case, 227–28, 234–36, 240
subsequent cases, 285n. 216 (see also *Sevince* case)
democracy, 10, 90–91, 95, 180, 260, 336–38, 438, 443, 451
"democratic deficit," 136, 161, 165, 253, 335–44 *passim*
democratization, 196, 428
restoration after fascist regime, 4
in U.S. and Germany, 386
Denmark, 117, 135, 139
Deringer, 64–68
Desert Storm, 434
diplomacy, 195–96, 210–12, 254, 305
direct effect. *See* Court of Justice of the European Communities
Directorate General (D.G.)
D.G. I (for external relations), 211
D.G. III, 52, 54
D.G. IV, 67
D.G. VIII (for development), 211
Disney Enterprises, 178
Doehring, Karl, 338
Dregger, 370, 372
Drouot L'Hermine, 68
Dubček, Alexander, 451
Dulles, John Foster, 5, 7
dumping, 162, 275n. 124
Durkheim, Emile, 426
Dutch. *See* Netherlands
Dutch Tax Administration, 18
Dutheillet de Lamothe (AG), 27, 34–35

Economic and Social Committee under EC treaty (ESC), 52, 54–57, 60–61, 65, 68–69, 71, 119
Specialized Section on Economic Questions, 57–58
Specialized Section on Non-Wage-Earning Activities and Services, 57
Elster, Jon, 438
employment discrimination, 29, 30–31, 126, 151–53
ENEL case, 24, 26–27, 35–37, 64, 125
Engelhard, 368–71
England. *See* United Kingdom
enumerated powers, 202, 208–9
See also United States, Constitution
environment, 117, 146, 174, 180, 192, 211, 221, 236, 288–89n. 254, 306
Erga omnes, 432
Eridania case, 169, 176
ERTA case, 32–36, 130, 208–9, 226, 229–32, 236
Ethiopian Civil Code, 94
EURATOM, 8, 163, 201, 233
European Central Bank, 194, 341
See also common currency
"The European Civil War 1917–1945: National Socialism and Bolshevism" (E. Nolte), 412
European Coal and Steel Community (ECSC), 163, 166, 201, 340, 472, 476
European Commission on Human Rights, 351
"Auschwitz lie" cases, 45n. 54, 380–82, 391–92n. 27, 406n. 179
European Convention for the Protection of Human Rights, 150, 163, 181n. 1, 209, 235, 381
art. 6(1): 381
art. 8: 235
art. 10: 381–82
European Council, 114, 119, 248, 251, 254, 304, 339
European Court of Human Rights, 253, 382
European Court of Justice (ECJ). *See* Court of Justice of the European Communities
European Defense Community, 201, 307

European Economic Community Treaty (EEC Treaty), 15–16, 22–23, 25, 36, 63, 116, 121, 124, 126–27, 129, 131–32, 137–38, 143–44, 146, 149–50, 152–55, 171–72, 202, 204, 223, 226, 241, 342
art. 3: 29–30
art. 7: 29
art. 12: 18–24, 39–40n. 12, 40n. 14, 41n. 19
art. 28: 214
art. 30: 145, 159n. 46
art. 36: 140, 237
art. 43: 236
art. 48: 229
art. 54: 54–55, 57–58, 63, 67
art. 58: 52
art. 85: 21, 476
art. 86: 21
art. 95: 28
art. 100: 59, 134
art. 103: 144, 214
art. 108: 144
art. 113: 33, 214, 225, 228–29, 236, 257–58
art. 115: 144
art. 119: 30–31
art. 169: 19–20, 24, 149, 241–42
art. 170: 19–20, 24, 149
art. 173: 124, 166–67, 172–74, 179, 476
art. 177: 19–21, 24, 32, 37, 124–27, 147, 149, 172–73, 476
art. 189: 31–32, 121
art. 210: 33, 204, 208
art. 224: 257–58
art. 225: 257–58
art. 226: 144
art. 228: 33, 230, 233
228 (2): 236–38, 242
as amended, 266–67n. 45
art. 229–231: 225
art. 234: 243
art. 235: 129, 134–35, 150, 209, 214, 229–30, 236
art. 236: 228, 229
art. 237: 229
art. 238: 33, 225, 227–31, 234
preamble, 338
Regulation 17: 166
European Foundation, 135
European Free Trade Association (EFTA), 221, 231, 250
European Integration, 9, 114, 116–17, 144–45, 201–2, 214, 253–54, 259–63, 304, 434
legal integration: EC law into national law, 16, 18, 25, 36
European Investment Bank, 256
European Monetary System, 136
European Parliament (EP), Common Assembly, Parliamentary Assembly, 28, 52, 55–56, 60
approval of Commission members, legislative codecision, other powers, 340–43
authority to approve association and accession agreements, 231, 233, 281n. 176
budget, legislation on non-economic issues, 135–36
composition, 61–62, 340
consultation on, approval of treaties, 222–23, 227
consultation on first coordination of company laws directive
in committees, 62–65
in plenary, 66–71
direct election for, 118, 340
EPC, with respect to, 252–53, 256–57, 262, 304, 338–39
in foreign affairs, 198, 204, 215, 221
Fouchet plan, 246
Legal Committee of, 65
as a parliamentary organ, 118, 132–33
Political Committee of, 253
sharing legislative power with Council under Maastricht Treaty, 114

supported by the Court (ECJ), 155, 171
European Political Community, 201
European Political Cooperation (EPC), 193–94, 197, 201, 210, 212, 215, 246, 250, 257–58, 263, 304
Cooperation of the Ambassadors, 249
COREU, 249, 252
Group of European Correspondents, 249, 252
Groups of Experts, 249
Political Committee, 248, 252, 254–56
Presidency, 249, 254–55
Secretariat established, 296n. 328
See also foreign affairs
European Road Transport Agreement (ERTA), 33
European Union, 114
See also Maastricht Treaty
European University Institute, 192

Falkland Islands, 257–58
family law
"child snatching," 321–22
child support, 322
divorce, 92, 94, 320–21
illegitimate children, 325, 327
marriage, 321, 324, 327
uniformity of in U.S., 319–26
"fast track" procedure, 41n. 19, 274n. 110
Faurisson, Robert, 357
Faust, 442
Federal Bar Association, 473
federalism, 9, 10, 113, 118, 154, 158, 161, 165, 196–97, 199, 207, 209, 217, 233, 309, 311, 323–24, 326, 421, 425, 444
Federal Rules of Civil Procedure, 314
Federation of Banks of the EEC, 56
Federation of Belgian Industries, 58
Fiji, 212
Ford Foundation, 161, 320
foreign affairs (external relations), 130–31, 193, 195–97
on diplomacy, 210–12, 305
EC succession
to GATT, 243, 280n. 167
to member state agreements, 242
not to UN Charter, 258
effects of EC agreements, 236
European Political Cooperation (EPC), 200, 245–63 (*see also* European Political Cooperation)
defense policy, 307–8
links to domestic policies, 306–7
organization, 247–50
recognition, 254
sanctions, 258
scope, activities, 253–58
in the UN, 255–56
U.S. as model 261–63, 264n. 12
Executive role in, 198, 204, 210, 304–5, 307
Foreign policy
in Amsterdam Treaty, 193
in EC, 339
in Maastricht Treaty, 304–8
international claims
in EC, 244–45
in U.S., 243
"mixed agreements," 223, 225
judicial review of, 234–36
with third states after 1988: 280n. 167
reach and limits of EC treaty powers, 225–34 (*see also* treaties)
treaty-making power, EC, 207–9, 220–21, 227–38, 269n. 69
U.S. and EC compared
allocation of powers, 197–10
autonomous acts, 212–15
communication and diplomacy, 210–12
differences, 197–99
treaty-making powers, 215–21
treaty-making process, 221–23

Foreign Affairs and the [*United States*] *Constitution* (L. Henkin), 192
Fouchet Plan, 246
France, 32, 37, 61, 68, 92, 96, 101, 117, 155, 201, 212, 235, 246, 250, 338, 350, 364, 412
  French Economic and Social Council, 57
  French law on Commercial Companies, 96
  French Parliament, 96
  French Senate, 67
  Secretariat of State for Economic Affairs, 54
  See also Conseil d'Etat
Franck, Thomas M., 216, 336
Frankfurter Allgemeine Zeitung, 16, 377, 411
Franz Grad case, 31–32, 35
freedom of establishment, 52, 113, 126
freedom of expression, 349, 377
  in U.S., 382–88
  in U.S. and Germany, compared, 348, 385, 388
  See also "Auschwitz lie"
free movement of goods and factors of production, 24, 113, 115, 137, 149
  cases, 137–41, 143–45, 152
free movement of workers, 126, 149–50, 228–29, 235
Freud, 472
Frowein, Jochen Abr., 341

Galli case, 149
Gand (AG), 28, 35, 171
Garcia v. San Antonio Met. Transp. Authority, 157n. 36
Gašparovič, Ivan, 435
Gaudet, Michel, 472–73, 476
Gaulle, Charles de, 7, 246
Geck, Wilhelm Karl, 347
Gellner, Ernest, 439, 454
General Agreement on Tariffs and Trade (GATT), 16, 193, 221, 239, 241–43, 258, 269n. 69, 291n. 276, 296n. 328, 474 (*see also* World Trade Organization)
Genocide, 368–70, 379–80, 411, 430
  ethnic cleansing, 430
Genscher, Hans-Dietrich, 308
Geofroy v. Riggs, 217, 233
Germany, 18–19, 25, 28, 60–61, 68–70, 92, 101, 117, 125, 164, 166–69, 192, 201, 228, 234
  Basic Law (Grundgesetz), 27–28, 349, 351–52, 366, 381, 387
  Civil Code
    art. 823: 366
    art. 1604: 366
  Criminal Code, 349, 351, 371, 376, 383, 410, 414
    art. 130: 351–52, 354–59, 361–66, 369, 379
    art. 131: 351, 353–55, 357–58, 362–63, 369, 379
    art. 185: 351, 353, 355–56, 361, 363–66, 381
    art. 189: 355, 361
    art. 194: 413
  Federal Administrative Court, 164, 173
  Federal Constitutional Court, 15–16, 28, 45n. 45, 46n. 54, 67, 125, 337, 348–49, 354–55, 380–81
  Federal Parliament, 67, 163, 347–48, 352
    See also Bundesrat; Bundestag
  Federal Supreme Court, 352, 356–59, 361, 363, 365–68, 371, 373–74, 376, 378–80, 388, 414
  Federation of Judges, 370
  Justice Ministry, 352
  Rahmengesetz (framework law), 121
  Reichsgericht (Supreme Court, pre-World War II), 353

Wehrstrafgesetz (Military Criminal Law), 352
Gessler, 54
Getreide-Import case, 169
Gibbons v. Ogden, 147
Glucoseries case, 170
Grabitz, Helge, 413–14
Greece, 6, 117, 221, 234, 257
Grundgesetz. *See* Germany, Basic Law
Guéhenno, J.M., 339

Haas, Ernst, 8
Hague
Hague Academy, 7
summit meeting of the Six, 247
Hallstein, 473
Haltern, Ulrich R., 343
Hamel Committee, 54
Hammarskjöld, Dag, 5
harmonization (coordination of laws)
of European company laws, 95–97
topics to coordinate, 52
European Company Statute, 96–97
first directive
in the Council of Ministers, 70–75
in European Parliament, 62–69
process: consultations, 51, 55–62
second draft, 69
generally, 50, 134–35, 253
harmony, 423
theoretical concern for, 318
health and safety regulations, 343
second coordination directive, 55–56
in U.S., 313
See also uniformity, legal
Havel, Václav, 417, 419–20, 438–39, 442, 444, 446, 451–53, 455
Hay, Peter, 8
Helsinki Watch, 419
Henkin, Louis, 192, 194, 205
Herder, 304
Hesse, 60
Heuss, Theodor, 372
Historikerstreit (quarrel among historians), 347, 411–13, 416
Hitler, 351, 358
The Hoax of the [*Twentieth*] *Century* (Butz), 362
Holmes, 153–54, 217, 475
Holocaust, 347–48, 354, 410–11, 413–14
See also "Auschwitz lie"
Holocaust (film), 361, 364
Horowitz, Donald L., 421, 423
Houin, 54
House of Lords, 136
human (basic) rights
basic rights in EC-EU, 8, 19, 27, 40n. 14, 44n. 48, 50, 150, 153, 163, 192, 209, 235, 254, 336–37
in Czecho-Slovakia
Charter 77: 419
in Czech and Slovak Republics, 433, 434
Federal Charter on Basic Rights and Freedoms, 444
in foreign policy, 305
free movement and equal treatment rights in EC and U.S., 150–253
in international law, 163
treaties, non-self-executing, 279n. 164
in UN, 6, 8
in U.S., protection of individual rights, 150, 218, 317
in U.S. Senate, treaties pending, ratified, 194, 220, 260–61, 277–78n. 137, 279n. 156
Hume, David, 337
Hungary, 6, 438

Immunity
functional, 211
sovereign, 274n. 115
Indonesia, 6
Industrial Revolution, 128
Institute for Advanced Legal Studies (London), 161

Institute for Advanced Studies (Berlin), 347
Institute for Historical Review and the Liberty Lobby (California), 382
intergovernmentalism, 341
Internal Market Committee, 62, 64–65, 67
International Agreement on Natural Rubber, 227
International Atomic Energy Agency, 6
international claims, 243–45
International Court of Justice, 6, 49n. 91, 171, 245, 294n. 304, 432
Internationale Handelsgesellschaft case, 27, 35
International Fruit case, 168, 170, 239, 242
International Labor Organization, 101, 319
international law, 3, 6, 7–8, 10, 16, 19–20, 23, 63, 89, 101–2, 162, 195, 198, 203, 206, 208
  effects of EC agreements in, 237–38
  international personality, 211, 243–44
  recognition in, 254, 326, 336
  successor states in, 431–32, 449, 472
  See also treaties
International Law Commission (ILC), 237
International Natural Rubber Agreement case, 232
International Trade Commission (U.S.), 211, 215
International Union of Attorneys, 56
Internet, 340
interpretation method, 32, 112, 116, 128–32, 291n. 276, 294n. 297
Iranian hostage situation, 250, 254, 257
Ireland, 30, 92, 94, 117, 250
Iron Curtain, 6
Israel, 254, 354, 358, 364, 372
  Parliament, 372
Italy 3–4, 24–26, 61, 68–69, 117, 125, 148, 164, 169
  Consiglio di Stato, 58
  Constitution, 24
  Constitutional Court, 24–26, 28, 36, 43n. 40, 125
  Northern League (Lega Norte), 428, 461n. 49
  Parliament, 26
  Senate, 68–69

Jackson, John, 474
Jacobs, Francis G. (AG), 161–62
Japan, 92, 103, 192, 221, 474
  Civil Code, 94
  Code of Criminal Procedure, 94
  Penal Code, 94
Jessup, Philip, 6
Jobert, 248
Joffe, Josef, 193
Jozeau-Marigné, 67
judicial notice, 356–57
  See also "Auschwitz lie"
judicial review, 15–16
  in EC, 18–37, 124–28
  in U.S., 122–23, 127, 174, 314–17, 324
  See also comparison of EC-U.S. systems; Court of Justice of the European Communities; standing to sue, review of administrative action

Kafka, 450
Kahn-Freund, Otto, 89–95, 98–99, 103, 474
Keck case, 159n. 46
Kirchoff, Paul, 16
Klaus, Václav, 428, 433, 449–50, 453
Klokočka, 452
Kohl, Helmut, 370–71, 415–16
Korean War, 201
Koskenniemi, Martti, 7
Kramer case, 226, 232

Kupferberg case, 237, 239
Kusín, Vladimír, 443

labor law, 92, 101, 146
  See also employment discrimination
labor and trade unions, 57, 59–60, 91–92
Lagrange (AG), 25, 35, 171, 173
Latin America
  administrative reorganization in Chile, 97
  integration, 9
Law Commission, English and Scottish, 99
Law Commission Act of 1965 (UK), 99
lawmaking process, 51–52
  in EC, 90–91, 99–101, 119, 335, 339–40
  in EC, U.S., 120
  making an EC directive, 55–75
  See also comparison of EC-U.S. systems; foreign affairs
Lay, 316
legal cultures, U.S. and Europe, 16, 38–39n. 4
legal education, 7–10, 89–90, 92, 101–4
legal transplants, 90–99
  See also comparison of EC-U.S. systems; foreign affairs
Legion for the Survival of Freedom, 382
legislative powers
  of Council in EC, 119
  in EC and U.S. generally, 128–36
  in free movement of goods, 136–45
  in free movement of persons, 149, 193
  in U.S., 157n. 36, 310, 312, 314–15
legitimacy, 36, 153–54, 165, 337, 342, 435, 437
Leleux, Paul, 474
Library of Congress, 101
Lincoln, 454, 456
Little Entente, 436
Lipstein, Kurt, 3
Lomé Convention, 221, 224
Lowack, 372
Lütticke case, 28, 35
Luxembourg, 16, 69, 70, 117, 247–48, 471, 473
Luxembourg Agreement, 119, 156

Maastricht Treaty, 114–15, 194, 281n. 176, 304, 307–8, 310, 342, 430, 447
MacChesney, 89
MacCormick, Neil, 342
Maistre, Joseph de, 304
Mancini, Federico, 16, 343
Mapp case, 100
Marbury v. Madison, 122–23, 472
Marshall, John, 113, 117, 122–23, 129–30, 146, 156, 193, 218, 271n. 78
Masaryk, T.G., 431, 435
Max Planck Institute for Foreign Public and International Law, 5, 99, 309
Mayras (AG), 32, 35
McCulloch v. Maryland, 127, 129, 271n. 78
Mečiar, Vladimír, 440, 442, 448–51, 453
media, 16
  in Czecho-Slovakia, 428–29
  in EU, 342–43
  in Germany, 362
Meehan, Gerard, 193
Meier, Christian, 414–16
membership in EC-EU, 117, 156n. 4
Metropolitan Life Insurance Co. v. Ward, 159n. 51
Minnesota v. Clover Leaf Co., 159n. 51
Miranda case, 100
Missouri v. Holland, 143, 217, 283n. 193, 285–86n. 227
Mitterand, François, 415
"mixed agreements," 223–25, 234–36
  See also foreign affairs

Mňačko Ladislav, 424, 456n. 2
Model Corporation Act, 100
Model Penal Code, 100
Molière, 113
Monnet, Jean, 201, 307, 340
  method of integration, 201
Monroe Doctrine, 213
Montesqieu, 90–91, 93, 118, 319
Morgenthau, Hans, 6
Morocco, 6
Mozambique, 254

Namibia, 254
Napoleon, 412
National Court of Appeals, 316
National Industrial Recovery Act, 175
nationalism, 5, 136, 307, 350, 420, 423, 427, 429, 435
"Nationalism and the Marketplace of Ideas" (J. Snyder and K. Ballentine), 428
National Labor Relations Act, 314
NATO. *See* North Atlantic Treaty Organization
neofunctionalism, 8
neo-Nazis
  Action Front of the National Socialists (ANS), 354
  in Germany, 349–50, 362, 368, 371–72, 375, 378
  in U.S., 384, 387
Netherlands, 19–20, 28, 37, 54, 59–62, 117, 168, 232
Neue Zürcher Zeitung, 379
New York Times v. Sullivan, 384
New York v. U.S., 159n. 36
New Zealand, 92
Nieland case, 351–52
Nietzsche, Friedrich, 425
Nixon Doctrine, 213
Nolte, Ernst, 411–13
North Atlantic Treaty Organization (NATO), 4, 246, 250, 307–8, 418, 430, 436, 440
  negotiation for, 7
Northwestern University Law School, 89
Nuremberg Laws, 365–67, 374

ombudsman, 264n. 13, 341
open-door doctrine, 213
Opinion 2/91, Opinion 1/94, Opinion 2/92 (ECJ), 269n. 69
Oregon Court of Appeals, 139
Organization for Economic Cooperation and Development (OECD), 226

Panama Canal Treaty, 216
Panorama of the World's Legal Systems (Wigmore), 101
Parental Kidnapping Prevention Act, 322
Paris University, 7
Parliament. *See* European Parliament; *and under individual country*
parliamentary diplomacy, 306
People's Republic of China, 192, 256
Permanent Court of Arbitration, 245
Permanent Court of International Justice, 23, 63
Permanent Missions of the Six to the Communities, 70
Pescatore, Pierre, 112, 119, 162
Pit'ha, Petr 435
Plaumann case, 166, 170
Pleven, 67–68
Poland, 23, 256–57, 438
political parties
  in Europe, 60, 62, 66–68, 92, 341–42
  in Czecho-Slovakia, 444, 446–48
  in Germany, 368–73
  in U.S., 120, 220
Polydor Ltd. v. Harlequin Record Shops Ltd., 239, 292n. 279
Pompidou, 247
Portugal, 145, 153, 256
positivism, 8, 15

Posner, Richard A., 438
post-Communist transformation, 4, 10, 427, 430, 437–38, 440–41
Précigout, 57, 59
preemption, 16, 145–49, 233
Prudential case, 143
Putnam, Robert, 440

Rahmengesetz (framework law), 121
Raiffa, Howard, 442, 448, 450
Reagan, 415
realists, 6, 341
recognition
  of states or governments, 274n. 115, 280n. 167, 430, 432
referendum
  elsewhere in Central-Eastern Europe, in the West, 434
  proposed in Czecho-Slovakia, 432
regionalism, 338
regions, 8, 310
  of Europe, 145, 422, 430
  of U.S., 132, 220, 311
Reischl (AG), 26, 35
Representative for Trade Negotiations (U.S.), 222
Revel, Jean-François, 474
Rey, Jean, 473
Reyners case, 29, 35
Rhodesia, 254, 257
Roemer (AG), 19, 27, 31, 35, 173
Roe v. Wade, 325–26
Roma (gypsies), 417, 436
Romania, 6, 438
Roman Law, 93–95
Roosevelt, Franklin Delano, 6
Ross, 456
Ruritania, 192
Russia, 436
  Soviet Union 6, 221, 257, 280n. 167, 435, 437
Rusk, Dean, 6

SABENA case, 30
sanctions, 258
  See also foreign affairs
Sandalow, Terrance, 112, 320, 324
Schermers, 141
Schlesinger, Arthur M., Jr., 455
Schlesinger, George B., 100, 318
Schmidt, Helmut, 368
Schwartz, Herman, 419
Seccombe, 192
secession, 421, 434
Seibel, 60
self-determination, 421, 431–35
separation, 421
  geo-political impact of Czecho-Slovak separation, 436–37
  movement for, in Belgium, Quebec, Italy, Czecho-Slovakia, 434–35
  other, 458n. 32, 460n. 45
  peaceful, 435
  Sweden and Norway, 434, 462n. 54
separation of powers, 26, 161, 196, 217, 241, 269n. 69, 278n. 142, 338
Serbo-Croatian-Bosnian conflict, 430
Seuffert, 64, 67
Sevince case, 240
Sierra Club, 178
Simma, Bruno, 474
Simmenthal case, 25–27, 35, 125
Single European Act, 114, 229, 296n. 328, 304
Skokie case, 348, 384–86, 388
Slovak National Council (Parliament), 40, 441, 445–47
Slovenia, 430
Smith, Adam, 426, 428
South Africa, 6, 254
sovereign immunity, 274n. 115
sovereignty, 19, 114, 171, 206–7, 213, 268n. 61, 338, 421, 429
Soviet Union. *See* Russia
Spaak, Fernand, 473
Spain, 145, 153, 192, 254
Staatenverbund, 342
Stalin, 418

standing to sue, review of administrative action
  before ECJ, 161–64, 165–74, 215
    of individuals, 19–20, 32
    of member states, 20
    requirement of "direct concern," 166–72, 179
  common law "legal right" test, 175–77, 181
  in domestic courts under EC treaty, 10, 23, 29
  in U.S., 174–79
  See also comparison of EC-U.S. systems
State Commissioners on Uniform State Laws, 320, 322
Stauder case, 27
Stein, Ted, 310
Stevens, Wallace, 9
Stewart, 154, 474
Strategic Arms Limitation Treaty I (SALT I), 216
Strauss (Prime Minister of Bavaria), 370
Strauss, Herbert A., 387, 410
subsidiarity, 235, 310, 342
succession, 242–43, 258, 431–32
Superintendencia de compañias de seguros, sociedades anónimas y bolsas de comercio, 97
supremacy of Community law, 16, 24–28, 36, 125–26, 145, 290n. 265, 290n. 266, 337
  See also Court of Justice of European Communities
Sutherland, 127, 206–7
Švejnar, Jan, 426
Sweden, 350
Sweden-Norway Union, 434, 460n. 45, 462n. 54
Switzerland, 343, 350, 428

Taiwan, 212
Taney, 156, 193
Tariefcommissie, 18–19
taxation, 10, 64, 113, 135, 138
  customs tariffs, duties, 18–20, 22, 131, 141
  directive for common VAT system, 31
  discrimination in, 20, 28, 41n. 19, 126, 129
  federal tax law (U.S.), 315
  power of, 116, 341, 200
Tennessee Valley Authority (TVA), 176
Themat, Pieter Verloren van, 473
Third Reich, National Socialist Regime (Nazi Germany), 347, 349–50, 354–55, 357, 360, 362, 365, 367, 369, 371, 373–74, 377–80, 411, 414, 418
Tocqueville, Alexis de, 309
Toepfer case, 167–70
Tolstoy, Lev, 425
Trabucchi (AG), 30–31, 35
treaties
  direct effect, 18–24, 28–32
  European Community Treaty. *See* European Economic Community Treaty; foreign affairs; mixed agreements
    "constitutionalization" of (*see* Court of Justice of the European Communities)
  generally, 10, 23
  status of forces (U.S.), 101
  succession to, 294n. 297
  supremacy, 24–28 (*see also* comparison of EC-U.S. systems; supremacy of Community law)
    over U.S. law, 218–20, 236–38
  Treaty Establishing the European Atomic Energy Community. *See* EURATOM
  Vienna Convention on the Law of Treaties, 22, 237
  WTO Agreements, 193–94, 261
  See also United Nations

Truman, 384
Truman Doctrine, 213
Tunisia, 6
Turkey, 153, 221, 228
Turkish Civil Code of 1926: 94

Uniform Abortion Act, 325
Uniform Child Custody Jurisdiction Act, 322
Uniform Commercial Code, 100, 134, 313
uniformity, legal
  in Europe, 309–10
  forces for uniformity, 318
    in continental Europe, 318
    in U.S., 311
  process toward uniformity generally in U.S., 21, 311–13
  through federal power, 314–18
  through voluntary action, 313, 327n. 11
  in U.S., 312–27
    in administrative and procedural rules, 92
    between courts, 312, 315–16
    in family law, 319
      marriage, divorce, property division, 92, 94, 320–21
      child-snatching and non-support, 322–23
    within states, 312–17
  in U.S. Supreme Court case law, 323–26
    abortion, 325–27
    classification on the basis of sex, 324
    contraceptive use, 324
    corporate securities law, 330n. 33
    criminal procedure, 330n. 33
    illegitimate children, 325
    interracial marriage, 324
  See also comparative law; comparison of EC-U.S. systems
Uniform Marital Property Act (Property Act), 321
Uniform Marriage and Divorce Act, 320–21
Uniform Reciprocal Enforcement of Support Act, 323
Union Démocratique Européenne (U.D.E.), 62, 68
Union of Industries of the European Community (UNICE), 56–57
United Kingdom, 15, 30, 32, 101, 117, 154, 161, 199, 228, 234, 250, 350
  England, 92, 103, 412
United Nations, 4–6, 9, 163, 237, 434, 448, 472
  administrative tribunals, 181n. 1
  Charter, 5
    art. 51: 7
  Conference on Trade and Development, 227
  Convention on the elimination of all forms of racial discrimination, 181n. 1
  Covenant on basic civil and political rights, 348, 392n. 27
  Covenants on human rights, 319
  Economic Commission for Europe, 226
  "failure" of, 9
  General Assembly, 5, 6, 248, 255–56, 299n. 357, 299n. 364, 302n. 370, 434
  Headquarters Agreement with U.S., 237
  Law of the Sea Convention, 223–24
  peace treaties with Bulgaria, Hungary, Romania case, 6
  principles, 433
  Relief and Works Agency Conventions, 236
  Security Council, 5, 250, 257–58
  Uniting for Peace Resolution, 5
  See also human (basic) rights
United States of America
  Articles of Confederation, 197, 199–200, 206

United States of America (*continued*)
  Congress, 120, 122, 126, 128, 131–35, 140, 143–44, 147, 153, 172, 176, 179–80, 200, 202, 204–5, 209–10, 212–15, 217, 219–20, 232, 243, 261, 309, 314–15, 317, 322, 326
    House of Representatives, 216–17, 223
    Senate, 194, 202–3, 216–17, 220, 234, 243, 262, 340–41
      Foreign Relations Committee, 216
  Constitution, 122–24, 126, 128–29, 137, 143, 150, 154, 179, 193, 197–98, 202, 204–6, 217–18, 258–59, 311, 314–17
    art. I, section 8: 203, 205
    art. II, 203, 205
    art. IV, section 2: 151
    Bill of Rights, 207, 218, 243, 317, 324
    Commerce Clause, 130, 135–36, 138–40, 142–43, 146–48, 153
    enumerated powers, 130, 133, 203–4, 206–7
    First Amendment, 385
    Fourteenth Amendment, 149, 324
    "necessary and proper" clause, 129, 134, 205
    spending power, 133
    "substantive due process," 138
    Supremacy Clause, 218, 322
    Tenth Amendment, 128, 130, 207
    treaty power provisions, 130, 215–20, 236
  Constitutional Convention, 127, 200, 202, 454
  Declaration of Independence, 206
  Department of Commerce, 222
  Department of State, 4, 6–7, 214, 219–20, 222, 243, 348, 471–72
  Bureau of UN Affairs, 4
  Federal Comptroller of Currency, 163
  President (executive branch), 120, 132, 172, 197, 197, 202–5, 207, 212–14, 216–17, 219–20, 222, 243, 261–62
  Supreme Court, 116, 122–24, 127, 129–32, 136–41, 143–48, 150–56, 163, 175–180, 206–8, 217–19, 232–33, 238, 261, 309–10, 312–17, 320, 323–25, 327, 349, 382–84
University of Florence, 192
University of London, 161
University of Michigan, 192, 475
  Law School, 3, 8, 9, 89, 473, 476–77
  Michigan Law Review, 347, 410, 412
Urban, Jan, 429
U.S. v. Lopez, 157n. 36

Valley Forge Christian College case, 189n. 71
van Binsbergen case, 29
van Duyn case, 29, 32, 35
van Gend case, 18, 20, 23–25, 27–28, 33–37, 125, 472
Vattel, 206
Verdam Commission Report, 60
Versailles Settlement, 216, 429
Viking Youth, 361
Vienna Convention on the Law of Treaties, 22, 237
Vining, Joseph, 161
Vogelaar, Theodor, 473
Vogelsang, 373, 414

Waelbroeck, 23, 146–48, 167, 233
Walrave case, 29–31, 35
Ward, 456
Warner (AG), 29, 35
War Powers Resolution of 1973: 213, 273n. 105
Warsaw Pact, 255, 418, 430

Washington, George, 340, 454
Watergate, 165
Watson, Alan, 89, 93–95, 97–98
Weber, Max, 319
Weiler, J.H.H., 192, 341, 343, 473–74
Weimar Republic, 349, 378
Weisband, 216
Weizmann, 412
Weizsäcker, Richard von, 380, 411
Western European Union, 307
Wigmore, 101
Winkler, Günther, 442
Woestijne, van de, 58, 60, 65
World Trade Organization, 16
Agreements, 193–94, 269n. 69
See also General Agreement on Tariffs and Trade (GATT)
World War I, 378
World War II, 3, 7, 104, 201, 317, 320, 434, 472

Yaoundé Convention, 221
Yeats, W.B., 471
Yeltsin, 454–55
Yntema, Hessel E., 102–3
Yugoslavia, 153, 305, 343, 377, 437

Zakaria, Fareed, 337
Zuckerfabrik Watenstadt case, 169